# elevate science

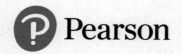 **Pearson**

**Boston, Massachusetts    Chandler, Arizona**
**Glenview, Illinois    New York, New York**

## You're an author!

As you write in this science book, your answers and personal discoveries will be recorded for you to keep, making this book unique to you. That is why you are one of the primary authors of this book.

✏ **In the space below, print your name, school, town, and state. Then write a short autobiography that includes your interests and accomplishments.**

YOUR NAME .............................................................................

SCHOOL ...................................................................................

TOWN, STATE ..........................................................................

AUTOBIOGRAPHY ...................................................................

.................................................................................................

.................................................................................................

.................................................................................................

.................................................................................................

.................................................................................................

.................................................................................................

Your Photo

The cover photo shows the Hubble Space Telescope.

Pearson Education, Inc.  330 Hudson Street, New York, NY 10013

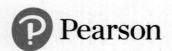

ISBN-13:   978-0-328-94855-0
ISBN-10:   0-328-94855-1
4   18

# Program Authors

**ZIPPORAH MILLER, Ed.D.**
*Coordinator for K-12 Science Programs, Anne Arundel County Public Schools*
Dr. Zipporah Miller currently serves as the Senior Manager for Organizational Learning with the Anne Arundel County Public School System. Prior to that she served as the K-12 Coordinator for science in Anne Arundel County. She conducts national training to science stakeholders on the Next Generation Science Standards. Dr. Miller also served as the Associate Executive Director for Professional Development Programs and conferences at the National Science Teachers Association (NSTA) and served as a reviewer during the development of Next Generation Science Standards. Dr. Miller holds a doctoral degree from the University of Maryland College Park, a master's degree in school administration and supervision from Bowie State University and a bachelor's degree from Chadron State College.

**MICHAEL J. PADILLA, Ph.D.**
*Professor Emeritus, Eugene P. Moore School of Education, Clemson University, Clemson, South Carolina*
Michael J. Padilla taught science in middle and secondary schools, has more than 30 years of experience educating middle-school science teachers, and served as one of the writers of the 1996 U.S. National Science Education Standards. In recent years Mike has focused on teaching science to English Language Learners. His extensive experience as Principal Investigator on numerous National Science Foundation and U.S. Department of Education grants resulted in more than $35 million in funding to improve science education. He served as president of the National Science Teachers Association, the world's largest science teaching organization, in 2005–6.

**MICHAEL E. WYSESSION, Ph.D**
*Professor of Earth and Planetary Sciences, Washington University, St. Louis, Missouri*
Author of more than 100 science and science education publications, Dr. Wysession was awarded the prestigious National Science Foundation Presidential Faculty Fellowship and Packard Foundation Fellowship for his research in geophysics, primarily focused on using seismic tomography to determine the forces driving plate tectonics. Dr. Wysession is also a leader in geoscience literacy and education; he is the chair of the Earth Science Literacy Initiative, the author of several popular video lectures on geology in the *Great Courses* series, and a lead writer of the *Next Generation Science Standards*\*.

# REVIEWERS

## Program Consultants

### Carol Baker
**Science Curriculum**

Dr. Carol K. Baker is superintendent for Lyons Elementary K-8 School District in Lyons, Illinois. Prior to this, she was Director of Curriculum for Science and Music in Oak Lawn, Illinois. Before this she taught Physics and Earth Science for 18 years. In the recent past, Dr. Baker also wrote assessment questions for ACT (EXPLORE and PLAN), was elected president of the Illinois Science Teachers Association from 2011–2013, and served as a member of the Museum of Science and Industry (Chicago) advisory board. She is a writer of the Next Generation Science Standards. Dr. Baker received her B.S. in Physics and a science teaching certification. She completed her master's of Educational Administration (K-12) and earned her doctorate in Educational Leadership.

### Jim Cummins
**ELL**

Dr. Cummins's research focuses on literacy development in multilingual schools and the role technology plays in learning across the curriculum. *Elevate Science* incorporates research-based principles for integrating language with the teaching of academic content based on Dr. Cummins's work.

### Elfrieda Hiebert
**Literacy**

Dr. Hiebert, a former primary-school teacher, is President and CEO of TextProject, a non-profit aimed at providing open-access resources for instruction of beginning and struggling readers, She is also a research associate at the University of California Santa Cruz. Her research addresses how fluency, vocabulary, and knowledge can be fostered through appropriate texts, and her contributions have been recognized through awards such as the Oscar Causey Award for Outstanding Contributions to Reading Research (Literacy Research Association, 2015), Research to Practice award (American Educational Research Association, 2013), and the William S. Gray Citation of Merit Award for Outstanding Contributions to Reading Research (International Reading Association, 2008).

## Content Reviewers

**Alex Blom, Ph.D.**
Associate Professor
Department Of Physical Sciences
Alverno College
Milwaukee, Wisconsin

**Joy Branlund, Ph.D.**
Department of Physical Science
Southwestern Illinois College
Granite City, Illinois

**Judy Calhoun**
Associate Professor
Physical Sciences
Alverno College
Milwaukee, Wisconsin

**Stefan Debbert**
Associate Professor of Chemistry
Lawrence University
Appleton, Wisconsin

**Diane Doser**
Professor
Department of Geological Sciences
University of Texas at El Paso
El Paso, Texas

**Rick Duhrkopf, Ph.D.**
Department of Biology
Baylor University
Waco, Texas

**Jennifer Liang**
University of Minnesota Duluth
Duluth, Minnesota

**Heather Mernitz, Ph.D.**
Associate Professor of Physical Sciences
Alverno College
Milwaukee, Wisconsin

**Joseph McCullough, Ph.D.**
Cabrillo College
Aptos, California

**Katie M. Nemeth, Ph.D.**
Assistant Professor
College of Science and Engineering
University of Minnesota Duluth
Duluth, Minnesota

**Maik Pertermann**
Department of Geology
Western Wyoming Community College
Rock Springs, Wyoming

**Scott Rochette**
Department of the Earth Sciences
The College at Brockport
  State University of New York
Brockport, New York

**David Schuster**
Washington University in St Louis
St. Louis, Missouri

**Shannon Stevenson**
Department of Biology
University of Minnesota Duluth
Duluth, Minnesota

**Paul Stoddard, Ph.D.**
Department of Geology and
  Environmental Geosciences
Northern Illinois University
DeKalb, Illinois

**Nancy Taylor**
American Public University
Charles Town, West Virginia

## Teacher Reviewers

**Jennifer Bennett, M.A.**
Memorial Middle School
Tampa, Florida

**Sonia Blackstone**
Lake County Schools
Howey In the Hills, Florida

**Teresa Bode**
Roosevelt Elementary
Tampa, Florida

**Tyler C. Britt, Ed.S.**
Curriculum & Instructional
 Practice Coordinator
Raytown Quality Schools
Raytown, Missouri

**A. Colleen Campos**
Grandview High School
Aurora, Colorado

**Ronald Davis**
Riverview Elementary
Riverview, Florida

**Coleen Doulk**
Challenger School
Spring Hill, Florida

**Mary D. Dube**
Burnett Middle School
Seffner, Florida

**Sandra Galpin**
Adams Middle School
Tampa, Florida

**Margaret Henry**
Lebanon Junior High School
Lebanon, Ohio

**Christina Hill**
Beth Shields Middle School
Ruskin, Florida

**Judy Johnis**
Gorden Burnett Middle School
Seffner, Florida

**Karen Y. Johnson**
Beth Shields Middle School
Ruskin, Florida

**Jane Kemp**
Lockhart Elementary School
Tampa, Florida

**Denise Kuhling**
Adams Middle School
Tampa, Florida

**Esther Leonard, M.Ed. and L.M.T.**
Gifted and talented Implementation Specialist
San Antonio Independent School District
San Antonio, Texas

**Kelly Maharaj**
Challenger K–8 School of Science
 and Mathematics
Spring Hill, Florida

**Kevin J. Maser, Ed.D.**
H. Frank Carey Jr/Sr High School
Franklin Square, New York

**Angie L. Matamoros, Ph.D.**
ALM Science Consultant
Weston, Florida

**Corey Mayle**
Brogden Middle School
Durham, North Carolina

**Keith McCarthy**
George Washington Middle School
Wayne, New Jersey

**Yolanda O. Peña**
John F. Kennedy Junior High School
West Valley City, Utah

**Kathleen M. Poe**
Jacksonville Beach Elementary School
Jacksonville Beach, Florida

**Wendy Rauld**
Monroe Middle School
Tampa, Florida

**Anne Rice**
Woodland Middle School
Gurnee, Illinois

**Bryna Selig**
Gaithersburg Middle School
Gaithersburg, Maryland

**Pat (Patricia) Shane, Ph.D.**
STEM & ELA Education Consultant
Chapel Hill, North Carolina

**Diana Shelton**
Burnett Middle School
Seffner, Florida

**Nakia Sturrup**
Jennings Middle School
Seffner, Florida

**Melissa Triebwasser**
Walden Lake Elementary
Plant City, Florida

**Michele Bubley Wiehagen**
Science Coach
Miles Elementary School
Tampa, Florida

**Pauline Wilcox**
Instructional Science Coach
Fox Chapel Middle School
Spring Hill, Florida

## Safety Reviewers

**Douglas Mandt, M.S.**
Science Education Consultant
Edgewood, Washington

**Juliana Textley, Ph.D.**
Author, NSTA books on school science safety
Adjunct Professor
Lesley University
Cambridge, Massachusetts

# Atoms and the Periodic Table...........xviii

 **Essential Question** How do atoms combine to form extended structures?

**Quest KICKOFF** Dessert Disaster ..................... 2

Go to **PearsonRealize.com**
to access your digital course.

▶ **VIDEO**
• Artist

↓ **INTERACTIVITY**
• Build an Atom • Models of Atoms
• Organization of the Periodic Table
• Interactive Periodic Table • Groups
of Elements • Valence Electrons
• Transferring Energy Through
Bonding • Build an Ionic Compound
• Ionic or Covalent Bonding
• Chemical Bonding • Properties and
Uses of Acids and Bases • Acids and
Bases in Careers • Acid Rain

📱 **VIRTUAL LAB**

☑ **ASSESSMENT**

📖 **eTEXT**

📱 **APP**

## HANDS-ON LABS

u**Connect** Modeling Matter

u**Investigate**
• How Far Away Is the Electron?
• Classifying Elements
• Element Chemistry
• Properties of Molecular Compounds
• Properties of Acids and Bases

u**Demonstrate**
Shedding Light on Ions

# TOPIC 2

# Chemical Reactions .........64

**The Essential Question** How can you determine when a chemical reaction has occurred?

**Quest** KICKOFF Hot and Cool Chemistry ..............66

MS-PS1-2, MS-PS1-3, MS-PS1-5, MS-PS1-6

Go to PearsonRealize.com to access your digital course.

**▶ VIDEO**
• Forensic Scientist

**👆 INTERACTIVITY**
• Separating a Mixture
• Inside a Water Treatment Plant
• Water Contaminants and Removal Methods
• Evidence of Chemical Reactions
• Analyze Exothermic and Endothermic Graphs
• Conservation of Matter
• Model a Chemical Reaction
• Reactants and Products
• Model the Conservation of Mass
• Describe the Impact of Synthetics
• The Impact of Synthetics

**📱 VIRTUAL LAB**

**☑ ASSESSMENT**

**📖 eTEXT**

**📱 APP**

# HANDS-ON LABS

**uConnect** What Happens When Chemicals React?

**uInvestigate**
• Particles in Liquids
• Changes in a Burning Candle
• Is Matter Conserved?
• Making Plastic from Starch

**uDemonstrate**
Evidence of Chemical Change

 Go to PearsonRealize.com to access your digital course.

▶ **VIDEO**
  • Mechanical Engineer

👆 **INTERACTIVITY**
  • Relative Motion • Balanced and Unbalanced Forces • Explore Forces • Falling for Velocity • Motion Graphs • How Forces Affect Motion • How are Mass, Motion, and Force Related? • Going, Going, Gone! • Fuel Efficient Vehicles • Exploring Gravity • The Pull of the Tides

📱 **VIRTUAL LAB**

☑ **ASSESSMENT**

📖 **eTEXT**

📱 **APP**

# HANDS-ON LABS

**иConnect** Identifying Motion

**иInvestigate**
  • Motion Commotion
  • Walking the Walk
  • Newton Scooters
  • Observing Friction
  • Sticky Sneakers

**иDemonstrate**
  Stopping on a Dime

# 4 Genes and Heredity ........168

Go to PearsonRealize.com
to access your digital course.

▶ **VIDEO**
- Genetic Counselor

**INTERACTIVITY**
- Making Copies
- Offspring Season
- Look Inside
- Colorful Chromosome
- The Role of DNA
- Making Proteins
- Sex-Linked Traits and Disorders
- Track Your Traits
- DNA Fingerprinting
- Solving Problems with Genetics

**VIRTUAL LAB**

**ASSESSMENT**

**eTEXT**

**APP**

HANDS-ON LABS

**иConnect** Making More

**иInvestigate**
- Observing Pistils and Stamens
- Chromosomes and Inheritance
- Modeling Protein Synthesis
- Extraction in Action

**иDemonstrate**
Make the Right Call!

TOPIC
**5**

# Natural Selection and Change Over Time .......... 234

**The Essential Question** How do characteristics change over time?

**Quest** KICKOFF A Migration Puzzle .................. 236

MS-LS4-1, MS-LS4-2, MS-LS4-3, MS-LS4-4, MS-LS4-5, MS-LS4-6

Go to PearsonRealize.com to access your digital course.

▶ **VIDEO**
• Evolutionary Biologist

👆 **INTERACTIVITY**
• Mystery on the Galapagos Islands
• Animal Feeding Adaptations
• Adaptations and Variations • Mice Selection on the Prairie • Species Adaptations • Lessons from the Potato Famine • Mutations Aren't All that Bad • Separated Species • Along the Canyon Wall • Legs, Arms, Wings, Flippers • Tiny Clues • Fossils Around the World • Tree of Life • Long Necks and Hoofed Feet

📱 **VIRTUAL LAB**

☑ **ASSESSMENT**

📖 **eTEXT**

📱 **APP**

**HANDS-ON LABS**

**иConnect** Fins and Limbs!

**иInvestigate**
• Nature at Work
• Variation in a Population
• Adaptations of Birds
• Finding Proof
• DNA Evidence

**иDemonstrate**
A Bony Puzzle

# TOPIC
# 6 History of Earth .............298

**The Essential Question** How can events in Earth's past be organized?

**Quest** KICKOFF The Big Fossil Hunt ............... 300

MS-ESS1-4

Go to PearsonRealize.com to access your digital course.

▶ **VIDEO**
  • Paleontologist

✋ **INTERACTIVITY**
  • Oldest to Youngest
  • Radiometric Dating
  • Know Your Index Fossils
  • On the Clock
  • A Very Grand Canyon
  • Going Away
  • How Old Are These Rocks?
  • Observation and Deduction
  • Big Changes

📱 **VIRTUAL LAB**

☑ **ASSESSMENT**

📖 **eTEXT**

📱 **APP**

# HANDS-ON LABS

**иConnect** Dividing History

**иInvestigate**
  • The Story in Rocks
  • Going Back in Time
  • Changes in the Water

**иDemonstrate**
Core Sampling Through Time

# TOPIC 7

# Energy in the Atmosphere and Ocean ............................... 338

**The Essential Question** How does energy move throughout Earth's atmosphere and ocean?

**Quest KICKOFF** Crossing the Atlantic .............. 340

MS-ESS2-6

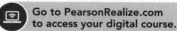

Go to PearsonRealize.com to access your digital course.

 **VIDEO**
- Ship Captain

**INTERACTIVITY**
- Fluids on the Move
- Patterns in the Wind
- Where the Wind Blows
- Winds Across the Globe
- Currents and Climate
- Ocean Habitats
- Keeping Current on Currents

**VIRTUAL LAB**

**ASSESSMENT**

**eTEXT**

**APP**

# HANDS-ON LABS

**иConnect** Does a Plastic Bag Trap Heat?

**иInvestigate**
- Heating Earth's Surface
- United States Precipitation
- Modeling Ocean Current Formation

**иDemonstrate**
Not All Heating Is Equal

# TOPIC
# 8  Climate ....................................380

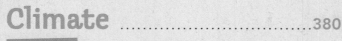
**The Essential Question** How have natural processes and human activities changed Earth's climate?

**Quest KICKOFF** Shrinking Your Carbon Footprint ... 382

MS-ESS2-6, MS-ESS3-5

Go to PearsonRealize.com
to access your digital course.

▶ **VIDEO**
• Science Writer

👆 **INTERACTIVITY**
• Two Sides of a Mountain
• Olympic Choices
• In the Greenhouse
• Human Impact on Climate Change
• Climate Change Q&A
• Methane Management
• Emission Reduction

📱 **VIRTUAL LAB**

☑ **ASSESSMENT**

📖 **eTEXT**

📱 **APP**

## HANDS-ON LABS

**иConnect** How Climates Differ

**иInvestigate**
• Classifying Climates
• What is the Greenhouse Effect?
• Thermal Expansion of Water

**иDemonstrate**
An Ocean of a Problem

# TOPIC 9 Earth-Sun-Moon System

The Essential Question  How do the sun and the moon affect Earth?

**Quest** KICKOFF  It's as Sure as the Tides............. 426

MS-ESS1-1

Go to PearsonRealize.com
to access your digital course.

▶ **VIDEO**
• Planetarium Technician

👆 **INTERACTIVITY**
• Discovery of the Solar System
• Interpreting the Night Sky
• Patterns in Earth's Rotation
  and Revolution
• What Keeps Objects in Motion?
• Seasons on Earth
• Our View of the Moon
• Eclipses
• Moon Phases and Eclipses

📱 **VIRTUAL LAB**

☑ **ASSESSMENT**

📖 **eTEXT**

📱 **APP**

## HANDS-ON LABS

u**Connect**  What Is at the Center?
u**Investigate**
• Watching the Skies
• Lighten Up!
• How Does the Moon Move?
u**Demonstrate**
Modeling Lunar Phases

# TOPIC 10

# Solar System and the Universe ...................468

**The Essential Question** What kind of data and evidence help us to understand the universe?

**Quest KICKOFF** Searching for a Star ............. 470

MS-ESS1-2, MS-ESS1-3

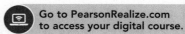
Go to PearsonRealize.com
to access your digital course.

▶ **VIDEO**
• Astrophysicist

👆 **INTERACTIVITY**
• Distance Learning
• Anatomy of the Sun
• Solar System
• How to Make a Solar System
• Space Exploration
• Telescopes
• Launch a Space Probe
• Eyes in Sky
• Star Systems
• Lives of the Stars
• Types of Galaxies
• Model a Galaxy

📱 **VIRTUAL LAB**

☑ **ASSESSMENT**

📖 **eTEXT**

📱 **APP**

**HANDS-ON LABS**

**ИConnect** Planetary Measures

**ИInvestigate**
• Pulling Planets
• Layers of the Sun
• Space Exploration Vehicle
• How Far Is That Star?
• Model the Milky Way

**ИDemonstrate**
Scaling Down the Solar System

# Elevate your thinking!

*Elevate Science* takes science to a whole new level and lets you take ownership of your learning. Explore science in the world around you. Investigate how things work. Think critically and solve problems! *Elevate Science* helps you think like a scientist, so you're ready for a world of discoveries.

## Explore Your World

Explore real-life scenarios with engaging Quests that dig into science topics around the world. You can:

- Solve real-world problems
- Apply skills and knowledge
- Communicate solutions

### Quest KICKOFF

**What do you think is causing Pleasant Pond to turn green?**

In 2016, algal blooms turned bodies of water green and slimy in Florida, Utah, California, and 17 other states. These blooms put people and ecosystems in danger. Scientists, such as limnologists, are working to predict and prevent future algal blooms. In this problem-based Quest activity, you will investigate an algal bloom at a lake and determine its cause. In labs and digital activities, you will apply what you learn in each lesson to help you gather evidence to solve the mystery. With enough evidence, you will be able to identify what you believe is the cause of the algal bloom and present a solution in the Findings activity.

## Make Connections

*Elevate Science* connects science to other subjects and shows you how to better understand the world through:

- Mathematics
- Reading and Writing
- Literacy

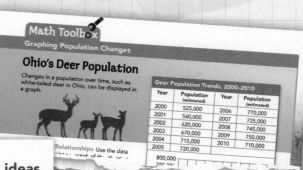

**Math Toolbox**

Graphing Population Changes

### Ohio's Deer Population

Changes in a population over time, such as white-tailed deer in Ohio, can be displayed in a graph.

**Deer Population Trends, 2000–2010**

| Year | Population (estimated) | Year | Population (estimated) |
|------|------------------------|------|------------------------|
| 2000 | 525,000 | 2006 | 770,000 |
| 2001 | 560,000 | 2007 | 725,000 |
| 2002 | 620,000 | 2008 | 745,000 |
| 2003 | 670,000 | 2009 | 750,000 |
| 2004 | 715,000 | 2010 | 710,000 |
| 2005 | 720,000 | | |

Relationships Use the data

800,000
750,000

**READING CHECK** **Determine Central Ideas**
What adaptations might the giraffe have that help it survive in its environment?

### Academic Vocabulary
Relate the term *decomposer* to the verb *compose*. What does it mean to compose something?

# Build Skills for the Future

- Master the Engineering Design Process
- Apply critical thinking and analytical skills
- Learn about STEM careers

## Focus on Inquiry

Case studies put you in the shoes of a scientist to solve real-world mysteries using real data. You will be able to:

- Analyze Data
- Test a hypothesis
- Solve the Case

**Case Study**

MS-LS2-1

THE CASE OF THE DISAPPEARING

# Cerulean Warbler

The cerulean warbler is a small, migratory songbird named for its blue color. Cerulean warblers breed in eastern North America during the spring and summer. The war blers spend the winter months in the Andes Mountains of Colombia, Venezuela, Ecuador, and Peru in northern South America.

## Enter the Lab

Hands-on experiments and virtual labs help you test ideas and show what you know in performance-based assessments. Scaffolded labs include:

- STEM Labs
- Design Your Own
- Open-ended Labs

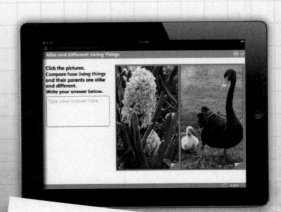

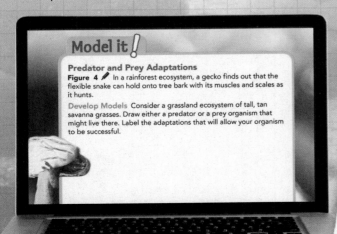

**Model it**

**Predator and Prey Adaptations**

**Figure 4** In a rainforest ecosystem, a gecko finds out that the flexible snake can hold onto tree bark with its muscles and scales as it hunts.

**Develop Models** Consider a grassland ecosystem of tall, tan savanna grasses. Draw either a predator or a prey organism that might live there. Label the adaptations that will allow your organism to be successful.

**HANDS-ON LAB**

**uInvestigate** Observe how once-living matter is broken down into smaller components in the process of decomposition.

**NGSS PERFORMANCE EXPECTATION**

**MS-PS1-1** Develop models to describe the atomic composition of simple molecules and extended structures.

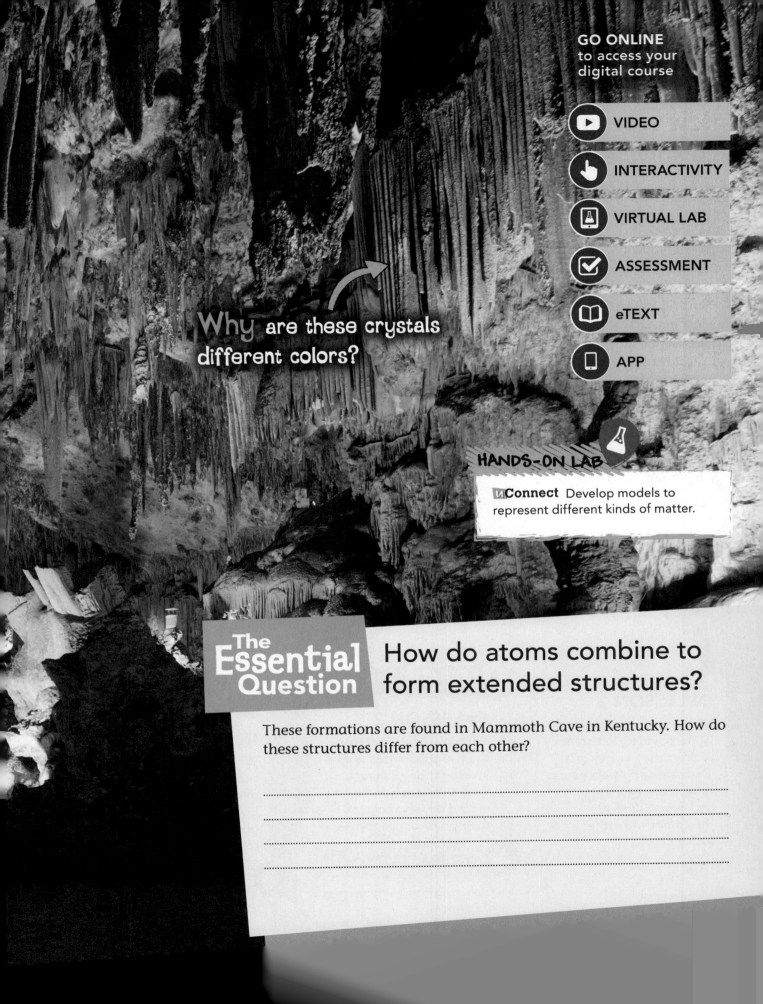

Why are these crystals different colors?

**GO ONLINE**
to access your
digital course

▶ VIDEO

👆 INTERACTIVITY

🧪 VIRTUAL LAB

☑ ASSESSMENT

📖 eTEXT

📱 APP

**HANDS-ON LAB**

иConnect Develop models to represent different kinds of matter.

## The Essential Question

How do atoms combine to form extended structures?

These formations are found in Mammoth Cave in Kentucky. How do these structures differ from each other?

................................................................................

................................................................................

................................................................................

................................................................................

# Quest KICKOFF

## How can you use chemistry to solve a culinary mystery?

**Phenomenon** The baking competition is in an uproar. A confident contestant's cake comes out of the oven in a disastrous state. She cries foul, claiming that her cake has been sabotaged by one of the other contestants. Could it be that one of the other bakers substituted one white powdery ingredient for another, resulting in the spoiled cake? In this problem-based Quest activity, you will be the chemist who determines what substance is in the spoiled cake and which contestant put it there. You will explore and identify the chemical properties of the substances in question. By applying what you learn, you will develop a report about the substance that ruined the cake and which contestant must be guilty.

**INTERACTIVITY**

Dessert Disaster

**MS-PS1-1** Develop models to describe the atomic composition of simple molecules and extended structures.

**NBC LEARN** ▶ VIDEO

After watching the Quest Kickoff video, answer the questions. Then turn and share with a partner.

**1** What are some culinary chemical reactions that you have seen?

..................................................................

..................................................................

..................................................................

**2** What culinary chemical reactions have you seen that didn't go well or that resulted in a culinary "disaster"?

..................................................................

..................................................................

..................................................................

## IN LESSON 1

Why does it matter which white powdery substance a baker uses in a cake? Think about how elements differ from each other and how differently they react with other substances.

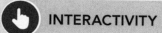
## Quest CHECK-IN

### IN LESSON 2

What elements make up the five substances under investigation? Examine each substance and record observations of their physical properties.

**INTERACTIVITY**

Examining Physical Properties of Powders

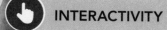
## Quest CHECK-IN

### IN LESSON 3

What are the chemical properties of the five substance under investigation? Examine, observe, and record results in a table.

**INTERACTIVITY**

The Iodine Test for Starch

Chemical reactions are critical to the outcome of all baked products. The ingredients used—and the exact amounts used—contribute to the taste, texture, and appearance of the final product. The wrong ingredient, or the wrong amount, can result in a culinary disaster.

## Quest CHECK-IN

### IN LESSON 4

How does each of the five substances react with vinegar? How does each respond to heat? Record observations and explain the results of each test.

👆 **INTERACTIVITY**

The Vinegar Test

## Quest CHECK-IN

### IN LESSON 5

STEM What is the mystery substance? Draw conclusions from the tests and solve the mystery of the dessert disaster.

🧪 **HANDS-ON LAB**

Solving the Mystery

## Quest FINDINGS

## Complete the Quest!

Present the findings of your investigation and explain how you arrived at your conclusion.

👆 **INTERACTIVITY**

Reflect on Your Investigation

## Guiding Questions

- What are the parts that make up an atom?
- What is atomic theory?
- What evidence supports the modern model of the atom?

## Connections

**Literacy** Determine Central Ideas

**Math** Interpret Diagrams

MS-PS1-1

## Vocabulary

atom
electron
nucleus
proton
neutron
atomic number
isotope
mass number

## Academic Vocabulary

theory

 **VOCABULARY APP**

Practice vocabulary on a mobile device.

**Quest CONNECTION**

Think about how elements differ from each other and how differently they react with other substances.

## Connect It !

✏️ **Circle one of the sea squirts in the image and read the photo's caption.**

**Infer** What gives a sea squirt its unique structure and shape?

......................................................................................

**Apply Information** How might nanowhiskers be used in fabrics to make them stain-resistant?

......................................................................................

......................................................................................

# Development of Atomic Theory

What's more than 16,000 times thinner than a human hair and can be used in fabrics to repel stains and odors? It's a nanowhisker!

Nanowhiskers are tiny threads that measure about 10 nanometers (1 nm = 0.000000001 m) in length and 1.5 nanometers in diameter. They are often made of carbon or silver. Scientists have found that the carbon-based material that makes up the structure of a sea squirt, shown in **Figure 1**, is made of nanowhiskers. These nanowhiskers are similar to the cellulose fibers that make up cell walls in plants.

What does a nanowhisker have to do with atoms? Both of these things are so small that it's difficult to imagine how tiny they are. However, as small as a nanowhisker is, its diameter is still about 10 times wider than the diameter of an atom.

Finding the smallest bits of matter that exist has always been a core question for scientists. For a long time, it was thought that atoms were the answer to this scientific puzzle. Now we know that atoms themselves are built from even smaller particles. The quest to find the absolute smallest bit of matter continues today.

☑ **READING CHECK** **Identify** Which two elements are nanowhiskers usually made of?

**HANDS-ON LAB**

Investigate how to determine the properties of an object without looking at it.

**Sea Squirts and Nanowhiskers**

**Figure 1** The structure of a sea squirt is made up of nanowhiskers, or tiny threads that are not much wider than atoms.

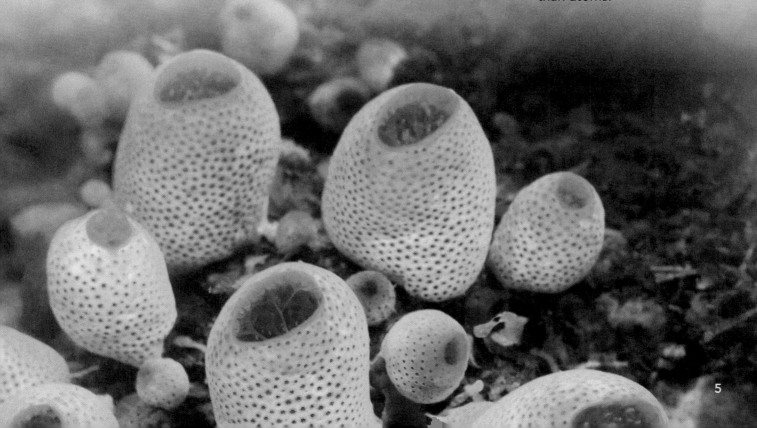

## The First Theories on Atoms

What, exactly, is an atom? Around 430 BCE, the Greek philosopher Democritus proposed that matter was formed of small pieces that could not be cut into smaller parts. He used the word *atomos*, meaning "uncuttable," for these smallest possible pieces. In modern terms, an **atom** is the smallest particle that still can be considered an element.

Because atoms are so tiny and therefore difficult to study, scientists have created models to describe them. Over the years, these models of atoms have evolved as scientists discovered more about them.

The study of atoms really gained speed in the 1600s. As people conducted various experiments, atomic **theory** began to take shape. Atomic theory grew as a series of models that developed from experimental evidence. As more evidence was collected, the theory and models were revised.

John Dalton, an English chemist, conducted many experiments centered on atoms. From these experiments, he inferred that all atoms had certain characteristics:

**Academic Vocabulary**

How does a scientific theory compare to a scientific law?

...............................................

...............................................

...............................................

...............................................

...............................................

**Literacy Connection**

**Determine Central Ideas**
Read about Dalton's atomic theory and write a brief summary of the main idea of his findings.

...............................................

...............................................

...............................................

...............................................

...............................................

## Dalton's Atomic Theory

- All elements consist of atoms that cannot be divided.

- All atoms of the same element are exactly alike and have the same mass. Atoms of different elements are different and have different masses.

- An atom of one element cannot be changed into an atom of a different element by a chemical reaction.

- Compounds are formed when atoms of more than one element combine in a specific ratio.

## Thomson's Model

We now know that atoms are made of parts that are even smaller than Dalton realized. In 1897, J. J. Thomson discovered that atoms contain negatively charged particles. Each of these particles is called an **electron**. Yet scientists knew that atoms themselves can have no electrical charge. So, Thomson reasoned that atoms must also contain some sort of positive charge.

Thomson proposed a model like the one shown in **Figure 2**. He described an atom that had electrons scattered throughout a ball of positive charge. His model looked similar to a scoop of chocolate chip ice cream.

## Rutherford's Model

In 1911, Ernest Rutherford found evidence that challenged Thomson's model. Rutherford's research team aimed a beam of positively-charged particles at a thin sheet of gold foil surrounded by a fluorescent-coated detector, as shown in **Figure 3**. Rutherford and his team predicted that, if Thomson's model were correct, the charged particles would pass straight through the foil. They also predicted that the paths of some particles would bend, or deflect, slightly because of the positive charge that was spread out in the gold atoms.

During the experiment, Rutherford observed that most of the particles passed straight through the foil with little or no deflection. But to everyone's surprise, a few particles were deflected at sharp angles by the gold foil.

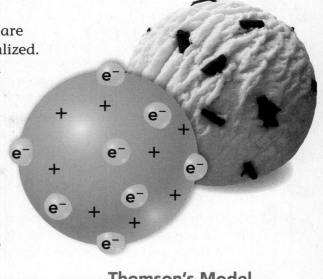

**Thomson's Model**

**Figure 2** Thomson suggested that atoms have negatively-charged electrons set in a positive sphere. Each electron is represented above by the symbol e⁻. What indicates that an atom has no overall charge?

.........................................................

.........................................................

.........................................................

.........................................................

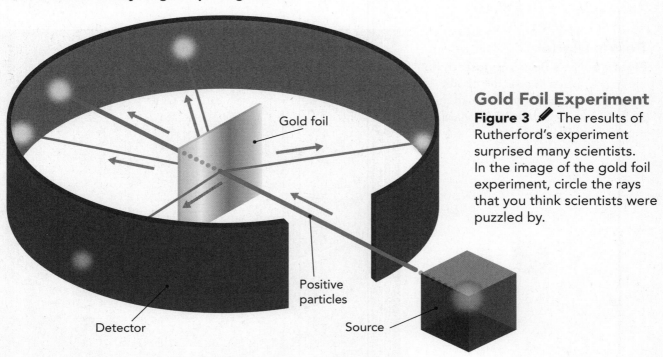

Gold foil

Positive particles

Detector

Source

**Gold Foil Experiment**

**Figure 3** 🖊 The results of Rutherford's experiment surprised many scientists. In the image of the gold foil experiment, circle the rays that you think scientists were puzzled by.

## Rutherford's Theory

**Figure 4** ✏ Write *A*, *B*, or *C* by each arrow to indicate how it supports Rutherford's model of an atom that is mostly empty space with a dense, positively-charged nucleus in the center.

A. Like charges repel each other. Any positive particle that passes near the nucleus of an atom is deflected from its path.

B. Most of an atom is empty space, so most positive particles pass straight through the foil.

C. The nucleus is small but dense. Any particle that actually hits the nucleus bounces back in about the same direction it came from.

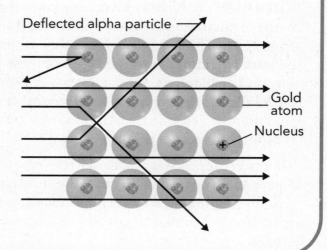

Deflected alpha particle

Gold atom

Nucleus

Based on his experiment, Rutherford concluded that the atom is mostly empty space but has a dense, positive charge at its center. This dense center is called the **nucleus**. (The plural of nucleus is nuclei.) Examine **Figure 4** to explore how the results of the gold foil experiment support Rutherford's conclusions. Rutherford called a positively-charged particle in an atom's nucleus a **proton**.

## Bohr's Model

Niels Bohr, a Danish scientist, was one of Rutherford's students. In 1913, Bohr revised the atomic model again. He suggested that electrons move only in specific orbits around an atom's nucleus. The orbits in Bohr's model look like moons orbiting a planet, as shown in **Figure 5**. Each possible electron orbit in Bohr's model has a fixed energy.

## Bohr's Model

**Figure 5** Niels Bohr suggested that electrons move in specific orbits around the nucleus of an atom, just as the moons of the planet Mars move in orbit around it.

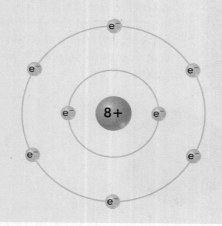

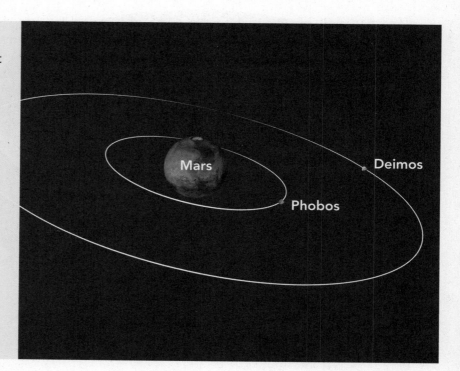

Mars

Deimos

Phobos

**Cloud Model** The atomic model changed again in the 1920s. Around that time, scientists determined that electrons do not move in specific orbits like planets do, as Bohr suggested. Instead, electrons move rapidly within a cloudlike region around the nucleus. The orange "cloud" in **Figure 6** is a visual model. It represents where electrons are likely to be found.

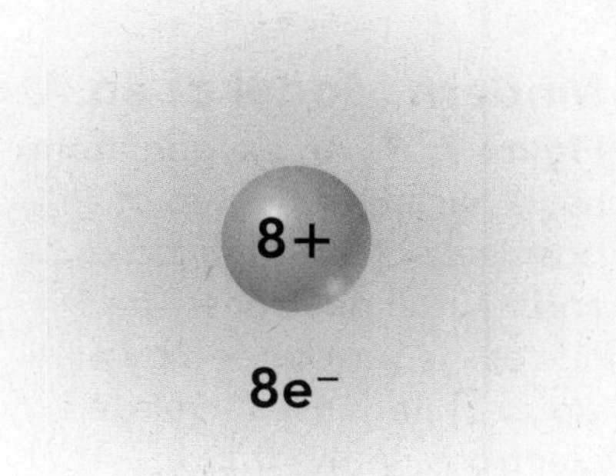

✓READING CHECK **Determine Central Ideas** How do later atomic theories differ from Dalton's atomic theory?

..................................................................................................

..................................................................................................

..................................................................................................

..................................................................................................

..................................................................................................

8+

8e⁻

**Cloud Model**
**Figure 6** In the cloud model of an atom, electrons move rapidly in all directions around the atom's nucleus.

# Model It

## Models of an Atom

The historic models of the atom can be compared to real-life objects. For example, Thomson's model was compared to chocolate chip ice cream, and Bohr's model was compared to the orbit of the moons of Mars around the planet.

**Develop Models** ✏ In each box below, draw a real-life example of something that can be used to represent that model of the atom. Do not use the examples used in this text.

| Dalton's Model | Thompson's Model |
|---|---|
| | |
| **Bohr's Model** | **Cloud Model** |
| | |

## Modern Model of an Atom

**Figure 7** ✏ An oxygen atom has a nucleus made up of positively-charged protons and neutral neutrons. The nucleus is surrounded by a cloud of negatively-charged electrons. In the figure, label the protons with a plus sign (+).

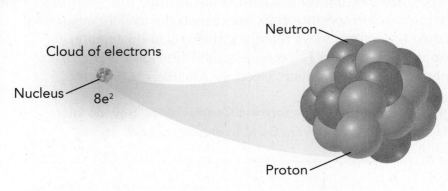

Cloud of electrons

Nucleus — 8e²

Neutron

Proton

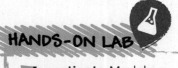

**HANDS-ON LAB**

☑**Investigate** Model an atom and its electrons to visualize their relative dimensions.

# A Modern Model of the Atom

In 1932, English scientist James Chadwick showed that another particle exists in the nucleus of atoms. This particle is called a **neutron**. It took scientists a long time to find this particle because it has no electric charge.

Since Chadwick's discovery, scientists have learned even more about atoms. One modern model of the atom is shown in **Figure 7**. At the center is a tiny, dense nucleus containing protons and neutrons. All around the nucleus is a cloudlike region of moving electrons. Neutrons, protons, and electrons are known as subatomic particles. A subatomic particle is any particle smaller than an atom.

Most of an atom is made up of the space in which the electrons move. This space is huge compared to the space taken up by the nucleus. Imagine holding a pencil while standing in the middle of a football stadium. If the pencil's eraser were the nucleus of an atom, its electrons would reach as far away as the top row of seats!

**Particle Charges** In most models of atoms, protons are shown by a plus sign (+). The symbol for a proton is $p^+$. Electrons are shown by the symbol $e^-$, and neutrons are represented by an $n$. According to the scale used for measuring charge in atoms, protons have a charge of +1 and electrons have a charge of –1. If you count the number of protons in **Figure 7**, you'll see there are eight. There are also eight electrons. Because these amounts are even, the charges balance, making the atom neutral. The number of neutrons present does not affect the charge of an atom because neutrons have a charge of zero.

**Comparing Particle Masses** When it comes to the masses of particles, protons and neutrons are about equal. Electrons, however, are much, much smaller. It takes almost 1,840 electrons to equal the mass of one proton or neutron. Therefore, protons and neutrons make up almost all the mass of an atom.

**Figure 8** compares the charges and masses of the three types of atomic particles. Atoms are much too small to be described by standard units of mass, such as grams. So, scientists usually measure atoms using atomic mass units (amu). A proton or a neutron has a mass equal to about one amu.

**Atomic Number** You have read that all atoms of an element are the same, and atoms of different elements are different. What can atoms tell us about elements?

The number of protons in the nucleus of an atom is the **atomic number** of that atom's element. The definition of an element is based on its atomic number. For example, every oxygen atom has eight protons, so the atomic number of oxygen is 8.

**INTERACTIVITY**

Explore how subatomic particles combine to form atoms.

**VIDEO**

Watch a video to learn about the isotopes of hydrogen.

**Masses of Atomic Particles**

**Figure 8** An adult rhino can have a mass of 1400 kg. The mass of a small egret is about 0.76 kg. What is the ratio of these two masses? How does this ratio compare to the ratio of the mass of a proton to the mass of an electron?

..................................................................................

..................................................................................

..................................................................................

..................................................................................

✏ **Complete the table.**

| Particle | Symbol | Mass (amu) |
|----------|--------|------------|
|          | $p^+$  |            |
| neutron  |        |            |
|          |        | $\dfrac{1}{1,840}$ |

11

**INTERACTIVITY**

Use what you have learned to design your own model of an atom.

**Isotopes** All atoms of an element have the same number of protons. The number of neutrons can vary. Atoms with the same number of protons and different numbers of neutrons are called **isotopes**.

An isotope is identified by its **mass number**, which is the sum of the protons and neutrons in the atom. The most common isotope of oxygen has a mass number of 16 (8 protons + 8 neutrons) and may be written as "oxygen-16." Most naturally-occurring oxygen is oxygen-16. The two other stable isotopes are oxygen-17 and oxygen-18.

Despite their different mass numbers, all three oxygen isotopes react the same way chemically. The number of electrons affects chemical reactivity, and neutrons generally do not affect chemical reactions very much. All isotopes of oxygen have the same number of electrons.

✓ READING CHECK **Infer** Why do you think the mass number includes only the numbers of protons and neutrons?

.........................................................................................................

.........................................................................................................

# Math Toolbox

## Exploring Isotopes

Most elements have several different isotopes, and they usually differ in abundance. For example, oxygen-16 makes up more than 99 percent of all oxygen atoms.

**1. Interpret Diagrams** ✏
Use the information you know about isotopes to complete the table with information about oxygen isotopes.

| Atom |  8e⁻ | 8e⁻ | 8e⁻ |
|---|---|---|---|
| **Isotope** | Oxygen-16 | Oxygen-17 | Oxygen-18 |
| **Protons** | 8 | | |
| **Neutrons** | | 9 | 10 |

**2. Analyze Data** ✏
Complete the table with the mass number, number of protons, number of neutrons, and number of electrons for the elements shown.

| Element | Mass Number | p⁺ | n | e⁻ |
|---|---|---|---|---|
| Fluorine | | | 10 | 9 |
| Argon | 40 | | 22 | |
| Calcium | 41 | | | 20 |

**1. Revise Information** How did the discovery of isotopes disprove one part of Dalton's atomic theory?

........................................................

........................................................

........................................................

........................................................

**2. Infer** In Rutherford's experiment, why were some particles deflected a small amount?

........................................................

........................................................

........................................................

........................................................

........................................................

........................................................

**3. Construct an Explanation** This diagram shows a hydrogen atom. Explain why it looks like it does.

........................................................

........................................................

........................................................

........................................................

........................................................

**4. Reason Quantitatively** An atom of chlorine has an atomic number of 17 and a mass number of 37. How many protons, neutrons, and electrons are in the atom?

........................................................

........................................................

**5. Develop Models** 🖊 An atom of carbon has six protons. In the space below, use the knowledge you gained in this lesson to draw a model of a carbon atom. Be sure to label the protons, neutrons, and electrons in your model, along with areas of positive and negative charge.

MS-PS1-1

# Unlocking the Power of the Atom

In the 20th century, scientists finally succeeded in splitting the atom. Splitting atoms into smaller atoms releases powerful energy. This process is called nuclear fission.

A nuclear reactor works on the principle of nuclear fission. The reactor splits uranium atoms, generating a great deal of energy. In a nuclear power plant, this energy is used to heat water, and the water produces steam. The steam turns turbines and thus produces electricity.

## Three Mile Island

Three Mile Island is near Harrisburg, the capital city of Pennsylvania. The island is home to a major nuclear power station. On March 28, 1979, a valve in the reactor closed by mistake, setting off a chain reaction of mechanical failures combined with human errors. This was the first time that a nuclear accident had taken place in the United States, and no one quite knew what the effects might be. Several anxious weeks went by as scientists examined what had happened.

| Pros | Cons |
| --- | --- |
| • Reduces dependency on fossil fuels | • Much more expensive than other renewable energy sources |
| • Uranium can be mined in U.S. | • Potential hazards from reactor malfunctions |
| • Nuclear power plants do not produce carbon dioxide | • Dangers in storing nuclear waste |

Three Mile Island near Harrisburg, Pennsylvania

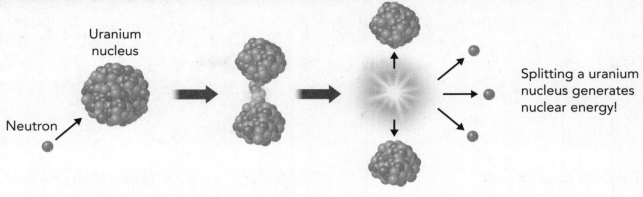

Uranium
nucleus

Neutron

Splitting a uranium
nucleus generates
nuclear energy!

Some people were terrified that radiation would spread, causing a
serious health crisis. Because the reactor had been so well designed,
however, very little radiation escaped during the accident. In the end,
neither the environment nor any people were harmed.

Largely because of public fear, the incident at Three Mile Island halted
further development of the U.S. nuclear power program. No new
reactors were commissioned for decades. In the end, though, people
understood and accepted that the original safety precautions had
functioned properly and protected them from harm.

1. **Engage in Argument** Do you think the
   benefits of nuclear power outweigh the
   potential drawbacks?

   .........................................................................

   .........................................................................

   .........................................................................

**Production of
Nuclear Power in the U.S.**

1980 U.S. nuclear industry produces
11% of U.S. electricity.

2001 U.S. nuclear industry produces
20% of U.S. electricity.

2015 U.S. nuclear industry produces
19.5% of U.S. electricity.

2. **Predict** Look at the data. To what degree do you
   think the U.S. will rely on nuclear energy for its
   electricity by 2026? By 2076?

   .........................................................................

   .........................................................................

   .........................................................................

3. **Construct Explanations** Why were people terrified by the Three Mile
   Island accident? Use evidence from the text to support your answer.

   .........................................................................

   .........................................................................

4. **Connect to Society** In the 1970s, people were reluctant to embrace
   nuclear power. What would it take for Americans today to favor a greater
   reliance on nuclear power as a source of electricity?

   .........................................................................

   .........................................................................

   .........................................................................

# ② The Periodic Table

## Guiding Questions

- Why do elements need to be organized?
- How was the periodic table developed?
- What information about elements is provided by the periodic table?

## Connections

**Literacy** Determine Central Ideas

**Math** Sequence

MS-PS1-1

## Vocabulary

atomic mass
periodic table
chemical symbol
period
group

## Academic Vocabulary

representation

 **VOCABULARY APP**

Practice vocabulary on a mobile device.

**Quest CONNECTION**

Find out what you can tell about an unknown substance by observing its physical properties.

## Connect It !

✏ **Circle and label the different types of recyclable materials you see in Figure 1.**

**Apply Concepts** What things in your home do you sort and organize?

.................................................................................................................

**Infer** What problems might it cause if a company tried to recycle materials without sorting them first?

.................................................................................................................

.................................................................................................................

.................................................................................................................

.................................................................................................................

# Organizing the Elements

Do you organize things according to their properties? Are all of your books together in your locker? Are your clothes organized according to whether they are winter clothes or summer clothes? **Figure 1** shows how sorting recyclable materials puts them into groups that are all recycled the same way.

Organizing things usually makes them easier to use because you can better know their properties, or characteristics. Items grouped together are likely to have some properties that are similar.

Scientists also had a need to organize elements. By 1869, a total of 63 elements had been discovered. A few were gases. Two were liquids. Most were solid metals. Some reacted explosively as they formed compounds. Others reacted slowly. Scientists wondered whether the properties of elements followed a pattern. One of these scientists, Dmitri Mendeleev (men duh LAY ef), discovered a set of patterns that applies to all the elements.

**HANDS-ON LAB**

Begin investigating the organization of the periodic table.

## Literacy Connection

**Determine Central Ideas** In the text, underline a reason that you might organize your DVDs into comedies, dramas, and action movies.

**Organizing with a Purpose**
**Figure 1** Recyclable items must be sorted into groups based on the properties of their materials.

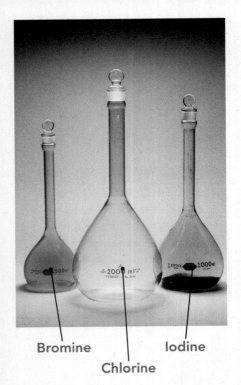

Bromine

Chlorine

Iodine

## Similar Properties

**Figure 2** At room temperature, chlorine is a gas, bromine is a liquid, and iodine is a solid. However, all three elements share some physical properties. They also have very similar chemical properties. They are grouped in the same column on the periodic table. What common property do you observe?

.............................................................

.............................................................

 **VIDEO**

Watch a video to observe patterns in daily life as they relate to the periodic table.

**Mendeleev's Work** Mendeleev knew that some elements had similar chemical and physical properties. For example, silver and copper are both shiny metals. Mendeleev thought these similarities were important clues to a hidden pattern. To find that pattern, Mendeleev noted each element's melting point, density, and color. He also included the element's atomic mass.

As you read in the previous lesson, scientists use atomic mass units (amu) to determine the mass of an element. An element's **atomic mass** is the average mass of all the isotopes of that element. Mendeleev noticed that a pattern of properties appeared when he arranged the elements in order of increasing atomic mass. He found that the pattern of the properties repeated regularly.

## The Periodic Table

The **periodic table** is a chart showing all of the elements arranged according to the repeating pattern of their properties. (The word *periodic* means "in a regular, repeated pattern.") Mendeleev created the first periodic table in 1869. He arranged his table according to each element's atomic mass. **Figure 2** shows three elements that have similar properties and were, therefore, grouped together.

In his periodic table, Mendeleev also left blank spaces. He predicted that the blank spaces would be filled by elements that had not yet been discovered. He even correctly predicted the properties of some of those new elements.

Mendeleev's table has indeed changed over time, as scientists discovered new elements and learned more about atomic structure. We now know that the number of protons in an atom's nucleus, indicated by the atomic number, is related to the chemical properties of an element. Therefore, modern periodic tables are arranged in order of increasing atomic number instead of by increasing atomic mass.

✓ **READING CHECK** **Explain** How is the modern periodic table different from Mendeleev's periodic table?

.....................................................................................

.....................................................................................

.....................................................................................

.....................................................................................

# Using the Periodic Table

The periodic table contains information about each of the known elements. It includes the name of each element, its atomic number, and its atomic mass. It also includes its **chemical symbol**. This symbol is a one- or two-letter abbreviation for the element. **Figure 3** shows the **representation** of the element phosphorus on the periodic table.

Look at the periodic table in **Figure 4** on the next two pages. Notice that the atomic numbers increase from left to right. Also notice that each color-coded region corresponds to a different class of elements—metals, nonmetals, and metalloids.

**Academic Vocabulary**
How are a symbol and a model both examples of a representation?

..............................................................

..............................................................

..............................................................

..............................................................

## Information in Each Cell

**Figure 3** 🖉 The periodic table contains one cell for each of the known elements. Each cell provides certain information about the element represented. Study the information shown for the element phosphorus. Then, using **Figure 4**, fill in the information for the element zinc on the cell shown, and label each piece of information.

**Atomic Number** One piece of information is the atomic number of the element, shown at the top of each cell. For phosphorus, that number is 15. Every phosphorus atom has 15 protons in its nucleus.

**Chemical Symbol** In the center of each cell is the chemical symbol for the element. A permanent chemical symbol contains either one or two letters. For phosphorus, that letter is "P." Chemical symbols with three letters are temporary and are used until permanent names are assigned to the elements.

**Atomic Mass** At the bottom of each cell is the average atomic mass of the element. For phosphorus, this value is 30.974 amu (atomic mass units). The atomic mass is an average because most elements consist of a mixture of isotopes.

15

P

30.974

Phosphorus

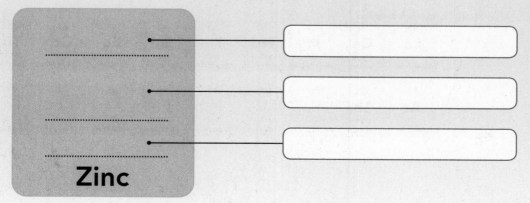

Zinc

# The Periodic Table

**Figure 4** The periodic table is one of a chemist's most valuable tools. Find the element identified by the atomic number 51 on the periodic table. Use the information to fill in the blanks below.

**Name of element** ....................................................

**Chemical symbol** ....................................................

**Atomic mass** ....................................................

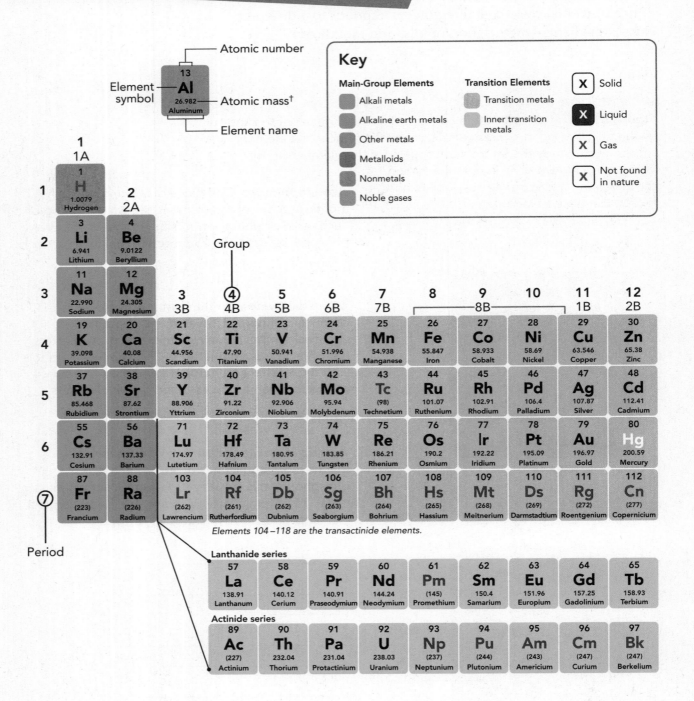

Elements 104–118 are the transactinide elements.

†*The atomic masses in parentheses are the mass numbers of the longest-lived isotope of elements for which a standard atomic mass cannot be defined.*

| | | | | | **18**<br>**8A** |
|---|---|---|---|---|---|
| | | | | | 2<br>**He**<br>4.0026<br>Helium |
| **13**<br>**3A** | **14**<br>**4A** | **15**<br>**5A** | **16**<br>**6A** | **17**<br>**7A** | |
| 5<br>**B**<br>10.81<br>Boron | 6<br>**C**<br>12.011<br>Carbon | 7<br>**N**<br>14.007<br>Nitrogen | 8<br>**O**<br>15.999<br>Oxygen | 9<br>**F**<br>18.998<br>Fluorine | 10<br>**Ne**<br>20.179<br>Neon |
| 13<br>**Al**<br>26.982<br>Aluminum | 14<br>**Si**<br>28.086<br>Silicon | 15<br>**P**<br>30.974<br>Phosphorus | 16<br>**S**<br>32.06<br>Sulfur | 17<br>**Cl**<br>35.453<br>Chlorine | 18<br>**Ar**<br>39.948<br>Argon |
| 31<br>**Ga**<br>69.72<br>Gallium | 32<br>**Ge**<br>72.59<br>Germanium | 33<br>**As**<br>74.922<br>Arsenic | 34<br>**Se**<br>78.96<br>Selenium | 35<br>**Br**<br>79.904<br>Bromine | 36<br>**Kr**<br>83.80<br>Krypton |
| 49<br>**In**<br>114.82<br>Indium | 50<br>**Sn**<br>118.69<br>Tin | 51<br>**Sb**<br>121.75<br>Antimony | 52<br>**Te**<br>127.60<br>Tellurium | 53<br>**I**<br>126.90<br>Iodine | 54<br>**Xe**<br>131.30<br>Xenon |
| 81<br>**Tl**<br>204.37<br>Thallium | 82<br>**Pb**<br>207.2<br>Lead | 83<br>**Bi**<br>208.98<br>Bismuth | 84<br>**Po**<br>(209)<br>Polonium | 85<br>**At**<br>(210)<br>Astatine | 86<br>**Rn**<br>(222)<br>Radon |
| 113<br>**Nh**<br>(284)<br>Nihonium | 114<br>**Fl**<br>(289)<br>Flerovium | 115<br>**Mc**<br>(288)<br>Moscovium | 116<br>**Lv**<br>(292)<br>Livermorium | 117<br>**Ts**<br>(294)<br>Tennessine | 118<br>**Og**<br>(294)<br>Oganesson |

| 66<br>**Dy**<br>162.50<br>Dysprosium | 67<br>**Ho**<br>164.93<br>Holmium | 68<br>**Er**<br>167.26<br>Erbium | 69<br>**Tm**<br>168.93<br>Thulium | 70<br>**Yb**<br>173.04<br>Ytterbium |
|---|---|---|---|---|
| 98<br>**Cf**<br>(251)<br>Californium | 99<br>**Es**<br>(252)<br>Einsteinium | 100<br>**Fm**<br>(257)<br>Fermium | 101<br>**Md**<br>(258)<br>Mendelevium | 102<br>**No**<br>(259)<br>Nobelium |

## Applying the Periodic Table

The order of elements on the periodic table enables scientists to predict properties about the elements. Answer these questions about the periodic table?

**1. Use Tables** What is the difference of the atomic masses of the heaviest and lightest elements in the table?

........................................................

**2. Sequence** Examine the periodic table. Which four pairs of elements would be reversed in order if the elements were listed by increasing atomic mass instead of increasing atomic number?

........................................................

........................................................

........................................................

**3. Predict** When Mendeleev developed the periodic table, the element gallium had not yet been discovered. Without looking at the periodic table on this page, examine the elements surrounding gallium in the diagram below, and predict the atomic number and atomic mass for this element. How does your prediction match the actual atomic number and atomic mass for gallium on the periodic table?

........................................................

........................................................

........................................................

| 13<br>**Al**<br>26.982<br>Aluminum | 14<br>**Si**<br>28.086<br>Silicon |
|---|---|
| 30<br>**Zn**<br>65.38<br>Zinc | *Ga*<br>Gallium | 32<br>**Ge**<br>72.59<br>Germanium |
| 48<br>**Cd**<br>112.41<br>Cadmium | 49<br>**In**<br>114.82<br>Indium | 50<br>**Sn**<br>118.69<br>Tin |

INTERACTIVITY

Explore how atomic mass and other properties of elements determine the organization of the periodic table.

# Periods in the Periodic Table

The rows in the periodic table are known as periods. Each **period** contains a series of different elements. Look at the period numbers on the left side of the periodic table in **Figure 4**. As you look from left to right across a period, you will notice that the properties of the elements change in a pattern. Metals are shown on the left of the table, and nonmetals are located on the right. Metalloids are found between the metals and nonmetals. This pattern is repeated in each period. An element's properties can be predicted by its location in the periodic table. This predictability is one reason that the periodic table is so useful to chemists.

**Lanthanides and Actinides** Under the bottom row of the main part of the periodic table, you can see two additional rows standing alone. These rows are placed off the table to save space and to make the rest of the table easier to read. Follow the line on **Figure 4** to see how these rows fit in the table.

The elements in the top row are the lanthanides. These elements are all found in nature and are sometimes called the "rare earth metals." The most commonly known element in this series is lanthanum (La), for which the series is named. Some uses for lanthanum are shown in **Figure 5**.

Under the lanthanides are the actinides. Uranium and thorium are the only two actinides that are found in significant quantities in nature. Most other actinides are not found in nature, but are made artificially in laboratories. One characteristic that all actinides have in common is that they are radioactive.

## La

### Lanthanum

**Uses of Lanthanum**
**Figure 5** 🖊 Lanthanum (La), like other lanthanides, is a soft, shiny metal. This lanthanide is a major component in batteries for hybrid cars and in permanent magnets. Label the lanthanum cell with the atomic number and atomic mass.

## Transuranium Elements

**Transuranium Elements** The elements that come after uranium (U) in the periodic table are known as transuranium elements. None of these elements is stable, and each of them decays radioactively into other elements. With the exception of small traces of neptunium and plutonium, these elements are not found in nature. They are made in a laboratory when nuclear particles are forced to crash into one another.

Scientists use particle accelerators to make atomic nuclei move at extremely high speeds. If these nuclei crash into the nuclei of other elements with enough energy, the particles can combine into a single nucleus.

In general, the higher the atomic number, the more difficult it is to synthesize new elements. So, this process has taken place only as more powerful particle accelerators have been built. Some of these newly discovered elements do not yet have permanent names or symbols. In the future, scientists around the world will agree on permanent names and symbols for these elements.

 **VIDEO**

See how art and science can come together in the work of an artist.

## Question It!

### Temporary Element Names

Until scientists assign permanent names to newly discovered elements, the elements are assigned temporary names based on their atomic number. Each digit in the atomic number is assigned the root name for that digit. Then the suffix *-ium* is added to the end of the name. For example, before element 116 got its permanent name, it was called ununhexium from the roots for the digits 1, 1, and 6, followed by the suffix *-ium*.

**Use Tables** Imagine that three new elements are discovered, and they need temporary names. Use the information in the table to name the yet-undiscovered elements with these atomic numbers. Then, write the three-letter chemical symbol for the element.

**Element 119** .................................................

**Element 120** .................................................

**Element 121** .................................................

| digit | root | symbol |
|-------|------|--------|
| 0 | nil | n |
| 1 | un | u |
| 2 | bi | b |
| 3 | tri | t |
| 4 | quad | q |
| 5 | pent | p |
| 6 | hex | h |
| 7 | sept | s |
| 8 | oct | o |
| 9 | en | e |

HANDS-ON LAB

⚗Investigate Practice arranging and classifying elements in the periodic table.

# Groups in the Periodic Table

The modern periodic table has seven periods, each of which follows a pattern. Because the pattern of properties repeats in each period, these patterns can be used to classify elements that have similar characteristics into a specific **group**, or family. There are 18 columns in the table, and so there are 18 groups.

## Groups Containing Metals
If you examine the periodic table, you can see that metals make up most of the elements. At least one metal is found in every group except Group 18. See **Figure 6** to examine some of the groups that contain metals.

### The Metal Groups

**Figure 6** ✏ The groups shaded on the periodic table below contain the alkali metals, the alkaline earth metals, and the transition metals. Next to each element's name and image, fill in its chemical symbol.

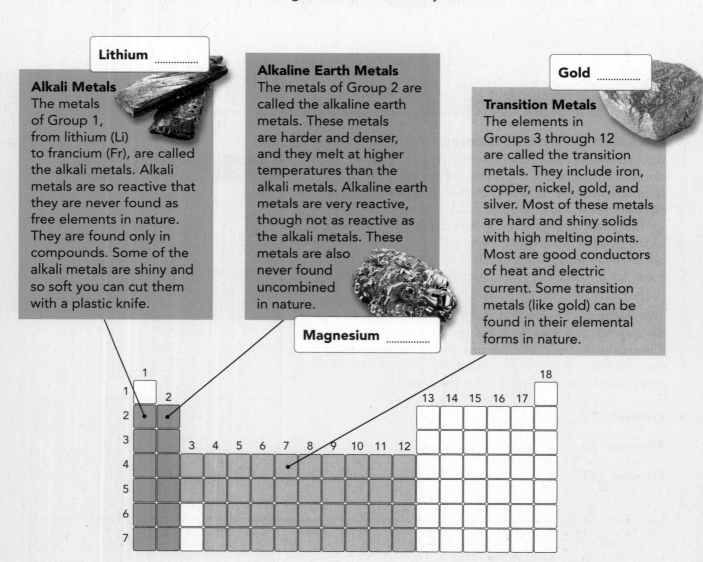

**Lithium** ...............

**Alkali Metals**
The metals of Group 1, from lithium (Li) to francium (Fr), are called the alkali metals. Alkali metals are so reactive that they are never found as free elements in nature. They are found only in compounds. Some of the alkali metals are shiny and so soft you can cut them with a plastic knife.

**Alkaline Earth Metals**
The metals of Group 2 are called the alkaline earth metals. These metals are harder and denser, and they melt at higher temperatures than the alkali metals. Alkaline earth metals are very reactive, though not as reactive as the alkali metals. These metals are also never found uncombined in nature.

**Magnesium** ...............

**Gold** ...............

**Transition Metals**
The elements in Groups 3 through 12 are called the transition metals. They include iron, copper, nickel, gold, and silver. Most of these metals are hard and shiny solids with high melting points. Most are good conductors of heat and electric current. Some transition metals (like gold) can be found in their elemental forms in nature.

## Groups Containing Metalloids and Nonmetals

Look back at the periodic table. There are nonmetals in Group 1 and in Groups 14 through 18. Examine **Figure 7**, which shows some groups that contain nonmetals (groups 13 through 16). These groups also contain metalloids, which have some properties of metals and some properties of nonmetals.

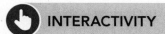
**INTERACTIVITY**

Analyze, identify, and classify elements based on their properties.

### Groups with Metalloids and Nonmetals

**Figure 7** 🖊 The groups shaded on the periodic table below contain metals, metalloids, and nonmetals. Write the chemical symbols of the representative elements next to each photo.

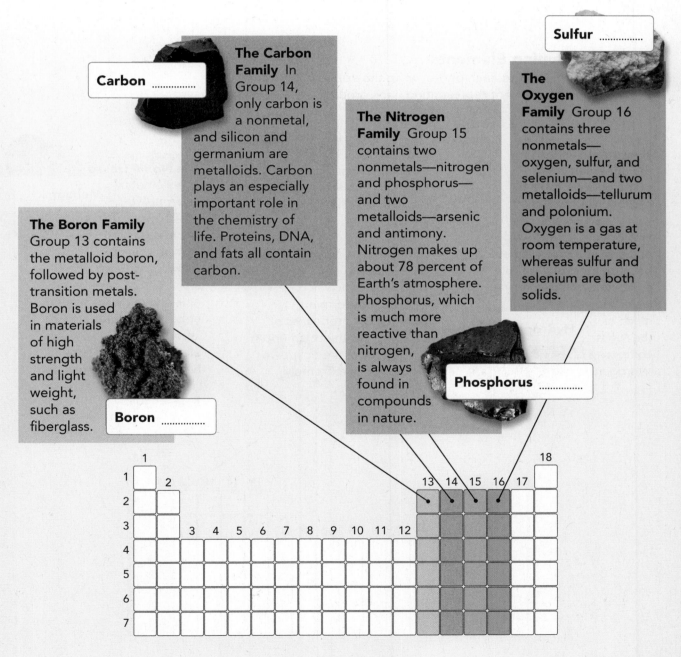

Carbon ................

**The Carbon Family** In Group 14, only carbon is a nonmetal, and silicon and germanium are metalloids. Carbon plays an especially important role in the chemistry of life. Proteins, DNA, and fats all contain carbon.

Sulfur ................

**The Oxygen Family** Group 16 contains three nonmetals—oxygen, sulfur, and selenium—and two metalloids—tellurum and polonium. Oxygen is a gas at room temperature, whereas sulfur and selenium are both solids.

**The Nitrogen Family** Group 15 contains two nonmetals—nitrogen and phosphorus—and two metalloids—arsenic and antimony. Nitrogen makes up about 78 percent of Earth's atmosphere. Phosphorus, which is much more reactive than nitrogen, is always found in compounds in nature.

**The Boron Family** Group 13 contains the metalloid boron, followed by post-transition metals. Boron is used in materials of high strength and light weight, such as fiberglass.

Boron ................

Phosphorus ................

**Reflect** How is the periodic table helpful to you? In your science notebook, describe one or two ways the periodic table might help you, and explain how.

# Halogens, Noble Gases, and Hydrogen

The shaded areas in **Figure 8** contain the halogens, the noble gases, and hydrogen. Halogens are the most reactive nonmetals, while noble gases are the least reactive nonmetals. Hydrogen is a nonmetal that does not fall into a family because its chemical properties are very different from other elements. It is the simplest element, containing only one proton and one electron.

✅ **READING CHECK** **Determine Central Ideas** What do alkali metals and alkaline earth metals have in common? How are they different?

..............................................................................................................

..............................................................................................................

..............................................................................................................

## The Remaining Elements

**Figure 8** ✏ Next to each photo, write the appropriate symbol of the element representing each group.

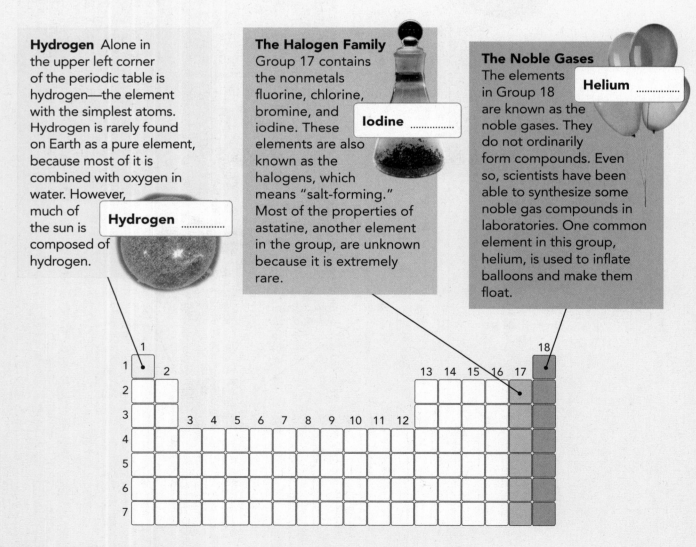

**Hydrogen** Alone in the upper left corner of the periodic table is hydrogen—the element with the simplest atoms. Hydrogen is rarely found on Earth as a pure element, because most of it is combined with oxygen in water. However, much of the sun is composed of hydrogen.

Hydrogen ..............

**The Halogen Family** Group 17 contains the nonmetals fluorine, chlorine, bromine, and iodine. These elements are also known as the halogens, which means "salt-forming." Most of the properties of astatine, another element in the group, are unknown because it is extremely rare.

Iodine ..............

**The Noble Gases** The elements in Group 18 are known as the noble gases. They do not ordinarily form compounds. Even so, scientists have been able to synthesize some noble gas compounds in laboratories. One common element in this group, helium, is used to inflate balloons and make them float.

Helium ..............

MS-PS1-1

1. **Distinguish Relationships** In addition to properties of elements, list at least two other things or events that are periodic.

.................................................................

.................................................................

.................................................................

.................................................................

.................................................................

2. **Construct Explanations** Assume that one particular atom of rhodium (Rh) has a mass of 102. Why does this number not exactly match the atomic mass of 102.91 listed on the periodic table for this element?

.................................................................

.................................................................

.................................................................

.................................................................

.................................................................

**Use Figure 4 to answer question 3.**

3. **Interpret Tables** What element is found in Group 6 and Period 4? Based on its location, is this element more similar to tungsten or to iron? Explain.

.................................................................

.................................................................

.................................................................

.................................................................

.................................................................

4. **Synthesize Information** The noble gases in Group 18 were some of the last natural elements to be discovered. Why do you think this is so?

.................................................................

.................................................................

.................................................................

.................................................................

.................................................................

.................................................................

# Quest CHECK-IN

**In this lesson, you learned how scientists use the periodic table as a tool to organize elements according to their physical and chemical properties.**

**Describe** If you were given five unknown substances and were asked to describe them by their physical properties, what would you look for? What should you **not** do while observing their physical properties?

.................................................................

.................................................................

.................................................................

.................................................................

.................................................................

## ⏺ INTERACTIVITY

Examining Physical Properties of Powders

**Go online** to learn more about the physical properties of some common elements and substances.

## Guiding Questions

- What causes atoms to bond together?
- How do valence electrons and bonding affect the properties of elements?

## Connection

**Literacy** Support Claims

MS-PS1-1

## Vocabulary

compound
valence electron
reactivity
malleable
ductile
luster
semiconductor

## Academic Vocabulary

interpretation
transfer

 **VOCABULARY APP**

Practice vocabulary on a mobile device.

**Quest CONNECTION**

Think about how you might go about discovering which elements make up an unknown substance.

## Connect It!

✏ **Circle the part of the image that shows the reactivity of hydrogen.**

**Predict** Use the periodic table to predict why krypton, another noble gas, is not used in airships.

..................................................................................................................................

..................................................................................................................................

**Infer** How would the results of the spark have been different if the Hindenburg had been filled with helium?

..................................................................................................................................

..................................................................................................................................

# Elements and the Periodic Table

Scientists might find it helpful to have elements organized in the periodic table, but is this helpful in everyday life? Does it really matter, for example, that the reactivity of elements changes in a predictable pattern across a period?

In **Figure 1,** you see the explosion of the airship known as the Hindenburg. On May 6, 1937, this hydrogen-filled airship left Frankfurt, Germany, on a flight to Lakehurst, New Jersey. As the Hindenburg attempted to land, a spark came into contact with the hydrogen used to fill the airship, causing an instantaneous explosion that killed 36 people.

Hydrogen is located in Group 1 of the periodic table. All of the elements in this group are very reactive, so hydrogen readily reacts with other elements. If hydrogen is so reactive, why was it used in the airship in the first place? The periodic table also tells you that hydrogen is the lightest element, and so the airship easily rose into the air when filled with this gas.

Is there another gas that would have been better? The next-lightest element is helium, a noble gas. Noble gases are in Group 18, and they are not reactive. Airships today, therefore, are filled with helium, with much safer results.

## Literacy Connection

**Support Claims** This page provides an example of how information from the periodic table is helpful in everyday life. Highlight the evidence that supports this claim.

## The Hindenburg Disaster

**Figure 1** Because of the explosion of the Hindenburg in 1937, manufacturers stopped making hydrogen-filled airships.

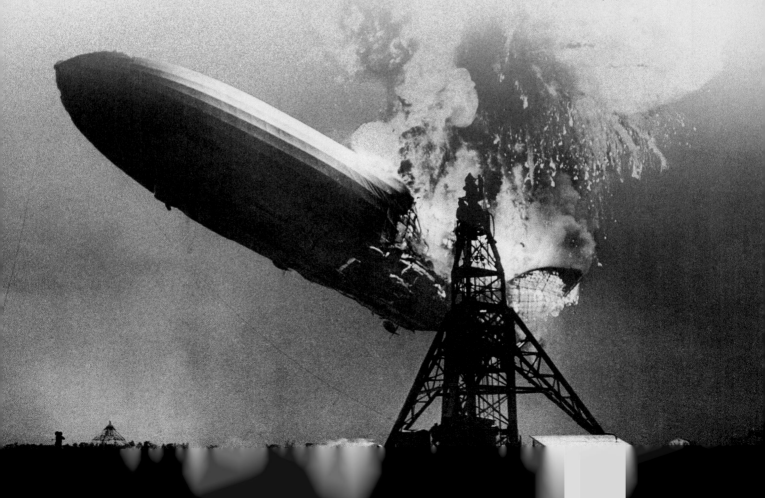

▶ **VIDEO**

Watch a video showing how you can use electron dot diagrams to model an atom.

# Bonding

Most things you see in the world around you are not made up of individual elements. They are made from **compounds**, or substances that form when atoms from two or more elements bond together. To understand how bonding works, you must first learn about valence electrons and the role they play in the bonding process.

**Valence Electrons** The electrons of an atom are found in different energy levels. The first energy level is the closest to the nucleus. It can hold a maximum of two electrons. The second energy level can hold up to 8 electrons. Larger atoms have even more energy levels that can hold different numbers of electrons. Electrons in higher energy levels have higher amounts of energy. The **valence electrons** of an atom are those electrons that have the highest energy. They are in the outermost energy level.

Each atom has a certain number of valence electrons. The number of valence electrons is specific to each element. An atom may have from one to eight valence electrons, depending on the element. One way to show the number of valence electrons in an element is to draw the electrons in an atom, as shown in **Figure 2**. This Bohr-model diagram shows the arrangement of electrons for a magnesium atom. The electrons in the outermost energy level are the valence electrons.

**Electron Dot Diagrams** Another way to show the number of valence electrons in an element is by drawing an electron dot diagram. An electron dot diagram includes the symbol for the element surrounded by dots, as shown in **Figure 3**. The top, bottom, left, and right parts of the diagram can each hold up to two dots. Each dot stands for one valence electron.

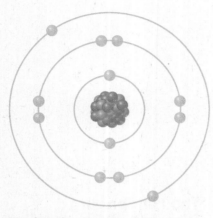

**Magnesium Atom**

**Figure 2** How many valence electrons does a magnesium atom have?

....................

**Electron Dot Diagrams**

**Figure 3** 🖊 The electrons in the outermost energy levels of these atoms are the valence electrons. The electron dot diagrams are drawn for hydrogen and oxygen. Draw electron dot diagrams for nitrogen and carbon.

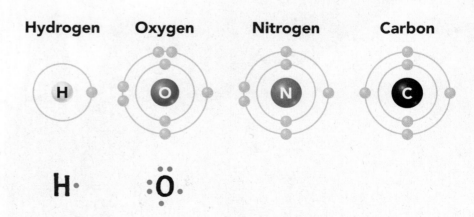

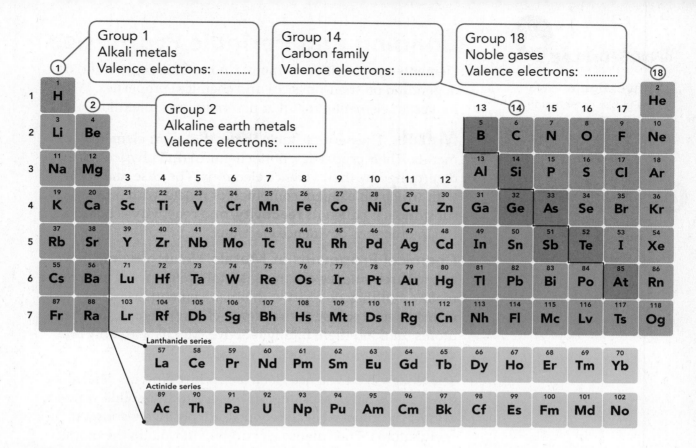

Group 1
Alkali metals
Valence electrons: ...........

Group 14
Carbon family
Valence electrons: ...........

Group 18
Noble gases
Valence electrons: ...........

Group 2
Alkaline earth metals
Valence electrons: ...........

Lanthanide series

Actinide series

**Valence Electrons and the Table** How do valence electrons relate to the periodic table? The periodic table is shown in **Figure 4**. An **interpretation** of the table gives you information about the valence electrons in atoms.

The elements are organized by increasing atomic number. Therefore, the number of valence electrons increases from left to right across each period. Each period begins with an element that has one valence electron and ends with an element that has eight electrons (except for Period 1, since helium has only two valence electrons). For Periods 2 and 3, Group 1 elements have one, Group 2 elements have two, Group 13 elements have three, Group 14 elements have four, and so on to Group 18, which has eight valence electrons.

Now, if you ignore helium and Groups 3 through 12, you may notice a pattern among the other groups. The elements within a group have the same number of valence electrons. As a result, the elements in each group have similar properties. Groups 3 through 12 follow a different pattern and are more difficult to predict.

✔**READING CHECK** **Support Claims** Choose an atom from Period 2 or 3. Do not choose an atom used in **Figure 3**. How many valence electrons does that atom have? Support your claim.

......................................................................................................

......................................................................................................

**Valence Electrons**

**Figure 4** 🖊 The number of valence electrons increases from left to right across a period. Fill in the number of valence electrons for each group circled in this periodic table. (note that helium is an exception)

**Academic Vocabulary**

Suppose someone gave you a picture of an electron dot diagram. What would be included in your interpretation of the diagram?

......................................................

......................................................

......................................................

......................................................

......................................................

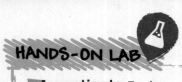

 **HANDS-ON LAB**

**Investigate** Explore how to use combustion levels to classify compounds.

**VIRTUAL LAB**

Analyze the properties of different elements in a virtual lab.

# Bonding and Periodic Properties

Elements are classified as metals, nonmetals, or metalloids, depending on their physical and chemical properties. What makes an element a metal, a nonmetal, or a metalloid?

**Metals** The periodic table shows that most elements are metals. Their properties, both chemical and physical, are determined by their valence electrons. The ease and speed with which an element combines, or reacts, with other substances is called its **reactivity**, and reactivity is based on the interactions of valence electrons.

**Chemical Properties of Metals** Metals generally have one to three valence electrons. Metals do not react with other metals, but they do react with other elements. Many of these elements tend to lose their valence electrons easily to other atoms, making them highly reactive. Metals with only one valence electron are especially reactive.

The loosely-held valence electrons in metal atoms determine how metals bond. Most metals are crystalline solids. A metal crystal is composed of closely-packed, positively-charged metal atoms. The valence electrons drift among the atoms. Each metal atom is held in the crystal by a metallic bond—an attraction between a positive metal atom and the electrons surrounding it. The activity below shows the metallic bonds that hold aluminum foil together.

# Question It!

**Metallic Bonding**
The positively-charged metal atoms are embedded in a "sea" of valence electrons. Aluminum atoms have three valence electrons.

Draw Conclusions How do you think the reactivity of aluminum compares to the reactivity of other metals?

...................................................................................
...................................................................................
...................................................................................
...................................................................................

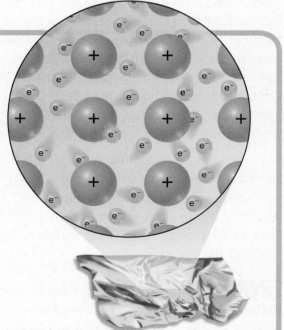

**Physical Properties of Metals** The physical properties of metals include malleability, ductility, and conductivity. A **malleable** material is one that can be hammered or rolled into flat sheets or other shapes. A **ductile** material is one that can be pulled out, or drawn, into long wires. The easy movement of valence electrons in metals is what makes metals malleable and ductile.

The movement of valence electrons also makes most metals good thermal and electrical conductors. Thermal conductivity is the ability of an object to **transfer** heat. Electrical conductivity is the ability of an object to carry electric current. You can see many of these physical properties of metals in **Figure 5**.

Other physical properties of metals include luster, low specific heat, high density, and solid state at room temperature. A material that has a high **luster** is shiny and reflective. Specific heat is the amount of energy required to raise the temperature of 1 gram of a material by 1 degree Celsius. Metals with low specific heats require only a small amount of heat energy to raise their temperatures. Most metals are solids at room temperature. Mercury is a metal that is liquid at room temperature. A few metals also share the property of magnetism. Iron, cobalt, and nickel are all magnetic metals.

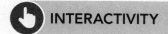

**INTERACTIVITY**

Learn more about the role of valence electrons in creating bonds between atoms.

**Academic Vocabulary**

Provide two examples of when you transferred something.

......................................

......................................

......................................

......................................

......................................

**Physical Properties of Metals**
**Figure 5** Metals have certain physical properties. Identify the property or properties of metals exhibited by each of the objects shown here.

Gold can be hammered into thin sheets known as gold leaf.

**Physical Properties**

......................................

......................................

Copper is sometimes used in electrical wiring.

**Physical Properties**

......................................

......................................

This item is made out of **iron**.

**Physical Properties**

......................................

......................................

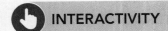

**INTERACTIVITY**

Explore electron sharing, crystal structures, and the conductive properties of elements.

**Nonmetals** Nonmetals have a much wider variety of properties than metals. Nonmetals have several properties in common.

**Chemical Properties** You know that atoms of metals do not react with atoms of other metals. Atoms of nonmetals, however, react with both metals and other nonmetals. For example, the metal sodium and the nonmetal chlorine react to form table salt (NaCl). The nonmetals nitrogen and oxygen react to form several different compounds. Some nonmetals form DNA, as shown in **Figure 6**.

While many compounds that contain nonmetals are essential to life, some nonmetals, such as the halogens, are poisonous and highly reactive. Still others, such as the noble gases, are nonreactive. These levels of reactivity, as with metals, are based on the number of valence electrons in the atoms of the elements.

**Physical Properties** A nonmetal is an element that lacks most of the properties of a metal. In general, nonmetals are poor conductors of electric current and heat. Solid nonmetals tend to be dull and brittle. If you were to hit most solid nonmetals with a hammer, they would break or crumble into a powder. Also, nonmetals usually have lower densities than metals.

Many nonmetals are gases at room temperature. The air you breathe contains mostly nitrogen and oxygen. Some nonmetal elements, such as carbon, sulfur, and iodine, are solids at room temperature. Bromine is the only nonmetal that is a liquid at room temperature.

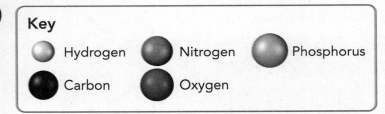

**Key**

○ Hydrogen    ● Nitrogen    ● Phosphorus

● Carbon    ● Oxygen

**DNA**

**Figure 6** DNA, which is made up of atoms of nonmetals, is essential to life. List at least two other substances essential to life that contain nonmetals.

.........................................................................

.........................................................................

## Metalloids

**Figure 7** 🖊 The metalloids are located along a stair-step line between the metals and the nonmetals on the periodic table. Referring to the periodic table as needed, draw the stair-step line on this table. Then, write the symbol for each metalloid in the correct location on this table.

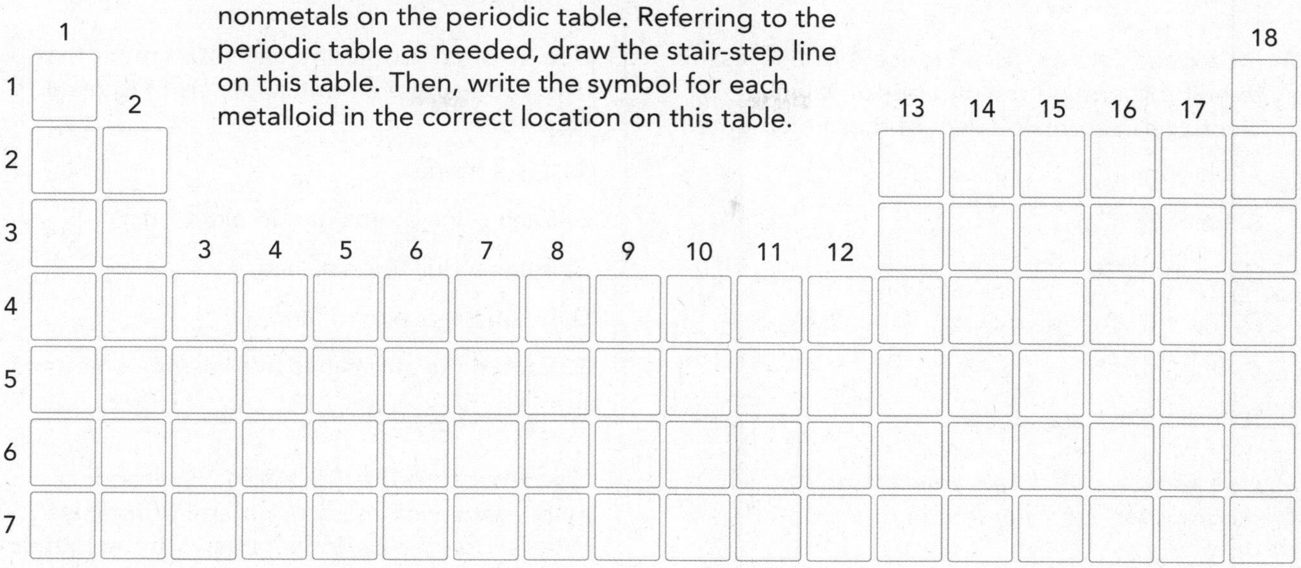

## Metalloids

The metalloids have some properties of metals and some properties of nonmetals. All metalloids are solids at room temperature. Metalloids are also brittle, hard, and somewhat reactive.

The most common metalloid is silicon (Si). Ordinary sand, which is a compound of silicon and oxygen, is the main component of glass. A compound of boron (B) and oxygen is added during the process of glassmaking to make heat-resistant glass.

A metalloid's most useful property is its ability to conduct electric current. The conductivity of a metalloid varies depending on temperature, exposure to light, or the presence of impurities. For this reason, metalloids such as silicon and germanium (Ge) are used to make semiconductors. A **semiconductor** is a substance that can conduct electric current under some conditions but not under other conditions. Semiconductors are used to make computer chips, transistors, and lasers. Semiconductors are also used in solar cells, such as the ones shown in **Figure 8**.

✔️READING CHECK **Infer** From the meaning of *semiconductor*, what does the prefix *semi-* mean?

...................................................................

...................................................................

### Planet Solar

**Figure 8** Planet Solar is the world's largest solar-powered boat. The solar panels on its deck contain silicon, which is a metalloid. List at least four properties of silicon and other metalloids.

...................................................................
...................................................................
...................................................................
...................................................................

1. **Interpret Tables** Use **Figure 4** of this lesson to help determine the number of valence electrons in atoms of each of these elements.

   A. chlorine (Cl) ........................

   B. calcium (Ca) ........................

   C. cesium (Cs) ........................

   D. neon (Ne) ........................

   E. tin (Sn) ........................

   F. indium (In) ........................

2. **Use Models** ✏ Draw an electron dot diagram for each element in question 1.

3. **Use Tables** Underline each statement that is true about the element sulfur. Use **Figure 4** to help you.

   A. It is a metal.

   B. Each of its atoms has 16 electrons.

   C. It has a dull appearance.

   D. It conducts electricity.

   E. Each of its atoms has five valence electrons.

   F. Its electron dot diagram has six dots.

4. **Construct an Explanation** Hydrogen is a nonmetal with many nonmetal properties. Why is it on the periodic table with the metals in Group 1?

   ............................................................
   ............................................................
   ............................................................
   ............................................................
   ............................................................
   ............................................................

# Quest CHECK-IN

In this lesson, you learned more about the physical and chemical properties of elements. You also learned more about how elements are sorted and grouped according to these properties.

**Analyze** How might you go about testing an unknown substance to determine its chemical properties?

............................................................
............................................................
............................................................
............................................................
............................................................

## INTERACTIVITY

The Iodine Test for Starch

**Go online** to learn more about how the elements in common substances react to exposure to various other elements and solutions.

# WHEN PARTICLES Collide

▶ **VIDEO**

Watch this video to find out more about the Large Hadron Collider.

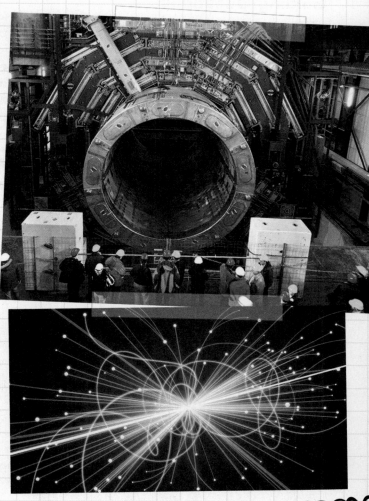

## The Large Hadron Collider,

or LHC, is the world's most powerful particle accelerator. It is named for the hadron, one of the subatomic particles that are the building blocks of atoms.

## The Challenge: To learn about the particles that make up an atom.

**Phenomenon** What is a particle accelerator? It is a machine that sends particles traveling faster and faster until they reach nearly the speed of light! Electrical fields provide the acceleration. Magnetic fields force the moving particles along a certain path. Scientists observe the accelerating particles to learn more about their nature. Two particles can be accelerated toward each other, and the high energy of their collision sometimes produces new particles!

The LHC is like a circular race track for particles, and it measures 27 kilometers around. It is located in an underground tunnel in Europe. The LHC has helped physicists to learn about the transuranium elements—those elements beyond uranium on the periodic table. These elements are very unstable, and some can exist only in a lab setting. Physicists also have detected a subatomic particle called the Higgs boson. Many believe that the Higgs boson may be responsible for giving matter its mass.

Scientists hope that future experiments using the LHC will help to answer questions about the universe and the matter within it.

## DESIGN CHALLENGE

Can you build a model of a particle accelerator? Go to the Engineering Design Notebook to find out!

# LESSON

# (4) Types of Bonds

## Guiding Questions

- How are electrons involved in bond formation?
- What types of bonds form between atoms?
- How do bonds determine certain properties of compounds?

## Connections

Literacy  Make Generalizations

Math  Construct Graphs

MS-PS1-1

## Vocabulary

ion
polyatomic ion
ionic bond
covalent bond
molecule
nonpolar bond
polar bond

## Academic Vocabulary

component

 **VOCABULARY APP**

Practice vocabulary on a mobile device.

### Quest CONNECTION

Why might an unknown substance react differently to vinegar than it does to water? How do you know?

## Connect It !

🖊 **Cyanoacrylate is a glue that can help reveal fingerprints. Read the figure caption, and underline the type of change that occurs for the cyanoacrylate compound to form.**

Compare and Contrast  How does cyanoacrylate compare to the elements that make it up?

......................................................................................................

......................................................................................................

# Bonding and Compounds

What do the elements carbon, hydrogen, oxygen, and nitrogen have in common? They are all nonmetals. And each element is a **component** of cyanoacrylate, a strong glue that is used to bind objects together, to connect skin after surgery, and to reveal fingerprints to help solve a crime.

**Figure 1** shows fingerprints resulting from cyanoacrylate fuming. Investigators place the object containing the fingerprints into fumes of cyanoacrylate. The fumes stick to the ridges of the fingerprints and make them visible. This method of fingerprinting is most often used when fingerprints are too faint to see or when the fingerprints need to be preserved.

How do carbon, hydrogen, oxygen, and nitrogen interact to make this new substance? You know that each of these elements has the chemical property of reactivity. You also know that the reactivity of each element is based on its valence electrons. In this lesson, you will explore how compounds are formed from different types of bonding and the role valence electrons play in this process.

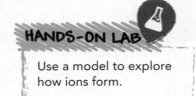

## HANDS-ON LAB

Use a model to explore how ions form.

## Academic Vocabulary

What might be some components of an electronic system?

..........................................................

..........................................................

..........................................................

..........................................................

### Cyanoacrylate

**Figure 1** The elements that make up cyanoacrylate undergo chemical changes to form the compound.

**Write About It** In your science notebook, write about a situation in life that models ionic bonding.

### Common Ions

**Figure 2** This table lists several common ions. The correct representation of an ion includes both its symbol and its charge.

| Common Ions and Their Charges | | |
|---|---|---|
| **Name** | **Charge** | **Symbol or Formula** |
| Sodium | 1+ | $Na^+$ |
| Potassium | 1+ | $K^+$ |
| Ammonium | 1+ | $NH_4^+$ |
| Calcium | 2+ | $Ca^{2+}$ |
| Magnesium | 2+ | $Mg^{2+}$ |
| Aluminum | 3+ | $Al^{3+}$ |
| Fluoride | 1– | $F^-$ |
| Chloride | 1– | $Cl^-$ |
| Iodide | 1– | $I^-$ |
| Oxide | 2– | $O^{2-}$ |

# Ionic Bonding

Ionic bonding is one way elements form compounds. Ionic bonding involves the attraction between ions of opposite charge.

**Ions** An **ion** is an atom or group of atoms that has either a positive or negative charge. When a neutral atom loses a valence electron, it loses a negative charge. It becomes a positive ion. When a neutral atom gains an electron, it gains a negative charge. It becomes a negative ion.

An atom is stable when its outermost energy level is filled with electrons. Metal atoms have few valence electrons. They are likely to lose those electrons, so that the next energy level becomes the outermost one. That level is already full of electrons. A potassium (K) atom easily loses its one valence electron to become more stable. Nonmetal atoms are likely to gain electrons. These atoms gain enough electrons so that they have eight valence electrons. A fluorine (F) atom gains one electron to achieve a stable arrangement of eight valence electrons.

**Common Ions** **Figure 2** lists the names of some common ions. Notice that some ions are made of several atoms. The ammonium ion is made of 1 nitrogen atom and 4 hydrogen atoms. An ion made of more than 1 atom is called a **polyatomic ion**. The prefix *poly-* means "many," so *polyatomic* means "many atoms." Like other ions, polyatomic ions have an overall positive or negative charge.

## Model It!

### How Ions Form

**Figure 3** An atom that loses one of its electrons becomes a positively charged ion. The atom that gains the electron becomes a negatively charged ion.

**Develop Models** Examine the diagram that shows how potassium (K) and fluorine (F) become ions. Then, complete the electron dot diagrams for the ionization of calcium (Ca) and oxygen (O).

**Example**

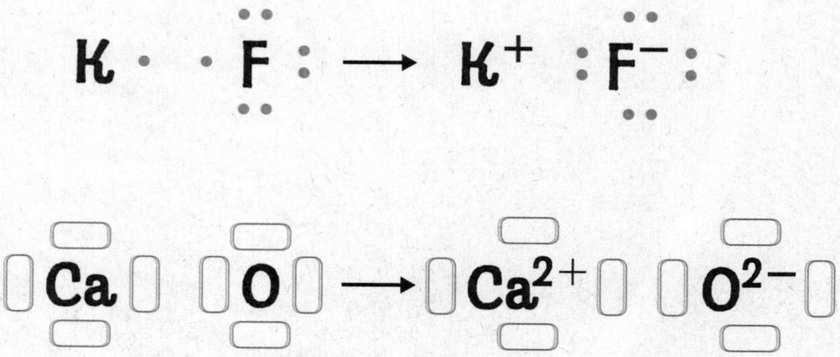

## Forming Ionic Bonds
When atoms that easily lose electrons react with atoms that easily gain electrons, they transfer valence electrons to form an **ionic bond.** The transfer gives each type of atom a more stable arrangement of electrons. Look at **Figure 4** to see how sodium atoms and chlorine atoms react to form sodium chloride (table salt).

**INTERACTIVITY**

Explore how to build ionic compounds by matching ionic charges.

### Formation of an Ionic Bond
**Figure 4** ✏ Follow the steps to see how an ionic bond forms between a sodium atom and a chlorine atom. Complete the electron dot diagrams for the sodium and chlorine atoms and their ions.

☑ **READING CHECK** **Make Generalizations** Look at **Figure 4**. Write a statement that shows how the charge on an ion relates to the number of electrons transferred.

........................................................................................................

........................................................................................................

**①** The sodium atom has one valence electron. The chlorine atom has seven valence electrons.

Sodium metal    Chlorine gas

**②** The valence electron of the sodium atom is transferred to the chlorine atom. Both atoms become ions. The sodium atom becomes a positive ion ($Na^+$). The chlorine atom becomes a negative ion ($Cl^-$).

Sodium ion    Chloride ion

**③** Particles with opposite charges attract, so the positive Na+ ion and the negative Cl− ion attract, forming an ionic bond. The resulting compound is called an ionic compound. It is made up of positive and negative ions. In an ionic compound, the total positive charge of all the positive ions equals the total negative charge of all the negative ions.

## Sharing Electrons

**Figure 5** ✏ By sharing two electrons in a covalent bond, each bromine atom gains a stable set of eight valence electrons. Circle the shared electrons that form a covalent bond between the two bromine atoms.

Bromine atom    Bromine atom

Bromine molecule

# Covalent Bonding

Just as bonds can form when two atoms transfer electrons, atoms can form a bond by sharing electrons. The chemical bond formed when two atoms share electrons is called a **covalent bond**. While ionic bonds usually form when a metal combines with a nonmetal, covalent bonds usually form between nonmetal atoms.

**Electron Sharing** Nonmetals can bond with other non-metals by sharing electrons. Sometimes, this sharing occurs between two atoms of the same element. **Figure 5** shows what happens when two bromine atoms share a pair of electrons. By sharing electrons, each bromine atom is surrounded by eight valence electrons. The attractions between the shared electrons and the protons in the nucleus of each atom hold the atoms together in a covalent bond. The two bonded bromine atoms form a molecule. A **molecule** is a neutral group of atoms joined by covalent bonds.

**Number of Bonds** Look at the electron dot diagrams in **Figure 6**. The diagram on the left shows the formation of a hydrogen sulfide molecule. Count the valence electrons around each hydrogen and sulfur atom. Hydrogen has one valence electron. Sulfur has six valence electrons. In a hydrogen sulfide molecule, sulfur forms one covalent bond with each of two hydrogen atoms. As a result, the sulfur atom has a stable arrangement of eight valence electrons. Each hydrogen atom forms one bond because it needs only two electrons to be stable.

## Covalent Bonds

**Figure 6** Atoms can form single, double, and triple covalent bonds by sharing one or more pairs of electrons. What type of covalent bond forms between two nitrogen atoms?

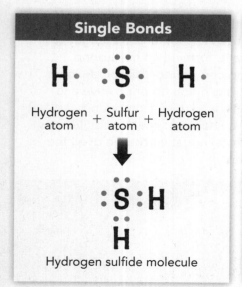

**Single Bonds**

Hydrogen atom + Sulfur atom + Hydrogen atom

Hydrogen sulfide molecule

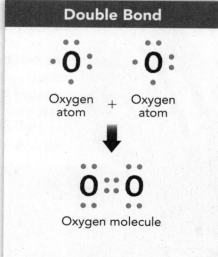

**Double Bond**

Oxygen atom + Oxygen atom

Oxygen molecule

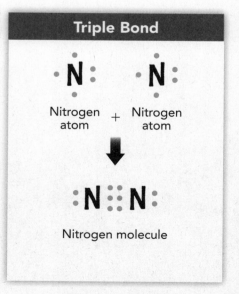

**Triple Bond**

Nitrogen atom + Nitrogen atom

Nitrogen molecule

Look at the electron dot diagram of the oxygen molecule (O₂) in **Figure 6**. This time the atoms share two pairs of electrons, forming a double bond. Atoms of some elements, such as nitrogen, share three pairs of electrons, forming a triple bond. The electron dot diagram for the nitrogen molecule (N₂) is also shown in the figure.

## Polarity

Have you ever played tug-of-war? If you have, you know that when one team pulls the rope with more force than the other team, the rope moves toward the side of the stronger team. The same is true of electrons in a covalent bond. Atoms of some elements pull more strongly on the shared electrons of a covalent bond than do atoms of other elements. As a result, the electrons are shared unequally. Unequal sharing of electrons causes covalently bonded atoms to have slight electric charges on different parts of the molecule. The overall molecule still has no charge.

If two atoms pull equally on the electrons, neither atom becomes charged. This happens when identical atoms are bonded. A covalent bond in which electrons are shared equally is a **nonpolar bond**. The iodine molecule (I₂) shown in **Figure 7** has a nonpolar bond.

When electrons in a covalent bond are shared unequally, the atom with the stronger pull gains a slightly negative charge. The atom with the weaker pull gains a slightly positive charge. A covalent bond in which electrons are shared unequally is a **polar bond**. Hydrogen chloride (HCl), also shown in **Figure 7**, has a polar bond.

## Nonpolar and Polar Bonds

**Figure 7** Just as the dogs equal in size exert equal forces on their toy (left), identical atoms exert equal forces on shared electrons, forming a nonpolar bond. Likewise, dogs of unequal size exert unequal forces on their toy (right), modeling what happens in a polar bond.

**Nonpolar Bond**

Iodine molecule

**Polar Bond**

Hydrogen chloride molecule

43

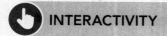
**INTERACTIVITY**

Use the properties of matter to distinguish an ionic substance from a covalent one.

## Polar Bonds in Molecules

Have you ever rubbed a balloon against your head, causing your hair to stand up? Positive and negative electrons in your hair and the balloon cause this phenomenon. Opposite charges attract each other, and charges that are the same repel each other.

A molecule is polar if it has a positively charged end and a negatively charged end. However, not all molecules containing polar bonds are polar overall. In a carbon dioxide molecule ($CO_2$), the oxygen atoms attract electrons more strongly than the carbon atom does. The bonds between the oxygen and carbon atoms are polar. But, as you can see in **Figure 8**, the two oxygen atoms pull with equal strength in opposite directions. The attractions cancel out, so the molecule is nonpolar.

A water molecule ($H_2O$), with its two polar bonds, is itself polar. In **Figure 8**, you can see that the two hydrogen atoms are at one end of the molecule, and the oxygen atom is at the other end. The oxygen atom attracts electrons more strongly than do the hydrogen atoms. As a result, the end of the molecule with the oxygen atom has a slight negative charge. The end of the molecule with the hydrogen atoms has a slight positive charge.

**READING CHECK** **Explain** Why can a molecule containing polar bonds be nonpolar overall?

.....................................................................................................

.....................................................................................................

.....................................................................................................

## Nonpolar and Polar Molecules
### Figure 8

**Part A** ✏ Both carbon dioxide and water molecules contain polar bonds. However, only water is a polar molecule. Draw a positive (+) sign next to the atoms that gain a slight positive charge. Draw a negative (–) sign next to the atoms that gain a slight negative charge.

**Part B** If a balloon is rubbed on your hair, it gains electrons and becomes negatively charged. When these charges come close to a stream of water, the stream of water bends. Use what you know about polar molecules to explain why the bending occurs.

.....................................................................................................

.....................................................................................................

.....................................................................................................

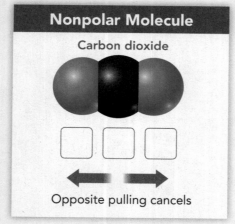

**Nonpolar Molecule**
Carbon dioxide
Opposite pulling cancels

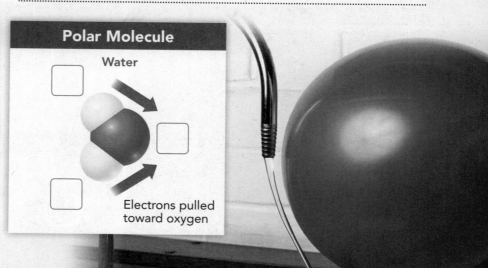

**Polar Molecule**
Water
Electrons pulled toward oxygen

## Quicklime

**Figure 9** The ions in ionic compounds are arranged in specific three-dimensional shapes called crystals. Some crystals have a cubic shape, like these crystals of quicklime, or calcium oxide.

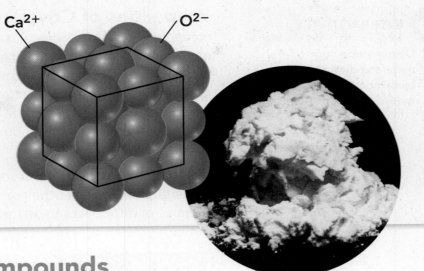

$Ca^{2+}$      $O^{2-}$

# Properties of Compounds

When bonding occurs, the resulting compounds have properties that are different from their component elements. Properties of ionic compounds differ from those of covalent compounds.

## Properties of Ionic Compounds

What are the properties of the ionic compounds that form when metals and nonmetals react? In general, ionic compounds form hard, brittle crystals that have high melting points. They conduct electric current when dissolved in water or melted.

**Ionic Crystals** Ionic compounds form solids by building up repeating patterns of ions. **Figure 9** shows a chunk of quicklime, which is how calcium oxide occurs naturally. Equal numbers of $Ca^{2+}$ and $O^{2-}$ ions in quicklime are attracted in an alternating pattern, as shown in the diagram. The ions form an orderly, three-dimensional arrangement called a crystal. Every ion in an ionic compound is attracted to ions of an opposite charge that surround it. The pattern formed by the ions is the same no matter what the size of the crystal.

**High Melting Points** The ions in the crystal have to break apart for an ionic compound to melt. It takes a huge amount of energy to separate the ions in a crystal because the attraction between the positive and negative ions is so great. As a result, many ionic compounds have very high melting points. For example, the melting point of calcium oxide is 2,613°C.

**Electrical Conductivity** Electric current involves the flow of charged particles. When ionic crystals dissolve in water or melt, the ions are free to move about, and the solution can conduct current. In contrast, ionic compounds in solid form do not conduct current well. The ions in a solid crystal are tightly bound to each other and cannot move from place to place. If charged particles cannot move, there is no current.

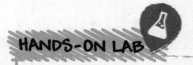

**HANDS-ON LAB**

**Investigate** Identify compounds as molecular or ionic, based on melting points.

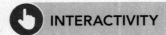
**INTERACTIVITY**

Demonstrate your understanding of bonding by categorizing and modeling various bonds.

## Properties of Covalent Compounds

Covalent compounds exist as molecules. Because of this, they are known as molecular compounds. Because bonds do not have to be broken for molecular compounds to melt, their melting points are relatively low. Have you ever noticed that some wires are covered in plastic or rubber insulation? These materials are made up of molecular compounds, which do not conduct heat or electricity.

Molecular compounds differ somewhat in their properties depending on whether they are polar or nonpolar. This is because of differences in attractions between their molecules.

☑ READING CHECK **Interpret Data** A compound has a melting point of 812°C. What type of bonding is in the compound?

........................................................................................................

# Math Toolbox

## Molecular and Ionic Properties

The table shows the melting and boiling points of a few molecular compounds and ionic compounds.

1. **Construct Graphs** ✏ Complete the bar graph below by drawing five bars showing the melting points of the compounds in the table. Arrange the bars in order of increasing melting point. Label each bar with the chemical formula of the compound.

| Substance | Formula | Melting Point (°C) | Boiling Point (°C) |
|---|---|---|---|
| Calcium chloride | $CaCl_2$ | 782 | 1,670 |
| Isopropyl alcohol | $C_3H_8O$ | −88.5 | 82.5 |
| Octane | $C_8H_{18}$ | −56.8 | 125.6 |
| Sodium chloride | $NaCl$ | 800.7 | 1,465 |
| Water | $H_2O$ | 0 | 100 |

2. **Interpret Data** ✏ Circle the correct answer: Ammonia ($NH_3$) has a melting point of −78°C and a boiling point of −34°C. These data suggest that ammonia is a(n) (molecular/ionic) compound.

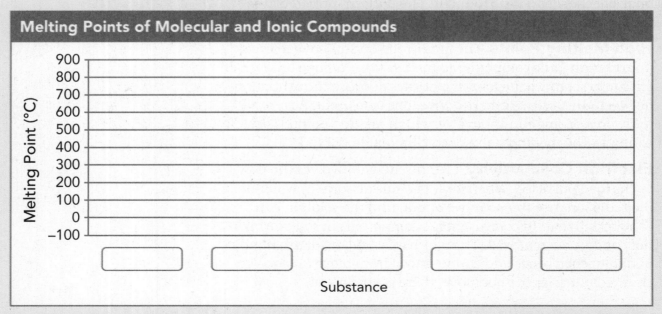

**Melting Points of Molecular and Ionic Compounds**

Melting Point (°C)

900
800
700
600
500
400
300
200
100
0
−100

Substance

**1. Construct Explanations** Why are some ions known as polyatomic ions?

........................................................

........................................................

**2. Integrate Information** In terms of valence electrons, explain the difference between an ionic bond and a covalent bond.

........................................................

........................................................

........................................................

........................................................

**3. Develop Models** 🖊 Draw an electron dot diagram to illustrate why noble gases are unreactive and do not in general form compounds. Use any noble gas except helium as your example.

**4. Explain Phenomena** Explain why it is important to life on Earth that water is a polar molecule rather than a nonpolar molecule.

........................................................

........................................................

........................................................

........................................................

**5. Use Tables** 🖊 Use the periodic table to determine the number of valence electrons in hydrogen (H) and in iodine (I). Then, draw an electron dot diagram showing the polar covalent bond that they form.

# 𝒬𝓊ℯ𝓈𝓉 CHECK-IN

**In this lesson, you learned about how different types of bonds determine certain properties of compounds. You also learned how processes such as melting or boiling affect a compound's properties.**

When a substance is heated, what causes its properties to change? What is one possible outcome of this process?

........................................................

........................................................

........................................................

........................................................

........................................................

## 👆 INTERACTIVITY

The Vinegar Test

**Go online** to learn more about how applying different forces, such as heat or extreme cold, can cause a substance to change.

# (5) Acids and Bases

## Guiding Questions

• What properties describe acids and bases?

• What happens when acids and bases interact?

## Connection

**Literacy** Evaluate Reasoning

MS-PS1-1

## Vocabulary

acid
corrosive
indicator
base
neutralization
salt

## Academic Vocabulary

process

 **VOCABULARY APP**

Practice vocabulary on a mobile device.

### Quest CONNECTION

Consider how you can use the properties of acids and bases to help identify unknown substances.

## Connect It !

✏ **Circle the part of the bog that you think is most acidic. Write a sentence to justify your response.**

.......................................................................................................

.......................................................................................................

.......................................................................................................

**Hypothesize** Why do bog acids react differently with the bones of the bodies than they do with the organs, hair, and skin?

.......................................................................................................

.......................................................................................................

.......................................................................................................

**Compare and Contrast** How are pickles similar to bog bodies?

.......................................................................................................

# Acids

Peat bogs exist in many locations worldwide. A peat bog is a wetland in which dead plant material, known as peat, accumulates. As the dead plant material decomposes, acids form. An **acid** is a compound that reacts with metals and carbonates, tastes sour, and turns blue litmus paper red. Almost all acids contain the element hydrogen as a positively-charged ion of a single hydrogen atom.

The photograph in **Figure 1** shows a bog body. Bog bodies are the remains of human bodies that have been preserved in the highly acidic conditions of peat bogs. The oldest discovered bog body is thousands of years old. Most of these bog bodies have been found in bogs in cold climates, such as northern Europe.

How do conditions in bogs preserve human bodies? They naturally pickle the bodies. The lack of oxygen in the water and the cold temperatures of regions such as northern Europe cause the acids to saturate body tissues before they decay. As a result, the organs, hair, and skin are all preserved. The acids dissolve the bones of the bog bodies, but details such as fingerprints and tattoos are still visible on some of the bodies. And to think, the bog acids that preserved the body in the photo are about the same strength as the vinegar found in most kitchens!

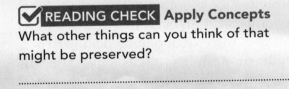

**READING CHECK** Apply Concepts
What other things can you think of that might be preserved?

........................................................................

........................................................................

## Literacy Connection

**Evaluate Reasoning**
As you read this page, underline the ways in which acids affect bog bodies. Choose the effect of acid you think is most important, and justify your choice.

........................................................................

........................................................................

........................................................................

........................................................................

........................................................................

........................................................................

........................................................................

## Acid in Action

**Figure 1** The soft tissues of this bog body have been preserved by acidic conditions in a wetland.

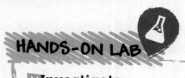

## HANDS-ON LAB

**Investigate**
Explore the properties of acids by studying their effects on litmus paper.

## INTERACTIVITY

Explore acids and bases through the eyes of people who use these substances in their careers.

# Properties of Acids

If you rode to school today, you were probably in a vehicle that has a battery. Most batteries depend on acids. Many other common items contain acids as well.

Acids are an important part of our lives. Folic acid, found in green, leafy vegetables, is important for human cell growth. Hydrochloric acid in your stomach helps with digestion. Phosphoric acid is an ingredient in plant fertilizers. Sulfuric acid drives many types of batteries, giving it the nickname "battery acid."

## Reactions With Metals

Acids react with certain metals to produce hydrogen gas. A few metals, such as platinum and gold, do not generally react with acids, but most other metals, such as aluminum, zinc, and iron, do. When they react, the metals seem to disappear in the solution. This is one reason acids are described as **corrosive**, meaning they "wear away" other materials.

The purity of precious metals can be determined by using acids. **Figure 2** shows a touchstone, which is used to test the purity of gold.

## Reactions With Carbonates

Acids also react with carbonate ions. Carbonate ions contain carbon and oxygen atoms bonded together with an overall negative charge ($CO_3^{-2}$). One product of the reaction of an acid with a carbonate is carbon dioxide, a common gas. Geologists use this property of acids to identify rocks. For example, if acid poured on a rock's surface produces carbon dioxide gas, then the rock may be made of limestone.

Objects that contain carbonate ions include limestone, seashells, eggshells, and chalk. Therefore, they can all be affected by acid. The oysters shown in **Figure 3** have been affected by the increasing acidity of ocean water in some areas.

## Testing for Gold

**Figure 2** The gold object being tested is scraped on the touchstone. Then, acid is poured onto the streak. Why do you think that the more gas bubbles the streak produces, the lower the purity of the gold?

..................................................................

..................................................................

..................................................................

**Sour Taste** If you've ever tasted a lemon, you've had firsthand experience with the sour taste of acids. Citrus fruits, such as lemons, grapefruit, and oranges, all contain citric acid. Many other foods, such as olives and tomatoes, also contain acids.

Although sour taste is a characteristic of many acids, it is not one you should use to identify a compound as an acid. It is not safe to taste unknown chemicals.

## Reactions With Indicators

Chemists use indicators to test for acids. Litmus paper is an example of an **indicator**, or a compound that changes color when it comes into contact with an acid. Acids turn blue litmus paper red. Litmus is a natural indicator. The hydrangea, a flower whose color varies according to the amount of acid in its soil, is another example of a natural indicator. See **Figure 4**.

☑ READING CHECK **Evaluate Reasoning** The text above says that many acids taste sour, but also states that oranges and tomatoes contain acid. Suggest at least one reason why these fruits don't taste sour.

..................................................................................................................

..................................................................................................................

### Oysters and Acids
**Figure 3** What effect do you think an increase of acidity of ocean water has on oyster shells?

..................................................................

..................................................................

..................................................................

..................................................................

..................................................................

### Hydrangeas and Acidity
**Figure 4** Some hydrangeas produce blue blossoms when they grow in acidic soil. What might you need to do to the soil if you prefer pink flowers?

..................................................................

..................................................................

51

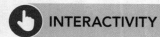

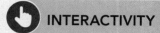

# Properties of Bases

Bases are another group of compounds that can be identified by their common properties. A **base** tastes bitter, feels slippery, and turns red litmus paper blue. The properties of bases are often described as the opposite of the properties of acids. In chemical reactions, acids are more likely to give up a positively charged hydrogen ion, which is really just a proton. Bases are more likely to accept a proton. Bases have many uses. Ammonia is a base and is used in fertilizers and household cleaners. Sodium hydroxide is used in some drain cleaners.

**Bitter Taste** Have you ever tasted tonic water? The base known as quinine causes the slightly bitter taste. Other foods that contain bases include almonds and cocoa beans.

**Slippery Feel** Many soaps and detergents contain bases. The slippery feeling of your shampoo is a property of the bases it contains. Just as you should avoid tasting an unknown substance, you should not touch one either. Strong bases can irritate your skin. A safer way to identify bases is by testing their properties with a litmus test.

☑ **READING CHECK** **Compare and Contrast** How are acids and bases similar? Why are they said to have "opposite" properties?

.................................................................................................................................

.................................................................................................................................

.................................................................................................................................

## Plan It!

### Acid or Base?

Imagine that you need to determine whether each liquid pictured is an acid or a base.

**Develop Possible Solutions** Plan an investigation to determine whether each liquid is an acid or a base. List any materials you will need, and predict your results.

.................................................................................................................................

.................................................................................................................................

.................................................................................................................................

.................................................................................................................................

.................................................................................................................................

Glass cleaner

Shampoo

Vinegar

Juice of an orange

# Neutralization of Acids and Bases

Acids and bases are used throughout our daily lives and in industry. However, they are not usually used in their purest forms or highest strengths. Instead, they are often mixed together to get a safer or specific strength.

If you mixed an acid and a base together and then tested the final result, you would find that the **process** produced a neutral solution of a salt and water, which is neither acidic nor basic. The salt is made from the positive ion of a base and the negative ion of an acid joining together. The reaction between an acid and a base is called a **neutralization** reaction. The reason for this reaction is because acids give off or donate protons, while bases take in or accept protons.

The results of a neutralization reaction are not always neutral. The final result depends on the volumes, concentrations, and strengths of the reactants. For example, if a small amount of strong base reacts with a large amount of strong acid, the solution will remain acidic, but closer to neutral than the original acid.

"Salt" may be the familiar name of the stuff you sprinkle on food, but to a chemist, the word refers to a specific group of compounds. A **salt** is any ionic compound that can be made from a neutralization reaction. Some common salts are shown in **Figure 5**.

☑ READING CHECK **Summarize** Why are the results of a neutralization reaction not always neutral?

.......................................................................

.......................................................................

.......................................................................

## Common Salts

**Figure 5** 🖉 Each of these salts is the result of a neutralization reaction. Complete the table with the formulas for the salts produced.

| Name of salt | Formula of acid | Formula of base | Formula of salt |
|---|---|---|---|
| Potassium iodide | HI | KOH | KI |
| Sodium fluoride | HF | NaOH | NaF |
| Sodium chloride | HCl | NaOH | |
| Lithium bromide | HBr | LiOH | |
| Potassium nitrate | $HNO_3$ | KOH | $KNO_3$ |
| Calcium chloride | HCl | $Ca(OH)_2$ | |

Sodium fluoride is one of several fluoride compounds used in toothpaste to help prevent cavities.

## Academic Vocabulary

How is the process of neutralization reaction like the process of mixing white and black paints to get gray?

.......................................................................

.......................................................................

.......................................................................

.......................................................................

.......................................................................

# ☑ LESSON 5 Check

MS-PS1-1

**1. Apply Concepts** 🖊 Draw a line to match each formula with the type of compound it represents.

KOH                    Acid

$NH_4Cl$               Base

$HNO_3$                Salt

**2. Construct Explanations** Why is vinegar stored in a plastic or glass container, rather than a metal one?

........................................................................

........................................................................

........................................................................

**3. Synthesize Information** What are the products of a neutralization reaction between hydrochloric acid (HCl) and magnesium hydroxide ($Mg(OH)_2$)?

........................................................................

........................................................................

........................................................................

**4. Explain Phenomena** Many stone buildings are made from limestone, which is primarily calcium carbonate. What happens to such buildings over time if they are exposed to acid rain?

........................................................................

........................................................................

........................................................................

**5. Design Your Solution** You are given an unknown solution and asked to determine whether it is an acid or a base. What properties of acids and bases could you use to classify the solution? What properties would you not use to make this determination?

........................................................................

........................................................................

........................................................................

........................................................................

# Quest CHECK-IN

**In this lesson, you learned about the properties of acids and bases. You also explored what happens when these substances interact with each other and with other substances.**

Make Observations Acids and bases interact with other substances in predictable ways. How do you think you can use the properties of acids and bases to help you identify unknown substances?

........................................................................

........................................................................

........................................................................

........................................................................

## HANDS-ON LAB

Solving the Mystery

**Go online** to test the mystery substance and then analyze the results. Then identify the individuals responsible for the crime.

MS-PS1-1

# ACIDS IN THE
*Human Body*

When chemists work with acids, they usually have to wear protective clothing such as safety goggles and gloves. Many acids are dangerously corrosive. But did you know that there are acids found in the human body that are essential to life?

**Nucleic acids** are found in every cell in your body in the form of DNA (deoxyribonucleic acid). DNA controls the growth, development, and functioning of each of your cells.

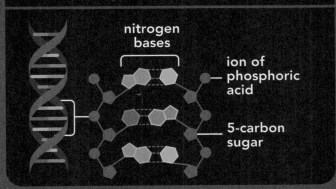

nitrogen bases

ion of phosphoric acid

5-carbon sugar

**Amino acids** are essential proteins that all cells need to function and survive. Proteins, which are coded by our DNA, are responsible for controlling and directing all the processes that occur in living cells.

**Gastric acid** is found in your stomach and is produced by special cells in the stomach lining. Gastric acid is mostly responsible for breaking down food so the stomach can digest it. One of the main components of gastric acid is hydrochloric acid, which is a corrosive acid.

hydrochloric acid

Cl

H

**Lactic acid** is a kind of acid produced in the human body as a result of intense exercise. This compound is responsible for the pain and soreness athletes feel in their muscles during strenuous activity.

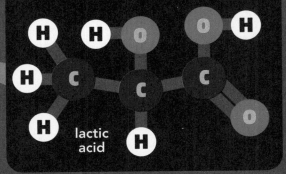

lactic acid

## MY DISCOVERY

Find out about other types of acids found in the human body. Type "acids in the human body" into an Internet search engine to find more information on this topic.

# ☑ TOPIC 1 Review and Assess

## ① Atomic Theory

MS-PS1-1

**1.** Which atomic particle has no charge?
- **A.** electron
- **B.** neutron
- **C.** nucleus
- **D.** proton

**2.** Which of these pairs of atoms are isotopes?
- **A.** scandium-46, titanium-46
- **B.** iron-56, sodium-24
- **C.** chlorine-35, chlorine-37
- **D.** sodium-24, magnesium-24

**3.** Which statement is a part of Dalton's atomic theory?
- **A.** Atoms are composed of protons, neutrons, and electrons.
- **B.** Elements can have atoms that are isotopes.
- **C.** One type of atom cannot be changed to another type by a chemical reaction.
- **D.** Electrons move around the nucleus in an electron cloud.

**4.** Rutherford predicted that an atom has a dense core called a(n) ............................................... .

**5. Develop Models** ✏ A carbon atom has an atomic number of 6, and a boron atom has an atomic number of 5. An atom of carbon-12 has the same mass number as an atom of boron-12. Sketch models that show the differences in the two atoms.

## ② The Periodic Table

MS-PS1-1

**Use a periodic table for reference, as needed.**

**6.** How are atoms arranged in the modern periodic table?
- **A.** by increasing atomic mass
- **B.** by decreasing atomic mass
- **C.** by increasing atomic number
- **D.** by decreasing atomic number

**7.** Who organized elements into the modern periodic table?
- **A.** Dalton
- **B.** Mendeleev
- **C.** Rutherford
- **D.** Thomson

**8.** Use a periodic table to choose the pair of elements whose properties are most similar.
- **A.** silicon (Si), phosphorus (P)
- **B.** neon (Ne), sulfur (S)
- **C.** potassium (K), magnesium (Mg)
- **D.** chlorine (Cl), iodine (I)

**9.** Scientists learn about the properties of some particles from the collisions that occur inside

a ...................................................................................... .

**10. Use Models** ✏ An element in Period 5 has eight valence electrons. Use a periodic table to figure out which element this is. Explain why you chose this element. Then, draw the information that the periodic table shows about the element.

...................................................................................

...................................................................................

...................................................................................

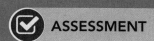

**3 Bonding and the Periodic Table**

MS-PS1-1

**11.** How many valence electrons are present in an atom of argon?
A. 0　　　　　　　B. 8
C. 18　　　　　　 D. 40

**12.** All the elements in Group 2 have the same
A. atomic mass.
B. number of valence electrons.
C. chemical symbol.
D. atomic number.

**13.** Why do metals have high conductivity?
A. All electrons are free to move.
B. All electrons are held in place.
C. Valence electrons are free to move.
D. Valence electrons are held in place.

**14.** One property of metalloids not shared with metals or nonmetals is that metalloids are

...............................................................................

**15. Use Tables** From the information provided, decide whether the element described is more likely to be a metal or nonmetal.

| Property | Data |
|---|---|
| Density | Low |
| Conductivity | Low |
| Appearance | Dull |
| Malleability | Low |
| Ductility | Low |

The element is more likely to be a

...............................................................................

**4 Types of Bonds**

MS-PS1-1

**16.** When do atoms form a covalent bond?
A. when they share electrons
B. when they give up electrons
C. when they accept additional electrons
D. when electrons remain with the same atoms

**17.** Most atoms gain, lose, or share electrons to end up with how many valence electrons?
A. 0　　　　　　　B. 8
C. 12　　　　　　 D. 16

**18. Identify** When a molecule has slight positive and negative charges at different locations, the molecule is

...............................................................................

**5 Acids and Bases**

MS-PS1-1

**19.** Which of these descriptions is a property of a base?
A. feels slippery
B. tastes sour
C. reacts with metals
D. reacts with carbonates

**20.** Which is most likely to be damaged by an acid?
A. a glass jar
B. a plastic bottle
C. a gold bracelet
D. an aluminum can

**21. Review** The products of a neutralization

reaction are ................................. and

...............................................................................

MS-PS1-1

## Evidence-Based Assessment

Suppose it is the year 2202 and a scientist named Abigail discovers a new element on another planet. Scientists agree to name the element abigailium after her and give it the chemical symbol Ab. The new element's relative position on the periodic table is shown in the diagram.

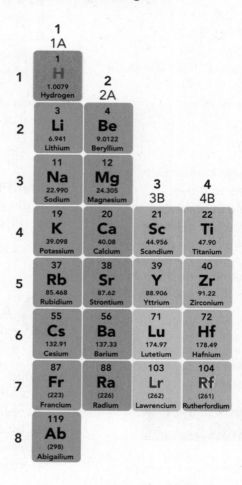

On the distant planet, this element is stable rather than radioactive. Abigail records the following information about the element:

- It is shiny and somewhat soft.
- It has a high thermal conductivity.

1. **Use Tables** Which element is most likely to have similar properties to abigailium?
   A. rubidium (Rb)  B. magnesium (Mg)
   C. lawrencium (Lr)  D. titanium (Ti)

2. **Interpret Data** How many protons and neutrons does isotope Ab-298 have?
   A. 119 protons and 180 neutrons
   B. 200 protons and 178 neutrons
   C. 119 protons and 179 neutrons
   D. 118 protons and 200 neutrons

3. **Analyze Data** Which of the following statements are true about the element? Select all that apply.
   ☐ It is in the 8th period on the periodic table.
   ☐ It has more protons than barium (Ba).
   ☐ It has zero valence electrons.
   ☐ It is a smaller atom than hydrogen (H).
   ☐ It has the same atomic number as magnesium (Mg).

4. **Draw Evidence** Based on Abigail's notes and the table, do you believe abigailium is a noble gas, an alkali metal, or a transition metal? Provide evidence for your choice.

........................................................................

........................................................................

........................................................................

........................................................................

........................................................................

........................................................................

........................................................................

........................................................................

........................................................................

........................................................................

........................................................................

........................................................................

5. **Construct an Argument** Chlorine has 7 valence electrons. Describe the type of bond that abigailium would have with chlorine. Write down the chemical formula of the compound these two elements would form together. Think about what the electron dot diagram would look like to help you.

........................................................................

........................................................................

........................................................................

........................................................................

........................................................................

........................................................................

........................................................................

........................................................................

# Quest FINDINGS

## Complete the Quest!

**Phenomenon** Present your findings about the mystery powder to your class. Explain how you arrived at your final conclusions.

**Summarize** How did your understanding of the periodic table, and your knowledge of acids and bases, help you figure out the mystery powder?

........................................................................

........................................................................

........................................................................

........................................................................

........................................................................

👆 **INTERACTIVITY**

Reflect on Your Investigation

MS-PS1-1

# Shedding Light on Ions

Can you design an **experiment** that demonstrates why **water** is a good **conductor** of **electricity**?

## Background

**Phenomenon** How do you keep safe if you are outside on a beach during a thunderstorm? Perhaps you have been told to keep away from the water. But pure water is a covalent compound, and covalent compounds don't conduct electricity. The water must contain dissolved ions. In this investigation, you will explore the kinds of compounds that produce ions when dissolved in a solution.

## Materials

(per pair)

- 100-mL beaker
- small plastic spoon
- sodium chloride (NaCl)
- salt substitute (KCl)
- sucrose (table sugar, $C_{12}H_{22}O_{11}$)
- sulfur (S)
- sample of pond, lake, or river water (or tap water)
- distilled water
- additional materials supplied by your teacher
- conductivity tester or probe

## Safety

Be sure to follow all safety guidelines provided by your teacher. The Safety Appendix of your textbook provides more details about the safety icons.

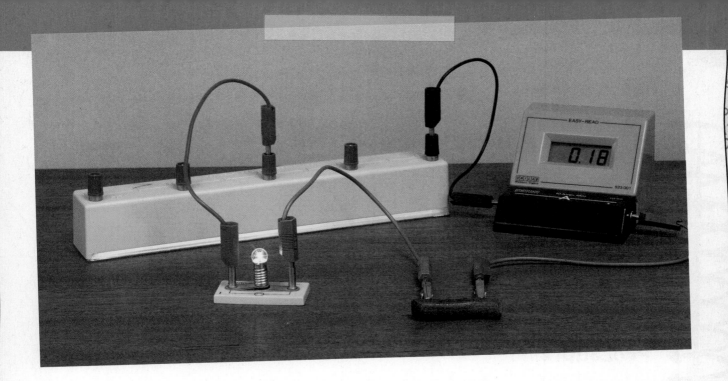

# Design an Experiment

**HANDS-ON LAB**

**иDemonstrate** Go online for a downloadable worksheet of this lab.

☐ **1.** You will design, develop, and conduct an experiment to determine the conductivity of different compounds and solutions using these compounds.

☐ **2.** Examine the materials supplied by your teacher. Think about how you can use them to conduct your investigation. Here are some important questions to consider:

- **What does the conductivity tester indicate and how does it work?**
- **How can you test the conductivity of each compound?**
- **How can you test the conductivity of each solution?**
- **How can you determine whether ions are present in a solution?**

☐ **3.** Develop a hypothesis that you can test about whether each substance and solution will conduct electricity.

☐ **4.** Use the space provided to develop and write your procedure.

☐ **5.** Use the data table to record your observations and results.

☐ **6.** Have your teacher review and approve your hypotheseis and procedure. Then conduct your experiment. Record your data in the table.

# uDemonstrate Lab

## Hypothesis

## Procedure

## Observations

| Sample | Conductivity Observations | Ions Present in Solution? |
|---|---|---|
| tap water (or pond/river water) | | |
| distilled water | | |
| table salt | | |
| salt substitute | | |
| sucrose | | |
| sulfur | | |

# Analyze and Interpret Data

1. **Control Variables** Did you test both tap water and distilled water before testing the sodium chloride solution? Why is it a good idea to do so?

...................................................................................................................

...................................................................................................................

...................................................................................................................

...................................................................................................................

2. **Interpret Data** Could you have used tap water in your experiment instead of distilled water? Explain.

...................................................................................................................

...................................................................................................................

...................................................................................................................

...................................................................................................................

3. **Infer** Sodium chloride (NaCl) is an ionic compound. How can you account for any observed differences in conductivity between dry and dissolved sodium chloride?

...................................................................................................................

...................................................................................................................

...................................................................................................................

...................................................................................................................

4. **Develop Models** Based on your results, how could you use your investigation to model why it is dangerous to swim outside during a thunderstorm?

...................................................................................................................

...................................................................................................................

...................................................................................................................

...................................................................................................................

...................................................................................................................

...................................................................................................................

...................................................................................................................

...................................................................................................................

...................................................................................................................

# Chemical Reactions

### NGSS PERFORMANCE EXPECTATIONS

**MS-PS1-2** Analyze and interpret data on the properties of substances before and after the substances interact to determine if a chemical reaction has occurred.

**MS-PS1-3** Gather and make sense of information to describe that synthetic materials come from natural resources and impact society.

**MS-PS1-5** Develop and use a model to describe how the total number of atoms does not change in a chemical reaction and thus mass is conserved.

**MS-PS1-6** Undertake a design project to construct, test, and modify a device that either releases or absorbs thermal energy by chemical processes.

HANDS-ON LAB

uConnect Explore what happens when chemicals react.

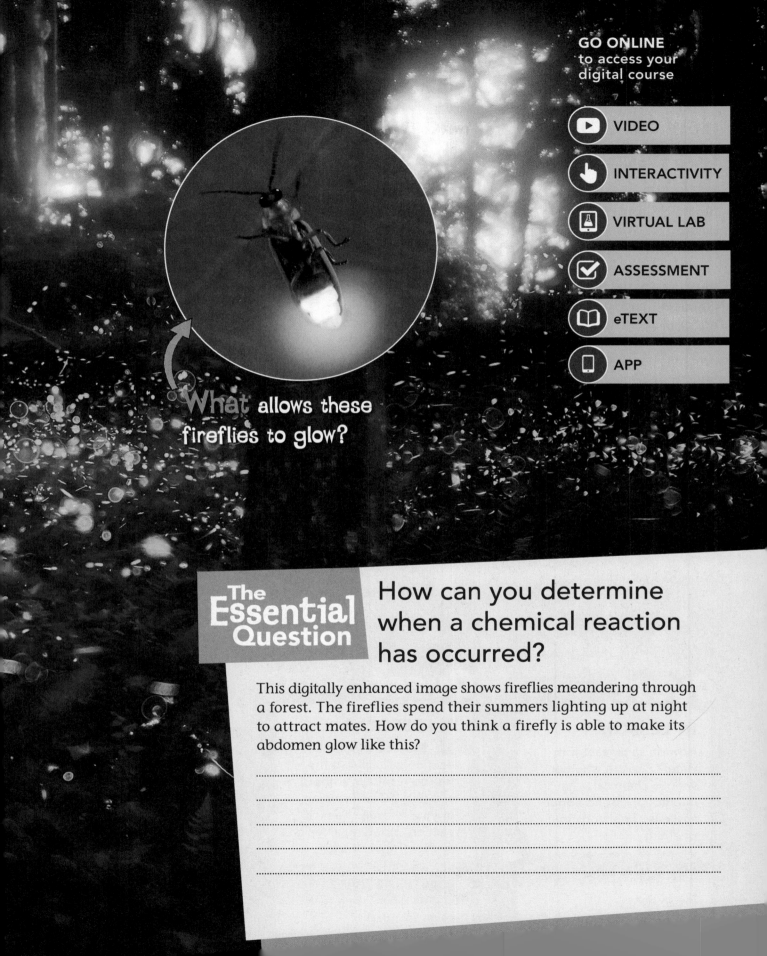

GO ONLINE
to access your
digital course

▶ VIDEO

👆 INTERACTIVITY

🧪 VIRTUAL LAB

☑ ASSESSMENT

📖 eTEXT

📱 APP

What allows these fireflies to glow?

## The Essential Question

# How can you determine when a chemical reaction has occurred?

This digitally enhanced image shows fireflies meandering through a forest. The fireflies spend their summers lighting up at night to attract mates. How do you think a firefly is able to make its abdomen glow like this?

.................................................................................................

.................................................................................................

.................................................................................................

.................................................................................................

.................................................................................................

# Quest KICKOFF

## How can you design and build hot packs and cold packs?

**Phenomenon** Every day, people test the strength, flexibility, and endurance of their bodies. They may be athletes, workers, or simply active kids and adults. When minor injuries occur, applying heat or cold can ease pain, reduce swelling, and help damaged muscle or tissue begin to heal. Chemists and product engineers have designed easy-to-use packs that get hot or cold because of chemical reactions that can activate when users are ready to use the packs. In this problem-based Quest activity, you will design and build a hot or cold pack for the treatment of minor injuries. You will determine which chemicals and materials best meet the criteria and constraints. After exploration, design, and testing, you will reflect on your product and its effectiveness.

👆 **INTERACTIVITY**

Hot and Cool Chemistry

**MS-PS1-6** Undertake a design project to construct, test, and modify a device that either releases or absorbs thermal energy by chemical processes.

**NBC LEARN** ▶ VIDEO

After watching the Quest Kickoff video, in which a chemist describes chemical processes that release or absorb heat, think of other uses for a product that heats up or cools down. Record three ideas.

**1**
........................................................
........................................................
........................................................

**2**
........................................................
........................................................
........................................................

**3**
........................................................
........................................................

# Quest CHECK-IN

### IN LESSON 1

How do salts react with water? Explore whether various chemical interactions bring about a release or absorption of energy.

**HANDS-ON LAB**

Energy Salts

# Quest CHECK-IN

### IN LESSON 2

STEM Which chemical reaction will achieve the desired results in a hot or cold pack? Devise a plan for your chosen chemical reaction, including a design plan for the pack itself.

👆 **INTERACTIVITY**

Design Your Pack

# Quest CHECK-IN

### IN LESSON 3

STEM How can you construct your hot or cold pack? Choose materials, build a prototype using ordinary salt or sugar, and test your product.

**HANDS-ON LAB**

Pack Building

Instant cold packs don't need to be kept in a freezer or cooler, so they are easier to transport than ice. They can be activated the moment an injury occurs.

## Quest CHECK-IN

### IN LESSON 4

STEM How can you construct a better prototype? Build an improved prototype using chemical salts and demonstrate the use of the product.

### HANDS-ON LAB

Heat It Up or Ice It Down

## Quest FINDINGS

## Complete the Quest!

Based on results and feedback from your demonstration, evaluate the effectiveness of your hot or cold pack. Reflect on your work.

INTERACTIVITY

Reflect on Your Pack

# LESSON 1 — Mixtures and Solutions

## Guiding Questions

- How can the properties of mixtures and solutions be used to classify them?
- What do the visible properties of mixtures reveal about their molecular and atomic properties?
- How can the different parts of a mixture be identified and separated?

## Connections

**Literacy** Draw Evidence

**Math** Use Ratio Reasoning

MS-PS1-2

## Vocabulary

mixture
colloid
suspension
solution
solvent
solute
solubility

## Academic Vocabulary

dissolve

 **VOCABULARY APP**

Practice vocabulary on a mobile device.

### Quest CONNECTION

Consider how solutes and solvents could be used to make hot packs and cold packs.

## Connect It!

🖊 **What are the components of the sand and the seawater? Write your answers in the boxes on the photograph.**

Plan an Investigation Suppose you are a researcher studying these components. You need to separate the shell fragments from the sand, and you must also extract the salt from the seawater. Describe how you would do this.

....................................................................................................................

....................................................................................................................

....................................................................................................................

# Types of Mixtures

Most materials we encounter consist of more than one element or compound, so they are mixtures. A **mixture** is made of two or more substances that are together in the same place, but their atoms are not chemically combined. Mixtures differ from compounds. Each substance in a mixture keeps its properties.

**Heterogeneous Mixture** The sand shown in **Figure 1** is a heterogeneous (het ur oh JEE nee us) mixture—one that features distinct components that can easily be seen and sorted. A plate of spaghetti with meatballs and a bowl of salad are other examples of heterogeneous mixtures. A characteristic of a heterogeneous mixture is that its components are not spread out evenly throughout the mixture. One portion of a heterogeneous mixture may consist of a relatively even balance of different things, while another portion is mostly one thing or another. One handful of this sand, for example, could contain a fossilized shark tooth, while a hundred handfuls around it do not.

**Homogeneous Mixture** Other mixtures are more difficult to analyze. Such homogeneous (hoh moh JEE nee ous) mixtures often look the same throughout the entire mixture. Their different components are difficult to see and are spread out uniformly throughout the entire mixture. Saltwater, honey, and soy sauce are examples of homogeneous mixtures that may be found in your kitchen.

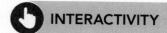
**INTERACTIVITY**

Take the poll about whether mixing certain substances will result in a chemical change.

**Reflect** As you read this lesson, build a T-chart in your science notebook of heterogeneous and homogeneous mixtures that you have seen, used, or even eaten today.

**Sea and Sand**
**Figure 1** At surf's edge, two different types of mixtures meet and mingle.

# Separating Mixtures

Remember that the individual components of a mixture keep their properties. This means that the properties of the components in a mixture can be used to separate them. Mixtures that contain particles of different sizes, for example, can be filtered so the larger particles are removed from the mixture. Mixtures that have magnetic components can be separated with a magnet. Liquid mixtures can be heated until some components evaporate and others are left behind as solids.

## Plan It!

### The Right Tool for the Job

**Figure 2** Three different mixtures need to be separated in order to analyze each component. You have three different tools available to get this job done: a magnet, a filter, and a hot plate. Identify which tool can be used to separate each mixture.

☑ READING CHECK **Explain** For each mixture, identify its components and explain how their properties can be used to separate the mixture.

**sand and iron filings**

Tool: ......................................

Components and how they are separated:

..................................................................................

..................................................................................

..................................................................................

**saltwater**

Tool: ......................................

Components and how they are separated:

..................................................................................

..................................................................................

..................................................................................

**muddy water**

Tool: ......................................

Components and how they are separated:

..................................................................................

..................................................................................

..................................................................................

## Classifying Mixtures

Honey, oil-and-vinegar salad dressing, and milk are examples of different types of mixtures that may be found on your dinner table. The three types are defined by the sizes of their particles and how the particles behave.

### Colloid
A **colloid** is a hetereogenous mixture containing small, undissolved particles that do not separate or settle out if the mixture is undisturbed. Think of a glass of milk. If you leave it on the table for hours, it remains consistently white throughout. The fat and water particles in it do not separate. The particles of a colloid are too small to be seen without a microscope, yet they are large enough to scatter a beam of light. This is why they are not clear. Paint, whipped cream, fog, and smoke are all colloids.

### Suspension
If you let a glass of cloudy liquid sit still for a while, and a distinct, cloudier layer accumulates at the top or bottom while the rest of the liquid seems to get more clear, you are likely looking at a **suspension** (suh SPEN shun). A suspension is a mixture with particles that can be seen and easily separated by settling or filtration. For example, a bottle of oil-and-vinegar salad dressing will settle out into its constituent parts if left undisturbed. Muddy river water, as shown in **Figure 4**, is another example of a suspension.

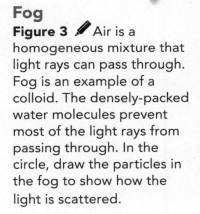

### Fog
**Figure 3** ✏ Air is a homogeneous mixture that light rays can pass through. Fog is an example of a colloid. The densely-packed water molecules prevent most of the light rays from passing through. In the circle, draw the particles in the fog to show how the light is scattered.

### Suspension
**Figure 4** Swiftly flowing river water may have a heavy "load" of suspended sediment. If collected in a jar and left undisturbed, the sediment will settle out.

**Academic Vocabulary**
Think of examples in everyday life of things that dissolve, such as hot chocolate mix in water. Record them below.

....................................................

....................................................

....................................................

....................................................

**HANDS-ON LAB**

Ⓤ**Investigate** Explore how different substances combine with water.

## Solutions

Grape juice is one example of a mixture called a solution. A **solution** is a homogenous mixture of a solvent and one or more solutes. The **solvent** is the part of the solution that is usually present in the largest amount. It **dissolves** the other substances in the solution. The **solute** is the substance that is dissolved by the solvent. Whether a solution is a solid, liquid, or gas, it forms when particles of the solute become separated and surrounded by particles of the solvent. This is what it means for a solute to dissolve. In grape juice, water is the solvent. Sugar and the other ingredients are the solutes.

Air and stainless steel are other examples of solutions. The air around us is a mixture of oxygen, nitrogen, and several other gases. Since nitrogen gas makes up most of the air, nitrogen is the solvent. Stainless steel is a solid solution made up of iron, chromium, and nickel. Because a solution is a homogenous mixture, it has the same properties throughout the entire mixture.

**Molecular Solutes** Molecular compounds, such as table sugar, break up into individual molecules in water. The sugar molecules are polar like water. The water molecules attract the sugar molecules, and the sugar molecules move away from one another. While the water molecules surround the sugar molecules, the chemical bonds do not break. Since polarity is so important to the dissolving process, most nonpolar molecules are not soluble in water.

**Ionic Solutes** Table salt is mostly made up of an ionic compound called sodium chloride (NaCl). Sodium chloride is made of positively charged sodium ions and negatively charged chloride ions. These charges allow salt to dissolve in water. Water is a polar molecule due to the arrangement of oxygen and hydrogen atoms. The oxygen side is slightly negative, while the hydrogen side is slightly positive. The attractions shown in **Figure 5** are what make salt soluble in water.

**Forming Saltwater**
**Figure 5** Observe what happens in each step as salt dissolves in water.

✓READING CHECK **Infer**
Many people refer to water as the "universal solvent." Why?

....................................................

....................................................

....................................................

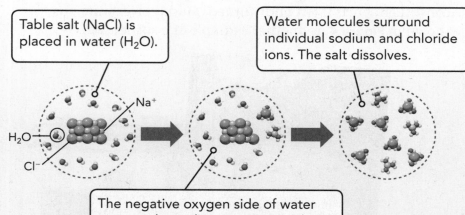

Table salt (NaCl) is placed in water ($H_2O$).

Water molecules surround individual sodium and chloride ions. The salt dissolves.

The negative oxygen side of water attracts the sodium ions ($Na^+$). The positive hydrogen side of water attracts the chloride ions ($Cl^-$).

# Concentration

Saltwater tastes salty, but it also has other properties that are different from pure water. Solutes raise the boiling point of a solution above that of the solvent. For example, under standard atmospheric pressure, pure water boils at 100°C, whereas saltwater boils at 102°C. Solutes also lower the freezing points of solutions. While the surface of a lake may freeze at 0°C, the salty ocean freezes at –1.8°C. More solute in water also makes water denser. You can experience this when swimming in the ocean. You will be extra buoyant in extra salty water.

Boiling point, freezing point, and density are physical properties of solutions that are affected by concentration. Concentration itself is also a physical property. The saltiness, or salinity, of seawater is due to the concentration of the solute (sodium chloride) in the solvent (water). A concentrated solution has a lot of solute. A solution with little solute is a dilute solution. Concentration increases by adding more solute or removing solvent. For example, a cup of tea will become more concentrated, or stronger, if it's left to sit so some of the water evaporates. The tea will also be more concentrated if the teabag is allowed to steep longer.

## Literacy Connection

**Draw Evidence** A friend is making vegetable soup. He adds some salt to the simmering broth. The salt dissolves, and your friend says the broth's saltiness is just right. After two more hours of cooking on the stovetop, the broth is way too salty. What happened?

.......................................................

.......................................................

.......................................................

.......................................................

.......................................................

.......................................................

.......................................................

## Math Toolbox

## Concentration of Salt in Seawater

Salinity, or the concentration of salt in seawater, varies in different parts of the ocean. The salinities of two seas are labeled on the map in ppt, or "parts per thousand." This means that the Baltic Sea has 10 units of dissolved salt in every 1000 units of seawater.

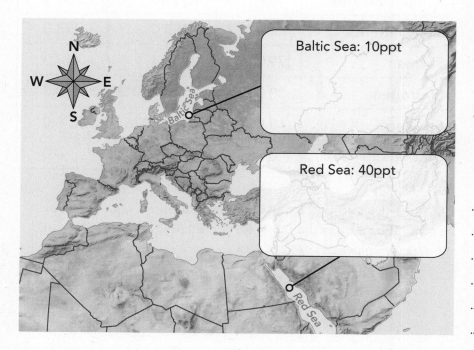

Baltic Sea: 10ppt

Red Sea: 40ppt

1. **Use Ratio Reasoning** Suppose you collected 100-gram samples of seawater from each of the two seas. Determine how many grams of dissolved salt you would expect to find in each of your seawater samples. Write the values in the appropriate boxes on the map.

2. **Apply Scientific Reasoning** From which sea could you take a water sample that would be easier to freeze? Explain.

.......................................................

.......................................................

.......................................................

.......................................................

.......................................................

.......................................................

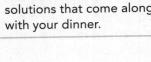

**VIDEO**

See the mixtures and solutions that come along with your dinner.

# Solubility

Imagine making lemonade by spooning powdered lemonade mix into a glass of water. At a certain point, there will be more lemonade mix than can possibly dissolve. This is where **solubility**, or the measure of how much solute will dissolve in a solvent, comes into play. A solution that can no longer dissolve a solute is saturated. The properties of the solute and solvent affect solubility, and temperature and pressure also play a role.

**Temperature** In general, raising the temperature of the solvent increases the solubility of a solid solute. This is one of the reasons we make soup broth on a hot stovetop—because the solid solutes, such as table salt, dissolve more easily if the solvent has a higher temperature. The higher temperature means the molecules of the solvent are moving faster. These more energetic particles can more easily break up the solid solute. However, unlike most solids, gases become less soluble when temperature is increases (see **Figure 6**). Gas particles are already separate from one another, so increasing the temperature increases the energy of the gas particles and causes them to escape from the liquid.

## Solubility and Temperature

**Figure 6** As temperature increases, solids become more soluble, but gases become less soluble. Because carbon dioxide is less soluble in warm water, a cold carbonated beverage is more bubbly than a warm one.

| Solubilities of Substances in Water | | | |
|---|---|---|---|
| | Solubility (g/100 g $H_2O$) | | |
| **Substance** | **0°C** | **50°C** | **100°C** |
| Sodium chloride | 35.7 | 37.0 | 39.2 |
| Silver nitrate | 122.0 | 455.0 | 733.0 |
| Sucrose | 179.0 | 260.4 | 487.0 |
| Hydrogen | 0.00019 | 0.00013 | 0.0 |
| Oxygen | 0.0070 | 0.0026 | 0.0 |
| Carbon dioxide | 0.335 | 0.076 | 0.0 |

✓**READING CHECK** **Draw Evidence** Based on what you have read and the data in the table, do you think silver nitrate is a solid or a gas? Explain.

......................................................................................................

......................................................................................................

......................................................................................................

**Pressure** While pressure has little effect on the solubility of solids, it does affect the solubility of gases. The solubility of a gaseous solute increases as pressure on the solution increases.

Scuba divers must learn the effects of pressure in order to avoid decompression sickness. Under normal atmospheric pressure, nitrogen from the air is not soluble in blood. However, under water, pressure increases as the diver swims deeper. The air that enters his or her lungs becomes more pressurized. Deeper than 18 meters (60 feet), the pressure of the air inside the diver's lungs and the compression of other body tissues makes nitrogen soluble in his or her blood.

As with a can of soda, a sudden release of that pressure can cause bubbles of gas to come out of solution. If the diver swims upward too quickly, nitrogen would suddenly come out of the blood and get lodged in blood vessels. The best way to avoid this painful condition is for the diver to swim up very slowly. That way, any dissolved nitrogen has time to leave the blood through the lungs.

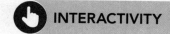

**INTERACTIVITY**

Discover what happens inside a water treatment plant.

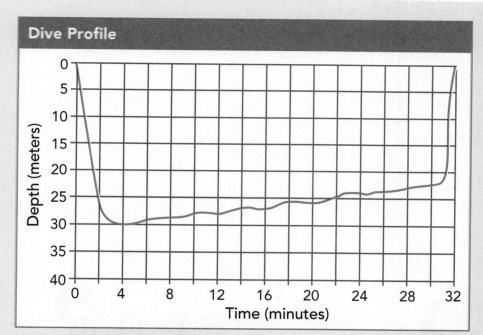

**Dive Profile**

*(Graph: Depth (meters) on y-axis from 0 to 40; Time (minutes) on x-axis from 0 to 32)*

**What Happened?**

**Figure 7** Picture yourself on a dive boat. Someone who has just climbed aboard the boat after an hour-longdive complains of pain in her joints. She loses consciousness. You check her dive computer, which appears to be flashing a warning sign about decompression stops. You click a button to reveal a dive profile—a graph that plots how long the diver spent at different depths over the course of her dive. The graph is shown here.

**Cite Evidence** ✏ Circle the area of the graph that represents the diver's rise to the surface. Based on the graph and figure caption, what do you think happened?

........................................................................................................

........................................................................................................

........................................................................................................

........................................................................................................

........................................................................................................

# ☑ LESSON 1 Check

**1. Determine Differences** Based on its physical properties, is a colloid a homogeneous mixture or heterogeneous mixture? How does it differ from a solution?

..................................................................
..................................................................
..................................................................
..................................................................
..................................................................

**2. Classify** The table shows the solubilities of three different substances in water at the same temperature and pressure.

| Substance | Solubility (g/100 g $H_2O$) |
|---|---|
| Aluminum chloride | 45.8 |
| Silver fluoride | 172.0 |
| Potassium bromide | 65.3 |

Which of the substances would have the greatest mass dissolved in 100 grams of water at the point of saturation? Explain your answer.

..................................................................
..................................................................
..................................................................
..................................................................
..................................................................

**3. Apply Scientific Reasoning** A carpenter has a mix of both iron nails and plastic nails in a jar. For a job, he needs only the iron nails. What physical properties could help him separate the nails?

..................................................................
..................................................................
..................................................................
..................................................................

**4. Plan an Investigation** You and a friend want to start a soda company. For ingredients, you have sucrose (table sugar), carbon dioxide gas, concentrated juices from different fruits, and water. Describe how you will experiment with these ingredients to develop a recipe for your soda. Consider the roles of temperature and pressure, and how to minimize the cost of energy in the production of your soda.

..................................................................
..................................................................
..................................................................
..................................................................
..................................................................
..................................................................
..................................................................
..................................................................

## Quest CHECK-IN

In this lesson, you learned about mixtures, especially solutions and the factors that affect their makeup and properties.

**Apply Scientific Reasoning** Why is it important to know the properties of both solutes and solvents when preparing a solution that is expected to meet a certain need?

..................................................................
..................................................................

## HANDS-ON LAB

Energy Salts

**Go online** to download the lab worksheet. Test different salts to determine whether they meet a specific design criterion for use in an instant hot pack or cold pack—the release or absorption of energy.

# MAKING WATER SAFE TO DRINK

**How do you** transform dirty water into water you can drink? You engineer it! A portable water purification system may be the answer.

**The Challenge:** To turn contaminated water into drinkable water in remote areas of the world.

**Phenomenon** Clean drinking water is essential for people to survive. However, in many places around the world, people have little or no access to clean water. Their water is a mixture of $H_2O$, particles of soil or waste, and other substances that are not safe to drink, such as lead. It is estimated that over 780 million people—or 1 in 9 people in the world—do not have access to clean water.

Water purification systems used to be large, heavy, and expensive to operate. But engineers have developed water systems that you can carry in your hand. Filters remove the large particles and other compounds that are dissolved or suspended in the water. Additionally, chemicals in these systems undergo chemical reactions that kill bacteria and viruses. These systems remove most of the contaminants from dirty water and make it safe and drinkable.

**DESIGN CHALLENGE** How can you build a simple water filter using sand and rocks? Go to the Engineering Design Notebook to find out!

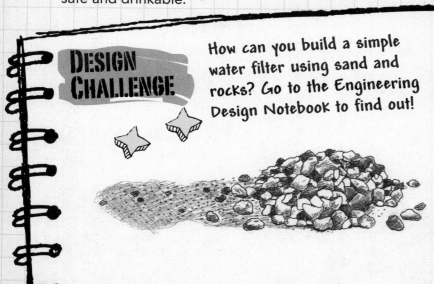

**INTERACTIVITY**

Find out more about different contaminants and the methods to remove them.

Water from a local stream is convenient, but it may contain solutes you would never want to drink! Water filtration systems can remove harmful solutes and cause chemical changes that kill bacteria.

77

# ② Chemical Change

## Guiding Questions

- How can data about the characteristic physical and chemical properties of substances be used to identify whether a physical or chemical change has occurred?
- What factors affect the rate at which a chemical change occurs?

## Connections

**Literacy** Cite Textual Evidence

**Math** Reason Quantitatively

MS-PS1-2

## Vocabulary

physical change
chemical change
reactant
product
exothermic
    reaction
endothermic
    reaction

## Academic Vocabulary

rate

 **VOCABULARY APP**

Practice vocabulary on a mobile device.

**Quest CONNECTION**

Think about whether a physical change or a chemical reaction will be part of your pack design.

## Connect It !

🖊 **Circle a place on the photograph where a color change is occurring.**

**Cause and Effect** What do you think causes this color change?

.............................................................................................................................

.............................................................................................................................

.............................................................................................................................

**Make Observations** When vegetables cook on a grill, what other changes occur? List three ways that the veggies change.

1. .........................................................................................................................

2. .........................................................................................................................

3. .........................................................................................................................

# Changing Matter

Think about the steps in grilling veggies. You slice some of them into smaller pieces. Then, you place them on the grill and turn on the heat. As the veggies cook, they become charred, turning black in some areas (**Figure 1**). The whole process involves both physical and chemical changes to matter.

### Physical Change
Slicing an onion is an example of a **physical change**—a change that alters the form or appearance of a substance without changing it into a different substance. The onion becomes smaller objects of different shape, but the onion pieces are made of the same matter as before. Water boiling is also a physical change. While the water may not be visible as vapor in the air, it is still water—molecules of two hydrogen atoms bonded to an oxygen atom. Bending, crushing, cutting, melting, freezing, and boiling are all physical changes.

While physical changes may alter some physical properties of an object, the characteristic physical properties of the matter remain the same. Some characteristic physical properties include density, conductivity, malleability, melting point, freezing point, and boiling point. For instance, the boiling point of water is 100°C. One drop of water or one liter will both boil at this temperature.

**HANDS-ON LAB**

See if you can identify whether a substance has changed into another substance.

## Physical and Chemical Changes
**Figure 1** Cooking any food, such as vegetables, can involve physical changes and chemical changes.

# Model It!

## Wood Work

**Figure 2** Cutting down a tree and burning the wood is part of a cycle that involves many physical and chemical changes. After a seed sprouts, the seedling uses energy from the sun to turn carbon dioxide and water from its surroundings into food and oxygen. The seedling uses this food to grow into a tree. Then, when the wood is burned, some of the carbon dioxide in the smoke may end up being used by other trees to make food to grow!

Develop Models ✏ Complete the model by drawing an image for the last step in the cycle. Identify whether each part of the cycle involves a physical and/or chemical change.

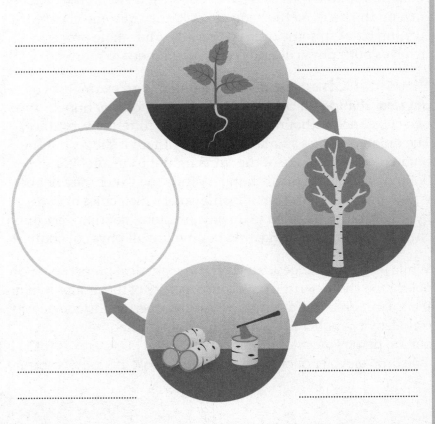

## Literacy Connection

**Cite Textual Evidence**
What is the difference between a physical change and a chemical change? Cite an example from the text that helped you understand this difference.

.......................................................
.......................................................
.......................................................
.......................................................
.......................................................
.......................................................
.......................................................
.......................................................

**Chemical Change** When veggies cook on the grill, they turn black in some places. Heat causes a chemical reaction that forms new compounds, resulting in the black color. A chemical reaction can also be called a **chemical change**—a change in matter that produces one or more new substances. In a chemical change, atoms and molecules rearrange to form new ones. Substances that undergo chemical changes are called **reactants**, and what they form are called **products**.

Burning and rusting are both examples of chemical changes. During these changes, characteristic chemical properties of the reactants can be observed. When a substance burns, you can observe the substance's flammability. When iron rusts, you can observe its reactivity with oxygen. During both of these chemical reactions, changes in color provide evidence that a chemical reaction has occurred.

# Building and Breaking Chemical Bonds

Chemical changes occur when existing bonds break and new bonds form. As a result, new substances are made. Atoms bond when they share or transfer electrons. **Figure 3** shows magnesium, a shiny metal, burning. It reacts with oxygen in the air to produce magnesium oxide, a white solid. Here is what happens to the atoms during the chemical reaction.

$$\ddot{O}::\ddot{O} \longrightarrow \ddot{O}: \; + \; :\ddot{O}$$

The electron dot diagram shows the letter O for each oxygen atom. The dots represent electrons. When the double bond breaks, each oxygen atom needs two more electrons to complete its outer shell. For each oxygen atom, an atom of magnesium provides the two electrons tht are needed.

$$Mg: \; + \; \ddot{O}: \longrightarrow Mg^{2+} \; \ddot{O}^{2-}$$

$$Mg: \; + \; \ddot{O}: \longrightarrow Mg^{2+} \; \ddot{O}^{2-}$$

Magnesium transfers two electrons to each of the original oxygen atoms. The magnesium ions are then bonded to the oxygen ions by the attraction of their opposite charges: 2+ and 2-.

▶ VIDEO

See the real-world effects of acid rain.

☑ READING CHECK

**Explain** Chemical changes are often represented by equations. Physical changes are not represented by equations. Why?

......................................................

......................................................

......................................................

......................................................

......................................................

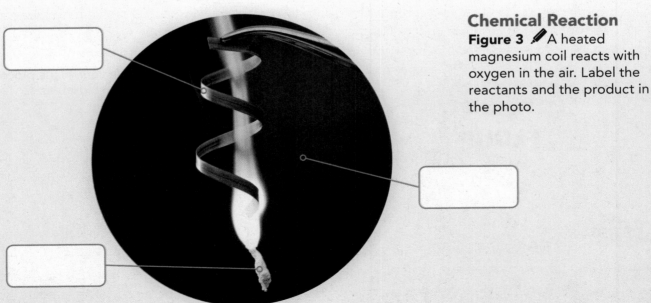

**Chemical Reaction**

**Figure 3** ✏ A heated magnesium coil reacts with oxygen in the air. Label the reactants and the product in the photo.

# HANDS-ON LAB

**Investigate** Explore the chemical changes of a burning candle.

# Evidence of Chemical Reactions

In the chemical changes you've just read about, there is some kind of movement of energy. For example, the reaction of magnesium and oxygen requires energy from the flame to get started, and then the chemical reaction releases energy. Changes in energy and changes in properties are both signs that a chemical reaction has occurred. In general, the only way to be absolutely certain that a chemical reaction has occurred is to confirm that a new substance has been created. However, there are other observable changes that can indicate that a chemical reaction has occurred.

**Color Change** A color change may signal that a new substance has formed in an otherwise unchanged object. A slice of bread that just popped up from a toaster is brown. This is because heat energy burns sugars in the bread, producing different carbon compounds that taste slightly different than the untoasted bread would taste.

## Chemistry in the Pizza Kitchen

**Figure 4** ✏ Three changes involved in making pizza are described in this figure. Label each change with the type of evidence that suggests there is a chemical reaction.

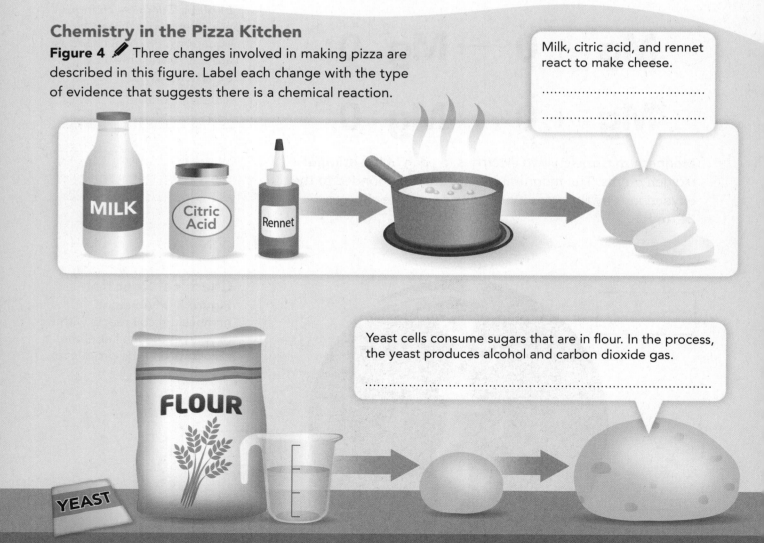

Milk, citric acid, and rennet react to make cheese.

...........................................

...........................................

Yeast cells consume sugars that are in flour. In the process, the yeast produces alcohol and carbon dioxide gas.

...........................................

**Gas Production** Another observable change that is evidence of a chemical reaction is the production of gas from solid or liquid reactants. For example, the chemical reaction between vinegar and baking soda produces carbon dioxide gas. However, the presence of bubbles is not always a sign of a reaction taking place. Bubbles of carbon dioxide appear in soda when the bottle is opened and pressure is released. The only way to be certain that any chemical reaction has taken place is the presence of one or more new substances.

**Formation of a Precipitate** Mixing two liquids may produce a precipitate, which is a solid that forms from liquids. When milk and lemon juice are mixed, a chunky precipitate forms. Some dairy products are made by taking advantage of similar reactions between milk and other substances.

✓ **READING CHECK** **Cite Textual Evidence** What is the only way to be certain that a chemical reaction has occurred?

.............................................................................................................

.............................................................................................................

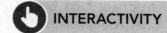
**INTERACTIVITY**

Watch a video of reactions and decide whether new substances have formed.

📓 **Write About It** What other physical or chemical changes might take place while making pizza? Write about them in your science notebook, noting whether each one is a physical or chemical change.

The cheese and pizza dough turn brown in some places when the pizza cooks.

.............................................

.............................................

## The Movement of Energy

**Figure 5** ✏ The reaction of baking soda and vinegar absorbs energy from its surroundings. A kerosene lamp is burned to release energy. On each image, draw an arrow to indicate the direction in which energy moves as a result of the reaction that is occurring.

☑READING CHECK

**Infer** What kind of chemical reaction occurs in a hand-warming product that is worn inside gloves? Explain your answer.

......................................

......................................

......................................

......................................

# Changes in Energy

You have seen that some chemical reactions, such as the browning that occurs on the surfaces of a pizza as it cooks, require energy in the form of heat. Other chemical reactions give off energy. Reactions are classified as exothermic or endothermic, based on the direction of heat flow.

## Exothermic Reaction
In an **exothermic reaction** (ex oh THUR mik), the energy released as the products form is greater than the energy required to break the bonds of the reactants. The energy is usually released as heat. For example, some ovens and stoves burn natural gas. When natural gas burns, it releases heat. This heat cooks your food. Similarly, the reactions between oxygen and other flammable fuels, such as wood, coal, wax, or oil (**Figure 5**), release energy in the form of light and heat.

## Endothermic Reaction
In an **endothermic reaction**, (en doh THUR mik), more energy is required to break the bonds of the reactants than is released by the formation of the products. Some endothermic reactions draw energy from the surroundings, leaving the surroundings feeling cold. Others require a continuous source of energy, like frying an egg in a pan on a stove. In **Figure 5**, baking soda undergoes an endothermic reaction when it is mixed with vinegar. The reaction absorbs heat from the surrounding air.

# Energy Graphs for Chemical Reactions

Reactants are a bit like kids on a swing set—they need an initial push to get going. The minimum amount of energy needed to start a chemical reaction is called activation energy. Once a reaction is underway, it will either need more energy to keep going, or it will release energy.

An exothermic reaction's energy is shown in **Figure 6A**. The dotted line marks the energy of the reactants before the reaction begins. The peak on the graph shows the activation energy. Notice that at the end of the reaction, the products have less energy than the reactants did.

An endothermic reaction is shown in **Figure 6B**. Endothermic reactions need activation energy to get started, and they also need energy to continue. Notice that the energy of the products is greater than the energy of the reactants. This means that the reaction must continually absorb energy to keep going.

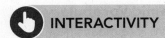

INTERACTIVITY

Analyze graphs of exothermic and endothermic reactions.

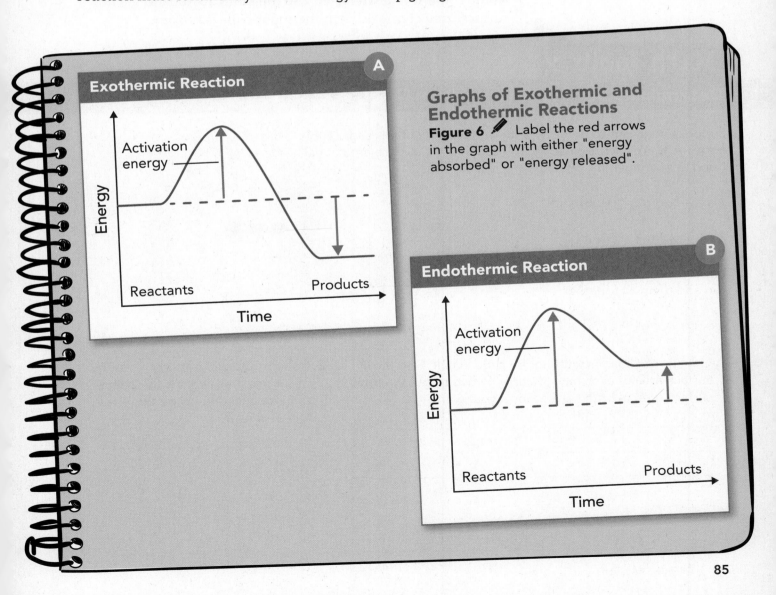

## Graphs of Exothermic and Endothermic Reactions

**Figure 6** ✏️ Label the red arrows in the graph with either "energy absorbed" or "energy released".

.......................................................

.......................................................

.......................................................

.......................................................

.......................................................

.......................................................

# Affecting Rates of Reactions

Chemical reactions don't all occur at the same **rate**. Some, such as explosions, are very fast. Others, like the rusting of iron in air, are slow. A particular reaction can occur at different rates depending on the conditions. If you want to make a chemical reaction happen faster, the particles of the reactants need to collide either more quickly or with more energy. Having more particles available to react is another way to make a reaction go faster. Factors that may affect rates of reactions include surface area, temperature, concentration, and the presence of catalysts and inhibitors.

## Surface Area
Think of a sugar cube. If held over a flame, the sugar will burn, but it will burn somewhat slowly. This is because only the surface of the cube can react with oxygen in the air and the ignition provided by the flame. All the grains of sugar underneath the surface can't react until they are exposed as well. Increasing the surface area of the sugar cube would allow it to burn faster. Use the Math Toolbox to see how surface area changes when the sugar cube is broken.

# Math Toolbox

## Determining Surface Area

Suppose you want to determine the surface area of this sugar cube. It has edges that are each 2 cm long. You can find the surface area of each side using this formula:

Area = Length × Width

**2 cm × 2 cm = 4 cm²**

The sides are all the same size, so you can add them all together:

4 cm² + 4 cm² + 4 cm² + 4 cm² + 4 cm² + 4 cm² = 24 cm²

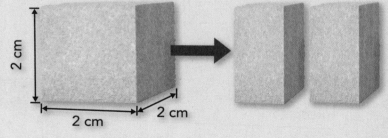

2 cm

2 cm

2 cm

**1. Calculate** Imagine cutting the cube in half. Find the surface area of each half. Multiply by two to get the total surface area of both halves. Show your work.

.................................................................................

.................................................................................

.................................................................................

.................................................................................

.................................................................................

.................................................................................

**2. Reason Quantitatively** In terms of surface area, what is the effect of cutting a cube-shaped object in half as shown?

.................................................................................

.................................................................................

**Temperature** Changing the temperature of a chemical reaction also affects the reaction rate. When you heat a substance, its particles move faster. Faster-moving particles have more energy, which helps reactions get started. Also, faster-moving particles come into contact more often, which means more chances for reactants to react. Reducing temperature slows down reaction rates because there is less energy in the movement of particles and particles interact less frequently. **Figure 7** explains how chemical reactions in a glow stick are affected by temperature.

**Other Factors** Another way to increase the rate of a chemical reaction is to increase the concentration of the reactants. Increasing the concentration of reactants supplies more particles to react. For example, an acidic solution whose concentration is 10 percent reacts more quickly with a base such as baking soda than would a 2 percent acidic solution.

Catalysts also help increase rates of reactions. Catalysts are substances that lower the activation energy needed to start a reaction. Although catalysts affect a reaction's rate, they are not permanently changed by a reaction and are not considered reactants. You can think of these as the parents who help get kids moving on a swing set.

Sometimes it is more useful to slow down a reaction rather than speed it up. A material used to decrease the rate of a chemical reaction is an inhibitor. For example, inhibitors called preservatives are added to food to prevent spoiling.

**Glow Sticks**
**Figure 7** The chemical reaction that takes place in a warm glow stick happens faster than in a cold glow stick. A glow stick becomes brighter more quickly if it is warm.

**▶ VIDEO**
Learn about the work that a forensic scientist does.

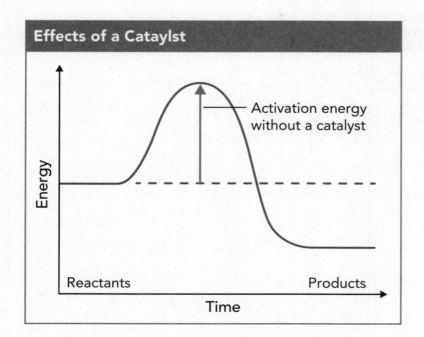

**Effects of a Cataylst**

Energy

Activation energy without a catalyst

Reactants          Products

Time

**Catalyzed Reaction**
**Figure 8** ✎ On this graph, draw a curve that shows how the activation energy would change if a catalyst were present. Use an arrow to indicate the activation energy with a catalyst.

**1. Summarize** How does reducing the temperature of a chemical reaction affect the rate at which it occurs?

........................................................

........................................................

........................................................

........................................................

........................................................

**2. Analyze and Interpret Data** While hiking in the woods, you see a brown, rotting apple lying on the ground. What changes in the physical properties of the apple are signs that a chemical reaction has occurred?

........................................................

........................................................

........................................................

........................................................

........................................................

**3. Cause and Effect** A clear liquid is poured into a beaker containing another clear liquid. A cloudy yellow substance forms, as if out of nowhere, but the rest of the liquid remains clear. What happened?

........................................................

........................................................

........................................................

........................................................

........................................................

**4. Ask Questions** Some silver coins are found inside an ancient shipwreck. They are coated with a black crust. Ask a question that could help you to determine whether the silver underwent a chemical change or a physical change. Explain.

........................................................

........................................................

........................................................

........................................................

........................................................

# Quest CHECK-IN

**In this lesson, you learned how to distinguish physical changes from chemical changes. You also discovered how specific chemical changes can be observed and even controlled by paying attention to energy and other evidence.**

**Apply Scientific Reasoning** What are some general rules or patterns you learned about in this lesson that you can apply when designing a device that will release or absorb heat?

........................................................

........................................................

........................................................

........................................................

........................................................

## 👆 INTERACTIVITY

Design Your Pack

**Go online** to brainstorm activation methods for your pack. Think about what materials you will use, and come up with your design plan.

# The Art of
# Chemical Change

**M**any artists paint landscapes or portraits. Others create multimedia works with sound and light. But some artists rely on chemical reactions to make their art. Acid etching is a process that some artists use to create beautiful artwork and jewelry, with metal as the canvas. Acid is used to etch designs into metals such as zinc, copper, brass, and even steel. When an acid reacts with a metal, it usually produces a salt and hydrogen gas. The metal loses atoms in the process. Hydrochloric acid, ferric nitrate, and sulfuric acid are some of the highly corrosive compounds used to produce this reactive art.

Film photographers also use chemical reactions when they process photographs. In photo processing, chemicals used to develop the photographs react with silver halides to create the darker areas of the image. Other artists use chemical reactions to create textiles, sculptures, and even movies.

## CONNECT TO YOU

You've been asked to create a work of art that demonstrates the beauty of chemical reactions. What kind of artwork would you create? What kinds of chemical reactions would you incorporate into your art?

A photograph is processed in a dark room, where a chemical reaction takes place on the photo paper.

Acid etching produced the patterns on this helmet.

89

# Modeling Chemical Reactions

## Guiding Questions

- How can a model be used to identify the components of a chemical reaction?
- How can a chemical equation be used to model the conservation of mass?

## Connections

**Literacy** Integrate With Visuals

**Math** Use Proportional Relationships

MS-PS1-5

## Vocabulary

law of
  conservation
  of mass
open system
closed system

## Academic Vocabulary

decomposition

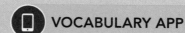 **VOCABULARY APP**

Practice vocabulary on a
mobile device.

**Quest CONNECTION**

Think about how chemical reactions apply
to your hot pack or cold pack.

## Connect It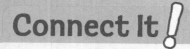

✏ **The rust on this ship formed from a chemical reaction between iron and oxygen. Label the rust, iron, and oxygen in the equation.**

Identify What are the sources of the iron and oxygen that form the rust on this ship?

........................................................................................................

........................................................................................................

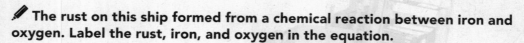

# Chemical Equations

When you communicate with friends using digital devices, you probably use symbols, abbreviations, and other ways to shorten your messages. This makes communication more efficient. Instead of typing "just kidding," you may type two letters—"jk"—to convey the same information. Science—and chemistry in particular—also makes use of shorthand language to convey information. A chemical equation is a way to describe a chemical reaction using symbols instead of words.

Chemical equations are shorter than sentences, but they contain all of the necessary pieces of information to summarize a chemical reaction. Just as a cell phone user who reads "jk" needs to learn what that stands for, a scientist needs to learn how to read and write chemical equations. The chemical equation that summarizes the reaction that makes rust is shown in the caption for **Figure 1**. The chemical equation conveys three things: the identities of the molecules involved in the reaction, the elements that make up those molecules, and whether the molecules are products or reactants.

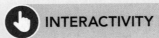

INTERACTIVITY

Write about the reaction that occurs when wood burns.

## Literacy Connection

**Integrate With Visuals**
Set up a two-column table in your notebook. As you read through this lesson, record examples of chemical reactions. In one column, write a description of the reaction. In the other column, write its chemical equation.

**Rusting Wreck**
**Figure 1** The process that transformed this ship's hull is a chemical reaction. Oxygen combines with iron to make iron oxide, which is commonly known as rust.

$$4\,Fe + 3\,O_2 \rightarrow 2\,Fe_2O_3$$

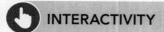
**Formulas** A chemical formula combines the symbols of different elements to represent molecules. For example, the formula for water is $H_2O$. H is the symbol for hydrogen, and O is the symbol for oxygen. The subscript number next to a letter shows how many atoms of that element are in the molecule. There are two hydrogen atoms in water. If there is no subscript, it means there is only one atom of that element. There is only one atom of oxygen in water.

## Structure of an Equation

All chemical equations share a basic structure. A chemical equation indicates the substances involved in a reaction and the substances that are formed as a result of the reaction. The formulas for the reactants are written on the left, followed by an arrow. The arrow means "yields," or "reacts to form." The formulas for the products are written to the right of the arrow. If there are two or more reactants, they are separated by a plus sign (+). If two or more products form, they are also separated by a plus sign.

**Reactant + Reactant ⟶ Product + Product**

The numbers in front of each component in the equation show how many particles of the reactants are needed and how many particles of the products are formed during the reaction. These numbers, called coefficients, balance the equation so that the number of atoms in the reactants equals the number of atoms in the products.

## Model It!

**Formation of Ammonia**

**Figure 2** The molecular model and chemical equation represent the formation of ammonia from nitrogen and hydrogen gas.

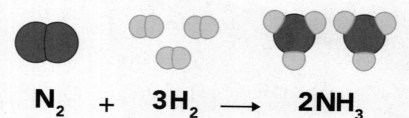

$$N_2 \;+\; 3H_2 \;\longrightarrow\; 2NH_3$$

1. **Identify** ✏ Circle the product and underline the coefficients in the chemical equation.

2. **Interpret Models** How many atoms of hydrogen are in one molecule of ammonia?

...........................................................

3. **Infer** Are any atoms created or destroyed in this reaction? Explain.

...........................................................

...........................................................

...........................................................

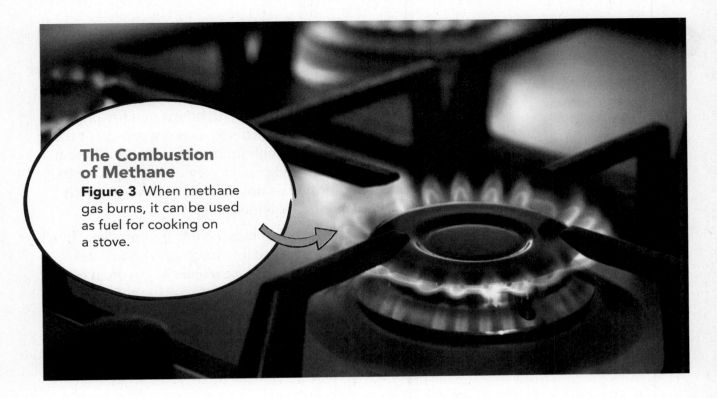

**The Combustion of Methane**

**Figure 3** When methane gas burns, it can be used as fuel for cooking on a stove.

**Chemical Reactions and Equations** The number of reactants and products can vary. Some reactions have only one reactant or product. Other reactions have two, three, or more reactants or products. For example, the reaction that occurs when limestone, or calcium carbonate ($CaCO_3$), is heated has one reactant and two products ($CaO$ and $CO_2$).

$$CaCO_3 \longrightarrow CaO + CO_2$$

The reaction that occurs when methane gas ($CH_4$) is burned in the presence of oxygen features two reactants and two products.

$$CH_4 + 2O_2 \longrightarrow CO_2 + 2H_2O$$

Note that the flame that provides the energy for the reaction as shown in **Figure 3** is not itself a reactant. Only the substances that are chemically rearranged in the reaction are shown in the equation.

☑ READING CHECK **Identify** Record the names and formulas of the reactants and products of methane combustion.

......................................................................................

......................................................................................

 **INTERACTIVITY**

Use models to help you understand chemical reactions.

 **HANDS-ON LAB**

☑**Investigate** Use nuts and bolts and their masses to model chemical reactions.

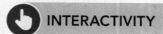

**INTERACTIVITY**

Perform a virtual experiment to compare the masses and colors of reactants and products.

# Law of Conservation of Mass

When reactants form new products, the new products always have the same amount of matter as the reactants. During a chemical reaction, matter is neither created nor destroyed. This is the **law of conservation of mass**. All atoms that are present at the beginning of a chemical reaction are present at the end of the reaction. Even though products may have different properties and may look and behave very differently from the reactants, the total mass does not change. This is why coefficients are used to balance equations.

For example, in the reaction such as the one that produces iron sulfide, the sum of the masses of iron and sulfur equals the mass of the iron sulfide they produce (**Figure 4**). An atom of iron bonds with an atom of sulfur, and the masses of the individual atoms combine when they form molecules. If there is more iron than can bind with sulfur, or more sulfur than can bind with iron, the leftover reactant will still be present, as will its mass.

## Mass Conserved

**Figure 4** ✏️ Iron and sulfur react to form iron sulfide. The masses of the reactants and the products are shown on the first set of scales. The second set of scales shows the masses of two liquid reactants. Fill in the expected mass of the liquid products for this second reaction.

$$Fe + S \longrightarrow FeS$$

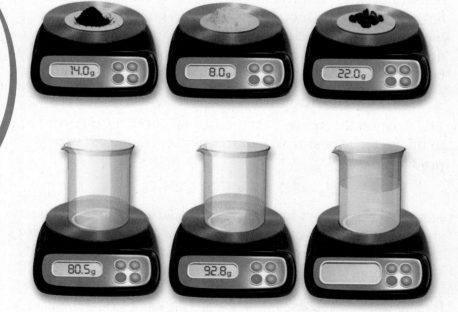

✅ READING CHECK **Integrate With Visuals** Explain how the masses on the scales in **Figure 4** demonstrate the law of conservation of mass.

........................................................................

........................................................................

## Balanced Equations

Because mass is conserved in a chemical reaction, chemical equations must be balanced.

**Use Proportional Relationships** Match each description shown with the chemical equation it describes.

none of the atoms in balance _____

oxygen atoms not balanced _____

iron atoms not balanced _____

all the atoms balanced _____

a. $2Fe + 3 O_2 \rightarrow 2Fe_2O_3$

b. $4Fe + 3 O_2 \rightarrow 2Fe_2O_3$

c. $2Fe + O_2 \rightarrow Fe_2O_3$

d. $Fe + O_2 \rightarrow Fe_2O_3$

## Open Systems
Some reactions may appear to violate the principle of conservation of mass. Recall that photosynthesis is a chemical reaction that plants use to make food. Carbon dioxide from the air, and water absorbed from soil, are reactants that produce sugar and oxygen, thanks to the energy provided by sunlight. But if you measure the mass of a plant as it grows, it will seem like a huge amount of mass is appearing out of nowhere. This is because most plants we see are in an **open system**, where matter can enter and escape. The flow and invisibility of the carbon dioxide gas that plants convert to food and structures—stems, trunks, leaves, and so on—makes it very difficult to know just how much carbon dioxide is involved (**Figure 5A**).

## Closed Systems
A **closed system** is a better place in which to measure the movement of matter and study reactions that involve gas. The sealed system in **Figure 5B** allows scientists to manipulate and analyze the contents of the system, including plants, without worrying that invisible gases may be moving into or out of the system.

### Open and Closed Systems
**Figure 5** Figure 5A shows an example of an open system, while Figure 5B shows an example of a closed system.

**VIDEO**

Watch a video to gain a better understanding of conservation of mass.

**INTERACTIVITY**

Demonstrate how matter is conserved in the formation of water and the burning of methane.

# Types of Chemical Reactions

There are three general types of chemical reactions. In each type, the reactants follow a characteristic behavior pattern.

**Synthesis** To synthesize is to put things together. When two or more elements or compounds combine to make a more complex substance, it's called a synthesis reaction, also known as a combination reaction. The reaction that produces magnesium oxide is a synthesis reaction.

$$2Mg + O_2 \longrightarrow 2MgO$$

**Decomposition** The opposite of a synthesis reaction is a **decomposition** reaction, in which compounds break down into simpler products. You may have a bottle of hydrogen peroxide ($H_2O_2$) in your house to clean cuts. If you keep such a bottle for a very long time, you'll have water instead. Hydrogen peroxide decomposes into water and oxygen gas.

$$2H_2O_2 \longrightarrow 2H_2O + O_2$$

**Replacement** When one element replaces another element in a compound, or if two elements in different compounds trade places, it's a replacement reaction. When potassium iodide and lead nitrate react, the potassium and lead change places.

$$2KI + Pb(NO_3)_2 \longrightarrow PbI_2 + 2KNO_3$$

Also note that a subscript is applied to the nitrate ($NO_3$) in the second reactant. This means there are two nitrates with a single lead (Pb) atom. On the product side of the equation, the coefficient is used because it applies to both the potassium (K) atom and the nitrate.

## Academic Vocabulary

In life science, the decomposition of matter occurs after something dies. Write a sentence that uses the word *decomposition*.

.................................................

.................................................

.................................................

## A Rusting Car

**Figure 6** Rust forms on this car as a result of a reaction between iron and oxygen. What kind of chemical reaction do you think produces this rust? Explain.

$$4Fe + 3O_2 \longrightarrow 2Fe_2O_3$$

.................................................

.................................................

.................................................

.................................................

**1. Identify** Aluminum (Al) and silver tarnish ($Ag_2S$) yield pure silver (Ag) in an aluminum sulfide solution.

$$3Ag_2S + 2Al \longrightarrow 6Ag + Al_2S_3$$

What are the reactants and products in this reaction?

........................................................................

........................................................................

........................................................................

**2. Interpret Data** Is the reaction above a replacement reaction? Explain.

........................................................................

........................................................................

**3. Infer** According to the law of conservation of mass, why must a chemical equation be balanced?

........................................................................

........................................................................

........................................................................

........................................................................

**4. Connect to Society** A neighbor wants to use his backyard garden to conduct an investigation of how tomato plants use specific amounts of carbon dioxide and water to grow at a certain rate. Is this a good idea? Explain.

........................................................................

........................................................................

........................................................................

........................................................................

........................................................................

........................................................................

........................................................................

**5. Interpret Models** ✏️ The chemical equation below is written with molecular models in place of chemical formulas. On the left is a carbon (C) atom and a molecule of oxygen. On the right is a molecule of carbon dioxide. Translate the visual model into a chemical equation.

# Quest CHECK-IN

In this lesson, you learned about the law of conservation of mass and how to model chemical reactions using equations. You also learned about different types of reactions and the impacts of open and closed systems.

**Draw Conclusions** What type of system should your pack use—an open system or a closed system? Explain.

........................................................................

........................................................................

........................................................................

## HANDS-ON LAB

Pack Building

**Go online** to download the lab worksheet. Build your pack from your design. Then test it to determine whether it is safe and easy to use.

# Producing Useful Materials

## Guiding Questions

- How are synthetic materials made from natural resources?
- How does the production and use of synthetic materials affect society?

## Connections

**Literacy** Evaluate Information

**Math** Analyze Quantitative Relationships

MS-PS1-3

## Vocabulary

synthetic
natural resource
polymer

## Academic Vocabulary

replicate

 **VOCABULARY APP**

Practice vocabulary on a mobile device.

### Quest CONNECTION

Consider the benefits and drawbacks of using synthetic materials, such as plastic bags, in your pack design.

## Connect It !

✏ **Many items we consume every day contain a yellow coloring agent called tartrazine—the powder shown here. Describe each item by writing *natural* or *artificial* under the image.**

**Construct Explanations** What other products do you think contain tartrazine? Explain your reasoning.

......................................................................................................................

......................................................................................................................

**Defend Your Claim** Some studies have indicated that tartrazine may complicate asthma and cause allergic reactions. Do you think that products containing tartrazine should be used by consumers? Why or why not?

......................................................................................................................

......................................................................................................................

# Synthetic Materials

Chemical reactions are constantly happening all around us in nature. Many of the products of naturally occurring reactions have properties that are useful to humans. For instance, plants perform photosynthesis, a chemical reaction that releases oxygen, which we need to survive.

However, not all of the chemicals and materials that humans use come directly from naturally occurring reactions. Instead, they are products of chemical reactions we induce. Such reactions start with substances found in nature, but they result in new materials being formed. For example, glass is made from sand and other minerals that are melted together.

Chemicals and resources made by humans are called **synthetic** materials. Synthetic materials, such as the tartrazine in **Figure 1**, have a wide variety of uses and have enabled great advances in engineering and technology. Chemists are always trying out new chemical reactions to produce new materials for our ever-changing needs.

### INTERACTIVITY

Engage in a class discussion about synthetic materials in your everyday life.

### Making Colors in the Lab
**Figure 1** Tartrazine is a synthetic coloring agent. It is used in products ranging from foods to medicines and cosmetics.

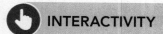

INTERACTIVITY

Explore the relationship between natural resources and synthetics in medicine.

**Academic Vocabulary**

*Replicate* means to copy or repeat. Use the word replicate in a sentence.

......................................................

......................................................

**Natural Resources as Building Blocks** All the useful materials we benefit from are synthesized from natural resources. A **natural resource** is anything naturally occurring in the environment that humans use. These resources may be pure elements, simple molecules, or complex molecules.

Chemists assemble synthetic materials in an ordered set of steps, using chemical reactions to create the desired material. The process can be **replicated** at a later time or by another lab to produce the same results. Just the way you would build a house one brick at a time, a chemist synthesizes a material by adding molecular "blocks" one step at a time. You build the house by moving the bricks into place by hand. The chemist relies upon chemical reactions to move molecules into place.

# Math Toolbox
## Nutrient Concentration

Vitamin C is an essential nutrient for a healthy, functioning body. This vitamin can be obtained from food sources or in a synthetic form in a tablet.

A tablet with a mass of 500 mg contains about 450 mg of synthetic vitamin C.

A 180-g (180,000-mg) orange contains about 106 mg of vitamin C.

**1. Analyze Quantitative Relationships** Compare the concentrations of vitamin C in the tablet and in the orange. To determine the concentration, calculate the percent of each object that is made up of vitamin C.

......................................................

......................................................

......................................................

......................................................

**2. Interpret Data** About how many oranges would you need to eat to get the same amount of vitamin C in one tablet?

......................................................

......................................................

......................................................

**Properties of Pure Substances** Every pure substance has characteristic physical and chemical properties that you use to identify it. Substances react in characteristic, predictable ways, forming new materials with physical and chemical properties different from the original substances. For example, sodium is a soft metal with a low melting point, and chlorine is a toxic gas. When sodium burns in chlorine gas, the product formed by the reaction is sodium chloride (NaCl). As you may recall, sodium chloride is table salt. The reaction of two substances produces a new material with completely different properties, and we can eat it!

With the knowledge of the physical and chemical properties of substances and how they chemically react with each other, chemists can combine substances to produce materials that have specific structures and that serve particular functions. This isn't to say that all synthetic materials are created on purpose, as shown in **Figure 2**.

 **VIDEO**

Watch a video to clear up misconceptions about synthetics.

## Accidental Synthetics

**Figure 2** Many synthetic materials were created accidentally in the lab. Use what you know about each of these products to write their properties.

Evaluate Information Use library or Internet resources to check your answers and find out more about each synthetic product. Make sure to evaluate the credibility of the sources you use.

| Synthetic and How It Was Discovered | Useful Properties |
|---|---|
| **Superglue** In the 1940s, a chemist working on plastic gun sights synthesized a material called cyanoacrylate that frustratingly stuck to everything it touched. A few years later, the chemist came up with an important purpose for the sticky material.  | |
|  **Non-stick Coating** In the 1930s, a chemist working on a new refrigerant came back to his lab to find small white flakes in a container instead of a gas he had been experimenting with. The chemist had unintentionally synthesized a new non-stick substance. | |
| **Artificial Sweetener** In the late 1800s, a chemist was working on an experimental compound. Forgetting to wash his hands before eating, he noticed that everything he ate tasted very sweet.  | |

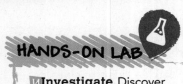

иInvestigate Discover how to make plastic from starch.

## Polymers

Many natural and artificial materials are made of **polymers**. Polymers are long chains of molecules that are made up of repeating units called monomers. Polymers occur naturally and have been used by people for centuries. They include wool, silk, rubber, and cellulose. Polymers have many different and important properties, such as strength, flexibility, and elasticity, all due to the structure of long molecule chains. Polymers that don't occur naturally are synthesized in large quantities to provide clothes, building materials, and most of our material goods. Plastic water bottles and toothbrushes (**Figure 3**) are made of polymers.

The most common synthetic polymers are plastics. Plastics are moldable substances that are strong but flexible. These synthetic materials are usually made from petroleum, a natural resource. While plastics have revolutionized our lives, they also are generally resistant to breaking down and biodegrading. They contribute to pollution when they are not recycled.

☑READING CHECK **Summarize** Why do chemists synthesize polymers in the lab?

.................................................................................................

.................................................................................................

.................................................................................................

## Model It!

### The Structure of Polymers

**Figure 3** The composition of a polymer such as plastic may be very simple, but the number of molecules may be huge, containing millions of atoms!

Develop Models ✏ Use the model of the monomer to create a model of a polymer.

Monomer

Polymer

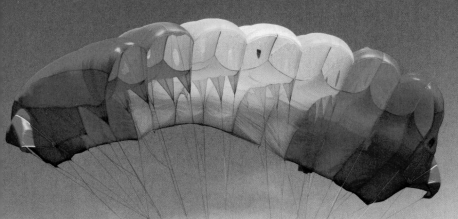

# Impact of Synthetic Materials

Synthetic materials allow very large numbers of people to be clothed, housed, and fed. Many of the medical, technological, and societal advances that have occurred during the last 200 years are due in large part to synthetic materials.

**Synthetic Fibers** Naturally occurring fibers such as cotton, wool, and silk have been used for thousands of years, but they can be expensive. In part, that is because each can be grown or raised only in certain parts of the world. Synthetic fibers, such as acrylic, nylon, polyester, spandex, and rayon, replicate or improve the characteristics of natural fibers. In addition, they generally are much less expensive to produce. Synthetic fibers last longer, dry more quickly, and clean more easily than natural fibers, although they often burn more easily.

**Synthetic Foods** Synthetic food products include flavorings, colorings, and preservatives. Many foods we eat would rot or decay quickly without synthetic preservatives. And yet, some preservatives have been found to cause health problems. Vanillin is a synthetic flavor designed as a substitute for the natural flavor of the vanilla bean. But the vanilla bean grows only on a few particular orchids in places such as Mexico and Madagascar. It would be too costly and time-consuming to meet the world demand for natural vanilla flavoring.

| Producing and Using Synthetic Food Products | |
|---|---|
| **Benefits** | **Drawbacks** |
| | |

**INTERACTIVITY**

Describe the impact of synthetics on society.

## Nylon
**Figure 4** The polymer nylon is used to make parachutes because of its strength and resistance to tearing.

## Literacy Connection
**Evaluate Information** Suppose you were asked to research information about a potentially dangerous synthetic food product. How would you evaluate the credibility of the sources you found?

...........................................................

...........................................................

...........................................................

## Preserving Food
**Figure 5** 🖋 Potassium sorbate is a synthetic food preservative often used in cheese, yogurts, and other dairy products to prevent mold growth. In the table shown, identify some benefits and drawbacks of producing and using synthetic food products.

**Write About It** How do you think the ability of chemists to synthesize compounds has affected the field of medicine? Write your thoughts in your science notebook.

**Synthetic Medicines** If you have ever taken medicine for an illness, you have likely benefited from chemical synthesis in the form of pharmaceuticals. Many synthetic chemicals are used to cure or reduce the effects of diseases and illnesses. Many medical compounds have been discovered in plants. Chemists can determine the chemical formula of these natural compounds and then produce them in large amounts and in safer forms through chemical synthesis. *Digitalis lanata,* shown in **Figure 6**, produces a compound that benefits cardiac patients. However, the plant is highly toxic to humans and animals. Chemists have isolated and synthesized the compound, called digoxin, that provides the benefits without the toxic side effects.

**Synthetic Fuels** One day, the world will run out of petroleum. Cars and trains can run on electricity, but how will we power planes and boats? Synthetic fuels of many kinds are made through chemical reactions. Chemists have been exploring how to synthesize resources such as plants, animal oils, coal, algae, or other materials into fuels.

✅ READING CHECK **Evaluate Information** A website publishes an article arguing that synthetic materials do not benefit society because they are created in a lab. Do you think the website is a reliable source? Explain.

.................................................................................................................................

.................................................................................................................................

.................................................................................................................................

.................................................................................................................................

### Safer Synthetics

**Figure 6** This plant is *Digitalis lanata,* also known as Grecian foxglove. Eating even a small portion of the plant itself can be fatal. However, a compound from this plant is used to help patients with heart conditions. Chemists synthesize the compound into digoxin tablets that are safe to consume.

Digoxin Tablets 125 micrograms 28 tablets For oral use

1. **Identify** What is a synthetic material?

...................................................................

...................................................................

...................................................................

2. **Write Informative Texts** What type of change must occur for pure substances to combine into new materials? Name a few kinds of synthetic materials that can be produced by this type of change.

...................................................................

...................................................................

...................................................................

...................................................................

...................................................................

3. **Describe Patterns** What is the difference between the structures of monomers and polymers?

...................................................................

...................................................................

...................................................................

...................................................................

4. **Relate Structure and Function** Describe how the structure of polymers helps to make them useful materials.

...................................................................

...................................................................

...................................................................

...................................................................

...................................................................

...................................................................

5. **Evaluate Claims** How would you respond to a friend's claim that chemists don't know what to expect when synthesizing new materials?

...................................................................

...................................................................

...................................................................

...................................................................

...................................................................

...................................................................

...................................................................

## Quest CHECK-IN

**In this lesson, you learned how chemists produce synthetic materials. You also investigated how synthetic materials have impacted society.**

**Evaluate** What are some of the benefits and drawbacks of using synthetic materials, such as plastic bags, in your pack design?

...................................................................

...................................................................

...................................................................

...................................................................

### HANDS-ON LAB

Heat It Up or Ice It Down

**Go online** to download the lab worksheet. Retest and refine your pack to make sure it meets the criteria of the challenge. Then demonstrate your final version.

# Is Plastic Really So Fantastic?

Chemists use crude oil to make plastics in a lab.

Look around your classroom or community, and you will likely see many things made from plastic.

Most plastic is synthesized from petroleum, or crude oil. This natural resource is a mixture of thousands of different compounds. To make plastic from it, these compounds have to be processed.

Oil is a mixture of carbon and hydrogen atoms, which differ in size and structure. These atoms form simple monomers. Through several chemical reactions, the monomers form large chains of polymers, and you end up with plastic.

## The Benefits of Plastic

Plastic has had a profound impact on society. It is very durable and fairly inexpensive to produce. Plastic is much lighter than metal, and it can be molded into just about any shape. These properties work to our advantage in a wide variety of applications. Many auto parts are plastic because they increase fuel efficiency by decreasing the mass of the car.

## The Drawbacks of Plastic

While plastic is a world-changing synthetic material, it has its share of problems. Plastic materials do not biodegrade readily. Landfills are overflowing with plastic items that will be around for many hundreds of years. Plastic refuse also has ended up in the oceans, impacting the survival of fish and other aquatic organisms.

One way to deal with the negative impacts of plastics is to recycle as much of it as possible. The table shows how the recycling of different types of plastic bottles has changed from 2013 to 2014.

| Postconsumer Plastics Recycled in U.S., 2013–2014 | | | |
| --- | --- | --- | --- |
| | Plastic Bottle Type | Plastic Recycled (millions of pounds) | Recycling Rate |
| 2013 | PET | 1798 | 31.2% |
| | HDPE Natural | 440.4 | 28.0% |
| | HDPE Pigmented | 605.0 | 34.9% |
| | Total Bottles | 1045.4 | 31.6% |
| 2014 | PET | 1812 | 31.0% |
| | HDPE Natural | 464.4 | 29.9% |
| | HDPE Pigmented | 643.0 | 36.8% |
| | Total Bottles | 1107.4 | 33.6% |

**Use the table to answer the following questions.**

1. **Identify Patterns** What patterns do you observe among the data in the table?

2. **Predict** What do you think the recycling data will look like in 2020? Explain. Do a calculation that predicts what the percentage will be.

3. **Apply Scientific Reasoning** Describe an experiment that could be conducted to investigate how long it takes different plastics to break down.

4. **Connect to Society** What are some ways you can think of to get people to recycle more plastic instead of allowing it to end up in a landfill or the ocean?

## 1 Mixtures and Solutions

MS-PS1-2

1. In a heterogeneous mixture, the substances
   A. can be physically separated.
   B. are chemically combined.
   C. can only be separated through chemical processes.
   D. break down into new substances.

2. Which of the following statements is true?
   A. A solution is a pure substance.
   B. A solution is a mixture.
   C. The solvent is dissolved in the solute.
   D. A solution has the same properties as a colloid.

3. Milk and sugar water are both (mixtures / pure substances). However, milk is a (colloid / solution) and sugar water is a (colloid / solution).

4. Analyze Data Examine the data table. Why is ethylene glycol used in de-icing fluid for airplanes and other vehicles?

| Ethylene Glycol in Water (%) | Freezing Point (°C) |
|---|---|
| 0 | 0 |
| 10 | 2 |
| 20 | 8 |
| 30 | 16 |
| 40 | 25 |

........................................................................

........................................................................

5. Apply Concepts What factors affect the properties of a solution?

........................................................................

........................................................................

........................................................................

........................................................................

## 2 Chemical Change

MS-PS1-2

6. Which of the following is an example of a chemical change?
   A. breaking a rock into smaller pieces
   B. burning a candle
   C. stirring butter and sugar together
   D. adding food coloring to water

7. In general, what happens to the rate of reaction when you decrease the temperature of a chemical reaction?
   A. it decreases
   B. it increases
   C. it is unaffected
   D. it increases, and then decreases

8. Burning a log is an example of
   A. an endothermic reaction.
   B. a solution.
   C. a catalyst.
   D. an exothermic reaction.

9. All chemical changes result in

........................................................................

10. Apply Concepts Milk contains bacteria that carry out chemical reactions to live and reproduce. Why is milk kept in the refrigerator?

........................................................................

........................................................................

........................................................................

........................................................................

........................................................................

........................................................................

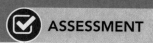 
## 3 Modeling Chemical Reactions

MS-PS1-5

**11.** In the chemical equation shown, what are the reactants?

$$4\,Al + 3\,O_2 \longrightarrow 2\,Al_2O_3$$

**A.** $Al_2O_3$

**B.** $Al_2O_3$ and $Al$

**C.** $Al$ and $O_2$

**D.** $Al_2O_3$ and $O_2$

**12.** You run an experiment in which two substances chemically react in a closed system. You run the same experiment in an open system. How would the masses of the products in each experiment compare? Explain.

..................................................................

..................................................................

..................................................................

..................................................................

**13.** Use Models ✏ A model of a reaction is shown below. In the reaction, 1 nitrogen molecule ($N_2$) and 3 hydrogen molecules ($H_2$) react to form 2 ammonia molecules ($NH_3$). Complete the model of the reaction. Then, explain how the model demonstrates the conservation of mass.

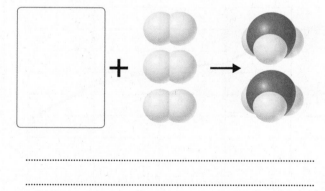

..................................................................

..................................................................

..................................................................

..................................................................

## 4 Producing Useful Materials

MS-PS1-3

**14.** Which of the following statements about synthetic materials is true?

**A.** Synthetic materials are never harmful to the environment.

**B.** Synthetic materials are pure substances found in nature.

**C.** Synthetic materials have properties that are different from those of the natural materials used to produce them.

**D.** Synthetic materials are not different from natural materials.

**15.** Which of the following is a valid explanation for why people produce synthetic materials?

**A.** Synthetic materials always biodegrade easily.

**B.** Synthetic materials do not require any natural resources to produce.

**C.** Synthetic materials are less artificial than natural resources.

**D.** Synthetic materials help meet societal demand for materials that are in short supply in nature.

**16.** Chemists can synthesize new materials using chemical reactions because pure substances form new materials that have (the same/ different) physical and chemical properties.

**17.** Relate Structure and Function Explain why the structure of a polymer such as plastic makes it such a useful material for society.

..................................................................

..................................................................

..................................................................

..................................................................

..................................................................

..................................................................

MS-PS1-2, MS-PS1-5

# Evidence-Based Assessment

Human industries and agriculture produce carbon dioxide ($CO_2$) gas that enters the atmosphere. About a quarter of the $CO_2$ is absorbed by Earth's ocean. Once the $CO_2$ dissolves in the seawater, it can react with water ($H_2O$) to produce carbonic acid ($H_2CO_3$). The equation shown below represents this reaction. The data table lists some of the properties of $CO_2$, $H_2O$, and $H_2CO_3$.

$$CO_2 + H_2O \rightarrow H_2CO_3$$

| Properties of Compounds | | | |
|---|---|---|---|
| | **Carbon Dioxide ($CO_2$)** | **Water ($H_2O$)** | **Carbonic Acid ($H_2CO_3$)** |
| **Density*** | $0.00198 g/cm^3$ | $1.000 g/cm^3$ | $2.54 g/cm^3$ |
| **Melting Point** | $-56.6°C$ | $0°C$ | $856°C$ |
| **Boiling Point** | $-78.5°C$ (sublimes) | $100°C$ | Not applicable |
| **Solubility** | Soluble in water | Not applicable | Soluble in water |

* Densities taken at standard temperature and pressure.

In water, carbonic acid produces hydrogen ions. The higher the concentration of these ions, the lower the pH of the seawater. The pH scale can be used to measure the acidity of a substance. If a substance has a lower pH, it is more acidic. This graph shows ocean pH levels near Hawaii.

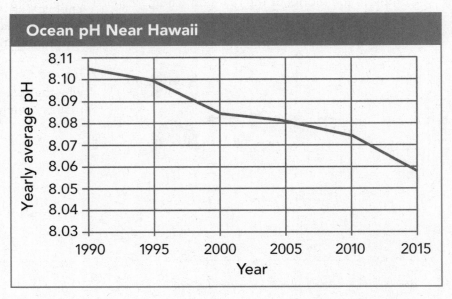

1. **Analyze Data** How did the pH of the ocean change from year 1990 to year 2015?
   A. It increased by about 0.05
   B. It decreased by about 0.05
   C. It increased by about 0.5
   D. It decreased by about 0.5

2. **Quantify Change** In which five-year period did ocean pH decline at the fastest rate?
   A. 1990–1995
   B. 2000–2005
   C. 2005–2010
   D. 2010–2015

3. **Use Models** Is mass conserved in the chemical equation shown? How can you tell?

   .........................................................................
   .........................................................................
   .........................................................................
   .........................................................................
   .........................................................................
   .........................................................................

4. **Cite Evidence** Based on the chemical equation and data table, provide two pieces of evidence that suggest a chemical change is occurring between dissolved $CO_2$ and $H_2O$ in the oceans.

   .........................................................................
   .........................................................................
   .........................................................................
   .........................................................................
   .........................................................................
   .........................................................................
   .........................................................................
   .........................................................................
   .........................................................................
   .........................................................................
   .........................................................................

5. **Construct an Argument** Since preindustrial times, the pH of the Earth's ocean has decreased significantly. Explain one reason why Earth's ocean is becoming more acidic and why you think this might be a problem.

   .........................................................................
   .........................................................................
   .........................................................................
   .........................................................................
   .........................................................................
   .........................................................................
   .........................................................................
   .........................................................................
   .........................................................................

# Quest FINDINGS

## Complete the Quest!

**Phenomenon** Determine the best way to present your design to the class and demonstrate the effectiveness of your pack.

Apply Concepts In this Quest, you dissolved salts in water to cause your pack to heat up or cool down. How might using different substances in the pack increase its effectiveness?

   .........................................................................
   .........................................................................
   .........................................................................
   .........................................................................
   .........................................................................
   .........................................................................

👆 **INTERACTIVITY**

Reflect on Your Pack

MS-PS1-2

# Evidence of Chemical Change

How can you **determine** when a **chemical reaction** has occurred?

## Background

**Phenomenon** Quiet on the set! You have been asked to create a video for a science channel to show and explain the differences between physical and chemical changes. In this investigation, you will observe how different substances interact. You will use this information to develop a script for the video that explains how to determine when a chemical change has occurred.

## Materials

(per group)
- 3 100-mL beakers
- baking soda (1 teaspoon)
- vinegar (10 mL)
- potato (2-cm cube)
- hydrogen peroxide (25 mL)
- sugar (1 teaspoon)
- iodine (10 mL)
- 3 plastic spoons
- graduated cylinder

## Safety

Be sure to follow all safety guidelines provided by your teacher. The Safety Appendix of your textbook provides more details about the safety icons.

# Design an Experiment

## HANDS-ON LAB

иDemonstrate Go online for a downloadable worksheet of this lab.

1. Design a procedure using the listed materials that lets you observe interactions of the pairs of substances listed in the table. Here are some questions that might help you to write your procedures:

   • At what points in each experiment might you need to make observations?

   • What evidence will you specifically look for?

   • When is the best time to make your prediction?

   • How will you determine whether the interaction has resulted in a physical or chemical change?

   • How might you determine when a reaction is complete?

| Interactions | | |
|---|---|---|
| **Interaction 1** | **Interaction 2** | **Interaction 3** |
| baking soda and vinegar | sugar and iodine | potato and hydrogen peroxide |

2. Record your predictions and observations in the data table.

3. Get your teacher's approval of your procedure. Then run your experiments.

## Procedure

_____
_____
_____
_____
_____
_____
_____
_____
_____
_____
_____
_____
_____
_____
_____
_____

## Data Table

| Interaction | Prediction | Observations |
|---|---|---|
| 1 | | |
| 2 | | |
| 3 | | |

# Analyze and Interpret Data

1. **Patterns** What similarities and differences did you observe among the three interactions?

   .................................................................................................
   .................................................................................................
   .................................................................................................

2. **Make Observations** In each case, how did the properties of the substances before the interaction compare to the properties of the substances after the interaction?

   Interaction 1:

   .................................................................................................
   .................................................................................................

   Interaction 2:

   .................................................................................................
   .................................................................................................

   Interaction 3:

   .................................................................................................
   .................................................................................................

3. **Apply Scientific Reasoning** Which of the three interactions result in chemical changes? Were your predictions correct? Explain how observing the properties of substances before and after the interactions helped you to determine whether a chemical change occurred.

   .................................................................................................
   .................................................................................................
   .................................................................................................
   .................................................................................................
   .................................................................................................
   .................................................................................................
   .................................................................................................

4. **Construct an Explanation** With your group, use the data and your observations from your experiment to develop a video script. Write it in your notebook. Your script should identify the substances in each interaction, demonstrate the interaction, and then explain how to determine whether a chemical reaction has occurred.

# TOPIC

# 3

# Forces and Motion

**LESSON 1**
Describing Motion
and Force
**uInvestigate Lab:** Motion Commotion

**LESSON 2**
Speed, Velocity,
and Acceleration
**uInvestigate Lab:** Walking the Walk

**LESSON 3**
Newton's Laws of Motion
**uInvestigate Lab:** Newton Scooters

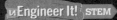 **uEngineer It!** STEM **Generating Energy from Potholes**

**LESSON 4**
Friction and Gravitational
Interactions
**uInvestigate Lab:** Observing Friction

**NGSS PERFORMANCE EXPECTATIONS**

**MS-PS2-1** Apply Newton's Third Law to design a solution to a problem involving the motion of two colliding objects.

**MS-PS2-2** Plan an investigation to provide evidence that the change in an object's motion depends on the sum of the forces on the object and the mass of the object.

**MS-PS2-4** Construct and present arguments using evidence to support the claim that gravitational interactions are attractive and depend on the masses of interacting objects.

**MS-PS3-2** Develop a model to describe that when the arrangement of objects interacting at a distance changes, different amounts of potential energy are stored in the system.

What forces act on these skydivers?

**HANDS-ON LAB**

**uConnect** Determine a reference point for two different observers.

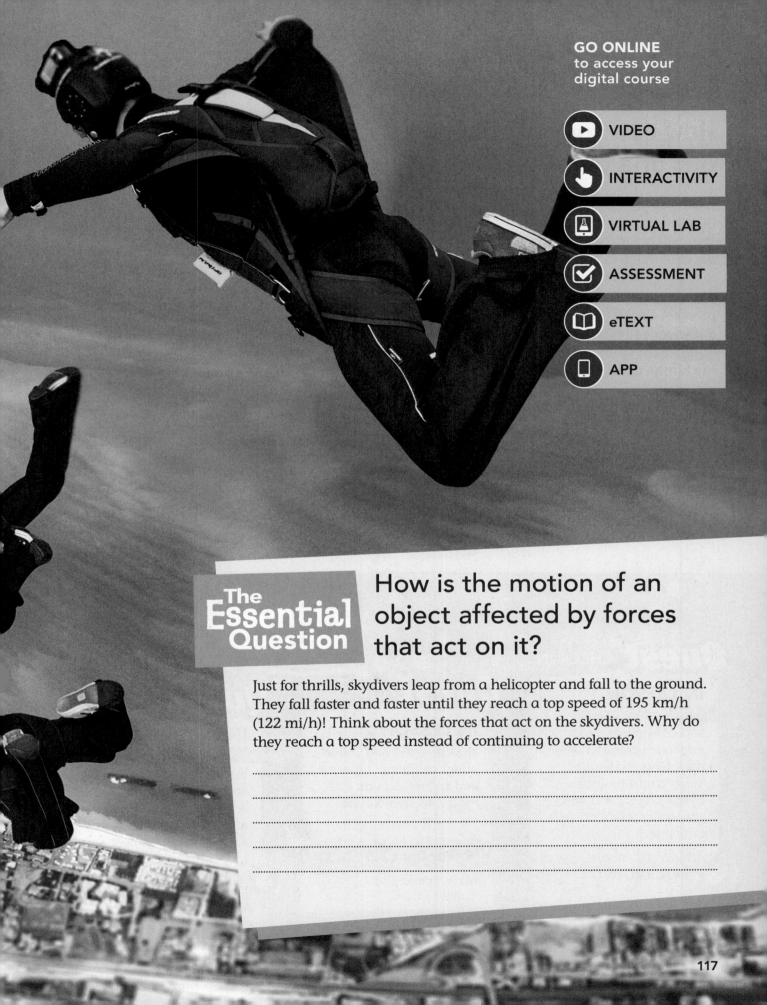

**GO ONLINE**
to access your
digital course

▶ VIDEO

👆 INTERACTIVITY

🧪 VIRTUAL LAB

☑ ASSESSMENT

📖 eTEXT

📱 APP

## The Essential Question

# How is the motion of an object affected by forces that act on it?

Just for thrills, skydivers leap from a helicopter and fall to the ground. They fall faster and faster until they reach a top speed of 195 km/h (122 mi/h)! Think about the forces that act on the skydivers. Why do they reach a top speed instead of continuing to accelerate?

.......................................................................................

.......................................................................................

.......................................................................................

.......................................................................................

.......................................................................................

## How can you take the crash out of a collision?

**Phenomenon** When engineers design amusement park rides, they have to consider all of the forces that will be acting on riders and make sure the rides are safe. Engineers test their designs with dummies to ensure that riders will not fall out of their seats and collisions will not be harmful to them. In this problem-based Quest activity, you will apply your knowledge of Newton's laws of motion to design a bumper car ride that is safe—for both the rider and the bumper car. You will explore forces and Newton's third law of motion as you design, build, test, and refine a model bumper car.

 **INTERACTIVITY**

Build a Better Bumper Car

MS-PS2-1 Apply Newton's Third Law to design a solution to a problem involving the motion of two colliding objects.

**NBC LEARN** ▶ VIDEO

After watching the Quest Kickoff video, which examines forces and the laws of motion, think about amusement park rides. Complete the 3-2-1 activity.

**3** things riders want to experience

.................................................

.................................................

.................................................

**2** ways that rides keep riders safe

.................................................

.................................................

**1** way in which riders sometimes get injured

.................................................

.................................................

.................................................

---

# Quest CHECK-IN

### IN LESSON 1

**STEM** What criteria and constraints must engineers consider when designing a safe ride? Think about the goals of the project and how you will ensure a positive outcome.

 **INTERACTIVITY**

Define Criteria and Constraints

# Quest CHECK-IN

### IN LESSON 2

How do mass and speed affect collisions? Observe and collect data on how mass and speed affect collisions.

**HANDS-ON LAB**

Mass, Speed, and Colliding Cars

# Quest CHECK-IN

### IN LESSON 3

**STEM** How do varying masses and rates of speed affect bumper cars and their riders? Develop and evaluate a design for a safe and fun bumper car.

 **INTERACTIVITY**

Apply Newton's Laws of Motion

Every time a bumper car moves forward and hits another car, there is an equal push in the opposite direction. That is part of what makes riding bumper cars fun.

## Quest CHECK-IN

### IN LESSON 4

STEM How do the action-reaction forces affect bumper cars and their riders? Build, test, evaluate, and improve your bumper car model.

### HANDS-ON LAB

Bumping Cars, Bumper Solutions

## Quest FINDINGS

### Complete the Quest!

Present your final design and explain how you applied Newton's third law of motion as you developed your design.

### INTERACTIVITY

Reflect on Your Bumper Car Solution

# Describing Motion and Force

## Guiding Questions

- When is an object in motion?
- How do different types of forces affect motion?

## Connections

**Literacy** Draw Evidence

**Math** Write an Inequality

MS-PS2-2

## Vocabulary

motion
reference point
force
newton
friction
gravity
net force

## Academic Vocabulary

relative

 **VOCABULARY APP**

Practice vocabulary on a mobile device.

### Quest CONNECTION

Think about how forces acting on amusement park rides might affect their motion.

## Connect It!

✎ **What part of the image indicates that there is motion? Label it with the word "motion."**

**Constructing Explanations** Why did you label that part of the image?

.................................................................................................

.................................................................................................

.................................................................................................

**Apply Scientific Reasoning** This image shows a car traveling down a road. Why do you think the dog in the car does not appear to be moving?

.................................................................................................

.................................................................................................

.................................................................................................

# An Object in Motion

How do you decide whether something is moving? For example, if you were the photographer riding in the car in **Figure 1**, would you say the dog is moving? Parts of it would seem to be. Its eyes blink, and its ears flap in the wind. But to you, the dog would appear to be staying in one position. You know, however, that the dog is in a car that is speeding down the road, so it must be moving. What determines whether the dog is moving or not?

**Reference Points** An object is in **motion** if its position changes when compared to another object. To decide whether the dog is moving, you might use yourself as a reference point. A **reference point** is a place or object used for comparison to determine whether something is in motion. Objects that are fixed to Earth—such as a tree, a stop sign, or a building—make good reference points. Suppose a tree along the road in **Figure 1** is used as a reference point. The car moves past the tree, as does the dog inside the car. In relation to the tree, the dog changes position, and therefore is in motion. However, if you are the photographer in **Figure 1**, and you are the reference point, your position relative to the dog does not change. You could say that, compared to you, the dog is not in motion.

☑ READING CHECK **Determine Conclusions** Suppose that you are in the car with the dog. What might be your reference point, other than yourself, if you determine that the dog is not moving?

....................................................................................

....................................................................................

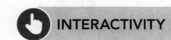
INTERACTIVITY

Discover how to use reference points.

**Movin' Along**
**Figure 1** The dog is moving in relation to the landscape, but it is not moving in relation to the car.

121

## HANDS-ON LAB

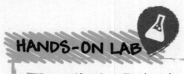

**🔍Investigate**  Explore how to tell whether an object you are observing is in motion.

### Academic Vocabulary

In this lesson, *relative* means "not fixed, not absolute." What does *relative* mean when you use it as a noun?

.................................................................

.................................................................

.................................................................

.................................................................

**Relative Motion**  Because motion is determined by a reference point that can change, motion is **relative**. Suppose you are relaxing on a beach. If you use your beach towel as your reference point, you are not moving. You and the beach towel are not changing positions relative to each other. Suppose you use the sun as a reference point instead of your beach towel. If you compare your position to the sun, you are moving quite rapidly, because you are on Earth and Earth revolves around the sun. Relative to the sun, you are moving, but relative to Earth, you are sitting still, so you don't feel as if you are in motion. See **Figure 2** for another example of relative motion.

**☑ READING CHECK  Draw Evidence**  What sources of information might you use to determine the relative motion of Earth compared to other planets in the solar system?

.................................................................................................................

.................................................................................................................

### Relative Motion

**Figure 2** ✏ Circle the person on the right side of the front car. In the table, list three reference points that could be used to show that the person is in motion. List three reference points that could be used to show that the person is stationary.

| In motion relative to... | Stationary relative to... |
|---|---|
|  |  |
|  |  |

# How Forces Affect Motion

While objects move relative to one another, they can also speed up, slow down, and change direction. The motion of an object can change when one or more forces act on the object. A **force** is a push or a pull. When one object pushes or pulls another object, the first object exerts a force on the second object. You exert a force on a book when you push it into your book bag. You exert a force on the sleeve of your jacket when you pull it off your arm.

**Describing Force**  A force is described by its strength and by the direction in which it acts. The force needed to lift a dinner plate requires less strength than the force needed to push a refrigerator. Pushing a faucet handle to the left is a different force from pushing it to the right. In an image, the direction and strength of a force acting on an object can be represented by an arrow. The arrow points in the direction of the force, as shown in **Figure 3**. The length of the arrow indicates the strength of the force—the longer the arrow, the greater the force. In the International System of Units (SI), the unit for the strength of a force is called a **newton** (N), after the scientist Sir Isaac Newton.

A bird sits on top of an elephant.

A horse starts pulling a man in a buggy.

A cat pushes a dog.

**Representing Forces**

**Figure 3** ✏ In the first image, a short arrow in a downward direction shows that the bird is exerting a small downward force on the elephant. Draw arrows on the other images to represent the size and direction of the forces applied by the animals in action.

**Infer** Which image shows a force that causes a change in motion? Why does this force cause a change in motion, but the forces in the other images do not?

.................................................................................................

.................................................................................................

.................................................................................................

123

**Types of Forces** Forces can be classified as either contact forces or noncontact forces. Contact forces are those applied only when one object actually touches another. When you push a box across the floor, your push is a contact force because the force only exists while you touch the box. The box may be difficult to push because there is another contact force acting on the box in the opposite direction of your push. It is the force of friction between the box and the floor. **Friction** is a contact force that two surfaces exert on each other when they rub against each other. Friction between your feet and the sidewalk prevents you from slipping as you walk. Ice on the sidewalk greatly reduces that friction.

A noncontact force is a force applied to an object whether it touches the object or not. One noncontact force that you experience every day is **gravity**—a force that pulls objects toward each other as a result of their masses. The force of gravity pulls your body toward Earth. Magnetism and electrical forces are also noncontact forces. **Figure 4** shows examples of contact forces and noncontact forces.

**READING CHECK** **Identify** What are three examples of noncontact forces?

......................................................

......................................................

**Contact and Noncontact Forces**
**Figure 4** You use contact and noncontact forces daily. Complete the sentence in each caption by underlining either "contact" or "noncontact."

This girl exerts a force on the pedals of this bicycle, and friction between the tires and the road help to keep the bike from slipping. Both the force on the pedals and friction are (contact/noncontact) forces.

Even when your feet don't touch the ground, gravity pulls you toward Earth's surface. Gravity is a (contact/noncontact) force.

**Balanced and Unbalanced Forces** More than one force can act on an object. If two forces acting on an object are equal in strength and opposite in direction, they are balanced forces. A single book resting on a shelf has two forces acting on it. The downward force of gravity is equal in strength and opposite in direction to the upward force of the shelf on the book. The forces are balanced.

What happens when someone pulls the book off the shelf? The pull of the person removing the book and the friction between the shelf and the book also act in opposite directions. These two forces, however are not equal in strength. The pull is stronger than the friction. These forces are unbalanced.

When the forces on an object are unbalanced, there is a nonzero net force acting on the object. The **net force** on an object is the combination of all the forces acting on that object. If the forces act in the same direction, the net force is the sum of the forces. If the forces act in opposite directions, the net force is the difference in the strengths of those forces. If the net force turns out to be zero, the forces are balanced. Otherwise, the forces are unbalanced. A nonzero net force acting on an object causes a change in the object's motion.

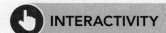
**INTERACTIVITY**

Explore balanced and unbalanced forces in action.

**Write About It!** In your science notebook, describe two examples of how unbalanced forces help you in your everyday life.

# Model It!

**Forces in Tug-of-War**

**Figure 5** A tug-of-war competition demonstrates the effects of balanced and unbalanced forces on motion. The people on the left side of the rope are experiencing a force from the rope pulling them to the right. They are also experiencing friction from the ground pushing them to the left. The winning team is the team that experiences the greater force of friction.

**Develop Models** ✎ Draw more people on the left side of the rope to increase the force of friction experienced by this team. Add arrows to the model to represent the force from the rope and the force of friction on the people.

# Math Toolbox

## Effects of Net Force

In each diagram, two animals push on an apple. The forces of gravity and friction acting on the apple in each scenario does not change, so the forces that may cause a change will come from the animals.

Two chipmunks push on the apple in opposite directions with forces of equal strength. The forces on the apple are balanced. The motion and position of the apple do not change.

A chipmunk and a squirrel push on the apple in opposite directions with forces of different strengths. The forces on the apple are unbalanced. In this case, the strength of the net force on the apple is found by subtracting the strength of the smaller force from the strength of the larger force. The net force is in the same direction as the larger force.

A chipmunk and a squirrel push on the apple in the same direction. The forces on the apple are unbalanced. The net force on the apple is the sum of these forces. The apple will start moving to the right.

2N ➡ ⬅ 2N

Net Force:

2N ➡ ⬅ 6N

Net Force:

6N ➡

2N ➡

Net Force:

1. **Write an Inequality** For each set of forces, write one of these signs to compare the forces: =, >, <.

   2 N ............. 2 N

   2 N ............. 6 N

   8 N ............. 0 N

2. **Apply Mathematical Concepts** 🖊 Label each diagram with the strength of the net force in newtons (N).

3. **Reason Quantitatively** In the center diagram, which direction will the apple start moving?

   ...................................................................

 **INTERACTIVITY**

Check your understanding of net force in this interactivity.

✔ **READING CHECK** **Infer** A girl picks up a bag of apples that are at rest on the floor. How does the force the girl applies compare to the force of gravity acting on the apples?

...................................................................

...................................................................

...................................................................

# ☑ LESSON 1 Check

MS-PS2-2

**1. Determine Differences** What is the difference between a contact force and a noncontact force?

.......................................................................

.......................................................................

.......................................................................

**2. Apply Scientific Reasoning** A child is riding in a wagon. What reference point might have been used if an observer said the child was not moving?

.......................................................................

.......................................................................

.......................................................................

**3. Calculate** Two children fight over a toy. One pulls with a force of 8 N to the right. The other pulls with a force of 6 N to the left. What is the strength and direction of the net force on the toy?

.......................................................................

.......................................................................

.......................................................................

**4. Identify Criteria** A cow is grazing in a field. Under what conditions does the cow have relative motion?

.......................................................................

.......................................................................

.......................................................................

.......................................................................

.......................................................................

**5. Synthesize Information** One man pushes on the front of a cart while another man pushes on the back of the cart. The cart begins to move forward. What are three things you know about these two applied forces?

.......................................................................

.......................................................................

.......................................................................

.......................................................................

.......................................................................

.......................................................................

# Quest CHECK-IN

**In this lesson, you learned about the motion of objects. You also learned about different types of forces and how these forces affect the movement of objects.**

**Identify** What are the forces that act upon amusement park rides? Why is it important for engineers to understand how motion and forces affect the rides they design?

.......................................................................

.......................................................................

.......................................................................

.......................................................................

.......................................................................

## INTERACTIVITY

Define Criteria and Constraints

**Go online** to identify the problem, consider criteria and constraints, and develop a design for your prototype.

127

# Speed, Velocity, and Acceleration

## Guiding Questions

- How do you determine speed from calculations and distance-versus-time graphs?
- How is velocity related to speed and acceleration?
- How can you interpret graphs to determine acceleration?

## Connections

**Literacy** Determine Conclusions

**Math** Solve Linear Equations

MS-PS2-2

## Vocabulary

speed
slope
velocity
acceleration

## Academic Vocabulary

average
variable

 **VOCABULARY APP**

Practice vocabulary on a mobile device.

### Quest CONNECTION

Think about what might cause bumper cars to speed up, slow down, or change direction.

## Connect It !

🖊 **Draw an arrow to show the strength and direction of the force applied to the sled by the people pushing the sled.**

**Construct Explanations** How does the snow help the sled move down the hill?

........................................................................................

........................................................................................

........................................................................................

**Describe** How would you describe the difference in the motion of the sled from when the people first start pushing to when the sled is halfway down the hill?

........................................................................................

........................................................................................

# Calculating Speed

You might describe the motion of the sled in **Figure 1** as slow when it starts moving and fast when it reaches the bottom of the hill. By using these words, you are describing the sled's speed. The **speed** of an object is the distance the object moves per unit of time. Speed is a type of rate. A rate tells you the amount of something that occurs or changes in one unit of time.

**Distance Over Time** To calculate the speed of an object, divide the distance the object travels by the amount of time it takes to travel that distance. This relationship can be written as an equation:

$$\text{Speed} = \frac{\text{Distance}}{\text{Time}}$$

Any unit that expresses distance over time is a unit of speed. Some examples of units of speed include kilometers per hour, miles per hour, and feet per minute. The SI unit for speed is meters per second, or m/s. For example, the sled might travel at a speed of 5 m/s near its starting point. This means that the sled travels a distance of 5 meters in 1 second. As it nears the bottom of the hill, the sled might be moving at a speed of about 15 m/s. This means that the sled travels a distance of 15 meters in 1 second. The greater the number of meters per second, the faster the speed at which the object is traveling.

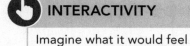

**INTERACTIVITY**

Imagine what it would feel like to ride on a very fast amusement park ride.

**Picking up Speed**
**Figure 1** Family members push each other on a sled from a stopped position at the top of the hill. As the sled glides down the hill, it moves faster and faster. This fast speed makes for a fun ride!

## HANDS-ON LAB

**ʋInvestigate** Experiment to find out how you can calculate your speed as you walk to your locker.

### Academic Vocabulary

In math, you find an average by dividing the sum of values by the number of values given. How might you use the word *average* in a situation that does not involve math?

..........................................................

..........................................................

..........................................................

..........................................................

..........................................................

**Instantaneous and Average Speeds** Think about the last time you rode in a car. Depending on road conditions and traffic, the speed of the vehicle varied. If you had looked at the speedometer for a moment in a traffic jam, it might have read 5 kilometers per hour. On the highway, at a particular instant, it might have read 88 kilometers per hour. The speed at a particular instant in time is called instantaneous speed.

Although you did not travel at the same speed for the whole trip, you did have an **average** speed throughout the trip. To calculate average speed, divide the total distance traveled by the total time. For example, suppose you drove a distance of 3 kilometers in 1 hour while in heavy traffic. Then, it took you 1 hour to drive 50 kilometers from one side of a city to the other. Finally, you traveled 211 kilometers on an interstate highway in 2 hours. The average speed of the car is the total distance traveled divided by the total time. In the equation below, you can see that your average speed on the road trip was 66 kilometers per hour.

Total distance = 3 km + 50 km + 211 km = 264 km

Total time = 1 h + 1 h + 2 h = 4 h

$$\text{Average speed} = \frac{264 \text{ km}}{4 \text{ h}} = 66 \text{ km/h}$$

☑ **READING CHECK** **Explain** How does instantaneous speed differ from average speed?

..........................................................

..........................................................

..........................................................

### Average Speed

**Figure 2** A racecar at the Daytona 500 zips around the track. It travels the first 80 kilometers in 0.4 hours. The next 114 kilometers take 0.6 hours. The following 80 kilometers take 0.4 hours. Calculate the racecar's average speed.

## Calculating Speed From a Graph

The graph you see on this page is a distance-versus-time graph. Time is shown on the horizontal axis, or *x*-axis. Distance is shown on the vertical axis, or *y*-axis. A point on the line represents the distance an object has traveled during a given time period. The *x* value of the point is time, and the *y* value is distance. The angle of a line on a graph is called **slope**. The slope tells you how one **variable** changes in relation to the other variable in the graph. In other words, slope tells you the rate of change. You can calculate the slope of a line by dividing the rise by the run. The rise is the vertical difference between any two points on the line. The run is the horizontal difference between the same two points.

$$\text{Slope} = \frac{\text{Rise}}{\text{Run}}$$

The points in the graph below show a rise of 50 meters and a run of 2 seconds. To find the slope, divide 50 meters by 2 seconds. The slope is 25 meters per second. What do you notice about the units of slope? On a distance-versus-time graph, the units of the slope of the line are the same as the units for speed. Because speed is the rate that distance changes in relation to time, the slope of a distance-versus-time graph represents speed. The steeper the slope is, the greater the speed. A constant slope represents motion at constant speed.

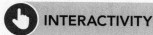

**INTERACTIVITY**

Explore the speed of a space probe using a distance-versus-time graph.

**Academic Vocabulary**

A variable is a letter or symbol that represents a number that can change. Use *variable* as an adjective in a sentence. Explain what it means.

........................................

........................................

........................................

........................................

........................................

## Math Toolbox

### Using a Distance-Versus-Time Graph

The cheetah in this photograph is running at a constant speed. The graph shows the distance the cheetah moves and the time it takes the cheetah to move that distance.

**Cheetah's Motion**

1. **Calculate** 🖉 Mark two new points on the line. Use these points to calculate the slope.

........................................

........................................

2. **Draw Conclusions** What is the average speed of the cheetah?

........................................

3. **Solve Linear Equations** The graph of a straight line that goes through the origin can be represented by the equation, $y = mx$. This equation describes the relationship between the two variables *x* and *y*. In this equation, *m* represents the constant slope of the line. Use this equation to determine the distance the cheetah traveled in 4 seconds.

........................................

## Velocity in Formations

**Figure 3** Each member in this marching band must move at a specific velocity to be in the correct place in the formation. What part of velocity that is important for this formation is not shown by a distance-versus-time graph?

........................................................

**Apply Scientific Reasoning** Do all of the members of the band have to move at the same velocity at all times? Explain your reasoning.

........................................................
........................................................
........................................................
........................................................
........................................................
........................................................
........................................................

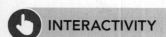 **INTERACTIVITY**

Investigate the speed, velocity, and acceleration of a skydiver.

# Describing Velocity

To describe an object's motion, you also need to know its direction. For example, suppose you hear that a thunderstorm is traveling at a speed of 25 km/h. Should you prepare for the storm? That depends on the direction in which the storm is moving. If it is traveling toward you, you might want to take cover. The speed at which an object travels in a given direction is called **velocity**. You know the velocity of a storm when you know that it is moving 25 km/h eastward.

In certain situations, describing the velocity of moving objects is important. For example, air traffic controllers must keep close track of the velocities of aircrafts. These velocities change as airplanes move overhead and on the runways. An error in determining a velocity, either in speed or in direction, could lead to a collision.

☑ **READING CHECK** **Determine Conclusions** How can understanding velocity help to prevent a mid-air collision?

........................................................
........................................................
........................................................
........................................................

# Determining Acceleration

Speed and velocity are not the only ways to describe motion. Suppose you are a passenger in a car stopped at a red light. When the light changes to green, the driver steps on the gas pedal. As a result, the car speeds up, or accelerates. But acceleration means more than just speeding up. Scientists define **acceleration** as the rate at which velocity changes. A change in velocity can involve a change in speed, direction, or both. In science, when an object accelerates, it increases speed, decreases speed, or changes direction.

**Change in Speed or Direction** When the term *acceleration* is used, it means one of two things—any change in speed or any change in direction. A dog that starts running to chase a squirrel is accelerating. You accelerate when you start walking faster to get to class on time. When objects slow down, they are also accelerating. A car accelerates as it comes to a stop at a red light. A water skier accelerates as the boat slows down. A decrease in speed is sometimes called deceleration.

Even an object that is traveling at a constant speed is accelerating when it changes direction. Therefore, a car accelerates as it follows a gentle curve in the road or changes lanes. Runners accelerate as they round the curve in a track.

## Model It!

### Acceleration

**Figure 4** This image shows a basketball player shooting a ball.

1. **Develop Models** ✏️ Label the two sections of the path to identify where the ball increases speed and decreases speed.

2. **Use Models** Besides the labels for changing speed, what is another way that you can tell from this model that the ball is accelerating?

..................................................
..................................................
..................................................

## Acceleration in Racing

**Figure 5** The pictures show different ways acceleration occurs in a race. Label each image as either increasing speed, decreasing speed, or changing direction.

**Starting Line**

**Curve**

**Finish Line**

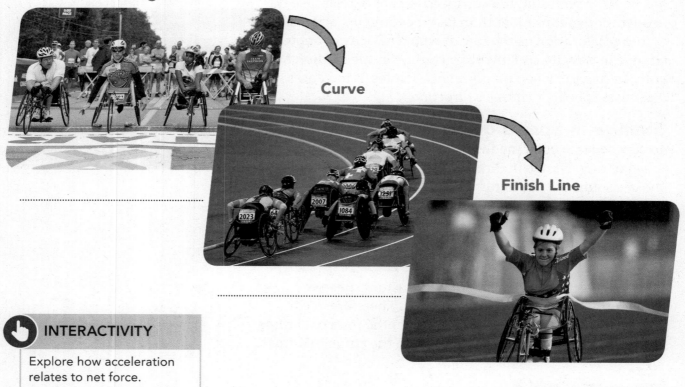

..........................................

..........................................

..........................................

👆 **INTERACTIVITY**

Explore how acceleration relates to net force.

## Acceleration of a Plane

**Figure 6** A plane speeds up and decelerates throughout its flight.

1. **Identify** As the plane travels down the runway for takeoff, is the plane speeding up or decelerating?

..............................................................................

| 0.0s | 1.0s | 2.0s | 3.0s |

| 0 m/s | 8 m/s | 16 m/s | 24 m/s |

## Calculating Acceleration

If an object is not changing direction, you can describe its acceleration as the rate at which its speed changes. To determine the acceleration of an object moving in a straight line, you calculate the change in speed per unit of time. This is summarized by the following equation:

$$\text{Acceleration} = \frac{\text{Final speed} - \text{Initial speed}}{\text{Time}}$$

Since speed is measured in meters per second (m/s) and time is measured in seconds, acceleration is meters per second per second, or $m/s^2$. This unit is the SI unit for acceleration.

To understand acceleration, imagine a small airplane moving down a runway, preparing for takeoff. **Figure 6** shows the airplane's speed after each second of its acceleration. To calculate the acceleration of the airplane during takeoff, you must first subtract the initial speed of 0 m/s from its final speed of 24 m/s. Then divide the change in speed by the time, 3 seconds.

$$\text{Acceleration} = \frac{24 \text{ m/s} - 0 \text{ m/s}}{3 \text{ s}}$$

$$\text{Acceleration} = 8 \text{ m/s}^2$$

The airplane accelerates at a rate of $8 \text{ m/s}^2$. This means that the airplane's speed increases by 8 m/s every second. Notice in **Figure 6** that after each second of travel during takeoff, the airplane's speed is 8 m/s greater than its speed in the previous second.

### Literacy Connection

**Determine Conclusions**
As you study the examples on this page, describe an example of your own that shows the three ways an object can accelerate.

.......................................................

.......................................................

.......................................................

.......................................................

.......................................................

.......................................................

2. **Calculate** On landing, the plane touches the runway with a speed of 65 m/s. The figure shows the speed of the plane after 1 second. Calculate the acceleration of the plane during its landing.

.......................................................

.......................................................

3. **Translate Information** What does a negative value for acceleration mean here?

.......................................................

.......................................................

0.0s    1.0s

65 m/s    60 m/s

**Graphing Acceleration** Suppose you bike down a long, steep hill. At the top of the hill, your speed is 0 m/s. As you start down the hill, your speed increases. Each second, you move at a greater speed and travel a greater distance than the second before. During the five seconds it takes you to reach the bottom of the hill, you are accelerating. Use the data provided in **Figure 7** to graph and analyze your motion on the accelerating bike.

✅ READING CHECK **Summarize** How are the speed, velocity, and acceleration of a moving object related?

...........................................................................................

...........................................................................................

...........................................................................................

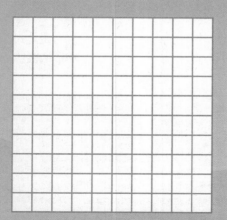

0s
1s
2s
3s
4s
5s

## Graphing Acceleration

**Figure 7** This table lists the distance the bike travels from the top of the hill and the speed of the bike at each second as it accelerates down the hill.

| Time (s) | Distance (m) | Speed (m/s) |
|---|---|---|
| 0 | 0 | 0 |
| 1 | 1 | 2 |
| 2 | 4 | 4 |
| 3 | 9 | 6 |
| 4 | 16 | 8 |
| 5 | 25 | 10 |

1. **Create a Graph** ✏️ Use the data in the table to create a distance-versus-time graph on the first grid. Plot distance on the vertical axis and time on the horizontal axis.

2. **Create a Graph** ✏️ On the second grid, create a speed-versus-time graph. Plot speed on the vertical axis and time on the horizontal axis.

3. **Apply Concepts** Compare the distance-versus-time graph in this figure to the distance-versus-time graph in the Math Toolbox in this lesson. Why does one graph have a straight line, while the other graph has a curved line?

...........................................................................

...........................................................................

...........................................................................

...........................................................................

# ☑ LESSON 2 Check

1. **Relate Change** What three changes in motion show that an object is accelerating?

..................................................................

..................................................................

2. **Calculate** What is the average speed of a train that covers 80 km in 1 h, 200 km in 2 h, and 420 km in 4 h?

..................................................................

..................................................................

..................................................................

3. **Evaluate Your Claim** A ball is pushed from a stop and rolls 6 m in 2 s. Student A says the average speed of the ball is 3 m/s. Student B says the average speed of the ball is 1.5 m/s². Which student is correct? Explain your answer.

..................................................................

..................................................................

..................................................................

..................................................................

..................................................................

4. **Interpret Data** A student graphed distance versus time for an object that moves 14 m every 2 s. What is the slope of the line on the graph? Explain.

..................................................................

..................................................................

..................................................................

..................................................................

5. **Apply Scientific Reasoning** If the line on a distance-versus-time graph and the line on a speed-versus-time graph are both straight lines going through the origin, can the two graphs be displaying the motion of the same object? Explain.

..................................................................

..................................................................

..................................................................

..................................................................

..................................................................

# Quest CHECK-IN

In this lesson, you learned how motion can be described by speed, velocity, and acceleration. You also learned how to use mathematical formulas to calculate and graph average speed and acceleration.

**Use Models** How might you use a model of a bumper car to determine how speed and acceleration affect the motion of the car? What materials might you use?

..................................................................

..................................................................

..................................................................

..................................................................

..................................................................

## HANDS-ON LAB

Mass, Speed, and Colliding Cars

**Go online** to download the lab worksheet. Learn about the features of bumper cars that affect acceleration, including positive acceleration, deceleration, and changes in direction. Brainstorm additional features that might affect speed in bumper cars.

# FINDING YOUR WAY WITH GPS

**B**efore the advent of the global positioning system (GPS), people had two choices if they were traveling in an unfamiliar area. They could either use a map or find someone to ask for directions.

Today, almost everyone relies on GPS, whether in car navigation systems or on smartphones and tablets. But what exactly is GPS, and how does it provide data about a moving object's location and speed?

The heart of this system is a network of more than 24 satellites orbiting Earth. These satellites form a "cloud" around the planet so that at least four of them are in the sky at any given place and time. System engineers monitor each satellite to keep careful track of its position.

## How GPS Works

Nearby satellites send radio signals to the GPS device, and the device calculates its position based on its distance from those satellites. Four satellites are needed for a GPS to calculate its latitude, longitude, and altitude with accuracy. If fewer satellites are used, only a relative position of the GPS device can be determined, not an exact location.

# How **GPS WORKS**

**Satellite**

**1** Each satellite transmits a radio signal in the form of electromagnetic waves. The signal contains data about the satellite's precise location and the time the signal was sent.

**2** The radio signal travels toward Earth at the speed of light.

**3** A GPS device receives the signals from the satellites overhead. The device uses the speed of light and the time it takes for the signal to reach the receiver to calculate its distance from each satellite. Using these distances, the device calculates its exact position.

DISTANCE

**GPS Receiver**

**Use the text and the diagram to answer the following questions.**

**1. Use Models** How does the GPS determine its distance from each satellite?

..............................................................................................................................................................

..............................................................................................................................................................

**2. Calculate** A radio signal from a GPS satellite takes only about 0.067 seconds to reach a GPS receiver. If the speed of light is about 300,000 km/s, then approximately how far away is the receiver from the satellite? Show your calculations.

..............................................................................................................................................................

..............................................................................................................................................................

**3. Apply Scientific Reasoning** Why is it necessary for engineers to know the precise location of each GPS satellite in the system?

..............................................................................................................................................................

..............................................................................................................................................................

..............................................................................................................................................................

**4. Construct Explanations** Explain how a GPS device can determine the speed at which it is moving. Provide a real-world example to support your response.

..............................................................................................................................................................

..............................................................................................................................................................

..............................................................................................................................................................

# Newton's Laws of Motion

## Guiding Questions

- How do Newton's laws of motion describe when and how objects move?
- How do an object's mass and the forces acting upon an object affect its motion?
- What are action and reaction forces, and how do they impact an object's motion?

## Connections

**Literacy** Use Information

**Math** Evaluate Expressions

MS-PS2-2

## Vocabulary

inertia

## Academic Vocabulary

derived

 **VOCABULARY APP**

Practice vocabulary on a mobile device.

**Quest CONNECTION**

Think about how the size of the bumper cars and the riders in the cars, along with the speed of the cars, might impact the safety of this ride.

## Connect It!

✎ **A hockey player hits a puck that was at rest on the ice. Mark an X on the point in the image where the hockey player first applied a net force to the puck.**

**Cause and Effect** How did the motion of the puck change as a result of being hit?

..................................................................................................................................

..................................................................................................................................

**Infer** After being hit, the puck travels along the ice at a constant speed. What might cause its motion to change?

..................................................................................................................................

..................................................................................................................................

# Newton's First Law of Motion

If you were watching an ice-hockey game, you would be surprised if a puck that was sitting still suddenly started moving without being hit. You would also be surprised if a moving puck suddenly stopped in the middle of the ice. Your surprise would be the result of knowing that a net force must act upon an object to cause a change in motion. This natural phenomenon that you observe in the world demonstrates Newton's first law of motion.

Newton's first law of motion states that an object at rest will remain at rest unless acted upon by a nonzero net force. Therefore, a hockey puck that is sitting still will remain at rest unless a player hits it, applying a net force. This law also states that an object moving at a constant velocity will continue moving at a constant velocity unless acted upon by a nonzero net force. You can see this law in action when a hockey puck slides in a straight line across the ice. The motion remains constant until it hits something like the net of the goal or another hockey stick.

A simple statement of Newton's first law of motion is that if an object is not moving, it will not start moving until a net force acts on it. If an object is moving, it will continue at a constant velocity until a net force acts to change its speed or its direction. If there is a net force acting on an object, it will accelerate.

## Literacy Connection

**Use Information** As you read these pages, underline information you can use to define Newton's first law.

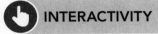

## INTERACTIVITY

Explore what causes a ball to stop rolling.

**Speeding Up**
**Figure 1** Just a moment ago, the puck was at rest on the ice. The net force that the player applied to the puck caused the puck to accelerate.

## Mass and Inertia

**Figure 2** Suppose each of these women wants to move the dog off of her lap.

Which dog has less inertia? .................................................................

Which dog is harder to move?

.................................................................................................................

**Inertia** Resistance to change in motion is called **inertia**. So Newton's first law is also called the law of inertia. Inertia explains many common events, including why seat belts and air bags are used in vehicles. If you are riding in a moving car, you are moving at the same speed the car is moving. When brakes apply a force to the car, the car decelerates. The brakes did not apply a force to you, however, so inertia keeps you moving forward at the same speed and direction you were going before the car decelerated. A force, such as the pull of a seat belt, is needed to pull you back.

**Inertia and Mass** Which object—you or the car—is harder to stop? Based on your own experience, you can probably figure out that the car is harder to stop. That is because it has more mass. The more massive object has a greater inertia, as in **Figure 2.** Once Newton had described the connection between inertia and mass, he next figured out how to find the acceleration of an object when a force acted on it.

☑ READING CHECK **Summarize** How does mass relate to inertia?

.................................................................................................................

.................................................................................................................

# Newton's Second Law of Motion

Newton's first law stated that inertia exists for an object. Newton then explained that an object's mass directly affects how much force is needed to accelerate the object.

**Changes in Acceleration and Mass** Suppose that you apply a constant net force on an object. How does changing the mass of the object affect its acceleration? You can see this with a horse-drawn sleigh, shown in **Figure 3**. The horses provide a steady force. If the sleigh is empty, it will accelerate quickly when the horses pull on it. If the sleigh is full of people, it has a greater inertia and will accelerate slowly. The acceleration of the sleigh will change depending on the mass of the load it carries. Newton understood these relationships and found a way to represent them mathematically.

**Calculating Force** Newton's second law of motion states that the size and direction of a net force equals the mass times the acceleration. The net force will have the same direction as the acceleration. This relationship can be written as follows:

$$\text{Net force} = \text{Mass} \times \text{Acceleration}$$

If the net force and mass are known, the resulting acceleration can be **derived** by using this equation:

$$\text{Acceleration} = \frac{\text{Net force}}{\text{Mass}}$$

**Academic Vocabulary**

Read the sentence in which the word *derived* is used, and infer its meaning.

........................................................

........................................................

........................................................

........................................................

**Newton's Second Law**

**Figure 3** The force applied by these two horses pulls the sleigh and the people it contains. This sleigh can contain up to 12 people.

1. **Reason Quantitatively** How might you change the number of people to increase the sleigh's acceleration?

........................................................

........................................................

........................................................

2. **Apply Scientific Reasoning** How might you change the number of people to decrease the sleigh's acceleration?

........................................................

........................................................

........................................................

143

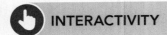
## Calculations with Newton's Second Law

As you have already seen, the formula for Newton's second law can be written to solve for force or acceleration. Newton's second law can also be written to solve for mass.

You already know that acceleration is measured in meters per second squared ($m/s^2$), and that mass is measured in kilograms (kg). When you multiply mass and acceleration according to Newton's second law, you find that force is measured in kilograms times meters per second squared ($kg\text{-}m/s^2$). This unit is also called a newton (N), which is the SI unit of force. One newton is the force required to give a 1-kg mass an acceleration of 1 $m/s^2$.

☑ **READING CHECK** **Apply Concepts** Based on what you've learned, derive another equation for Newton's second law that is written to solve for mass.

......................................................................................................

# Math Toolbox

## Using Newton's Second Law

Use the equations for Newton's second law to understand how mass and force affect the motion of a volleyball.

**Evaluate Expressions** Show your calculations for each problem.

**a.** A volleyball is hit and experiences a net force of 2 N, which causes it to accelerate at 8 $m/s^2$. What is the mass of the volleyball?

**b.** The same ball is hit again and experiences a net force of 3.5 N instead. What is the acceleration of the volleyball?

**c.** The same ball rolls horizontally along the sand and decelerates at a rate of 6 $m/s^2$. Calculate the force of friction that caused this deceleration.

# Newton's Third Law of Motion

A library is full of shelves of books. Gravity pulls each book down. If the shelf did not push upward on each book with equal force, the books would fall through the shelf. The force exerted by the shelf is equal in strength and opposite in direction to the force the books exert on the shelf. Newton's third law of motion states that if one object exerts a force on another object, then the second object exerts a force of equal strength in the opposite direction on the first object. Another way to state Newton's third law is that for every action there is an equal (in strength) but opposite (in direction) reaction.

## HANDS-ON LAB

☑ **Investigate** Use Newton's third law to design a vehicle that moves forward by pushing backward.

▶ **VIDEO**

Examine how action-reaction pairs cause motion in real-world scenarios.

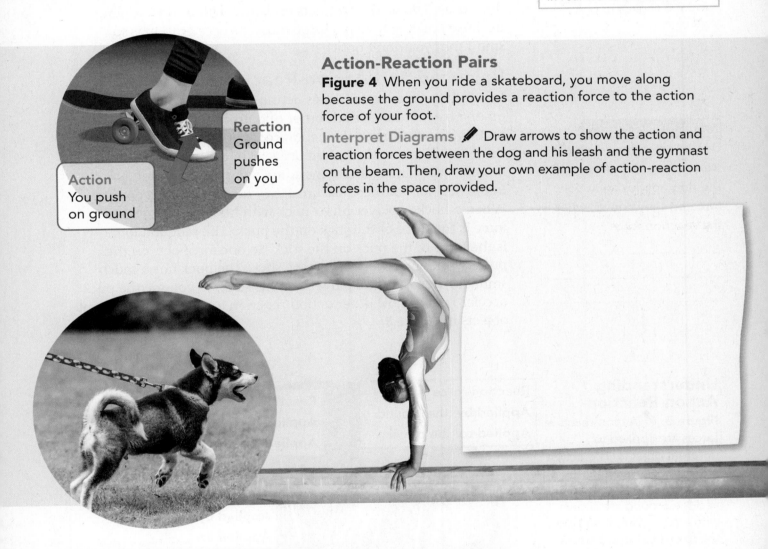

**Reaction** Ground pushes on you

**Action** You push on ground

## Action-Reaction Pairs

**Figure 4** When you ride a skateboard, you move along because the ground provides a reaction force to the action force of your foot.

**Interpret Diagrams** ✎ Draw arrows to show the action and reaction forces between the dog and his leash and the gymnast on the beam. Then, draw your own example of action-reaction forces in the space provided.

**Action-Reaction Pairs** An action force is always paired with a reaction force. Pairs of action and reaction forces are all around you. When you walk, you push backward on the ground with your feet. Think of this as an action force. The ground pushes forward on your feet with an equal and opposite force. This is the reaction force. You can walk only because the ground pushes you forward!

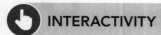

INTERACTIVITY

Use Newton's laws to discover how a baseball player can hit more home runs.

▶ VIDEO

Discover how a mechanical engineer uses science to solve engineering problems.

☑ READING CHECK

**Use Information** A dog walks along the ground. If the dog applies an action force on the ground, what is the reaction force?

..........................................................

..........................................................

..........................................................

**Detecting Forces and Motion** Some results of action-reaction forces are easily observed. If you were the skateboarder in **Figure 4**, you could feel the force of the ground on your foot. You could see and feel the skateboard accelerate. If you drop your pen, gravity pulls the pen downward and you can see it fall.

But some changes caused by action-reaction forces are not as easily detected. When you drop your pen, the pen pulls Earth upward with an equal and opposite reaction force, according to Newton's third law. You see the pen fall, but you don't see Earth accelerate toward the pen. Remember Newton's second law. If mass increases and force stays the same, acceleration decreases. The same force acts on both Earth and your pen. Because Earth has such a large mass, its acceleration is so small that you don't notice it.

**Balanced and Action-Reaction Forces** You have learned that two equal forces acting in opposite directions on an object balance each other and produce no change in motion. So why aren't the action-reaction forces in Newton's third law of motion balanced as well? In order for forces to balance, they must act on the same object. Action-reaction forces are not balanced because they act on different objects. When a hockey player hits a puck with his stick, the action force is the force of the stick on the puck. The reaction force is the force of the puck on the stick. So one force acts on the puck, while the other acts on the stick. The puck has a much smaller mass than the player and his stick, so you see the puck accelerate. See how other action-reaction forces act on different objects in **Figure 5**.

**Understanding Action-Reaction**

**Figure 5** 🖊 Action-reaction forces are applied to different objects. The action and reaction forces acting on a soccer player, a soccer ball, and the ground are shown with arrows. Finish labeling the forces to describe how they are being applied.

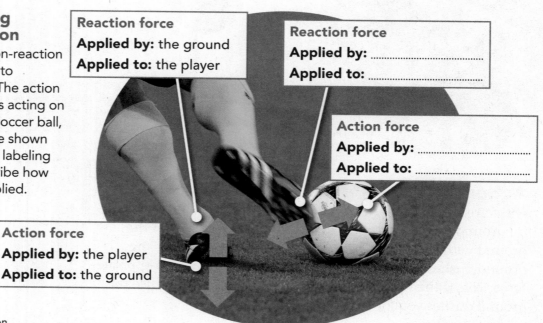

Reaction force
**Applied by:** the ground
**Applied to:** the player

Reaction force
**Applied by:** ..............................
**Applied to:** ..............................

Action force
**Applied by:** ..............................
**Applied to:** ..............................

Action force
**Applied by:** the player
**Applied to:** the ground

# Question It !

## Applying Newton's Laws

Kirsten has a parakeet that likes to sit on a swing. Sometimes the bird makes the swing move back and forth.

**Ask Questions** You want to investigate the bird and his swing and how they relate to Newton's laws of motion. List at least two questions you might ask.

..........................................................................................................................................

..........................................................................................................................................

**Newton's Laws Together** When you have a situation involving force, acceleration, and mass, it usually involves two or even all three of Newton's laws! Look at **Figure 6** to see how Newton's laws apply to an amusement park ride.

**Reflect** Describe how Newton's laws of motion are involved in an activity in your daily life.

| Newton's First Law: | Newton's Second Law: | Newton's Third Law: |
|---|---|---|
| | | |

**Newton's Laws**

**Figure 6** ✏ In each space provided, give an example of a way that one of Newton's laws is shown in this amusement park ride.

# ☑ LESSON 3 Check

MS-PS2-2

1. **Communicate** In your own words, what is Newton's second law of motion?

.................................................................
.................................................................
.................................................................
.................................................................

2. **Apply Concepts** What is inertia? Use an example in your description.

.................................................................
.................................................................
.................................................................
.................................................................

3. **Integrate Information** What is the difference between balanced forces and action-reaction forces?

.................................................................
.................................................................
.................................................................
.................................................................

4. **Explain Phenomena** You push on a door and it opens. Explain what happens in terms of action-reaction forces.

.................................................................
.................................................................
.................................................................
.................................................................
.................................................................
.................................................................
.................................................................

5. **Calculate** A 12-N net force acts on a 4-kg jug of water. What is the resulting acceleration of the jug? Show your calculations.

.................................................................
.................................................................
.................................................................
.................................................................

# Quest CHECK-IN

In this lesson, you learned how Newton's laws explain the motions of moving objects and how mass affects acceleration. You also learned that every action has an equal and opposite reaction.

**Apply Concepts** How would Newton's laws of motion relate to the movement of bumper cars? How might the mass of the riders and the speed of the cars affect this movement?

.................................................................
.................................................................
.................................................................
.................................................................
.................................................................
.................................................................

## 👆 INTERACTIVITY

Apply Newton's Laws of Motion

**Go online** to learn about how action-reaction forces affect the movement of vehicles in collisions. Then brainstorm how these forces would affect bumper cars.

**148** Forces and Motion

# GENERATING ENERGY from Potholes

INTERACTIVITY

Explore how Newton's laws can be used to design more fuel-efficient vehicles.

**Traveling in a car** over uneven road surfaces and potholes can make for a bouncy ride. How can you capture the energy generated by that bouncing motion? You engineer it!

**The Challenge:** To convert the motion of a car into electrical energy.

**Phenomenon** When a car travels down the road, the car exerts an action force on the road, and the road exerts a reaction force on the wheels of the car. A bumpy road occasionally exerts a stronger force than a smooth road, which means an uncomfortable ride for passengers. That's where shock absorbers come in. Shock absorbers are part of a car's suspension system, and they cause the body of the car to react slowly to bumps. This decreases the force exerted on a car by the road.

With traditional shock absorbers, the energy that is absorbed is then released as heat. Auto engineers have now found a way to use their understanding of the Law of Conservation of Energy to harness this energy. They have developed electromechanical shock absorbers that use a lever arm to capture the up-and-down motion of the wheels. A device called an alternator transforms this kinetic energy into electricity. The engineers hope that this electrical energy can be used to increase the fuel efficiency of cars.

With electromechanical shock absorbers, the energy generated by bumps and potholes can be transformed into electrical energy.

**DESIGN CHALLENGE** Can you build a shock absorber? Go to the Engineering Design Notebook to find out!

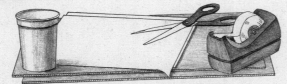

# Friction and Gravitational Interactions

## Guiding Questions

- What factors affect the different types of friction?
- What factors affect gravity?
- How are gravity and friction related to motion and energy?

## Connections

**Literacy** Write Arguments

**Math** Analyze Relationships

MS-PS2-4, MS-PS3-2

## Vocabulary

weight

## Academic Vocabulary

associate

 **VOCABULARY APP**

Practice vocabulary on a mobile device.

**Quest CONNECTION**

Think about how different road conditions affect the movement of a car. How might the surface upon which bumper cars move affect their motion?

## Connect It!

🖊 **Circle two areas that show what causes the bike to slow down.**

**Identify** What force is responsible for stopping the bike?

......................................................................................................................

**Classify** Is this force a contact or noncontact force? Explain.

......................................................................................................................

......................................................................................................................

......................................................................................................................

# Factors That Affect Friction

Recall that the force two surfaces exert on each other when they rub against each other is the contact force called friction. For example, if you slide a book across a table, the surface of the book rubs against the surface of the table. The resulting force is friction. This force acts in a direction opposite to the motion of the book and eventually stops the book.

**Two Factors** Both the types of surfaces involved and how hard the surfaces are pushed together affect the friction between two surfaces. The bicyclist in **Figure 1** is using friction to slow his bicycle. One place where friction occurs on the bicycle is between the tires and the ground. Have you ever examined the surface of a tire? The tread on the tire results in more friction between the tire and the ground. A tire on a mountain bike has more tread on it than a regular bike tire, so a lot of friction is produced between a mountain bike tire and the ground. In general, smoother surfaces produce less friction than rougher surfaces.

In this instance, friction also occurs between the brake pads and the wheels. This friction prevents the tire from turning. The harder the bicyclist applies the brakes, the more quickly the bike will come to a stop. Friction increases as surfaces push harder against each other.

Friction acts in a direction opposite to the direction of the object's motion. Without friction or some other force acting in the opposite direction, a moving object will not stop until it strikes another object.

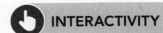

**INTERACTIVITY**

Describe your experiences riding a bicycle on different surfaces.

**Skidding to a Stop**
**Figure 1** This mountain biker applies his brakes and skids to slow down.

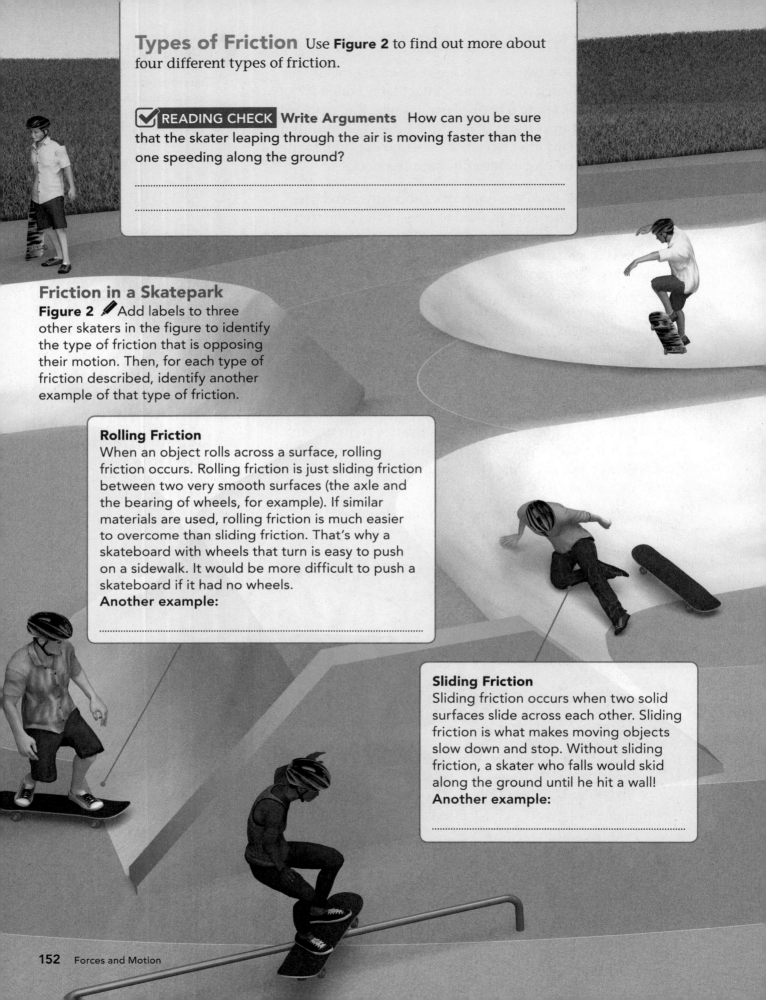

## Types of Friction Use **Figure 2** to find out more about four different types of friction.

☑ READING CHECK **Write Arguments** How can you be sure that the skater leaping through the air is moving faster than the one speeding along the ground?

..................................................................................................................

..................................................................................................................

### Friction in a Skatepark

**Figure 2** ✏️ Add labels to three other skaters in the figure to identify the type of friction that is opposing their motion. Then, for each type of friction described, identify another example of that type of friction.

### Rolling Friction

When an object rolls across a surface, rolling friction occurs. Rolling friction is just sliding friction between two very smooth surfaces (the axle and the bearing of wheels, for example). If similar materials are used, rolling friction is much easier to overcome than sliding friction. That's why a skateboard with wheels that turn is easy to push on a sidewalk. It would be more difficult to push a skateboard if it had no wheels.

**Another example:**

..................................................................................................................

### Sliding Friction

Sliding friction occurs when two solid surfaces slide across each other. Sliding friction is what makes moving objects slow down and stop. Without sliding friction, a skater who falls would skid along the ground until he hit a wall!

**Another example:**

..................................................................................................................

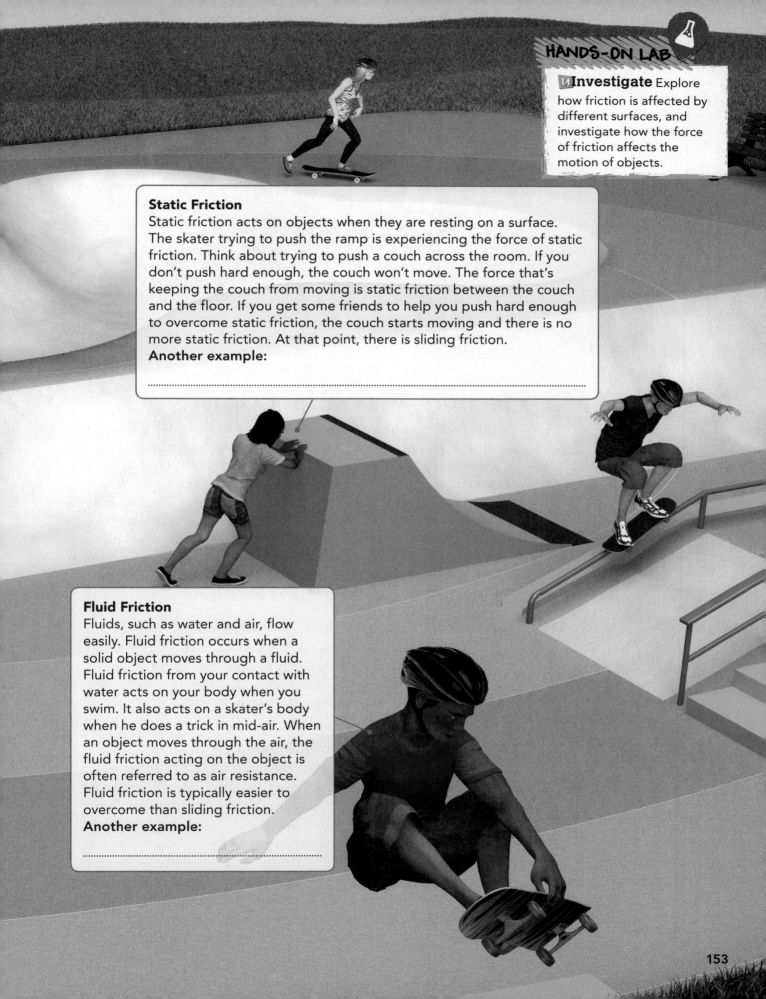

HANDS-ON LAB

и**Investigate** Explore how friction is affected by different surfaces, and investigate how the force of friction affects the motion of objects.

### Static Friction

Static friction acts on objects when they are resting on a surface. The skater trying to push the ramp is experiencing the force of static friction. Think about trying to push a couch across the room. If you don't push hard enough, the couch won't move. The force that's keeping the couch from moving is static friction between the couch and the floor. If you get some friends to help you push hard enough to overcome static friction, the couch starts moving and there is no more static friction. At that point, there is sliding friction.

**Another example:**

.................................................................................................................................................................................

### Fluid Friction

Fluids, such as water and air, flow easily. Fluid friction occurs when a solid object moves through a fluid. Fluid friction from your contact with water acts on your body when you swim. It also acts on a skater's body when he does a trick in mid-air. When an object moves through the air, the fluid friction acting on the object is often referred to as air resistance. Fluid friction is typically easier to overcome than sliding friction.

**Another example:**

......................................................................

153

**Universal Gravitation**
**Figure 3** How does the gravitational attraction between these people compare to the gravitational attraction between the people and Earth?

..................................................

..................................................

 **VIDEO**

Explore why the moon is able to circle Earth without falling toward it.

✓ READING CHECK

**Summarize** What is the law of universal gravitation?

..................................................

..................................................

..................................................

..................................................

# Factors That Affect Gravity

While friction is an example of a contact force, gravity is an example on a non-contact force. Remember that gravity is a force that pulls objects toward each other. How is gravity experienced on Earth? You could name many examples. A basketball player shoots a ball toward the basket, and the ball falls toward Earth. Rain falls from the sky to Earth. We are so familiar with objects falling that we may not think much about why they fall. One person who thought about this was Sir Isaac Newton. He concluded that a force called gravity acts to pull objects straight down toward the center of Earth.

**Universal Gravitation** Newton realized that gravity acts everywhere in the universe, not just on Earth. It is the force that causes the tides in Earth's ocean and keeps all the planets in our solar system orbiting around the sun. On Earth, gravity is the force that makes the jumpers in **Figure 3** fall toward the water.

Newton's realization is now called the law of universal gravitation. This law states that the force of gravity acts between all objects in the universe that have mass. So, any two objects in the universe that have mass attract each other. You are attracted not only to Earth but also to your school desk, the other planets in the solar system, and the most distant star you can see. Earth and the objects around you are attracted to you as well. You can clearly see the gravitational effect of Earth on an object. However, you do not notice the attraction between objects on Earth because these forces are extremely small compared to the attraction between the objects and Earth itself.

## Factors Affecting Gravity

What factors control the strength of the gravitational force between two objects? These factors are the mass of each object and the distance between them.

The more mass an object has, the greater the gravitational force between it and other objects. Earth's gravitational force on nearby objects is strong because the mass of Earth is so large. Gravitational force also depends on the distance between the objects' centers. As distance increases, gravitational force decreases. What happens when you drop your cell phone? You see your cell phone fall to Earth because Earth and your cell phone are close together. If your cell phone were on the moon, Earth would not exert a visible gravitational attraction to it because Earth and the phone would be so far apart. The phone would be visibly attracted to the moon instead.

## Weight and Mass

Mass is sometimes confused with weight. Mass is a measure of the amount of matter in an object. **Weight** is a measure of the force of gravity on an object. Since weight is a measure of force, the SI unit of weight is a newton (N). If you know the mass of an object in kilograms, you can calculate its weight on Earth using Newton's second law. The acceleration due to gravity at Earth's surface is 9.8 m/s². The force is the weight of the object.

Net force = Mass × Acceleration

When you stand on a bathroom scale, it displays your weight—the gravitational force that Earth is exerting on you. On Earth, 1 pound equals 4.45 newtons. If you could stand on the surface of Jupiter, which has a mass around 300 times the mass of Earth, your mass would remain the same, but your weight would increase. This is because the gravitational force exerted on you is greater on Jupiter than on Earth.

### Describing g-Forces

**Figure 4** A lowercase g is used as the symbol for acceleration due to gravity at Earth's surface (9.8 m/s²). This symbol is used in the field of space engineering, where acceleration is often measured in "g"s. Engineers must design space shuttles considering the acceleration and forces that the crew and the shuttle itself would experience during flight.

**INTERACTIVITY**

Investigate how gravity affects falling objects.

## Literacy Connection

**Write Arguments** Write an argument supported by evidence that explains why the pencil and notebook resting on your desk are not being pulled together by the force of gravity between them.

........................................
........................................
........................................
........................................
........................................
........................................

# Math Toolbox

## The Relationship Between Weight and Mass

Weight varies with the strength of the gravitational force. This baby elephant weighs 480 pounds on Earth, and its mass is 218 kilograms. On the moon, he would weigh about one-sixth of what he does on Earth. On Mars, he would weigh just over one-third of what he does on Earth. On Jupiter, he would weigh approximately 2.5 times as much as he does on Earth.

**Analyze Relationships** ✏ Complete the table using the information about the baby elephant.

| Location | Earth | Moon | Mars | Jupiter |
|---|---|---|---|---|
| **Mass (kg)** | | | | |
| **Weight (lbs)** | | | | |

# Energy, Forces, and Motion

By now, you can see how forces such as gravity and friction relate to motion. Recall that forces and motion are also related to energy.

**Gravitational Potential Energy** As you know, the potential energy of an object is the energy stored in the object. There are several different types of potential energy, based on different types of forces. The type of potential energy that we **associate** with gravity is called gravitational potential energy. On Earth, gravitational potential energy (GPE) is based on an object's position. In general, the higher up an object is, the greater its GPE. For example, as a diver climbs the ladder to a diving board, her GPE increases. The GPE of a skydiver increases as he rides the helicopter to his jumping point. You can calculate the GPE of an object on Earth based on the mass of the object, the acceleration due to gravity (9.8 m/s²), and the height of the object above Earth's surface.

$$\text{Gravitational potential energy (GPE)} = \text{Mass} \times \text{Acceleration due to gravity} \times \text{Height}$$

**Academic Vocabulary**

Used as a verb, *associate* means to connect something to something else in one's mind. Write a sentence using *associate* as a noun.

..............................................

..............................................

..............................................

..............................................

**Forces and Motion** When a skydiver jumps from a helicopter, a net force acts on his body as he falls. This net force is a combination of gravity and friction. Gravity pulls him down toward the ground, and fluid friction acts on him in the opposite direction as he falls through the air. However, these forces are unbalanced—the force of gravity is stronger than the air resistance, so he accelerates downward. Net force works on him as he falls, so his GPE transforms to kinetic energy, the energy of motion. As a result, his speed increases throughout his fall. As the skydiver accelerates, the force of air resistance increases until it is equal to the force of gravity. At this point, the forces on the skydiver are balanced and he falls at a constant speed the rest of the way down. This top speed is called terminal velocity. It only takes about 15 seconds for skydivers to reach 99% of their terminal velocity of 195 km/h (122 mi/h)! When skydivers open a parachute, air resistance increases. This causes the forces acting on the skydiver to balance at a much slower terminal velocity.

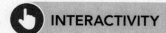

**INTERACTIVITY**

Explore the relationships among friction, gravity, tides, and Earth's rotation.

## Model It

**Develop Models** ✏ Use what you know about energy, forces, and motion to develop a model of a falling object. Add labels to your sketch to show locations of maximum and minimum gravitational potential energy, kinetic energy, and speed. Label areas of acceleration. Draw arrows to represent the forces acting on the object. Write a caption to explain what your model shows.

# ☑ LESSON 4 Check

MS-PS2-4, MS-PS3-2

1. **Synthesize Information** What is the difference between weight and mass?

.......................................................
.......................................................
.......................................................
.......................................................

2. **Identify** Snow has been lying on a mountainside. Suddenly, it starts to move down the mountain. Which types of friction are observed in this avalanche? Where does each type occur?

.......................................................
.......................................................
.......................................................
.......................................................
.......................................................

3. **Apply Scientific Reasoning** Give a real-life example of fluid friction.

.......................................................
.......................................................
.......................................................
.......................................................

4. **Explain Phenomena** A 4-kg ball is 2 cm away from one 1-kg ball and 6 cm away from another 1-kg ball. Use the relationships among the balls to describe two factors that affect gravity. Also explain why the balls do not move toward each other unless acted upon by another force.

.......................................................
.......................................................
.......................................................
.......................................................
.......................................................
.......................................................
.......................................................
.......................................................
.......................................................

5. **Construct Explanations** Rather than push a heavy box from one room to another, a worker chooses to place the box on a wheeled cart. In terms of friction, explain why moving the box on the wheeled cart is easier than pushing.

.......................................................
.......................................................
.......................................................
.......................................................

# Quest CHECK-IN

**In this lesson, you learned how different types of friction affect the movement of objects. You also learned about universal gravitation and how this scientific law applies to objects on Earth and elsewhere in the universe.**

**Evaluate** How might friction affect the movement of bumper cars? What role does gravity play in how bumper cars move? How might you use these concepts to make bumper cars safer?

.......................................................
.......................................................
.......................................................
.......................................................

## HANDS-ON LAB

Bumper Cars, Bumper Solutions

**Go online** to download the worksheet for this lab. Learn how friction and gravity affect vehicles on different surfaces. Then brainstorm how these factors influence the speed and direction of bumper cars.

MS-PS2-2

# Spacetime Curvature and Gravitational Waves

How does mass cause objects to attract one another? The famous scientist Albert Einstein explored this question and came up with a revolutionary theory of gravity. It explains the existence of gravitational waves, while Newton's theory could not!

In Einstein's theory, space and time are not separate from one another. They make up a four-dimensional fabric that can warp and curve. Imagine that a ball is placed on a puffy comforter. The ball sinks into the comforter so that the comforter curves around it. Objects with mass sit in spacetime in a similar way. If you roll a marble past the ball, the marble circles around the ball. The marble gets caught in a groove created by the ball. That's basically how gravity works—objects attract one another by falling into grooves of spacetime.

Now, add acceleration into the picture, and you get ripples in the fabric of spacetime! For example, when two stars circle each other, they accelerate faster and faster. This acceleration produces ripples in spacetime similar to ripples of water on a pond.

Scientists detected gravitational waves for the first time on September 14, 2015. By detecting gravitational waves, we can learn about events all around the universe, such as black holes colliding!

As these stars accelerate, they create ripples in spacetime called gravitational waves.

**MY-DISCOVERY**

Check out magazine articles on gravitational waves at your local library.

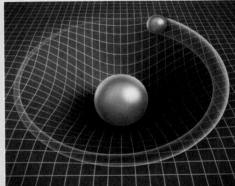

Any object with mass, such as Earth, causes the fabric of spacetime to curve. The result of this curvature is gravitational attraction.

# ☑TOPIC 3 Review and Assess

## 1 Describing Motion and Force

MS-PS2-2

**1.** A girl pushes on the classroom door to open it. Which two terms accurately describe the net force acting on the door?
A. contact and balanced
B. contact and unbalanced
C. noncontact and balanced
D. noncontact and unbalanced

**2.** A dog is pulling on a leash while walking down the sidewalk. What frame of reference would indicate that the dog is not moving?
A. A nearby building    B. A tree
C. The leash    D. The sidewalk

**3.** Two dogs pull on a rope. One dog pulls with a force of 5 N to the left, and the other dog pulls with a force of 3 N to the right. What is the result?
A. The rope remains in place.
B. The rope moves to the left.
C. The rope moves to the right.
D. The rope has a balanced force applied to it.

**4. Develop Models** Using pictures, labels, and arrows, model a box that has two forces acting on it, 12 N to the right and 4 N to the left. Also show the net force on the box.

## 2 Speed, Velocity, and Acceleration

MS-PS2-2

**5.** A bus driver drove from Philadelphia to Washington D.C. He drove the first 100 km in 2 hours, the next 55 km in 1 hour, and the final 75 km in 2 hours. What is the average speed of the bus throughout the trip?
A. 46 km/h
B. 50 km/h
C. 77 km/h
D. 81 km/h

**6.** Which statement about acceleration is always true?
A. The unit m/s is the SI unit of acceleration.
B. For objects to accelerate, they must speed up.
C. Either a change in speed or a change in direction causes acceleration.
D. Both speed and direction must change for acceleration to occur.

**7.** A cross-country runner runs 4 km in 15 minutes. What can you calculate using this information?
A. acceleration
B. force
C. speed
D. velocity

**8.** You can find the speed on a distance-versus-time graph by finding the ............................................. of the line.

**9. Identify Criteria** A woman is taking a walk, moving at a rate of 80 m/min. What additional information would you need to determine her velocity?

...............................................................................

...............................................................................

...............................................................................

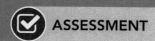 
## 3 Newton's Laws of Motion

MS-PS2-2

**10.** A soccer player kicks a ball. Which of the following describes the reaction force to this kick?
  A. friction between the ball and the foot
  B. friction between the ball and the ground
  C. force applied to the ground by the foot
  D. force applied to the foot by the ball

**11.** Which term describes resistance to change in motion?
  A. Acceleration
  B. Inertia
  C. Net force
  D. Velocity

**12.** The acceleration of a baseball after it is hit by a bat depends on the mass of the ball and the net force on the ball. This example best illustrates what law?
  A. Newton's first law of motion
  B. Newton's second law of motion
  C. Newton's third law of motion
  D. Newton's law of universal gravitation

**13. Integrate Information** Describe how each of Newton's laws may be observable during a car trip.

..........................................................................
..........................................................................
..........................................................................
..........................................................................
..........................................................................
..........................................................................
..........................................................................
..........................................................................

## 4 Friction and Gravitational Interactions

MS-PS2-4, MS-PS3-2

**14.** When is there static friction between your desk chair and the floor?
  A. when the chair sits still
  B. when the chair falls to the floor
  C. when you lift the chair
  D. when you slide your chair under your desk

**15.** The amount of matter an object contains is ............................................, and the force of gravity on that matter is ............................................ .

**16.** A group of skydivers are riding in a helicopter up to the spot from which they will jump. As they ride upward, their gravitational potential energy _____.
  A. decreases
  B. remains constant
  C. increases
  D. changes to kinetic energy

**17. Apply Concepts** Using examples, explain how each of the four types of friction are present during lunch time in the school cafeteria.

..........................................................................
..........................................................................
..........................................................................
..........................................................................
..........................................................................
..........................................................................
..........................................................................
..........................................................................
..........................................................................
..........................................................................

MS-PS2-1, MS-PS2-2,
MS-PS2-4

## Evidence-Based Assessment

In 2005, NASA sent a robotic spacecraft called DART to a satellite that was orbiting Earth. DART was supposed to demonstrate that it could move around the satellite and communicate with it, without a human on board. The spacecraft was supposed to come close to the satellite without actually touching it.

Here is how the DART system works: The spacecraft's navigation system estimates its position and speed. Then, commands are sent to the thrusters to keep the spacecraft along its intended path. Force from the thrusters causes a change in motion. If the GPS system communicates incorrect navigation data to the spacecraft, then it will travel incorrectly and use up its fuel.

DART made it into space, but then its navigation system failed, providing incorrect data on its position and speed. This failure caused DART to bump into the satellite. The force of the collision changed the motion of the satellite. Luckily it remained in orbit around Earth, but the mission was deemed a failure. Though NASA has had many successes, the science and engineering work involved with space exploration is extremely complex, and sometimes even the best-planned projects fail.

The diagram below shows the relative positions of DART, and the satellite before the collision.

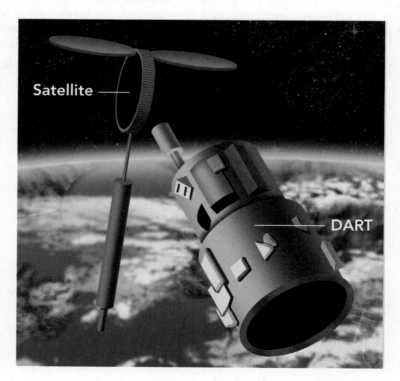

1. **Apply Scientific Reasoning** If the satellite had less mass, but the force of the collision was the same, then the collision would have
   - (A.) caused the satellite to accelerate more quickly.
   - B. caused the satellite to accelerate more slowly.
   - C. caused the satellite to accelerate at the same rate.
   - D. had no effect on the satellite's original motion.

2. **Cite Evidence** Did DART apply a balanced or unbalanced force to the satellite during the collision? What evidence supports your answer?

   .............................................................

   .............................................................

   .............................................................

   .............................................................

   .............................................................

3. **Draw Comparative Inferences** Describe the action-reaction forces during the collision between DART and the satellite.

   .............................................................

   .............................................................

   .............................................................

   .............................................................

   .............................................................

4. **Distinguish Relationships** Which do you think is stronger—the gravitational attraction between DART and Earth, or the gravitational attraction between DART and the satellite? Explain your answer.

   .............................................................

   .............................................................

   .............................................................

   .............................................................

   .............................................................

   .............................................................

5. **Synthesize Information** What labels and symbols could you add to an image to represent the forces acting on DART and the satellite during the collision? Describe what you would draw and write.

   .............................................................

   .............................................................

   .............................................................

   .............................................................

   .............................................................

   .............................................................

   .............................................................

   .............................................................

# Quest FINDINGS

## Complete the Quest!

**Phenomenon** Design a way to present your new bumper car design and the results of your testing to your class. Be sure to include how you applied Newton's third law of motion to your design.

**Synthesize Information** Bumper cars have safety features to protect both the riders and the cars themselves. These features are built around how forces and the laws of motion affect the movement of the cars. What is another example of how forces and laws of motion impact your safety in your daily life?

.............................................................

.............................................................

.............................................................

👆 **INTERACTIVITY**

Reflect on Your Bumper Car Solution

MS-PS2-1, MS-PS2-2, MS-PS2-4, MS-PS3-2

# Stopping on a Dime

## Background

**Phenomenon** Imagine your school is hosting a championship basketball game, and the school band will be playing at the game. The band director wants the band to set up its instruments very close to the out-of-bounds line of the basketball court, so that the band will be front and center during the game. Some people at the school, however, have raised concerns about this plan. They feel that having band members so close to the court is unsafe because the members might be hit by players running off the court.

You and some of your fellow science students have been asked to design and conduct an experiment to determine whether or not the band director's plan is safe for both the band members and the players. In this experiment, you will investigate how time, distance, and average speed relate to changes in motion, and you will apply these concepts to the players on the basketball court.

How can you **design** a **basketball court** so that players don't run into band members and other spectators near the court lines?

## Materials

(per group)

- tape measure
- 2 stopwatches or watches with second hands

## Design Your Investigation

To model the basketball players running off the court, you will determine the speed of someone running a distance of 10 meters. Your will also determine how far it takes the runner to come to a complete stop after hitting the 10-meter mark. Discuss with your group how you will design and conduct the investigation. As you plan, consider the following questions with your group:

### HANDS-ON LAB

⊔**Demonstrate** Go online for a downloadable worksheet of this lab.

1. What three properties of the players in motion do you need to consider?

2. What do you need to know to calculate the speed of a runner?

3. What tests will you perform?

4. How many trials of each test will you perform?

5. What type of data will you be collecting? How will you collect, record, and organize your data?

6. What evidence will you need to present after your investigation?

7. How will you present your evidence to communicate your results effectively?

Write your plan in the space provided on the next page. After getting your teacher's approval, conduct your investigation. Record the data you collect in your group data table.

## Procedure

.......................................................................................................
.......................................................................................................
.......................................................................................................
.......................................................................................................
.......................................................................................................
.......................................................................................................
.......................................................................................................
.......................................................................................................
.......................................................................................................
.......................................................................................................

## Data Table

**Speed (m/s)**



**Stopping Distance (m)**

# Analyze and Interpret Data

1. **Characterize Data** Why was it important to carry out the steps of your procedure multiple times with each participant?

.............................................................................................................................

.............................................................................................................................

.............................................................................................................................

.............................................................................................................................

2. **Apply Concepts** How are unbalanced forces at work when a runner attempts to stop quickly after reaching the 10-m mark?

.............................................................................................................................

.............................................................................................................................

.............................................................................................................................

.............................................................................................................................

3. **Interpret Data** Do your data seem reasonable for representing speeds and distances traveled by basketball players on a court? Explain why or why not.

.............................................................................................................................

.............................................................................................................................

.............................................................................................................................

.............................................................................................................................

4. **Provide Critique** Compare your procedure with the procedure of another group. What did that group do differently? What would you suggest to improve that group's procedure?

.............................................................................................................................

.............................................................................................................................

.............................................................................................................................

5. **Construct Arguments** Write a proposal to the school that explains the importance of making sure the basketball court has enough space around it. In your proposal, suggest a strategy for making the court safer. Cite data from your investigation as evidence to support your points.

.............................................................................................................................

.............................................................................................................................

.............................................................................................................................

.............................................................................................................................

.............................................................................................................................

# TOPIC
# 4

# Genes and Heredity

### NGSS PERFORMANCE EXPECTATIONS

**MS-LS3-1** Develop and use a model to describe why structural changes to genes (mutations) located on chromosomes may affect proteins and may result in harmful, beneficial, or neutral effects to the structure and function of the organism.

**MS-LS3-2** Develop and use a model to describe why asexual reproduction results in offspring with identical genetic information and sexual reproduction results in offspring with genetic variation.

**MS-LS4-4** Construct an explanation based on evidence that describes how genetic variations of traits in a population increase some individuals' probability of surviving and reproducing in a specific environment.

**MS-LS4-5** Gather and synthesize information about the technologies that have changed the way humans influence the inheritance of desired traits in organisms.

HANDS-ON LAB

uConnect Explore the effects of different methods of reproduction.

How can these horses be the parents of the foal?

**GO ONLINE**
to access your
digital course

▶ VIDEO

👆 INTERACTIVITY

🧪 VIRTUAL LAB

☑ ASSESSMENT

📖 eTEXT

📱 APP

## The Essential Question

# How do offspring receive traits from their parents?

You might expect a foal to look just like at least one parent, but offspring can vary greatly in appearance. How do you think this foal ended up looking so different from both parents?

.......................................................................................................

.......................................................................................................

.......................................................................................................

.......................................................................................................

.......................................................................................................

# Quest KICKOFF

## How can you sell a new fruit?

**Phenomenon** Consumers are often open to new ideas—especially tasty new ideas. But it may take some convincing. What new fruit sensation can you develop, and how will you get growers and consumers to buy in? In this Quest activity, you will explore reproduction, heredity, and genetics as you choose desirable traits and figure out how to ensure their consistent appearance in your product. Once your new fruit is characterized, you will create a brochure to help growers understand your product, why it is desirable, and how they can grow it successfully.

## 🐾 NBC LEARN ▶ VIDEO

After watching the Quest Kickoff video about different kinds of fruit hybrids, think about the qualities you desire in your fruit. In the table below, identify the characteristics you want your new fruit to have.

| Color | |
|---|---|
| **Taste** | |
| **Size** | |
| **Shape** | |
| **Texture** | |

👆 **INTERACTIVITY**

Funky Fruits

**MS-LS3-1** Develop and use a model to describe why structural changes to genes (mutations) located on chromosomes may affect proteins and may result in harmful, beneficial, or neutral effects to the structure and function of the organism.

**MS-LS3-2** Develop and use a model to describe why asexual reproduction results in offspring with identical genetic information and sexual reproduction results in offspring with genetic variation.

**MS-LS4-5** Gather and synthesize information about the technologies that have changed the way humans influence the inheritance of desired traits in organisms.

# Quest CHECK-IN

## IN LESSON 1

How can you use both sexual and asexual reproduction to develop your new fruit? Explore how farmers benefit from using both types of reproduction to establish and maintain a consistent product.

👆 **INTERACTIVITY**

An Apple Lesson

# Quest CHECK-IN

## IN LESSON 2

What role do chromosomes and genes play in fruit reproduction? Make a chromosome map and locate genes that carry desirable traits.

👆 **INTERACTIVITY**

About Those Chromosomes

## IN LESSON 3

What do DNA and protein synthesis have to do with the traits exhibited by an organism? Consider how genes will affect the characteristics of your fruit.

These white strawberries, called pineberries, taste somewhat like pineapples.

## Quest CHECK-IN

### IN LESSON 4

How are dominant and recessive traits inherited? Examine data tables for trait inheritance and complete Punnett squares to determine the probable outcomes of crosses.

**HANDS-ON LAB**

All in the Numbers

### IN LESSON 5

How do growers ensure consistency in their product? Consider how you might use genetic technologies to develop your new fruit.

## Quest FINDINGS

### Complete the Quest!

Create a brochure for prospective growers of your new fruit. Convince readers that your fruit will be a delicious success!

 **INTERACTIVITY**

Reflect on Funky Fruits

# Patterns of Inheritance

## Guiding Questions

- How did Gregor Mendel advance the fields of genetics and inheritance?
- How are inherited alleles related to an organism's traits?
- How is probability related to inheritance?

## Connections

**Literacy** Determine Conclusions

**Math** Use a Probability Model

MS-LS3-2

## Vocabulary

heredity
dominant allele
recessive allele
probability
genotype
phenotype

## Academic Vocabulary

quantify
factor

 **VOCABULARY APP**

Practice vocabulary on a mobile device.

**Quest CONNECTION**

Think about how favorable traits can be used to develop the most desirable fruit.

## Connect It !

✏️ **Male northern cardinals express the trait for bright red feather color. Circle the male cardinal.**

**Predict** ✏️ List four more visible characteristics that these birds will pass on to their offspring. Then list the inherited trait that their offspring will possess.

| Visible Characteristics | Inherited Traits |
| --- | --- |
| reddish bill color | bill color |
| | |
| | |
| | |
| | |

**Apply Concepts** Will their offspring look exactly like the parents? Explain.

.................................................................................................................................

.................................................................................................................................

# Mendel's Observations

Like all other organisms, the cardinals in **Figure 1** pass their traits to their offspring. To better understand **heredity**, the passing of traits from parents to offspring, it is important to learn about the history behind the science. In the 1800s, a European monk named Gregor Mendel studied heredity. Mendel's job at the monastery was to tend the garden. After several years of growing pea plants, he became very familiar with seven possible traits the plants could have. Some plants grew tall, while others were short. Some produced green seeds, while others produced yellow.

## Mendel's Experiments

Mendel's studies became some of the most important in biology because he was one of the first to **quantify** his results. He collected, recorded, and analyzed data from the thousands of tests that he ran.

The experiments Mendel performed involved transferring the male flower part of a pea plant to the female flower part to get a desired trait. Mendel wanted to see what would happen with pea plants when he crossed different traits: short and tall, yellow seeds and green seeds, and so on. Because of his detailed work with heredity, Mendel is often referred to as the "father of modern genetics."

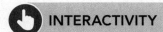

**INTERACTIVITY**

Examine different methods of passing on genes to offspring.

**Academic Vocabulary**

In Latin, *quantus* means "how much." Have you heard the word quantify used before? Does it remind you of any other words?

........................................................

........................................................

........................................................

........................................................

........................................................

........................................................

**Passing on Traits**
**Figure 1** Male and female northern cardinals share many traits, but also have several that make them unique.

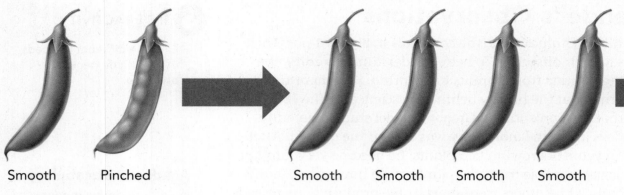

Smooth    Pinched          Smooth    Smooth    Smooth    Smooth

**P generation**                    **F₁ generation**

## Pea Pod Shape

**Figure 2** 🖊 Circle the pod shape in the P generation that has the dominant trait.

**Parents and Offspring** When Mendel cross-pollinated, or crossed, a tall plant with a short one, all of the offspring were tall. The tall plant and short plant that were crossed are called the parent plants, or P generation. The offspring are called the $F_1$, or first filial generation. The term *filial* originates from the Latin terms *filius* and *filia*, which mean "son" and "daughter," respectively.

Mendel examined several traits of pea plants. Through his experimentation, he realized that certain patterns formed. When a plant with green peas was crossed with one with yellow peas, all of the $F_1$ offspring were yellow. However, when he crossed these offspring, creating what is called the second filial generation, or $F_2$, the resulting offspring were not all yellow. For every four offspring, three were yellow and one was green. This pattern of inheritance appeared repeatedly when Mendel tested other traits, such as pea pod shape shown in **Figure 2**. Mendel concluded that while only one form of the trait is visible in $F_1$, in $F_2$ the missing trait sometimes shows itself.

## Plan It!

**Develop a Procedure**
Consider five other traits that Mendel investigated. Explain how you could repeat Mendel's procedure for one of these traits and what the likely results would be.

| Trait | Dominant | Recessive |
|---|---|---|
| seed shape | round | wrinkled |
| seed color | yellow | green |
| pod color | green | yellow |
| flower color | purple | white |
| pod position on stem | side of stem | top of stem |

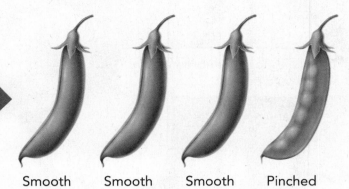

Smooth     Smooth     Smooth     Pinched

**F₂ generation**

# Alleles Affect Inheritance

In Mendel's time, people had no knowledge of genetic material or its ability to carry the code for an organism's traits. However, Mendel was still able to formulate several ideas about heredity from his experiments. He called the information that carried the traits **factors**, because they determined what was expressed. He also determined that for every trait, organisms receive one factor from their mother and one factor from their father. He concluded that one factor can mask the expression of the other even if both are present at the same time.

**Genes and Alleles** Today, the term *factor* has been replaced with *gene* or *allele*. Alleles are the different forms of a gene. Pea plants have one gene that controls the color of the seeds. This gene may express itself as being either yellow or green through a combination of yellow alleles and green alleles. When crossed, each parent donates one of its alleles for seed color to the offspring. The allele that each parent donates is random. An offspring's seed color is determined by the combination of both alleles.

An organism's traits are controlled by the alleles it inherits. A **dominant allele** is one whose trait always shows up in the organism when the allele is present. A **recessive allele**, on the other hand, is hidden whenever the dominant allele is present. If one parent donates a dominant allele and the other donates a recessive allele, only the dominant trait will be expressed.

✓ READING CHECK **Determine Conclusions** What conditions would have to occur for an offspring to express the recessive trait?

.........................................................................................

.........................................................................................

HANDS-ON LAB

Explore cross-pollination by examining the parts of a flower.

**Academic Vocabulary**

How is factor used differently in math and science?

.........................................................................................

.........................................................................................

.........................................................................................

.........................................................................................

.........................................................................................

.........................................................................................

## Dominating Color

**Figure 3** 🖉 Mendel discovered that yellow is the dominant pea seed color, while recessive pea seed color is green. Complete the statements. Use the letters *G* and *g* as needed.

**Apply Concepts** What are the alleles for the green pea seed? Would it be a pure-bred or a hybrid?

.................................................................

.................................................................

The alleles for a purebred yellow seed would be ..................

The alleles for a hybrid yellow seed would be ....................

## Literacy Connection

**Determine Conclusions** How did Mendel come to the conclusion that an organism's traits were carried on different alleles? Underline the sentence that answers this question.

**Writing Alleles** The traits we see are present because of the combination of alleles. For example, the peas in **Figure 3** show two different colors. Pea color is the gene, while the combinations of alleles determines how the gene will be expressed. To represent this, scientists who study patterns of inheritance, called geneticists, use letters to represent the alleles. A dominant allele is represented with a capital letter (G) and a recessive allele with a lowercase letter (g).

When an organism has two of the same alleles for a trait, it is called a purebred. This would be represented as GG or gg. When the organism has one dominant allele and one recessive allele, it is called a hybrid. This would be represented as Gg. Remember that each trait is represented by two alleles, one from the mother and one from the father. Depending upon which alleles are inherited, the offspring may be a purebred or a hybrid.

Mendel's work was quite revolutionary. Prior to his work, many people assumed that all traits in offspring were a mixture of each parent's traits. Mendel's experiments, where traits appeared in the $F_2$ generation that were not in the $F_1$ generation, disproved this idea.

# Probability and Heredity

When you flip a coin, what are the chances it will come up heads? Because there are two options (heads or tails), the probability of getting heads is 1 out of 2. The coin has an equal chance of coming up heads or tails. Each toss has no effect on the outcome of the next toss. **Probability** is a number that describes how likely it is that an event will occur. The laws of probability predict what is likely to happen and what is not likely to happen.

**Probability and Genetics** When dealing with genetics and inheritance, it is important to know the laws of probability. Every time two parents produce offspring, the probability of certain traits getting passed on is the same. For example, do you know any families that have multiple children, but all of them are the same sex? Picture a family where all the children are girls. According to the laws of probability, a boy should have been born already, but there is no guarantee of that happening. Every time these parents have a child, the probability of having a boy remains the same as the probability of having a girl.

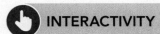

**INTERACTIVITY**

Collect data to determine whether a trait is genetic or acquired.

## Math Toolbox

### Determining Probability

Probability is an important part of the science of genetics. Answer the questions on probability below.

1. **Predict** The probability of a specific allele from one parent being passed on to an offspring is 1 in 2, or ½. This is the same probability as predicting a coin toss correctly. How often would you expect a coin to show tails if you flip it 100 times?

   .........................................................................................

2. **Identify Patterns** A die is a six-sided cube with dots representing the numbers 1 through 6. What is the probability of rolling a 3?

   .........................................................................................

3. **Use a Probability Model** You and a friend both roll a die at the same time. On the first roll, the dots on the two dice add up to 7. On the second roll, they add up to 2. Which do you think was more likely, rolling a total of 2 or a total of 7? Explain your answer.

   .........................................................................................

   .........................................................................................

   .........................................................................................

   .........................................................................................

   .........................................................................................

## Making a Punnett Square

**Making a Punnett Square** To determine the probability of inheriting alleles, geneticists use a tool called a Punnett square. To construct a Punnett square, it is important to know what trait is being considered and whether the parents are purebred or hybrid.

The following steps demonstrate how to use a Punnett square to calculate the probability of offspring having different combinations of alleles. The example describes the procedure for a cross between two hybrid parents; however, this procedure will work for any cross.

### Using a Punnett Square

Mendel's experiments involved crossing two hybrid pea plants in the F$_1$ generation. Most plants in the F$_2$ generation showed the dominant trait, but some showed the recessive trait. A Punnett square uses the laws of probability to demonstrate why those results occurred. Consider the question of what the offspring of two hybrid pea plants with yellow seed color will be.

**1** **Draw a square box** divided into four square parts.

One parent's alleles go on top and the other parent's alleles go on the left.

**2** **Determine the alleles** of each of the parents. You know that they are both hybrids, so they have one dominant allele (represented as a capital letter) and one recessive allele (represented as a lowercase letter). Place one set of alleles on top of the columns of the box, and one set of alleles next to the rows of the box, as shown.

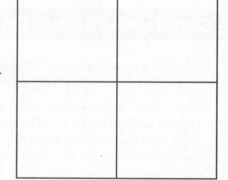

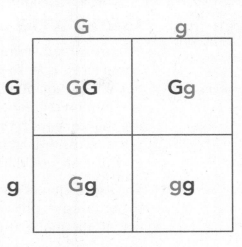

|     | G | g |
|-----|-----|-----|
| **G** | **GG** | **Gg** |
| **g** | **Gg** | **gg** |

**3** **Do the cross!** Inside each box, combine the letter at the top of the column with the letter to the left of the row the box is in. Always write a dominant allele before a recessive allele.

**4** **Determine the likelihood** of different combinations of alleles. As you can see from the Punnett square, the combination GG occurs ¼ of the time, the combination Gg occurs ²⁄₄, or ½ of the time, and the combination gg occurs ¼ of the time.

**5** **Determine which trait is expressed** for each combination of alleles. In this example, the combination GG and Gg result in the dominant yellow seed color, while the combination gg results in the green seed color. Therefore, the dominant allele will be expressed ¾ of the time. This matches the results of Mendel's experiments.

**Use a Probability Model** ✎ You cross a pea plant that is hybrid for yellow seed color (Gg) with a purebred green seed color (gg) plant. Draw a Punnett square to show the results of the cross. What is the probability that the offspring will have green seed color?

........................................................................................

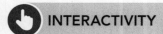

**INTERACTIVITY**

Use models to describe how sexual reproduction leads to genetic variation.

# Genotype

You are already familiar with the terms *purebred* and *hybrid*. These terms refer to **genotype**, an organism's genetic makeup or combination of alleles. As shown in **Figure 4**, the genotype of a purebred green seed pea plant would be gg. Both alleles are the same (purebred) and they are recessive because green is the recessive trait in terms of seed color. The hybrid genotype for this trait would be Gg.

The expression of an organism's genes is called its **phenotype**, the organism's physical appearance or visible traits. The height, the shape, the color, the size, the texture—whatever trait is being expressed, is referred to as the phenotype. So, a pea plant with the phenotype of yellow seed color could have two possible genotypes, GG or Gg.

## Genotypes and Phenotypes for Seed Color

**Figure 4** The phenotype of an organism is explained as physical characteristics we see, while the genotype describes the combination of alleles that are inherited.

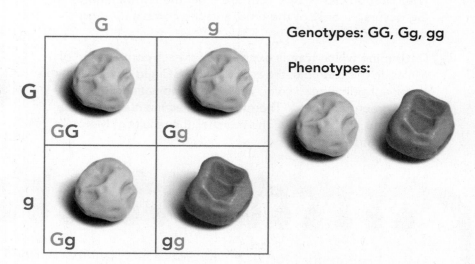

There are two other terms geneticists use to describe genotypes. Instead of saying purebred, they refer to an organism with two identical alleles as homozygous (*homo*- means "the same"). When the alleles are both dominant, as in the yellow seed plant (GG), the genotype is called homozygous dominant. However, when the alleles are both recessive, as in the green seed color (gg), the genotype is called homozygous recessive. When an organism is a hybrid, as in yellow seed color (Gg), the genotype is called the heterozygous condition (*hetero*- means "different").

✓ READING CHECK **Determine Differences**
Explain how genotypes and phenotypes are different.

........................................................................................................

........................................................................................................

1. **Identify** The dominant allele for dimples is D and the recessive allele is d. What genetic condition does an individual with the alleles dd have?

.................................................................

**Use the information you calculated in the Punnett square activity to answer questions 2 and 3.**

2. **Interpret Data** How did the probabilities of yellow seeds and green seeds compare with each other?

.................................................................

.................................................................

.................................................................

.................................................................

3. **Cause and Effect** What would happen to the probabilities of yellow and green seeds if one parent were homozygous recessive and the other were homozygous dominant?

.................................................................

.................................................................

.................................................................

.................................................................

4. **Construct an Explanation** Why were Mendel's experiments with pea plants so important toward advancing current knowledge of genetics and inheritance?

.................................................................

.................................................................

.................................................................

.................................................................

.................................................................

.................................................................

5. **Predict** For plant stem length, the dominant allele for height is T and the recessive allele is t. What would be the genotypes, phenotypes, and offspring probabilities of a cross between a heterozygous parent for tall stem length and one that was homozygous recessive for short stem length?

.................................................................

.................................................................

.................................................................

.................................................................

## Quest CHECK-IN

**In this lesson, you learned how inherited alleles determine traits and how probability is related to inheritance. You also explored the factors that determine an organism's genotype and phenotype.**

**Apply Concepts** How can you increase the likelihood that the desired trait will be inherited in your fruit?

.................................................................

.................................................................

.................................................................

### 👆 INTERACTIVITY

An Apple Lesson

**Go online** to explore how you can utilize both sexual and asexual reproduction to develop your new fruit.

MS-LS3-1, MS-LS3-2, MS-LS4-4

# CEPHALOPODS
## SPECIAL EDITION

Octopuses, squids, and cuttlefish are a type of mollusk called cephalopods. These soft-bodied invertebrates reproduce sexually. They are fast swimmers and aggressive predators. With prominent heads and multiple tentacles, cephalopods are known for their complex behaviors and for being extremely intelligent.

Cephalopods also have a remarkably large genome— it's even larger than the human genome! Their genome stands out because it has many genes related to neuron connectivity, which might explain their unusually large brains and intelligence. Cephalopods are so smart that they can solve puzzles, use tools, and even open jars.

## Adding Variation

Sexual reproduction is not the only process that contributes to making offspring different from their parents. Squids and octopuses, for example, have developed a clever mechanism that increases variation in traits without really having to make changes to their genetic information.

Some genetic information becomes traits by means of a messenger molecule called RNA. RNA is the molecule that allows the expression of genetic information.

In a process called RNA editing, squids and octopuses can make changes to RNA, the messenger molecule. RNA editing leads to a change in traits that are expressed, regardless of the information coded in the genome. The highest rate of RNA-editing takes place in nervous system cells.

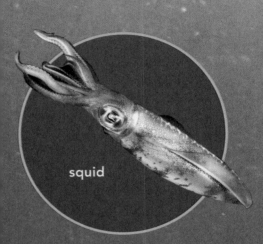

squid

octopus

RNA editing in cephalopods is triggered by environmental factors. It could be turned on when the cephalopod travels from the tropics from the arctic. Or it will turn off the RNA editing when the cephalopod remains in one location.

cuttlefish

One fascinating feature of RNA editing is that not all of the messenger molecules are edited the same way. As a result, many different RNA messenger molecules can come out of one single gene.

Scientists think that this increase in variation may also explain cephalopods' complex brains and high intelligence. They also wonder whether there could be a trade off. By relying on RNA editing to adapt to such influences in the environment as temperature changes and experiences, could these special cephalopods be losing something else?  After all, these specific changes are not passed down to their offspring.

**Read the case study and answer the following questions.**

1. **Analyze Data**  Suppose the ability to edit RNA is a dominant trait. A male squid with two dominant alleles for RNA editing sexually reproduces with a female squid that has two recessive alleles for RNA editing. Will their offspring be able to edit their RNA? Explain.

   ...................................................................................................................

2. **Apply Scientific Reasoning**  If there is a change in a squid's messenger RNA, will this change appear in its genetic material? Will it be inherited by its offspring?

   ...................................................................................................................
   ...................................................................................................................

3. **Construct Explanations**  How can changes in RNA be beneficial for squids?

   ...................................................................................................................
   ...................................................................................................................

4. **Explain Phenomena**  What do you think could happen if humans had the same RNA-editing ability as cephalopods? What might be the result?

   ...................................................................................................................
   ...................................................................................................................
   ...................................................................................................................

## Guiding Questions

- What is the relationship among genes, chromosomes, and inheritance?
- How is a pedigree used to track inheritance?
- How does the formation of sex cells during meiosis differ from the process of cell division?

## Connections

**Literacy** Read and Comprehend

**Math** Model With Mathematics

MS-LS3-2

## Vocabulary

chromosome
cell cycle
pedigree
meiosis
chromatids
mitosis

## Academic Vocabulary

structure
function

 **VOCABULARY APP**

Practice vocabulary on a mobile device.

### Quest CONNECTION

Think about how chromosomes are passed down from parents to offspring.

## Connect It !

✏️ **Circle the traits that are similar between the parents and the offspring.**

**Apply Concepts** How were the traits transferred from the parents to the ducklings during reproduction? Where were those traits found?

.............................................................................................................

.............................................................................................................

.............................................................................................................

**Apply Scientific Reasoning** Each duckling came from these parents. They look similar, but they are not exactly the same. Why are they not identical? Explain.

.............................................................................................................

.............................................................................................................

# Chromosomes and Genes

Gregor Mendel's ideas about inheritance and probability can be applied to all living things. Mendel determined that traits are inherited using pieces of information that he called factors and we call genes. He observed and experimented with genes in pea plants. He discovered how genes, such as those in ducks (**Figure 1**), were transferred from parents to offspring and how they made certain traits appear. However, Mendel did not know what genes actually look like.

Today, scientists know that genes are segments of code that appear on structures called **chromosomes**. These thread-like **structures** within a cell's nucleus contain DNA that is passed from one generation to the next. These threadlike strands of genetic material have condensed and wrapped themselves around special proteins. This provides support for the chromosome structure.

Chromosomes are made in the beginning of the **cell cycle**, the series of events in which a cell grows, prepares for division, and divides to form daughter cells. During this time, the chromosome gets its characteristic X shape.

## HANDS-ON LAB

Investigate genetic crosses in imaginary creatures.

## Academic Vocabulary

Identify and describe something that has a particular structure.

...................................................

...................................................

...................................................

...................................................

...................................................

**Parents Pass Traits to Their Offspring**

**Figure 1** Each baby mallard duck receives some traits from the mother and some from the father.

## Scales of Genetic Material

**Figure 2** ✏ Order the structures from smallest to largest by writing the numbers 1 through 5 in the blank circles. Number 1 is the smallest.

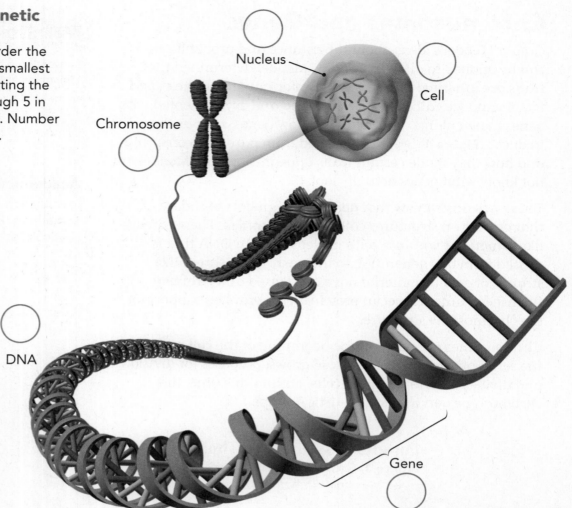

Nucleus

Cell

Chromosome

DNA

Gene

📓 **Make Meaning** Why do sex cells contain only half the number of chromosomes needed for offspring? In your science notebook, explain what would happen if sex cells contained the same number of chromosomes as body cells.

**Academic Vocabulary**

What is the difference between an object's structure and its function?

..............................

..............................

..............................

### Number of Chromosomes
Every cell in your body other than the sex cells has the same number of chromosomes. In humans, this number is 46. Other organisms have different numbers of chromosomes, and there is a great variety. For example, mallard ducks have 80 chromosomes. All sexually-reproducing organisms form sex cells, which have half the number of chromosomes that body cells have.

### Genes on Chromosomes
Every living thing needs instructions to live. Without these instructions, living things would not be able to grow and **function**. These instructions are located on genes. As you can see in **Figure 2,** genes are located on chromosomes.

In humans, between 20,000 and 25,000 genes are found on the 46 chromosomes. Chromosomes are different sizes. Larger chromosomes contain more genes than smaller chromosomes. Each gene contains instructions for coding a particular trait. There are hundreds to thousands of genes coding traits on any given chromosome. For many organisms, these chromosomes come in sets.

**Chromosome Pairs** During fertilization, you receive 23 chromosomes from your father and 23 chromosomes from your mother. These chromosomes come in pairs, called homologous chromosomes, that contain the same genes. Two alleles—one from the mother and one from the father— represent each trait. However, the alleles for these genes may or may not be the same. Some of the alleles for how the gene is expressed may be dominant or recessive. In **Figure 3**, the offspring that received these chromosomes inherited two different forms of a gene—allele *A* from one parent and allele *a* from the other. The individual will be heterozygous for that gene trait. Because more than one gene is present on the 23 pairs of chromosomes, there is a wide variety of allele combinations.

☑ READING CHECK **Read and Comprehend** How would geneticists—people who study genes—know whether an organism is homozygous or heterozygous for a certain trait by examining its chromosomes?

........................................................................................................

........................................................................................................

........................................................................................................

........................................................................................................

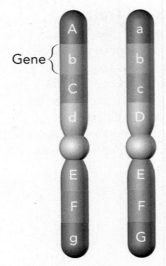

Chromosome pair

**A Pair of Chromosomes**
**Figure 3** ✏ Circle all the pairs of alleles that would be homozygous for a trait.

Math Toolbox

## Counting on Chromosomes

1. **Model with Mathematics** ✏ Fill in the table with the appropriate chromosome number for the missing body cell or sex cell.

| Organisms | Number of Chromosomes | |
|---|---|---|
| | Body Cells | Sex Cells |
| House cat | 38 | |
| Mallard duck | | 40 |
| Corn | 20 | |
| Peanut | 40 | |
| Horse | | 32 |
| Oak tree | | 12 |
| Sweet potato | 90 | |
| Camel | | 35 |
| Chicken | 78 | |

2. **Construct Graphs** ✏ Complete the line plot below. Place an *X* for each organism whose body cell chromosome number falls within the given range.

**Body Cell Chromosome Distribution**

0–21    21–40    41–60    61–80    81–100
Number of chromosomes

## Tracking Traits

**Figure 4** 🖍 Sickle cell anemia is a genetic disease that changes the structure of red blood cells. In the pedigree, affected members are shaded. Circle any individuals on the pedigree who are definitely carriers for the trait.

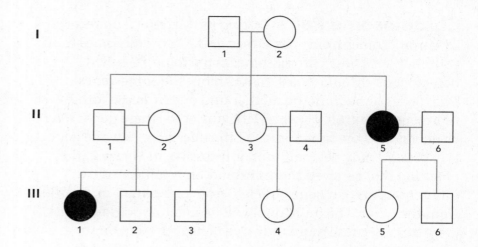

**INTERACTIVITY**

Take a look inside the formation of sex cells through meiosis.

## Using a Pedigree

Alelles can sometimes recombine to produce traits that are not favorable, such as a genetic disease. Geneticists study how traits are inherited in order to trace their genetic origin and predict how they may be passed on to future generations.

A **pedigree** is a tool that geneticists use to map out the inheritance of traits. The diagram shows the presence or absence of a trait according to the relationships within a family across several generations. It is like a family tree. **Figure 4** shows multiple generations represented by Roman numerals I, II, and III. Most pedigrees show which family members express a particular trait (shaded figures) as well as the individuals who carry the trait but do not express it (half-shaded figures). In a pedigree, males are represented with squares and females with circles. One horizontal line connects the parent couple and another line leads down from the parents to their children.

## Model It

**Develop Models** 🖍 Think of a trait that you admire. How can that trait get passed through a family? Create a pedigree that outlines the transmission of this trait through a family. Consider who has the trait, who is a carrier for it, and who does not have it.

# Forming Sex Cells

In an organism that is reproduced sexually, a body cell has twice as many chromosomes a sex cell. Why is this important? Well, it is through the sex cells that parents pass their genes on to their offspring. When the sperm and egg fuse, they form a zygote, or fertilized egg. The zygote gets two sets of chromosomes—one set from the sperm and one set from the egg. Human eggs, for example, contain 23 total chromosomes in a set and sperm contain 23 total chromosomes in a set. So, each of your body cells contains one set of chromosomes from your mother and another set from your father for a total of 46 chromosomes.

Sex cells (sperm and egg) are formed through a very specialized process called **meiosis**, during which the number of chromosomes is reduced by half. It is through meiosis that homologous chromosomes separate into two different cells. This creates new cells with half as many chromosomes as the parent cell.

Homologous chromosomes have one chromosome from each parent. While the two chromosomes share the same sequence of genes, they may have different alleles. Before the chromosomes separate and move into separate cells, they undergo a process called crossing over. Notice in **Figure 5** that a small segment of one chromosome exchanges places with the corresponding segment on the other chromosome. By exchanging this genetic information, the new cells that form will have a slightly different combination of genes. This allows for minor variations in traits to form, which means there is a higher likelihood that offspring with desirable traits will form within the larger population.

## Swapping Genetic Material

**Figure 5** 🖊 During crossing over, a segment of the gene from the mother changes places with a segment of the same gene from the father. Circle the gene segments that exchanged places.

**Cause and Effect** What would happen to offspring if crossing over did not occur during the first part of meiosis?

....................................................

....................................................

....................................................

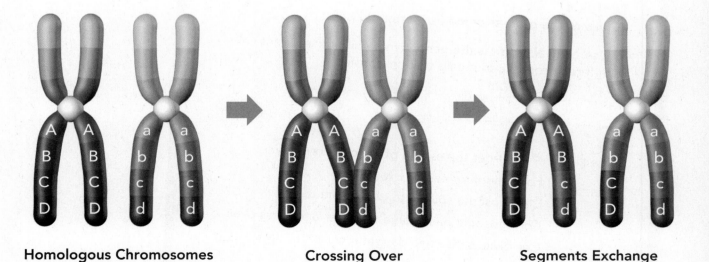

**Homologous Chromosomes**       **Crossing Over**       **Segments Exchange**

**VIDEO**

Observe the process of meiosis in action.

**INTERACTIVITY**

Trace the path of a particular trait through meiosis.

**Meiosis** Before a cell can divide, the genetic material condenses into chromosomes. **Figure 6** shows how meiosis starts with the genetic material being copied and condensing into chromosomes. After crossing over, the chromosomes separate and the cell divides into two cells. Each new cell, now containing half the number of chromosomes, then divides again, making a total of four daughter cells. Meiosis II in **Figure 6** shows how this second division occurs. Each chromosome splits into two rod-like structures called **chromatids**. Each chromatid contains a double helix of DNA. Note that each of the four daughter cells has one distinct chromatid.

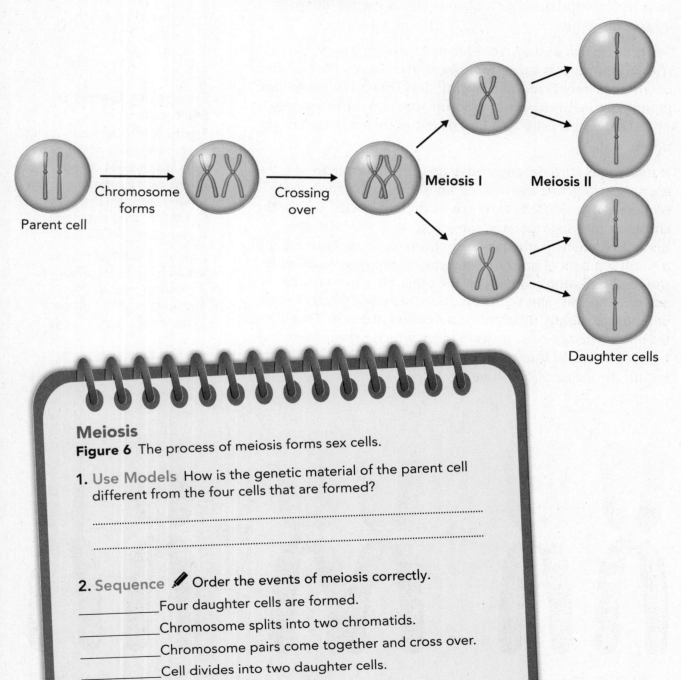

Parent cell — Chromosome forms — Crossing over — Meiosis I — Meiosis II — Daughter cells

**Meiosis**
**Figure 6** The process of meiosis forms sex cells.

1. **Use Models** How is the genetic material of the parent cell different from the four cells that are formed?

.................................................................................................................

.................................................................................................................

2. **Sequence** ✏ Order the events of meiosis correctly.

_____ Four daughter cells are formed.

_____ Chromosome splits into two chromatids.

_____ Chromosome pairs come together and cross over.

_____ Cell divides into two daughter cells.

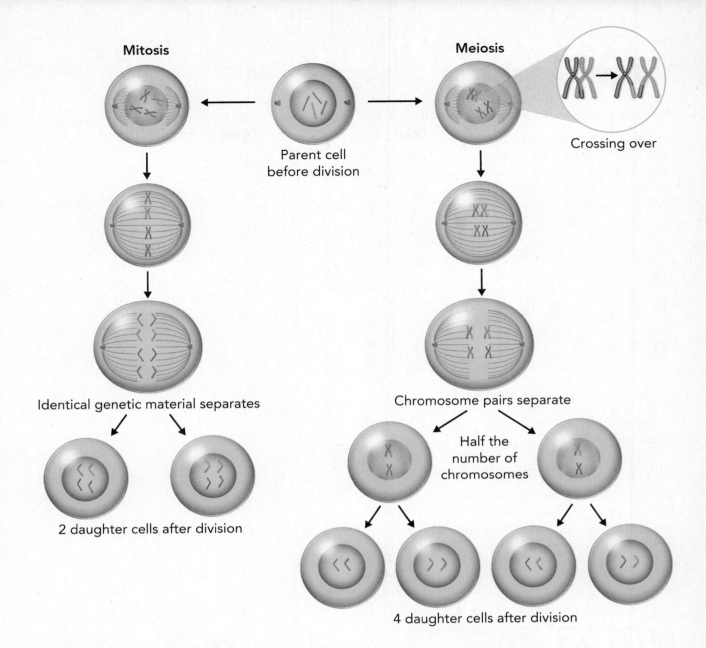

**Mitosis**

Parent cell before division

**Meiosis**

Crossing over

Identical genetic material separates

2 daughter cells after division

Chromosome pairs separate

Half the number of chromosomes

4 daughter cells after division

**Comparing Meiosis and Mitosis** The two main types of cell division are meiosis and mitosis. The majority of our body cells divide to make two genetically identical new cells in a process called **mitosis**: The cell's nucleus divides into two new nuclei, and identical copies of the parent cell's genetic material are distributed into each daughter cell.

Compare the processes of meiosis and mitosis shown in **Figure 7**. Mitosis produces two identical daughter cells with the same DNA as the parent cell. The sex cells produced by meiosis, however, are not genetically identical. There are two reasons for this difference. First, crossing over exchanges genetic material between homologous chromosomes. Secondly, the two cell divisions that occur in meiosis produce four daughter cells and each cell has half its parent cell's DNA. As a result, each sex cell has different genetic information.

**Meiosis versus Mitosis**
**Figure 7** While meiosis forms sex cells, mitosis forms new body cells.

MS-LS3-2

**Use the pedigree to answer questions 1 & 2.**

In humans, free earlobes are dominant and attached earlobes are recessive. The pedigree shows the transmission of attached earlobes through four generations of a family.

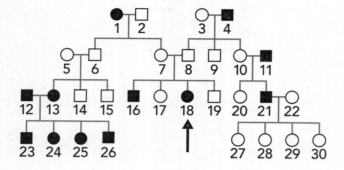

**1. Interpreting Diagrams** Which male members of the family have attached earlobes?

......................................................................

**2. Predict** If the female marked by the arrow (individual 18) has a child with a male carrier, what is the probability their child will have attached earlobes?

......................................................................

......................................................................

**3. Analyze Data** Is chromosome number a good predictor of organism complexity? Explain.

......................................................................

......................................................................

......................................................................

......................................................................

**4. Calculate** A male king crab has 104 chromosomes in a sperm cell. How many chromosomes does it have in each of its body cells?

......................................................................

**5. Cause and Effect** How can crossing over lead to the expression of new traits?

......................................................................

......................................................................

......................................................................

......................................................................

......................................................................

# Quest CHECK-IN

In this lesson you learned how chromosomes carry genes and how chromosomes come in pairs that you receive from each parent. You explored how combinations of alleles are passed down in families. You also learned how cells can divide to create genetically similar cells or to create sex cells.

**Apply Concepts** A domestic cat has 38 chromosomes in its skin cells, while a dog has 78 chromosomes. How does this fact help to explain why dogs and cats cannot interbreed?

......................................................................

......................................................................

......................................................................

......................................................................

 **INTERACTIVITY**

About Those Chromosomes

**Go online** to begin your chromosome map.

Genetic Counselor

# Chromosome COUNSELORS

**VIDEO**

Watch what's involved with being a genetic counselor.

Sometimes it runs in the family, as they say. We get traits such as eye color from genes passed on to us by our parents, but we can inherit diseases, too.

Genetic counselors help people who are at risk for a disease or a genetic disorder. Thexy are experts in genetics, so they know better than anyone how genes work. And they are trained counselors, too. They give emotional support and help families make health decisions.

For example, a genetic counselor might help new parents of a baby with Down syndrome. Or the counselor might meet with a patient whose family has a history of Alzheimer's.

Genetic counselors study a family's health history, order genetic tests, and help people to live with a genetic disease. They even advise doctors. They're the genetic experts, and they share their knowledge to help people.

**MY CAREER**

Want to help people understand their genes? Do an online search for "genetic counselor" to learn more about this career.

Genetic counselors complete a four-year bachelor's degree in biology or a healthcare field. After graduating, they work on completing a master's degree. This degree will focus on human genetics and counseling. They also complete extensive research. In addition, excellent communication and decision-making skills are required.

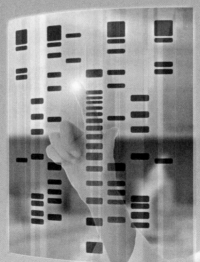

Genetic counselors help others understand the complex world of DNA, genes, and chromosomes.

## LESSON 3

# Genetic Coding and Protein Synthesis

## Guiding Questions

- Why do cells undergo DNA replication?
- How do cells make proteins?
- Why do cells undergo protein synthesis?

## Connection

**Literacy** Draw Comparative Inferences

MS-LS3-1

## Vocabulary

DNA
protein synthesis
messenger RNA
transfer RNA

## Academic Vocabulary

sequence

 **VOCABULARY APP**

Practice vocabulary on a mobile device.

### Quest CONNECTION

Think about how you might change a fruit's DNA to alter its traits.

## Connect It!

🖊 **A blueprint is a plan to build something. Circle the blueprint.**

**Make Connections** When have you used instructions to build something?

...................................................................................................

...................................................................................................

**Construct Explanations** How did the instructions help you with building the structure?

...................................................................................................

...................................................................................................

# The Genetic Code

Just as the couple in **Figure 1** need a blueprint to renovate a house, your body needs a plan to carry out daily functions. Your "blueprint" is found in the nucleus of each cell in the form of **DNA**. DNA (deoxyribonucleic acid) is the genetic material that carries information about an organism and is passed from parent to offspring.

In 1953, almost 100 years after DNA was discovered, scientists realized that DNA was shaped like a double helix—a twisted ladder. The structure of DNA consists of sugars, phosphates, and nitrogen bases. The sides of the ladder are made of sugar molecules, called deoxyribose, alternating with phosphate molecules. The rungs of the ladder are made of nitrogen bases. DNA has four nitrogen bases: adenine (A), thymine (T), guanine (G), and cytosine (C).

Genes are sections of DNA found on chromosomes. Each gene consists of hundreds or thousands of nitrogen bases arranged in a **sequence**. And it's this order that forms the instructions for building proteins — long chains of amino acids. Genes direct the construction of proteins, which in turn affect the traits that individuals receive from their parent(s). In other words, proteins trigger cellular processes that determine how inherited traits get expressed.

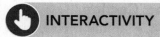

## INTERACTIVITY

Explore the role of DNA in cellular processes and reproduction.

## Academic Vocabulary

List some other contexts in which you have seen the word sequence.

..................................................

..................................................

..................................................

..................................................

## Using a Blueprint

**Figure 1** A blueprint is a plan for a building. DNA is the blueprint for constructing an organism.

## Making Copies

**Figure 2** ✏ In the circles, label the five nitrogen bases that would pair with the bases between the two arrows on the bottom strand.

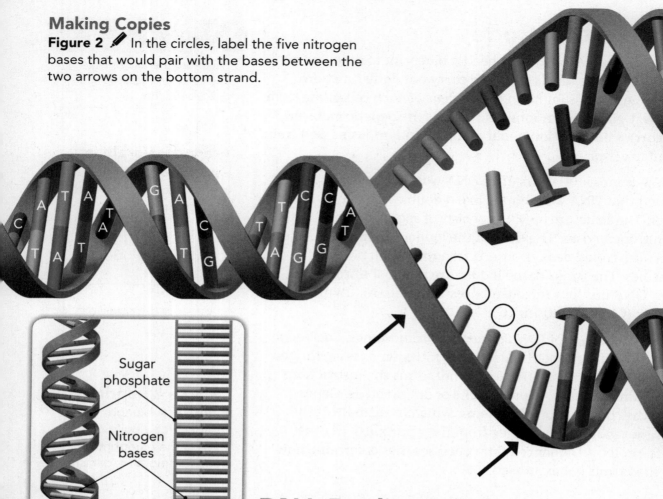

Sugar phosphate

Nitrogen bases

▶ **VIDEO**

Learn how the simplicity of DNA's four-letter code leads to the complexity of life.

## DNA Replication

Scientists estimate that humans are made of approximately 37 trillion cells. As you grow and age, new cells form to build and repair structures or to replace cells that have died. For this to happen, cells need to replicate, and this requires making copies of DNA.

As shown in **Figure 2**, DNA replication begins when the double helix untwists. Then, a protein breaks the DNA strand in half—at the structure's weakest point—between the nitrogen bases. This separation actually looks like a zipper (**Figure 3**), and is often referred to as "unzipping the DNA." Next, nitrogen bases with a sugar and phosphate attached pair up with the bases on each half of the DNA. Because nitrogen bases always pair in the same way, adenine with thymine and guanine with cytosine, the order of the bases on both strands are identical. At the end of replication, a chromosome with two identical DNA strands is formed.

☑ **READING CHECK** **Draw Comparative Inferences** How is the separation of DNA like a zipper?

..................................................................................................

..................................................................................................

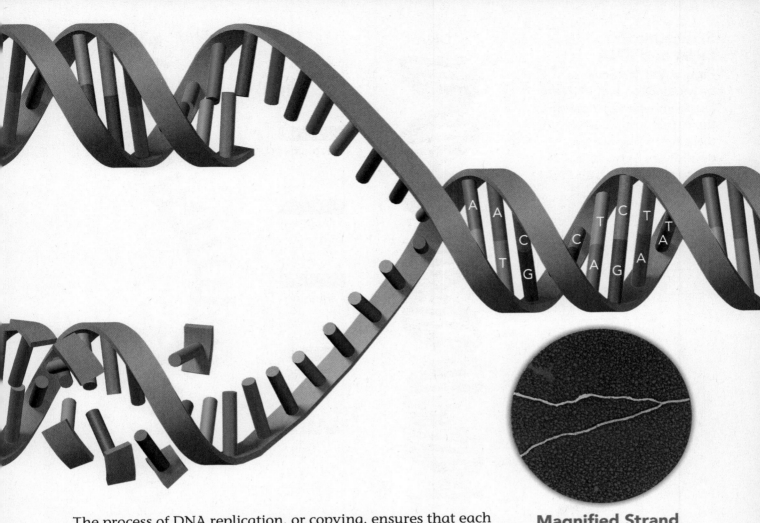

The process of DNA replication, or copying, ensures that each chromatid of a chromosome has identical DNA. During cell division, chromosomes split. During mitosis, the identical chromatids separate, resulting in identical DNA in each daughter cell. During meiosis, crossing over occurs before the chromatids split. No matter the type of cell division, DNA replication ensures that each cell contains the correct amount of DNA to carry out life processes.

**Magnified Strand of DNA**

**Figure 3** This photograph taken by an electron microscope shows DNA replication in action.

# Design It!

**Develop Models** ✏ Sketch how you would model DNA replication using household materials such as beads and pipe cleaners. How do the pipe cleaners and beads relate to the structure and function of DNA?

## Structure of DNA and RNA

**Figure 4** Differences between DNA and RNA are apparent when comparing their structure. Use the diagram to identify two differences between a DNA molecule and an RNA molecule.

...................................

...................................

...................................

...................................

...................................

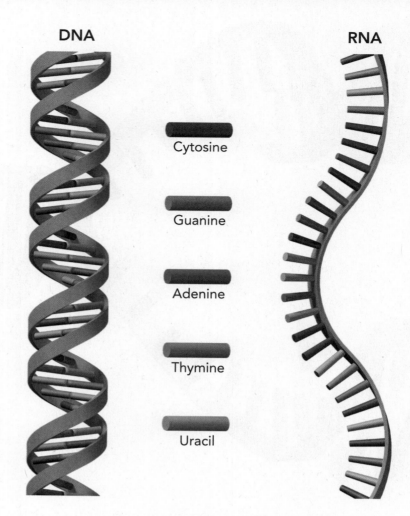

DNA

RNA

Cytosine

Guanine

Adenine

Thymine

Uracil

HANDS-ON LAB

Make a model of the process of protein synthesis.

Literacy Connection

**Draw Comparative Inferences** Identify locations in both the diagram and the text that describe the similarities and differences between DNA and RNA.

# Making Proteins

Proteins are made from building blocks called amino acids. There are only 20 amino acids in the human body, but your body can combine them in thousands of ways to make many different types of proteins needed to carry out cell processes. Inside the cell, amino acids link to form proteins through a process called **protein synthesis**. Once the protein is made, the cell will express the trait or perform a function.

**RNA** The process of protein synthesis starts in the nucleus, where the DNA contains the code for the protein. However, the actual assembly of the protein occurs at an organelle called the ribosome. Before a ribosome can assemble a protein, it needs to receive the blueprint to assemble the right protein from the nucleus.

The blueprint is transferred from the nucleus to the ribosome by a different nucleic acid called RNA (ribonucleic acid). Even though both RNA and DNA are nucleic acids, they have some differences. One difference is that RNA contains the sugar ribose instead of deoxyribose. **Figure 4** shows two other differences.

**How RNA Is Used** There are two main types of RNA involved in protein synthesis: messenger RNA and transfer RNA. **Messenger RNA** (mRNA) carries copies of instructions for the assembly of amino acids into proteins from DNA to ribosomes in the cytoplasm. **Transfer RNA** (tRNA), shown in **Figure 5**, carries amino acids to the ribosome during protein synthesis.

The order of the nitrogen bases on a gene determines the structure of the protein it makes. In the genetic code, a group of three nitrogen bases codes for one specific amino acid. For example, the three-base DNA sequence C-G-T (cytosine-guanine-thymine) always codes for the amino acid alanine. The order of the three-base code units determines the order in which amino acids are put together to form a protein. (**Figure 6**). See **Figure 7** for a summary of the entire process of protein synthesis.

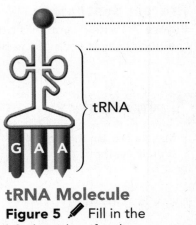

**tRNA Molecule**
**Figure 5** 🖉 Fill in the label to identify what tRNA molecules carry.

## Knowing the Code

**Figure 6** A codon is a sequence of three bases that codes for one amino acid. For the DNA sequence C-T-A, the complementary mRNA codon would be G-A-U. Since RNA does not have thymine, the RNA complement to adenine will always be uracil. Scientists use an mRNA codon table to determine which codons will code for each amino acid. The highlighted parts of the table show you how the codon G-A-U codes for aspartic acid, also known as aspartate.

### mRNA Codon Table

| First position | | Second position | | | | Third position |
|---|---|---|---|---|---|---|
| | | U | C | A | G | |
| U | | phenyl-alanine | serine | tyrosine | cysteine | U |
| | | | | | | C |
| | | leucine | | stop | stop | A |
| | | | | stop | tryptophan | G |
| C | | leucine | proline | histidine | arginine | U |
| | | | | | | C |
| | | | | glutamine | | A |
| | | | | | | G |
| A | | isoleucine | threonine | asparagine | serine | U |
| | | | | | | C |
| | | | | lysine | arginine | A |
| | | methionine/start | | | | G |
| G | | valine | alanine | aspartic acid | glycine | U |
| | | | | | | C |
| | | | | glutamic acid | | A |
| | | | | | | G |

1. **Synthesize** What is the mRNA sequence for the DNA sequence A-C-C?

   ....................................................................

2. **Use Tables** What amino acid is that mRNA sequence coding for?

   ....................................................................

3. **Construct an Explanation** Why would it be incorrect to say that the DNA sequence A-C-G codes for the amino acid threonine?

   ....................................................................

   ....................................................................

   ....................................................................

   ....................................................................

   ....................................................................

# Protein Synthesis

**Figure 7** Protein synthesis begins in the nucleus and ends at the ribosome.

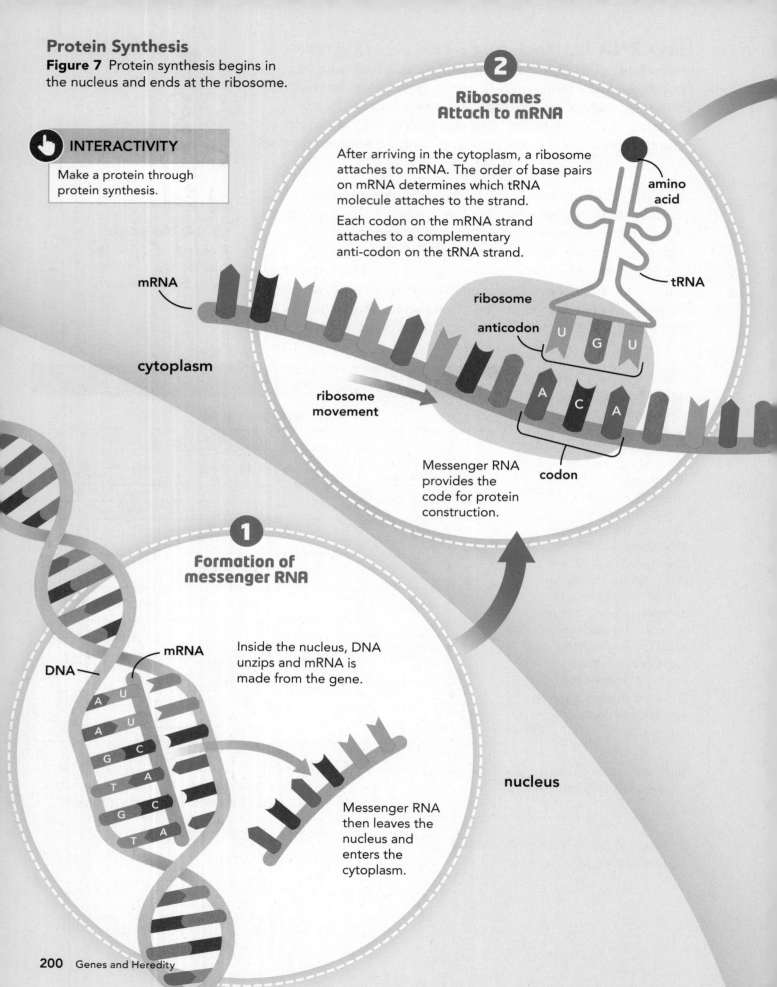

👆 **INTERACTIVITY**

Make a protein through protein synthesis.

**2**

## Ribosomes Attach to mRNA

After arriving in the cytoplasm, a ribosome attaches to mRNA. The order of base pairs on mRNA determines which tRNA molecule attaches to the strand.

Each codon on the mRNA strand attaches to a complementary anti-codon on the tRNA strand.

amino acid

tRNA

mRNA

cytoplasm

ribosome

anticodon

U G U

A C A

ribosome movement

Messenger RNA provides the code for protein construction.

codon

**1**

## Formation of messenger RNA

Inside the nucleus, DNA unzips and mRNA is made from the gene.

mRNA

DNA

A U
A U
A C
G A
T C
G A
T A

nucleus

Messenger RNA then leaves the nucleus and enters the cytoplasm.

## 3
### tRNA Brings the Correct Amino Acid

The order of base pairs on tRNA determines the type of amino acid it carries.

amino acid

As the ribosome moves along the mRNA strand, molecules of tRNA bring their attached amino acids.

## 4
### Protein Chain Is Formed

protein chain

As tRNA anti-codons line up with mRNA codons, the amino acids bond at the ribosome and form a long protein chain.

## Model It

Use Models ✏ Use the steps in **Figure 7** as a guide to fill in the missing molecules that drive each step of the process. Then complete the flowchart with the complementary nitrogen bases or amino acids (refer to codon table in **Figure 6**).

| Step | Molecules | | | | | | |
|---|---|---|---|---|---|---|---|
| **1** _____ | | T | G | T | G | A | A |
| **2** _____ | | | | | | | |
| **3** _____ | | | | | | | |
| **4** **Protein** | | | | | | | |

MS-LS3-1

1. **Identify Patterns** List the six nitrogen bases that would pair with the following sequence of bases in a strand of DNA: T C G A C A

........................................................................

2. **Analyze Structures** DNA replication begins when the double helix untwists and breaks in half between the nitrogen bases. What are the next two steps in the process of DNA replication?

........................................................................

........................................................................

........................................................................

........................................................................

........................................................................

........................................................................

3. **Identify** What carries the genetic information in DNA from the nucleus to the cytoplasm during protein synthesis?

........................................................................

........................................................................

4. **Explain Phenomena** What function does DNA serve during protein synthesis?

........................................................................

........................................................................

........................................................................

5. **Construct an Explanation** Explain the relationship of making proteins to inheritance of traits.

........................................................................

........................................................................

........................................................................

........................................................................

........................................................................

6. **Determine Differences** What are three differences between RNA and DNA in humans?

........................................................................

........................................................................

........................................................................

........................................................................

........................................................................

........................................................................

7. **Make Models** ✏ Sketch the general process of protein synthesis below.

MS-LS3-1

# REINVENTING DNA AS
# Data Storage

👆 **INTERACTIVITY**

Understand existing models to use them in new ways.

## How much digital space

do you need for all your texts, emails, photos, and music? Digital information can take up lots of space.

| Code | P | l | a | y |
|---|---|---|---|---|
| Binary data | 01010000 | 01101100 | 01100001 | 01111001 |
| DNA nucleotides | GCGAG | ATCGA | AGAGC | TGCTCT |

**The Challenge:** To provide storage solutions for the data storage needs of everyone on Earth.

**Phenomenon** Some estimates state that the world has 40 trillion gigabytes (GB) of data. Forty trillion GB equals about 40 million petabytes (PB). Ten billion photos on social media sites use about 1.5 PB. So, if every star in our Milky Way galaxy were one byte of data, then we would need 5,000 Milky Ways, each with 200 billion stars, to amass one PB of data. How can we possibly store all of our data?

Nature may offer an answer: DNA. Our entire genetic code fits within the nucleus of a single cell. Scientists have figured out how to convert digital data (in 1s and 0s) into DNA's A-C-T-G code. Then they constructed synthetic DNA in a lab. So far, scientists have been able to encode and store images and videos within a single strand of DNA. If current cost constraints are overcome, DNA could be the next microchip. Someday, the data currently stored on computers in enormous buildings may fit in the palm of your hand!

Scientists can store documents and photos by converting digital code to DNA code and then making synthetic DNA. To retrieve a file, the DNA code gets converted back to digital code.

**DESIGN CHALLENGE** Can you design your own code to store information? Go to the Engineering Design Notebook to find out!

# 4 Trait Variations

## Guiding Questions

- How do genes on sex chromosomes determine different traits?
- How do mutations affect protein synthesis and increase variation?
- How does the environment influence genetic traits?

## Connections

**Literacy** Integrate with Visuals

**Math** Construct a Scatter Plot

MS-LS3-1, MS-LS4-4

## Vocabulary

variation
sex chromosomes
autosomal chromosomes
mutation
sex-linked genes

## Academic Vocabulary

sequence

 **VOCABULARY APP**

Practice vocabulary on a mobile device.

**Quest CONNECTION**

Think about the likelihood that the desired traits for your fruit will be passed on to the next generation.

## Connect It !

✏️ **Circle a trait that distinguishes the male elephant seal from the female.**

**Determine Differences** What other differences do you notice between the male and female elephant seals?

......................................................................................................

......................................................................................................

**Apply Scientific Reasoning** What traits allow the elephant seal to live in water? Explain your reasoning.

......................................................................................................

......................................................................................................

......................................................................................................

# Diversity of Life

Organisms from the same species tend to have many similarities. The Northern elephant seals in **Figure 1**, however, show that very different traits can exist in two individuals. Some differences are visible traits, such as wrinkled skin or brown hair. Others are invisible, such as type I diabetes or sickle-cell anemia. Differences have the potential to be passed on from one generation to the next, and change the population.

The diversity of life on Earth relies in part on the variety of traits within a species. Any difference between individuals of the same species is a **variation**. Two friends with different eye color have a variation (green, brown) of the same trait (eye color). Variations may be due to DNA inherited from the parents, exposure to certain environmental factors, or a combination of both inheritance and environmental factors.

Variations can be helpful, harmful, or neutral. Consider a population of butterflies avoiding predators. Some have the same wing color pattern as a poisonous species. When this variation is passed from one generation to the next, the offspring are more likely to survive and reproduce. A harmful variation, on the other hand, threatens a population's survival. For example, low blood oxygen levels can be found in individuals with sickle-cell anemia. Neutral variations, such as different eye color, do not benefit or harm the population.

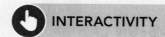

**INTERACTIVITY**

Identify traits found on a dog.

**Northern Elephant Seals**

**Figure 1** Seals of the same species share most of the same DNA, yet there are differences in their appearance. This male (left) and female (right) relax near the ocean.

## HANDS-ON LAB

**ηInvestigate** Observe physical traits found in a group of individuals.

## INTERACTIVITY

Explore how some genetic disorders are carried on sex chromosomes.

# Chromosomes and Variation

You received 23 chromosomes from your mother and 23 chromosomes from your father. The combination of genes found on these chromosomes codes for the proteins that determine your traits.

**Types of Chromosomes** There are two types of chromosomes found in every one of your cells. Of the 23 pairs of chromosomes, one pair is sex chromosomes, while the other 22 pairs are autosomal chromosomes. **Sex chromosomes** are the pair of chromosomes carrying genes that determine whether a person is biologically male or female.

The combination of sex chromosomes determines the sex of the offspring. A human female inherits one X chromosome from her mother and one X chromosome from her father. A male receives one X chromosome from his mother and one Y chromosome from his father. **Figure 2** compares the X and Y chromosomes.

The 22 pairs of chromosomes that are not sex chromosomes are **autosomal chromosomes**. You inherit half of your autosomal chromosomes from your mother and half from your father. All the pairs of autosomal chromosomes are homologous chromosomes. This means that the genes for a trait are located at the same place on each chromosome in the pair, even though the alleles may be different. Females also have homologous sex chromosomes, while males do not.

## Inheriting Sex Chromosomes

**Figure 2** ✏ Using the genotype given for the mother and father, complete the Punnett square to show the genotype of their offspring.

**Use Models** Which parent contributes the sex chromosome that determines the sex of the offspring? Explain.

..............................................................
..............................................................
..............................................................
..............................................................
..............................................................
..............................................................
..............................................................

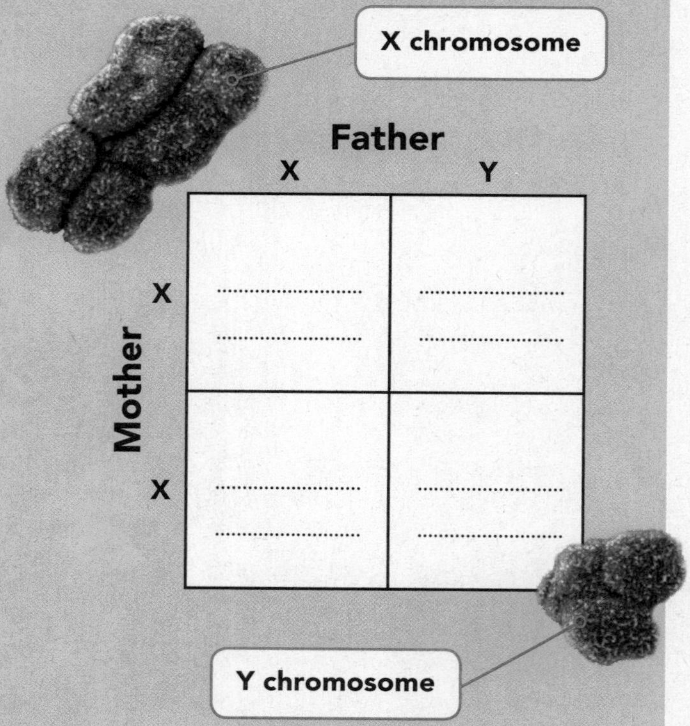

**X chromosome**

**Father**

|  | X | Y |
|---|---|---|
| **X** | .......... .......... | .......... .......... |
| **X** | .......... .......... | .......... .......... |

**Mother** (left side label)

**Y chromosome**

**Chromosomes Size** Chromosomes contain DNA, and each section of DNA that codes for a protein is a gene. For every trait, there is a gene or group of genes that controls the trait by producing proteins through the process of protein synthesis. Because the number of genes found on each chromosome and the length of each gene varies, chromosomes come in different sizes. For example, the X chromosome is almost three times the size of the Y chromosome and contains close to 16 times as many genes. Thus, it codes for more proteins, and determines more traits.

✓ READING CHECK **Cite Textual Evidence** Why does the X chromosome express more traits than the Y chromosome?

........................................................................................

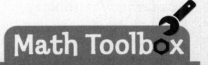

# Math Toolbox

## Chromosome and Gene Relationship

This data shows chromosome size as number of base pairs in the millions (Mbp) and estimated number of genes found on each one.

1. **Construct a Scatter Plot** ✏ Complete the scatter plot. Each dot represents the relationship between the total base pairs and the estimated number of genes for each chromosome.

**Human Chromosome Size vs. Number of Genes**

(Scatter plot with y-axis "Estimated Number of Genes" from 0 to 2,000 and x-axis "Millions of Base Pairs (Mbp)" from 0 to 250.)

2. **Identify Patterns** What relationship do you see between chromosome size and number of genes?

........................................................................................

........................................................................................

| Chromosome | Mbp | Genes |
|---|---|---|
| 1 | 248.96 | 2000 |
| 2 | 242.19 | 1300 |
| 3 | 198.3 | 1000 |
| 4 | 190.22 | 1000 |
| 5 | 181.54 | 900 |
| 6 | 170.81 | 1000 |
| 7 | 159.35 | 900 |
| 8 | 145.14 | 700 |
| 9 | 138.4 | 800 |
| 10 | 133.8 | 700 |
| 11 | 135.09 | 1300 |
| 12 | 133.28 | 1100 |
| 13 | 114.36 | 300 |
| 14 | 107.04 | 800 |
| 15 | 101.99 | 600 |
| 16 | 90.34 | 800 |
| 17 | 83.26 | 1200 |
| 18 | 80.37 | 200 |
| 19 | 58.62 | 1500 |
| 20 | 64.44 | 500 |
| 21 | 46.71 | 200 |
| 22 | 50.82 | 500 |
| X | 156.04 | 800 |
| Y | 57.23 | 50 |

# Types of Mutations

An organism can develop traits due to changes in their genetic code. A **mutation** is any change in the DNA of a gene or chromosome. Mutations can be inherited from a parent or acquired during an organism's life. Inherited mutations occur when the parent passes on the mutation during reproduction. These mutations are present throughout the life of the organism, and are in every cell of the body. Acquired mutations occur at some point during an organism's lifetime. Acquired mutations can only be passed on from parent to offspring if the mutations occur in sex cells.

**Genetic Mutations** Many mutations are the result of small changes in the organism's DNA. Just one small change to a base pair is a mutation and may cause an incorrect protein to be made during protein synthesis. For example, the DNA **sequence** ATG is complimentary to the mRNA sequence UAC and codes for the amino acid tyrosine. If the second base were replaced, making the DNA sequence AGG (mRNA compliment UCC), it would code for the wrong amino acid, serine. As a result, the trait may be different from what was expressed before. Genetic mutations can occur between one base pair or several base pairs. **Figure 4** shows genetic mutations that can result when a base pair is deleted, added, or exchanged for different base pairs. **Figure 5** shows an example of a substitution mutation.

## Academic Vocabulary

Explain a situation where you restated a sequence of events.

............................................

............................................

............................................

............................................

## Literacy Connection

**Integrate with Visuals** 🖉
Find the three examples of mutation. Draw an arrow to show where a base pair was deleted. Circle where a base pair was added. Draw an X on the base pair that was substituted.

### Genetic Mutations

**Figure 4** The diagram shows three types of single base pair mutations.

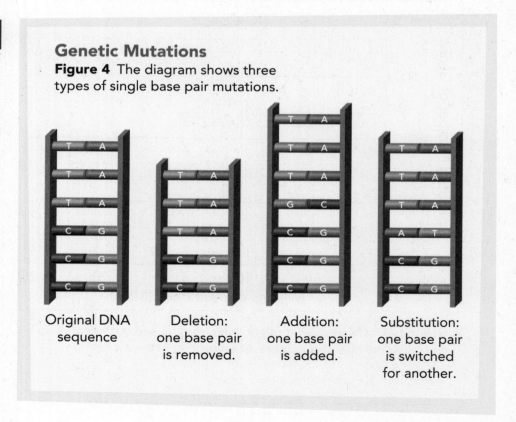

Original DNA sequence

Deletion: one base pair is removed.

Addition: one base pair is added.

Substitution: one base pair is switched for another.

**Sex-Linked Mutations** A mutation can occur on any chromosome. Some mutations occur on **sex-linked genes**, which are genes carried on a sex chromosome. Because the X chromosome has more genes than the Y chromosome, most sex-linked mutations occur on the X chromosome. In addition, many sex-linked mutations are recessive. Hemophilia is a recessive sex-linked mutation, where the individual's ability to clot blood is reduced. Males are more likely to exhibit hemophilia because they have only one X chromosome.

# Model It !

## Mutations and Protein Construction

**Figure 5** Sickle cell anemia results from a substitution mutation. The mutation alters the shape of red blood cells. Sickled cells can get stuck in blood vessels, blocking the flow of oxygenated blood cells.

**Develop Models** ✎ Not all mutations result in new traits. Fill in the normal and mutated amino acid in the diagram below. Then, using the normal red blood cell DNA sequence, create a model that has one mutation, but will still make a normal protein. Refer to the mRNA Codon Table in Lesson 3, Genetic Coding and Protein Synthesis.

**DNA sequence**

| C A C | G T G | G A C | T G A | G G A | C T C | C T C |
| G T G | C A C | C T G | A C T | C C T | G A G | G A G |

| Valine | Histidine | Leucine | Threonine | Proline | | Glutamic acid |

**Amino acid sequence**　　　　　　　　　　　　　　normal

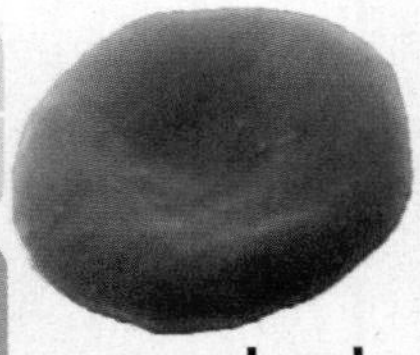

normal red blood cell

**DNA sequence**

| C A C | G T G | G A C | T G A | G G A | C A C | C T C |
| G T G | C A C | C T G | A C T | C C T | G T G | G A G |

| Valine | Histidine | Leucine | Threonine | Proline | | Glutamic acid |

**Amino acid sequence**　　　　　　　　　　　　　　mutation

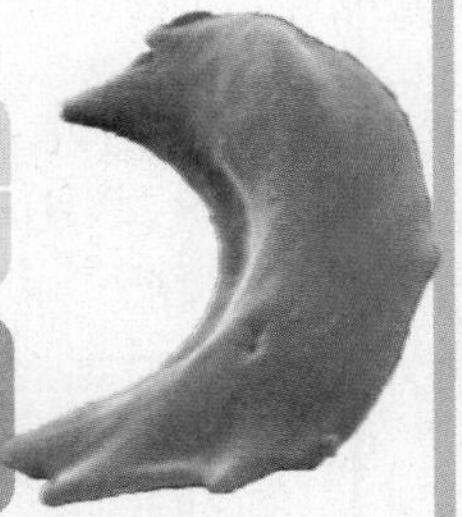

sickled red blood cell

**DNA sequence**

| | | | | | |
| | | | | | |

| | | | | | |

**Amino acid sequence**

# Environmental Factors

Interactions with our surroundings and the conditions in which we live have the potential to change the way genes are normally expressed. First, environment factors can change nucleotides, the building blocks of nucleic acids—DNA and RNA. Secondly, the chemicals found on DNA can be changed.

Organisms come in contact with harmful chemicals and radiation on a regular basis. These agents are called mutagens because they can damage DNA in such way that it causes mutations. Some mutagens naturally occur, while others are synthetic. For example, radiation in the form of ultraviolet (UV) or X-rays are naturally occurring mutagens. Synthetic mutagens can be found in pesticides, asbestos, and food additives.

**Gene Expression** Changes in the way genes are expressed may occur naturally or because of the environment. An example of natural change is when a caterpillar transitions to a butterfly. As the organism develops, the DNA does not change, but the genes are read and expressed differently.

The environment can change the way genes are expressed. Identical twins have the same DNA, but can acquire different traits when they grow up in different environments. Activities such as smoking and unhealthy eating habits can also alter the way genes are expressed, which changes a person's traits. **Figure 6** shows another way genes can be expressed differently.

## Damage from Sun Exposure

**Figure 6** 🖊 UV radiation from the sun harms skin cells. UVA radiation penetrates into the deep layers of the skin. UVB radiation penetrates only the top layer of the skin. Draw arrows in the first diagram to show how deep UVA and UVB penetrate into the skin. Then, identify the radiation type—UVA or UVB—in the box next to the picture that shows a possible effect of the radation.

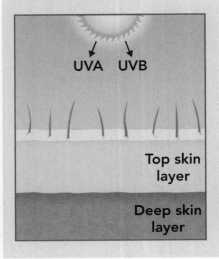

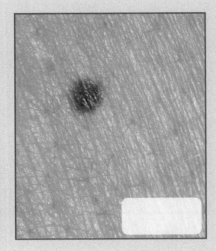

**Camouflage**
**Figure 7** ✏ Sometimes mutations benefit to survival of a species. Predators will likely not see this animal, passing it as they swim. Circle the animal that is camouflaged.

**Mutation Effects** Mutations may be harmful, helpful, or neutral. Helpful mutations are those that benefit the survival of the species and are often passed on to offspring. Harmful mutations do not benefit the species and often decrease the likelihood of survival. Neutral mutations are those that do not affect an organism's chance of survival.

**Helpful Mutations** Some mutations can help an organism survive in their environment. One example of a helpful mutation is camouflage. Possessing the ability to blend in with the environment, **Figure 7**, protects an organism from predators that may be looking for a meal. In humans, a mutation in a gene controlling fast-twitch muscles produces sprinters who are world class athletes.

**Harmful Mutations** Genetic disorders and cancer are both the result of harmful mutations. A genetic disorder is an abnormal condition that a person inherits through genes or chromosomes. Cystic fibrosis is a genetic disorder that causes the body to make thick mucus in the lungs and digestive system. The mucus builds up in the lungs and blocks air flow. Cancer is a disease in which some body cells grow and divide uncontrollably, damaging the parts of the body around them. Few cancers are inherited. Most cancers are caused by acquired mutations that occur from damage to genes during the life of an organism.

**Neutral Mutations** Not all mutations are helpful or harmful. Some mutations, such as human hair color, may be neutral and have no impact on the survival of an organism. There may also be mutations that still code for the same protein. Even though the DNA sequence has changed, the amino acid that is produced remains the same.

☑ READING CHECK **Distinguish Facts** In what ways can the environment impact the traits of an organism?

.................................................................................................

.................................................................................................

.................................................................................................

# Mutations in Reproduction

Not all mutations are the result of small changes in an organism's DNA. Some mutations occur when chromosomes do not separate correctly during the formation of sex cells. When this happens, a sex cell can end up with too many or too few chromosomes. When a chromosomal mutation occurs, either additional proteins are created or fewer proteins are created.

During meiosis, sometimes DNA does not separate normally, instead staying together as the cell divides. This abnormal distribution of DNA is called a nondisjunction, shown in **Figure 8**.

## Nondisjunction

**Figure 8** DNA can separate abnormally during Meiosis I or Meiosis II.

1. **Calculate** Normal human sex cells have 23 chromosomes. Use the art to determine the number of chromosomes a sex cell may have if the nondisjuction occured during Meiosis I. Include all possible chromosome totals.

   ...........................................................

   ...........................................................

2. **Use Models** What is the difference between the sex cells of a nondisjunction that occurred during meiosis I and the sex cells of a nondisjunction that occurred during meiosis II?

   ...........................................................

   ...........................................................

   ...........................................................

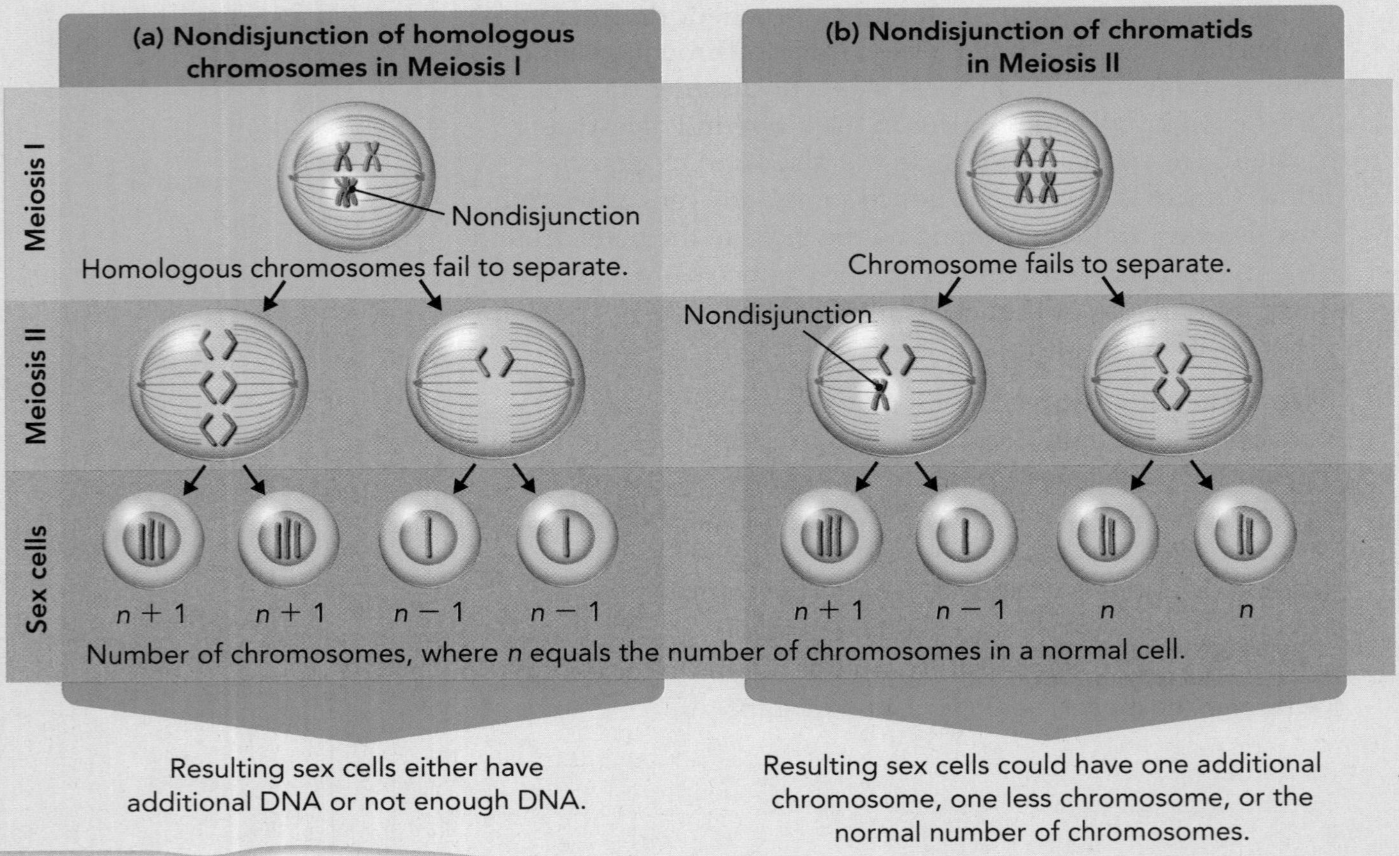

| (a) Nondisjunction of homologous chromosomes in Meiosis I | (b) Nondisjunction of chromatids in Meiosis II |
|---|---|

**Meiosis I**

Homologous chromosomes fail to separate.

Nondisjunction — Chromosome fails to separate.

**Meiosis II**

Nondisjunction

**Sex cells**

$n + 1$  $n + 1$  $n - 1$  $n - 1$    $n + 1$  $n - 1$  $n$  $n$

Number of chromosomes, where *n* equals the number of chromosomes in a normal cell.

Resulting sex cells either have additional DNA or not enough DNA.

Resulting sex cells could have one additional chromosome, one less chromosome, or the normal number of chromosomes.

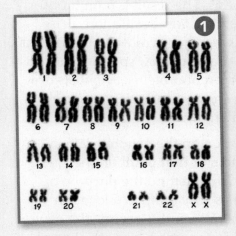

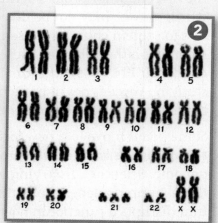

## Comparing Karyotypes

**Figure 9** 🖊 Karyotype 1 shows what chromosomes would look like without a nondisjunction. Circle the chromosomes in the second, third, and forth karyotypes that indicate a nondisjunction occurred.

1. **Use Models** What is the sex of the individual found represented in the first karyotpe?

..................................................

2. **Apply Concepts** How would a scientist name the disorder represented by the third karyotype?

..................................................

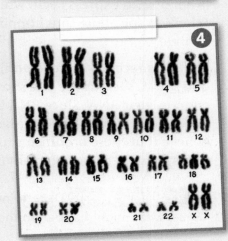

**Karyotypes** Sometimes, doctors suspect that an individual has a genetic disorder based on observable traits. To accurately determine if an individual has a chromosomal mutation, a scientist will create a karotype **(Figure 9)**, which is a picture of all the chromosomes in a person's cell and then arrange the chromosomes by size and matching chromosome patterns. Homologous chromosomes are paired to provide a quick overview. The karyotypes on this page compare a normal individual and three individuals with genetic disorders. If there is an additional chromosome, the grouping is called a trisomy (*tri-* means "three" and *somy*, from Greek *soma* for *body*, indicates a chromosome). If one chromosome is missing, it is a monosomy (*mono-* means "one"). In addition, scientists include the homologous number and often assign a common name to the disorder. For example, trisomy 18 is Edward's Syndrome, while trisomy 21 is Down's Syndrome.

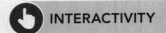

INTERACTIVITY

Explore patterns of
inheritance in offspring.

**Protein Changes** Amino acids are the building blocks of proteins, which can be considered the architects of cell function. A change in the amino acid sequence can alter the directions for protein synthesis. The result is a mutation, which may or may not be detectable. Some mutations arise due to protein changes caused when genes move to a different location on the genome. There are also a few species that can alter their RNA to synthesize different proteins. Scientists are studying these types of protein changes to understand any benefits they might bring to an organism.

Some genes move to a new location on the genome. When this occurs, it produces the protein at that point on the genome. Scientists are trying to understand the purpose of these 'jumping genes'. Sometimes they jump to a location that disrupts a functioning gene. When this occurs, the gene is not able to express itself, which can cause traits to change. Scientists speculate that jumping genes may cause a species to change.

Scientists recently discovered that some species of octopus and squid, such as the one shown in **Figure 10**, are able to change their RNA. Since RNA is needed for the construction of proteins, they are able make different proteins. Scientists believe that these organisms are able to create specific proteins in response to a changing environment.

## Changing RNA

**Figure 10** Organisms, like this squid, are able to change their RNA, thus changing the proteins that are constructed.

Synthesize Information Why is it beneficial for scientists to understand how other organisms are able to edit their RNA?

READING CHECK **Determine Central Ideas** When a gene jumps, what might happen to the organism's traits?

................................................................................

................................................................................

................................................................................

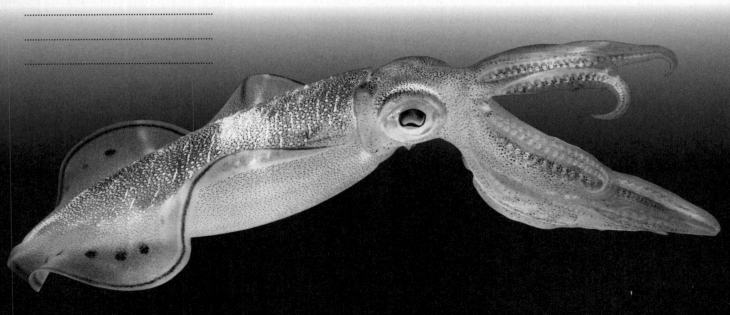

# ☑ LESSON 4 Check

MS-LS3-1, MS-LS4-4

**1. Identify Knowns** How many and what types of chromosomes are found in every one of your cells?

...........................................................

...........................................................

**2. Determine Differences** How are inherited mutations different from acquired mutations?

...........................................................

...........................................................

...........................................................

...........................................................

**3. Explain Phenomena** How is an organism's ability to produce offspring affected by changes to a chromosome?

...........................................................

...........................................................

...........................................................

...........................................................

...........................................................

...........................................................

**4. Evaluate Claims** A student states that only a male human offspring can express a recessive sex-linked X chromosome mutation. Is this statement accurate? Explain.

...........................................................

...........................................................

...........................................................

...........................................................

...........................................................

**5. Develop Models** ✏ Red-green color blindness is a sex-linked recessive condition. Its gene is located on the X chromosome. Most people with red-green color blindness cannot see the difference in shades of red and green. Suppose a heterozygous female ($X^N X^n$) has offspring with a male who is color blind ($X^n Y$). Draw a Punnett square. Label each offspring as applicable: normal vision, carrier, or color blind. ($X^N$ indicates normal vision; $X^n$ indicates color blindness.)

# Quest CHECK-IN

**In this lesson, you learned that organisms can inherit traits, acquire traits, and some organisms can change their traits.**

**Support Your Explanation** Why are the desired traits you selected for your fruit not always a guarantee that your fruit will have those traits? Provide support.

...........................................................

...........................................................

...........................................................

...........................................................

...........................................................

## HANDS-ON LAB

All in the Numbers

**Do the hands-on lab** to complete the investigation and discover how experimental results may vary from probability. You will make observations and test the crossing of traits.

## Guiding Questions

- How do humans use artificial selection to produce organisms with desired traits?
- How do scientists engineer new genes?
- How can genetic information be used?

## Connection

**Literacy** Corroborate

MS-LS4-5

## Vocabulary

artificial selection
genetic engineering
gene therapy
clone
genome

## Academic Vocabulary

manipulation

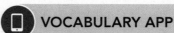 **VOCABULARY APP**

Practice vocabulary on a mobile device.

**Quest CONNECTION**

Consider how genetic technologies can help you design your new fruit.

## Connect It !

🖋 **Dogs come in many different shapes, sizes, and colors. Which of the ones shown here would you prefer as a pet? Circle your choice.**

Apply Concepts  Many purebred dogs have problems later in life, such as joint or eye diseases. Why are purebred dogs more likely to develop problems later in life?

........................................................................................................................

........................................................................................................................

Make Inferences  What can be done to decrease the likelihood of these problems appearing?

........................................................................................................................

........................................................................................................................

# Artificial Selection

When consumers make choices, they are often attracted to products with the highest quality. We want the healthiest and best-tasting fruits and vegetables. We want the right amount of fat and flavor in our meats. We even want the best traits in our pets, such as the dogs you see in **Figure 1**. These high-quality products do not appear only in nature. Scientists and breeders have influenced the traits that other organisms inherit through the process of selective breeding.

**Selective Breeding** In the natural world, individuals with beneficial traits are more likely to survive and successfully reproduce than individuals without those traits. This is called natural selection. **Artificial selection** is also known as selective breeding. It occurs when humans breed only those organisms with desired traits to produce the next generation. It's important to note that desired traits are not necessarily the traits that benefit the organism's chances for survival. Instead, they are traits that humans desire.

Dogs, cats, and livestock animals have all been selectively bred. Cows, chickens, and pigs have been bred to be larger so that they produce more milk or meat. Breeding and caring for farm animals that have certain genetic traits that humans desire is called animal husbandry. The many different breeds of dogs shown in **Figure 1** have also been bred over time for very specific functions.

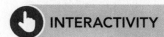

**INTERACTIVITY**

Consider how artificial selection affects the traits of dogs.

**Literacy Connection**

**Corroborate** Find statements in the text that support the claim that artificial selection is not a natural process and does not necessarily help the organism's survival.

**Purebred Dogs**
**Figure 1** Each type of purebred dog shown here is the result of selective breeding over the course of many generations.

# Genetic Engineering

With the discovery of DNA and its relationship to genes, scientists have developed more methods to produce desired traits. Through a process called **genetic engineering**, modern geneticists can transfer a gene from the DNA of one organism into another. Genetic engineering is used to give organisms genes they could not acquire through breeding.

Scientists use genetic engineering techniques to insert specific desired genes into animals. By **manipulating** a gene, scientists have created a fish that glows when under a black light **(Figure 2)**. A jellyfish gene for fluorescence was inserted into a fertilized fish egg to produce the glowing fish. Scientists are hoping that further research on this gene will lead to a method that helps track toxic chemicals in the body.

Genetic engineering is also used to synthesize materials. A protein called insulin helps control blood-sugar levels after eating. People who have diabetes cannot effectively control their blood-sugar levels, and many must take insulin injections. Prior to 1980, some diabetics were injecting themselves with insulin from other animals without getting the desired results. To help diabetics, scientists genetically engineered bacteria to produce the first human protein — insulin. The process they used, and still use today, is shown in **Figure 3**. Furthermore, bacteria can reproduce quickly, so large amounts of human insulin are produced in a short time.

## Glowing Fish
**Figure 2** Genetic engineering made glowing fish possible.

## Academic Vocabulary
Explain the difference between manipulating a tool and manipulating another person.

........................................................

........................................................

........................................................

........................................................

........................................................

........................................................

........................................................

# Plan It

### Synthesize a New Trait
🖊 Create a trait that has never been seen before in an animal. Identify a trait you would like an animal to have. Then, sketch the animal and describe a process by which you could achieve your desired result.

........................................................

........................................................

........................................................

........................................................

........................................................

........................................................

........................................................

........................................................

## Bacteria Make Human Insulin

**Figure 3** 🖊 Bacteria can be used to produce insulin in humans. Complete the diagram by showing the process for Step 5.

❶ Small rings of DNA, or plasmids, are found in some bacteria cells.

❷ Scientists remove the plasmid and cut it open with an enzyme. They then insert an insulin gene that has been removed from human DNA.

❸ The human insulin gene attaches to the open ends of the plasmid to form a closed ring.

❹ Some bacteria cells take up the plasmids that have the insulin gene.

❺ When the cells reproduce, the new cells contain copies of the "engineered" plasmid. The foreign gene directs the cells to produce human insulin.

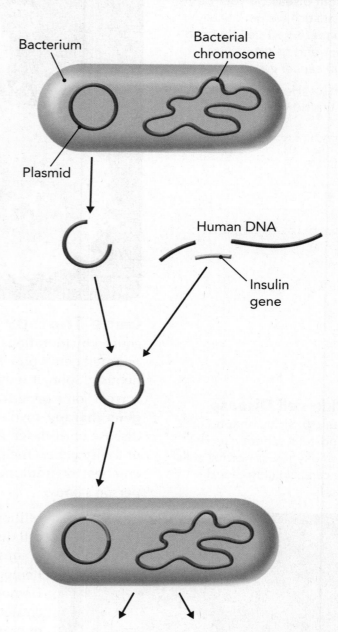

219

## T-cell Destroys Cancer Cell

**Figure 4** T-cells are a type of white blood cell that help to fight disease in your body. Scientists have genetically engineered a T-cell that can attack and destroy up to 1,000 cancer cells.

**Predict** How might doctors use this new T-cell?

.................................................

.................................................

.................................................

.................................................

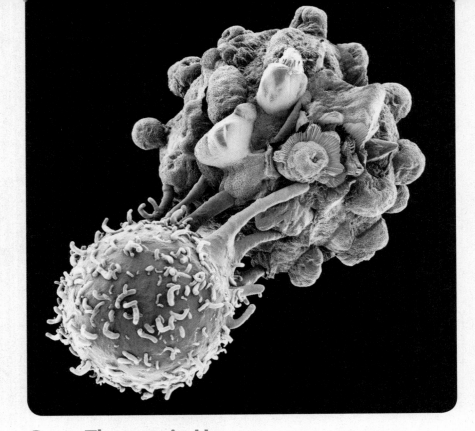

## Sickle-cell Disease

**Figure 5** Sickle-shaped red blood cells cannot carry as much oxygen as normal cells and can also clog blood vessels.

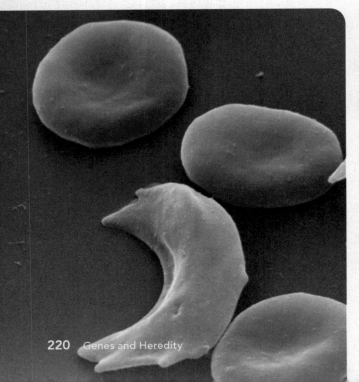

### Gene Therapy in Humans

Genetic diseases are caused by mutations, or changes in the DNA code. Some mutated genes pass from parent to child; others occur spontaneously. Soon, it may be possible to use genetic engineering to correct some genetic disorders in humans. This process, called **gene therapy**, involves changing a gene to treat a medical disease or disorder. A normal working gene replaces an absent or faulty gene. One promising therapy involves genetically engineering immune-system cells and injecting them into a person's body.

Millions of people worldwide suffer from sickle cell disease. This painful genetic disorder is caused by a singe mutation that affects hemoglobin, a protein in red blood cells. Hemoglobin carries oxygen. The mutation causes the blood cells to be shaped like a sickle, or crescent, as shown in **Figure 5.**

CRISPR is a gene-editing tool that can help people with sickle cell disease. CRISPR uses a "guide RNA" and an enzyme to cut out the DNA sequence causing the dangerous mutation. The "guide RNA" takes the enzyme to the DNA sequence with the sickle cell mutation, and the enzyme then removes that sequence. Then another tool pastes a copy of the normal sequence into the DNA.

**Cloning Organisms** A **clone** is an organism that has the same genes as the organism from which it was produced. The process of cloning involves removing an unfertilized egg and replacing its nucleus with the nucleus of a body cell from the same species. Because this body cell has a full set of chromosomes, the offspring will have the same DNA as the individual that donated the body cell. The egg is then implanted into a female so it can develop. If the process is successful, the clone is born.

Cloning is used to develop many of the foods we eat. Many plants are cloned simply by taking a small piece of the original and putting it in suitable conditions to grow. For example, the Cavendish banana (see **Figure 6**) is the most common banana for eating. All these bananas are clones of the original plant. Cloning helps to produce crops of consistent quality. But a population with little genetic diversity has drawbacks.

☑ **READING CHECK** **List** List the steps to creating a clone.

...............................................................................................

...............................................................................................

...............................................................................................

...............................................................................................

▶ **VIDEO**

Learn how selective breeding and cloning can lead to populations with desired traits.

**Cloned Bananas**

**Figure 6** A fungus that causes bananas to rot is spreading across the globe. The Cavendish banana is particularly vulnerable.

**Construct Explanations** Why is a disease more damaging to cloned crops?

...........................................................

...........................................................

...........................................................

...........................................................

...........................................................

## Genetic Cousins

**Figure 7** Humans and modern-day chimpanzees share about 99 percent of their DNA.

**Infer** How does knowing we are close genetically to chimpanzees help humans?

...........................................

...........................................

...........................................

...........................................

...........................................

 **INTERACTIVITY**

Gather fingerprints and identify who committed a crime.

# Practical Uses for DNA

Due to new technologies, geneticists now study and use genes in ways that weren't possible before. Modern geneticists can now determine the exact sequence of nitrogen bases in an organism's DNA. This process is called DNA sequencing.

**Sequencing the Human Genome** Breaking a code with six billion letters may seem like an impossible task to undertake. But scientists working on the Human Genome Project did just that. The complete set of genetic information that an organism carries in its DNA is called a **genome**. The main goal of the Human Genome Project was to identify the DNA sequence of the entire human genome. Since sequencing the human genome, scientists now research the functions of tens of thousands of human genes. Some of these genes also allow scientists to better understand certain diseases.

Our genome can also help us understand how humans evolved on Earth. All life on Earth evolved from simple, single-celled organisms that lived billions of years ago, and we still have evidence of this in our DNA. For example, there are some genes that exist in the cells of almost every organism on Earth, which suggests we all evolved from a common ancestor. Some organisms share a closer relationship than others. By comparing genomes of organisms, scientists continue to piece together a history of how life on Earth evolved.

**DNA Technologies** Before the Human Genome Project, scientists such as Gregor Mendel used experimentation to understand heredity. Since the project's completion in 2003, the use of technologies to understand heredity and how DNA guides life processes has increased greatly. For example, DNA technologies help diagnose genetic diseases.

Genetic disorders typically result from one or more changed genes, called mutations. Medical specialists can carry out a DNA screening to detect the presence of a mutation. To complete a DNA screen, samples of DNA are analyzed for the presence of one or more mutated genes. This information is then used to help those individuals whose DNA includes mutated genes.

DNA comparisons determine how closely related you are to another person. To do this, DNA from a person's cell is broken down into small pieces, or fragments. These fragments are put into a machine that separates them by size. When this happens, a pattern is produced creating a DNA fingerprint, like the one shown in **Figure 8**. Similarities between patterns determine who contributed the DNA. Genetic fingerprints can be used to tie a person to a crime scene, prevent the wrong person from going to jail, identify remains, or identify the father of a child.

**INTERACTIVITY**

Consider using technology to solve the world's food problem.

**DNA Fingerprint**
**Figure 8** Circle the suspect that left his or her DNA at the crime scene.

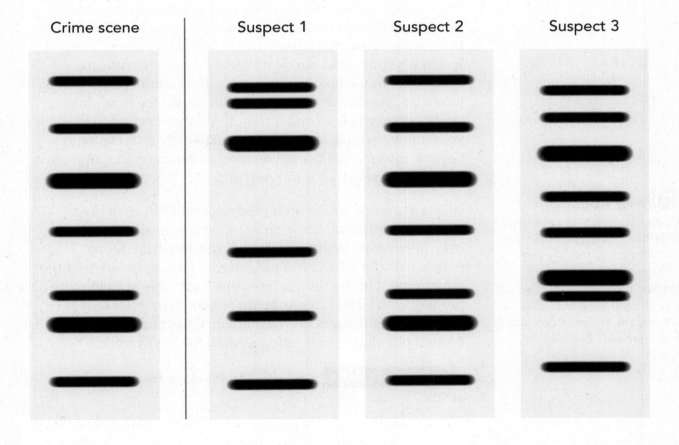

| Crime scene | Suspect 1 | Suspect 2 | Suspect 3 |

## Using Genetic Information

**Figure 9** Some people fear that medical insurance companies will not cover their medical expenses if they have been genetically tested and results show a genetic disorder.

**Evaluate Reasoning** Why is this a fear of many people? What can we do to protect our privacy?

..................................................

..................................................

..................................................

..................................................

..................................................

..................................................

..................................................

..................................................

**Write About It**

Organ transplants save lives. Scientists have learned how to genetically modify pigs in order to grow human organs for transplant. Do you think it's a good idea to transplant organs from pigs into humans? Explain.

## Controversies of DNA Use

As genetic research advances, some people are concerned about how genetic information will be used or altered. Some people are concerned about the use of genetically modified organisms (GMOs) in our food supply. Others worry about who can access their DNA information, and how this information will be used.

Your genetic information is a big part of your identity, and many people want to keep it as private as possible. The Genetic Information Nondiscrimination Act (GINA) was signed into law in 2008. This act makes it illegal for health insurance companies and employers to discriminate against individuals based on genetic information. Health insurance companies cannot deny you care and a company cannot refuse to hire you simply because of the results of a genetic test (**Figure 9**). Genetic information cannot be used without consent, and must be used in a way that is fair and just.

GMOs are made by changing the original DNA so desired traits are expressed. Growing our food from seeds that have been genetically modified is highly controversial. Many people fear the impact it could have on human health and the environment in the future. Yet farmers are able to yield more product with GMO crops that are not eaten by pests or overcome by weeds. Scientists must balance sustaining a growing human population with safeguarding the environment.

**READING CHECK** **Corroborate** What are the pros and cons of GMO foods?

..................................................................................

..................................................................................

1. **Identify** Shortly after World War II, chickens were bred to grow much more quickly and to produce much more meat. What is this an example of?

........................................................................

2. **Compare and Contrast** What are some positive and negative ways that genetic information may be used?

........................................................................

........................................................................

........................................................................

3. **Cause and Effect** Some genetically engineered organisms can mate with wild species. For example, farm-raised fish are often genetically modified. What can happen to the wild species of fish if this mating occurs?

........................................................................

........................................................................

........................................................................

4. **Construct Explanations** Gorillas and humans evolved from a common ancestor. Geneticists found that they may be more closely related than previously thought. How can DNA sequencing of the gorilla and human genomes determine this?

........................................................................

........................................................................

........................................................................

........................................................................

5. **Draw Conclusions** Consider natural selection and artificial selection. Why is artificial selection not necessarily helpful to an organism?

........................................................................

........................................................................

........................................................................

........................................................................

........................................................................

6. **Relate Structure and Function** How can changes to the structure of DNA lead to the development of new traits in a species?

........................................................................

........................................................................

........................................................................

........................................................................

........................................................................

........................................................................

........................................................................

........................................................................

........................................................................

........................................................................

7. **Design a Solution** The procedure used to make insulin in bacteria can also be used to synthesize other biological materials. Think of a chemical or material inside the human body that could be synthesized within bacteria. What would be the potential benefits of this process? What would be the potential drawbacks?

........................................................................

........................................................................

........................................................................

........................................................................

........................................................................

........................................................................

........................................................................

........................................................................

........................................................................

........................................................................

........................................................................

........................................................................

## ① Patterns of Inheritance

MS-LS3-2

1. Genes are carried from parents to offspring on structures called
   A. alleles.
   B. chromosomes.
   C. phenotypes.
   D. genotypes.

2. Which of the following represents a heterozygous genotype?
   A. GG
   B. gg
   C. Gg
   D. none of the above

3. An organism's phenotype is the way its .......................... is expressed.

4. **Use a Model** ✏ Fill in the Punnett Square to show a cross between two guinea pigs who are heterozygous for coat color. *B* is for black coat color and *b* is for white coat color.

5. **Interpret Tables** What is the probability that an offspring from the cross in Question 9 has the genotype *bb*?

.............................................................................

.............................................................................

## ② Chromosomes and Inheritance

MS-LS3-2

6. Chromosomes are long, thread-like structures of
   A. cells.
   B. proteins.
   C. genes.
   D. DNA.

7. Which process results in the formation of sex cells?
   A. crossing over
   B. meiosis
   C. separation
   D. transfer

8. Geneticists use a ..............................
   to map the inheritance of particular traits.

9. **Apply Concepts** Each body cell in the American black bear has 74 chromosomes. How many chromosomes are in the black bear's sex cells? Explain your answer.

.............................................................................

.............................................................................

.............................................................................

10. **Construct Explanations** In sexual reproduction, if each chromosome in a pair has the same genes, how is genetic variety possible?

.............................................................................

.............................................................................

.............................................................................

.............................................................................

.............................................................................

.............................................................................

.............................................................................

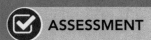 
## 3 Genetic Coding and Protein Synthesis

MS-LS3-1

**11.** A gene is a section of DNA within a chromosome that codes for a(n)
**A.** amino acid.         **B.** specific protein.
**C.** ribosome.          **D.** double helix.

**12.** Proteins are long-chain molecules made of
**A.** nitrogen bases.    **B.** chromosomes.
**C.** amino acids.       **D.** organisms.

**13. Draw Conclusions** How does the pairing of nitrogen bases in a DNA molecule make sure that a replicated strand is exactly the same as the original strand?

...........................................................................................

...........................................................................................

...........................................................................................

...........................................................................................

...........................................................................................

## 4 Trait Variations

MS-LS3-1, MS-LS4-4

**14.** A female human has
**A.** one X chromosome.
**B.** two X chromosomes.
**C.** one Y chromosome.
**D.** two Y chromosomes.

**15. Apply Scientific Reasoning** A friend says that all genetic mutations are harmful. Do you agree or disagree with this statement? Why?

...........................................................................................

...........................................................................................

...........................................................................................

## 5 Genetic Technologies

MS-LS4-5

**16.** Genetic diseases are caused by
**A.** X chromosomes.     **B.** modified cells.
**C.** plasmids.          **D.** mutations.

**17.** Which of the following is the best example of a possible future technology that could be used to eliminate sickle cell disease in humans?
**A.** a genetically engineered virus which can eliminate sickle-shaped cells in human blood
**B.** genetic screening which matches sickle cell carriers to people with AA genotypes
**C.** the ability to replace all S alleles in human red blood cells
**D.** the ability to replace all S alleles in fertilized eggs

**18.** Scientists created a new variety of rice. They modified a common strain of rice by inserting the carotene gene from carrots. The addition of this gene resulted in a rice enriched with vitamin-A, a crucial vitamin for humans. What technology does this example represent?
**A.** meiosis
**B.** genetic engineering
**C.** artificial selection
**D.** cloning

**19. Support Your Explanation** The technology of genetic engineering holds great promise, yet it frightens some people. What are the advantages and disadvantages of genetic engineering?

...........................................................................................

...........................................................................................

...........................................................................................

...........................................................................................

...........................................................................................

227

MS-LS3-1, MS-LS4-4, MS-LS4-5

## Evidence-Based Assessment

Scientists have figured out a way to insert the genes of one organism into another. A genetically modified organism, GMO, expresses desired traits that prove to be beneficial to many farmers. Reliance on GMO crops has been increasing in the United States for many years.

The graph shows three genetically modified crops—corn, soybeans, and cotton. In each crop, the DNA has been engineered for a desired trait. New DNA sequences that code for specific proteins are inserted into a crop's DNA.

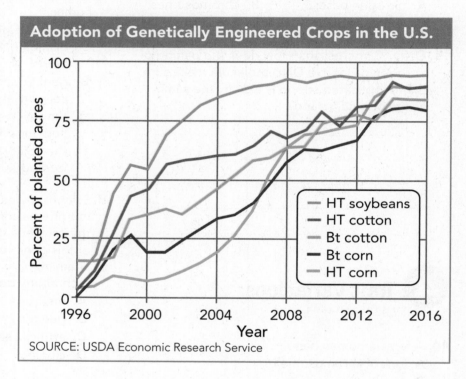

**Adoption of Genetically Engineered Crops in the U.S.**

- HT soybeans
- HT cotton
- Bt cotton
- Bt corn
- HT corn

SOURCE: USDA Economic Research Service

For example, some crops have been engineerd to resist droughts. The gene for drought resistance is spliced from the DNA of a desert-dwelling species and then inserted into the crop species. The resistance-to-drought trait will be expressed when these genetically engineered crop plants reproduce. Another desirable trait that has been produced through genetic engineering is improved herbicide tolerance (HT). This trait protects the GMO crop when herbicides are sprayed on the fields to kill weeds. In the case of the Bt crops, the desired gene comes from the *Bacillus thuringiensis* bacterium. The gene produces a protein that destroys the corn borer larvae. Farmers can grow Bt crops instead of spraying insecticides that could also kill helpful insects, such as bees.

1. **Analyze Data** Which genetically engineered crop has shown the greatest increase in usage from 2006 to 2016?
   - (A.) HT Corn
   - **B.** Bt Corn
   - **C.** HT Cotton
   - **D.** HT Soybeans

2. **Patterns** What patterns do you observe in the line graphs for the crops that are herbicide tolerant, HT? Support your claim.

...............................................................
...............................................................
...............................................................
...............................................................
...............................................................
...............................................................
...............................................................
...............................................................
...............................................................
...............................................................

3. **Connect to the Environment** What would be an advantage and a disadvantage to increased reliance on genetically engineered crops?

...............................................................
...............................................................
...............................................................
...............................................................
...............................................................
...............................................................
...............................................................
...............................................................
...............................................................
...............................................................

4. **Construct Arguments** Based on the data, will genetically engineered crops continue to be used in the future? Explain.

...............................................................
...............................................................
...............................................................
...............................................................
...............................................................
...............................................................
...............................................................
...............................................................
...............................................................
...............................................................
...............................................................
...............................................................

# Quest FINDINGS

## Complete the Quest!

**Phenomenon Create a brochure for prospective growers of your new fruit. Convince readers that your fruit will be a delicious success!**

**Construct Arguments** How will you know which traits are most beneficial to the general public so you can use them to create your fruit?

...............................................................
...............................................................
...............................................................
...............................................................

### INTERACTIVITY

Reflect on Funky Fruits

MS-LS3-2

# Make the Right Call!

How can you design and use a **model** to make **predictions** about the possible results of **genetic crosses**?

## Background

**Phenomenon** Suppose your neighbors tell you that their cat is going to have kittens. They can't stop talking about what color they think the kittens will be and whether their hair will be long or short. Using the suggested materials and your knowledge of genetic crosses, how can you make a model to show your neighbors the probabilities of the possible color and hair length combinations for the kittens?

Your neighbors got both the mother and father cat from a respected breeder. The index card shows background information about the two cats.

Max, male cat, short hair, homozygous black hair.

Willa, female cat, heterozygous short hair, heterozygous black hair.

## Materials

(per pair)

- 4 small paper bags
- 12 red marbles
- 12 blue marbles
- 12 green marbles
- 12 yellow marbles
- marking pen

# Design Your Investigation

**1.** In the space below, use Punnett squares to determine the possible outcomes from a cross between the male and female cats.
**TIP: First identify each parent's alleles, noting that all of them are known.**

**Demonstrate** Go online for a downloadable worksheet of this lab.

**Homozygous** — parent or offspring has either two dominant or two recessive alleles.

**Heterozygous** — parent or offspring has one of each allele (one dominant and one recessive)

| Dominant Trait | Recessive Trait |
|---|---|
| Short Hair | Long Hair |
| Black Hair | Brown Hair |

**2.** Design a way to model these crosses using the marbles and bags. The bags should contain the alleles of the male and female parent cats—two bags for each parent (one bag for hair color, the other bag for hair length).
**TIP: Use four marbles for each allele in each cat.**

**3.** In the space provided in the Procedure section, describe or sketch a procedure for modeling the crosses. Have your teacher review and approve the procedure before you carry it out. If necessary, make adjustments based on your teacher's feedback.

**4.** Use your model. Record your observations in the data tables.

# μDemonstrate Lab

## Procedure

........................................................................................

........................................................................................

........................................................................................

........................................................................................

........................................................................................

........................................................................................

........................................................................................

........................................................................................

........................................................................................

........................................................................................

## Observations

| Data Table 1 Hair Length | | | |
|---|---|---|---|
| Trial Cross | Allele from Bag 1 (Max) | Allele from Bag 2 (Willa) | Offspring's Alleles |
| 1 | | | |
| 2 | | | |
| 3 | | | |
| 4 | | | |
| 5 | | | |
| 6 | | | |
| 7 | | | |
| 8 | | | |
| 9 | | | |
| 10 | | | |
| 11 | | | |
| 12 | | | |

| Data Table 2 Hair Color | | | |
|---|---|---|---|
| Trial Cross | Allele from Bag 3 (Max) | Allele from Bag 4 (Willa) | Offspring's Alleles |
| 1 | | | |
| 2 | | | |
| 3 | | | |
| 4 | | | |
| 5 | | | |
| 6 | | | |
| 7 | | | |
| 8 | | | |
| 9 | | | |
| 10 | | | |
| 11 | | | |
| 12 | | | |

# Analyze and Interpret Data

1. **Develop a Model** How did you use the materials? What did the different parts of the model represent?

   ..............................................................................................................................
   ..............................................................................................................................
   ..............................................................................................................................

2. **Characterize Data** Refer to your Punnett squares. What percentages of black kittens (BB or Bb) and brown kittens (bb) did you predict? What percentages of shorthair kittens (SS or Ss) and longhair (ss) kittens did you predict?

   ..............................................................................................................................
   ..............................................................................................................................
   ..............................................................................................................................

3. **Use a Model to Evaluate** Refer to your data table. Did the percentages of offspring with a given genotype match the percentages that you obtained by completing the Punnett squares? Explain.

   ..............................................................................................................................
   ..............................................................................................................................
   ..............................................................................................................................
   ..............................................................................................................................

4. **Compare Data** How did using a Punnett square differ from using your model? Which did you prefer?

   ..............................................................................................................................
   ..............................................................................................................................
   ..............................................................................................................................
   ..............................................................................................................................
   ..............................................................................................................................

5. **Form an Opinion** Was your model effective at showing the neighbors all of the possible combinations of hair color and length to expect in their kittens? Explain.

   ..............................................................................................................................
   ..............................................................................................................................
   ..............................................................................................................................
   ..............................................................................................................................

# TOPIC
# 5

# Natural Selection and Change Over Time

**NGSS PERFORMANCE EXPECTATIONS**

**MS-LS4-1** Analyze and interpret data for patterns in the fossil record that document the existence, diversity, extinction, and change of life forms throughout the history of life on Earth under the assumption that natural laws operate today as in the past.

**MS-LS4-2** Apply scientific ideas to construct an explanation for the anatomical similarities and differences among modern organisms and between modern and fossil organisms to infer evolutionary relationships.

**MS-LS4-3** Analyze displays of pictorial data to compare patterns of similarities in the embryological development across multiple species to identify relationships not evident in the fully formed anatomy.

**MS-LS4-4** Construct an explanation based on evidence that describes how genetic variations of traits in a population increase some individuals' probability of surviving and reproducing in a specific environment.

**MS-LS4-5** Gather and synthesize information about the technologies that have changed the way humans influence the inheritance of desired traits in organisms.

**MS-LS4-6** Use mathematical representations to support explanations of how natural selection may lead to increases and decreases of specific traits in populations over time.

Has this dragonfly changed from its fossilized ancestor?

**GO ONLINE** to access your digital course

 VIDEO

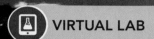 INTERACTIVITY

 VIRTUAL LAB

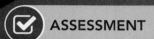 ASSESSMENT

eTEXT

 APP

**HANDS-ON LAB**

**uConnect** Analyze evidence that whales may have walked on land.

## The Essential Question   How do characteristics change over time?

At first glance, this modern-day dragonfly and its fossilized ancestor probably don't look very different. Both seem to have long, slender bodies, two sets of wings, and large eyes. Would it surprise you to know that the dragonfly ancestor, *Meganeura*, lived about 300 million years ago and had a wingspan of 75 cm? It's the largest known flying insect! In comparison, the largest modern dragonfly has a wingspan of only 16 cm. Think about why we don't see such large insects anymore. List your ideas below.

.............................................................................................................................

.............................................................................................................................

.............................................................................................................................

.............................................................................................................................

# Why is the migration pattern changing for some European bird populations?

**NBC LEARN** ▶ VIDEO

After watching the Quest Kickoff video about migrating golden eagles, list some of the factors that might affect the birds' migration patterns and routes.

**Phenomenon** To understand how bird populations change over time in response to environmental conditions, ornithologists (scientists who study birds) analyze long-term data. In this problem-based Quest activity, you will investigate factors that may be influencing changes in two populations of European blackcaps. By applying what you learn from each lesson, digital activity, and hands-on lab, you will determine what is causing the changes to the bird populations. Then in the Findings activity, you will prepare a multimedia report to communicate what you have learned and to explain the changes in the blackcap populations.

......................................................

......................................................

......................................................

......................................................

......................................................

......................................................

......................................................

 **INTERACTIVITY**

A Migration Puzzle

**MS-LS4-1** Analyze and interpret data for patterns in the fossil record that document the existence, diversity, extinction, and change of life forms throughout the history of life on Earth under the assumption that natural laws operate today as in the past.

**MS-LS4-2** Apply scientific ideas to construct an explanation for the anatomical similarities and differences among modern organisms and between modern and fossil organisms to infer evolutionary relationships.

**MS-LS4-3** Analyze displays of pictorial data to compare patterns of similarities in the embryological development across multiple species to identify relationships not evident in the fully formed anatomy.

**MS-LS4-4** Construct an explanation based on evidence that describes how genetic variations of traits in a population increase some individuals' probability of surviving and reproducing in a specific environment.

## Quest CHECK-IN

### IN LESSON 1
What differences exist between the UK and Spanish blackcaps? Determine evidence for variations in the European blackcap population.

 **INTERACTIVITY**

Meet the Blackcaps

### IN LESSON 2
What are the roles of genes and mutations in natural selection? Think about how you can include these factors in your report.

## Quest CHECK-IN

### IN LESSON 3
How can natural selection and inherited variations influence a population? Investigate factors that may have caused the variations in the European blackcaps.

 **INTERACTIVITY**

Evolution of the Blackcaps

In the 1960s, some European blackcaps started migrating to the United Kingdom from Central Europe during the winter. Over time, they have formed a distinct population of blackcaps.

## IN LESSON 4
What can you learn from the fossil record? Think about how the fossil record of the European blackcap might provide information on how the bird has adapted over time.

## Quest CHECK-IN

### IN LESSON 5
What else would be helpful to know about European blackcaps? Research your questions and gather information to include in your report.

👆 **INTERACTIVITY**

Prepare Your Report

## Quest FINDINGS

## Complete the Quest!

Create a multimedia report about the two populations of European blackcaps and what caused them to be so different from each other.

👆 **INTERACTIVITY**

Reflect on Blackcap Migration

# Early Study of Evolution

## Guiding Questions

- What processes explain how organisms can change over time?
- What observations and evidence support the theory of evolution?

## Connection

**Literacy** Determine Central Ideas

MS-LS4-4

## Vocabulary

species
evolution
fossil
adaptation
scientific theory

## Academic Vocabulary

hypothesize

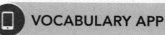 **VOCABULARY APP**

Practice vocabulary on a mobile device.

**Quest CONNECTION**

Think about what factors might cause variations in two different populations of European blackcaps.

## Connect It!

✏ **Draw an arrow pointing to the squirrel that you think is better suited for the environment.**

**Construct Explanations** Why do you think that squirrel is better suited for the environment? Explain your reasoning.

......................................................................................................................

......................................................................................................................

......................................................................................................................

......................................................................................................................

# Observing Changes

Suppose you put a birdfeeder outside your kitchen or classroom window. You enjoy watching birds and gray squirrels come to get a free meal. The squirrels seem to be perfectly skilled at climbing the feeder and breaking open seeds. One day, you are surprised to see a white squirrel, like the squirrel in **Figure 1**, visiting the feeder. This new white squirrel and the gray squirrel appear to be the same **species**—a group of similar organisms that can mate with each other and produce offspring that can also mate and reproduce. You would probably have a few questions about where this squirrel came from and why it is white!

**Curiosity About How Life Changes** Scientists such as Charles Darwin were also curious about the differences they observed in natural populations. A variation is any difference between individuals of the same species. Some scientists asked how life on Earth got started and how it has changed over time throughout the planet's history. The scientists wondered what dinosaurs were like and why they disappeared. Darwin and others worked to develop a theory of **evolution**—the process by which modern organisms have descended from ancient organisms.

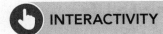
**INTERACTIVITY**

Explore feeding adaptations of animals in a coral reef ecosystem.

## Surprise at the Birdfeeder!

**Figure 1** In Brevard, North Carolina, about one-third of the Eastern gray squirrel population is white. In 1949, a resident received a pair of white squirrels as a gift. When one squirrel escaped, the other was released to join its friend. Soon after, people began to spot more white squirrels in town.

239

## Organizing Life

**Figure 2** Linnaeus classified life based on the structures of each organism.

**Classify** ✎ Identify three characteristics that you can observe in the image and list them below. Assign each characteristic a shape: a circle, square, or triangle. Using the characteristics you have identified, organize the organisms in the image into three groups by drawing the appropriate shapes around them.

.....................................................
.....................................................
.....................................................
.....................................................
.....................................................
.....................................................
.....................................................
.....................................................
.....................................................

**Make Meaning** What problem or question have you had that required you to make observations and gather evidence to figure out?

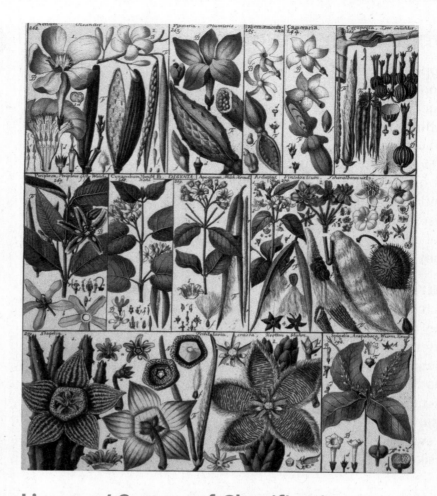

## Linnaeus' System of Classification

Recall that Carolus Linnaeus (1707–1778) developed the first scientific system for classifying and naming living things. Linnaeus collected samples of organisms from around the world. When classifying the organisms according to shared characteristics like those shown in **Figure 2**, he observed that there were variations of traits within a species. He was able to describe the variations and diversity of life, but not explain what caused that variation and diversity. No one was yet exploring how organisms came to be the way they are. In fact, many people still believed that organisms could appear out of the air as if by magic.

## Lamarck's Idea

The first serious attempts to explain evolution began in the late 1700s. A French scientist, Jean-Baptiste Lamarck (1744–1829), was put in charge of a museum department of "Insects and Worms," which also included all the invertebrates, or animals without backbones. Lamarck devoted himself to learning everything he could about invertebrates. Unlike Linnaeus, Lamarck wasn't satisfied with describing what the animals looked like. Instead, Lamarck attempted to figure out how the organisms came to be. After much study, Lamarck developed the first attempt at a scientific theory of evolution.

**Lamarck's Theory of Transformation** Lamarck mistakenly believed that organisms could change during their lifetimes by selectively using or not using various parts of their bodies. For example, moles could develop long, strong claws by digging through dirt. Lamarck **hypothesized** that if two adult moles with long claws mated, their offspring would inherit those claws, as shown in **Figure 3**. In the next generation, the individuals who used their claws would pass even longer claws on to their offspring. In this way, the whole population of moles would gradually grow bigger, stronger claws, until they reached the form we see today.

Unfortunately, Lamarck's theory of transformation doesn't hold up when investigated further. His theory doesn't explain how features such as eyes could have developed. The theory also does not work when tested with experiments. For example, you can force a plant to grow sideways. However, the offspring of the plant grow straight up toward the light. While his theory was not correct, Lamarck did contribute some important new ideas. First, he suggested that evolution takes place by small, gradual steps. Second, he proposed that simple organisms could develop over many generations into more complex organisms.

**Academic Vocabulary**

*Hypothesize* comes from the Greek word for *foundation*. To hypothesize means to propose a hypothesis—a possible explanation to a question that can be investigated. A hypothesis can be based on limited evidence. Why is it helpful to hypothesize in subjects like history and science?

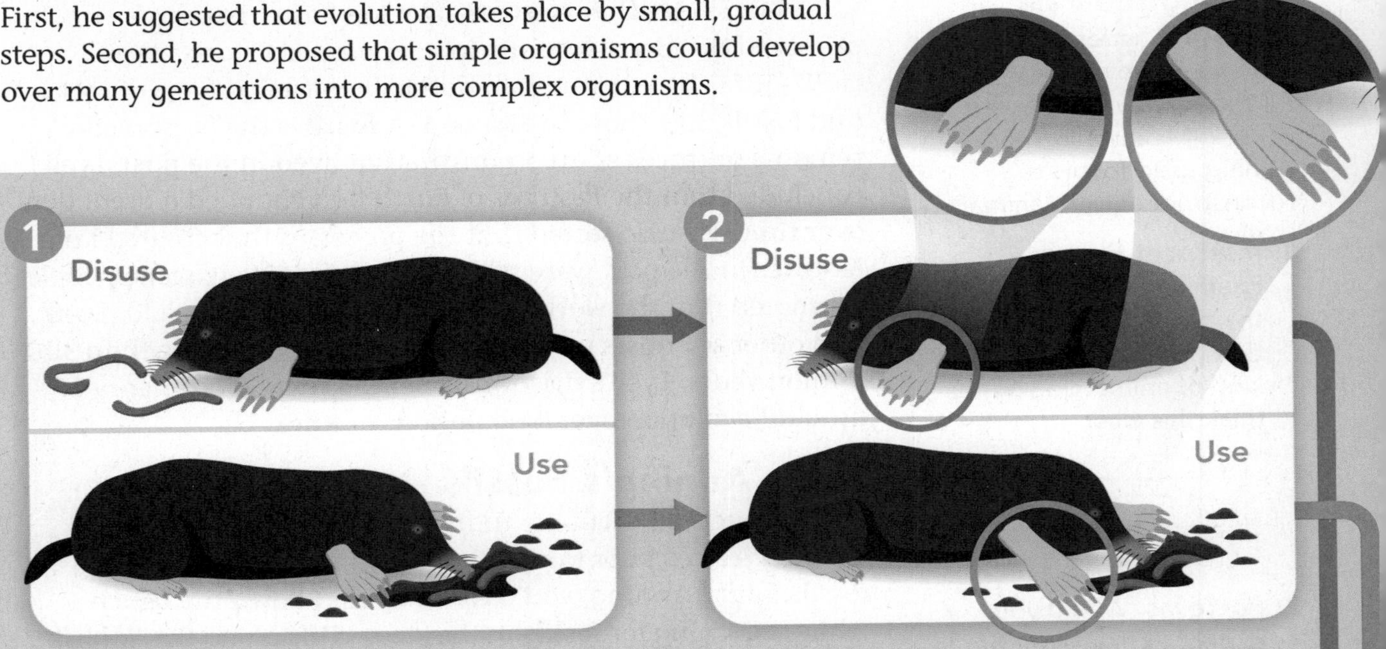

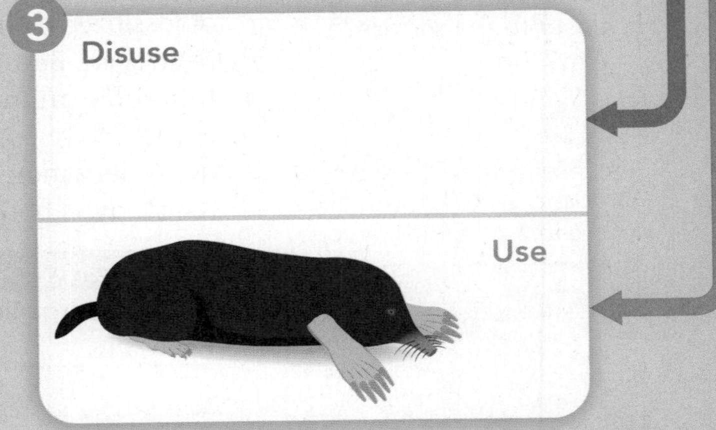

......................................................

......................................................

......................................................

......................................................

**Theory of Transformation**

**Figure 3** ✎ In the open space, draw what you think the offspring of the mole that did not dig for food will look like, based on Lamarck's theory.

☑ **READING CHECK** Draw Conclusions Why was Lamarck's theory not supported?

......................................................

......................................................

......................................................

## Reading the Past

**Figure 4** Charles Lyell discovered how to read Earth's history from layers of rock. Meanwhile, Mary Anning used fossils to reconstruct ancient animals.

1. **Interpret Photos** Examine the fossil. List the parts of the animal that you recognize. What kind of animal do you think this was?

..........................................................

..........................................................

..........................................................

2. **Patterns** Would you expect to find older or newer fossils in rock layers closer to the surface? Why?

..........................................................

..........................................................

..........................................................

..........................................................

..........................................................

**Charles Lyell's Rocks** Not long after Lamarck proposed his ideas, a young lawyer named Charles Lyell (1797–1875) began studying naturally-formed layers of rocks and fossils, like those in **Figure 4**. A **fossil** is the preserved remains or traces of an organism that lived in the past. Lyell concluded that the features of Earth had changed a great deal over time. He also stated that the processes that created land features in the past were still active. Before Lyell, some people estimated that the world was less than 6,000 years old. Lyell and other scientists pushed that estimate back more than 300 million years. Lyell's discoveries set the stage for a theory of gradual evolution over long periods of time.

**Mary Anning's Fossils** Mary Anning (1799–1847) lived a much different life than Linnaeus, Lamarck, or Lyell. Coming from a poor family that made money by collecting fossils, Mary Anning would roam up and down the beach while searching for fossils in the steep cliffs along the English Channel. Anning taught herself how to reconstruct the bodies of fossilized animals. Many of these animals had never before been seen. Because of Anning's work, scientists began to realize that some animals had lived in the ancient past but no longer existed. While Anning had no formal training as a scientist, her observations and discoveries made her a key contributor in the study of both fossils and geology.

☑ **READING CHECK** **Summarize Text** How did the scientists show that organisms and Earth changed over time?

..........................................................................................

..........................................................................................

# Darwin's Journey

In 1831, 22-year-old Charles Darwin set out on a five-year trip around the world aboard a British navy ship, the HMS *Beagle*. Darwin was a naturalist—a person who observes and studies the natural world. The captain of the *Beagle* wanted someone aboard who could make and record observations as the crew explored South America. One of Darwin's professors suggested inviting Darwin. And thus was launched a brilliant career!

Darwin was surprised to see the diversity of living things he encountered during the voyage. He saw insects that looked like flowers. He also saw armadillos digging insects from the ground. These mammals with a leathery shell that looks like a small suit of armor would have been very strange creatures to see. Today, scientists know that organisms are even more diverse than Darwin thought. Scientists have calculated that there are millions of species on Earth—and new ones are being identified all the time. Scientists have no way to estimate how many undiscovered species exist, but they believe the numbers are very high.

**Fossils** On his journey aboard the *Beagle*, Darwin also saw fossils of animals that had died long ago. Some of the fossils he observed confused him. **Figure 5** shows fossils Darwin found that resembled the bones of living armadillos but were much larger in size. Darwin wondered what had happened to the ancient, giant armadillos. Over long periods of time, could the giant armadillos have evolved into the smaller species we see today?

## Armored Animals

**Figure 5** Darwin thought that the fossil bones of giant Glyptodons (right) resembled the bones of modern armadillos (left).

1. **Determine Similarities** List two common features that the animals share.

.................................................

.................................................

2. **Infer** Why might these features be important to both ancient and modern armadillos?

.................................................

.................................................

.................................................

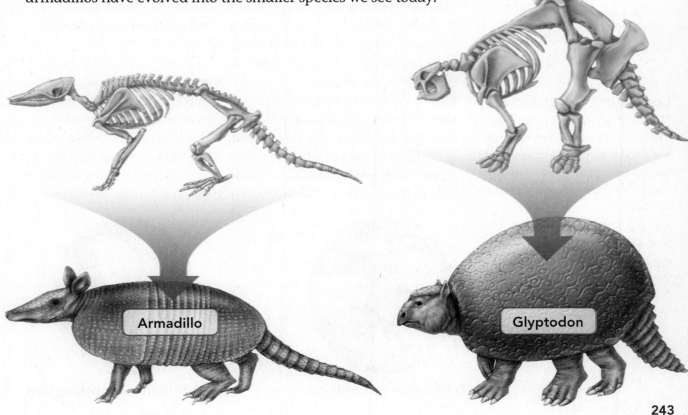

Armadillo

Glyptodon

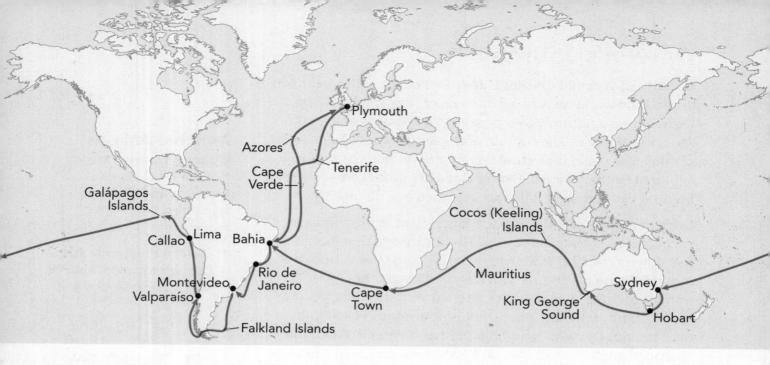

## Voyage of the HMS Beagle, 1831–1836

**Figure 6** Darwin sailed 40,000 miles around the world during his five-year voyage.

## Galápagos Organisms
The *Beagle* sailed to many different locations, as shown in **Figure 6**, and made several stops along the coast of South America. From what is now Ecuador on the Pacific coast, the ship traveled west to the Galápagos Islands. Darwin observed many different life forms there. He compared organisms from the Galápagos Islands to organisms that lived elsewhere. He also compared organisms living on the different islands.

## Comparisons to the Mainland
Darwin discovered similarities between Galápagos organisms and those found in South America. Some of the birds and plants on the islands resembled those on the mainland. However, Darwin also noted important differences between the organisms. You can see differences between island and mainland mockingbirds in **Figure 7**. Darwin became convinced that species do not always stay the same. Instead, he thought species could change and even produce new species over time. Darwin began to think that the island species might be related to South American species. After much reflection, Darwin realized that the island species had become different from their mainland relatives over time.

## Long-Lost Relatives?

**Figure 7** ✏ Mockingbirds on the South American mainland are similar to mockingbirds on the Galápagos Islands. Circle and label the features that are not similar.

**Relate Structure and Function** Why do you think these birds have different traits?

....................................................

....................................................

....................................................

....................................................

**Galápagos mockingbird**

**South American mockingbird**

## Comparisons Among the Islands

Darwin collected birds from several of the Galápagos Islands. The birds were a little different from one island to the next. Darwin would learn that the birds were all types of finches. He concluded that the finch species were all related to a single common ancestor species that came from the mainland. Over time, different finches developed different beak shapes and sizes that were well suited to the food they ate. Beak shape is an example of an **adaptation**—an inherited behavior or physical characteristic that helps an organism survive and reproduce in its environment. Look at **Figure 8**. Birds with narrow, prying beaks can grasp insects. Those with long, pointed, sharp beaks can pick at cacti. Short, hooked beaks tear open fruit, while short, wide beaks crush seeds.

☑ **READING CHECK** **Determine Central Ideas** What convinced Darwin that species can change over time?

...............................................................................................

...............................................................................................

## Galápagos Finches

**Figure 8** 🖋 Draw a line from each finch matching it to the type of food you think it eats based on its beak adaptations.

**Interpret Diagrams** What do you think explains the variation in bird beaks?

...............................................................

...............................................................

...............................................................

...............................................................

...............................................................

...............................................................

👆 **INTERACTIVITY**

Observe organisms that Darwin encountered in the Galápagos Islands.

# Question It !

## We Got the Beak!

**Identify Knowns** The finches in **Figure 8** show variations due to adaptation. Suppose someone asks you what caused a bird's beak to change to begin with. How would you answer the person?

...............................................................................................

...............................................................................................

...............................................................................................

...............................................................................................

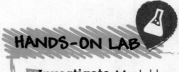

**HANDS-ON LAB**

ⵏ**Investigate** Model how species change over time.

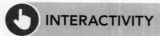
INTERACTIVITY

Identify plant and animal adaptations and how they help the organisms survive.

## Literacy Connection

**Determine Central Ideas**
As you read, underline the elements that are needed to develop a scientific theory.

**Darwin's Hypothesis** Darwin thought about what he had observed during his voyage on the *Beagle*. By this time, while Darwin was convinced that organisms change over time, he wanted to know how the organisms changed. Darwin consulted other scientists and gathered more information. Based on his observations, Darwin reasoned that plants or animals that arrived on the Galápagos Islands faced conditions different from those on the nearby mainland. Darwin hypothesized that species change over many generations and become better adapted to new conditions. Darwin's hypothesis was an idea that contributed important new knowledge. Later, he and other scientists used it to test and develop a scientific theory.

**Developing a Theory** In science, a theory explains why and how things happen in nature. A **scientific theory** is a well-tested explanation for a wide range of observations and experimental results. Based on a body of facts, scientific theory is confirmed repeatedly through observation and experimentation. Darwin's ideas are often referred to as the theory of evolution. From the evidence he collected, and from all the discoveries of the scientists who had come before him, Darwin concluded that organisms on the Galápagos Islands had changed over time, or evolved.

✓ **READING CHECK Cite Textual Evidence** Why do you think theories, like Darwin's theory of evolution, are important to science?

.................................................................

.................................................................

.................................................................

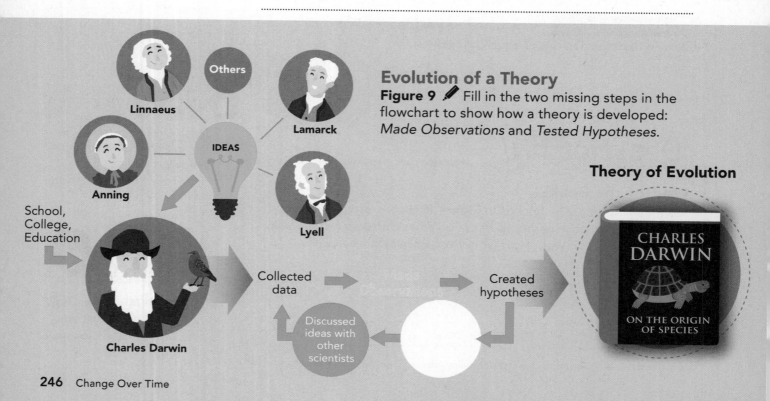

**Evolution of a Theory**

**Figure 9** ✐ Fill in the two missing steps in the flowchart to show how a theory is developed: *Made Observations* and *Tested Hypotheses*.

# ☑ LESSON 1 Check

1. **Identify** Name four people, other than Darwin, whose work contributed to the study of evolution.

......................................................

2. **Apply Scientific Reasoning** Why are fossils important to developing a theory of evolution?

......................................................
......................................................
......................................................
......................................................

3. **Compare and Contrast** How are variations and adaptations similar? How are they different?

......................................................
......................................................
......................................................
......................................................
......................................................
......................................................

4. **Integrate Information** Which two ideas of Lamarck contributed the most to Darwin's theory of evolution?

......................................................
......................................................
......................................................
......................................................
......................................................

5. **Construct Explanations** If the finches on the Galápagos Islands had such different beaks, how could Darwin think they shared a common ancestor from the mainland?

......................................................
......................................................
......................................................
......................................................
......................................................

# Quest CHECK-IN

In this lesson, you learned about adaptations and variations as well as the people whose ideas and activities contributed to understanding how organisms change over time. You also learned how Darwin developed his theory of evolution.

**Apply Scientific Reasoning** Consider what you learned about variation and how species change over time. Why is it important to understand how a different migration route might be affecting the blackcaps' physical traits?

......................................................
......................................................
......................................................
......................................................

## INTERACTIVITY

Meet the Blackcaps

**Go online** to draw conclusions about the variations between the two groups, based on what you've learned about where the birds migrate in winter.

# LESSON 2 Natural Selection

## Guiding Questions

- How does natural selection lead to change over time in organisms?
- What are the roles of genes, mutations, and the environment in natural selection?

## Connections

**Literacy** Cite Textual Evidence

**Math** Graph Proportional Relationships

MS-LS4-4, MS-LS4-5, MS-LS4-6

## Vocabulary

mechanism
natural selection
competition

## Academic Vocabulary

expression

 **VOCABULARY APP**

Practice vocabulary on a mobile device.

### Quest CONNECTION

Think about how natural selection might cause differences in the traits and characteristics of the two blackcap populations.

## Connect It !

✏️ **Estimate how many dead fish are shown here. Write your estimation on the photograph.**

**Explain Phenomena** Some fish survived this event, known as a fish kill. What might be different about the fish that survived?

.........................................................................................................................

.........................................................................................................................

**Apply Scientific Reasoning** If low oxygen levels occur every year and cause fish kills, how might the population of fish change over time?

.........................................................................................................................

.........................................................................................................................

# Evolution by Natural Selection

Living in a small body of water can be dangerous for fish. If water conditions become unhealthy, there is nowhere for the fish to go. Too little rain, too many fish, and an overgrowth of algae can work together to reduce oxygen levels in water. **Figure 1** shows what happened when oxygen levels fell too low. A "fish kill" can wipe out most of the local population of a species of fish. Some individuals, however, usually survive the disaster. These fish will live to reproduce, thus ensuring the species survives.

**Darwin's Search for a Mechanism** After his return to England, Darwin was not satisfied with his theory of evolution. He struggled to determine evolution's mechanism. A **mechanism** is the natural process by which something takes place. Darwin asked himself how organisms could change over time. And how could a species become better adapted to new conditions? To solve this mystery, Darwin performed experiments and read the works of other naturalists and scientists.

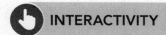

**INTERACTIVITY**

Investigate how a species of butterflyfish adapts to changes in its environment.

## Fish Kill
**Figure 1** Fish can survive only in water with dissolved oxygen. When oxygen levels fall too low, thousands of fish can perish at once.

Rock dove
(*Columba livia*)

Fantail pigeon

Silky fantail pigeon

## Fancy Pigeons

**Figure 2** Through artificial selection, Darwin helped to create the fantail pigeon (center) from the wild rock dove, commonly known as a pigeon (left). Silky fantails (right) were then bred from the fantail pigeon.

**Make Observations** List the differences you see between the three different pigeon types.

## Literacy Connection

**Cite Textual Evidence** As you read about natural selection, underline sentences or parts of sentences that you can refer to later to help you support your explanations about this process.

**Artificial Selection** Darwin studied farm and pet animals produced by artificial selection. In artificial selection, only individuals with a desired trait, such as color, are bred by humans in the hope that the next generation will inherit the desired trait. Darwin himself bred pigeons with large, fan-shaped tails (see **Figure 2**). He repeatedly allowed only those pigeons with many tail feathers to mate. In this way, Darwin produced pigeons with two or three times the usual number of tail feathers. Darwin thought that a process similar to artificial selection might happen in nature. But he wondered what natural process performed the selection.

**Natural Selection** Darwin understood how evolution could work when he read an essay by Thomas Malthus. Malthus noted that both animals and humans can produce many offspring. If all the offspring survived, the world would quickly become overpopulated. There would not be enough food for everyone, and part of the population would starve. Darwin realized that some individuals have traits that help them to survive and reproduce. If these traits are hereditary, they can be passed on to the next generation. Gradually, over many generations, more and more individuals will have the helpful traits.

***The Origin of Species*** Darwin waited a long time to publish his ideas. He thought they might be too revolutionary for the public to accept. Then, in 1858, Alfred Russel Wallace sent Darwin a letter. Wallace had also read Malthus' work and discovered the same mechanism for evolution! The next year, Darwin published his theory in *The Origin of Species*. In his book, Darwin proposed that evolution occurs by means of **natural selection**, a process by which individuals that are better adapted to their environment are more likely to survive and reproduce than other members of the same species.

## How Natural Selection Works
Darwin identified three factors that affect the process of natural selection: overproduction, variaton, and competition. First, there must be overproduction, shown in **Figure 3** below. Darwin knew that most species produce more offspring than can possibly survive. Secondly, there must be variation. Members of a population differ from one another in many of their traits. For example, sea turtles may differ in color, size, the ability to crawl quickly on sand, and shell hardness. Such variations are hereditary, passed from parents to offspring through genetic material. Finally, there must be **competition**—the struggle among living things to get the necessary amount of food, water, and shelter. In many species, so many offspring are produced that there are not enough resources—food, water, and living space—for all of them.

✓READING CHECK **Summarize** What are the factors that affect the process of natural selection?

HANDS-ON LAB

Investigate Measure variation in plant and animal populations.

## Overproduction
**Figure 3** Brown rats can give birth up to 12 times each year with about 6 to 11 pups in each litter. The young rats are ready to breed when they are 12 weeks old.

1. **Analyze Data** About how many pups can each female rat produce every year?

2. **Draw Conclusions** Why can't every rat survive and reproduce at its maximum rate?

**Selection** Darwin observed that some variations make individuals better adapted to their environment. Those individuals were more likely to survive and reproduce, and their offspring would inherit the helpful characteristic. The offspring, in turn, would be more likely to survive and reproduce and pass the characteristic to their offspring. After many generations, more members of the population would have the helpful characteristic. **Figure 4** shows an example of selection in a sea turtle population. In effect, conditions in the environment select the sea turtles with helpful traits to become parents of the next generation. Darwin proposed that, over a long time, natural selection can lead to change. Helpful variations may accumulate in a population, while unfavorable ones may disappear.

**Adaptations and Selection**

**Figure 4** Once sea turtles hatch from a nest, they must be fast and strong enough to reach the ocean before predators arrive.

☑️ READING CHECK **Cite Textual Evidence** Considering the environment, what helpful traits do you think would be passed on to increase the turtle population?

.......................................................................................................................

.......................................................................................................................

# Math Toolbox

## Hatching for Success

Sea turtles play an important role in maintaining Florida's coastal ecosystem.

1. **Analyze Proportional Relationships** ✏️ Complete the data table by calculating the percent of nests that hatched. Circle the location(s) where sea turtles have the highest probability of hatching.

2. **Graph Proportional Relationships** ✏️ Complete the graph to compare the total number of sea turtle nests at each beach to the number of nests that hatched sea turtles. Create a key next to the graph.

| Beach | Total Nests | Hatched Nests | Percent Hatched |
|---|---|---|---|
| **Barefoot Beach** | 174 | 50 | |
| **City of Naples** | 148 | 14 | |
| **Delnor Wiggins** | 46 | 6 | |
| **Marco Island** | 52 | 15 | |
| **10,000 Islands** | 87 | 13 | |

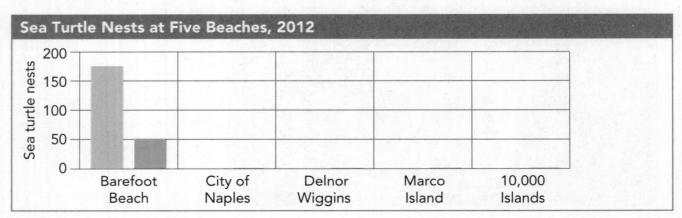

**Sea Turtle Nests at Five Beaches, 2012**

(Graph: y-axis "Sea turtle nests" from 0 to 200; x-axis beaches: Barefoot Beach, City of Naples, Delnor Wiggins, Marco Island, 10,000 Islands)

**Environmental Change** A change in the environment can affect an organism's ability to survive and may therefore lead to natural selection. For example, a storm can topple many trees in a forest. Trees that are better able to withstand strong winds have a survival advantage. In **Figure 5** you can see how natural selection might result in a shift in the population toward storm-resistant trees.

## Natural Selection in Action

**Figure 5** Natural events can lead to selection for favorable traits in a population. Read each image caption and use evidence to answer each question.

1990: Biologists survey a forest.

**Use Models** List your observations related to the variation, competition, and overproduction of this tree population.

........................................................................

........................................................................

........................................................................

1991: Same forest after a windstorm.

**Explain Phenomena** What helpful trait did most of the surviving trees have?

........................................................................

........................................................................

........................................................................

2010: Same forest is surveyed again.

**Make Observations** How is the population different now compared to 1990?

........................................................................

........................................................................

2017: Another windstorm hits.

**Develop Models** ✏ In the space provided, draw the effect of the storm on the forest.

**Draw Conclusions** How will natural selection have changed the forest from 1990 to 2030?

........................................................................

........................................................................

INTERACTIVITY

Analyze data on how a mouse population changes.

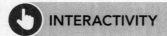

**Genes and Natural Selection** Darwin did a brilliant job of explaining natural selection, but he was never able to figure out where variations come from. He also did not understand how traits were passed from parents to offspring. Darwin hypothesized that tiny particles from around the parents' bodies passed into the developing offspring. Even at the time, Darwin realized that this explanation was flawed. Yet he did not have enough information to formulate a better explanation. You may recall Gregor Mendel and his study of heredity and genetics. Mendel's experiments in plant breeding took place during Darwin's life. His work showed that parents pass genes to their offspring. Genes are units of genetic material that provide instructions for a specific protein or function. Inherited variations result from individuals having different combinations of genes, as shown in **Figure 6**. Your hair color, eye color—and dimples, if you have them—are all determined by the genes your parents passed to you. Only traits controlled by genes can be acted upon by natural selection. Genetic variations contribute to the diversity of organisms.

### Inherited Traits

**Figure 6** Variations in traits depend on who the parents are.

1. Make Observations List several inherited variations you can observe in this group of students.

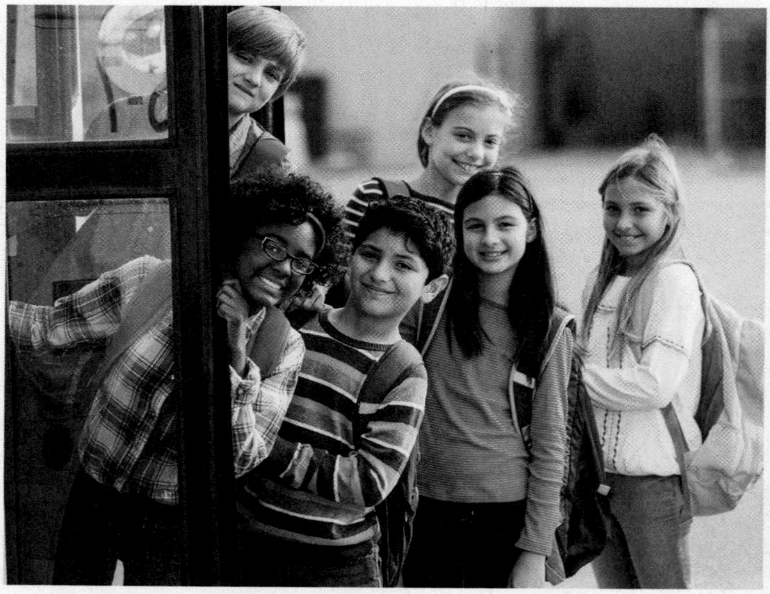

2. Draw Conclusions How did the students in **Figure 6** get such variations in traits?

**Figure 7** A mutation caused the flower on the right to grow in an unusual way.

**Explain Phenomena** Describe how the mutation changed the flower.

.........................................................

.........................................................

.........................................................

**Mutations** Sexual reproduction causes existing gene variations to be recombined in each member of a population. To get a new variation, there must be a gene mutation. A mutation is any change to the genetic material. **Figure 7** shows a flower with an obvious mutation. Only mutations to reproductive cells can be passed on to offspring. In humans, new genetic variations are introduced by mutations to egg or sperm cells. A mutation to a body cell, such as a heart or brain cell, only affects the individual and is not passed on to offspring. If offspring are born with a mutation, natural selection will determine whether that mutation gets passed on to the next generation.

**Epigenetic Changes** Epigenetics is the study of small changes to DNA that turn genes on or off but do not change the genetic code itself. All the cells in your body have identical DNA, but functions vary greatly. Gene **expression** determines how a cell acts—whether it will function as a bone cell or a skin cell. In your lifetime, there will be small chemical changes to your DNA affecting how genes get expressed. Your offspring can inherit these changes.

Inherited changes can affect multiple generations. For example, smoking makes small changes to DNA. Due to epigenetics, a grandmother who smokes is more likely to have a grandchild with asthma. The grandchild will inherit the same epigenetic changes that smoking caused in his or her grandmother. Epigenetics is challenging the idea that natural selection acts on genetic variation alone. Scientists are working to understand how a gene that gets turned on or off in a body cell could show up two generations later.

**☑ READING CHECK Distinguish Facts** A mutation can be inherited only if it occurs in which type of cell?

.........................................................................................

**👆 INTERACTIVITY**

Explore how a lack of genetic variations can impact crops.

**Academic Vocabulary**

Your friends may be able to tell what you are thinking based on your expression. How is a facial expression similar to gene expression?

.............................................

.............................................

.............................................

.............................................

.............................................

# ✓ LESSON 2 Check

MS-LS4-4, MS-LS4-5, MS-LS4-6

1. **Identify** Darwin identified three factors affecting the process of natural selection. What are they?

.................................................................................

2. **Determine Differences** The terms *mechanism* and *natural selection* both refer to natural processes. What makes them different?

.................................................................................

.................................................................................

.................................................................................

.................................................................................

3. **Evaluate Claims** A classmate claims that all mutations are both bad and inheritable. Is this true? Explain.

.................................................................................

.................................................................................

.................................................................................

.................................................................................

.................................................................................

4. **Apply Scientific Reasoning** How does natural selection help a species to evolve?

.................................................................................

.................................................................................

.................................................................................

5. **Construct Explanations** How does the genetic variation of traits within a population affect its probability for survival? Explain.

.................................................................................

.................................................................................

.................................................................................

.................................................................................

.................................................................................

.................................................................................

6. **Develop Models** ✏ Sea turtles can lay 50 to 200 eggs in a nest. Some eggs get destroyed or eaten by other animals. The young turtles that do hatch face many challenges as they head to the ocean. They may have to crawl up and down steep slopes, through seaweed, or around obstacles. Raccoons, foxes, crabs, birds, fish, and sharks may also eat the young turtles. Most sea turtle populations have declined and are listed as threatened or endangered species. Draw a young turtle and the variations you think could make it more successful. Label the variations and explain how they would benefit the turtle.

**256**   Change Over Time

# Fossils from Bedrock

▶ VIDEO

Explore the techniques and technologies that scientists use to extract fossils.

Do you know how to get a fossil out of a rock? You engineer it! Scientists use several methods to extract these remains of the past.

**The Challenge:** To remove fossils from bedrock without damaging them or the surrounding area.

**Phenomenon** Fossils stay trapped under layers of rock for millions of years. When the geology of an area changes, these layers are sometimes exposed. This offers a great opportunity to search for evidence of how adaptation by natural selection contributes to the evolution of a species.

Scientists carefully brush away dirt and debris from bones discovered in dig sites to gather fossil evidence of how organisms have changed over time.

Removing a fragile fossil from rock takes skill, time, and special tools. Sometimes fossil collectors have to dig out the larger section of rock holding a fossil. Until recently, extracting a fossil meant slowly and carefully chipping away at the rock with a small chisel and hammer, then sweeping away rock dust with a small brush. The latest technology is the pneumatic drill pen. Vibrating at 30,000 times each minute, the drill pen carves out a fossil more quickly and with greater control. Another method is the acid wash. While it takes much longer than the mechanical methods, and can only be used on fossils found in limestone and chalk, an acid wash is the safest way to remove a fossil.

**DESIGN CHALLENGE** How would you modify the process for removing fossils from bedrock? Go to the Engineering Design Notebook to find out!

# LESSON 3

# The Process of Evolution

## Guiding Questions

- How do natural selection and inherited variations influence a population?
- How does sexual selection influence a population's genetic variation?
- How is species interaction a factor in evolution?

## Connection

**Literacy** Determine Conclusions

MS-LS4-4, MS-LS4-6

## Vocabulary

fitness
sexual selection
coevolution

## Academic Vocabulary

randomly
interactions

 **VOCABULARY APP**

Practice vocabulary on a mobile device.

**Quest** CONNECTION

As you learn about evolution, consider what factors may be causing changes in the two blackcap populations.

## Connect It!

✏️ **Label each duck as either male or female.**

**Support Your Explanation**   Do you think that both ducks' appearance could be a result of natural selection? Explain your reasoning.

........................................................................................................

........................................................................................................

........................................................................................................

# Processes of Evolution

Charles Darwin's theory of natural selection is straightforward. Any population of living things has inherited variations. In addition, the population produces more young than can survive. According to natural selection, only the individuals that are well-adapted to their environments will survive and reproduce. An organism's **fitness** describes how well it can survive and reproduce in its environment. According to Darwin's theory, the fittest individuals survive to reproduce and pass their traits to the next generation. Organisms with low fitness are not as well-adapted to their environment and may die without reproducing or may not have as many offspring. Over time, as individual organisms successfully respond to changing conditions in the environment, the population evolves and its fitness increases.

**Beyond Natural Selection** Observe the male and female mandarin ducks in **Figure 1**. Both ducks have many adaptations that help them survive and reproduce in their watery habitat. Oily feathers keep the ducks dry. Webbed feet propel the ducks quickly through the water. Nesting in trees keeps ducklings safe from predators. Dull colors help the female duck blend in with her background. Now, look at the male duck. He seems to be calling for attention! His brightly colored face and the bold black and white stripes on his sides surely attract predators. How could natural selection result in traits that hurt the male duck's chance of survival? Answer: There is more to evolution than "survival of the fittest."

**HANDS-ON LAB**

**Investigate** Explore how different birds' feet help them survive in their environments.

**Opposites Attract**
**Figure 1** Believe it or not, these ducks are both from the same species. Male and female mandarin ducks have evolved to look very different!

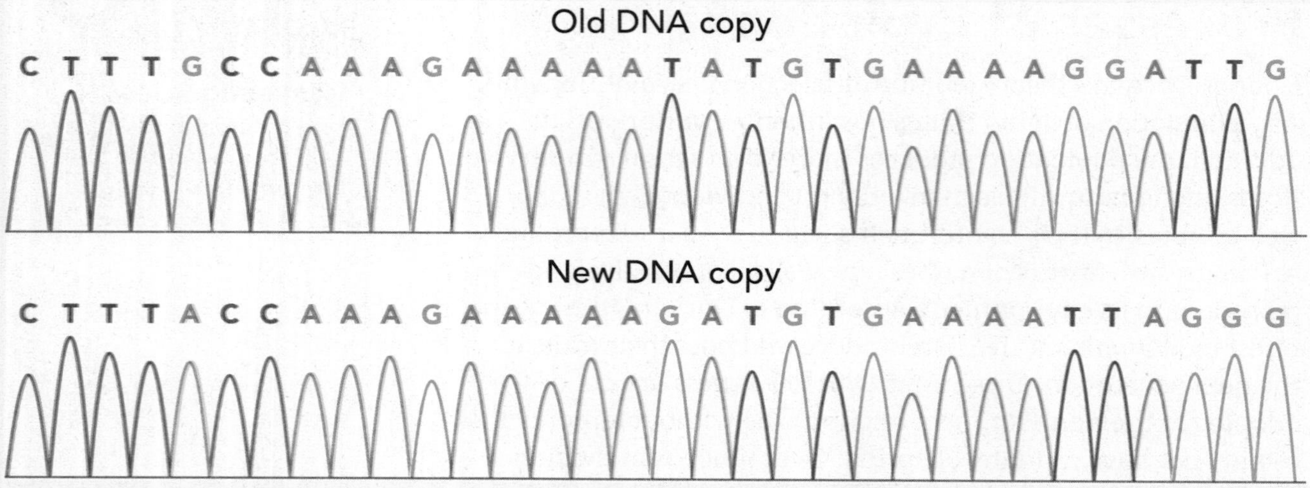

## Old DNA copy

C T T T G C C A A A G A A A A A T A T G T G A A A A G G A T T G

## New DNA copy

C T T T A C C A A A G A A A A A G A T G T G A A A A T T A G G G

## Spellcheck, Please!

**Figure 2** 🖊 A mutation is like a spelling error in a gene's DNA sequence of nucleotides—A, C, G, and T. Any change in the sequence results in a mutation. Here, each nucleotide has its own color. Observe how the sequence of nucleotides changes. Compare the sequences of the two DNA copies. Circle any differences you observe in the new DNA copy.

**Explain Phenomena** What do you think may have caused the differences between the two DNA copies?

...............................................................................................

...............................................................................................

## Literacy Connection

**Determine Conclusions**
Why is it that mutations to body cells do not affect offspring?

...............................................

...............................................

...............................................

...............................................

...............................................

...............................................

**INTERACTIVITY**

Analyze mutations and how they can impact evolution.

**Mutations** One reason for Darwin's oversimplification of evolution was that he did not yet know about mutations. You've already learned that a mutation is any change to an organism's genetic material. Mutations can create multiple alleles, or forms of a gene. Different alleles cause variations in traits such as eye color, ear shape, and blood type.

**How Mutations Happen** Mutations are created in two ways. First, a dividing cell can make an error while copying its DNA (see **Figure 2**). There are approximately six billion units in one copy of human DNA. Imagine copying by hand a book that had six billion letters. Think how easy it would be to make a mistake! Researchers estimate that each human child inherits an average of 60 new mutations from his or her parents. That sounds like a lot, doesn't it? But it means that the body makes only one mistake out of every 100 million units of DNA copied. Secondly, mutations also occur when an organism is exposed to environmental factors such as radiation or certain chemicals that damage the cell's DNA. While the cell has mechanisms to repair damaged DNA, that repair is not always perfect. Any mistake while fixing the DNA results in a mutation.

**Effects of Mutations** Most mutations have no effect on the individual organism. The mutation may be in a part of the DNA that is inactive. Or the mutation may not cause a difference in the function of the body. Out of the mutations that do affect function, most are harmful to the individual. **Randomly** changing a process in the body typically results in decreased function. Only mutations to sex cells can get passed on and affect the fitness of offspring. A mutation that increases fitness tends to grow more common in a population. A mutation that decreases fitness tends to disappear because the individuals with that mutation die or reproduce less successfully.

**Need for Mutations** People often think of mutations as harmful. It's true that mutations can lead to cancer and genetic defects. At the same time, however, mutations are necessary for evolution to occur. Mutations create all the variations among members of a species and account for the diversity of organisms on Earth. **Figure 3** shows how mutations can change plant leaf shapes. Imagine if the first single-celled organisms had never experienced mutation! That first species would have been the only life that ever existed on the planet.

☑ **READING CHECK** **Summarize Text** How are mutations both harmful and helpful?

.......................................................................................................

.......................................................................................................

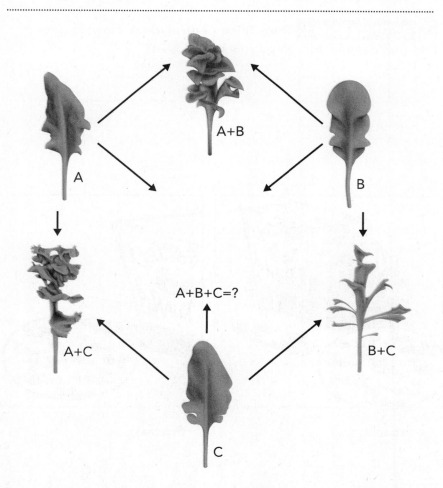

A

A+B

B

A+C

A+B+C=?

B+C

C

**Academic Vocabulary**

List where you may have heard the word *random* used before. What does *randomly* mean as it's used here?

.........................................................

.........................................................

.........................................................

.........................................................

.........................................................

**Variations from Mutations**

**Figure 3** Scientists studied how three mutations in mustard plant DNA (labeled A, B, and C in the image) affect leaf shape.

**Use a Model to Predict**
🖊 Examine the effects of the mutations on leaf shape. In the center of the image, draw what you think the leaves would look like if a plant had all three mutations.

**INTERACTIVITY**

Investigate how populations of organisms evolve due to gene flow and genetic drift.

## Gene Flow

Mutations are not the only source of new alleles in a population. Alleles also enter a population through gene flow. As you know, a gene is a unit of genetic material that acts as instructions for a specific protein or function. Gene flow occurs when individuals with new alleles physically move from one population to another. Gene flow can increase the genetic variation of a population.

How do individuals move between populations? Sometimes birds and insects are blown to a new continent by a storm. Plant seeds and pollen can stick to animal fur and travel long distances, too. Humans are often accidentally responsible for gene flow. Animals, seeds, and microorganisms can hitch a ride on trucks or in the water in the bottom of ships.

## Genetic Drift

The last mechanism of evolution is a random, directionless process. Just by chance, some alleles may be lost to a population. Think of a small population of birds living on an island. The only bird that carries an allele for light-colored feathers could be hit by lightning and die. It will pass no genes on to the next generation. Through random chance, the genetic variation of the population shrinks over time. This process is called genetic drift. **Figure 4** shows how gene flow and genetic drift affect the level of variation in a population of snakes.

**READING CHECK** **Determine Central Ideas** How do gene flow and genetic drift play a role in evolution?

.............................................................................................

.............................................................................................

.............................................................................................

## Gene Flow and Genetic Drift

**Figure 4** ✎ Examine how snakes enter or leave the snake population in each of the images and label the process taking place as either *genetic drift* or *gene flow.*

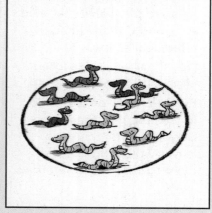

**Original Snake Population**

**Process:** ...................

**Process:** ...................

**Figure 5** Stag beetles compete to control the best territory. A good territory gives the winning beetle access to females for mating.

1. **Identify** 🖊 Circle the feature of the beetles that has grown due to male competition.

2. **Relate Structure and Function** Do you think that female stag beetles also have the same large feature?

......................................................

......................................................

......................................................

......................................................

......................................................

# Sexual Selection

The measure of an individual's fitness is its ability to survive and reproduce. An organism that reproduces asexually can reproduce all on its own. An organism that reproduces sexually, however, must blend its genes with those of a mate. **Sexual selection** is natural selection that acts on an organism's ability to get the best possible mate. The fitness of the offspring depends on the fitness of both the parents. Therefore, sexually-reproducing organisms try to choose mates with specific traits that have higher fitness.

**Female Choice** In some species, females choose which males will father their offspring. Natural selection favors traits that help females choose mates with high fitness. Consider the ducks in **Figure 1**. Suppose that male ducks with bright feathers have better fitness. Females may evolve a trait that causes them to choose males with bright feathers. Over time, male ducks will grow brighter and fancier feathers. Even after the bright colors start to hurt the males' survival, the females may continue to select males with ever-brighter feathers.

**Male Competition** In other species, males compete to control a territory with access to females. Any trait that gives males an advantage in the competition will be favored by natural selection. Male competition can lead to exaggerated horns, pincers, or body size, as shown in **Figure 5**. The need to reproduce can cause males to evolve characteristics that make them less likely to survive!

☑ READING CHECK **Determine Conclusions** Why do you think bright feathers make a male duck a desirable mate?

......................................................................................

......................................................................................

......................................................................................

📓 **Reflect** What is a difference that you have observed between male and female members of the same species in a zoo, aquarium, or in your local community?

## Coevolution and Cooperation

**Figure 6** The acacia tree and ants both evolved features that help them work together.

**Infer** What features do you think the acacia tree and the ants might have that would help one another?

........................................

........................................

........................................

........................................

**Academic Vocabulary**

If you break down the word *interactions*, it means "the actions between." How would you define interactions between two species?

........................................

........................................

........................................

........................................

## Coevolution

Two or more species with close **interactions** can affect each other's evolution. **Coevolution** is the process by which two species evolve in response to changes in each other over time. Coevolution can happen when species cooperate with each other, as shown in **Figure 6**. Several acacia trees in Central America have coevolved with select species of ants. The acacias trees evolved hollow thorns and nectar pores because of their close interactions with the ants. Likewise, the ants evolved defense behaviors to protect "their" trees. A queen ant lays her eggs in the hollow thorns of an acacia tree. In return for the shelter and food from the tree, the ants protect the tree. They attack when other insects or animals try to devour the acacia leaves. Other examples of interactions that can lead to coevolution include species that compete for resources and species involved in a prey-predator relationship.

**Mimicry in Coevolution**

**Figure 7** Tiger-wing butterflies evolved to absorb and store toxins from plants they ate when they were caterpillars. This makes them taste bad. Birds avoid eating tiger-wing butterflies and other butterflies that mimic, or closely resemble, them.

**Develop Models** ✏ Sketch the progression of how a butterfly's wing patterns may have changed over time to mimic that of the tiger-wing butterfly.

MS-LS4-4, MS-LS4-6

1. **Define** What does fitness mean in terms of evolution?

...........................................................................

...........................................................................

2. **Describe** How does gene flow affect a population's genetic variation?

...........................................................................

...........................................................................

3. **Infer** Is sexual selection a form of natural selection? Explain.

...........................................................................

...........................................................................

...........................................................................

...........................................................................

4. **Use Evidence** What are the two ways in which mutations are created? Give at least one example of an environmental factor.

...........................................................................

...........................................................................

...........................................................................

...........................................................................

5. **Construct Explanations** Explain the role of mutations in genetic variation and in the diversity of living things. Support your explanation with evidence.

...........................................................................

...........................................................................

...........................................................................

...........................................................................

...........................................................................

...........................................................................

...........................................................................

...........................................................................

6. **Explain Phenomena** How is species interaction a factor in evolution? Use the ant and the acacia tree as an example.

...........................................................................

...........................................................................

...........................................................................

...........................................................................

...........................................................................

# Quest CHECK-IN

**In this lesson, you learned how a population can be influenced by natural selection, species interactions, and genetic variations due to mutations, gene flow, genetic drift, and sexual selection.**

Why is it important to consider the role of genetic variations when trying to determine what caused the changes to the European blackcaps?

...........................................................................

...........................................................................

...........................................................................

...........................................................................

👆 **INTERACTIVITY**

Evolution of the Blackcaps

**Go online** to investigate factors that may have caused the variations in the European blackcaps.

# LESSON 4 Evidence in the Fossil Record

## Guiding Questions

- What supports evidence for the scientific theory of evolution?
- How do fossils show change over time?
- What does the early development of different organisms tell us about evolution?
- How does failure to adapt to a changing environment lead to a species' extinction?

## Connections

**Literacy** Summarize Text

**Math** Analyze Proportional Relationships

MS-LS4-1, MS-LS4-2, MS-LS4-3, MS-LS4-6

## Vocabulary

fossil record
embryo
homologous
  structures
extinct

## Academic Vocabulary

evidence

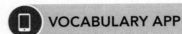
**VOCABULARY APP**

Practice vocabulary on a mobile device.

## Quest CONNECTION

Think about how the fossil record of the European blackcap might provide information on how the bird has adapted over time.

## Connect It !

✏️ **Draw arrows to connect similar features between the fossil and the modern animal.**

**Interpret Photos** Which parts of the crinoid's tentacles are best preserved in the fossils? Which parts were not preserved?

...............................................................................................................

...............................................................................................................

...............................................................................................................

# The Fossil Record

Fossils are preserved remains or traces of living things. **Figure 1** shows fossils of crinoids, relatives of modern-day starfish. All the fossils that have been discovered and what we have learned from them make up the **fossil record**. The patterns in the fossil record are like data that scientists can analyze and interpret. The fossil record documents the diversity of the life forms, many now extinct, and shows how life forms existed and changed throughout Earth's history. The fossil record is a treasure trove of **evidence** about how organisms of the past evolved into the forms we see today.

## Microevolution and Macroevolution

Scientists can observe evolution taking place within populations of organisms. Small, gradual changes in the color or size of a certain population is called microevolution. *Micro-* means very small, and *evolution* means change through time. One example of microevolution is the northern population of house sparrows. They adapted to a colder climate by growing larger bodies than the southern population. This small change took less than 100 years. Usually, for multicellular organisms, it takes years to thousands of years for a new species to develop. Scientists turn to the fossil record to learn about macroevolution, or major evolutionary change.

**A Glimpse of the Past**
**Figure 1** Crinoids are relatives of starfish. We can learn a lot about the evolution of crinoids by looking at fossils of their extinct relatives. Some ancient crinoids grew more than 40 meters long!

A. As rock erodes, the fossil is exposed on the surface.

B. An organism dies and sinks to the bottom of a lake.

## Forming a Fossil

**Figure 2** A fossil may form when sediment quickly covers a dead organism.

**Relate Text to Visuals**

✏ Are the images matched with the correct captions? Or are there some mistakes? Match up each image with the right caption by writing the correct letters in the blank circles.

## Many Kinds of Fossils

**Figure 3** A fossil may be the preserved remains of an organism's body, or the trace of an organism—something it leaves behind.

1. **Classify** ✏ Label each image as either a body fossil or a trace fossil.

2. **Evaluate Evidence** Why did you classify them that way?

.................................................

.................................................

.................................................

.................................................

.................................................

**How Fossils Form** A fossil is the impression that an organism or part of an organism leaves in rock. That impression comes about in one of two ways. A mold creates a hollow area in the rock that is the shape of an organism or part of an organism. Or, a cast makes a solid copy of an organism's shape, sometimes containing some of the original organism.

Most fossils form when living things die and sediment buries them. Sediment is the small, solid pieces of material that come from rocks or the remains of organisms and settle to the bottom of a body of water. Over time, the sediment slowly hardens into rock and preserves the shapes of the organisms. Fossils can form from any kind of living thing, from bacteria to dinosaurs.

Many fossils come from organisms that once lived in or near still water. Swamps, lakes, and shallow seas build up sediment quickly and bury remains of living things. In **Figure 2**, you can see how a fossil might form. When an organism dies, its soft parts usually decay quickly or are eaten by other organisms. Only hard parts of an organism typically leave fossils. These hard parts include bones, shells, teeth, seeds, and woody stems. It is rare for the soft parts of an organism to become a fossil. People often see fossils after erosion exposes them. Erosion is the wearing away of Earth's surface by natural processes such as water and wind.

Snail shells

Turtle dropping

C. Over millions of years, the sediment hardens into rock, preserving the remains.

D. Over time, sediment covers the organism.

## Kinds of Fossils

There are two types of fossils: body fossils and trace fossils. Each one gives us different information about the ancient organism it represents.

**Body Fossils** Body fossils preserve the shape and structure of an organism. We can learn about what a plant or animal looked like from a body fossil. Body fossils of trees are called petrified wood. The term *petrified* means "turned into stone." Petrified fossils are fossils in which minerals replace all or part of an organism. In petrified wood, the remains are so well preserved that scientists can often count the rings to tell how old a tree was when it died millions of years ago. Ancient mammoths frozen into ice, petrified dinosaur bones, and insects trapped in amber are other examples of body fossils.

**Trace Fossils** We can learn what an animal did from trace fossils. Footprints, nests, and animal droppings preserved in stone are all trace fossils, as shown in **Figure 3**.

HANDS-ON LAB

☑**Investigate** Model how different fossils form.

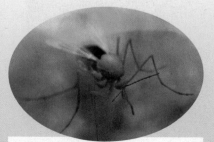

**Mosquito in amber**

**Smilodon, cat skull**

**Dinosaur tracks**

# Fossil Evidence of Evolution

Most of what we know about ancient organisms comes from the fossil record. The fossil record provides evidence about the history of life and past environments on Earth. The fossil record also shows how different groups of organisms have changed over time. Each new discovery helps to fill holes in our understanding of evolution.

**Early Earth** When Earth first formed, more than 4.5 billion years ago, it was extremely hot. Earth was likely mostly melted. As Earth cooled, solid rocks became stable at Earth's surface. The oldest known fossils are from rocks that formed about a billion years after Earth formed. **Figure 4** shows a rock made of these fossils. Scientists think that all other forms of life on Earth arose from these simple organisms.

Scientists cannot yet pinpoint when or where life first evolved. Scientists hypothesize that life first evolved in Earth's ocean. The early ocean contained reactive chemicals. Under the right conditions, sunlight and lightning can change those chemicals into molecules similar to those found in living cells. More research will help scientists to settle the question of the origin of life on Earth.

## Literacy Connection

**Summarize Text** At the end of each two-page spread, stop to see if you can summarize what you just read.

**Fossils Reveal Early Life**

**Figure 4** Stromatolites are rock-like structures formed by layers of fossilized bacteria. Dating as far back as 3.4 billion years ago, they are the oldest evidence of life forms on Earth. Ancient bacteria in water produced thin sheets of film that trapped mud. Over time, these thin sheets formed microfossils—fossils too small to see without a microscope. Eventually, the sheets built up into the layers you see here.

**Interpret Photos** Draw a scale next to the fossil stromatolite to show which are the oldest layers and which are the youngest.

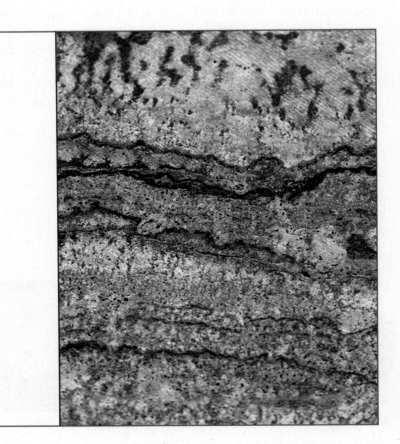

**Gomphotherium**
24–5 mya

**Moeritherium**
36 mya

**Platybelodon**
23–5.3 mya

**Mammut americanum**
(American mastodon)
4 mya–11,500 ya

**Mammuthus**
(Woolly Mammoth)
Pliocene, from
750,000–11,500 ya

**Loxodonta**
(African elephant)
1.8 mya–present

ya = years ago; mya = millions of years ago

**Fossils and Evolution Through Time** The fossil record shows that life on Earth has evolved. Rock forms in layers, with newer layers on top of older layers. When we dig deeper, we see older rocks with fossils from earlier time periods. The oldest rocks contain fossils of only very simple organisms. Younger rocks include fossils of both simple organisms and also more complex organisms. Looking at fossils in rocks from different time periods, scientists can reconstruct the history of evolution. **Figure 5** shows the evolution of the elephant, reconstructed from the fossil record.

The fossil record also shows how Earth's climate has changed. Some plant fossils reveal surprises, such as palm trees in Wyoming and giant tropical ferns in Antarctica. Fossils and preserved remains are also evidence of how climate change influences evolution.

**Evolution of the Modern Elephant**
**Figure 5** Scientists have reconstructed the evolutionary history of the elephant with evidence from the fossil record.

✓ READING CHECK
**Determine Conclusions** Would you expect to find fossils related to the evolution of the elephant in the oldest rocks in the fossil record? Why?

..................................................
..................................................
..................................................

# Question It!

Kyle has very limited vision and needs someone to explain the evolution of elephants to him. Suppose you are going to work with Kyle to help him understand the changes elephants have undergone.

**Interpret Diagrams** Using **Figure 5**, what features of the animals have stayed the same? What features have changed?

..................................................
..................................................
..................................................
..................................................
..................................................

# Comparisons of Anatomy

The structure of an organism's body is called its anatomy. Similarities in anatomy are clues that organisms evolved from a common ancestor. Evidence from the fossil record and observations of modern organisms help us to reconstruct evolutionary history.

### Embryological Development

An **embryo** is a young organism that develops from a fertilized egg (called a zygote). The growing embryo may develop inside or outside the parent's body. The early development of different organisms in an embryo shows some striking similarities. For example, chickens, fish, turtles, and pigs all resemble each other during the early stages of development. These similarities in early development suggest that organisms are related and share a common ancestor.

Scientists can also analyze fossilized eggs to learn about development in species from long ago. **Figure 6** shows the model of a duck-billed dinosaur embryo, known as a Hadrosaur, compared to an x-ray of a chicken embryo. You can see many similarities in their early development.

### Homologous Structures

Similar structures that related species have inherited from a common ancestor are known as **homologous structures** (hoh MAHL uh gus). Bats, dogs, dolphins, and even flying reptiles have homologous structures in their limbs. Although the structures look very different now, in the Math Toolbox you can see the bones that these animals all have in common.

**READING CHECK** **Determine Conclusions** If two organisms have homologous structures and similar early development, what can you infer about them?

....................................................................................................................................

....................................................................................................................................

**Birds and Dinosaurs**

**Figure 6** 🖉 Draw lines and label the features that look similar in both the Hadrosaur and chicken embryos.

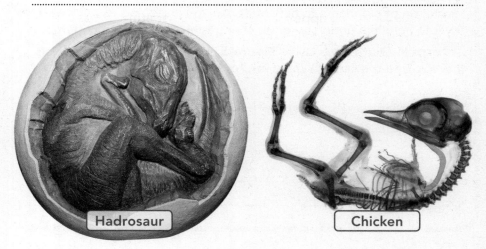

Hadrosaur   Chicken

## Homologous Anatomical Structures

The wings, flipper, and leg of these organisms all have similar anatomical (body) structures. Note that the structures are not drawn to scale.

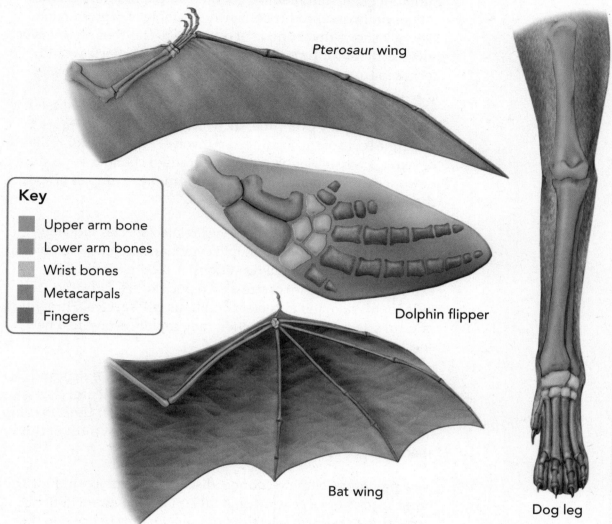

*Pterosaur* wing

Dolphin flipper

Bat wing

Dog leg

**Key**
- Upper arm bone
- Lower arm bones
- Wrist bones
- Metacarpals
- Fingers

1. **Construct Tables** ✏ Choose two of the animals shown above to examine closely. Using a metric ruler, measure the upper arm bone, the lower arm bone, and the fingers. Create a data table at right and record the measurements in millimeters.

2. **Analyze Proportional Relationships** In each species, compare the upper arm to lower arm, or compare fingers to metacarpals. Can you find any equivalent ratios?

..............................................................................................

..............................................................................................

..............................................................................................

..............................................................................................

INTERACTIVITY

Interpret data from the fossil record that supports species extinction.

# Beginning and End of a Species

Natural selection explains how variations can lead to changes in a species. A new species forms when one population remains isolated from the rest of its species long enough to evolve such different traits that members of the two populations can no longer mate and produce offspring capable of reproduction. **Figure 7** shows an example of a turtle species that has evolved seven different subspecies. Over time, the subspecies could form separate species.

**Gradual Change** Some species in the fossil record seem to change gradually over time, such as the elephants in **Figure 5**. The time scale of the fossil record involves thousands or millions of years. There is plenty of time for gradual changes to produce new species. The fossil record contains many examples of species that are halfway between two others.

**Rapid Change** At times, new, related species suddenly appear in the fossil record. Rapid evolution can follow a major change in environmental conditions. A cooling climate, for example, can put a lot of stress on a population. Only the individuals adapted to cooler conditions will survive. Through natural selection, the population may rapidly evolve to a new species.

**Extinction** A species is **extinct** if it no longer exists and will never again live on Earth. A rapid environmental change is more likely to cause a species to become extinct than to bring about a new species. The fossil record shows that most of the species that ever lived on Earth are now extinct.

New predators, climate change, disease, and competition with other species are a few factors that can lead to extinction. According to natural selection, if a species fails to develop the adaptations necessary to survive the changing conditions in an environment, that species will not survive and reproduce. Small populations that breed slowly and cannot relocate are more likely to become extinct. The fossil record shows that volcanic eruptions, asteroids striking Earth, and sudden climate change can kill off many species in a short time.

**READING CHECK Translate Information** How do you know that the animals whose limbs are depicted in the Math Toolbox had a common ancestor at one point? What question could you ask to find out more and why would you ask it?

......................................................................

......................................................................

......................................................................

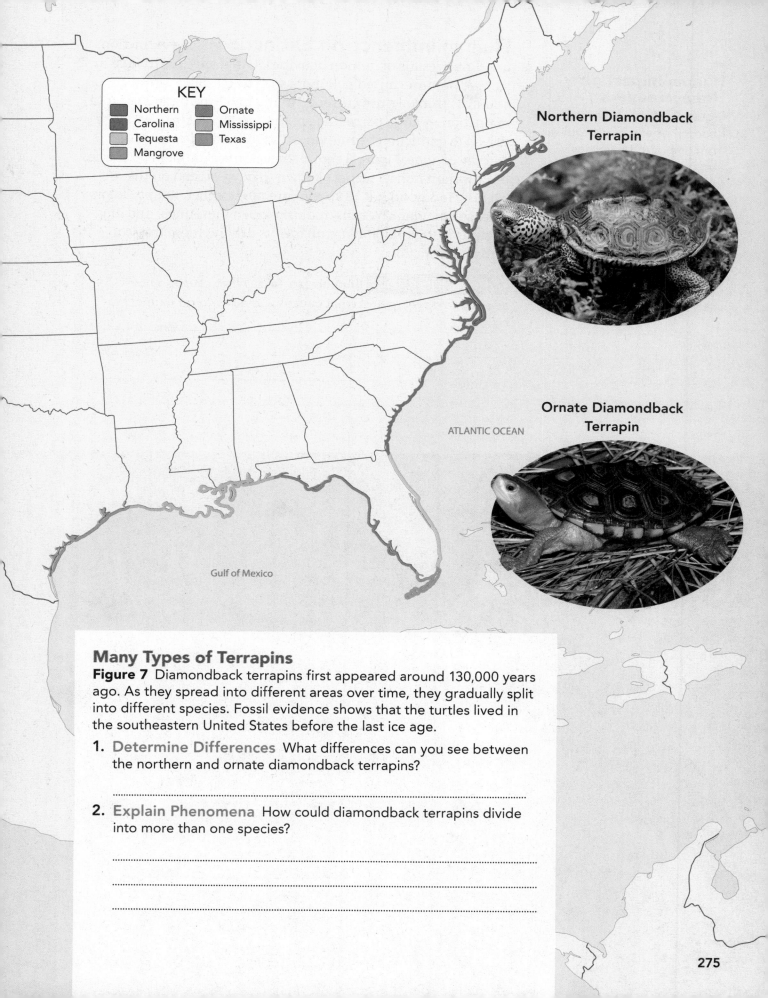

KEY

Northern
Carolina
Tequesta
Mangrove

Ornate
Mississippi
Texas

Northern Diamondback Terrapin

Ornate Diamondback Terrapin

ATLANTIC OCEAN

Gulf of Mexico

## Many Types of Terrapins

**Figure 7** Diamondback terrapins first appeared around 130,000 years ago. As they spread into different areas over time, they gradually split into different species. Fossil evidence shows that the turtles lived in the southeastern United States before the last ice age.

1. **Determine Differences** What differences can you see between the northern and ornate diamondback terrapins?

   ........................................................................................

2. **Explain Phenomena** How could diamondback terrapins divide into more than one species?

   ........................................................................................
   ........................................................................................
   ........................................................................................

## Human Impact on Honeycreepers

**Figure 8** Many Hawaiian honeycreeper species evolved from one or more finches that traveled to the islands thousands of years ago. Most honeycreeper species are now extinct or endangered.

**Construct Explanations** How could the honeycreepers' island habitat make them more likely to go extinct?

..................................................

..................................................

..................................................

..................................................

..................................................

**Human Influence on Extinction** Some extinctions are direct results of human activities. Other species struggle to survive human-caused pollution, such as oil spills. Many scientists think we are currently living in a time period of rapid extinction. A large percentage of the species on Earth could be driven to extinction by human activities and human-caused climate change. **Figure 8** shows some of the estimated 56 species of Hawaiian honeycreepers known to have existed on the islands. Today, all but 18 species are now extinct. Rat predators, disease-carrying chickens, malaria-laden mosquitos, and pigs trampling their habitat are all factors driving these tropical birds to extinction.

✓ **READING CHECK** **Summarize Text** What causes a new species to develop and what causes a species to go extinct?

..................................................

..................................................

..................................................

..................................................

MS-LS4-1, MS-LS4-2, MS-LS4-3, MS-LS4-6

**1. Make Generalizations** What sort of information can you get from a body fossil that you can't get from a trace fossil?

..................................................................

..................................................................

..................................................................

**2. Analyze Data** According to the fossil record, which level in the rock layers shown in the diagram will have the oldest organisms? Explain.

..................................................................

..................................................................

..................................................................

..................................................................

..................................................................

..................................................................

**3. Construct an Explanation** How do you account for differences between the bat's wing and the dolphin's flipper?

..................................................................

..................................................................

..................................................................

Dolphin flipper

Bat wing

**4. Construct Explanations** What does the fossil record show and how does it support the theory of evolution?

..................................................................

..................................................................

..................................................................

..................................................................

**5. Patterns** If you were a scientist trying to determine if an organism evolved gradually or rapidly, how would patterns in the fossil record help you? Explain how the pattern would provide evidence to support the rate of evolution for that organism.

..................................................................

..................................................................

..................................................................

..................................................................

..................................................................

..................................................................

..................................................................

..................................................................

..................................................................

..................................................................

**6. Apply Scientific Reasoning** Why is a sudden change in the environment more likely to cause a species to go extinct rather than to cause a new species to develop?

..................................................................

..................................................................

..................................................................

..................................................................

..................................................................

*Vegavis* is not the direct ancestor of modern-day ducks or chickens, but it is closely related to waterfowl such as geese.

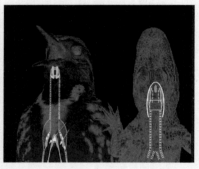

**Location of syrinx in living songbird compared to larynx in an alligator**

The presence of a syrinx in the *Vegavis iaai* fossil strongly suggests that the bird was capable of producing sounds. In the songbird, as in *Vegavis*, the syrinx is located in the chest. In the alligator, the larynx is located in the throat.

**Photo Credit:** Dr. Julia Clarke, University of Texas at Austin

# Could DINOSAURS Roar?

So many movies have dinosaurs roaring as they roam across the landscape shredding trees and devouring prey the size of SUVs. Fossil evidence, however, supports a more silent world. In fact, it wasn't until about 65 to 68 million years ago that a very important piece of anatomy developed—the syrinx. Think of it as a voice box.

In 1992, on an Antarctic island, scientists found a fossil of *Vegavis iaai*, a bird that lived between 68 and 65 million years ago. At that time in Earth's history, Antarctica had a tropical climate. It wasn't until recently that technology revealed the most important find in the fossil: a syrinx.

## Connections to Modern-Day Birds

The presence of a syrinx helps us to understand the ancestry of modern birds. Because of the asymmetrical structure of the syrinx, scientists speculate that the bird may have honked like a goose. Scientists analyzed the same structures in 12 living birds and compared them to the next oldest fossilized syrinx that was available. They found similarities in structure across the samples. Their findings supported the claim that *Vegavis iaai* was related to modern birds, but not an ancestor of modern reptiles, who are also able to vocalize through the larynx.

It would take a large brain to produce a selection of noises that meant something. If dinosaurs were able to vocalize or utter any sounds at all, then the sounds they made would have been a far cry from what you hear in the movies.

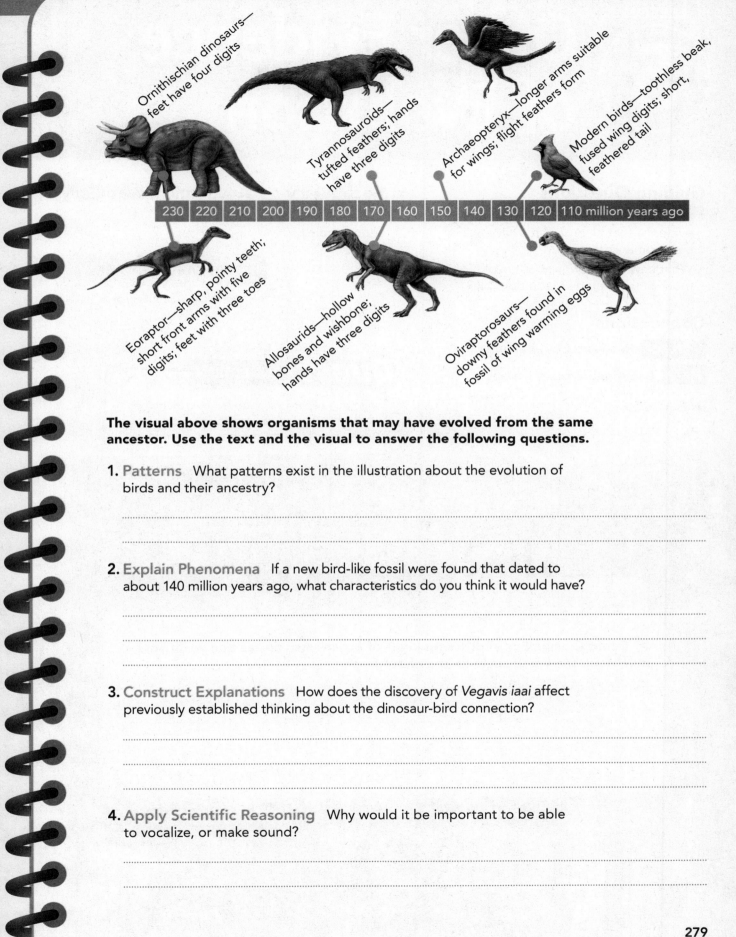

Ornithischian dinosaurs—feet have four digits

Tyrannosauroids—tufted feathers; hands have three digits

Archaeopteryx—longer arms suitable for wings; flight feathers form

Modern birds—toothless beak, fused wing digits; short, feathered tail

| 230 | 220 | 210 | 200 | 190 | 180 | 170 | 160 | 150 | 140 | 130 | 120 | 110 million years ago |

Eoraptor—sharp, pointy teeth; short front arms with five digits; feet with three toes

Allosaurids—hollow bones and wishbone; hands have three digits

Oviraptorosaurs—downy feathers found in fossil of wing warming eggs

**The visual above shows organisms that may have evolved from the same ancestor. Use the text and the visual to answer the following questions.**

1. **Patterns**   What patterns exist in the illustration about the evolution of birds and their ancestry?

.........................................................................................................................

.........................................................................................................................

2. **Explain Phenomena**   If a new bird-like fossil were found that dated to about 140 million years ago, what characteristics do you think it would have?

.........................................................................................................................

.........................................................................................................................

.........................................................................................................................

3. **Construct Explanations**   How does the discovery of *Vegavis iaai* affect previously established thinking about the dinosaur-bird connection?

.........................................................................................................................

.........................................................................................................................

.........................................................................................................................

4. **Apply Scientific Reasoning**   Why would it be important to be able to vocalize, or make sound?

.........................................................................................................................

.........................................................................................................................

# Other Evidence of Evolution

## Guiding Questions

- How does modern technology provide evidence that all organisms have a common ancestor?
- What new discoveries about evolution has modern technology made possible?

## Connections

**Literacy** Read and Comprehend

**Math** Use Algebraic Expressions

MS-LS4-2, MS-LS4-6

## Vocabulary

protein
endosymbiosis

## Academic Vocabulary

transfer

 **VOCABULARY APP**

Practice vocabulary on a mobile device.

### Quest CONNECTION

As you prepare your report, consider what factors might be causing the genetic variations. Look for evidence of change.

## Connect It !

✎ **Count the number of different kinds of organisms you see and write your number in the white circle on the photograph.**

**Evaluate Evidence** What do all the organisms in the photo have in common?

.......................................................................................................................................

.......................................................................................................................................

.......................................................................................................................................

# Using Technology to Study Evolution

Advances in technology have led to new knowledge about evolution. Darwin and scientists of his time used their eyes, hand tools, and simple microscopes to study evolution. Darwin's microscope had less than 200x magnification. Modern scientists have much better tools. We now have such powerful microscopes and imaging devices that computers can show us the shapes of individual molecules. Future advances may further our understanding of evolution.

**Genetic Material and Evolution** The coral reef in **Figure 1** contains an amazing variety of living things. The diverse shapes, body structures, and lifestyles are all due to differences in genetic material, the set of chemical instructions that guide the function and growth of an organism. Evolution results from changes in genetic material. Small changes in genetic material lead to microevolution within species. An accumulation of small changes causes macroevolution, or the creation of new species.

**INTERACTIVITY**

Discuss how a device or object you use every day has changed over time.

## Literacy Connection

**Read and Comprehend**
As you work your way through this lesson, stop frequently to see if you understand what you just read. Each paragraph has key information. Try to restate it in your own words.

**Rainbow of Life on a Reef**
**Figure 1** All of the differences among Earth's organisms result from evolutionary changes in genetic material.

281

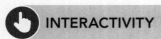 INTERACTIVITY

Explore how technological advances have helped to determine ancestral relationships.

## Genetic Evidence for a Common Ancestor

Every living thing uses DNA for genetic material. Mosquitoes, humans, plants, and bacteria all have cells with the same system of genetic material. The shared use of DNA is one piece of evidence that every organism on Earth has a common ancestor. This common ancestor, called LUCA for Last Universal Common Ancestor, was most likely a single-celled organism similar to modern bacteria or archaea.

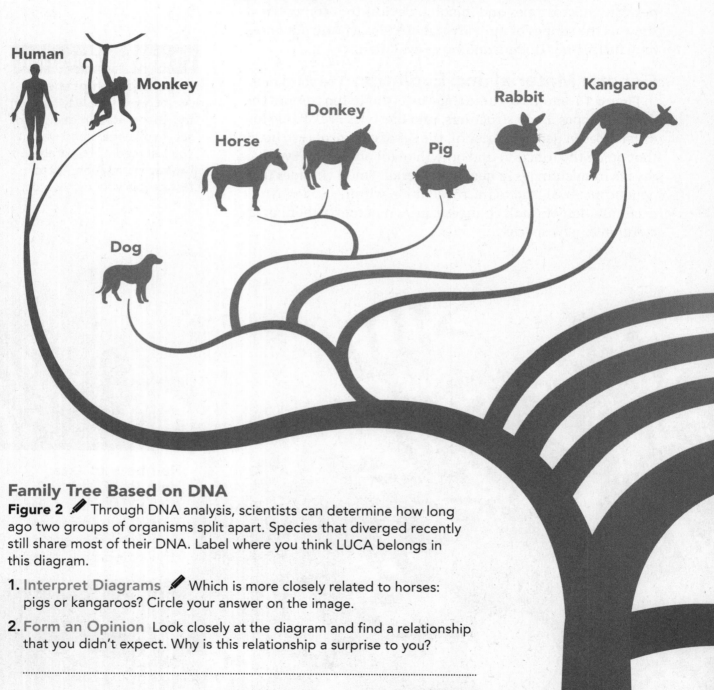

### Family Tree Based on DNA

**Figure 2** 🖊 Through DNA analysis, scientists can determine how long ago two groups of organisms split apart. Species that diverged recently still share most of their DNA. Label where you think LUCA belongs in this diagram.

1. **Interpret Diagrams** 🖊 Which is more closely related to horses: pigs or kangaroos? Circle your answer on the image.

2. **Form an Opinion** Look closely at the diagram and find a relationship that you didn't expect. Why is this relationship a surprise to you?

..................................................................................................

..................................................................................................

..................................................................................................

**Dawn of Evolution** DNA is a complex molecule, difficult to copy without making any mistakes. LUCA started to change as it accumulated mutations, or changes to its DNA. Natural selection and other processes shaped LUCA's evolution. The original population of LUCA split and diverged, evolving into all the species that live or have ever lived on Earth. The traces of this evolution are recorded in the DNA of every organism. Shared DNA between species provides evidence of the evolutionary past. The more similar the DNA between two species, the more closely related they are. **Figure 2** shows a family tree based on differences in one stretch of DNA.

**HANDS-ON LAB**

**Investigate** Explore how DNA provides evidence for evolution.

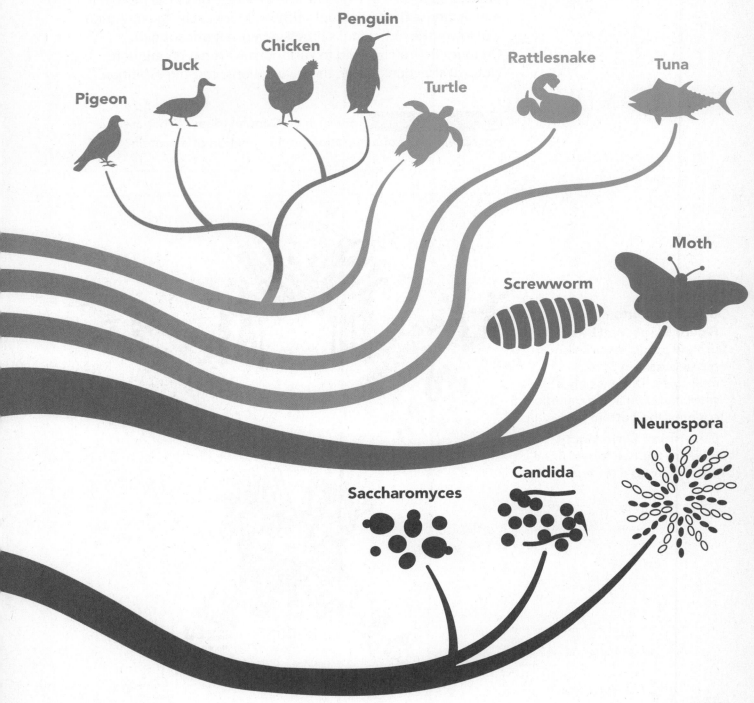

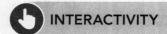

**INTERACTIVITY**

Explore how different types of evidence help to establish evolutionary relationships.

**Proteins** Recall that genes code for different **proteins**, which are complicated molecules that carry out important cellular functions. Proteins can act as the building blocks for cell materials and carry out important cellular functions. For example, some muscle fibers are made of chains of the protein actin. Other proteins act as messengers, fight diseases, carry out chemical reactions, or carry materials around the body.

**Proteins and Evolution** Consider what could happen to the function of a protein if the gene for it contains a mutation. The mutant genetic material may code for a different form of the protein, as shown in **Figure 3**. The new version of the protein may increase the individual's fitness. More likely, the mutation will lower the individual's fitness or leave it unchanged. Changes in proteins lead to variations within a population. Natural selection acts on those variations, causing evolution.

✓ **READING CHECK** **Determine Central Ideas** What are the possible effects of a mutation on the function of a protein?

...................................................................................................................

...................................................................................................................

## Mutations and Proteins

**Figure 3** The Mre11-Rad50 protein group helps cells to repair breaks in DNA molecules. There is only a small mutation in the genetic code for the bottom form.

**Determine Differences** How are the two forms of the protein group different?

.............................................

.............................................

.............................................

.............................................

.............................................

.............................................

.............................................

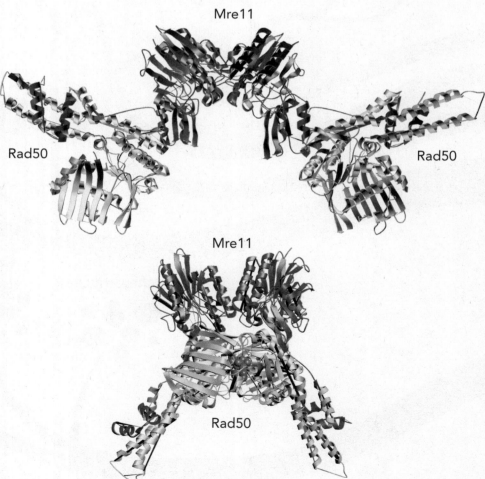

**Protein Analysis and Evolution** Scientists compare proteins to see how closely any two species are related. In most cases, evidence from DNA and protein structure confirms conclusions based on fossils, embryos, and body structure. For example, DNA comparisons show that dogs are more similar to wolves than to coyotes. This confirms an earlier conclusion based on similarities in the structure and development of the three species.

## Math Toolbox

## All in the Family

Humans, apes, and monkeys are all members of the order Primates. Bonobos, chimpanzees, gorillas, and orangutans are all considered apes, but monkeys are not. Humans and monkeys share about 93 percent of their DNA.

| Primate | Genetic Difference with Humans |
|---------|-------------------------------|
| Bonobo | 1.2% |
| Chimpanzee | 1.3% |
| Gorilla | 1.6% |
| Orangutan | 3.1% |
| Monkey | 7.0% |

1. **Use Algebraic Expressions** Write an expression representing the percentage of DNA that gorillas share with humans. Let $g$ = gorilla.

2. **Draw Comparative Inferences** What can you say about the evolutionary relationship between the apes and monkeys compared to humans?

## An Evolutionary Leap

**Figure 4** Normally, a new trait evolves over thousands of generations. In this case, bacteria species 2 gets a fully formed gene from a different species.

1. **Identify** ✏ Label the transferred gene in Species 2.

2. **Predict** Will the transferred gene be passed on to the next generation? Explain.

..............................................
..............................................
..............................................
..............................................

### Academic Vocabulary

You transfer your books from your locker into your school bag. How does this example help you understand what gene transfer is?

..............................................
..............................................
..............................................
..............................................

Species 1        Species 2

DNA

Antibiotic-resistance gene

## Gene Transfer Between Species

Individuals usually inherit DNA from their parent or parents. Surprisingly, scientists have discovered that genes can also pass between individuals from different species! The **transfer** of genes can happen when one cell engulfs another or when bacteria share their DNA with other cells. The transferred DNA is almost always destroyed. But occasionally, a cell adds the new genes to its DNA.

Bacteria use gene transfer to pass on adaptive traits. **Figure 4** shows how one bacterium can pass the trait of antibiotic resistance to a different species of bacteria. Being immune to antibiotics could provide a big boost for the bacterium in fitness for the bacterium. DNA analysis shows scientists which genes have passed from one species to another.

**Design It!**

### Designer Genes

By transferring helpful genes from one species directly into cells of another species, scientists can produce desired traits in an organism. This creates genetically modified organisms, or GMOs. Scientists have modified eggplant genes to produce an insect-resistant plant. Insects attacked the plants on the left, but not those that were modified on the right.

**Design Your Solution** ✏ Draw an organism that you think could benefit from gene transfer and modification to become the next GMO. Label its features and describe the benefits.

**Symbiosis** Two organisms of different species that have a close relationship that involves living with each other is called symbiosis. In endosymbiosis, shown in **Figure 5**, one organism actually moves inside the other organism's cell. Scientists have theorized that endosymbiosis may be the mechanism that allowed life to generate on Earth. Mitochondria (the cell's power house) and chloroplasts (they capture the sun's energy and store it as food) are both organelles. Just as a bacterium cell contains its own DNA and ribosomes, so do mitochondria and chloroplasts. Bacteria, mitochondria, and chloroplasts are also similar in size. Over millions of years of evolution, one type of bacteria became mitochondria and another type of bacteria became chloroplasts. At first, many scientists rejected the idea that mitochondria and chloroplasts had evolved from bacteria. Finally, advances in technology led to DNA sequencing that gave evidence supporting the hypothesis.

☑ READING CHECK **Read and Comprehend** What are two ways that genetic material can move from one species to another?

..................................................................................................

..................................................................................................

## Endosymbiosis

**Figure 5** Evidence supports the idea that both mitochondria and chloroplasts evolved through endosymbiosis.

1. **Integrate with Visuals** 🖉 Label what happens in the two missing steps.

2. **Relate Structure and Function** Chloroplasts are parts of plant cells that turn sunlight into chemical energy for food. Consider how bacteria became chloroplasts. How might the bacteria have benefited from the arrangement?

..................................................................................................

..................................................................................................

..................................................................................................

❶ There are two different bacteria cells.

❷ ..................................................................................................
..................................................................................................

❸ Now the larger cell has the smaller one living inside it.

❹ Both bacteria cells benefit.

❺ ..................................................................................................
..................................................................................................

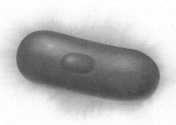

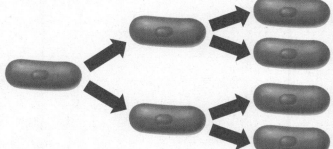

# ☑ LESSON 5 Check

MS-LS4-2, MS-LS4-6

1. **Identify** What evidence is there that every organism on Earth once had a common ancestor?

........................................................................

........................................................................

2. **Compare and Contrast** What do microevolution and macroevolution have in common? How do they differ?

........................................................................

........................................................................

........................................................................

........................................................................

3. **Synthesize Information** How have advances in technology supported the theory of evolution?

........................................................................

........................................................................

........................................................................

........................................................................

........................................................................

4. **Construct Explanations** How does natural selection influence evolution through mutations?

........................................................................

........................................................................

........................................................................

........................................................................

........................................................................

5. **Support Your Explanation** What does LUCA stand for and how did it evolve into all the life forms we see today?

........................................................................

........................................................................

........................................................................

........................................................................

........................................................................

........................................................................

........................................................................

........................................................................

# Quest CHECK-IN

**In this lesson, you learned more about how genetics drives evolution and how mutations to proteins lead to variations within a population.**

**Apply Scientific Reasoning** What caused changes to the blackcap populations? How was natural selection at work here?

........................................................................

........................................................................

........................................................................

........................................................................

........................................................................

## 👆 INTERACTIVITY

Prepare Your Report

**Go online** to investigate the European blackcaps. Look for new information to add to your report. Brainstorm ideas for different ways to represent information.

MS-LS4-2, MS-LS4-4, MS-LS4-5

# DNA, Fossils, and
# Evolution

**A**ll living things contain DNA. This blueprint carries the codes for every trait an organism expresses. We now have the technology to extract DNA from living things, as well as fossils, and then map out the locations of all the genes. By comparing modern DNA with that of fossils, it is possible to determine which traits similar species have in common.

Scientists are able to remove and analyze DNA from fossils using a process called an assay. DNA is removed from the center of a fossil and then prepared using an assortment of different chemicals. The DNA sample is then amplified and run through a process called gel electrophoresis. This separates different pieces of the DNA. The results are then compared to known DNA to see how similar they are.

One of the interesting things DNA research has discovered is that the domestication of dogs has changed their diet. While ancestral wolves ate mostly meat, modern dogs have more genes to help them digest starch and other carbohydrates. This suggests that the early dogs who could handle the starches in the human diet had an advantage.

## MY DISCOVERY

With a classmate, research how dogs were domesticated from wolves. Engage in a classroom debate about the evidence that supports and refutes the descent of dogs from wolves.

DNA evidence from wolf fossils, like the one shown here, helps to determine the similarities and differences between domestic dogs and their wolf ancestors.

# ☑ TOPIC 5 Review and Assess

## 1 Early Study of Evolution

MS-LS4-4

1. Adaptations and variations show evidence of past
   A. evolution.
   B. offspring.
   C. diversity.
   D. fossils.

2. Who made the first attempt at developing a theory of evolution?
   A. Anning
   B. Darwin
   C. Lamarck
   D. Lyell

3. On his five-year journey sailing around the world, Darwin was amazed by the ............................................ of living things that he saw.

4. A species is a group of similar ............................................ that can mate with each other and produce offspring capable of

   ............................................ .

5. **Construct Explanations** Consider what caused the variation in finch beaks on the Galápagos Islands. How did it bring about new species of birds?

   ................................................................................
   ................................................................................
   ................................................................................
   ................................................................................
   ................................................................................
   ................................................................................
   ................................................................................
   ................................................................................
   ................................................................................
   ................................................................................
   ................................................................................

## 2 Natural Selection

MS-LS4-4, MS-LS4-5, MS-LS4-6

6. Darwin was able to create the fantail pigeon from the wild rock dove by using
   A. artificial selection.
   B. mechanisms.
   C. natural selection.
   D. overproduction.

7. Darwin observed that some variations make individuals better adapted
   A. to accumulate traits.
   B. to their environment.
   C. for population change.
   D. for more mutations.

8. Helpful variations may ............................................ in a population, while unfavorable ones may disappear.

9. Natural selection is affected by three factors: ............................................ , variations among members of the population, and

   ............................................ .

10. **Explain Phenomenon** How do environmental factors contribute to evolution by natural selection?

    ................................................................................
    ................................................................................
    ................................................................................
    ................................................................................
    ................................................................................
    ................................................................................
    ................................................................................
    ................................................................................
    ................................................................................
    ................................................................................
    ................................................................................

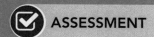

# ③ The Process of Evolution

MS-LS4-4, MS-LS4-6

**11.** Unlike an organism with low fitness, an organism with high fitness has the ability to survive and
   **A.** mutate.
   **B.** coevolve.
   **C.** reproduce.
   **D.** interact.

**12.** Because they create multiple alleles, mutations can cause
   **A.** cell division.
   **B.** damaged DNA to repair itself.
   **C.** overproduction of offspring.
   **D.** variations in traits.

**13.** ........................................................, a mechanism of evolution, is a random, directionless process.

**14.** Mutations can occur when an organism is exposed to ........................................ or certain chemicals that damage the cell's ........................................ .

**15. Distinguish Relationships** Consider two species that compete for the same resources. Might their interactions affect each other's evolution? Explain.

........................................................................
........................................................................
........................................................................
........................................................................
........................................................................
........................................................................
........................................................................
........................................................................

# ④ Evidence in the Fossil Record

MS-LS4-1, MS-LS4-2, MS-LS4-3, MS-LS4-6

**16.** Evidence supporting biological evolution is found in the fossil record and in
   **A.** adaptations to changing environments.
   **B.** similar anatomies and embryos.
   **C.** offspring with various traits.
   **D.** layers of sediment.

**17. Support Your Explanations** What can you infer about this fossilized organism and its environment?

........................................................................
........................................................................
........................................................................
........................................................................
........................................................................
........................................................................
........................................................................

# ⑤ Other Evidence of Evolution

MS-LS4-2, MS-LS4-6

**18.** Evolution results from changes in
   **A.** genetic material.     **B.** migration patterns.
   **C.** habitats and climate.   **D.** the fossil record.

**19. Apply Scientific Reasoning** DNA comparisons show that dogs are more similar to wolves than to coyotes. How else could scientists confirm their close relationship?

........................................................................
........................................................................
........................................................................

MS-LS4-1, MS-LS4-4,
MS-LS4-6

## Evidence-Based Assessment

A group of scientists was researching evolutionary relationships. They decided to investigate a particular protein called cytochrome-c. They compared the amino acid sequence that codes for the protein among several species. They made a surprising discovery. In moths, whales, and Baker's yeast—organisms that do not look at all related—almost half of the positions in the cytochrome-c amino acid sequence were identical.

Cytochrome-c is a very important protein when it comes to releasing energy from food. Like other proteins, cytochrome-c is made of a sequence of amino acids that may or may not vary among organisms. The analysis of cytochrome-c in different organisms provides strong evidence for determining which organisms are closely related. Scientists can predict evolutionary relationships by looking at the amino acid sequences in cytochrome-c that different organisms have in common.

The data table shows ten positions where there are different amino acids in the sequence that codes for the cytochrome-c protein from five different species. In all other positions, the amino acids are the same.

| Species | Amino Acid, Position Number in Sequence | | | | | | | | | |
|---|---|---|---|---|---|---|---|---|---|---|
| | 20 | 23 | 52 | 55 | 66 | 68 | 70 | 91 | 97 | 100 |
| human | M | S | P | S | I | G | D | V | E | A |
| horse | Q | A | P | S | T | L | E | A | T | E |
| kangaroo | Q | A | P | T | I | G | D | A | G | A |
| pig | Q | A | P | S | T | G | E | A | G | E |
| whale | Q | A | V | S | T | G | E | A | G | A |

SOURCE: National Center for Biotechnology Information

### Amino Acid Symbols

A = Alanine          M = Methionine
D = Aspartic Acid    P = Proline
E = Glutamic Acid    Q = Glutamine
G = Glycine          S = Serine
I = Isoleucine       T = Threonine
L = Lysine           V = Valine

1. **Analyze Data** According to cytochrome-c analysis, to which other species is the pig most closely related?
   A. human
   B. horse
   C. kangaroo
   D. whale

2. **Support Your Explanation** How did you determine the pig's closest relation among the four species? Use evidence from the data table to support your claim.

   ........................................................
   ........................................................
   ........................................................
   ........................................................
   ........................................................
   ........................................................
   ........................................................
   ........................................................
   ........................................................
   ........................................................
   ........................................................
   ........................................................
   ........................................................
   ........................................................

3. **Cite Evidence** According to cytochrome-c analysis, which organism is least like the others? Cite evidence to support your claim.

   ........................................................
   ........................................................
   ........................................................
   ........................................................
   ........................................................
   ........................................................
   ........................................................
   ........................................................
   ........................................................

4. **Construct Arguments** Cows and sheep have the same sequence of amino acids in their cytochrome-c protein. How is it possible that they can be different species?

   ........................................................
   ........................................................
   ........................................................
   ........................................................
   ........................................................
   ........................................................
   ........................................................
   ........................................................
   ........................................................
   ........................................................
   ........................................................

# Quest FINDINGS

## Complete the Quest!

**Phenomenon** Create a multimedia report about the two populations of European blackcaps and what caused them to be so different from each other.

**Draw Conclusions** If evolution continues, what can be said about the common ancestry of both populations of European blackcaps?

........................................................
........................................................
........................................................
........................................................

**INTERACTIVITY**

Reflect on Blackcap Migration

MS-LS4-2, MS-LS4-4

# A Bony Puzzle

How can you analyze **patterns** in structures to **show** evolutionary **relationships?**

## Materials

(per group)
- Activity Sheets 1, 2, and 3
- ruler

## Background

**Phenomenon** A new museum of natural history is opening in your community. The director of the museum has asked your class to help with an exhibit about evolutionary history. The director hopes you can show how patterns in skeletons provide clues about common ancestors.

In this investigation, you will analyze and compare the internal and external structures of a pigeon, a bat, and a rabbit. Then you will use the similarities and differences you observe to describe a possible common ancestor and infer evolutionary relationships among these organisms.

Rock pigeon (*Columba livia*)

Eastern cottontail rabbit (*Sylvilagus floridanus*)

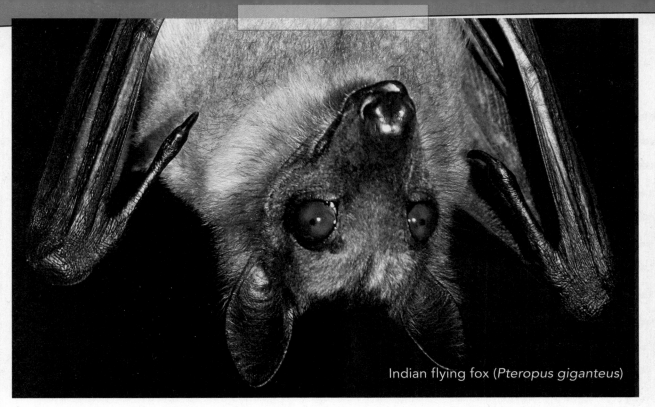

Indian flying fox (*Pteropus giganteus*)

## Plan Your Investigation

☐ 1. Using the photographs and the diagrams, you will compare the features and structures of the pigeon, bat, and rabbit. You will look for patterns in the skeletons and note similarities and differences among the three animals.

☐ 2. Work with your group to plan a procedure for comparing the skeletons of the three animals. Write out your plan in the space provided. Consider the following questions as a guide for planning your procedure:

- Should we compare all the bones shown in the diagrams or select a few important features that they all have in common to compare?

- Do we also want to include our observations from the photographs of the animals?

- What's the best way to record and organize our observations so we can analyze them more easily? Should we write notes summarizing what we see? Or should we use only data tables to organize the data?

☐ 3. After receiving your teacher's approval, follow the procedure your group developed. Remember that you may need to revise the plan as you carry it out. Record your observations about the three skeletons in the data tables.

### HANDS-ON LAB

и**Demonstrate** Go online for a downloadable worksheet of this lab.

## Procedure

## Observations

| Skeleton | Similarities | Differences |
|----------|--------------|-------------|
| Spine | | |
| Skull | | |
| Limbs | | |

| Photos | Similarities | Differences |
|--------|--------------|-------------|
| covering | | |
| faces | | |
| other | | |

# Analyze and Interpret Data

1. **Identify Patterns** What evidence did you find that will help you describe how these three skeletons are alike?

   ....................................................................................................................
   ....................................................................................................................
   ....................................................................................................................
   ....................................................................................................................

2. **Evaluate Evidence** How does the skeleton pattern that you identified provide evidence for a common ancestor among the pigeon, bat, and rabbit?

   ....................................................................................................................
   ....................................................................................................................
   ....................................................................................................................
   ....................................................................................................................

3. **Explain Phenomena** Which bones of the common ancestor do you think might have changed the most in its descendants? Which bones remained about the same? Cite evidence from the skeleton diagrams to support your answer.

   ....................................................................................................................
   ....................................................................................................................
   ....................................................................................................................
   ....................................................................................................................

4. **Apply Scientific Reasoning** How are the wings of the bat and the bird, and the rabbit's front legs, all examples of homologous structures? Use evidence from your investigation to support your answer.

   ....................................................................................................................
   ....................................................................................................................
   ....................................................................................................................
   ....................................................................................................................

5. **Construct Explanations** The museum exhibit will include information to explain evolutionary relationships. What evidence can you use to show that bats share a more recent common ancestor with rabbits than they do with birds?

   ....................................................................................................................
   ....................................................................................................................
   ....................................................................................................................

**NGSS PERFORMANCE EXPECTATION**

**MS-ESS1-4** Construct a scientific explanation based on evidence from rock strata for how the geologic time scale is used to organize Earth's 4.6-billion-year-old history.

### HANDS-ON LAB

uConnect Develop a timeline of the major events in the life of a family member.

What do these fossils reveal about Earth's past?

GO ONLINE
to access your digital course

▶ VIDEO

👆 INTERACTIVITY

🧪 VIRTUAL LAB

☑ ASSESSMENT

📖 eTEXT

📱 APP

## The Essential Question

# How can events in Earth's past be organized?

Earth has changed a lot since these ammonites swam the ocean. Our planet has changed even more since it first formed. How do scientists find out about events in Earth's history? Identify several things that you think scientists study to find out how Earth has changed over time.

.................................................................................................

.................................................................................................

.................................................................................................

.................................................................................................

.................................................................................................

# Quest KICKOFF

## How do paleontologists know where to look for fossils?

**Phenomenon** Dr. Digg is the head paleontologist at a museum. She has hired you to help the museum set up a new exhibit on an extinct genus of ancient animal called *Dimetrodon*. Where in the world can you find *Dimetrodon* fossils to form the centerpiece of the exhibit? Fossils are found all over Earth, and you can't dig up the entire planet. In this problem-based Quest activity, you will choose a dig site that is likely to produce fossils of *Dimetrodon*. You will evaluate information about four sites, using information about rock layers and other fossils found at those sites to narrow the choices down. In a final report, you will share your evaluations of each site and give reasons for choosing one site and rejecting the other three.

 INTERACTIVITY

The Big Fossil Hunt

**MS-ESS1-4** Construct a scientific explanation based on evidence from rock strata for how the geologic time scale is used to organize Earth's 4.6-billion-year-old history.

 NBC LEARN ▶ VIDEO

After viewing the Quest Kickoff video and watching a paleontologist at work, complete the concept map by recording four things that you should consider when exploring for fossils.

How to Find Fossils

---

# Quest CHECK-INS

## IN LESSON 1

What do paleontologists learn from layers of rock and the organisms found within those layers? Gather clues to find the best dig site.

 INTERACTIVITY

Clues in the Rock Layers

 INTERACTIVITY

Fossils Around the World

# Quest CHECK-IN

## IN LESSON 2

How do paleontologists use the geologic time scale to help find fossils? Explore how scientists use information from already-discovered fossils to predict where other fossils might be.

 HANDS-ON LAB

A Matter of Time

The Carnegie Dinosaur Quarry is a dig site within the Dinosaur National Monument in Utah. Paleontologists excavate and preserve dinosaur fossils that range from 148 to 155 million years old.

## Quest CHECK-IN

### IN LESSON 3

How do paleontologists use information about ancient organisms to determine where to search for fossils? Conduct research and make a final selection of a dig site for *Dimetrodon*.

👆 **INTERACTIVITY**

Time to Choose the Dig Site

## Quest FINDINGS

### Complete the Quest!

Prepare a report in which you evaluate each site and give reasons for choosing or rejecting that site.

👆 **INTERACTIVITY**

Reflect on the Big Fossil Hunt

# 1 Determining Ages of Rocks

## Guiding Questions

- How do geologists describe the ages of rocks?
- How do geologists determine the relative ages of rocks?
- How do geologists determine the absolute ages of rocks?

## Connections

**Literacy** Write Explanatory Texts

**Math** Write an Expression

MS-ESS1-4

## Vocabulary

relative age
absolute age
law of superposition
fossil
unconformity
radioactive decay
radioactive dating

## Academic Vocabulary

relative
infer

 **VOCABULARY APP**

Practice vocabulary on a mobile device.

### Quest CONNECTION

Consider how knowing more about the ages of rocks and fossils can help you decide where to look for another fossil.

## Connect It!

✏ **How many rock layers do you see? Draw an arrow pointing from the youngest rock to the oldest rock.**

**Construct Explanations** How did you decide which rocks are the youngest and oldest?

.................................................................................................................

.................................................................................................................

.................................................................................................................

**Apply Scientific Reasoning** Suppose you were the first person to study the canyon. How could you find out exactly how old the oldest rock is?

.................................................................................................................

.................................................................................................................

.................................................................................................................

# Describing the Ages of Rocks

If you visit the Painted Desert in Arizona, you will find rock layers that look grey, red, green, blue, and even purple. If you're curious, you might start by asking "How did these colorful rocks form?" Your next question would probably be "How old are these rocks?" In other words, you would want to describe the ages of the rocks. Geologists have two ways to describe the age of a rock: age **relative** to another rock and age in number of years since the rock formed.

## Relative Age

The **relative age** of a rock is its age compared to the ages of other rocks. You probably use the idea of relative age when you compare your age with someone else's. For example, if you say that you are older than your brother but younger than your sister, you describe your relative age.

## Absolute Age

The relative age of a rock does not provide its absolute age. The **absolute age** of a rock is the number of years that have passed since the rock formed. It may be impossible to know the exact absolute age of some rocks, so geologists often use both absolute and relative ages.

Why do geologists want to analyze and describe the ages of rocks? Evidence of past events occurs in rocks. That evidence shows that Earth has changed and evolved over time due to natural processes. Rock layers like those in **Figure 1** form a record of Earth's history of change, known as the geologic record. By studying clues in Earth's rocks and determining their ages, geologist can organize past events in sequence to better understand Earth's history.

✔ **READING CHECK** **Summarize** What is the difference between relative age and absolute age?

...............................................................................................

...............................................................................................

...............................................................................................

### Academic Vocabulary

Describe your location relative to an object or another person in the room.

...............................................................

...............................................................

...............................................................

## Rainbow of Rock Layers

**Figure 1** Many colorful rock layers make up the hills of Arizona's Painted Desert. These rock layers represent many millions of years of Earth's history.

INTERACTIVITY

Examine a sequence of rock layers to learn their relative ages.

# Determining Relative Ages of Rocks

Geologists use many methods to determine the age of Earth's rocks. To find a rock's relative age, they analyze the position of rock layers. They also look for a variety of clues in rocks, such as fossils. These methods provide ways to find relative ages, but not absolute ages, of rocks.

**Position of Rock Layers** Sedimentary rock usually forms in horizontal layers, or strata. Geologists use the **law of superposition** to determine the relative ages of sedimentary rock layers. According to the law of superposition, in undisturbed horizontal sedimentary rock layers, the oldest layer is at the bottom and the youngest layer is at the top. The higher you go, the younger the rocks are. The lower or deeper you go, the older the rocks are.

**Clues from Igneous Rocks** Magma is molten material beneath Earth's surface. Lava (magma that reaches the surface) can harden on the surface to form an igneous extrusion. Magma can also push into layers of rock below the surface. The magma can harden and form an igneous intrusion, like the one shown in **Figure 2**. An extrusion is younger than the rock it covers. An intrusion is younger than the rock around it.

**Clues from Faults** More clues come from the study of faults. A fault, like the one shown in **Figure 2**, is a break in Earth's crust. Forces inside Earth cause movement of the rock on opposite sides of a fault. A fault is always younger than the rock it cuts through. To determine the relative age of a fault, geologists find the relative age of the youngest layer cut by the fault.

**Clues Within Rocks**

**Figure 2** ✏ Intrusions and faults can help to determine a sequence of events within rock layers. Draw an X over the igneous intrusion. Draw a line along a fault.

**Compare and Contrast** ✏ The rock layers are (older/younger) than any faults or intrusions that run through them.

Igneous Intrusion

Faults

**Using Fossils** The preserved remains or traces of living things are called **fossils**. They most often occur in layers of sedimentary rock. Fossils preserved in rock layers provide physical evidence about the history of life on Earth and how Earth has changed over time.

Certain fossils, called index fossils, help geologists to match and date rock layers, even if those layers are far apart or in different locations. An index fossil is a fossil of an organism that was widely distributed and existed for a geologically short period of time. Fossils from organisms that lived for a long geologic time might show up in multiple rock layers, but index fossils show up in only a few layers. Index fossils are useful because they tell the relative ages of the rock layers in which they occur. Geologists **infer** that layers with matching index fossils are the same age.

You can use index fossils to match rock layers and find their relative age. Look at the diagram in **Figure 3,** which shows rock layers from four different locations. Notice that two of the fossils are found in only one rock layer. These are index fossils.

**INTERACTIVITY**

Use index fossils to decode Earth's history.

**Academic Vocabulary**

Think about a pet you saw recently. What can you infer about the animal's age? Explain your answer.

..............................................

..............................................

..............................................

..............................................

# Model It!

## Using Fossils to Match Rock Layers

**Figure 3** You can model how scientists use index fossils to match rock layers separated by distance.

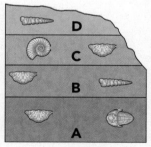 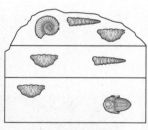 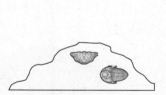 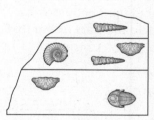

Location 1          Location 2          Location 3          Location 4

1. **Interpret Diagrams** 🖊 At Location 1, circle the fossils that you can use as index fossils.

2. **Use Models** 🖊 Use the index fossils at Location 1 to label the matching layers at Locations 2–4. Then, draw a line to connect each matching layer across all locations and shade them the same color.

3. **Apply Concepts** At Location 4, what can you infer about the ages of rocks and history? Cite evidence to support your inference.

.............................................................................

.............................................................................

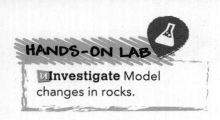

☐ **Investigate** Model changes in rocks.

## Changes in Rocks

The geologic record of sedimentary rock layers is not complete. In fact, erosion destroyed most of Earth's geologic record over billions of years. Gaps in the geologic record and folding can change the position in which rock layers appear. As was shown in **Figure 2**, motion along faults can also change how rock layers line up. These changes make it harder for scientists to reconstruct Earth's history. **Figure 4** shows how the order of rock layers may change.

**Gaps in the Geologic Record** When rock layers erode, an older rock surface may be exposed. Then deposition begins again, building new rock layers. The surface where new rock layers meet a much older rock surface beneath them is called an unconformity. An **unconformity** is a gap in the geologic record. It shows where rock layers have been lost due to erosion.

**Folding** Sometimes, forces inside Earth fold rock layers so much that the layers are turned over completely. In this case, the youngest rock layers may be on the bottom!

Samples from many different areas are needed to give a complete geologic record. Geologists compare rock layers in many places to understand a complete sequence.

☑ **READING CHECK** **Write Explanatory Texts** In you own words, explain one of the methods that geologists use to find the relative ages of rocks.

..........................................................................................................

..........................................................................................................

..........................................................................................................

### Literacy Connection

**Write Explanatory Texts** Underline the sentences in the text that explain how the rock layers in **Figure 4** changed.

### Unconformity and Folding

**Figure 4** 🖊 Shade the oldest and youngest layers in the last two diagrams. Label the unconformity. Circle the part of the fold that is overturned.

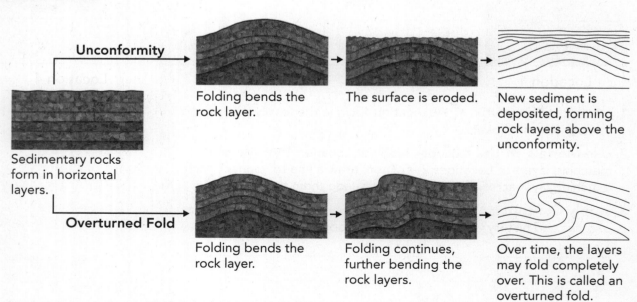

Sedimentary rocks form in horizontal layers.

Unconformity

Folding bends the rock layer.

The surface is eroded.

New sediment is deposited, forming rock layers above the unconformity.

Overturned Fold

Folding bends the rock layer.

Folding continues, further bending the rock layers.

Over time, the layers may fold completely over. This is called an overturned fold.

# Determining Absolute Ages of Rocks

Geologist use different methods to determine the absolute age of Earth's rocks. To find a rock's absolute age, they use certain elements in rocks that change over time.

**Radioactive Decay** An element is said to be radioactive when its particles become unstable and release energy in the form of radiation. This process is called radioactive decay. During **radioactive decay**, the atoms of one element break down to form atoms of another element.

Radioactive elements occur naturally in some igneous rocks. As an unstable radioactive element decays, it slowly changes into a stable element. The amount of the radioactive element decreases, but the amount of the new element increases, causing the overall composition of elements in the rock to change.

Each radioactive element decays at its own constant rate, represented by its half-life. The half-life of a radioactive element measures the time it takes for half of the radioactive atoms to decay. You can see in **Figure 5** how a radioactive element decays over time. Scientists use the half-life ratio to calculate the age of the rock in which a radioactive element is found.

**Reflect** Think about rocks you have collected, or buildings, statues, or landforms made of rock that you have seen. For which rock would you like to find the absolute age? Record this in your science notebook.

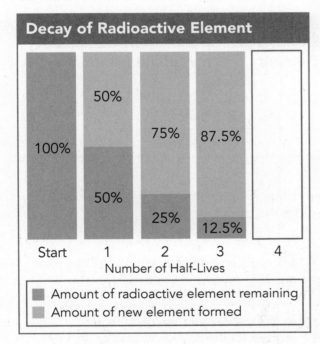

**Decay of Radioactive Element**

100% | 50% | 75% | 87.5% |
 | 50% | 25% | 12.5% |

Start | 1 | 2 | 3 | 4
Number of Half-Lives

■ Amount of radioactive element remaining
■ Amount of new element formed

## Radioactive Decay and Half-Life
**Figure 5** This is a sample element that illustrates radioactive decay.

**Radioactive Decay**

Unstable atom → Energy and particles / Energy and particles → New atom

1. **Analyze Graphs** ✎ What pattern do you see in the graph? Use the pattern to complete the last bar.

2. **Analyze Proportional Relationships** ✎ The graph shows that as the amount of the old radioactive element (increases/decreases), the amount of the new stable element (increases/decreases).

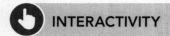

INTERACTIVITY

Use radioactive dating to determine the absolute age of different objects.

✓ READING CHECK

**Determine Central Ideas**
Underline the main idea in the first paragraph.

**Radioactive Dating** Geologists use **radioactive dating**, or radiometric dating, to determine the absolute ages of rocks. In radioactive dating, scientists first determine the amount of a radioactive element in a rock sample. Then they compare that with the amount of the stable element into which the radioactive element decays. They use this information and the half-life of the element to calculate the age of the rock.

**Potassium-Argon Dating** Scientists often date rocks using potassium-40. This form of potassium decays to stable argon-40 and has a half-life of 1.3 billion years. Potassium-40 is useful in dating the most ancient rocks because of its long half-life.

**Carbon-14 Dating** Scientists can date plant and animal remains using carbon-14. All organisms contain carbon, including this radioactive form. Carbon-14 decays to stable nitrogen-14 and has a half-life of only 5,730 years. Therefore, this method can't be used to date remains older than about 50,000 years because the amount of carbon-14 left would be too small to measure accurately.

# Math Toolbox

## Using Radioactive Dating to Calculate Absolute Age

A rock contains 25 percent of the potassium-40 it started with. Use radioactive dating to calculate the absolute age.

**Step 1. Determine how many half-lives have passed.** After one half-life, 50 percent of the potassium would remain. After two half-lives, 25% of the potassium would remain.

**Step 2. Find the half-life of potassium-40.** The half-life of potassium-40 is 1.3 billion years.

**Step 3. Multiply the half-life by the number of half-lives that have passed to calculate the rock's age.** 1.3 billion years × 2 half-lives = 2.6 billion years old.

| Elements Used in Radioactive Dating | |
| --- | --- |
| **Radioactive Element** | **Half-life (years)** |
| Carbon-14 | 5,730 |
| Potassium-40 | 1.3 billion |
| Uranium-235 | 713 million |

1. Calculate  A bone contains 12.5 percent of the carbon-14 it began with. How old is the bone?

..................................................................

2. Interpret Data  A rock is determined to be 1.426 billion years old. How much uranium-235 remains in the rock?

..................................................................

3. Write an Expression  If X represents the half-life of potassium–40 and Y represents the half-life of carbon-14, write an expression that correctly compares the two half-lives.

..................................................................

1. **Identify** What method do geologists use to find the absolute ages of rocks?

........................................................................

2. **Explain** How could a geologist match the rock layers in one area to rock layers found in another area?

........................................................................

........................................................................

........................................................................

........................................................................

3. **Compare and Contrast** A layer of sandstone sits above two other layers of rock. A fault cuts through the two lower layers of rock. How does the age of the fault compare with the ages of all three rock layers?

........................................................................

........................................................................

........................................................................

........................................................................

4. **Construct an Explanation** A geologist observes rock layers that are folded. She determines that a layer of siltstone is younger than the layer of limestone above it. How can you explain the geologist's findings?

........................................................................

........................................................................

........................................................................

........................................................................

........................................................................

5. **Apply Scientific Reasoning** A scientist finds tools made of rock in the ruins of an ancient home. He also finds burned wood likely cut by the tools in the home's fire pit. How could the scientist estimate when the tools were made?

........................................................................

........................................................................

........................................................................

........................................................................

# Quest CHECK-INS

**In this lesson, you learned how geologists find the ages of rocks and how events and fossil histories are recorded within the rock layers.**

**Explain** How can information from rock layers give you clues about where to look for additional fossils?

........................................................................

........................................................................

........................................................................

........................................................................

........................................................................

### INTERACTIVITIES

• Clues in the Rock Layers
• Fossils Around the World

**Go online** to think about the layers of rock at the dig sites and to consider how knowing more about the ages of rocks and fossils can help you to choose where to look for another fossil.

MS-ESS1-4

# REWRITING THE HISTORY OF
# Your Food

Modern tomatillos

If you have ever eaten salsa verde with your tacos, then you have likely eaten a tomatillo (toh mah TEE yoh). Related to husk tomatoes and ground cherries, modern tomatillos have a paper-thin husk covering their berry-shaped fruit.

Tomatillos are members of the plant genus *Physalis*, a small part of the nightshade family. This family includes many plants that we eat, including peppers, eggplants, and potatoes, and some too dangerous to eat, such as the poisonous belladonna plant.

Until recently, the evolution of these plants was poorly understood. Because many parts of the plants decompose easily, the fossil record is limited. Based on those limited fossils, scientists inferred that plants similar to tomatillos and ground cherries evolved fairly recently, about 9 to 11 million years ago.

However, scientist rewrote the tomatillo's history with a recent discovery from Patagonia, a region that covers southern Argentina and Chile. An international team collected thousands of fossils to study the evolutionary relationship between extinct and living organisms. Among the samples, they found two fossils of husked fruit, ancestors of the modern tomatillo.

The fossils were preserved in sediment deposited in an ancient lake near a volcano. Based on radioactive, or radiometric, dating of volcanic rocks found with the fossils, scientists concluded that ancestral tomatillos are actually more than 50 million years old! These plants existed in southern South America when the region was close to Antarctica and had a warm and wet climate—very different from its modern dry, cool climate. So enjoy some salsa verde and appreciate just how long the ancestors of those tomatillos have been growing on Earth!

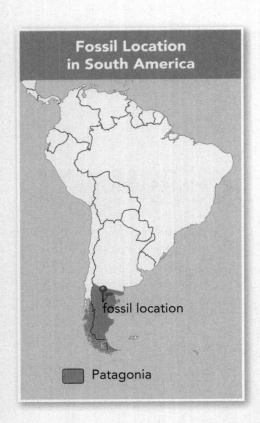

**Fossil Location in South America**

fossil location

Patagonia

## Tomatillo Group Fossil Record

| | Previously-Discovered Fossils | Newly-Discovered Fossils |
|---|---|---|
| **Plant Parts Preserved** | Tiny seeds and wood | Husks and fruit |
| **Approximate Age** | 9 to 11 million years old | 52 million years old |
| **Dating Method Used** | Molecular dating (uses rates of change and DNA to determine when organisms evolved) based on modern plants and fossils | Argon-argon dating (a newer variation of potassium-argon dating) of volcanic rocks found with the fossils |

**Use the text and table to answer the following questions.**

1. **Summarize** Based on new data, what conclusion did scientists draw about the tomatillo and nightshade plant family?

2. **Calculate** About how much older are the newly-discovered plant fossils compared to the age of previously discovered fossils?

3. **Cite Evidence** What evidence supports the scientists' conclusion about the age of the husk fruits and the nightshade family overall?

4. **Construct Explanations** How has radioactive dating helped to change our understanding of Earth's history? Use evidence from the fossil discovery to support your answer.

## Guiding Questions

- What is the purpose of the geologic time scale?
- How do events help geologists define and divide geologic time?

## Connection

**Literacy** Write Informative Texts

MS-ESS1-4

## Vocabulary

geologic time scale
era
period

## Academic Vocabulary

organize
refine

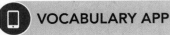 **VOCABULARY APP**

Practice vocabulary on a mobile device.

**Quest** CONNECTION

Think about how you could use the geologic time scale to organize information about fossils and narrow down the potential dig sites.

## Connect It !

✏ **Circle the unconformity. What does it tell you about the history of this location?**

**Interpret Photos** What can you infer about the history based on these rocks?

.................................................................................................

.................................................................................................

**Explain** How could you use the information in these rocks to organize events in Earth's history?

.................................................................................................

.................................................................................................

.................................................................................................

# The Geologic Time Scale

When you speak of the past, what names do you use for different spans of time? You probably use names such as century, decade, year, month, week, and day. But these units aren't very helpful for thinking about much longer periods of time—such as the 4.6 billion years of Earth's history.

To **organize** this vast number of years into manageable periods, scientists created the geologic time scale. The **geologic time scale** is a record of the geologic events and the evolution of life forms as shown in the rock and fossil records. Notice that it is a timeline—a model of the relative order of events over a long period of time that might otherwise be difficult to study.

Scientists first developed the geologic time scale by studying rock layers and index fossils worldwide. They gathered evidence using methods of determining the relative ages of rocks, such as evidence from unconformities as in **Figure 1**. With this evidence, scientists placed Earth's rocks in order by relative age. Later, they used radioactive dating to help them determine the absolute age of the divisions in the geologic time scale.

✅ **READING CHECK** **Summarize Text** How do scientists organize Earth's history and what evidence do they use?

........................................................................

........................................................................

........................................................................

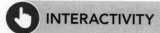

👆 **INTERACTIVITY**

Consider the best way to represent the geologic time scale.

**Academic Vocabulary**

Describe how you organize something in your life. Compare the state of that thing before and after you organized it.

........................................................................

........................................................................

........................................................................

........................................................................

........................................................................

**A Gap in Time**
**Figure 1** This unconformity represents a gap in geologic time of about 65 million years. The remaining rocks tell the story of how Earth evolved over geologic time.

313

## The Geologic Time Scale

**Figure 2** The geologic time scale is based on physical evidence from rock and fossil records that show how Earth has evolved over geologic time. The divisions of the geologic time scale are used to organize events in Earth's history.

1. **Calculate** 🖊 After you read the rest of the lesson, calculate and fill in the duration of each period.

2. **Use Models** 🖊 Use the time scale to identify the period in which each organism pictured below lived.

3. **Develop Models** 🖊 Draw lines from each fossil or rock pictured on the right to the part of the time scale that represents when it formed.

### Precambrian Time

### Paleozoic Era

| Period | | Cambrian | Ordovician | Silurian | Devonian | Carboniferous |
|---|---|---|---|---|---|---|
| **Began** (Millions of Years Ago) | 4,600 | 541 | 485 | 444 | 419 | 359 |
| **Duration** (Millions of Years) | 4,059 | | 41 | 25 | 60 | |

**Organism:** *Velociraptor*

**Age:** about 80 million years

**Period:** ........................

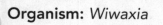

**Organism:** *Wiwaxia*

**Age:** about 500 million years

**Period:** ........................

▶ Limestone and shale containing fossil coral from Kentucky and Indiana provide evidence that a shallow sea covered much of North America during the Silurian period.

▼ Geologic evidence such as these deposits from an ancient glacial lake in Washington suggest that a period of major global cooling began about 2.6 million years ago.

◀ Fossilized cyanobacteria that date to about 3.5 billion years ago provide evidence that single-celled organisms actually appeared during the Precambrian.

## Mesozoic Era                    Cenozoic Era

| | Permian | | Triassic | Jurassic | Cretaceous | | Paleogene | Neogene | Quarternary |
|---|---|---|---|---|---|---|---|---|---|
| | 299 | | 252 | 201 | 145 | | 66 | 23 | 2.6 |
| | ............ | | ............ | 56 | 79 | | ............ | 20.4 | 2.6 |

**Organism:** *Smilodon*

**Age:** between about 2.5 million and 10,000 years

**Period:** ............................................

315

## Microscopic Fossil Evidence

**Figure 3** This image, produced by a scanning electron microscope, shows the microscopic shells of fossil foraminifera. Information recorded in the shells of these ancient single-celled ocean organisms provides evidence with which scientists track past changes in Earth's climate and refine the geologic time scale.

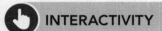

## INTERACTIVITY

Review how geologists learn about Earth's history.

## HANDS-ON LAB

**Investigate** Model the geologic time scale.

## ✓ READING CHECK

**Write Informative Texts** Provide an example of a defining event for a geologic time division.

...................................

...................................

...................................

# Dividing Geologic Time

As geologists studied the rock and fossil records, they found major changes in life forms at certain times. Fossils are widely distributed in Earth's rocks. They occur in rocks in a definite order, with new species appearing and old species disappearing. In this way, fossils provided evidence of change on Earth. Geologists used these changes to help identify major events in Earth's history and mark where one unit of geologic time ends and the next begins. Therefore, most divisions of the geologic time scale depend on events in the history of life on Earth. **Figure 2** shows the major divisions of the geologic time scale.

**Precambrian Time** Geologic time begins with a long span of time called Precambrian (pree KAM bree un) time. Precambrian time covers about 88 percent of Earth's history, from 4.6 billion years ago to 541 million years ago. Few fossils survive from this time period.

**Eras** Geologists divide the time between the Precambrian and the present into three long units of time called **eras**. During the Paleozoic era, life increased in complexity and Pangaea formed. The Mesozoic era is defined by the dominance of dinosaurs and Pangaea breaking apart. During the Cenozoic era, mammals evolved to become the dominant land animals and the continents moved to their present-day positions.

**Periods** Eras are subdivided into units of geologic time called **periods**. You can see in **Figure 2** that the Mesozoic era includes three periods: the Triassic period, the Jurassic period, and the Cretaceous period. Each period is defined by certain events. For example, at the end of the Cretaceous period, major volcanic eruptions coincided with the impact on Earth of a huge asteroid. These events significantly changed the global environment.

**Refining Earth's History** Our understanding of Earth's history changes with each newly-discovered fossil (see **Figure 3**) or rock. Our understanding also changes as the technology used to analyze rocks and fossils advances. That's why geologists continually **refine** the geologic time scale. For example, geologists use the start of a period of major global cooling to mark the beginning of the Quaternary period. Recently, evidence from ocean floor sediments and other sources led scientists to move that boundary from 1.8 to 2.6 million years ago. The new boundary, based on new physical evidence, more accurately reflects a major change in Earth's climate.

**Academic Vocabulary**
Describe how you might refine something you make or do.

.................................................

.................................................

.................................................

.................................................

# Question It!

## Modeling Geologic Time
Suppose your friend makes his own model of the geologic time scale. He decided to use a scale of 1 m = 1 million years. Would your friend's model work?

1. **Compare and Contrast** How would your friend's model differ from the geologic time scale shown in **Figure 2**?

.................................................................

.................................................................

2. **Identify Limitations** What would be one advantage and one disadvantage of your friend's model?

.................................................................

.................................................................

.................................................................

.................................................................

**Literacy Connection**

**Write Informative Texts** After you read this page, explain in your own words why scientists constantly refine the geologic time scale.

.................................................

.................................................

.................................................

.................................................

.................................................

.................................................

**1. Summarize** What is the geologic time scale?

..........................................................................

..........................................................................

..........................................................................

..........................................................................

**Use Figure 2 in the lesson to help you answer Questions 2 and 3.**

**2. Identify** How is Precambrian Time different from the other divisions of the geologic time scale?

..........................................................................

..........................................................................

..........................................................................

**3. Describe** How is the geologic time scale divided?

..........................................................................

..........................................................................

..........................................................................

..........................................................................

**4. Predict** Explain why you think the geologic time scale will or will not change over the next 20 years.

..........................................................................

..........................................................................

..........................................................................

..........................................................................

..........................................................................

..........................................................................

..........................................................................

**5. Construct an Explanation** Give an example of physical evidence used to organize Earth's history on the geologic time scale.

..........................................................................

..........................................................................

..........................................................................

..........................................................................

..........................................................................

..........................................................................

## Quest CHECK-IN

**In this lesson, you learned about the purpose of the geologic time scale and how the segments of the geologic time scale are defined.**

**Evaluate** How could you organize the fossils of potential dig sites using the geologic time scale?

..........................................................................

..........................................................................

..........................................................................

..........................................................................

..........................................................................

👆 **INTERACTIVITY**

| A Matter of Time |
| --- |

**Go online** to learn about fossils found at each potential dig site and plot them on the geologic time scale.

# Tiny Fossil, BIG ACCURACY

### INTERACTIVITY

Determine which absolute dating method will return the most accurate result.

**How can you** determine the age of a small geologic sample with the greatest precision? You engineer it! An accelerator mass spectrometer is designed for accurate dating with less material.

**The Challenge:** To develop ways to determine more precisely the absolute age of a geologic event using smaller samples.

**Phenomenon** Representing a technological leap in absolute dating methods, the accelerator mass spectrometer (AMS) is one of the most important tools scientists use when dating events in Earth's past. Whereas traditional radioactive dating methods might require a 100-gram sample of material, an AMS can help to determine the absolute ages of samples with as little as 20 milligrams. These sensitive devices are also more accurate and can return results in less time than traditional radioactive dating methods. These improvements help geologists organize events in the geologic time scale more accurately and faster. The AMS is particularly helpful when dating more recent events of the Quaternary period, from which only small samples of organic remains may be available for carbon-14 dating.

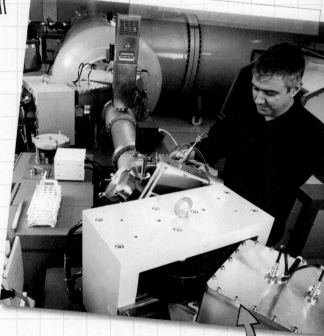

The accelerator mass spectrometer helps scientists to refine the geologic time scale.

**DESIGN CHALLENGE** Can you make a model of the geologic time scale? Go to the Engineering Design Notebook to find out!

# LESSON 3

# Major Events in Earth's History

## Guiding Questions

- How did Earth change in the Paleozoic era?
- How did Earth change in the Mesozoic era?
- How did Earth change in the Cenozoic era?

## Connections

**Literacy** Cite Textual Evidence

**Math** Represent Quantitative Relationships

MS-ESS1-4

## Vocabulary

invertebrate
vertebrate
amphibian
reptile
mass extinction
mammal

## Academic Vocabulary

factors
hypothesize

 **VOCABULARY APP**

Practice vocabulary on a mobile device.

**Quest CONNECTION**

Consider how knowing about Earth's history can help you choose a dig site.

## Connect It!

✎ **Circle any organisms you recognize in this Carboniferous swamp.**

**Determine Similarities** How was life during the Carboniferous period similar to life today?

........................................................................................

........................................................................................

........................................................................................

**Make Observations** What do you think conditions were like in this Carboniferous period dragonfly's habitat?

........................................................................................

........................................................................................

........................................................................................

# Major Events in the Paleozoic Era

Earth has a long history of change, starting 4.6 billion years ago when the planet formed. The geologic time scale, interpreted from the rock and fossil records, provides a way to organize that long history of change. The development and evolution of organisms is just one example of the changes that have taken place. For example, **Figure 1** shows how different life was on Earth 300 million years ago.

Through most of Earth's history, during Precambrian time, the only living things were single-celled organisms. Near the end of the Precambrian, more complex living things evolved. Feathery, plantlike organisms anchored themselves to the seafloor. Jellyfish-like organisms floated in the oceans. Then, a much greater variety of living things evolved during the next phase of geologic time—the Paleozoic era.

**The Cambrian Explosion** During the first part of the Paleozoic era, known as the Cambrian period, life took a big leap forward. Many different kinds of organisms evolved, including some that had hard parts such as shells and outer skeletons. This evolutionary event is called the Cambrian explosion because so many new life forms appeared within a relatively short time. To date these changes, scientists use the law of superposition and other methods to find relative ages and radioactive dating to find absolute ages in the geologic record.

At this time, all animals lived in the sea. Many were animals without backbones, or **invertebrates**. Common invertebrates included jellyfish, worms, sponges, clam-like brachiopods, and trilobites.

HANDS-ON LAB

☑**Investigate** Analyze changes in biodiversity over time.

**Ancient Swamp Life**
**Figure 1** This artist's drawing shows life in a swampy forest during the Carboniferous period, which occurred about 200 million years after the Cambrian period.

**Figure 2** 🖊 These fossils provide evidence of the evolution of organisms during the Paleozoic era. Write the period during which the organism appeared in the fossil record.

Jawless Fish _____

## First Vertebrates and Land Plants
The Ordovician period is the second segment of the Paleozoic era. The first vertebrates, including jawless fish, evolved during the Ordovician. A **vertebrate** is an animal with a backbone. The first insects may have evolved at this time, along with land plants.

Plants grew abundantly during the next period, the Silurian. These simple plants grew low to the ground in damp areas. By the Devonian period that followed, plants evolved that could grow in drier areas. Among these plants were the earliest ferns.

Both invertebrates and vertebrates lived in the Devonian seas. Even though the invertebrates were more numerous, the Devonian is often called the Age of Fish. Every main group of fish, including sharks, was present in the oceans. Most fish had jaws, bony skeletons, and scales on their bodies.

## Animals Reach Land
The Devonian period was also when vertebrates began to live on land. The first land vertebrates were lungfish with strong, muscular fins. The first amphibians evolved from these lungfish. An **amphibian** (am FIB ee un) is an animal that lives part of its life on land and part of its life in water.

**Literacy Connection**

**Cite Textual Evidence**
Underline the evidence that supports the statement "Animals and plants evolved further during the Carboniferous Period."

## Animals and Plants Evolve Further
The Carboniferous period followed the Devonian in the late Paleozoic era. During this period, the amniote egg (an egg filled with special fluids) evolved. This important adaptation allowed animals to lay eggs on land without the eggs drying out. This adaptation coincides with the appearance of reptiles in the fossil record. **Reptiles** have scaly skin and lay eggs that have tough, leathery shells.

During the Carboniferous, winged insects evolved into many new forms, including huge dragonflies and cockroaches. Giant ferns, mosses, and cone-bearing plants formed vast swampy forests. These plants resembled plants that live in tropical and temperate areas today.

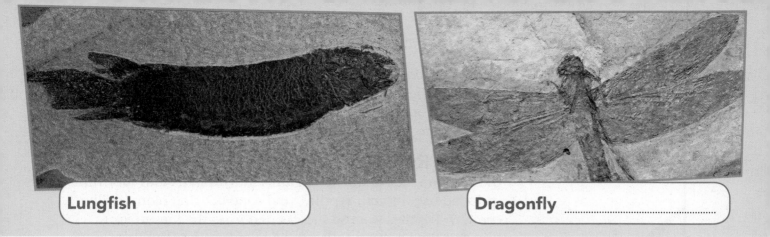

Lungfish ........................................

Dragonfly ........................................

**Pangaea** Over the course of the Paleozoic era, Earth's continents slowly moved together to form a great landmass, or supercontinent, called Pangaea (pan JEE uh). The formation of Pangaea caused deserts to expand in the tropics and sheets of ice to cover land closer to the South Pole.

**Mass Extinction** The organisms in **Figure 2** represent the huge diversity of life that evolved during the Paleozoic era. However, during the Permian period at the end of the Paleozoic, a major change occurred and most species of life on Earth died out during the worst extinction event in Earth's history. This was a **mass extinction**, an event during which many types of living things became extinct at the same time. Scientists estimate that about 90 percent of all ocean species and 70 percent of species on land died out. Even widespread organisms such as trilobites became extinct.

Scientists aren't sure what caused this extinction. Some scientists think multiple volcanoes erupted so much dust and debris that the energy from the sun was blocked. This would have prevented plants from performing photosynthesis. Other scientists think a rise in global temperatures was to blame. Scientists have also found that the amount of carbon dioxide in the oceans increased and the amount of oxygen declined. It would have been difficult for organisms to quickly adjust to these changes. All of these **factors** likely contributed to the mass extinction.

☑ READING CHECK **Cite Textual Evidence** According to the text, what impact did the amniote egg have on lifeforms on Earth?

........................................................................

........................................................................

........................................................................

........................................................................

........................................................................

 **INTERACTIVITY**

Observe fossils to make deductions about the organisms and their environments.

**Academic Vocabulary**
What two factors determined what you did over the weekend?

........................................................................

........................................................................

........................................................................

........................................................................

........................................................................

........................................................................

323

**Reflect** Which major event or time in Earth's history would you most like to witness? In your science notebook, describe the event or time period and why you would like to experience it.

Dimorphodon

## Mesozoic Winged Animals

**Figure 3** This illustration shows an artist's idea of what a *Dimorphodon* (a type of pterosaur) and an *Archaeopteryx* looked like.

1. **Compare** List three similarities between the *Dimorphodon* and the *Archaeopteryx*.

   ....................................................

   ....................................................

2. **Contrast** Examine the wings of both animals. How are they different? Support your answer with evidence from the images.

   ....................................................

   ....................................................

   ....................................................

   ....................................................

   ....................................................

# Major Events in the Mesozoic Era

Mass extinctions are followed by increases in evolution and variation. The mass extinction at the end of the Paleozoic era became an opportunity for many new life forms, including dinosaurs, to develop in the Mesozoic era.

**Age of Reptiles** Some living things managed to survive the Permian mass extinction. Plants and animals that survived included fish, insects, reptiles, and cone-bearing plants called conifers. Reptiles were so successful during the Mesozoic era that this time is often called the Age of Reptiles. The first dinosaurs appeared during the first period of the Mesozoic era, called the Triassic period.

**First Mammals** Mammals also first appeared during the Triassic period. A **mammal** is a vertebrate that controls its own body temperature and feeds milk to its young. Mammals in the Triassic period were very small—about the size of a mouse.

**Reptiles and Birds** During the Jurassic period, the second segment of the Mesozoic era, dinosaurs were the dominant land animals. Scientists have identified several hundred different kinds of dinosaurs, including some that ate plants and some that were predators. One plant-eating dinosaur, *Brachiosaurus*, was 26 meters long!

The ocean and seas during this period were also filled with diverse life forms, including sharks, rays, giant marine crocodiles, and plesiosaurs. Plesiosaurs had long necks and paddle-like fins.

Late in the Jurassic, the first known birds appeared in the skies. *Archaeopteryx,* which means "ancient winged one," is thought to have evolved from a dinosaur. The sky also had flying reptiles, called pterosaurs, and many varieties of insects. Use **Figure 3** to compare *Archaeopteryx* and a type of pterosaur called *Dimorphodon*.

Archaeopteryx

**Flowering Plants** The Cretaceous period is the final and longest segment of the Mesozoic era. Reptiles, including dinosaurs, were still widespread throughout the Cretaceous. Ancient birds evolved better adaptations for flying and began to replace flying reptiles.

One of the most important events of the Cretaceous period was the evolution of flowering plants, or angiosperms. Unlike conifers, flowering plants produce seeds that are inside a fruit. Many flowering plants you may recognize today first appeared during this time, such as magnolias, figs, and willows.

**Another Mass Extinction** At the end of the Cretaceous, another mass extinction occurred. Scientists **hypothesize** that this mass extinction occurred when an asteroid struck Earth at a time when extreme volcanic activity in the area that is now India had weakened environments. This mass extinction wiped out more than half of all plant and animal groups, including the dinosaurs. Use **Figure 4** to illustrate the event.

✔ READING CHECK **Use Information** How did organisms from the Mesozoic era differ from organisms of the Paleozoic?

..............................................................................................

..............................................................................................

..............................................................................................

👆 **INTERACTIVITY**

Examine evidence that shows major changes over time.

**Academic Vocabulary**

Use *hypothesize* in a sentence about a subject other than science.

..............................................................

..............................................................

..............................................................

..............................................................

# Model It !

**The End of the Dinosaurs**

**Figure 4** Scientists hypothesize that an asteroid hit Earth near present-day southeastern Mexico. Show how this event, combined with the environment at the time, contributed to the mass extinction.

**Develop Models** ✏ Complete the comic strip. Draw events that led to the extinction of the dinosaurs. Label each stage. Add a title.

**Title:** ..........................................................................................................

Many giant mammals evolved in the Cenozoic era. The *Megatherium* is related to the modern sloth but is much taller.

**1. Measure** Use the ruler to measure the height of each sloth.

*Megatherium* height: about ..................

Modern sloth height: about ..................

**2. Represent Quantitative Relationships** About how many times taller was *Megatherium* than a modern sloth? Complete the equation below, in which $m$ is the height of *Megatherium* and $s$ is the height of the modern sloth.

$m = s \times$ ..................

Modern Sloth

Megatherium

# Major Events in the Cenozoic Era

During the Mesozoic era, small mammals had to compete with dinosaurs and other animals for food and places to live. The mass extinction at the end of that era created an opportunity for the species that did survive, including some mammals. During the Cenozoic era that followed, mammals evolved to live in many different environments—on land, in water, and even in the air. Geologists have found evidence for the spread of mammals in the fossils, rocks, and sediment of the early Cenozoic era.

**Mammals Thrive** The Cenozoic begins with the Paleogene and Neogene periods. During these periods, Earth's climate became gradually cooler over time. As the continents drifted apart, ocean basins widened and mammals such as whales and dolphins evolved. On land, mammals flourished. Some birds and mammals became very large. Forests thinned, making space for flowering plants and grasses to become more dominant.

**Ice Ages** At the start of the Quaternary period, large sheets of ice began to appear on Earth's surface. Earth's climate continued to cool and warm in cycles, causing a series of ice ages followed by warmer periods. During an ice age, about 30 percent of Earth's surface was covered in thick glaciers. The latest warm period began between 10,000 and 20,000 years ago. During that time, sea levels rose and most of the glaciers melted.

**Humans** The Quaternary period is sometimes referred to as the "Age of Humans." *Homo erectus*, an ancestor of modern humans, appears in the fossil record near the start of the period, while modern humans appeared about 190,000 years ago. By about 12,000 to 15,000 years ago, humans had migrated to every continent except Antarctica.

## How Scientists Organize Earth's History

**Figure 5** 🖊 This timeline shows major events in Earth's history. It is a model that you can use to study events that occur over geologic time. (Note that, to make the timeline easier to read, periods are not drawn to scale.) Circle the periods during which mass extinctions occurred.

| Events | Period | Began (Millions of Years Ago) | |
|---|---|---|---|
| Earth forms. First single-celled and multi-celled organisms evolve. | | 4,600 | PRECAMBRIAN TIME |
| "Explosion" of new forms of life occurs. Invertebrates such as trilobites are common. 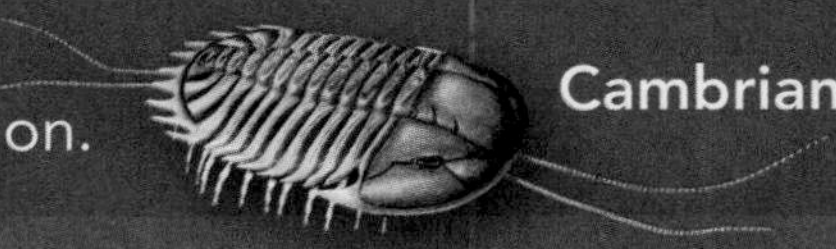 | Cambrian | 541 | PALEOZOIC ERA |
| First vertebrates, insects, and land plants evolve. | Ordovician | 485 | PALEOZOIC ERA |
| Early fish are common in seas. | Silurian | 444 | PALEOZOIC ERA |
| "Age of Fish" occurs, with many different kinds of fish. Lungfish and amphibians first reach land. | Devonian | 419 | PALEOZOIC ERA |
| Appalachian Mountains form. Reptiles and giant insects evolve. Ferns and cone-bearing plants form forests. | Carboniferous | 359 | PALEOZOIC ERA |
| Pangaea forms. Mass extinction kills most species. | Permian | 299 | PALEOZOIC ERA |
| Reptiles flourish, including the first dinosaurs. First mammals evolve. 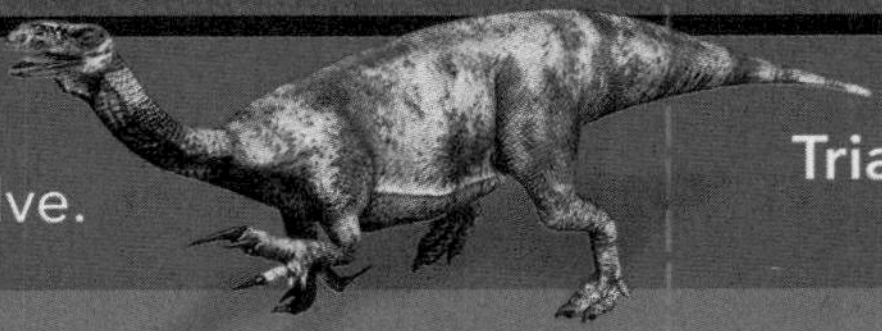 | Triassic | 252 | MESOZOIC ERA |
| Dinosaurs become common. First birds evolve. | Jurassic | 201 | MESOZOIC ERA |
| Dinosaurs are widespread. Birds begin to replace flying reptiles. Flowering plants appear. Mass extinction occurs. | Cretaceous | 145 | MESOZOIC ERA |
| Mammals flourish. Grasses first spread widely. | Paleogene | 66 | CENOZOIC ERA |
| The Andes and Himalayas form. Some mammals and birds become very large. | Neogene | 23 | CENOZOIC ERA |
| Ice ages occur. Many kinds of animals thrive. First modern humans evolve.  | Quarternary | 2.6 | CENOZOIC ERA |

MS-ESS1-4

1. **Identify** During which era was the "Age of Reptiles"?

..................................................................

..................................................................

2. **Sequence** Arrange the following organisms in order from earliest to latest appearance: amphibians, jawless fish, trilobites, bony fish.

..................................................................

..................................................................

..................................................................

..................................................................

3. **Cause and Effect** Name two possible causes of the mass extinction at the end of the Paleozoic.

..................................................................

..................................................................

..................................................................

..................................................................

4. **Construct an Explanation** What factors allowed new organisms to evolve and thrive during the Cenozoic era?

..................................................................

..................................................................

..................................................................

..................................................................

..................................................................

..................................................................

..................................................................

..................................................................

5. **Identify Evidence** Identify a major event in Earth's past and describe the supporting evidence for that event you would expect to observe in the fossil record.

..................................................................

..................................................................

..................................................................

..................................................................

..................................................................

## Quest CHECK-IN

**In this lesson, you learned about major events that help to define and organize Earth's history.**

**Evaluate** How can knowing about Earth's history help you to choose your dig site?

..................................................................

..................................................................

..................................................................

..................................................................

..................................................................

### 👆 INTERACTIVITY

Time to Choose the Dig Site

**Go online** to conduct research about *Dimetrodon* to make the final site selection.

MS-ESS1-4

# A New Mass Extinction?

When a species dies out, we say it is extinct. When large numbers of species die out at the same time, scientists use the term *mass extinction*. Scientists know of multiple mass extinctions in Earth's history. Some suggest that another mass extinction is approaching.

One factor that can lead to extinctions is the introduction of plant and animal species into new environments. Some of this is due to species migration. Animals and plants can move into new areas where temperature and climate patterns have become more favorable due to global warming. However, most species are brought to new areas by humans. In many cases, this leads to the disappearance of native species.

Habitat loss is another factor that leads to extinctions. When habitats are lost, the species that live within them no longer have the space or resources to live. As the human population increases, so has the human need for resources, such as fuel, land, and food. Habitats are cleared or changed to meet those needs, and the organisms that lived there may die off. For example, burning and clearing tropical forests threatens many endangered primates.

Climate change caused by global warming may also lead to extinctions. Our increased use of fossil fuels and the accompanying rise in carbon dioxide in the atmosphere has led to a steady increase in global temperatures. As temperatures rise, environments change. Species that cannot adapt to the changes may die out.

Most scientists agree that there is a real threat of another mass extinction. However, there are still steps people can take to prevent or minimize the loss of our biodiversity.

Urban development to accommodate a growing human population leads to habitat loss.

## MY COMMUNITY

What steps can you take in your community to change our path away from mass extinction? Use the library and the Internet to find facts and evidence that will support your ideas.

# ✅ TOPIC 6 Review and Assess

## 1 Determining Ages of Rocks

MS-ESS1-4

1. Which term describes a gap in the geologic record that occurs when sedimentary rocks cover an eroded surface?
   - A. extrusion
   - B. fault
   - C. intrusion
   - D. unconformity

2. Which term describes the time it takes for half of a radioactive element's atoms to decay?
   - A. absolute age
   - B. half-life
   - C. radioactive decay
   - D. relative age

3. Which statement **best** describes one rule for determining the relative age of a rock layer?
   - A. A fault is always younger than the rock it cuts through.
   - B. An extrusion is always older than the rocks below it.
   - C. An index fossil is always younger than the rock layer it occurs in.
   - D. An intrusion is always older than the rock layers around it.

4. Which of the following conclusions can geologists draw about a limestone rock layer based on the law of superposition?
   - A. The limestone layer is 2 million years old.
   - B. The limestone layer contains 2 million fossils.
   - C. The limestone layer is younger than the sandstone layer below it.
   - D. The limestone layer is the same age as another layer 100 hundred kilometers away.

5. A geologist finds an area of undisturbed sedimentary rock. The ................................. layer is most likely the oldest.

6. Radioactive dating is a method used by geologists to determine the ................................. age of rocks.

7. **Construct Explanations** A geologist finds identical index fossils in a rock layer in the Grand Canyon in Arizona and in a rock layer 675 kilometers away in Utah. What can she infer about the ages of the two rock layers?

   ...........................................................................

   ...........................................................................

   ...........................................................................

8. **Sequence** Using the numbers and letters, list the rock layers and formations in the diagram in order from oldest to youngest. Cite evidence from the diagram to explain your answer.

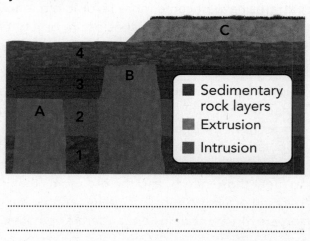

   ...........................................................................

   ...........................................................................

   ...........................................................................

   ...........................................................................

   ...........................................................................

   ...........................................................................

   ...........................................................................

   ...........................................................................

   ...........................................................................

   ...........................................................................

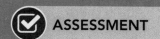

## 2 Geologic Time Scale

MS-ESS1-4

9. Into which units is the geologic time scale subdivided?
   A. relative ages       B. absolute ages
   C. months and days     D. eras and periods

10. What do geologists **mostly** study to develop the geologic time scale?
    A. Earth's rotation
    B. tectonic plate motions
    C. volcanoes and earthquakes
    D. rock layers and index fossils

11. How do geologists use radioactive dating in developing the geologic time scale?
    A. to identify index fossils
    B. to identify types of rocks
    C. to place rocks in order by relative age
    D. to determine the absolute age of rocks

12. The geologic time scale is a record of
    ........................................ and ..........................:

13. **Construct Explanations** Why do geologists need the geologic time scale? Give two reasons.

    ................................................................................

    ................................................................................

    ................................................................................

    ................................................................................

    ................................................................................

    ................................................................................

    ................................................................................

    ................................................................................

## 3 Major Events in Earth's History

MS-ESS1-4

14. Which event occurred in the Cenozoic era?
    A. first mammals
    B. spread of mammals
    C. first flowering plants
    D. spread of ferns and conifers

15. What were Earth's earliest multicellular organisms?
    A. bacteria        B. land plants
    C. vertebrates     D. invertebrates

16. The first birds evolved during the
    ........................................ era.

17. **Develop Models** 🖉 Draw what the Devonian period of the Paleozoic era might have looked like. Think about the events that define the Devonian period when making your model.

# ☑TOPIC 6 Review and Assess

MS-ESS1-4

## Evidence-Based Assessment

A team of geologists explores an area of land that was once an ancient sea. They dig for fossils of marine organisms at three locations. The geologists collect and record information about the fossils they have discovered and the rock layers that the fossils were found in. The data are summarized in the diagram.

The geologists attempt to identify an index fossil to help them analyze the relative ages of the rock layers and to determine how the layers at the three sites correspond to each other. The researchers attempt to determine the relative ages of the layers and the marine organisms whose fossils they have dug up.

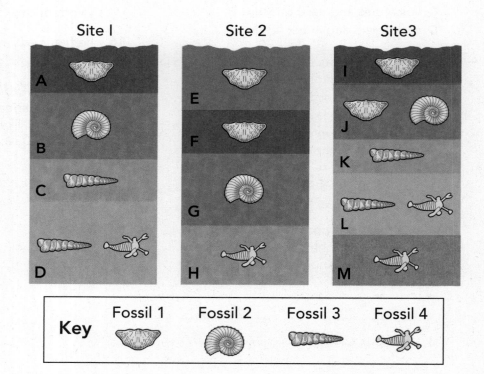

Site 1, Site 2, Site3

Key — Fossil 1, Fossil 2, Fossil 3, Fossil 4

1. **Interpret Data** Which of the following is an index fossil?
   A. Fossil 1
   B. Fossil 2
   C. Fossil 3
   D. Fossil 4

2. **Evaluate Scale** Which of the following statements about the relative ages of the rock layers is true? Select all that apply.
   ☐ Layers B, G, and J are the same age.
   ☐ Layer E is the youngest layer.
   ☐ Layers D, H, and J are the same age.
   ☐ Layer M is the oldest layer.
   ☐ Layer A is the youngest layer.
   ☐ Layers D and H are the oldest layers.

3. **Apply Scientific Reasoning** Based on the data, what can you conclude about the relative ages of Fossils 1 and 2? What scientific law can you use to support your response?

   ...........................................................................
   ...........................................................................
   ...........................................................................
   ...........................................................................
   ...........................................................................
   ...........................................................................
   ...........................................................................
   ...........................................................................
   ...........................................................................
   ...........................................................................
   ...........................................................................
   ...........................................................................
   ...........................................................................
   ...........................................................................
   ...........................................................................
   ...........................................................................

4. **Construct Explanations** Fossil 2 is about 300 million years old. Testing reveals that Layer M is about 400 million years old. The geologists conclude that Fossil 3 is an organism that likely lived about 350 million years ago. Do you agree? Support your answer using evidence from the diagram.

   ...........................................................................
   ...........................................................................
   ...........................................................................
   ...........................................................................
   ...........................................................................
   ...........................................................................
   ...........................................................................

# Quest FINDINGS

## Complete the Quest!

**Phenomenon Present your choice of dig site in a report to the head of the science museum that is sponsoring the *Dimetrodon* exhibit. In your report, include evidence and scientific reasoning that supports your choice.**

Explain What roles did the rock and fossil record play in determining your choice of dig site?

...........................................................................
...........................................................................
...........................................................................
...........................................................................
...........................................................................

👆 **INTERACTIVITY**

Reflect on the Big Fossil Hunt

MS-ESS1-4

# Core Sampling Through Time

How can you **determine** the **relative ages of rock layers** in different locations?

## Materials

(per group)

- four models positioned around the classroom representing rock layers
- plastic gloves
- metric ruler
- large-diameter drinking straw
- long dowel or rod that fits into the straw
- several sheets of paper
- colored pencils

## Safety

Be sure to follow all safety guidelines provided by your teacher. The Safety Appendix of your textbook provides more details about the safety icons.

## Background

**Phenomenon** Visitors to a local state park see a variety of rocks and fossils on the surface in different locations. They often ask: Are the rocks here the same age as those over there? In your role as volunteer park ranger, how will you answer? You will need to find out how the ages of the rocks throughout the park compare.

You know that you can learn about the order of events in Earth's history by studying rocks. However, geologists cannot simply flip through layers of sedimentary rock like the pages in a magazine to study them. Instead, they must analyze samples taken from deep below the surface. In a process called coring, hollow tubes are driven into sedimentary rock layers. When the tubes are pulled out, they contain samples of each layer.

In this activity, you will illustrate the geologic history of the park using the data you gather through core sampling.

# Plan Your Investigation

### HANDS-ON LAB

**иDemonstrate** Go online for a downloadable worksheet of this lab.

1. Your teacher positioned four models around the classroom. The models represent sedimentary rock layers, some with index fossils, in different locations throughout the park.

2. Design an investigation to discover the geologic history of the park by drilling and analyzing core samples. Think about the following questions as you form your plan:

   - In which locations should you drill to get a complete picture of the rocks throughout the park so you can compare their ages?

   - How many core samples will you drill in each location?

   - How will you record what you observe in the core samples?

   - How will you compare the locations of sediment layers and index fossils?

   - How will you present your findings?

3. Use the space provided to summarize your investigation. Show your plan to your teacher for approval.

4. Conduct your investigation, record your observations, and report your findings according to your plan.

### Procedure

_____

_____

_____

_____

_____

_____

_____

_____

_____

_____

_____

_____

### Evidence Gathered from Core Samples

# Analyze and Interpret Data

1. **Develop Models** Use your observations and analysis to make a diagram of the complete geologic history of the park.

2. **Use Models** Compare the geologic record at the different locations represented by your model core samples. Explain any differences you observe.

   ........................................................................................................................

   ........................................................................................................................

3. **Construct Explanations** Which rock layers at the different locations do you think are the same age? Explain your answer using evidence.

   ........................................................................................................................

   ........................................................................................................................

4. **Apply Scientific Reasoning** Choose two core samples that represent different locations in the park. Compare the ages of the rocks on the surface. Explain how you determined their relative ages.

   ........................................................................................................................

   ........................................................................................................................

   ........................................................................................................................

   ........................................................................................................................

   ........................................................................................................................

# TOPIC
# 7

# Energy in the Atmosphere and Ocean

**NGSS PERFORMANCE EXPECTATION**

**MS-ESS2-6** Develop and use a model to describe how unequal heating and rotation of the Earth cause patterns of atmospheric and oceanic circulation that determine regional climates.

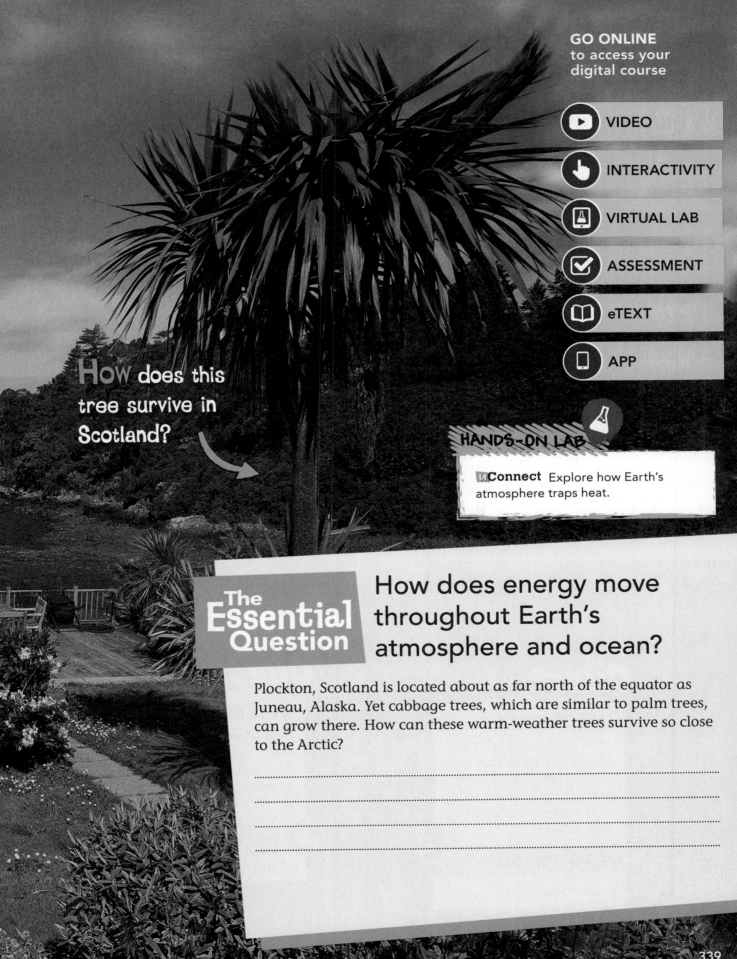

GO ONLINE
to access your
digital course

VIDEO

INTERACTIVITY

VIRTUAL LAB

ASSESSMENT

eTEXT

APP

HANDS-ON LAB

иConnect Explore how Earth's atmosphere traps heat.

How does this tree survive in Scotland?

## The Essential Question

# How does energy move throughout Earth's atmosphere and ocean?

Plockton, Scotland is located about as far north of the equator as Juneau, Alaska. Yet cabbage trees, which are similar to palm trees, can grow there. How can these warm-weather trees survive so close to the Arctic?

........................................................................................

........................................................................................

........................................................................................

........................................................................................

339

# Quest KICKOFF

## What is the most efficient way for a container ship to cross the Atlantic?

**Phenomenon** Shipping is a very cost-effective mode of transporting goods. But trips across the ocean can be dangerous, and it is up to the ship's captain and its officers to plan and follow safe navigation routes. In this problem-based Quest activity, you will plot a round-trip ocean journey across the Atlantic Ocean for a container ship. In digital activities and labs, you will evaluate data on fuel consumption and the effects of wind patterns and ocean currents. Finally, you will develop and present a recommended route.

 **INTERACTIVITY**

Crossing the Atlantic

MS-ESS2-6 Develop and use a model to describe how unequal heating and rotation of the Earth cause patterns of atmospheric and oceanic circulation that determine regional climates.

**NBC LEARN** ▶ VIDEO

After watching the Quest Kickoff video about the work involved in navigating a ship, identify three dangers a container ship might face at sea.

**1**
..................................................................
..................................................................
..................................................................

**2**
..................................................................
..................................................................
..................................................................

**3**
..................................................................
..................................................................
..................................................................

# Quest CHECK-IN

## IN LESSON 1

How does the speed of a ship affect the cost of the trip? Determine the most cost-effective speed for a ship traveling across the Atlantic.

### HANDS-ON LAB

Choose Your Speed

# Quest CHECK-IN

## IN LESSON 2

How does wind affect a ship's speed? Consider how using wind can help to decrease the time of the ship's journey.

 **INTERACTIVITY**

Wind at Your Back

Each container on this ship is equivalent to the back of a semi-trailer truck.

## Quest CHECK-IN

### IN LESSON 3

How do global ocean currents affect navigation routes? Analyze the patterns of currents in the northern Atlantic Ocean, and then finalize your route.

 **INTERACTIVITY**

Find Your Advantage

## Quest FINDINGS

## Complete the Quest!

Present your recommended route and explain the factors that you considered when planning the route.

 **INTERACTIVITY**

Reflect on Crossing the Atlantic

341

# Energy in Earth's Atmosphere

## Guiding Questions

- How does the sun's energy reach and move through Earth's atmosphere?
- How is heat transferred in Earth's atmosphere?
- What role does the atmosphere play in allowing life to thrive on Earth?

## Connections

**Literacy** Determine Central Ideas

**Math** Convert Measurement Units

MS-ESS2-6

## Vocabulary

electromagnetic wave
greenhouse effect
thermal energy
convection
conduction
radiation

## Academic Vocabulary

absorb

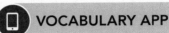 **VOCABULARY APP**

Practice vocabulary on a mobile device.

### Quest CONNECTION

Think about the most cost-effective speed for a ship crossing the Atlantic.

## Connect It!

✏ **Circle the correct terms to complete the statement in the box.**

Draw Conclusions Suppose you observe puddles on the ground after a brief rainstorm. A few hours after the sun comes out, the puddles are no longer there. What has happened to them?

...........................................................................................................................

...........................................................................................................................

...........................................................................................................................

# Energy from the Sun

Most of the energy that is moving within Earth's atmosphere and across Earth's surface comes from the sun. The sun's energy travels to Earth as electromagnetic radiation, a form of energy that can move through the vacuum of space. **Electromagnetic waves** consist of an electric field and a magnetic field.

When you use a microwave oven or watch television, you are using the energy created by electromagnetic waves. The waves are classified according to wavelength, or distance between wave peaks. Most of the electromagnetic waves that travel from the sun and reach Earth are in the form of visible light, which you can see in **Figure 1,** and infrared radiation. A smaller amount arrives as ultraviolet (UV) radiation.

**INTERACTIVITY**

Investigate how sand and water absorb light energy.

## Electromagnetic Waves

**Figure 1** Energy from the sun travels to Earth in the form of radiation.

Sunlight (warms / cools) the ice, causing it to (freeze / melt).

**Academic Vocabulary**
What other things can be absorbed?

........................................

........................................

........................................

........................................

........................................

## Literacy Connection

**Determine Central Ideas**
As you proceed through the lesson, keep track of how energy moves and changes by underlining relevant sentences or passages.

## Sunlight and the Atmosphere

In order for the sun's energy to reach Earth's surface and sustain life, it must first get through the atmosphere. Earth's atmosphere is divided into layers based on temperature. Some sunlight is **absorbed** or reflected by the different levels of the atmosphere before it can reach the surface, as shown in **Figure 2**.

Some UV wavelengths are absorbed by the topmost layer of the atmosphere, called the thermosphere. More UV energy, along with some infrared energy, is absorbed in the next layer, the mesosphere. Below that, in the stratosphere, ozone absorbs more infrared and UV energy. Without the ozone layer, too much UV radiation would reach Earth's surface and threaten the health of organisms. However, the amount of UV radiation that reaches Earth's surface can still be damaging, which is why humans benefit from wearing clothing, sunscreen, and sunglasses.

By the time sunlight reaches the troposphere, there is some infrared radiation, some UV radiation, and visible light. Some light has been reflected into space by clouds. The daytime sky on a cloudless day appears blue because gas molecules scatter short wavelengths of visible light, which are blue and violet, more than the longer red and orange wavelengths.

**Layers of Atmosphere**
**Figure 2** Much of the energy in sunlight that reaches the atmosphere does not reach Earth's surface.

**Make Inferences** What would happen if all of the sun's energy were to reach Earth?

........................................

........................................

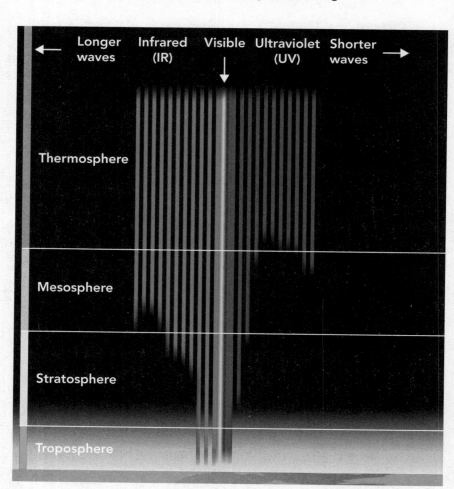

**Earth's Energy Budget** Of the radiation that travels from the sun to the troposphere, only about 50 percent is absorbed by land and water and converted, or transformed, to heat. The rest, as shown in **Figure 3**, is reflected by clouds and other particles in the atmosphere (25%), absorbed by gases and particles (20%), or reflected by the surface itself (5%). Snow, ice, and liquid water reflect some sunlight back into the atmosphere, where some will be absorbed by clouds and particles that the energy missed on the way down.

Only a tiny fraction of the visible light that reaches Earth's surface is transformed to chemical energy in plants and other photosynthetic organisms. The rest is absorbed by Earth and re-emitted into the atmosphere as infrared radiation. Earth's surface absorbs and re-emits equal amounts of energy so that its energy remains in balance over time.

☑ READING CHECK **Determine Central Ideas** Describe the atmosphere's role in moderating the amount of electromagnetic radiation necessary to sustain life on Earth.

......................................................................................

......................................................................................

**The Sun's Energy**
**Figure 3** ✐ Label the different percentages of energy that are absorbed or reflected.

**Make Meaning**

When the sun goes down, a real-world greenhouse may need an alternative source of light or heat to keep the plants alive. How is this similar to Earth's surface at night?

## The Greenhouse Effect

Have you ever been to a greenhouse to buy plants? The glass walls and roof of a greenhouse allow sunlight inside. Some sunlight is absorbed by plants and transformed into chemical energy. Most of the sunlight is converted to heat. Much of the heat is contained by the glass panes of the greenhouse, keeping the interior at an acceptable temperature for plant growth.

Earth's atmosphere plays a similar role. Sunlight is absorbed and transformed into heat within the atmosphere and in the materials at Earth's surface, such as rock and water. The surface reradiates all of that energy, and Earth's total energy remains in balance over time. (Otherwise, Earth would continually heat up and turn into molten rock.) Gases in the atmosphere trap some of the heat near Earth's surface, while some heat escapes into space. This **greenhouse effect** is shown in **Figure 4**.

Overall, Earth's atmosphere keeps our planet at a temperature that is adequate to support life. Organisms are adapted to specific ranges of temperatures. Surface features such as the sea level and the amounts of trapped ice have been relatively constant for thousands of years. However, changes to the composition of the atmosphere—those gases that absorb the infrared energy radiated from Earth's surface—can result in changes in temperature. Most scientists who study the atmosphere and the climate think that humans have been enhancing the greenhouse effect by increasing the amounts of carbon dioxide and methane in the atmosphere. This has caused an increase in the average temperature of Earth, which in turn is causing changes to sea level and melting ice in polar regions and in glaciers.

**Earth as a Greenhouse**

**Figure 4** 🖉 Fill in the boxes in the diagram to describe how the atmosphere, Earth's surface, sunlight, and space interact.

## Daily Air Temperature

**Convert Measurement Units** 🖊

Grace records the air temperature throughout the day in a table. Convert Grace's measurements from degrees Fahrenheit (°F) to degrees Celsius (°C) using the formula shown below.

**(Temp °F – 32) × $\frac{5}{9}$ = Temp °C**

| Time | Temperature | |
| --- | --- | --- |
| | °F | °C |
| 8:00 AM | 52 | |
| 11:00 PM | 56 | |
| 2:00 PM | 60 | |
| 5:00 PM | 55 | |
| 8:00 PM | 50 | |

# Heat Transfer in the Atmosphere

All matter is made up of particles that are constantly moving. The faster the particles move, the more energy they have. Temperature is the *average* amount of energy of motion of each particle of a substance. **Thermal energy** is the total energy of motion in the particles of a substance.

It may seem odd to think that particles in solids are moving, but they are vibrating in place. Even the water molecules in a block of ice, or the atoms of iron and carbon in a steel beam, are moving ever so slightly.

When a substance reaches its melting point, the substance has enough energy of motion to reach a new state—liquid. And when the substance reaches its boiling point, it changes into a gas, which has even more energy of motion. The energy that first reaches Earth as sunlight drives many processes on Earth, including the freezing, melting, and evaporation of water.

✔**READING CHECK** **Determine Conclusions** Which has more thermal energy: a 1-kilogram block of ice or a 1-kilogram volume of water vapor? Why?

..............................................................................................

..............................................................................................

**INTERACTIVITY**

Find out how convection currents form in the atmosphere.

**HANDS-ON LAB**

⚗**Investigate** Develop and test a hypothesis about the heating and cooling rates of land and water.

**VIDEO**

Explore radiation, conduction, and convection.

## Methods of Heat Transfer
We often talk about heat as though it is the same as thermal energy. Heat is actually energy that transfers into an object's thermal energy. Heat only flows from a hotter object to a cooler one. Heat transfers in three ways: **convection**, **conduction**, and **radiation,** as shown in **Figure 5**.

### Things Are Heating Up
**Figure 5** A campfire can illustrate all three types of heat transfer.

### Convection
In fluids such as a hot campfire's smoke, particles move easily from one place to another, taking energy with them. Convection is the transfer of heat by the movement of a fluid.

**Convection**

### Radiation
The transfer of energy by electromagnetic waves is called radiation. The energy that is transferred from the sun to Earth is radiation. Likewise, the light and heat that are emitted by a campfire to toast a marshmallow or cook a hot dog is radiation.

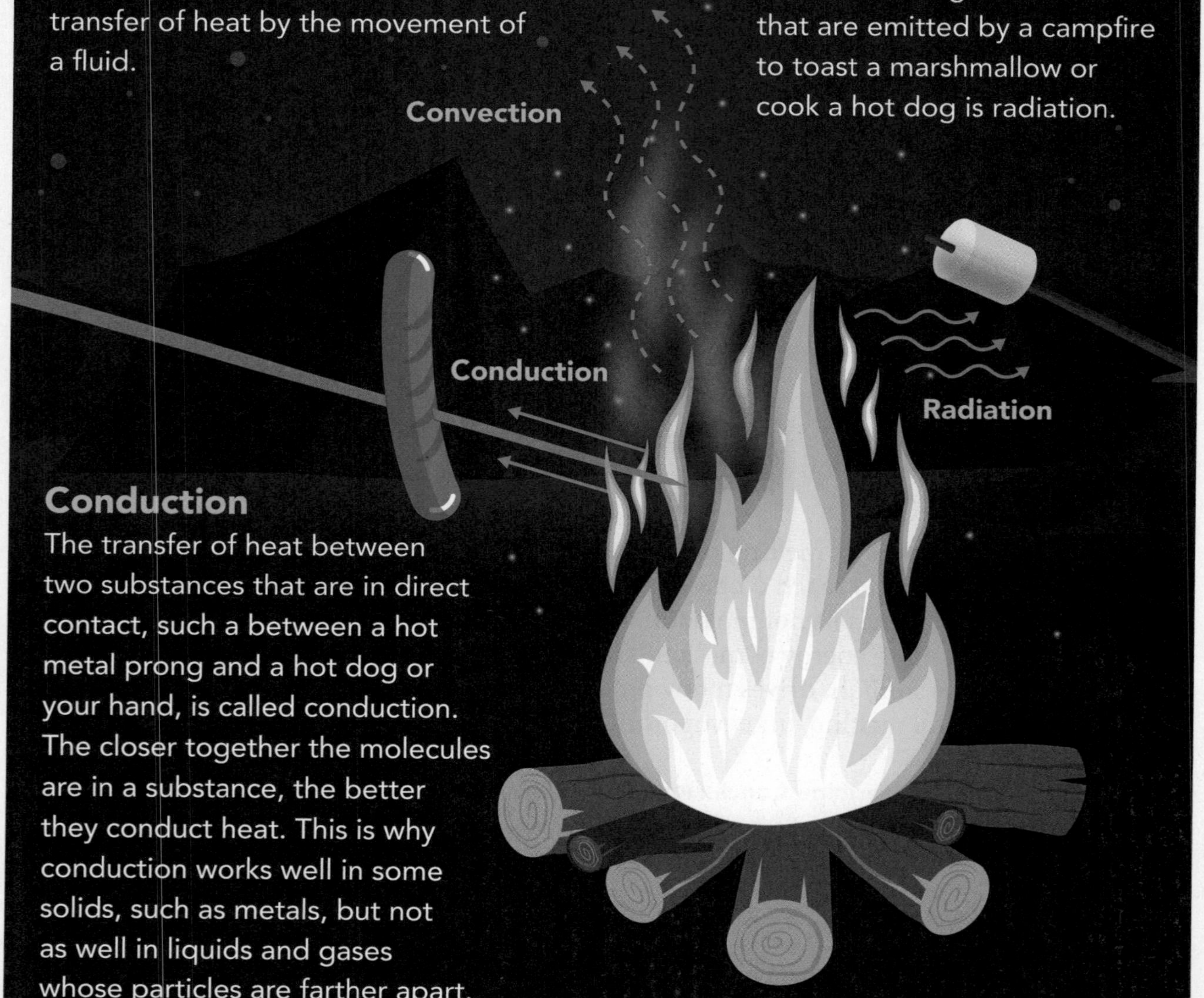

**Conduction**

**Radiation**

### Conduction
The transfer of heat between two substances that are in direct contact, such a between a hot metal prong and a hot dog or your hand, is called conduction. The closer together the molecules are in a substance, the better they conduct heat. This is why conduction works well in some solids, such as metals, but not as well in liquids and gases whose particles are farther apart.

## Heat Transfer at Earth's Surface

The sun's radiation is transformed at Earth's surface into thermal energy. The surface may get warmer than the air above it. Air doesn't conduct heat well. So only the first few centimeters of the troposphere are heated by conduction from Earth's surface to the air. When ground-level air warms up, its molecules move more rapidly. As they bump into each other, they move farther apart, making the air less dense. The warmer, less-dense air rises, and cooler, denser air from above sinks toward the surface.

The cool air then gets warmed by the surface, and the cycle continues. If the source of heat is isolated in one place, a convection current can develop. This occurs in Earth's atmosphere as a result of radiation, conduction, and convection working together. The horizontal movement of the convection current in the atmosphere is what we call wind. Convection currents are especially powerful if Earth's radiant surface is much warmer than the air above it. This is related to why storms can arise much more suddenly and be more severe in warmer regions of Earth. For example, hurricanes tend to form in tropical areas where the sea is very warm and the air above it is relatively cool.

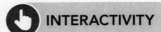
**INTERACTIVITY**

Discover patterns in the wind and how they relate to energy transfer in the atmosphere.

✓ **READING CHECK** **Translate Information** Explain how a pot of heated water could demonstrate convection.

...................................................................................................

...................................................................................................

...................................................................................................

## Model It!

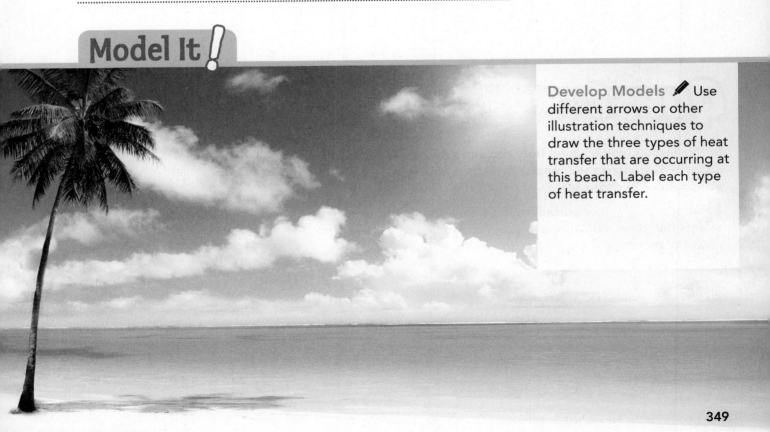

**Develop Models** ✏ Use different arrows or other illustration techniques to draw the three types of heat transfer that are occurring at this beach. Label each type of heat transfer.

**1. Identify** What are the three types of heat transfer that occur on Earth?

........................................................................

........................................................................

**2. Predict** If the amounts of greenhouse gases such as carbon dioxide and methane continue to increase in the atmosphere, what will happen to the average temperature of Earth? Explain.

........................................................................

........................................................................

........................................................................

........................................................................

**3. Summarize** How is the amount of sunlight absorbed by Earth's surface and the amount of energy released by Earth kept in balance?

........................................................................

........................................................................

........................................................................

........................................................................

**4. Construct an Explanation** You place a metal spoon in a pot of soup. After a few minutes, you touch the end of the spoon and notice that it is hot. Which type of heat transfer caused this to happen? Explain.

........................................................................

........................................................................

........................................................................

........................................................................

........................................................................

**5. Cause and Effect** What causes sunburn? Why do we have difficulty perceiving the energy that causes it?

........................................................................

........................................................................

........................................................................

........................................................................

........................................................................

........................................................................

# Quest CHECK-IN

**In this lesson, you learned how the sun's energy is reflected, absorbed, transformed, and transferred by Earth's atmosphere and surface.**

**Evaluate** Why is it important to know how the sun's energy affects the lower atmosphere if you are planning to harness the power of moving air?

........................................................................

........................................................................

........................................................................

........................................................................

## HANDS-ON LAB

Choose Your Speed

**Do the Hands-On Lab** to determine the most cost-effective speed for a ship traveling across the Atlantic and how the sun's energy affects moving air.

MS-ESS2-6

# Measure Radiation with a Cube

**R**ight now, satellites the size of toasters are circling Earth. Each one is collecting data about the planet's atmosphere. These small cube satellites, or CubeSats, give scientists a new way to measure changes in Earth's climate. Different teams have built their own CubeSats, even students.

One team launched a CubeSat called RAVAN to measure the amount of radiation energy leaving Earth's atmosphere. Data from the satellite will allow the team to compare the amount of energy coming in from the sun with the amount of energy leaving Earth. This energy balance reveals a lot about Earth's climate. So tracking the energy balance will help scientists to predict future climate changes.

RAVAN is only the beginning. The team hopes to launch 30 to 40 cubes that will collect data from every part of Earth's atmosphere.

This RAVAN can measure incoming energy from the sun and outgoing energy from Earth in the form of radiation. A difference in the amounts, called Earth's radiation imbalance, can affect the planet's climate.

## MY DISCOVERY

Anyone can submit an idea for a CubeSat to NASA. Elementary students at St. Thomas More Cathedral School in Arlington, Virginia, built, tested, and launched their own CubeSat. Everyone in the entire school participated for more than three years to launch it. Search the Internet to learn more about the St. Thomas More CubeSat. Can you think of a school project where a CubeSat would come in handy?

CubeSats are so small that most of their scientific instruments are about the size of a deck of cards.

# Patterns of Circulation in the Atmosphere

## Guiding Questions

- What causes winds?
- How does the sun's energy affect wind characteristics?
- How do winds redistribute energy around Earth?

## Connections

Literacy Translate Information

Math Analyze Relationships Using Tables

MS-ESS2-6

## Vocabulary

wind
sea breeze
land breeze
Coriolis effect
jet stream

## Academic Vocabulary

area
model

 **VOCABULARY APP**

Practice vocabulary on a mobile device.

**Quest CONNECTION**

Consider how wind might affect a container ship on the ocean.

## Connect It!

✏ **Without wind, there wouldn't be any kite surfing. Draw an arrow to show the direction you think the wind is blowing.**

Construct Explanations What are some ways that you rely on the wind?

......................................................................................................

......................................................................................................

......................................................................................................

# Winds

The surfer in **Figure 1** is moving over the top of a fluid, water. But the surfer is also moving through another fluid, called air. Air, like water, flows from place to place and does not have a fixed shape. But what causes air to flow?

**Causes of Winds** Air, like most things, moves away from high pressure **areas** to low pressure areas. When there is a difference in air pressure, air moves and wind is created. **Wind** is the movement of air parallel to Earth's surface.

Higher and lower pressure areas are results of the unequal heating of the atmosphere. Air over the heated surface expands, becomes less dense, and rises. As the warm air rises, its air pressure decreases. Meanwhile, if another area is not heated as much, then the air in that area is cooler and denser. The denser air sinks and air pressure increases. The cool, dense air with a higher pressure flows underneath the warm, less dense air. This difference in pressure forces the warm air to rise.

**INTERACTIVITY**

Explore how Earth's rotation affects wind.

**Academic Vocabulary**

The word *area* is used in mathematics and in everyday life. How are the two ways to use the word *area* related?

..............................................

..............................................

..............................................

..............................................

**Catching the Wind**
**Figure 1** Kite surfers need wind to move across the water.

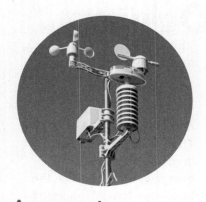

**Anemometer**

**Figure 2** The higher the wind speed, the faster the cups spin around on the anemometer, shown in the top left side of the image.

**Measuring Wind** Wind is a valuable resource, and understanding wind can put this resource to work for us. To identify winds, they are named using the direction from which they originate and their speed. A wind vane is helpful in seeing which way the wind is blowing. The arrow on the wind vane points in the direction from which the wind is blowing. Winds can blow from any of the four directions: north, south, east, and west, and they are named by the direction from which they are blowing. For example, a north wind blows from the north to the south.

Wind speed and pressure can be measured with an anemometer like the one in **Figure 2**. An anemometer has three or four cups mounted at the ends of horizontal spokes that spin on an axle. The force of the wind against the cups turns the axle. The anemometer tracks the number of rotations, and that number is used to calculate wind speed.

 **READING CHECK** **Summarize Text** What causes wind?

.............................................................................................

.............................................................................................

# Math Toolbox

## Windchill Factor

The wind blowing over your skin removes body heat. The increased cooling that a wind causes is called the windchill factor.

1. **Analyze Relationships Using Tables** A weather reporter says, "It is 20 degrees Fahrenheit. But with a wind speed of 30 miles per hour, the windchill factor makes it feel much colder." Use the table to determine how cold the air will feel with the windchill factor accounted for.

...............................................................

2. **Predict** Will it feel colder with an air temperature of 15°F with wind speeds of 40 mph or with an air temperature of 10°F with wind speeds of 25 mph? Explain.

...............................................................

**Windchill Factor**

| Wind (mph) | 35 | 30 | 25 | 20 | 15 | 10 | 5 | 0 | −5 |
|---|---|---|---|---|---|---|---|---|---|
| 5 | 31 | 25 | 19 | 13 | 7 | 1 | −5 | −11 | −16 |
| 10 | 27 | 21 | 15 | 9 | 3 | −4 | −10 | −16 | −22 |
| 15 | 25 | 19 | 13 | 6 | 0 | −7 | −13 | −19 | −26 |
| 20 | 24 | 17 | 11 | 4 | −2 | −9 | −15 | −22 | −29 |
| 25 | 23 | 16 | 9 | 3 | −4 | −11 | −17 | −24 | −31 |
| 30 | 22 | 15 | 8 | 1 | −5 | −12 | −19 | −26 | −33 |
| 35 | 21 | 14 | 7 | 0 | −7 | −14 | −21 | −27 | −34 |
| 40 | 20 | 13 | 6 | −1 | −8 | −15 | −22 | −29 | −36 |
| 45 | 19 | 12 | 5 | −2 | −9 | −16 | −23 | −30 | −37 |

Temperature (°F)

.............................................................................................

# Local Winds and Global Winds

Because of Earth's shape, surfaces, and tilt, the sun cannot evenly warm all of Earth at the same time. Different parts of Earth are warmed at different times and rates. This unequal heating and Earth's rotation affect wind and weather conditions on land, both in local areas and over global regions. Scientists use this understanding to make a **model**, such as a diagram or a map, to describe and predict wind patterns and their effects.

**Local Winds** Have you ever noticed a breeze at the beach on a hot summer day? Even if there is no wind inland, there may be a cool breeze blowing in from the water. Winds that blow over short distances and affect local weather are called local winds. The unequal heating of Earth's surface within a local area causes local winds. These winds form only when the global winds in an area are weak.

Two types of local winds are sea breezes and land breezes, which are illustrated in **Figure 3** below. When sunlight reaches the surface of Earth, land warms up faster than water. The air over the land gets warmer than the air over the water. As you know, warm air is less dense, and it rises, creating a low-pressure area. Cool air blows inland from over the water and moves underneath the warm air, causing a sea breeze. A **sea breeze** or a lake breeze is a local wind that blows from an ocean or lake.

At night, the land cools faster than water. The air above the land begins to cool and move under the warm air rising off the water. The flow of air from land to a body of water forms a **land breeze**.

**Sea Breeze and Land Breeze**

**Figure 3** Fill in the labels to indicate how a sea breeze and a land breeze develop.

The ............... air rises.

The ............... air moves to take ............... air's place.

The ............... air rises.

At night, the ............... air moves off land.

355

**INTERACTIVITY**

Construct a model to show atmospheric cirulation.

**VIDEO**

Learn about general circulation and wind belts.

**Global Winds** The patterns of winds moving around the globe are called global winds. Like local winds, global winds are created by the unequal heating of Earth's surface. However, unlike local winds, global winds occur over a large area.

**Figure 4** models how the sun's radiation strikes Earth. Direct rays from the sun heat Earth's surface intensely near the equator at midday. Near the poles, the sun's rays strike Earth's surface less directly. The sun's energy is spread out over a larger area, so it heats the surface less. As a result, temperatures near the poles are much lower than they are near the equator.

Global winds form from temperature differences between the equator and the poles. These differences produce giant convection currents in the atmosphere. Warm air rises at the equator, and cold air sinks at the poles. Therefore, air pressure tends to be lower near the equator and greater near the poles. This difference in pressure causes winds at Earth's surface to blow from the poles toward the equator. Away from Earth's surface, the opposite is true. Higher in the atmosphere, air flows away from the equator toward the poles. Those air movements produce global winds.

## Model It

### Earth Is Heating Up

**Figure 4** Depending on where you are on Earth's surface, the sun's rays may be stronger or weaker and you may be hotter or colder. These temperature differences produce convection currents in the atmosphere.

1. **Identify** Label the areas where the sun hits Earth most directly (M) and least directly (L).

2. **Identify** Describe how cool and warm air moves in the atmosphere.

........................................................................

........................................................................

3. **Develop Models** Draw a convection current in the atmosphere north of the equator. Use arrows to show the direction of air movement.

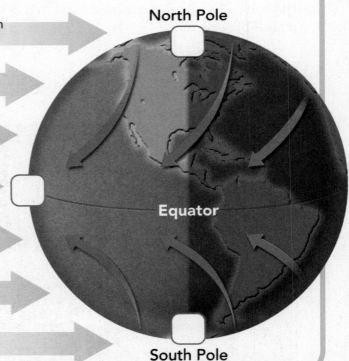

North Pole

Equator

South Pole

## The Coriolis Effect

If Earth did not rotate on its axis, global winds would blow in straight lines. Instead, global winds get deflected or shifted by Earth's rotation. As the winds blow, Earth rotates from west to east underneath them, making it seem as if the winds curve. The way Earth's rotation makes winds curve is called the **Coriolis effect** (kawr ee OH lis ih FEKT) as shown in **Figure 5**. Because of the Coriolis effect, global winds in the Northern Hemisphere gradually turn toward the right. A wind blowing toward the south gradually turns toward the southwest. In the Southern Hemisphere, winds curve toward the left.

**INTERACTIVITY**

Explain how local wind patterns form.

☑ READING CHECK **Translate Information** How do **Figure 5** and the text support the concept that winds do not follow a straight path due to the Coriolis effect?

.................................................................

.................................................................

.................................................................

.................................................................

**No rotation**

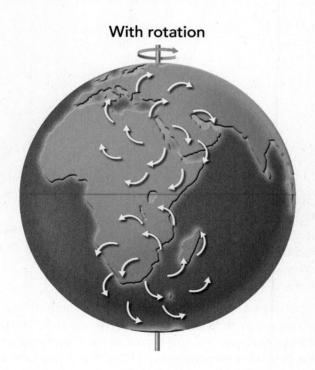

### Modeling the Coriolis Effect

**Figure 5** The Coriolis effect is the result of Earth's rotation. Without it, global winds would travel in straight lines away from their sources. With it, global winds turn to the right in the Northern Hemisphere and to the left in the Southern Hemisphere.

**With rotation**

# Global Wind Patterns

The Coriolis effect, global convection currents, and other factors combine to produce a pattern of calm areas and global wind belts around Earth, as shown in **Figure 6**. The calm areas where air rises or sinks include the doldrums and the horse latitudes. The major global wind belts are the trade winds, the polar easterlies, and the prevailing westerlies. These wind belts are not stationary and can shift about from month to month.

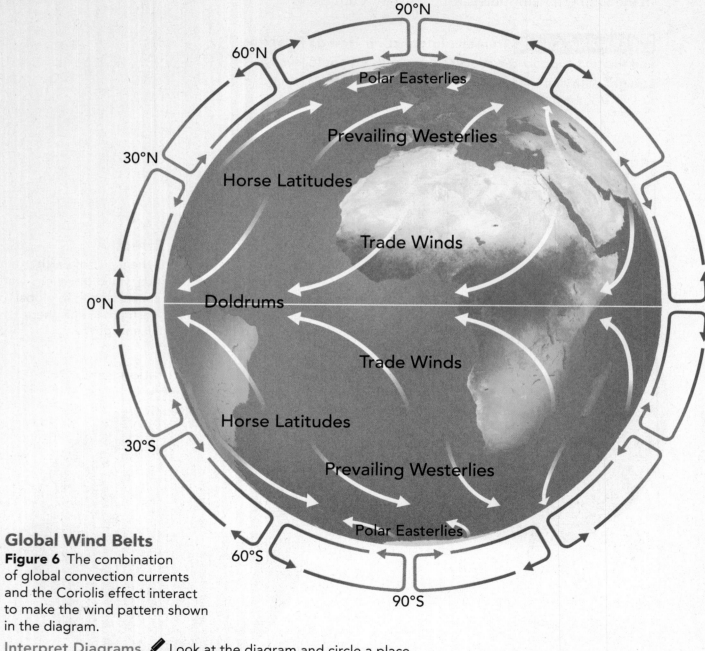

**Global Wind Belts**

**Figure 6** The combination of global convection currents and the Coriolis effect interact to make the wind pattern shown in the diagram.

Interpret Diagrams ✏ Look at the diagram and circle a place where warm air is rising. Draw a square around a place where cool air is sinking. Draw a triangle on a place that shows winds turning right in the Northern hemisphere. Place a check mark on a place where winds along Earth's surface are calm.

**Effects of Global Wind Belts** Global winds affect local weather by moving masses of air from one place to another. The air masses affect the temperature, rainfall, and air pressure. Overall, the global wind belts move energy away from the equator and toward the poles. This helps to equalize the temperature, allowing life to survive in a larger range of latitudes on Earth.

**Jet Streams** About 10 kilometers above Earth's surface are bands of high-speed winds called **jet streams**. They generally blow from west to east at speeds of 200 to 400 kilometers per hour. As jet streams travel around Earth, they wander north and south along wavy paths that vary over time.

The jet streams greatly affect local weather. As shown in **Figure 7**, the jet streams traveling over North America bring a variety of weather conditions. Weather forecasters track the jet streams to predict temperature and precipitation. If the polar jet stream wanders farther south than usual in winter, it could mean colder temperatures and snowy conditions for areas north of the jet stream. If the jet stream wanders farther north than usual, then warmer air moves up from the south and warmer temperatures are predicted for areas south of the jet stream.

HANDS-ON LAB

✐ **Investigate** Explore precipitation in the United States.

**Literacy Connection**

**Translate Information** As you read, underline the text that describes how the jet stream pictured in **Figure 7** can be used to predict weather.

**Jet Streams**

**Figure 7** ✎ The changing positions of the jet streams over the United States influence local weather, particularly in winter. The map shows the position of the polar jet stream on a winter day.

1. Interpret Diagrams The weather in Boise, Idaho, is most likely (colder/warmer) than usual.

2. Interpret Diagrams The weather in Cheyenne, Wyoming, is most likely (colder/warmer) than usual.

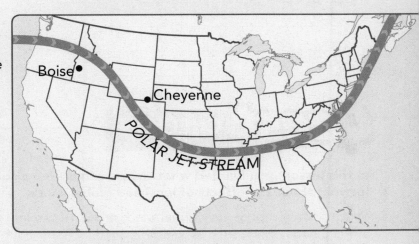

✓ READING CHECK **Integrate With Visuals** How does the map help you to understand the path of the jet stream?

.................................................................................................

.................................................................................................

# ☑LESSON 2 Check

MS-ESS2-6

**1. Identify** What is wind?

......................................................................

......................................................................

......................................................................

**2. Describe Patterns** What pattern occurs in the prevailing westerlies and polar easterlies of the Northern Hemisphere because of the Coriolis effect?

......................................................................

......................................................................

......................................................................

**3. Construct Explanations** How is the sun's energy related to winds?

......................................................................

......................................................................

......................................................................

......................................................................

......................................................................

......................................................................

......................................................................

**4. Develop Models** Describe how you could use a globe and your hand to model the path of a global convection current in the atmosphere.

......................................................................

......................................................................

......................................................................

......................................................................

......................................................................

......................................................................

......................................................................

......................................................................

**5. Predict** How might the jet stream affect the weather in your town this winter? Explain your prediction.

......................................................................

......................................................................

......................................................................

......................................................................

......................................................................

......................................................................

......................................................................

# Quest CHECK-IN

**In this lesson, you learned what causes winds. You also learned about the effects of local and global winds.**

**Predict** Think about how global winds move. How might they affect a large object such as a ship?

......................................................................

......................................................................

......................................................................

......................................................................

......................................................................

## 👆 INTERACTIVITY

Wind at Your Back

**Go online** to explain why a container ship's captain might want to travel in the direction the wind is blowing rather than against the wind.

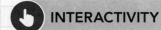

# Windmills of the **Future**

**Windmills** are great when winds are steady and strong. But how can you capture energy from swirling winds? You engineer it!

**The Challenge:** To make a wind turbine that produces electricity from swirling winds.

A company in Spain has come up with a way to capture swirling winds. As wind moves around a tall, slim mast, it vibrates. Magnets located inside a cone at the top of the mast amplify this movement. When wind pushes the mast one way, the magnets push it in the opposite direction so that the whole turbine swirls. The energy of this movement is then converted to electricity. The turbine works no matter the wind direction or speed.

This new turbine needs only a mast, which means no spinning blades, so it doesn't pose a danger to birds and is totally silent. It also costs less, because there are fewer parts to make and maintain. And many more bladeless turbines can fit in one area, so they won't take up as much space. One day soon, forests of these windmills of the future may capture wind energy in a location near you!

**INTERACTIVITY**

Visualize the inner workings of a turbine.

The circular mast is light enough to oscillate due to the wind.

The carbon-fiber rod is strong, but also flexible.

The generator housed inside the bottom of the mast converts the mast's motion into electricity.

**DESIGN CHALLENGE** Can you design and build a wind turbine? Go to the Engineering Design Notebook to find out!

# Patterns of Circulation in the Ocean

## Guiding Questions

- What causes ocean currents?
- How do ocean currents redistribute Earth's energy?

## Connections

**Literacy** Integrate With Visuals

**Math** Analyze Quantitative Relationships

MS-ESS2-6

## Vocabulary

current
El Niño
La Niña

## Academic Vocabulary

gradually

 **VOCABULARY APP**

Practice vocabulary on a mobile device.

**Quest CONNECTION**

Think about how global ocean currents might affect a container ship's navigation route.

## Connect It !

✎ **In the space provided, identify how you think ocean currents, water temperature, and weather might affect a sea turtle.**

**Apply Scientific Reasoning** How do factors such as ocean currents, water temperature, and weather affect you in your daily life?

........................................................................................................

........................................................................................................

........................................................................................................

# Surface Currents

You probably know that ocean water moves as waves. It also flows as currents. A **current** is a large stream of moving water that flows through the ocean. Both waves and currents can affect ocean ecosystems, such as the one shown in **Figure 1**. Unlike waves, currents carry water from one place to another. Some currents move water deep in the ocean. Other currents, called surface currents, move water at the surface of the ocean.

Surface currents are driven mainly by global winds and affect water to a depth of several hundred meters. They follow Earth's global wind patterns. Surface currents move in circular patterns in the five major ocean basins.

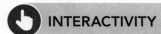
**INTERACTIVITY**

Describe what it would be like to swim against a current.

**Riding the Currents**
**Figure 1** Sea turtles travel long distances by riding ocean currents.

weather

ocean currents

water temperature

363

**Reflect** Along which surface current in **Figure 2** would you most like to float in a boat? In your science notebook, explain why.

## Factors Affecting Surface Currents

Global wind belts affect surface currents. Unequal heating and the rotation of Earth combine to produce global wind belts. Because global winds drive surface currents, unequal heating and Earth's rotation also drive patterns of ocean circulation. Warm currents moving away from the equator redistribute energy to keep temperatures moderate. Cold currents move toward the equator to complete the circle, as shown in **Figure 2**.

You learned that as Earth rotates, the paths of global winds curve. This effect, known as the Coriolis effect, also applies to surface currents. In the Northern Hemisphere, the Coriolis effect causes the currents to curve to the right. In the Southern Hemisphere, the Coriolis effect causes the currents to curve to the left.

As ocean currents are moved by the winds, the continents stop the movements and redirect the currents. Winds push currents, but once the currents meet land, they have to find a new path.

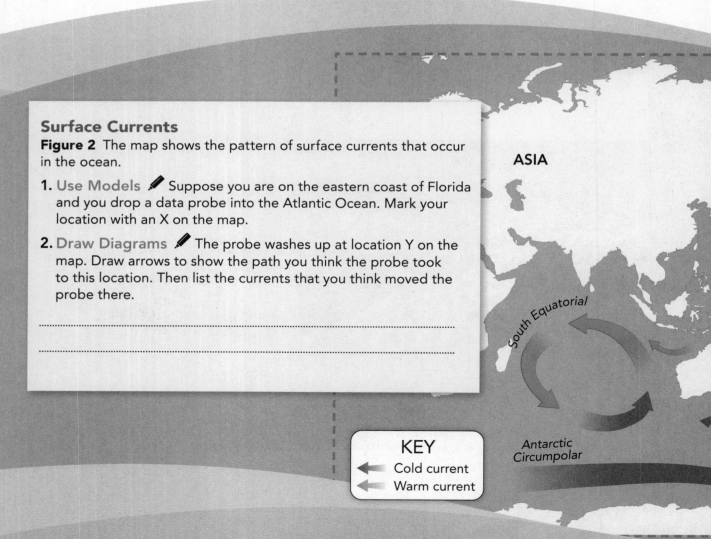

### Surface Currents

**Figure 2** The map shows the pattern of surface currents that occur in the ocean.

1. Use Models ✏️ Suppose you are on the eastern coast of Florida and you drop a data probe into the Atlantic Ocean. Mark your location with an X on the map.

2. Draw Diagrams ✏️ The probe washes up at location Y on the map. Draw arrows to show the path you think the probe took to this location. Then list the currents that you think moved the probe there.

...................................................................................................................

...................................................................................................................

ASIA

South Equatorial

Antarctic
Circumpolar

KEY
← Cold current
← Warm current

**Effects on Climate** The Gulf Stream is the largest and most powerful surface current in the North Atlantic Ocean. It originates from the Gulf of Mexico and brings warm water up the east coast of North America and across the Atlantic. This large, warm current is caused by powerful winds from the west and is more than 30 kilometers wide and 300 meters deep. When the Gulf Stream crosses the Atlantic, it becomes the North Atlantic Drift.

The Gulf Stream and other surface currents redistribute heat from the equator to the poles. These currents have a great impact on local weather and climates. Climate is the temperature and precipitation typical of an area over a long period of time. For example, the North Atlantic Drift brings warm water to Northern Europe. The warm water radiates heat and brings warm temperatures and wet weather. This is why England is warmer and wetter than other countries at the same latitude, such as Canada and Russia. In a similar way, when cold surface currents bring cold water, they cool the air above them. Because cold air holds less moisture than warm air, it results in a cool and dry climate for the land areas.

**Literacy Connection**

**Integrate With Visuals**
Use information from **Figure 2** and the text to explain the effects of warm and cold surface currents on climate.

.................................................

.................................................

.................................................

.................................................

.................................................

.................................................

.................................................

.................................................

.................................................

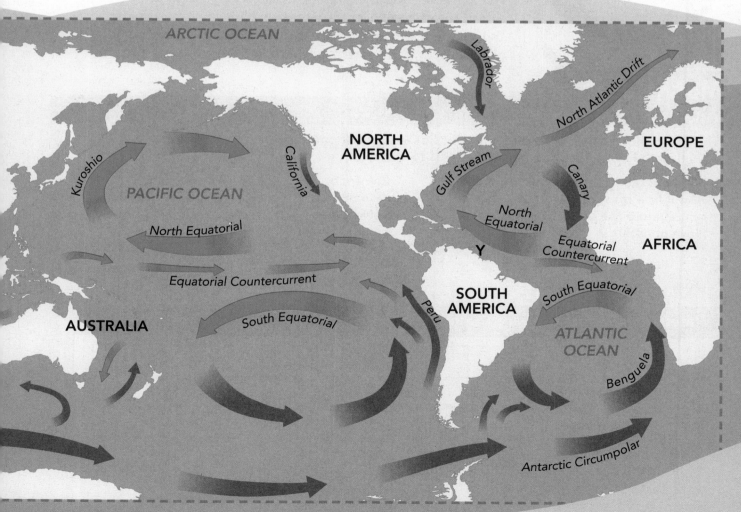

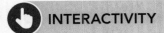
## El Niño

**Figure 3** The image shows the surface temperatures of water in the Pacific Ocean during the 2015–2016 El Niño. Red indicates the warmest temperatures and blue the coolest.

## El Niño and La Niña

Changes in wind patterns and ocean currents can have major impacts on weather conditions on nearby land. One example is **El Niño**, a climate event that occurs every two to seven years in the Pacific Ocean.

Near the equator, winds usually blow east to west. During El Niño, the winds along the equator weaken and reverse direction. This change allows warm, tropical water from the Pacific Ocean to flow east toward the South American coast and prevents the cold, deep water from moving to the surface. El Niño conditions can last for one to two years.

El Niño's effects on the atmosphere and ocean cause shifts in weather patterns. The most recent El Niño in 2015 and 2016, shown in **Figure 3**, was one of the three strongest on record. It increased rainfall and snowfall in California and caused flooding in California and Texas.

When surface waters in the eastern Pacific are colder than normal, a climate event known as **La Niña** occurs. A La Niña event is the opposite of an El Niño event. During a La Niña, stronger winds blow above the Pacific Ocean, causing more warm water to move west. This allows lots of cold water to rise to the surface. This change in the ocean temperature affects weather all over the world. La Niña can cause colder than normal winters and greater precipitation in the Pacific Northwest and the north central United States.

## Math Toolbox

### Analyzing El Niño Data

The graph shows how much warmer the Pacific Ocean was from 2015 to 2016 than the average temperature from 1981 to 2010.

1. **Analyze Quantitative Relationships** About how many degrees did water temperature rise between January and November 2015?

...............................................................

...............................................................

2. **Interpret Diagrams** Why does the temperature most likely decrease between November 2015 and April 2016?

...............................................................

...............................................................

...............................................................

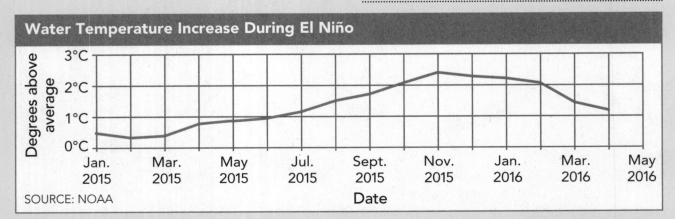

**Water Temperature Increase During El Niño**

SOURCE: NOAA

# Deep Ocean Currents

Deep below the ocean surface, another type of current causes the movement of cold waters across the ocean floor. Deep currents are caused by differences in the density of ocean water.

**Temperature, Salinity, and Density** The density of ocean water varies with its temperature and salinity. Water is dense if it is cold or salty. Dense water sinks, which drives deep ocean currents. When a warm surface current moves from the equator toward one of the poles, it **gradually** gets denser because it both cools and becomes saltier as water evaporates. As ice forms near the poles (see **Figure 4**), the salinity of the water increases even further. This is because the ice contains only fresh water, leaving the salts in the water. The cold salty water sinks and flows along the ocean floor as a deep current. Like surface currents, deep currents are affected by the Coriolis effect, which causes them to curve.

Deep currents move and mix water around the world. They carry cold water from the poles toward the equator. Deep currents flow slowly. They may take longer than 1,000 years to make one full trip around their ocean basins.

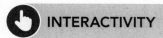

INTERACTIVITY

Explore ocean habitats.

## Academic Vocabulary
Use the term *gradually* in a sentence describing Earth's movements.

.......................................................

.......................................................

.......................................................

.......................................................

## Sea Ice
**Figure 4** Sea ice forms different shapes. This ice is called pancake ice.

## Plan It !

### Sea Ice and Salinity
**Plan Your Investigation** How can you use the set up below to investigate how ice formation affects the salinity of ocean water? Summarize your plan.

.......................................................................................................

.......................................................................................................

**Make Observations** 🖊 Each glass of water contains the same amount of salt. Circle the glass that contains water with the greatest salinity?

## INTERACTIVITY

Learn what causes Earth's patterns of ocean currents.

## ▶ VIDEO

Discover how global currents affect the United States.

## Global Ocean Conveyor

The ocean currents move in a loop around Earth's bodies of water. The movement looks like a conveyor belt, as shown in **Figure 5**, and results from density differences due to variations in temperature and salinity. The movement of the currents circulates oxygen that is essential for marine life.

The ocean's deep currents mostly start as cold water in the North Atlantic Ocean. This is the same water, called the North Atlantic Deep Water, that moved north across the Atlantic as part of the Gulf Stream. It sinks and flows southward toward Antarctica. From there it flows northward into both the Indian and Pacific oceans. There, deep cold water rises to the surface, warms, and eventually flows back along the surface into the Atlantic.

This system circulates water and transfers heat throughout the interconnected ocean basins and thus around Earth from the equator to the poles and back again.

☑ READING CHECK **Integrate With Visuals** How does the map in **Figure 5** relate to the text on this page?

.................................................................................................

.................................................................................................

## Global Conveyor Belt

**Figure 5** Deep currents and surface currents form a global system of heat distribution through Earth's interconnected ocean basins.

1. **Develop Models** 🖉 Draw arrows on the conveyor to indicate the direction of both cold and warm water movement.

2. **Predict** What might happen if the global conveyor stopped?

.................................................................................................

.................................................................................................

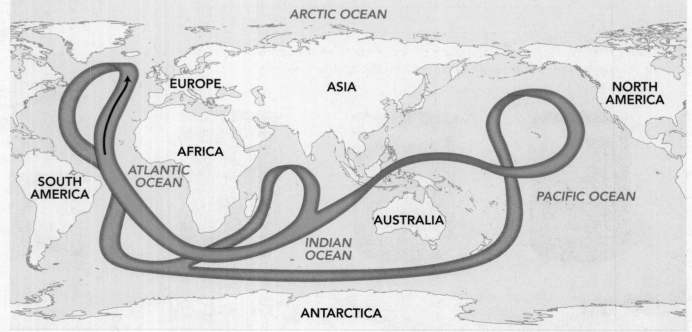

MS-ESS2-6

**1. Cause and Effect**  What causes surface currents?

......................................................................

**2. Patterns**  What pattern of movement do both warm and cold surface currents share?

......................................................................

......................................................................

......................................................................

......................................................................

**3. Apply Concepts**  Explain why cities located on the western coast of Norway in northern Europe near the cold Artic Circle have a milder climate compared to other places located farther inland at the lower latitudes.

......................................................................

......................................................................

......................................................................

......................................................................

......................................................................

**4. Develop Models**  ✏ Draw a diagram or flow chart to show how variations in ocean water properties result in a deep ocean current forming.

# Quest CHECK-IN

**In this lesson, you learned about how surface currents and deep ocean currents form. You also discovered how they affect weather and climate.**

**Apply Concepts**  Which ocean currents are most likely to affect your container ship? Why?

......................................................................

......................................................................

......................................................................

......................................................................

......................................................................

## 👆 INTERACTIVITY

Find Your Advantage

**Go online** to analyze the path of the Gulf Stream.

MS-ESS2-6

# HURRICANES in the Making

You've probably seen images of enormous hurricanes swirling over the Atlantic Ocean. Where will the next one strike? Thankfully, these giant storms often follow predictable patterns. That's because the development and movement of hurricanes is affected by air and ocean currents.

## How Hurricanes Form

Hurricanes form over the southern Atlantic Ocean where the water temperature is at least 80°F. As the warm ocean air rises, it leaves an area of low air pressure in its place. Air rushes in to fill the low pressure area, and then it heats up and rises, too, which makes the air begin to swirl and spin.

Hurricanes move with Earth's air currents. Most hurricanes form in a current of westward-flowing air near the equator called the trade winds. If a low pressure area forms off the coast of Africa, it can then catch a ride on the trade winds. As the low pressure area moves westward across the warm ocean waters, it grows in strength. By the time it reaches the southern United States, the low pressure area has become a hurricane.

## Tracking Hurricanes

A hurricane may take different paths. A hurricane moving northward might run into westerly winds that blow across the United States. These winds will cause the hurricane to turn eastward, back out to sea. Sometimes a northward hurricane also lines up with the Gulf Stream, the warm ocean current running northward up the coast. When that happens, a hurricane can travel up to New England.

Other hurricanes may take a path westward across Florida. Some travel into the Gulf of Mexico, where westerly winds may turn a hurricane back eastward, across Louisiana, Alabama, or Florida.

Hurricanes that impact the eastern United States usually form off the western coast of Africa or in the Caribbean Sea.

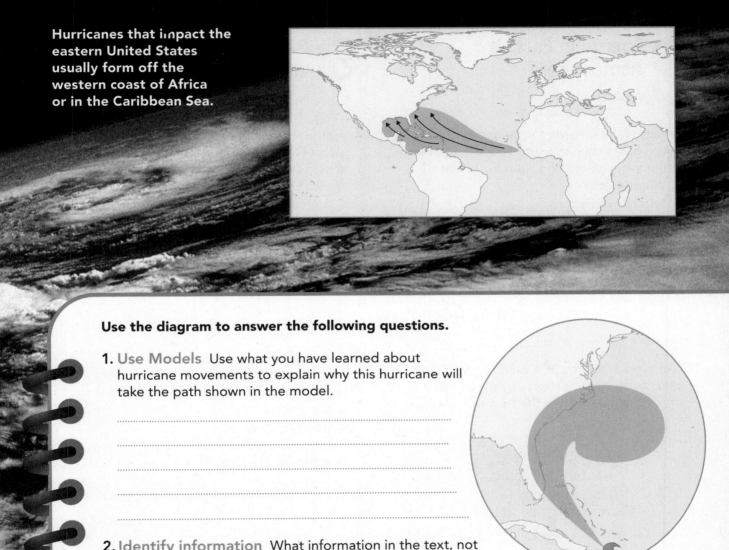

**Use the diagram to answer the following questions.**

1. **Use Models** Use what you have learned about hurricane movements to explain why this hurricane will take the path shown in the model.

........................................................................................

........................................................................................

........................................................................................

........................................................................................

........................................................................................

2. **Identify information** What information in the text, not shown in the model, helps to explain the hurricane's track?

........................................................................................

........................................................................................

........................................................................................

3. **Construct Explanations** Explain why using models to track hurricanes is important.

........................................................................................

........................................................................................

........................................................................................

........................................................................................

4. **Develop Models** ✏ Meteorologists now predict calmer westerly winds for the next few days. Draw a new track for the hurricane based on this information.

371

# ☑TOPIC 7 Review and Assess

## 1 Energy in Earth's Atmosphere

MS-ESS2-6

1. Which of the following is the process through which gases such as water vapor hold energy in the atmosphere and keep Earth warm?
   A. condensation
   B. infrared radiation
   C. ultraviolet radiation
   D. the greenhouse effect

2. When land absorbs sunlight, some energy is directly transferred to the air by
   ............................................. waves in the form of
   .............................................

3. **Develop Models** ✏ Complete the flow chart to show the process by which the transfer of heat within the troposphere occurs.

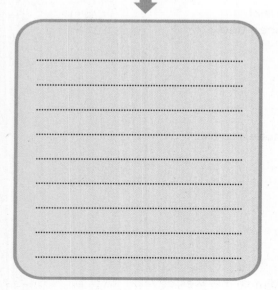

The sun's energy heats the Earth's land surface.

## 2 Patterns of Circulation in the Atmosphere

MS-ESS2-6

4. A student makes a model of global winds that affect North America. Which of the following should the student's model include?
   A. doldrums          B. sea breezes
   C. land breezes      D. polar easterlies

5. Which unequal condition causes a sea breeze to develop?
   A. dryer air over land than water
   B. dryer air over water than land
   C. warmer air over land than water
   D. warmer air over water than land

6. Which global wind pattern can wander farther south than usual in winter causing temperatures in the U.S. to decrease?
   A. trade winds
   B. polar jet stream
   C. prevailing westerlies
   D. subtropical jet stream

7. In the Southern Hemisphere, global winds turn
   to the ................................................. because of the
   .................................................

8. **Cause and Effect** How does unequal heating and the movement of warm air at the equator and cold air at the poles produce global wind patterns?

   ...........................................................................
   ...........................................................................
   ...........................................................................
   ...........................................................................
   ...........................................................................
   ...........................................................................
   ...........................................................................
   ...........................................................................
   ...........................................................................

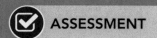

# ③ Patterns of Circulation in the Ocean

MS-ESS2-6

**9.** What makes ocean currents move in a curved path?
**A.** Earth's rotation
**B.** unequal density
**C.** unequal heating
**D.** Earth's revolution

**10.** What causes deep ocean currents to flow?
**A.** local winds
**B.** global winds
**C.** unequal heating
**D.** density differences

**11.** Which of the following can bring heavy rains and flooding to California and an especially warm winter in the northeastern United States?
**A.** El Niño
**B.** La Niña
**C.** Coriolis effect
**D.** North Atlantic Drift

**12.** Which effect does the Gulf Stream have on the climates of nearby land?
**A.** calming
**B.** drying
**C.** freezing
**D.** warming

**13.** Deep ocean currents slowly carry cold water from the ............................................... to the

...............................................

**14.** **Analyze Systems** What is the role of the global conveyor system?

...........................................................................

...........................................................................

...........................................................................

**15.** **Develop Models** ✏ Draw a diagram of a major warm ocean surface current flowing along a coastal area. Label the current and type of climate you would most likely find in the area. Show how the current influences the area's climate.

MS-ESS2-1, MS-ESS2-4

## Evidence-Based Assessment

An oceanographic research team is investigating patterns in surface ocean currents around the globe. After collecting the data, they develop a map to record information about major surface currents in the ocean.

Their map shows both the directions of the surface currents and the temperature of the water carried by the currents.

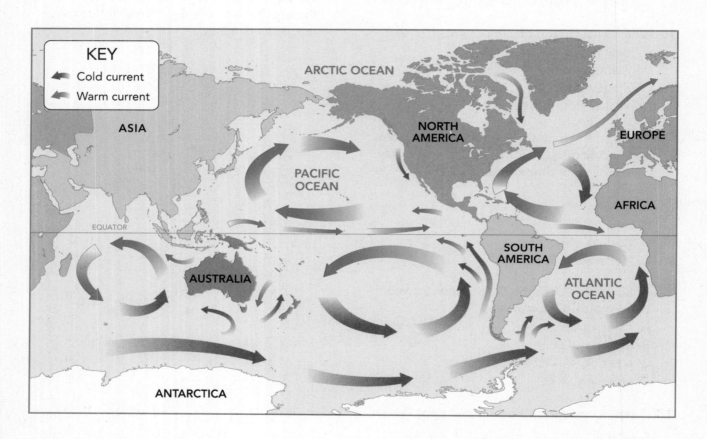

**1. Analyze Systems** According to the research team's map, the longest cold surface currents
(A) travel around the South Pole.
B. are found in the Atlantic Ocean.
C. do not interact with warm surface currents.
D. travel down the eastern coasts of South America and Africa.

**2. Analyze Data** Which continent is mostly surrounded by surface currents carrying cold water?
A. Africa
(B.) Antarctica
C. Asia
D. Europe

3. **Develop Models** Suppose the team decides to add arrows to indicate the circulation of winds in the atmosphere. How would these wind circulations compare to the ocean currents? What explains this relationship?

.......................................................................................

.......................................................................................

.......................................................................................

.......................................................................................

.......................................................................................

.......................................................................................

.......................................................................................

.......................................................................................

.......................................................................................

.......................................................................................

.......................................................................................

.......................................................................................

.......................................................................................

.......................................................................................

.......................................................................................

4. **Patterns** Which of the following patterns of ocean circulation are supported by data in the map? Check all that apply.

☐ Warm water is carried by currents from the equator to the poles, where it cools.

☐ Currents move in large circles between continents and landmasses.

☐ Cool water is carried from the west coast of Africa to the north coast of South America, where it is warmed.

☐ Cool water travels from the poles to the equator, where it is warmed.

☐ Ocean currents move in a clockwise direction in the Northern Hemisphere and counterclockwise in the Southern Hemisphere.

☐ Warm water moves from the poles to the equator, where it cools.

5. **Cause and Effect** Explain how Earth's rotation and the sun's uneven heating of the planet are responsible for the patterns of ocean circulation detailed on the map.

.......................................................................................

.......................................................................................

.......................................................................................

.......................................................................................

.......................................................................................

.......................................................................................

.......................................................................................

.......................................................................................

.......................................................................................

.......................................................................................

.......................................................................................

# Quest FINDINGS

## Complete the Quest!

**Phenomenon** Write a report that recommends a speed and route for the container ship crossing the Atlantic Ocean. Be sure to include evidence that justifies your recommendations and explain the factors that affect your recommendations.

**Construct Explanations** Explain why you think your recommendations will or will not still be valid in a year.

.......................................................................................

.......................................................................................

.......................................................................................

.......................................................................................

👆 **INTERACTIVITY**

Reflect on Crossing the Atlantic

MS-ESS2-6

# Not All Heating Is Equal

How can you use a model to **demonstrate** the amount of **solar energy** that different places on **Earth** receive?

## Background

**Phenomenon** As an engineer at a solar energy company, you must help choose a location for a new solar farm. The company has identified three possible sites: near Yellowknife, Canada; La Paz, Mexico; or Quito, Ecuador. In this investigation, you will model how sunlight hits Earth to determine the best location for the solar farm.

# Design and Plan Your Investigation

HANDS-ON LAB

☑ **Demonstrate** Go online for a downloadable worksheet of this lab.

☐ 1. Look at the diagram. Then predict how you think the amount of solar energy received at each of the three spots is related to its location. Which of the three locations do you think is best suited for a solar farm? Record your prediction in the space provided.

☐ 2. Design your model to test your predictions. Sketch your model and identify the materials you will use. Use your model to measure the temperature of surfaces that face a light source at different angles. (Hint: Assume that the temperature of black construction paper will increase after about 15 minutes when a light shines on it from 30 cm away.) Consider the following questions as you design and plan your investigation:

- How will you represent the sun and Earth in your model?
- What two variables will you investigate?
- How will you make sure that you test only one variable?
- How will you measure the amount of solar energy each location receives?

☐ 3. Write a detailed procedure describing how you will use your model to test your predictions about how the amount of solar energy received at each of the three spots is related to its location. (Hint: Plan to use some of the available materials to determine how the temperature of the black paper is affected by its position on your model.) Record your procedure in the space provided.

☐ 4. Have your teacher approve your procedure. Then make your model and conduct the investigation to test your prediction. Use the data table to record your data.

## Prediction

........................................................................

........................................................................

## Sketch of Model

## Procedure

........................................................................

........................................................................

........................................................................

........................................................................

........................................................................

## Data Table

| Location | Temperature after 15 minutes (°C) |
|---|---|
| A (Yellowknife) | |
| B (La Paz) | |
| C (Quito) | |

# Analyze and Interpret Data

1. **Develop Models** Summarize how you developed your model to test your prediction.

   ...........................................................................................................................
   ...........................................................................................................................
   ...........................................................................................................................
   ...........................................................................................................................

2. **Interpret Data** In which locations did you observe the highest and lowest temperatures?

   ...........................................................................................................................
   ...........................................................................................................................
   ...........................................................................................................................
   ...........................................................................................................................

3. **Cause and Effect** How does the temperature of each location relate to the amount of solar energy it receives? Explain.

   ...........................................................................................................................
   ...........................................................................................................................
   ...........................................................................................................................
   ...........................................................................................................................

4. **Patterns** Based on your results, explain how the location of an area on Earth affects the amount of solar energy it receives. Then describe how your results compare to your prediction.

   ...........................................................................................................................
   ...........................................................................................................................
   ...........................................................................................................................
   ...........................................................................................................................

5. **Construct Explanations** Based on your results, which of the three locations is the best site for the new solar farm? Use evidence from your observations to support your answer.

   ...........................................................................................................................
   ...........................................................................................................................
   ...........................................................................................................................
   ...........................................................................................................................

# Climate

NGSS PERFORMANCE EXPECTATIONS

**MS-ESS2-6** Develop and use a model to describe
how unequal heating and rotation of the Earth
cause patterns of atmospheric and oceanic
circulation that determine regional climates.

**MS-ESS3-5** Ask questions to clarify evidence of
the factors that have caused the rise in global
temperatures over the past century.

HANDS-ON LAB

u**Connect** Make observations about
the factors that determine climate
regions.

What is happening to this glacier?

**GO ONLINE** to access your digital course

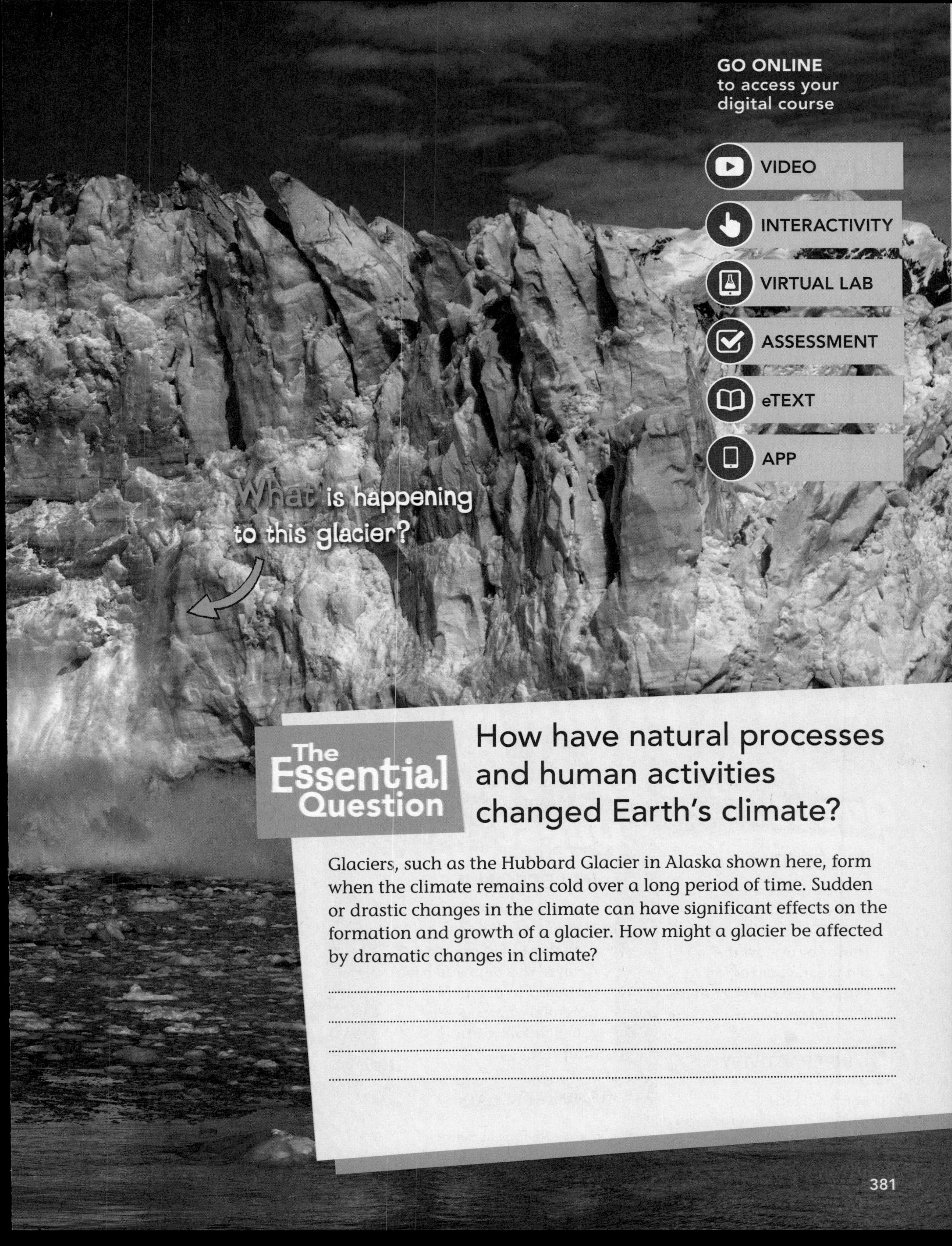

- VIDEO
- INTERACTIVITY
- VIRTUAL LAB
- ASSESSMENT
- eTEXT
- APP

**The Essential Question**

# How have natural processes and human activities changed Earth's climate?

Glaciers, such as the Hubbard Glacier in Alaska shown here, form when the climate remains cold over a long period of time. Sudden or drastic changes in the climate can have significant effects on the formation and growth of a glacier. How might a glacier be affected by dramatic changes in climate?

..........................................................................................

..........................................................................................

..........................................................................................

..........................................................................................

## How can I help reduce my school's carbon footprint?

**Phenomenon** The construction of new schools often involves the work of energy engineers. These specialists review architectural plans to improve the energy efficiency of buildings. They also recommend equipment that helps to reduce energy usage.

In this Quest activity, you will explore how the climate of your region affects energy usage at your school. In digital activities and labs, you will investigate ways to increase the efficiency of energy usage at your school. By applying what you have learned, you will develop a plan to reduce your school's carbon footprint.

**INTERACTIVITY**

Shrinking Your Carbon Footprint

**MS-ESS3-5** Ask questions to clarify evidence of the factors that have caused the rise in global temperatures over the past century.

**NBC LEARN** ▶ VIDEO

After watching the video, which examines how to make homes more energy efficient, think about ways you use energy sources, such as gas and electricity, in your daily life. List three activities you do each day that use the greatest amount of energy.

**1**
..................................................................
..................................................................

**2**
..................................................................
..................................................................

**3**
..................................................................
..................................................................

# Quest CHECK-IN

### IN LESSON 1
How does the climate of a region affect the people who live there? Think about how the climate in your region impacts the energy needs of your school.

**INTERACTIVITY**

Footprint Steps

# Quest CHECK-IN

### IN LESSON 2
How can small changes result in significant cutbacks in energy usage? Analyze the data you have gathered to estimate potential reductions to your school's carbon footprint.

**HANDS-ON LAB**

Energy Savings at School

# Quest CHECK-IN

### IN LESSON 3
How can your school effectively reduce its energy usage? Develop a school-wide plan for reducing your school's carbon footprint.

**INTERACTIVITY**

Make a Difference

The Green School in Bali, Indonesia, admits students up through high school. The design of the buildings and classrooms allows the school to maintain a small carbon footprint.

## Quest FINDINGS

### Complete the Quest!

Apply what you've learned by developing and delivering a presentation that outlines your proposals and clearly communicates your data.

👆 **INTERACTIVITY**

Reflect on Shrinking Your Carbon Footprint

# Climate Factors

## Guiding Questions

- How does climate differ from weather?
- How do latitude, altitude, and land distribution affect patterns of circulation in the atmosphere and ocean?
- How do patterns of circulation in the atmosphere and ocean determine regional climates?

## Connections

**Literacy** Integrate With Visuals

**Math** Analyze Proportional Relationships

MS-ESS2-6

## Vocabulary

climate

## Academic Vocabulary

describe

 **VOCABULARY APP**

Practice vocabulary on a mobile device.

**Quest CONNECTION**

Consider how climate affects the energy usage in a particular area.

## Connect It!

✏️ **Label the parts on the image that indicate what kind of temperature and precipitation are present in Antarctica.**

**Make Generalizations** From what you see in the image, how would you describe conditions in Antarctica?

.................................................................................

**Infer** How do you think humans would adapt to this climate?

.................................................................................

.................................................................................

.................................................................................

# Factors That Affect Temperature

No matter where you live, the weather changes every day. In some areas, the temperature might change just one degree from one day to the next. In other areas, a cold, rainy day might be followed by a warm, sunny one.

While weather describes the short-term conditions in an area, **climate** is the long-term weather pattern in an area. Specifically, climate refers to the average, year-after-year conditions of temperature, precipitation, wind, and clouds. So, while "it's snowing" **describes** the current weather, you need more information to describe the climate.

How water cycles in different areas determines climate patterns. For example, year-round freezing temperatures in Antarctica prevent snow from melting and limit evaporation from the ocean. **Figure 1** shows that Antarctica has a cold, dry climate.

Another example is California's Mojave Desert, where the limited precipitation evaporates rapidly. The climate there is hot and dry. But, if you move west from the Mojave Desert toward California's coast, you would notice a cooler, more humid climate. Why does this happen?

An area's climate is affected by its latitude, altitude, distance from large bodies of water, ocean currents, and global prevailing winds. These factors are continuously changing, but an area's climate does remain relatively stable. However, if these factors change too quickly or drastically, then the area's climate can change as well.

 **INTERACTIVITY**

Explore how moving north or south on Earth affects the climate of the region.

**Academic Vocabulary**

How might you describe your favorite food?

.......................................................

.......................................................

.......................................................

.......................................................

**Temperature and Climate**

**Figure 1** Polar climates have certain patterns of temperature and precipitation, as shown in this image of Antarctica.

## Latitude and Temperature

**Figure 2** ✏ Label the temperature zones *polar*, *temperate,* or *tropical*, based on the latitudes shown. In which temperature zone is most of the United States located?

........................................................

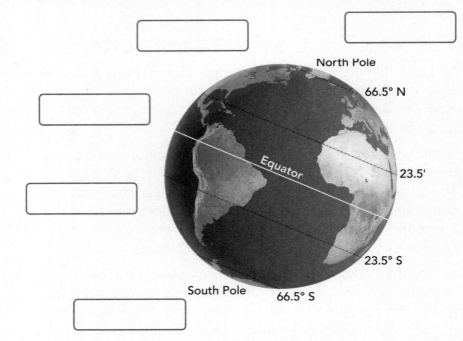

North Pole

66.5° N

Equator

23.5°

23.5° S

South Pole    66.5° S

### Latitude
Towns and cities in the northern United States tend to have snowy winters, while those in the south have mild, warm winters. This is because areas closer to the equator have warmer climates. The sun's rays hit Earth's surface more directly at the equator than at the poles. At the poles, the same amount of solar radiation hits at a greater angle, which brings less warmth. Based on latitude, Earth's surface is divided into three types of temperature zones **(Figure 2)**.

The tropical zone includes all of the locations on Earth that can possibly see the sun directly overhead. The polar zones extend from about 66.5° to 90°N and 66.5° to 90°S latitudes. Between them are the temperate zones. In summer, the sun's rays strike the temperate zones quite directly. In winter, the sun's rays strike at a lower angle.

### Altitude
In the case of high mountains, altitude is a more important climate factor than latitude. Near Earth's surface, temperature decreases as altitude increases. Thus, many mountainous areas have cooler climates than the lower areas around them.

## Math Toolbox

### Temperature and Altitude

For every 1-kilometer increase in altitude in the lower atmosphere, temperature decreases about 6.5°C.

**Analyze Proportional Relationships** A researcher releases a weather balloon to study the atmosphere. The air temperature at the ground is 27°C. If the sensors read an air temperature of 17°C, then about how far up has the balloon traveled?

........................................................

## Distance from Large Bodies of Water

The ocean and other large bodies of water, such as lakes, can affect the weather and climate of nearby land by moderating local air temperatures. Water heats up and cools down about five times more slowly than land. As a result, the air above water heats up and cools down more slowly than air over land. When winds blow across oceans onto land, they moderate temperatures in coastal areas, bringing mild winters and cool summers. The centers of most continents, however, are too far from the ocean to be warmed or cooled by it. These areas have continental climates, with colder winters and warmer summers.

## Ocean Currents

Marine climates are strongly influenced by the temperature of nearby ocean currents—streams of water within the ocean that move in regular patterns caused by different amounts of solar energy striking Earth at different latitudes. As shown in **Figure 3**, most warm ocean currents move toward the poles. Conversely, cold water currents tend to move toward the equator. Cold currents affect climate by carrying cold water from the polar zones toward the equator, cooling local air masses.

✔ READING CHECK **Determine Conclusions** How does the North Atlantic Drift most likely affect the climate in Europe?

..................................................................................................

## Major Ocean Currents

**Figure 3** Major currents circulate warm and cold ocean water between the poles and the equator. Compare and contrast the major ocean currents north and south of the equator.

.............................................

.............................................

.............................................

.............................................

.............................................

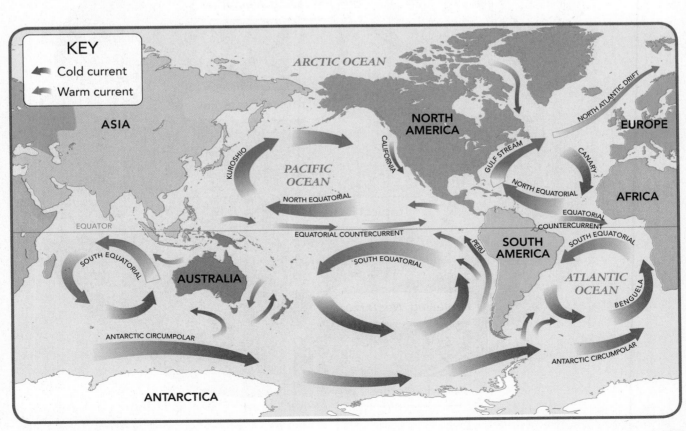

**INTERACTIVITY**

Learn how topography affects precipitation in an area.

**VIDEO**

Watch how ocean currents help to regulate the climate.

# Factors That Affect Precipitation

The amount of precipitation a particular area experiences from month to month and year to year can vary greatly. By analyzing the amount of precipitation an area has received over many years, meteorologists determine the average yearly precipitation for that area. The main factors that affect the amount of precipitation an area receives are prevailing winds, presence of mountains, and seasonal winds.

**Prevailing Winds** Prevailing winds are winds that usually blow in one direction over large distances on Earth. As shown in **Figure 4,** these winds are organized into belts that can move air masses with different temperatures and humidities over long distances. The amount of water vapor an air mass carries affects how much rain or snow it can produce.

## Prevailing Winds

**Figure 4** 🖊 The globe shows Earth's prevailing global winds. Circle the name of the wind belt that most affects Europe.

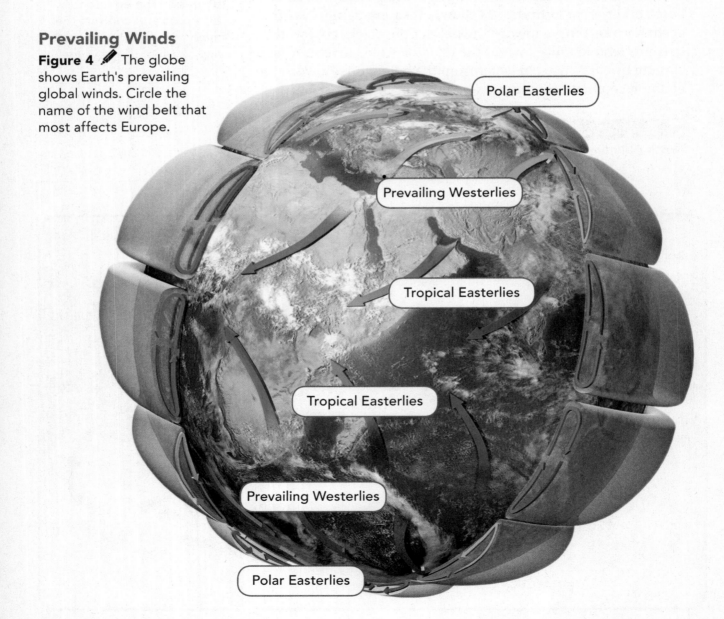

Polar Easterlies

Prevailing Westerlies

Tropical Easterlies

Tropical Easterlies

Prevailing Westerlies

Polar Easterlies

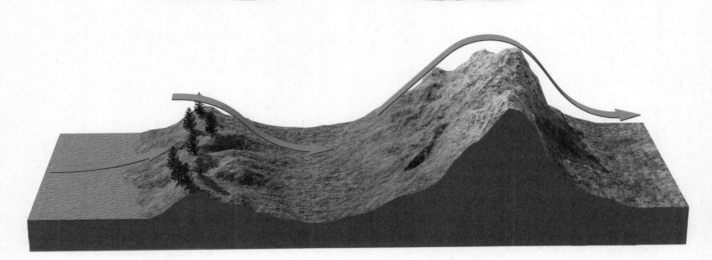

1. Warm, moist air is carried from the Pacific Ocean by the prevailing Westerlies.

2. Somewhat drier air continues to move eastward, rising along with the slope of the land.

3. Now dry air continues to move East after passing the mountains.

## Mountain Ranges

The presence of a mountain range can affect the type and location of precipitation any air masses may produce as they pass over the area **(Figure 5)**. Humid air masses blown in from the ocean are forced to rise as they encounter coastal mountains, producing clouds and precipitation on the side of the mountain facing the wind. After passing over the mountains, the air mass is cooler and dryer, having lost much of its water vapor. This leaves the side of the mountain facing away from the wind in a rain shadow, where little precipitation falls.

## Seasonal Winds

A seasonal change in wind patterns and precipitation, called a monsoon, occurs in some parts of the world. Monsoons are caused by different rates of heating and cooling between the ocean and nearby land. During the summer in southern Asia, when the land gradually gets warmer than the ocean, warm and humid winds constantly blow in from the ocean, producing heavy rains. In winter, the opposite occurs as the land becomes colder than the ocean. Cool, dry winds constantly blow out to sea from the land.

### Mountains and Precipitation

**Figure 5** 🖊 This image shows what happens when a mountain range is in the path of a prevailing wind. Draw rain and snow where they are most likely to occur. Add a redwood tree and a cactus in the locations that you think favor the growth of these plants.

 **INTERACTIVITY**

Demonstrate how the atmosphere and ocean circulations affect climate.

✅ READING CHECK **Integrate With Visuals** If the area shown in Figure 5 were located in a region where monsoons occur, would the figure represent a summer monsoon or a winter monsoon? Explain.

........................................................................................

........................................................................................

........................................................................................

## Major Climates

**Figure 6** ✏ The locations of major climate regions covering Earth's surface are influenced by many factors. Draw a circle around the area on the map where you live. What type of climate exists where you live?

........................................................

........................................................

........................................................

........................................................

........................................................

........................................................

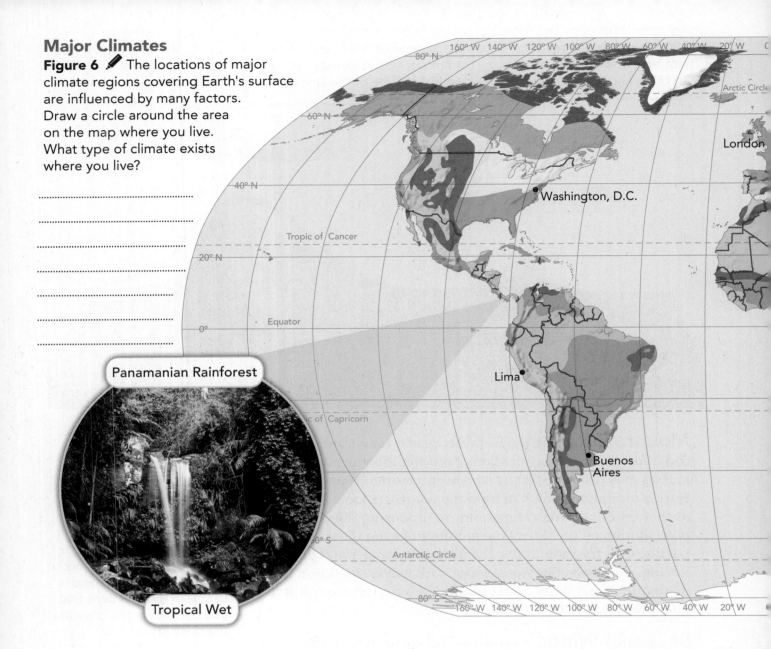

Panamanian Rainforest

Tropical Wet

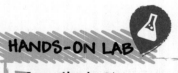

☐**Investigate** Observe some of the factors that help to distinguish among climate regions.

# World Climates

Imagine winning a vacation to the Australian Outback! The Outback is a region near the central area of Australia. What type of clothes should you take on the trip? The best way to find out is to learn more about your destination's climate.

**Classifying Climates** Scientists classify climates by taking into account an area's average temperature, average annual precipitation, and the vegetation found growing there. The major climate regions of Earth each have their own smaller subdivisions **(Figure 6).** Recall that local climates can be affected by changes in natural climate factors, such as ocean currents and winds. Human activities that affect the atmosphere and ocean can also impact local climates. So Earth's climate regions can change over time.

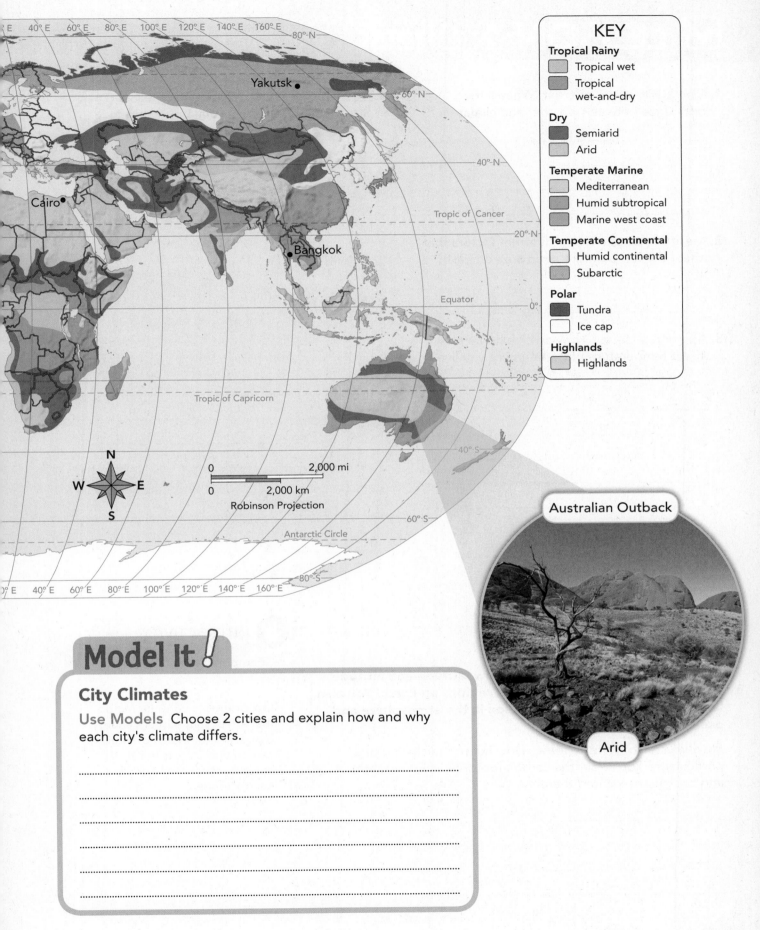

## KEY

**Tropical Rainy**
Tropical wet
Tropical wet-and-dry

**Dry**
Semiarid
Arid

**Temperate Marine**
Mediterranean
Humid subtropical
Marine west coast

**Temperate Continental**
Humid continental
Subarctic

**Polar**
Tundra
Ice cap

**Highlands**
Highlands

Yakutsk

Cairo

Bangkok

N
W E
S

0          2,000 mi
0     2,000 km
Robinson Projection

Tropic of Cancer
Equator
Tropic of Capricorn
Antarctic Circle

Australian Outback

Arid

# Model It!

## City Climates

Use Models  Choose 2 cities and explain how and why each city's climate differs.

..........................................................................................

..........................................................................................

..........................................................................................

..........................................................................................

..........................................................................................

..........................................................................................

MS-ESS2-6

**1. Compare and Contrast** What is the difference between weather and climate?

........................................................

........................................................

........................................................

........................................................

**2. Identify** What are four different factors that affect the temperature of an area on Earth?

........................................................

........................................................

**3. Apply Concepts** How do climate factors affect temperature patterns where you live?

........................................................

........................................................

........................................................

........................................................

........................................................

........................................................

........................................................

........................................................

**4. Use Models** How do you think the Gulf Stream influences the climate of northern Europe?

........................................................

........................................................

........................................................

........................................................

........................................................

........................................................

........................................................

........................................................

........................................................

# Quest CHECK-IN

**In this lesson, you learned about how latitude and altitude can affect the climate of different regions on Earth. You also learned how patterns of circulation in the atmosphere and ocean affect climate.**

**Apply Scientific Reasoning** How might the climate of a particular region affect the carbon footprint of homes, schools, and businesses located there?

........................................................

........................................................

........................................................

........................................................

........................................................

## 👆 INTERACTIVITY

Footprint Steps

**Go online** to consider factors that affect your school's energy usage and calculate how much carbon dioxide was released by your school based on its energy usage.

# Urban Heat Islands

For years, people have observed that cities are often much warmer than less-developed surrounding areas—even at night. Scientists can now precisely measure this phenomenon, which they call the urban heat island effect.

Many of the materials used to build cities absorb a great deal of sunlight, which causes them to become warmer. This makes surface temperatures in many cities higher than they would be if the environment consisted of trees and soil instead of asphalt, granite, and glass. For example, surface temperatures in Providence, Rhode Island, are about 12°C (22°F) warmer than in surrounding towns that are less developed.

As you have probably noticed when walking across a parking lot on a sunny day, the hot surface warms the air above it. This is why the heat island effect can make a city's downtown air feel as hot at night as it was during the day. All the thermal energy absorbed by the streets and buildings during the day is radiated back out into the air at night.

## MY DISCOVERY

Search *urban heat island* in an online search engine and find out about the ways that cities are attempting to reduce the effects of this phenomenon.

Satellite images showing temperatures in Providence and the surrounding area (top) and land development (bottom). In the top image, the lighter color indicates warmer areas, while the darker color indicates colder areas.

# 2 Climate Change

## Guiding Questions

- What effects do greenhouse gases in the atmosphere have on global temperatures?
- How do natural processes and human activities affect patterns of change in global temperatures?

## Connections

**Literacy** Cite Textual Evidence

**Math** Reason Quantitatively

MS-ESS3-5

## Vocabulary

greenhouse gas
greenhouse effect
climate change
global warming
fossil fuel

## Academic Vocabulary

impact

 **VOCABULARY APP**

Practice vocabulary on a mobile device.

### Quest CONNECTION

Think about how your school's carbon footprint may contribute to climate change.

## Connect It!

✏️ **Label the image with a "W" where you predict the air would be warmer and a "C" where you predict the air would be cooler.**

Construct Explanations  Why do these areas have different air temperatures?

.......................................................................................................................

.......................................................................................................................

.......................................................................................................................

# Studying Earth's Climate

Earth has an amazing variety of climates, from the dry, cold polar regions to the wet, hot tropics. Scientists study climates to better understand how the atmosphere, water, land masses, and solar energy all interact within a climate. They look at causes of changes in climates in the past and predict how climates may change in the future.

**Greenhouse Effect** While the differences between climates may seem extreme, Earth's overall climate patterns remain fairly stable compared to conditions in space. This is because of gases in the atmosphere, which help to regulate energy in the system.

The greenhouse in **Figure 1** absorbs thermal energy from the sun to warm the air inside. Gardeners add water and soil to create the special climate conditions the plants inside the greenhouse need to survive. Certain gases in the atmosphere, called **greenhouse gases**, such as water vapor, carbon dioxide, methane, and nitrous oxide, absorb much of the heat leaving Earth's surface. The **greenhouse effect** is the process by which these gases trap heat, keeping Earth warm. Without greenhouse gases, thermal energy would radiate from Earth's surface and escape directly into space, making our planet too cold to support life.

**INTERACTIVITY**

Investigate the different greenhouse gases in Earth's atmosphere.

**Reflect** Does the climate in which you live remain relatively stable? In your science notebook, describe the how patterns in your climate stay the same or change over time.

**Trapping the Sun's Energy**
**Figure 1** The glass of this greenhouse in Brazil lets sunlight in and keeps the warmed air from escaping.

**Investigate** Model and observe the greenhouse effect in action.

## Earth's Climate History

By studying the data from yearly climate patterns in an area, scientists can observe that some years are cooler and wetter, while others are hotter and drier. However, how do scientists study the climate of the distant past? Scientists use a wide variety of methods to gather data about past conditions.

Fossils found in an area not only indicate organisms living in the past, but what conditions were like. Fossils of warm-weather plants found in Antarctica suggest that, at some time earlier, Antarctica's climate was much warmer. Rock deposits from glaciers in now-warm regions suggest colder conditions.

Scientists collect ice cores by drilling down through layers of ice, sometimes kilometers thick. The ice cores, which look like glass rods, contain air bubbles and particles such as volcanic ash, sea salt, and dust. By analyzing these materials, scientists can reconstruct climate factors in Earth's past and how they have changed. Similarly, the growth rings of trees record climate conditions as the tree lived and grew each year. The tree rings shown in **Figure 2** show how events and climate conditions in the past shaped the tree's growth.

**Climate change** is a sudden or gradual change in Earth's climate. By studying Earth's climate history in the past, scientists can better understand how conditions change over time, and the effects of gradual or sudden climate changes.

## Model It!

### Climate History in Tree Rings

**Figure 2** The growth rings of trees record data about climate conditions during the tree's life.

**Develop Models** ✏ Consider the growth of a tree during a period of time when the climate conditions were cold and dry over several years, and then conditions changed and the climate became warmer and wetter. Draw a model of the tree rings to represent these conditions. Label the rings representing the different climate conditions.

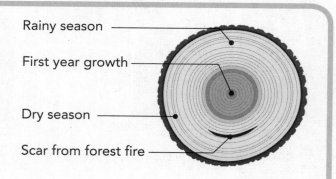

Rainy season

First year growth

Dry season

Scar from forest fire

## Natural Processes

Evidence shows that the overall climate of Earth has changed in the past, both gradually and suddenly. Natural processes that affect climate and may cause climate change include the movements of continents, fluctuations in solar radiation, and volcanic eruptions that disturb the atmosphere.

Recall that landmasses and bodies of water are factors that regulate climate. Earth's continents gradually shift and move. As the size and position of continents and oceans have changed, so too has the climate. This process occurs very slowly, and continues to this day.

Significant climate changes in the past resulted from fluctuations in solar radiation. Like all stars, our sun goes through cycles of energy production. The energy output of the sun varies, as does Earth's tilt and orbit around the sun. Small changes over large periods of time can have big impacts on the climate.

Volcanic eruptions may cause sudden changes in climate by disturbing the atmosphere. In the past, major eruptions have caused short-term global cooling when ash and aerosol particles, or tiny particles suspended in gas, temporarily blocked solar energy. Some scientists theorize that large-scale volcanic eruptions could cause long-term warming by releasing massive amounts of greenhouse gases into the atmosphere.

**Volcanic Eruptions**

**Figure 3** The eruption of Mount Pinatubo in 1991 caused the global temperature to drop 1°F for nearly two years.

Cause and Effect ✎
Label the picture with different substances released by the volcano that could impact climate change.

**Ice Ages** The most researched examples of dramatic climate change in Earth's past are ice ages. During these periods, Earth's climate was 5 to 15 degrees Celsius cooler, causing huge glaciers to extend well beyond the ice caps. Scientists have used evidence from cores of ice and the ocean floor to estimate that there have been about 40 cooling cycles in the past 2.5 million years.

Variations in the tilt of Earth's axis and orbit around the sun occur at regular intervals, and this can **impact** climate. A mathematician named Milutin Milankovitch discovered the pattern. Every 40,000 to 100,000 years, variations in Earth's tilt and orbit result in a period of unusually cool summers in the Northern Hemisphere. Milankovitch theorized the lack of snow melt in the cool summer caused a build-up of reflective ice and snow. This, in turn reflected solar energy even more, causing the cooling trend to escalate. The most recent ice age, which ended about 10,000 years ago, coincided with one of these intervals in which Earth received and retained less energy from sunlight.

☑ READING CHECK **Cite Textual Evidence** How do scientists gather information about climate conditions millions of years ago?

........................................................................................

........................................................................................

### Academic Vocabulary

What are some familiar words that are similar in meaning to *impact*?

........................................................................

........................................................................

........................................................................

# Math Toolbox

## Ice Age Cooling Cycles

The graph shows cooling and warming cycles that have occurred during the past 425,000 years on Earth.

**1. Reason Quantitatively** ✏
Circle areas on the graph where you think the ice ages occurred.

**2. Evaluate Change** What do the data in the graph indicate about the stability of Earth's climate?

........................................................

........................................................

........................................................

........................................................

........................................................

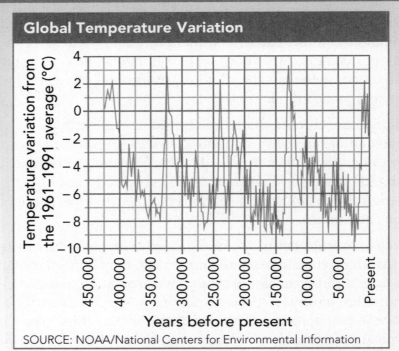

**Global Temperature Variation**

SOURCE: NOAA/National Centers for Environmental Information

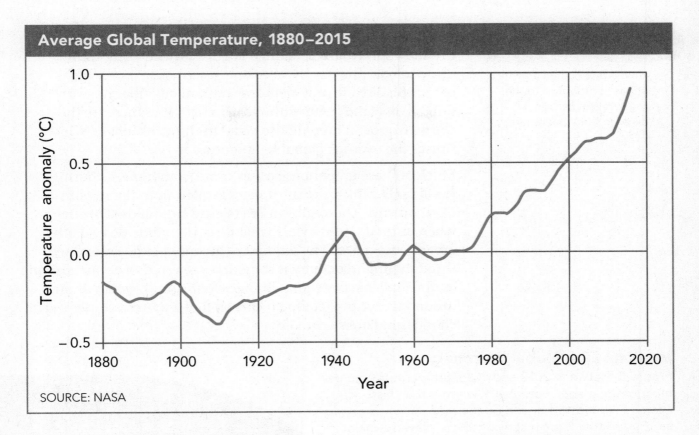

**Average Global Temperature, 1880–2015**

SOURCE: NASA

## Recent Climate Change

Evidence of Earth's past suggests that most climate change takes place over long periods of time—thousands or even tens of thousands of years. However, over the past century, scientists studying the climate have observed a clear and alarming trend in the data. Global surface temperature measurements from the past 140 years indicate that the average global temperature has been rising. This gradual increase in temperature is called **global warming**.

In addition to measuring average temperature changes, scientists also gather data about the concentration of greenhouse gases, such as carbon dioxide and methane, in the atmosphere. They also measure changes in annual Arctic sea ice coverage and overall sea levels around the world. All of these data suggest that global warming is occurring at a surprisingly fast rate.

In the Earth's overall geologic timescale, massive climate changes that happen over millions of years have different causes and different impacts on the planet. Even small changes can have a huge impact on Earth when they happen in such a short amount of time. The graph in **Figure 4** measures temperature changes in only the past 140 years. By studying Earth's climate past, scientists hope to predict some of the impacts of the current climate change.

**Global Temperature Change**

**Figure 4** The graph represents how the average global temperature each year has deviated from a historical norm (shown as 0.0 on the y-axis). Circle the 20-year interval on the graph that shows the most rapid increase in temperature.

**Literacy Connection**

**Cite Textual Evidence** As you read, underline evidence in the text that you think supports the central idea that recent data show a rapid rise in global temperatures.

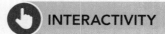

Examine one human activity
that has contributed to the
rising levels of carbon
dioxide in the atmosphere.

**Human Activities** Human activities, some of which
are shown in **Figure 5**, change Earth's surface faster than
any geologic process. By releasing greenhouse gases, such
as carbon dioxide and methane, human activities have an
impact on global temperatures. Our activities increase the
concentration of greenhouse gases in the atmosphere, which
causes the average global temperature to rise.

Much of these greenhouse gases come from humans burning
**fossil fuels**, which are substances formed from the remains
of organisms. These substances release a great deal of energy
when burned. But they also release carbon dioxide and other
greenhouse gases. The amount of greenhouse gases emitted
through human activity is sometimes referred to as our carbon
footprint. When we make changes to the land, water, or air
around us, we are leaving a carbon footprint that causes major
changes in Earth's climate.

## Humans and Global Warming

**Figure 5** Between 2012 and 2016, temperatures across
most of the planet were 2–4°F warmer than historical
averages (indicated by red on the map). Scientists have
concluded that human activities have played a major
role in these temperature changes.

**Cite Evidence** As you read, identify
examples of evidence to support the
claims made about the human
causes of global warming.

**Agriculture** Raising livestock, producing
feed for them, and managing waste produced
from agriculture contribute to greenhouse gas
emissions, such as nitrous oxide and methane.
It is estimated nearly 9 percent of all
greenhouse gas emissions in the United States
come from agricultural activities.

Evidence
...........................................................................

...........................................................................

...........................................................................

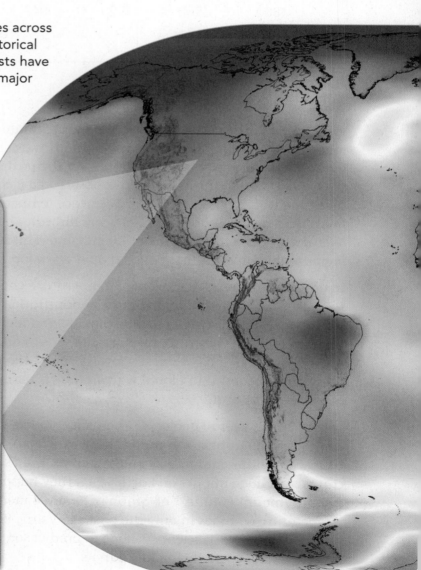

**Mining and Burning Fossil Fuels** For years, fossil fuels, such as coal and petroleum, have powered factories, automobiles, and trains. Chemists have used petroleum to develop revolutionary plastics. However, the mining and burning of fossil fuels have released more greenhouse gases into the atmosphere in the past 150 years than in any other time in human history.

Evidence
........................................................................
........................................................................
........................................................................

**Industry** Industries do not only burn fossil fuels to manufacture and transport goods. They also produce some materials that result in greenhouse gas emissions. Manufacturing processes, such as making cement, produce carbon dioxide from certain chemical reactions that are used to process raw materials.

Evidence
........................................................................
........................................................................
........................................................................

**Deforestation** Trees play an important role in regulating climate by naturally absorbing carbon dioxide from the air for photosynthesis. Removing trees for logging, agriculture, or development results in more carbon dioxide in the atmosphere.

Evidence
........................................................................
........................................................................
........................................................................

Temperature Difference (Fahrenheit)

−4 −3 −2 −1 0 1 2 3 4

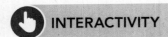

**INTERACTIVITY**

Determine if natural causes can explain the climate change occurring in Antarctica.

**Carbon Dioxide Concentrations** Carbon, like other forms of matter such as water, moves through the land and ocean in a natural cycle. Photosynthetic organisms absorb carbon dioxide from the atmosphere. That carbon is stored and used through life processes until it is released again as carbon dioxide into the atmosphere. Because carbon dioxide is a greenhouse gas, its levels in the atmosphere regulate Earth's global temperature. If there is very little carbon dioxide in the atmosphere, then Earth will not retain enough solar energy to have a stable climate. When carbon dioxide levels are high, global temperatures can rise.

Carbon dioxide concentrations in the atmosphere are constantly being exchanged through natural processes, absorbed by Earth's oceans and locked up in the biosphere in substances such as fossil fuels. Human activities in the past century have upset the balance of these processes. As a result, they have directly impacted the rising concentrations of carbon dioxide in the atmosphere, as shown in **Figure 6**.

**Carbon Dioxide Concentrations**

**Figure 6** Quantify Change ✏ The graph shows levels of carbon dioxide in the atmosphere during the last 400,000 years. Draw a line across the graph at 300 ppm. What does this line represent?

.............................................

.............................................

.............................................

.............................................

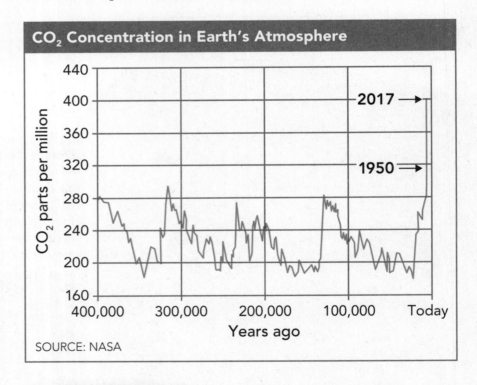

**CO₂ Concentration in Earth's Atmosphere**

SOURCE: NASA

✓ READING CHECK **Integrate with Visuals** Study the graph in **Figure 6**. How have human activities affected concentrations of carbon dioxide in the atmosphere?

.............................................

.............................................

.............................................

.............................................

# ☑ LESSON 2 Check

MS-ESS3-5

1. **Define** What are greenhouse gases? List examples.

........................................................

........................................................

........................................................

........................................................

........................................................

2. **Apply Concepts** How have variations in Earth's tilt and orbit affected its climate conditions in the past?

........................................................

........................................................

........................................................

........................................................

........................................................

........................................................

3. **Identify Patterns** What patterns of climate change have scientists observed in the past?

........................................................

........................................................

........................................................

........................................................

4. **Interpret Data** How do scientists use changes in carbon dioxide concentrations as evidence that human activities affect Earth's climate?

........................................................

........................................................

........................................................

........................................................

5. **Ask Questions** How could scientists collect data about the impact of deforestation on global warming?

........................................................

........................................................

........................................................

........................................................

6. **Relate Change** Why has the concentration of carbon dioxide been increasing so rapidly since the 1950s?

........................................................

........................................................

........................................................

........................................................

........................................................

## Quest CHECK-IN

**In this lesson, you learned how different natural and human factors interact with one another to affect climate change. You observed data showing how human activities release greenhouse gases that have caused the rise in global temperatures.**

**Evaluate** Why is it important to consider your school's carbon footprint when making day-to-day decisions about energy use and waste production?

........................................................

........................................................

........................................................

### HANDS-ON LAB

Energy Savings at School

**Do the hands-on lab** to conduct a school energy audit and identify ways for your school to save energy.

MS-LS2-5

# THE CARBON CYCLE

Every year, 120 gigatons of carbon are taken up by plants and other photosynthetic organisms on land. In turn, 60 gigatons are released into the atmosphere by those organisms through respiration. The other 60 gigatons are released by microbes through decomposition. This cycle is detailed in the diagram. Numbers in parentheses represent estimated stores of carbon. These include trees and other plants, seafloor sediments, and carbon in the atmosphere that does not cycle through the biosphere or hydrosphere. It also includes carbon that is locked underground in coal, petroleum, and natural gas. These stores do not enter the carbon cycle until humans mine and burn them.

Human activities that add carbon to the cycle are represented by red numbers. For example, land-use, burning fossil fuels, and cement production add a total of 9 gigatons of carbon to the atmosphere every year.

Like the terrestrial part of the carbon cycle, the marine part is relatively balanced. Ninety gigatons of carbon are exchanged between the ocean and atmosphere through photosynthesis, respiration, and the decomposition of marine organisms. Two of the 9 gigatons of carbon that humans add to the atmosphere are taken up by the ocean.

The 6,000 gigatons of carbon in sediments stored in the ocean floor are made up of substances that contain frozen methane. These solids, called methane hydrates, can melt into methane gas and water if the temperature of the ocean floor rises. Microbes then convert the methane into carbon dioxide. The carbon dioxide will dissolve into the water and eventually move into the atmosphere.

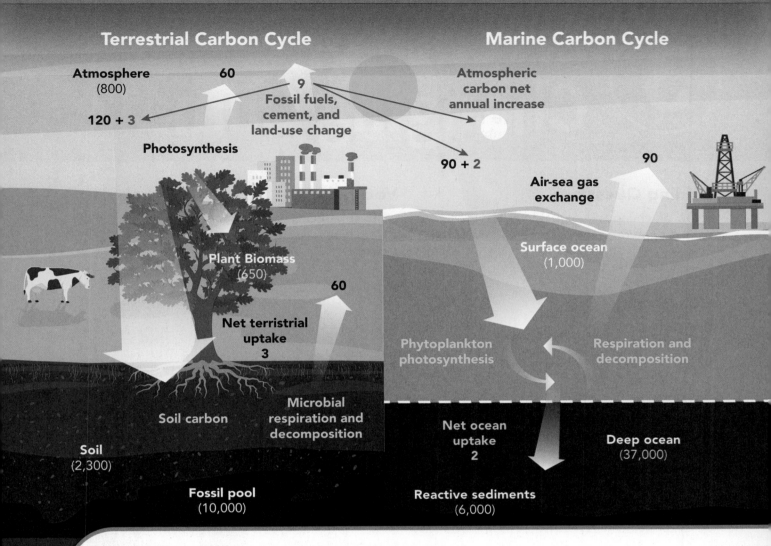

## Terrestrial Carbon Cycle

Atmosphere
(800)

60

9
Fossil fuels, cement, and land-use change

120 + 3

Photosynthesis

Plant Biomass
(650)

60

Net terristrial uptake
3

Soil carbon

Microbial respiration and decomposition

Soil
(2,300)

Fossil pool
(10,000)

## Marine Carbon Cycle

Atmospheric carbon net annual increase

90 + 2

Air-sea gas exchange

90

Surface ocean
(1,000)

Phytoplankton photosynthesis

Respiration and decomposition

Net ocean uptake
2

Deep ocean
(37,000)

Reactive sediments
(6,000)

---

**Study the diagram to answer the following questions.**

1. **Calculate** What is the net annual increase in atmospheric carbon dioxide? To calculate the answer, follow the movement of the 9 gigatons of carbon released by human activity. Fill in the empty circle on the diagram.

2. **Interpret Diagrams** How much of the carbon released by human activity ends up being taken up by photosynthesis on land?

3. **Construct Explanations** What do you think will happen to ocean floor sediments if the atmosphere and ocean continue to warm?

# Effects of a Changing Climate

## Guiding Questions
- How do changes in global temperatures impact natural systems on Earth?
- What can be done to mitigate climate change and its effects?

## Connections
**Literacy** Support Author's Claim

**Math** Represent Quantitative Relationships

MS-ESS3-5

## Vocabulary
cascade effect
alternative
 energy

## Academic Vocabulary
argument

 **VOCABULARY APP**

Practice vocabulary on a mobile device.

**Quest CONNECTION**

Think about ways you and your classmates can reduce or offset the carbon dioxide emissions caused by your school.

## Connect It !

✎ **Look closely at the city's coastline. Imagine if the level of the water rose by three meters. Draw a line where the new water level would be.**

**Cause and Effect** How would the lives of the people in this city be affected if the water level rose?

........................................................................................................

........................................................................................................

........................................................................................................

# Impact of Rising Temperatures

Earth's climate is a complex system, acting in ways that scientists can't always predict. There is some **argument** among scientists about how much human activities have impacted global temperatures. However, scientists are certain that global warming will affect our planet in a number of significant ways. Warming temperatures result in changing weather patterns and new environmental conditions in which organisms must adapt quickly or perish.

Humans are vulnerable to the changes that are occurring and will continue to occur as a result of global warming. Millions of people across the United States live in coastal communities, such as downtown Miami in **Figure 1.** Rising sea levels around the world threaten people's homes, businesses, and lives.

Humans have played a role in causing climate change. Some climate models predict global temperatures will continue to rise several more degrees over the next century. We can play an important role in Earth's climate history by trying to reduce our impact on climate change and to minimize its effects.

## 👆 INTERACTIVITY

Identify an everyday action you can take to reduce your impact on climate change.

## Academic Vocabulary

How is a scientific argument different from a fight or disagreement?

........................................................

........................................................

........................................................

........................................................

**Rising Sea Levels**

**Figure 1** Downtown Miami, Florida, stands right where land and water meet.

## Predicting Sea-Level Changes

**Figure 2** By 2100, sea levels are expected to rise by about 1 meter. In the next 600 years, sea levels are predicted to rise at least 6 meters.

**Cause and Effect** Why is a city like New Orleans especially vulnerable to rising sea levels?

..........................................................

..........................................................

..........................................................

..........................................................

..........................................................

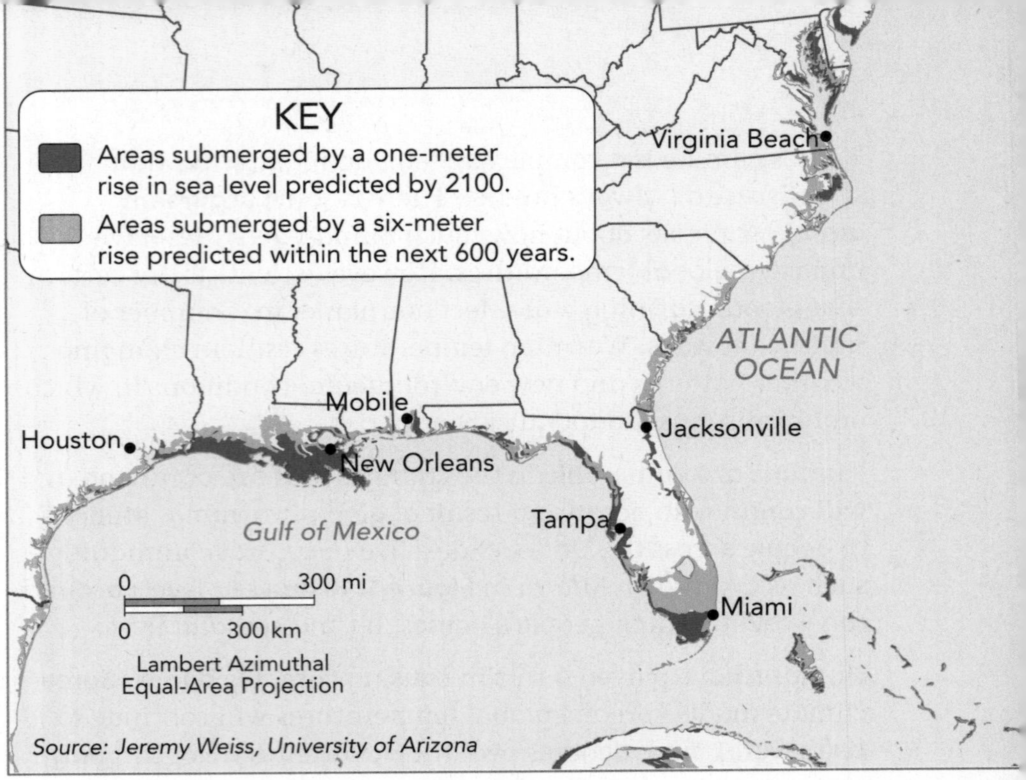

**KEY**

- Areas submerged by a one-meter rise in sea level predicted by 2100.
- Areas submerged by a six-meter rise predicted within the next 600 years.

Houston
Mobile
New Orleans
Jacksonville
Tampa
Miami
Virginia Beach
ATLANTIC OCEAN
Gulf of Mexico

0       300 mi
0       300 km
Lambert Azimuthal Equal-Area Projection

Source: Jeremy Weiss, University of Arizona

**Literacy Connection**

**Support Author's Claim** As you read, underline evidence in the text that you think supports the author's claim that rising sea levels are a result of global warming.

**Rising Sea Levels** Approximately 71 percent of Earth's surface is covered with water. Most of that water is oceans, but up to two percent of that water is stored as sea ice, glaciers, and permanent snow. The polar regions are particularly vulnerable to global warming because even slight increases in temperature cause huge areas of stored ice to melt and flow into Earth's oceans. As global temperatures rise, so does the global sea level.

Glaciers, huge areas of ice in mountain regions, store fresh water in the form of solid ice. Scientists studying glaciers over the past 50 years observe not only that glaciers are retreating as temperatures rise, but the rate at which they melt is steadily increasing. Melting glaciers carry massive amounts of fresh water and sediment from the land to the ocean. Alaska's glaciers have lost nearly 50 gigatons of ice each year since 2003.

Rising sea levels have devastating effects on coastal areas. In the past century, the global sea level has risen approximately 20 centimeters (8 inches). Low-lying land areas near the coast would be completely submerged in ocean water, resulting in habitat loss for humans and wildlife. The map in **Figure 2** illustrates areas in North America that would be completely submerged by rising sea levels over the next 100 years. Scientists estimate Earth's sea level has risen more than 120 meters (about 394 feet) since the last ice age, and will continue to rise.

**Polar Regions Under Threat** In addition to causing a rise in global sea levels, melting conditions in polar regions appear to have set off a chain reaction of other negative climate effects. Higher temperatures allow the atmosphere above the ice caps to hold more water vapor, which acts as a greenhouse gas. The loss of reflective ice covering the northern ocean also allows solar energy to be absorbed by ocean waters, increasing temperatures even more.

Scientists are now observing unexpected side-effects of global warming in arctic and tundra climates. Near Earth's polar regions, a thin layer of soil supports plant life during the brief summer thaw, while the soil below, called permafrost, is frozen year-round. As rising global temperatures melt permafrost, decomposing plant matter that has been covered for thousands of years releases carbon dioxide and methane gases. The concentration of these greenhouse gases increases in the atmosphere, which further accelerates global warming.

**HANDS-ON LAB**

**Investigate** Model the effects of thermal expansion on water.

**Math Toolbox**

## Rising Sea Levels

Since 1993, NASA uses satellites to monitor sea level changes caused by melting land ice and the expansion of sea water as it warms.

| Sea Level Changes Observed By Satellite | |
| --- | --- |
| Year | Sea Height Variation (mm) |
| 1995 | 6 mm |
| 2000 | 26 mm |
| 2005 | 42 mm |
| 2010 | 58 mm |
| 2015 | 80 mm |

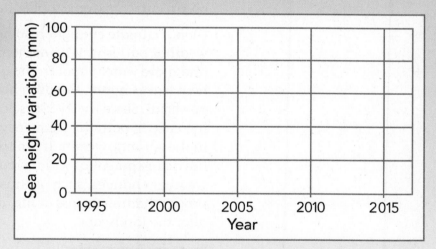

1. **Represent Quantitative Relationships** 🖊 Create a line graph of the data in the table.

2. **Cause and Effect** How does your graph provide evidence of rising sea levels? What are some factors that may be causing this phenomenon?

.................................................................................................

.................................................................................................

.................................................................................................

**Write About It** Imagine having to deal with extreme changes such as droughts, floods, or stronger storms. In your science notebook, describe what extreme change would have the biggest impact on your local community.

**Adapt or Perish** All living organisms have adaptations to survive in their environments. These adaptations usually develop over very long periods of time as organisms thrive or perish. When conditions in an environment change rapidly, organisms must adapt or move into new locations for food. As global warming accelerates, mass die-offs are predicted.

Global warming has a **cascade effect**, an unforeseen chain of events caused by a disturbance in a system, on Earth's organisms. Scientists estimate 75 percent of the world's coral reefs are under threat due to rising ocean temperatures. Certain types of algae necessary for the survival of reef-building coral are affected by rising temperatures, causing coral to lose all its coloring in a process called bleaching. Entire reefs can die off due to coral bleaching, resulting in the destruction of habitats and many more negative impacts.

**Extreme Weather Change** Global warming refers to the overall warming of Earth's temperatures, but it may not mean all areas of Earth experience warmer conditions. Parts of Earth, such as Europe, could start to experience colder temperatures because of disturbed ocean currents. The world's oceans act as a conveyor belt, circulating cold water from the poles and warm water from the equator. Due to melting ice, that process is gradually being disrupted, and it could prevent ocean currents from stabilizing global climates.

Global climate changes also have cascading effects on regional weather patterns. Warmer temperatures result in more energy and more water vapor in the atmosphere. This can make heat waves hotter, flooding heavier, and severe storms more powerful. Since the 1980s, scientists have measured an increase in both the frequency and intensity of hurricanes in the Atlantic Ocean. If the trend continues, they predict hurricane potential will increase 20 percent by 2100. Extreme weather changes, such as those shown in **Figure 3**, cause property damage, loss of life, and sometimes permanently alter the landscape.

☑ **READING CHECK** **Support Author's Claim** What evidence does the author provide to support the idea that global temperatures and organisms' adaptations are connected?

......................................................................................................

......................................................................................................

......................................................................................................

......................................................................................................

......................................................................................................

## Cascading Effects of Climate Change

**Figure 3** For every change in climate, there are cascading effects for ecosystems and organisms trying to adapt to the changes.

**Cause and Effect** Read each image caption describing a phenomenon caused by climate change. Identify possible cascading effects of each phenomenon.

Global warming causes atmosphere changes that lead to more extreme storms and flooding.

Effects: .................................................
.................................................
.................................................

Disruptions in precipitation patterns cause heat waves and droughts.

Effects: .................................................
.................................................
.................................................

Rising ocean temperatures cause coral bleaching when vital algae die off.

Effects: .................................................
.................................................
.................................................

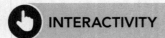

**INTERACTIVITY**

Examine the effects of industrialization on levels of carbon dioxide in the atmosphere.

# Dealing with Climate Change

The effects of climate change may look grim, but there are many ways humans can alter their behaviors to reduce or counteract the increasingly harmful effects of global warming. Scientists, lawmakers, engineers, and other creative minds are working together to find new solutions to reduce the extent of climate change and human vulnerability to its effects. Because these changes have accumulated over time, it will also take time to slow or reverse the effects.

**Alternative Energy** Human activities require energy, and 91 percent of all greenhouse gases emitted by human activities comes from burning fossil fuels. By developing **alternative energy**, or clean energy sources that do not come from fossil fuels, we can reduce the mining and burning of fossil fuels. This will greatly reduce the levels of greenhouse gases being released into the atmosphere. Alternative energy sources such as solar, wind, geothermal, and tidal power do not require fossil fuels and have no greenhouse gas emissions.

**Energy-Efficient Technologies** In addition to developing new sources of energy, we can focus on developing more efficient technologies. In the short term, these technologies might reduce emissions and reliance on traditional forms of energy. And for long-term solutions, engineers might develop technology that changes how we consume energy—from batteries powered by nitrogen in the air to new super-efficient hybrid cars.

# Design it !

### Adapting for Climate Change
Through careful design and consideration of energy use, we can reduce our impact on global climate change, while adapting to the changes already occurring.

Design Solutions ✏ Develop a design for a house that sits on beachfront property. Consider ways to use alternative energy and energy-efficient technologies. The design must also allow for the house to withstand the effects of a rising sea level.

**Engineering New Solutions** Reducing carbon emissions may not be enough to slow climate change. Many scientists think a proactive approach of removing carbon from the atmosphere may be needed. Using nature as a guide, engineers are developing ways to remove carbon dioxide from the atmosphere. This is done through using the natural process of photosynthesis to remove carbon dioxide from the air, or filtering carbon directly and storing it underground. Other engineers are working on solutions to help deal with the effects of climate change by helping communities be less vulnerable to effects such as rising sea levels.

**The Role of Government** Realizing that climate change is a global issue, governments from nations around the world have been coming together to discuss evidence and make plans to wisely counteract global warming. In 2012, the Solomon Islands **(Figure 4)** led the world by passing a comprehensive climate change policy in response to the challenges they are already facing.

Following the example of tiny nations in crisis, over 190 nations joined together in 2016 to commit to controlling greenhouse gas emissions. The Paris Climate Agreement, as it is called, outlines long-term goals and legislation to unite the world in mitigating climate change. By understanding climate science and making informed decisions, people and their governments can reduce human vulnerability to a changing planet.

**Disappearing Islands**
**Figure 4** In recent years, some of the small islands that make up the Solomon Islands have been lost to rising sea levels.

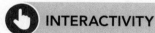

**INTERACTIVITY**

Help a city planner determine how to reduce emissions.

☑ READING CHECK **Summarize** What are some ways the government can play a role in dealing with climate change?

.................................................................................

.................................................................................

.................................................................................

.................................................................................

MS-ESS3-5

1. **Identify** What factors are contributing to rising sea levels?

.................................................................

.................................................................

.................................................................

2. **Compare and Contrast** How are localized droughts and increased flooding both related to global warming?

.................................................................

.................................................................

.................................................................

.................................................................

3. **Cause and Effect** What impact does climate change have on organisms that are well-adapted to their environments?

.................................................................

.................................................................

.................................................................

.................................................................

4. **Analyze Systems** What are some possible cascade effects of the melting of sea ice in the Arctic Ocean due to global warming?

.................................................................

.................................................................

.................................................................

5. **Describe** How could using alternative energy sources help slow the process of global warming?

.................................................................

.................................................................

.................................................................

6. **Construct Arguments** How might national governments have a positive impact on the world's climate change crisis?

.................................................................

.................................................................

.................................................................

.................................................................

.................................................................

# Quest CHECK-IN

**In this lesson, you learned about the effects of climate change. You explored ways that people and governments are working to reduce greenhouse gas emissions that have caused the rise in global temperatures.**

**Evaluate Feedback** Why is it important to consider the cascade effects of global warming when evaluating ways to reduce energy usage at your school?

.................................................................

.................................................................

.................................................................

.................................................................

## 👆 INTERACTIVITY

Make a Difference

**Go online** to record data that will help you evaluate your school's energy use.

# CHANGING
# Climate Change

How do you reduce the amounts of greenhouse gases and lessen severity of climate change? You engineer it!

**The Challenge:** Reduce the level of carbon dioxide in the atmosphere to fight global warming.

**Phenomenon** Efforts are underway to reduce the amount of carbon dioxide released as a result of human activities. Limiting the burning of fossil fuels is one approach. But that method alone is not enough to solve the problem. Another way is to capture the carbon that is released when fuels are burned. The process is known as carbon capture and storage technology, or CCS. The goal is to capture carbon dioxide released during the production and burning of fuels, and then pump it deep underground.

In 2017, one of the country's largest industrial CCS facilities opened in Decatur, Illinois. The company produces ethanol, which is fuel made from corn. Carbon dioxide produced when making ethanol is injected into a saltwater reservoir nearly two kilometers below the surface of the ground. The facility is permitted to run for five years and can bury about one million tons of carbon dioxide each year.

**VIDEO**

Explore how engineers use technology to help reduce levels of carbon dioxide in the atmosphere.

## DESIGN CHALLENGE

Can you design a house to reduce its carbon footprint? Go to the Engineering Design Notebook to find out!

CO₂ source (power plant)

CO₂ injection

CO₂ transport

CO₂ compression unit

CO₂ capture & separation plant

CO₂ storage

# ☑TOPIC 8 Review and Assess

## 1 Climate Factors

MS-ESS2-6

1. Which of the following terms refers to long-term weather patterns in an area?
   A. climate
   B. weather
   C. altitude
   D. prevailing winds

2. Why do areas near the equator have warmer climates than areas near the poles?
   A. There are fewer mountains near the equator than in areas near the poles.
   B. Sunlight strikes Earth's surface more directly at the equator than at the poles.
   C. Ocean currents carry warm water from the poles to the equator.
   D. Areas near the equator are generally at higher altitudes than areas near the poles.

3. Ocean currents traveling from the equator toward the polar zones carry ........................... water, which helps to ........................... air masses at the poles.

4. **Apply Concepts** Why do most tall mountains have cooler climates than the areas at their bases?

   ...............................................................................
   ...............................................................................
   ...............................................................................
   ...............................................................................

5. **Describe** What factors do you think are responsible for the differences in temperatures found in a temperate marine climate and a temperate continental climate?

   ...............................................................................
   ...............................................................................
   ...............................................................................
   ...............................................................................
   ...............................................................................

## 2 Climate Change

MS-ESS3-5

6. Why is carbon dioxide considered a greenhouse gas?
   A. It is found in high concentrations in greenhouses that contain lots of plants.
   B. It is produced as a result of human activity.
   C. It traps radiated energy in the atmosphere, which causes air temperatures to rise.
   D. It is necessary for plants to survive.

7. Which of the following is *not* a natural process that can affect Earth's climate?
   A. volcanoes
   B. changes in solar radiation
   C. lunar eclipses
   D. shifting continents

8. **Integrate Information** Why do climate scientists study tree rings and ice cores?

   ...............................................................................
   ...............................................................................
   ...............................................................................
   ...............................................................................

9. **Relate Change** How has Earth's average global temperature changed in the last 140 years? What is the main cause of this change?

   ...............................................................................
   ...............................................................................
   ...............................................................................
   ...............................................................................

10. **Cause and Effect** How does raising livestock contribute to global warming?

    ...............................................................................
    ...............................................................................
    ...............................................................................
    ...............................................................................

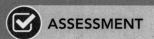

# 3 Effects of a Changing Climate

MS-ESS3-5

**11.** What do most climate models predict about Earth's global temperature in the near future?
A. It will stop rising and remain constant.
B. It will rise several more degrees.
C. It will drop before slowly rising again.
D. It will drop quickly and bring about an ice age.

**12.** As global temperatures rise, the global sea level is expected to rise in part because
A. more precipitation is falling.
B. permafrost is thawing.
C. greenhouse gases cause water to expand.
D. glaciers are melting at a faster rate.

**13.** Which of the following is an effect of the loss of sea ice covering northern oceans?
A. More solar energy is absorbed by ocean water.
B. Sea levels decrease.
C. Earth's global temperature drops.
D. Ocean water becomes saltier.

**14. Engage in Argument** When dealing with climate change, do you think it is more important for us to figure out ways to deal with its effects, figure out ways to reduce climate change, or both? Explain.

..................................................................
..................................................................
..................................................................
..................................................................
..................................................................
..................................................................
..................................................................
..................................................................
..................................................................

**15. Develop Models** ✎ Complete the flow chart to identify cascading effects of global warming.

> Rising temperatures cause glacier ice to melt.

⬇

[ ]

⬇

[ ]

⬇

[ ]

⬇

[ ]

**16. Construct Explanations** Identify one way that technology might be used to mitigate the effects of climate change. Explain how the technology works to reduce the impact of human activity on climate change.

..................................................................
..................................................................
..................................................................
..................................................................
..................................................................
..................................................................
..................................................................
..................................................................
..................................................................
..................................................................
..................................................................

MS-ESS3-5C

## Evidence-Based Assessment

A group of students investigates how levels of methane in the atmosphere have changed over time and how this factor contributes to global warming.

From their research, the students learn the following information:

- Methane accounts for about 10 percent of the greenhouse gases in the atmosphere. But its ability to trap heat is 25 times as great as carbon dioxide.

- Some methane is released by natural processes, but over 60 percent of methane emissions are the result of human activities.

- Agricultural activities, such as raising livestock and managing livestock waste, are a major source of methane emissions.

- The production of natural gas and petroleum is another major source of methane emissions.

The students display some of the data collected during research in the graph and tables shown here.

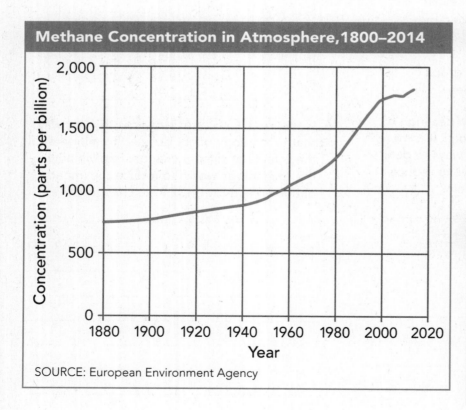

Methane Concentration in Atmosphere, 1800–2014

SOURCE: European Environment Agency

### Global Beef Production

| Year | 1,000 Metric Tons |
|------|-------------------|
| 2000 | 49,775 |
| 2005 | 52,374 |
| 2010 | 57,043 |
| 2015 | 60,022 |

Source: USDA

### Global Natural Gas Production

| Year | Billion Cubic Meters |
|------|----------------------|
| 2000 | 2,421,0 |
| 2005 | 2,790.9 |
| 2010 | 3,208.5 |
| 2015 | 3,538.6 |

Source: BP Statistical Review of World Energy, June 2016

1. **Analyze Data** What trend is shown in the data collected by the students?
   - (A.) Methane levels are increasing, as are the levels of beef and natural gas production.
   - B. Methane levels are decreasing, as are the levels of beef and natural gas production.
   - C. Methane levels are increasing, while the levels of beef and natural gas production are decreasing.
   - D. Methane levels are decreasing, while the levels of beef and natural gas production are increasing.

2. **Ask Questions** Which of the following questions are the students attempting to answer in their investigation? Select all that apply.
   - ☐ How much do human activities contribute to methane emissions?
   - ☐ Why was more natural gas produced in 2005 than in 2000?
   - ☐ Why is methane considered a factor in rising global temperatures?
   - ☐ How are beef and gas production related to the levels of methane in the atmosphere?
   - ☐ How much beef did people consume each year from 2000 to 2015?

3. **Cite Evidence** What is the relationship between the data in the tables and in the graph? Support your answer with evidence.

   ............................................................
   ............................................................
   ............................................................
   ............................................................
   ............................................................
   ............................................................
   ............................................................
   ............................................................
   ............................................................
   ............................................................

4. **Construct Arguments** How are recent trends in beef and natural gas production tied to the rise in global temperatures? Use evidence to support your argument.

   ............................................................
   ............................................................
   ............................................................
   ............................................................
   ............................................................
   ............................................................
   ............................................................
   ............................................................
   ............................................................

# Quest FINDINGS

## Complete the Quest!

**Phenomenon** Determine the best way to present your proposals for reducing your school's carbon footprint and to display the supporting data you have collected.

**Evaluate** What are some important factors to consider when evaluating the effectiveness of ideas for reducing carbon emissions?

............................................................
............................................................
............................................................
............................................................

👆 **INTERACTIVITY**

Reflect on Shrinking Your Carbon Footprint

MS-ESS3-5

# An Ocean of a Problem

How can you determine what is responsible for reducing the size of oysters in the ocean?

## Background

**Phenomenon** As a science expert on an advisory panel, you are charged with examining a complaint from oyster fishers. Oysters caught in the Northwest Pacific and Mid-Atlantic regions of the ocean are smaller than in the past and their numbers are decreasing. The oyster fishers blame the problem on the increased acidity of seawater, which they believe is the result of increased levels of carbon dioxide in the atmosphere. According to the fishers, acidic water prevents the oysters from producing normal shells by dissolving new shell growth. This results in oysters that are smaller and more vulnerable to predators.

In this investigation, you will participate in one of two research teams. Your common goal will be to determine whether ocean acidification could be responsible for the problems with the oysters. You will also investigate whether carbon dioxide in the atmosphere is to blame.

## Safety

Be sure to follow all safety guidelines provided by your teacher. The Safety Appendix of your textbook provides more details about the safety icons.

## Materials

(per group)

### For Research Team 1
- universal indicator solution or strips
- eggshell from one egg
- 200-mL beaker (2)
- 100 mL vinegar
- 100 mL distilled water

### For Research Team 2
- 50 mL universal indicator solution
- small plastic cup (2)
- 300-mL beaker (2)
- 30 mL distilled water
- 30 mL carbonated water
- plastic wrap
- rubber band

According to recent estimates, harvests of oysters in the Chesapeake Bay are less than 1 percent of what they were 100 years ago.

# Design Your Experiment

1. Divide your group into two research teams.

2. ![icon] ![icon] **Research Team 1** should design an experiment using the materials provided to explore the effects of acid on shells. Make sure the experiment you develop uses a control and that you measure and record the pH of the substances you use. Record your team's procedure in the space provided. Include a sketch of your set up. Consider the following questions as you develop and design your experiment:

   • What will the eggshell represent in your tests?

   • How can you model the effects of an acid on the eggshell?

   • How can you use the distilled water as a control in your investigation?

   • What observations will you make? What data will you collect?

   • How can you measure the pH of each substance you use in your experiment? When should you measure the pH?

3. After getting your teacher's approval, carry out your team's experiment. Make a table to record your observations and data in the space provided.

4. ![icon] ![icon] **Research Team 2** should design an experiment using the materials provided to determine the effect of carbon dioxide on the acidity of water. Your experiment should use a control to help you analyze your results. Record your team's procedure in the space provided. Include a sketch of your set up. Consider the following questions as you develop your experiment:

   • How can you use the carbonated water to test whether carbon dioxide in the air can change the pH of a substance?

   • How can you design your experiment so that only carbon dioxide in the air—and not the carbonated water—will come into contact with the indicator solution?

   • How can you use the distilled water as a control in your investigation?

   • What observations will you make? What data will you collect?

5. After getting your teacher's approval, carry out your team's experiment. Make a table to record your observations and data in the space provided.

6. When both research teams have completed their experiments, meet as a group to share and discuss the evidence that has been collected.

A pH scale uses both color and number scales to indicate the acidity or alkalinity of a substance. A pH indicator can be used to test the pH of a substance.

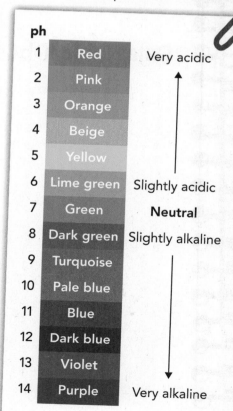

| ph | | |
|---|---|---|
| 1 | Red | Very acidic |
| 2 | Pink | |
| 3 | Orange | |
| 4 | Beige | |
| 5 | Yellow | |
| 6 | Lime green | Slightly acidic |
| 7 | Green | **Neutral** |
| 8 | Dark green | Slightly alkaline |
| 9 | Turquoise | |
| 10 | Pale blue | |
| 11 | Blue | |
| 12 | Dark blue | |
| 13 | Violet | |
| 14 | Purple | Very alkaline |

Observations

Data Table/Observations

# Analyze and Interpret Data

1. **Communicate** Why were there two research teams for this investigation? Why is it important for the two teams to share their results before drawing any conclusions about the complaint?

.............................................................................................................

.............................................................................................................

.............................................................................................................

.............................................................................................................

.............................................................................................................

.............................................................................................................

2. **Quantify Change** What observations did each team make?

.............................................................................................................

.............................................................................................................

.............................................................................................................

.............................................................................................................

3. **Ask Questions** What evidence can you provide to support the claim that increased levels of carbon dioxide in the atmosphere are responsible for the changes seen in the oysters?

.............................................................................................................

.............................................................................................................

.............................................................................................................

.............................................................................................................

.............................................................................................................

.............................................................................................................

4. **Evaluate Feedback** Based on your results and what you know about carbon dioxide levels in the atmosphere and ocean, what recommendations or advice would you give to the oyster fishers?

.............................................................................................................

.............................................................................................................

.............................................................................................................

.............................................................................................................

.............................................................................................................

.............................................................................................................

# TOPIC
# 9

# Earth-Sun-Moon System

**NGSS PERFORMANCE EXPECTATION**

**MS-ESS1-1** Develop and use a model of the
Earth-sun-moon system to describe the cyclic
patterns of lunar phases, eclipses of the sun and
moon, and seasons.

HANDS-ON LAB

**uConnect** Model systems showing
both Earth and the sun at the center.

What is happening to the sun?

**GO ONLINE**
to access your
digital course

 VIDEO

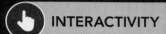 INTERACTIVITY

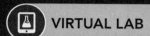 VIRTUAL LAB

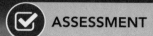 ASSESSMENT

eTEXT

APP

## The Essential Question

## How do the sun and the moon affect Earth?

As the moon travels around Earth and Earth travels around the sun, the three objects interact with each other. What are some of the patterns you can observe in the interactions among Earth, the sun, and the moon?

........................................................................................

........................................................................................

........................................................................................

........................................................................................

........................................................................................

........................................................................................

# Quest KICKOFF

## How are tides related to our place in space?

**Phenomenon** The ebb and flow of the ocean's tides are as steady and sure as the passage of time. Engineers are investigating how to put the power of the tides to work as an alternative to the burning of fossil fuels. In this Quest activity, you will produce a model to help visitors to a tidal power company understand why tidal power is a reliable source of renewable energy. You will explore how and why our position within the solar system causes tides and their patterns. The model that you produce will demonstrate how tides happen.

 **INTERACTIVITY**

It's as Sure as the Tides

**MS-ESS1-1** Develop and use a model of the Earth-sun-moon system to describe the cyclic patterns of lunar phases, eclipses of the sun and moon, and seasons.

**NBC LEARN** ▶ VIDEO

After watching the Quest Kickoff video about tidal energy, think about this source of energy. Complete the diagram by identifying some benefits and drawbacks of tidal energy.

### Benefits and Drawbacks of Tidal Energy

| Benefits | Drawbacks |
|----------|-----------|
|          |           |

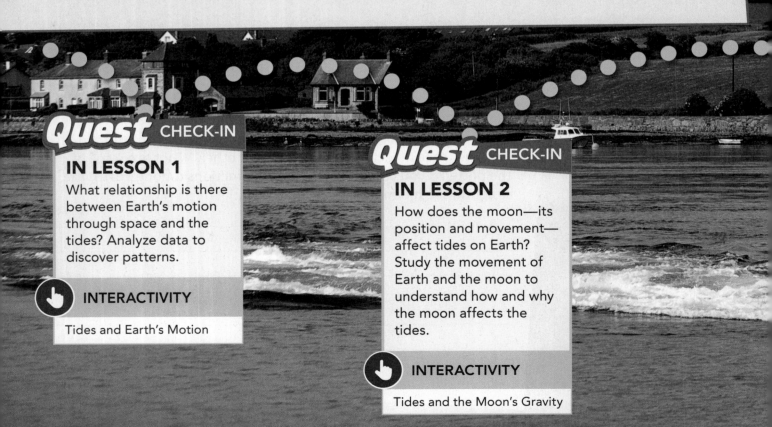

# Quest CHECK-IN

## IN LESSON 1

What relationship is there between Earth's motion through space and the tides? Analyze data to discover patterns.

**INTERACTIVITY**

Tides and Earth's Motion

# Quest CHECK-IN

## IN LESSON 2

How does the moon—its position and movement—affect tides on Earth? Study the movement of Earth and the moon to understand how and why the moon affects the tides.

**INTERACTIVITY**

Tides and the Moon's Gravity

This tidal turbine in Northern Ireland provides enough electricity to power hundreds of homes.

## Quest CHECK-IN

### IN LESSON 3

**STEM** What makes the tides and tidal ranges vary? Investigate how the relative positions of the moon, Earth, and the sun affect the tides.

### HANDS-ON LAB

The Moon's Revolution and Tides

## Quest FINDINGS

### Complete the Quest!

Apply what you've learned to create a model that demonstrates why tides occur and how and why they provide a reliable source of energy.

### INTERACTIVITY

Reflect on It's as Sure as the Tides

## Guiding Questions

- What objects can you see in the night sky?
- Why do stars in the night sky seem to move?
- How do objects in the solar system move?

## Connections

**Literacy** Integrate With Visuals

**Math** Create an Equation

MS-ESS1-1

## Vocabulary

satellite
star
planet
meteor
comet
constellation
geocentric
heliocentric
ellipse

## Academic Vocabulary

observations

 **VOCABULARY APP**

Practice vocabulary on a mobile device.

**Quest CONNECTION**

Use what you have learned about Earth's movements in space to analyze information about tides and look for patterns.

## Connect It !

✎ **Circle the meteors in this photo.**

**Apply Scientific Reasoning** Why do you think meteors leave a trail of light as they move through the sky?

.......................................................................................................................

.......................................................................................................................

# The Night Sky

Why do the stars appear to move? What makes the moon shine through the darkness? Aryabhata I (ar yah BAH tah) was an early astronomer who thought about these questions. He was born in 476 CE in what is now India. Aryabhata I wrote that the moon and the planets shine because they reflect light from the sun. He came up with these conclusions based solely on his **observations** of the sky with his naked eye.

**Stars, Planets, and the Moon** You may look up on a clear night, such as the one shown in **Figure 1**, and see stars, the moon, planets, meteors, and comets, much as Aryabhata I did. Earth's moon is the brightest and largest object in our night sky. The moon is Earth's only natural satellite. A **satellite** is a body that orbits a planet. By contrast, stars appear as tiny points of light. However, a **star** is a giant ball of superheated gas, or plasma, composed of hydrogen and helium. As seen from Earth, the positions of stars relative to each other do not seem to change.

Have you ever noticed objects that change position from night to night against the background of the stars? These are planets. A **planet** is an object that orbits the sun, is large enough to have become rounded by its own gravity, and has cleared the area of its orbit of any debris. There are eight planets in our solar system.

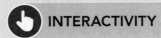

INTERACTIVITY

Answer a poll about things you have seen in the night sky.

**Academic Vocabulary**
How does making observations help scientists come up with new ideas?

........................................................

........................................................

........................................................

........................................................

........................................................

**Objects in the Sky**
**Figure 1** On a clear night, you can often see meteors in the night sky.

429

**HANDS-ON LAB**

*Investigate* Model how stars' positions change relative to a night sky observer on Earth.

**Meteors and Comets** Have you ever seen a shooting star? These sudden bright streaks are called meteors. A **meteor** is a streak of light produced when a small piece of rock or ice, known as a meteoroid, burns up as it enters Earth's atmosphere. You can see a meteor on almost any clear night.

Comets are rarer sights than meteors. A **comet** is a cold mixture of dust and ice that develops a long trail of light as it approaches the sun. When a comet is far from the sun, it is frozen. As it gets close to the sun, the cloud trailing behind the comet forms a glowing tail made up of hot dust and gases.

Perhaps the most famous comet is Halley's Comet. This highly visible comet was documented by Edmund Halley, who calculated its orbit and predicted its next appearance in the sky. Sure enough, the comet appeared as he predicted in 1758, although Halley didn't live to see it. It has continued to appear about every 75 years, last appearing in 1986.

# Math Toolbox

## Halley's Comet

In 1910, Halley's Comet traveled close to Earth—about 1/7 of the distance from Earth to the sun. Earth's distance from the sun is 149.6 million kilometers.

1. **Create an Equation** How close was Halley's Comet to Earth in 1910? Create an equation to answer the question.

...................................................................................

2. **Interpret Data** Estimate the next three years when Halley's Comet will appear.

...................................................................................

...................................................................................

3. **Use Proportional Reasoning** The core of Halley's comet is oblong in shape, with its longest dimension 16 km long. Earth's diameter is about 12,700 km. How many times larger in diameter is Earth than Halley's comet?

...................................................................................

...................................................................................

## Finding Constellations

**Figure 2** ✏️ Star charts can help you to find constellations in the night sky. This is a summer chart for the Northern Hemisphere. Find these constellations in the star chart. Then write each constellation's name by its picture.

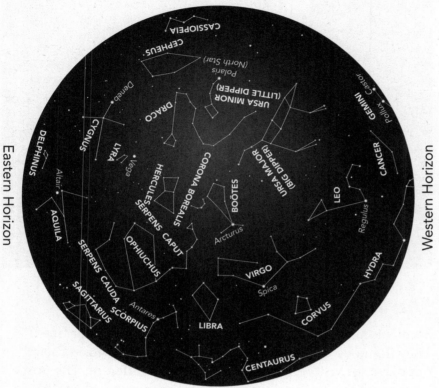

Northern Horizon

Eastern Horizon

Western Horizon

Southern Horizon

........................................

........................................

........................................

## Constellations

For thousands of years, human beings in many cultures have seen patterns in groups of stars and given them names. A pattern or group of stars that people imagine represents a figure, animal, or object is a **constellation**. Often, as in the ancient Roman and Greek cultures, constellations supported specific mythologies. Today, scientists divide the sky into 88 constellations. Some constellations are named for people or animals from Greek myths. Pegasus and Perseus, for example, are both mythological characters and constellations. Study the constellations shown in **Figure 2**.

☑️ **READING CHECK** **Integrate With Visuals** How do the pictures in **Figure 2** help you remember the constellations?

...............................................................

...............................................................

...............................................................

...............................................................

📔 **Reflect** In your science notebook, write about the patterns of stars you see in the night sky.

431

**VIDEO**

Explore how apparent motion can affect perception.

### Star Trails

**Figure 3** 🖊 A time-lapse photo taken over the course of minutes or hours captures the movements of stars. The North Star happens to be aligned with the axis of Earth, directly "above" the North Pole. Circle the North Star in the photo.

# Movement in the Sky

Stars, planets, and other objects appear to move over time. They do move in space, but those actual motions and their apparent, or visible, motions may be very different. The positions of objects in the sky depend on the motions of Earth.

Stars generally appear to move from east to west through the night. Toward the poles, stars appear to take a circular path, as shown in **Figure 3**. As Aryabhata I thought, this apparent motion is caused by Earth rotating toward the east. The sun's apparent motion is also caused by Earth's rotation.

**Seasonal Changes** Constellations and star patterns remain the same from year to year, but the constellations visible to you vary from season to season. For example, you can find the constellation Orion in the eastern sky on winter evenings. But by spring, you'll see Orion in the west, disappearing below the horizon shortly after sunset.

These seasonal changes are caused by Earth's revolution, or orbit, around the sun. Each night, the position of most stars shifts slightly to the west. After a while, you no longer see stars once visible in the west, and previously unseen stars appear in the east. After six months, Earth is on the other side of the sun. Constellations that used to appear in the night sky are now behind the sun, where the sun's bright light blocks them from our vision during the day.

**Planets** Planets appear to move against the background of stars. In fact, the word *planet* comes from a Greek word meaning "wanderer." Because the planets all orbit the sun in about the same plane, they appear to move through a narrow band in the sky. This band is called the zodiac.

Some planets are visible all night long. Mars, Jupiter, and Saturn are all farther from the sun than Earth is. When Earth passes between them and the sun, these three planets are visible after sunset, once the sun's bright light no longer blocks the view. You can see Venus and Mercury only in the evening or morning. They are closer to the sun than Earth, and so they always appear close to the sun, as shown in **Figure 4**.

> ✓ **READING CHECK** **Cite Textual Evidence** Why would you need two different star charts for finding constellations in the summer and the winter?

......................................................................................................................

......................................................................................................................

......................................................................................................................

......................................................................................................................

......................................................................................................................

## Mercury and Venus
**Figure 4** The planets Mercury and Venus never appear far from the sun in the sky.

**Use Models** ✏ Where in this image is Venus farthest from the sun? Place a dot on the image to indicate the spot.

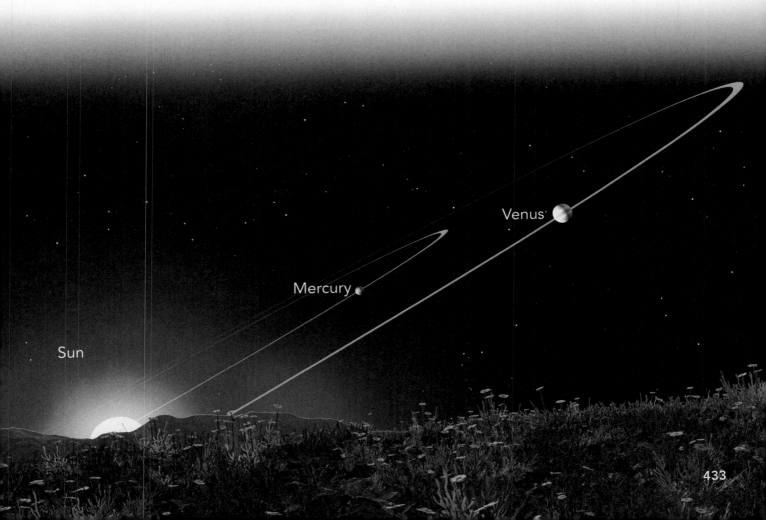

Sun

Mercury

Venus

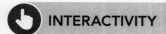
# Models of the Solar System

From here on Earth, it seems as if our planet is stationary and that the sun, moon, and stars are moving around Earth. Ancient peoples such as the Greeks, Chinese, and Mayans noticed that although the stars seemed to move, they stayed in the same position relative to one another.

**Geocentric Model** Many early observers, including the Greek philosopher, Aristotle, thought Earth was the center of the universe, with all the planets and stars circling it, as shown in **Figure 5**. Because *ge* is the Greek word for "Earth," an Earth-centered model is known as a **geocentric** (jee oh SEN trik) model.

In about 140 C.E., the Greek astronomer Ptolemy further developed Aristotle's geocentric model. In Ptolemy's model, the planets made small circles called epicycles as they moved along their orbital paths. This model seemed to explain the motions observed in the sky. As a result, Ptolemy's geocentric model was widely accepted for nearly 1,500 years after his death.

## Literacy Connection

**Integrate With Visuals** As you look at **Figure 5**, think about why this diagram was included on this page. Highlight the portion of the text that relates to the diagram. How does this diagram add to the information you gained by reading the text?

.................................................

.................................................

.................................................

.................................................

.................................................

.................................................

.................................................

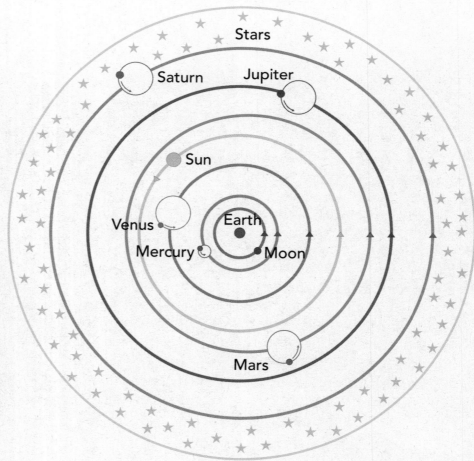

**The Geocentric Model**

**Figure 5** This geocentric model shows our solar system, with Earth in the center. The other planets orbit Earth and move along their epicycles at the same time.

## Heliocentric Model

Not everybody believed in the geocentric system. An ancient Greek scientist named Aristarchus, who lived over 400 years before Ptolemy, developed a sun-centered or **heliocentric** (hee lee oh SEN trik) model. *Helios* is Greek for "sun." In a heliocentric system, Earth and the other planets revolve around the sun. This model was not well received. Many people insisted that Earth had to be at the center of the universe.

**Figure 6** lists four scientists who worked to expand and prove the heliocentric model of the solar system. The Polish astronomer Nicolaus Copernicus further developed the heliocentric model. Copernicus proposed that Earth's rotation and revolution around the sun explained the observed movements of the stars and planets. He published his work in 1543. Copernicus's theory would eventually revolutionize the science of astronomy, the study of space.

Early heliocentric models assumed that planets moved in perfect circles. Their models fit existing observations fairly well. But in the late 1500s, the Danish astronomer Tycho Brahe (TEE koh BRAH huh) made much more accurate observations. Brahe's assistant, Johannes Kepler, used the observations to figure out the shape of the planets' orbits. When he used circular orbits, his calculations did not fit the observations. After years of detailed calculations, Kepler found that the orbit of each planet is actually an **ellipse**, an oval shape, rather than a perfect circle.

## Galileo's Discovery

For many years, people continued to believe the geocentric model. However, evidence collected by the Italian scientist Galileo Galilei gradually convinced others that the heliocentric model was correct. In 1610, Galileo, using a telescope that he constructed himself, discovered moons orbiting Jupiter. These Galilean moons showed that not everything in the sky travels around Earth.

**1500**

**1550**

**1600**

**1650**

**Heliocentric Timeline**

**Figure 6** Explain what each scientist added to our understanding of the heliocentric model of the solar system.

**Copernicus**

..........................................
..........................................
..........................................
..........................................
..........................................
..........................................
..........................................

**Brahe and Kepler**

..........................................
..........................................
..........................................
..........................................
..........................................
..........................................
..........................................
..........................................

**Galileo**

..........................................
..........................................
..........................................
..........................................
..........................................
..........................................
..........................................

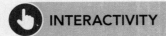
INTERACTIVITY

Determine how seasonal changes in our perception of stars support a specific model of the solar system.

**Confirming the Heliocentric Model** Galileo also made other observations that supported Copernicus's theory that the sun was the center of the solar system. For example, Galileo discovered that Venus goes through phases similar to the moon's phases. But, since Venus is never too far away from the sun in the sky, it would not have a full set of phases if both it and the sun circled around Earth. Therefore, Galileo reasoned, the geocentric model did not hold true.

☑ READING CHECK **Cite Textual Evidence** How does the development of the heliocentric model show how scientific ideas change over time?

........................................................................................

........................................................................................

........................................................................................

........................................................................................

## Model It

### Models of the Universe

Develop Models ✏ Draw Galileo's heliocentric system. Show and label the evidence he produced to support his model.

**1. Predict** Two photographers take time-lapse photos of the night sky. One of them is at the equator. The other is at the South Pole. Which photo will show stars that never rise or set? Explain.

........................................................................

........................................................................

........................................................................

........................................................................

**2. Summarize Text** Explain the two theories about how Earth and the sun move in space relative to each other.

........................................................................

........................................................................

........................................................................

........................................................................

........................................................................

........................................................................

........................................................................

**3. Infer** What observations made by Galileo supported Copernicus's theory about the solar system?

........................................................................

........................................................................

........................................................................

........................................................................

........................................................................

........................................................................

........................................................................

**4. Construct an Explanation** Which patterns in space are predictable? Why?

........................................................................

........................................................................

........................................................................

........................................................................

**5. Cause and Effect** What causes the stars to appear to move across the night sky?

........................................................................

........................................................................

........................................................................

# Quest CHECK-IN

In this lesson, you learned why the stars in the night sky seem to move. You learned that various objects move, or seem to move, in space. You also discovered how Earth and the other planets move in relation to the sun.

**Evaluate** If the relative positions of the sun and moon affect the ocean's tides, why would it be smart for sailors and other people who work on the ocean to understand patterns in the Earth-sun-moon system?

........................................................................

........................................................................

........................................................................

........................................................................

👆 **INTERACTIVITY**

Tides and Earth's Motion

**Go online** to analyze images and data about tides and look for connections in the patterns you see.

MS-ESS1-1

# THE PTOLEMAIC MODEL:
# Explaining
# the Unexplained

**B**efore there were satellites and telescopes, ancient Greek and Roman astronomers relied on their eyes to learn about the solar system. Their observations led them to an understanding of the solar system in which the sun, moon, and planets revolved around Earth.

## Theory from Observation

Believing he was standing at the center of the universe, astronomer Claudius Ptolemy watched planets march across the sky. But he made a few observations that intrigued him. The planets grew brighter or dimmer at times, and they seemed to speed up and slow down. Even more puzzling, some planets—such as Mars—occasionally appeared to move *backward* across the sky. If the planets circled Earth as everyone believed, how could they move so irregularly?

Ptolemy developed a theory to explain this retrograde, or backward, motion of the planets. The planets still revolved around Earth, but he argued that they moved in small circles as they traveled through a circular orbit.

Astronomer Claudius Ptolemaeus, or Ptolemy (100 CE – 170 CE), lived in Alexandria, Egypt.

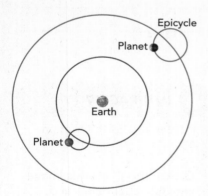

Ptolemy developed the concept of epicycles to explain why some planets appeared to move backward in their orbits. Depending on where a planet was in its epicycle, it would seem to move one way and then the other from Earth.

# Advances in Technology

The Ptolemaic model was the dominant model for centuries. But astronomical instruments improved and provided more accurate measurements. Astronomers began to find errors in Ptolemy's model. In the 1500s, Copernicus proposed a heliocentric model in which the sun was the center of the solar system. Finally, Galileo used newly developed technology—a telescope—to disprove Ptolemy's model. Ptolemy hadn't been standing at the center of the universe after all.

**Use the diagrams to answer the following questions.**

1. **Compare** How does the geocentric model of the solar system differ from the heliocentric model?

2. **Construct Explanations** Explain how our evolving model of the solar system shows why scientists need to keep an open mind as they gather more data.

3. **Connect to Technology** Astronomers continue to refine their understanding of the solar system. How might advances in technology help to add to our knowledge?

**Ptolemaic or geocentric model**

**Copernican or heliocentric model**

# Earth's Movement in Space

## Guiding Questions

- How does Earth's motion affect the amount of daylight and the seasons?
- Why do Earth and the moon remain in orbit?

## Connections

**Literacy**  Cite Textual Evidence

**Math**  Analyze Quantitative Relationships

MS-ESS1-1

## Vocabulary

axis
rotation
revolution
orbit
solstice
equinox
gravity
law of universal
  gravitation
inertia

## Academic Vocabulary

hypothesize

 **VOCABULARY APP**

Practice vocabulary on a mobile device.

### **Quest** CONNECTION

Study the motions of Earth and the moon and observe how these motions affect the tides on Earth's surface.

## Connect It !

✏ **Draw an X on the image to indicate the position of the sun.**

**Apply Scientific Reasoning**  Which part of Earth is experiencing daytime in the image?

...............................................................................................................................................

...............................................................................................................................................

...............................................................................................................................................

# How Earth Moves

The apparent motion of the sun, moon, and stars in the sky is a result of the way Earth itself moves through space. Earth, as well as the other planets, moves around the sun in two separate ways: rotation and revolution.

**Rotation** To help describe Earth's movement, scientists have named an imaginary line that passes from the North Pole, through the Earth's center, to the South Pole. This line is known as Earth's **axis**, and the spinning of Earth on its axis is called **rotation**.

Look at **Figure 1**. You can see that half of Earth is lit and half is in darkness. Earth rotates from west to east (see **Figure 2**.) As it rotates, objects in the sky appear to move in the direction opposite of Earth's rotation.

As Earth rotates eastward, the sun appears to move west across the sky. As Earth continues to turn to the east, the sun appears to set in the west. Because sunlight can't reach the side of Earth facing away from the sun, it is night there. It takes Earth about 24 hours to rotate once. As you know, each of these 24-hour cycles is called a day.

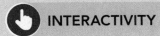

**INTERACTIVITY**

Investigate the patterns in Earth's rotation and revolution.

**Day and Night**
**Figure 1** Day occurs on the part of Earth that is turned toward the sun. Night occurs on the part of Earth that is turned away from the sun.

## Earth's Axis

**Figure 2** ✏ Earth spins on its axis, rotating from west to east to cause day and night. Shade the part of Earth that is experiencing night.

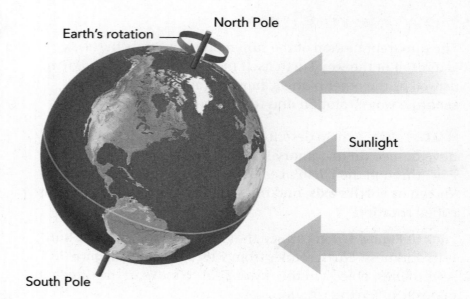

Earth's rotation

North Pole

Sunlight

South Pole

▶ **VIDEO**

Consider the difference between rotating and revolving.

## Revolution

**Revolution** As you read this page, do you feel as if you are moving? You may not feel it, but as Earth rotates, it is traveling around the sun. **Revolution** is the movement of one object around another. One revolution of Earth around the sun takes one year. Like other planets, Earth's path, or **orbit**, around the sun is an ellipse, an oval shape. The ellipse brings the planet closest to the sun in January.

## Design It ✏

**Develop Models** ✏ How could you model Earth's movements? Design a model using real objects to represent Earth and the sun. Explain how you could use these objects to illustrate Earth's motions. Include both Earth's rotation and revolution in your design and explanation.

..........................................................................................................................

..........................................................................................................................

..........................................................................................................................

..........................................................................................................................

# The Seasons

The extent of seasonal change in any given place on Earth depends on how far away that place is from the equator. The farther away a place is from the equator, the more widely its seasonal temperatures vary. This is because of how sunlight hits Earth.

When we look at areas near the equator, we see that sunlight hits Earth's surface very directly. This sunlight is concentrated in the smallest possible area. Near the North and South Poles, sunlight hits Earth at a steep angle, so the same amount of sunlight spreads over a greater area. That's why it is warmer near the equator than near the poles.

Seasonal differences in temperature are dependent on the tilt of Earth's axis. If the axis were straight up and down relative to Earth's orbit, temperatures in a given area would remain constant year-round, and there would be no seasons. However, Earth's axis is tilted at an angle of 23.5° from the vertical. Therefore, as Earth revolves around the sun, the north end of its axis is tilted away from the sun for part of the year and toward the sun for part of the year. Earth has seasons because its axis is tilted as it revolves around the sun.

**Figure 3** shows how Earth moves during the year. In June, the Northern Hemisphere is tilted toward the sun and we experience summer. The sun's rays are more concentrated and the temperatures are warmer. In December, the Northern Hemisphere is tilted away from the sun and we experience winter. The sun's rays are less concentrated, so temperatures are lower. During March and September, sunlight strikes both hemispheres equally, causing the mild temperatures felt in spring and autumn.

## Seasons

**Figure 3** Earth's tilted axis affects the strength of sunlight in different places throughout the year. Which month labels the part of the diagram showing the South Pole in complete darkness?

..............................................

..............................................

..............................................

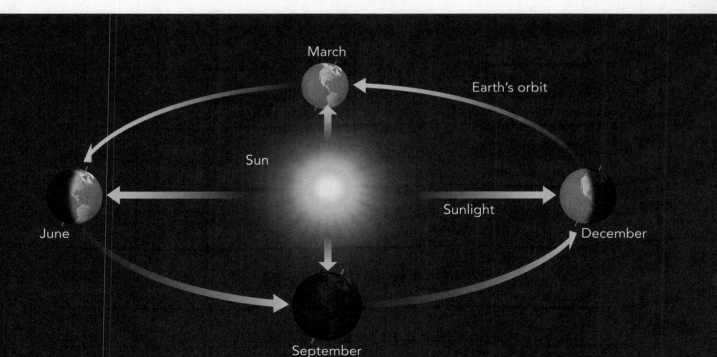

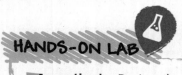
**Investigate** Review the differences between mass and weight and how weight is affected by gravity.

**Day Length** The tilt of Earth's axis also affects day length. The hemisphere that is tilted toward the sun has more hours of day than night. Points on Earth near the poles have the most drastic changes in day length. In Kiruna, Sweden, shown in **Figure 4**, the sun remains below the horizon throughout the day for most of January. However, in June the sun never fully sets.

## Solstices and Equinoxes

In each hemisphere, there is one day per year when the sun appears highest in the sky. Each of these days is called a **solstice**. Solstices occur when either the Northern or Southern Hemisphere is at its strongest tilt towards the sun.

Halfway between the solstices, neither hemisphere is tilted toward the sun. Each of these days is called an **equinox**, which means "equal night." This day occurs when the sun passes directly overhead at the equator at noon, and night and day are both 12 hours long.

The solstices and equinoxes occur at opposite times in the Northern and Southern Hemispheres. In the Northern Hemisphere, the summer solstice occurs around June 21, and the winter solstice occurs around December 22. However, in the Southern Hemisphere, these dates are opposite of what they are in the Northern Hemisphere. Equinoxes occur in both the Northern and Southern Hemispheres around September 22 and March 21.

**Short Days**

**Figure 4** At noon in January, the sun is still low in the sky in Sweden.

# Gravity and Orbits

The force that keeps Earth in orbit around the sun and the moon in orbit around Earth is the same force that prevents you from flying away when you jump. That force is gravity.

**Gravity** In the 1600s, an English scientist named Isaac Newton was curious about why the moon orbits Earth. In his work *Principia,* Newton contended that there must be a force, or a push and pull, acting between Earth and the moon.

Newton **hypothesized** that the same force that pulls the moon toward Earth also pulls apples to the ground when they fall from a tree. This force that attracts all objects toward each other is called **gravity**. Newton's **law of universal gravitation** states that every object in the universe attracts every other object. The strength of the force of gravity between two objects depends on two factors: the masses of the objects and the distance between them. Mass is the amount of matter in an object. Because Earth is so massive, it exerts a much greater force on you than your textbook exerts on you.

The measure of the force of gravity on an object is called weight. Mass doesn't change, but an object's weight can change depending on its location. On the moon, you would weigh about one-sixth as much as on Earth. The moon has less mass than Earth, so the pull of the moon's gravity on you would also be less. In space, as shown in **Figure 5**, you have no weight at all.

Gravity is also affected by the distance between two objects. The force of gravity decreases as distance increases. If the distance between two objects doubles, the force of gravity decreases to one-fourth of its original value.

**Academic Vocabulary**
How have you heard the term *hypothesize* used before?

.................................................................

.................................................................

.................................................................

.................................................................

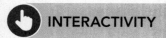
**Inertia** If the sun and Earth are constantly pulling on one another because of gravity, why doesn't Earth fall into the sun? The fact that such a collision has not occurred shows that a factor called inertia is at work.

**Inertia** is the tendency of an object to resist a change in motion. You feel the effects of inertia when you are riding in a car and it stops suddenly, but you keep moving forward. The more mass an object has, the greater its inertia. An object with greater inertia is more difficult to start or stop.

Isaac Newton stated his ideas about inertia as a scientific law. Newton's first law of motion says that an object at rest will stay at rest and an object in motion will stay in motion with a constant speed and direction, unless acted on by a force.

# Math Toolbox

## Gravity vs. Distance

Imagine that a spacecraft is leaving Earth's surface. How does the force of gravity between the rocket and the planet change?

| Distance from Earth's Center (planet's radius = 1) | 1 | 2 | 3 | 4 |
|---|---|---|---|---|
| Force of Gravity on the Spacecraft (million newtons) | 4 | 1 | 0.44 | 0.25 |

1. **Construct Graphs** ✏ Create a line graph of the data above.

2. **Analyze Quantitative Relationships** What is the force of gravity on the spacecraft at twice the planet's radius from its center?

   ....................................................

3. **Make Predictions** What would the force of gravity on the spacecraft be at a distance of 8 radii?

   ....................................................

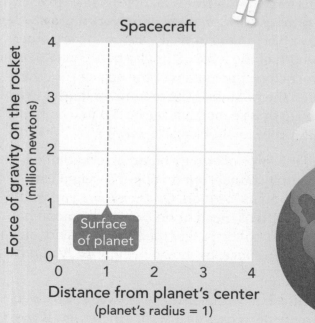

Spacecraft

Surface of planet

Force of gravity on the rocket (million newtons)

Distance from planet's center (planet's radius = 1)

**Orbital Motion** So, the moon travels through space at the same speed because of its inertia. But, it is constantly changing direction to remain in orbit around Earth. Newton concluded that inertia and gravity combine to keep the moon in orbit around Earth. You can see how this occurs in **Figure 6**.

Without Earth's gravity, the moon would veer away from Earth in a straight line. Earth's gravity pulls the moon inward and prevents it from moving away in a straight line. The combination of these two factors results in a curved orbital path. Similarly, planets are held in their elliptical orbits around the sun by the combined forces of gravity and inertia.

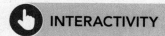

**INTERACTIVITY**

Explore how Earth's tilted axis and revolution influence the seasons.

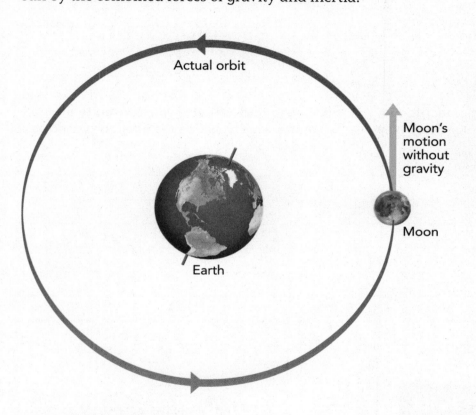

Actual orbit

Moon's motion without gravity

Moon

Earth

**Orbital Motion**

**Figure 6** 🖉 Gravity and inertia keep the moon in orbit around Earth. Complete the diagram by drawing an arrow to indicate the force of gravity Earth exerts on the moon as it orbits Earth.

✅ **READING CHECK Cite Textual Evidence** What factors affect the strength of the pull of gravity between two objects?

.................................................................................................

.................................................................................................

.................................................................................................

.................................................................................................

.................................................................................................

.................................................................................................

.................................................................................................

.................................................................................................

.................................................................................................

MS-ESS1-1

**1. Identify** What are the two ways Earth moves?

..................................................................

..................................................................

**2. Patterns** What causes the pattern of day and night? What causes the pattern of the seasons?

..................................................................

..................................................................

..................................................................

**3. Draw Conclusions** What happens to the length of the day during the solstices? Why does this occur?

..................................................................

..................................................................

..................................................................

..................................................................

..................................................................

..................................................................

..................................................................

..................................................................

**4. Construct an Explanation** What parts of Earth generally have the highest temperatures? Which have the lowest? What causes this difference?

..................................................................

..................................................................

..................................................................

..................................................................

..................................................................

..................................................................

**5. Cause and Effect** If you traveled to the moon, what would be the effect on your mass and weight?

..................................................................

..................................................................

..................................................................

..................................................................

..................................................................

..................................................................

..................................................................

# Quest CHECK-IN

In this lesson, you learned about the way that the sun interacts with Earth to produce day, night, and the seasons. You also discovered how gravity, mass, and inertia affect the movement of Earth and the moon.

**Infer** When the sun, moon, and Earth are aligned, ocean tides are larger—high tide is higher, low tide is lower—than when they are not aligned. How might this relate to gravity?

..................................................................

..................................................................

..................................................................

..................................................................

..................................................................

## 👆 INTERACTIVITY

Tides and the Moon's Gravity

**Go online** to study models of the motions of Earth and the moon and observe how these motions affect the tides on Earth's surface.

# Tracking
# Time in the Sky

**W**ill your birthday fall on a weekend this year? Better check the calendar! A calendar organizes time into days, months, and years. It may seem like a simple grid of squares, but a calendar is actually a measurement of time based on patterns of movement among Earth, the sun, and the moon.

### Egyptian Calendar (3rd Millenium BCE)
The ancient Egyptians created one of the first calendars. They figured out that a year—the time it takes for Earth to orbit the sun—was 365 days long. They used the repeating phases of the moon to divide a year into 12 months of 30 days each and tacked on five extra days at the end of the year.

### Julian Calendar (46 BCE)
The Romans borrowed the Egyptian calendar, but they noticed that it didn't always line up with the first day of spring. It actually takes 365 ¼ days for Earth to orbit the sun. So, Julius Caesar added an extra day every four years to keep the calendar on track. This extra day is inserted into a "leap year," so that February has 29 days instead of 28.

### Gregorian Calendar (1582 CE)
After a few centuries, it became clear that the Roman calendar also wasn't quite right. In fact, it was almost 11 minutes off each year. That may not sound like much, but by the year 1582, the first day of spring was a full ten days too early. To fix the problem, Pope Gregory XIII reset and tweaked the calendar, giving us the one we still use today.

**CONNECT TO YOU**

Divide this year by 4. If the year is evenly divisible by 4, it's a leap year. Years that end in 00 are exceptions. They must be divisible by 400!

The ancient Egyptians created a calendar to keep track of civic events such as festivals. Archeologists discovered this calendar in the Temple of Karnak in Luxor.

# 3 Phases and Eclipses

## Guiding Questions

- Why does the moon appear to change shape?
- What causes solar and lunar eclipses?
- How do the sun and moon affect the tides?

## Connections

Literacy Summarize Text

Math Interpret Data

MS-ESS1-1

## Vocabulary

phase
eclipse
umbra
penumbra
tide
spring tide
neap tide

## Academic Vocabulary

significant

📱 VOCABULARY APP

Practice vocabulary on a mobile device.

## Quest CONNECTION

Think about how the position of the moon relative to Earth and the sun affects tides.

## Connect It !

🖊 **Observe the image of the moon in Figure 1. Draw several other shapes that you have seen the moon take.**

Construct Explanations   What might be causing these changes?

........................................................................................................................................

........................................................................................................................................

........................................................................................................................................

Determine Conclusions   How is Earth affected by the moon?

........................................................................................................................................

........................................................................................................................................

# The Appearance of the Moon

When the moon is full, it shines so brightly that it makes the night sky significantly brighter. At these times, when viewed from Earth, the moon is round or almost round. Other times, the moon is just a thin crescent in the sky, seeming to emit a small strand of light, as in **Figure 1**. The different shapes of the moon you see are called **phases**. Phases are caused by the motions of the moon around Earth.

## The Two Sides of the Moon

When you look at the moon when it's full, you may see what looks like a face. You are actually seeing some of the most dramatic features of the moon, a pattern of light-colored and dark-colored areas on the moon's surface. The dark-colored areas are low, flat plains of lava called *maria*. You may also be able to detect brighter patterns that indicate highland areas, often dotted with craters.

For observers from Earth these distinctive patterns on the moon never move. The side of the moon that always faces Earth is called the near side. The side of the moon that always faces away from Earth is the far side, or dark side. To find out why the same side of the moon always faces Earth, you must study the motion of the moon around Earth.

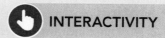

INTERACTIVITY

Investigate why the moon is sometimes visible during the day.

**Reflect** Look up at the sky tonight. What phase of the moon do you see? In your science notebook, track the phases of the moon. Based on your observations, what is the position of the moon in relation to the sun and Earth?

## Moon Phases

**Figure 1** This crescent moon appeared over the horizon shortly before sunrise.

## Lunar Motion

**Figure 2** ✏️ This diagram shows the rotation and revolution of the moon. Add a drawing of a face on the two remaining images of the moon to show how the moon is facing Earth at each phase. How would the moon appear from Earth if the moon did not rotate?

...........................................................................................................................................

...........................................................................................................................................

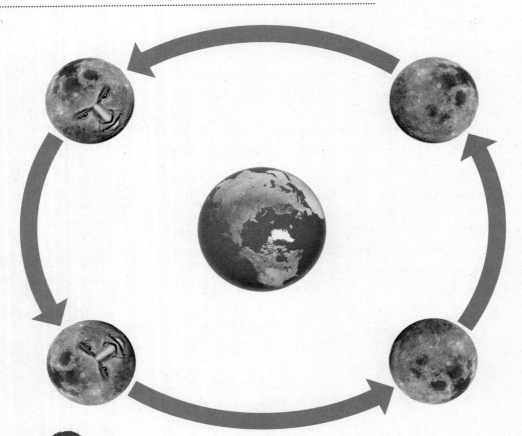

### HANDS-ON LAB

☐ **Investigate** Research to find out why we don't see the dark side of the moon from Earth.

## Literacy Connection

**Summarize Text** Underline the sentences that, if gathered together, best summarize how the sun, the moon, and Earth affect one another.

**Motions of the Moon** The moon, like Earth, rotates and revolves. The moon revolves around Earth and also rotates on its own axis. The moon rotates once on its axis in the same time that it takes to revolve once around Earth, as shown in **Figure 2**. Thus, a "day" on the moon is the same length as a "year" on the moon. This also explains why you always see the same side of the moon from Earth.

If you could look at the moon from space, you would see that half of the moon is always lit by the sun. The amount of the moon's surface that is lit is constant. But because the moon orbits Earth, the part of the lit surface that is visible from Earth changes. The phase of the moon you see depends on how much of the sunlit side of the moon faces Earth. These periods of light and darkness occur in predictable patterns, as shown in **Figure 3**.

**Phases of the Moon** During the new moon phase, the moon is between Earth and the sun. The side of the moon facing Earth is dark and the opposite side of the moon is facing the sun. As the moon revolves around Earth, the side of the moon you see gradually becomes more illuminated by direct sunlight.

After about a week, the angle formed by the sun, moon, and Earth is about 90 degrees. This is called the first quarter moon and it is half lit and half dark. About halfway through the moon's revolution, you see the full sunlit side of the moon, called a full moon. About a week later, the sun is shining on the other half of the moon, creating a third quarter moon. At this time you see half of the lit side. After about 29.5 days, the pattern begins again and a new moon occurs.

 **READING CHECK** **Translate Information** Use **Figure 3** to describe what is happening during a waning crescent.

..................................................................................................

..................................................................................................

..................................................................................................

..................................................................................................

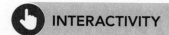 **INTERACTIVITY**

Explore why the moon sometimes appears as a crescent in the sky.

▶ **VIDEO**

Find out more about the changing appearance of the moon as we see it from Earth.

**Moon Phases**
**Figure 3** ✎ In the empty circle, draw what a waning crescent moon looks like from Earth.

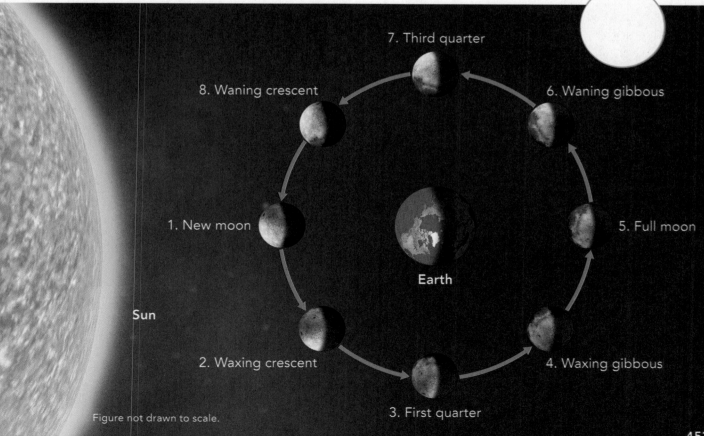

7. Third quarter

8. Waning crescent

6. Waning gibbous

1. New moon

5. Full moon

Earth

Sun

2. Waxing crescent

4. Waxing gibbous

3. First quarter

Figure not drawn to scale.

## Two Types of Eclipses

**Figure 4** ✏ Draw an X on each diagram to show a spot where each eclipse can be seen. Add labels for the Earth's penumbra and umbra in the lunar eclipse diagram. Mark a *P* to show the places a moon could be during a partial lunar eclipse.

👆 **INTERACTIVITY**

Use a virtual activity to learn more about eclipses.

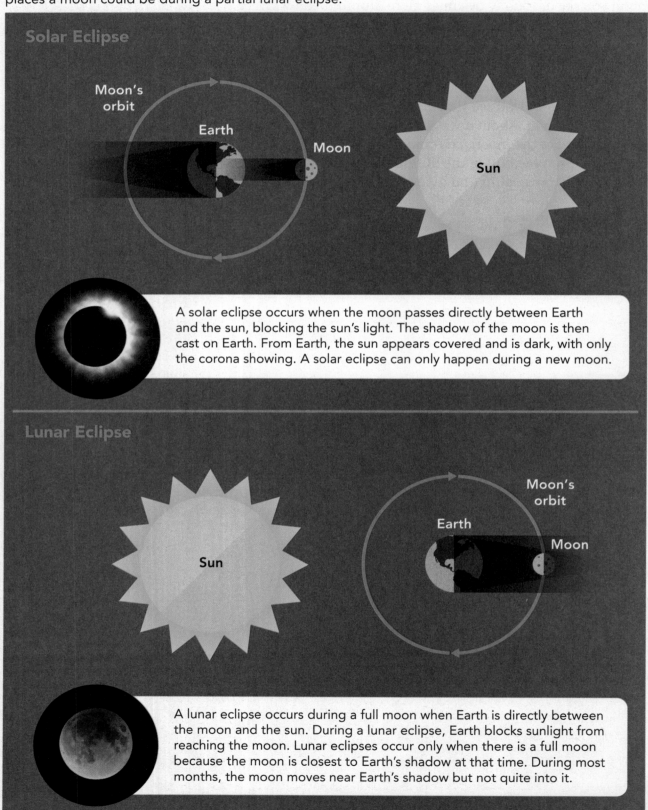

### Solar Eclipse

Moon's orbit

Earth

Moon

Sun

A solar eclipse occurs when the moon passes directly between Earth and the sun, blocking the sun's light. The shadow of the moon is then cast on Earth. From Earth, the sun appears covered and is dark, with only the corona showing. A solar eclipse can only happen during a new moon.

### Lunar Eclipse

Sun

Moon's orbit

Earth

Moon

A lunar eclipse occurs during a full moon when Earth is directly between the moon and the sun. During a lunar eclipse, Earth blocks sunlight from reaching the moon. Lunar eclipses occur only when there is a full moon because the moon is closest to Earth's shadow at that time. During most months, the moon moves near Earth's shadow but not quite into it.

# Eclipses

When an object in space comes between the sun and a third object, it cases a shadow on the third object, causing an **eclipse**. There are two types of eclipses, solar eclipses and lunar eclipses, as shown in **Figure 4**.

Every month there is a new moon and a full moon, but eclipses don't occur every month. The plane of the moon's orbit around Earth is off by about 5 degrees from the plane of Earth's orbit around the sun. During most months, the shadow cast by Earth or the moon misses the other object.

During an eclipse, the very darkest part of the shadow where the light from the sun is completely blocked is the **umbra**. Only people within the umbra experience a total solar eclipse. The moon's umbra is fairly narrow, while Earth's is much broader. Because Earth's shadow is larger than the moon's, it can be seen from many more places, and more people have a view of a total lunar eclipse than of a total solar eclipse.

The area of the shadow where the sun is only partially blocked is called the **penumbra**. During a solar eclipse, people in the penumbra see only a partial eclipse. A partial lunar eclipse occurs when the moon passes partly into the umbra of Earth's shadow. The edge of the umbra appears blurry, and you can watch it pass across the moon for two or three hours.

☑ READING CHECK **Determine Central Ideas** Why isn't there an eclipse every month?

...................................................................................................................

...................................................................................................................

...................................................................................................................

INTERACTIVITY

Learn more about the phases of the moon and eclipses.

VIDEO

Discover what it's like to work in a planetarium.

## Model It!

### Solar and Lunar Eclipses

Solar and lunar eclipses occur when the sun, moon, and Earth are perfectly aligned.

Develop Models 🖊 How could you represent Earth, the moon, and the sun during an eclipse? Use real objects to create a model of a solar eclipse and a lunar eclipse. Think about what you could use as a light source to represent the sun. What positions would your objects need to be in to illustrate each type of eclipse? Draw and label the plan for your models.

# Tides

**Tides** are the rise and fall of ocean water that occur approximately every 12.5 hours. Tides result from gravitational differences in how Earth, the moon, and the sun interact at different alignments. The water rises for about 6 hours, then falls for about 6 hours.

**The Moon and Sun** The moon's gravity pulls more strongly on the side of Earth facing the moon. This pull causes the ocean water to bulge on that side of Earth. Another bulge forms on the side of Earth that is farther from the moon, where the moon's pull is weakest. This causes the formation of high tides in both locations and low tides in between. As Earth rotates, the bulges shift to remain oriented with the moon. As a result, a full rotation will result in two high-tides and two low-tides at a given location.

The sun also affects the ocean tides. Even though the sun's gravitational pull on Earth is much stronger than the moon's, the sun is so far away that the differences at the near side and far side of Earth are small. As a result, the sun's effect cannot cancel out the moon's effect, but it does influence it. Changes in the relative positions of the moon and sun affect the changing levels of the tides over the course of a month.

## Math Toolbox

Tides are measured at different locations by choosing a reference height and then determining how far above that height the water rises. The table shows approximate data for high and low tides in Nag's Head, North Carolina, in November 2016.

| High and Low Tides, Nag's Head, NC | | |
|---|---|---|
| Date | High Tide (cm) | Low Tide (cm) |
| Nov. 21 | 99.9 | 20.3 |
| Nov. 23 | 101.6 | 25.4 |
| Nov. 25 | 109.2 | 17.8 |
| Nov. 27 | 116.8 | 10.2 |

**1. Interpret Data** Which tide has the greatest change in centimeters? What was the difference?

......................................................................................................

......................................................................................................

**2. Infer** Which of the dates was most likely the closest to a new moon? Explain.

......................................................................................................

......................................................................................................

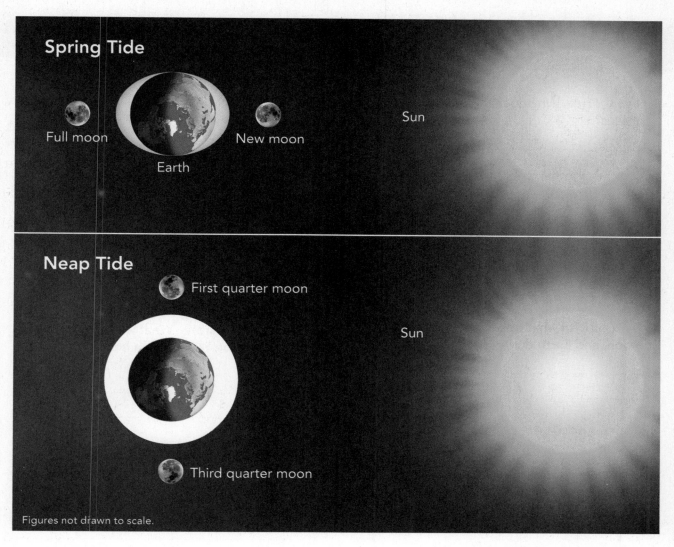

Spring Tide

Full moon — Earth — New moon — Sun

Neap Tide

First quarter moon — Sun

Third quarter moon

Figures not drawn to scale.

**Spring and Neap Tides** The sun, the moon, and Earth line up during the new moon and full moon phases as is shown in **Figure 5**. The gravitational pulls from both the sun and moon combine to produce a tide with the most **significant** difference between consecutive low and high tides, called a **spring tide**.

During the moon's first quarter and third quarter phases, the line between Earth and the sun is at a right angle to the line between Earth and the moon. Because the sun and the moon are pulling in different directions, their gravitational pulls partially cancel each other. This arrangement produces more moderate tides, called neap tides. A **neap tide** is a tide with the least difference between consecutive low and high tides.

☑ **READING CHECK Summarize Text** What causes high and low tides?

......................................................................................

......................................................................................

......................................................................................

**Spring and Neap Tides**

**Figure 5** 🖊 Spring and neap tides occur twice a month. Shade in the bulges that occur during the neap tide.

**Academic Vocabulary**

Can you use the word *significant* in a sentence about the weather?

......................................................

......................................................

......................................................

......................................................

......................................................

MS-ESS1-1

**1. Summarize** Why does the moon have phases?

.......................................................
.......................................................
.......................................................
.......................................................
.......................................................
.......................................................

**2. Describe** In what positions are the sun, moon, and Earth during a full moon?

.......................................................
.......................................................

**3. Cause and Effect** What causes a total lunar eclipse?

.......................................................
.......................................................
.......................................................
.......................................................
.......................................................

**4. Construct an Explanation** Under what circumstances might you be able to view a partial solar eclipse instead of a full solar eclipse?

.......................................................
.......................................................
.......................................................
.......................................................
.......................................................
.......................................................

**5. Draw Conclusions** What would you expect the tides to be like during a first quarter moon?

.......................................................
.......................................................
.......................................................
.......................................................
.......................................................
.......................................................
.......................................................
.......................................................

# Quest CHECK-IN

In this lesson, you learned about how Earth, the moon, and the sun interact to create the phases of the moon, eclipses, and tides.

**Evaluate** What does the pattern among the moon's phases and the cycle of tides suggest about how reliable tidal power would be?

.......................................................
.......................................................
.......................................................
.......................................................

## HANDS-ON LAB

The Moon's Revolution and Tides

**Go online** for a downloadable worksheet of this lab. Investigate how the position of the moon relative to Earth and the sun affects tides and to explore why some tidal ranges vary over time.

# Power From THE TIDES

▶ VIDEO

Explore the mechanics of a turbine and how it generates usable energy.

**How do you** generate electricity from tides? You engineer it!

**The Challenge:** To harness tidal power to generate electricity.

**Phenomenon** If you've ever had to move your beach towel further up the sand as you notice the tide coming in, you've witnessed one of Earth's greatest renewable resources. Twenty-four hours a day, the tides move millions of gallons of water along coastlines around the world.

Engineers are applying an existing technology—turbines—in a new way to generate power from moving tides. Turbines look like large fans. When placed in shallow water where the tide is strong, moving ocean water turns the turbine's blades. The spinning blades power generators to make electricity. The world's first tidal energy plant, in France, produces enough electricity to power a small city.

Tidal energy doesn't create pollution, and tides are reliable and powerful. But the technology used to harness the tides is expensive. Engineers are looking for ways to make tidal turbines more cost-effective. When that happens, harnessing tidal energy may become the wave of the future.

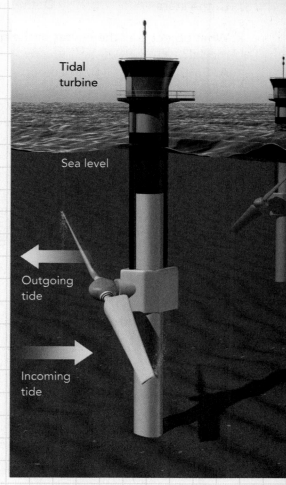

Tidal turbine

Sea level

Outgoing tide

Incoming tide

A tidal turbine generates power both when the tide comes in and when the tide goes out.

**DESIGN CHALLENGE** Can you design a tidal turbine? Go to the Engineering Design Notebook to find out!

# ☑ TOPIC 9 Review and Assess

## ① Movement in Space

MS-ESS1-1

**1.** Planets appear to move in the sky against the backdrop of
  **A.** other planets.   **B.** the sun.
  **C.** the stars.   **D.** the moon.

**2.** What object is at the center of the geocentric model?
  **A.** Earth   **B.** the moon
  **C.** the sun   **D.** a star

**3.** What discovery by Galileo supported the heliocentric model?
  **A.** the phases of Venus
  **B.** the elliptical orbits of planets
  **C.** the moon's orbiting of Earth
  **D.** the movement of planets in the night sky

**4.** Objects in the sky appear to move due to Earth's .................................................. and ....................................

**5. Cause and Effect** Why do stars appear to move from east to west in the night sky?

**6. Patterns** The constellation Hercules is visible in the sky in September. Why isn't Hercules visible in the sky in March?

## ② Earth's Movements in Space

MS-ESS1-1

**7.** The imaginary line that runs through Earth's pole is its
  **A.** axis.   **B.** orbit.
  **C.** revolution.   **D.** rotation.

**8.** Which of the following is responsible for the cyclic pattern of day and night on Earth?
  **A.** the tilt of Earth's axis
  **B.** the rotation of Earth on its axis
  **C.** Earth's revolution around the sun
  **D.** the revolution of the moon around Earth

**9.** Earth has seasons because
  **A.** its axis is tilted as it revolves around the sun.
  **B.** it rotates on its axis as it revolves.
  **C.** the moon exerts a gravitational force on it.
  **D.** the relative positions of Earth, the sun, and the moon do not change.

**10.** The two times of the year in which the sun is directly overhead at the equator are the .......................................... and the ......................

**11. Patterns** How does the distance between two objects affect the force of gravity between them?

**12. Apply Concepts** Why is it generally warmer in the Northern Hemisphere in June than it is in December?

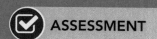 

Evaluate your understanding by taking a Topic Test.

# 3 Phases and Eclipses

MS-ESS1-1

**13.** Which of the following occurs when the moon moves through Earth's shadow?
**A.** high tide
**B.** a solar eclipse
**C.** a lunar eclipse
**D.** the phases of the moon

**14.** When the sun, the moon, and Earth line up during a new moon, which of the following is produced?
**A.** low tide
**B.** high tide
**C.** spring tide
**D.** neap tide

**15. Apply Scientific Reasoning** Suppose you traveled to the moon during a lunar eclipse. From your vantage point on the moon, what astronomical event would you be witnessing?

...................................................................

**16. Cause and Effect** Why does the moon have phases?

...................................................................

...................................................................

...................................................................

**17. Use Models** Does the diagram show a solar eclipse or a lunar eclipse? Explain.

...................................................................

...................................................................

...................................................................

...................................................................

**18. Apply Concepts** Which event would be less widely visible from Earth: a partial lunar eclipse or a total lunar eclipse? Explain.

...................................................................

...................................................................

...................................................................

...................................................................

...................................................................

**19. Develop Models** ✏ Draw a diagram of Earth, the sun, and the moon to demonstrate the phases of the moon: new, first quarter, full, and last quarter. In your diagram, label the four different positions of the moon and sketch what the corresponding phases look like from Earth.

461

MS-ESS1-1

## Evidence-Based Assessment

Gita is constructing a model to help her younger sister in science class. She hopes to use the model to demonstrate how the sun, Earth, and the moon interact so that her sister can describe and explain patterns in the cycles of this system. Gita wants her sister to be able to describe the following phenomena using the model:

- the phases of the moon

- the seasons on Earth

- solar and lunar eclipses

Gita's model is shown here. Gita labels E1, E2, E3, and E4 to show four positions of Earth in its orbit around the sun. She labels M1, M2, M3, and M4 to show four positions of the moon in its orbit around Earth.

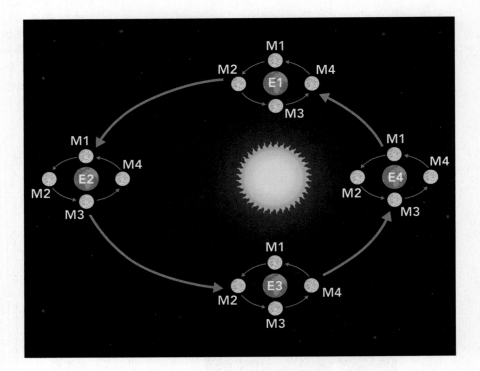

1. **Analyze Data** If Earth is at position E1 on the model and there is a new moon, then what is the moon's position?

A. M1

B. M2

C. M3

D. M4

2. **Patterns** Complete the table to identify the positions of Earth and the moon in their respective orbits for each phenomenon listed.

| Phenomenon | Earth's Position | Moon's Position |
|---|---|---|
| lunar eclipse | | M4 |
| solar eclipse | E3 | |
| full moon | E1 | |

3. **Use Models** Evaluate Gita's model and explain whether her sister can use it to correctly describe the patterns of the seasons on Earth.

....................................................................
....................................................................
....................................................................
....................................................................
....................................................................
....................................................................
....................................................................
....................................................................
....................................................................
....................................................................
....................................................................
....................................................................
....................................................................
....................................................................
....................................................................

4. **Construct an Explanation** Explain how Gita's sister can also use the model to show how patterns in the interactions among the sun, Earth, and the moon allow us to predict when lunar phases and eclipses occur.

....................................................................
....................................................................
....................................................................
....................................................................
....................................................................
....................................................................
....................................................................
....................................................................
....................................................................
....................................................................
....................................................................

# Quest FINDINGS

## Complete the Quest!

**Phenomenon** Think about ways to develop your model to demonstrate how the tides occur.

**Identify Limitations** What are some of the limitations of your model for the visitor center? How could you make your model more accurate?

....................................................................
....................................................................
....................................................................

👆 **INTERACTIVITY**

Reflect on It's as Sure as the Tides

463

MS-ESS1-1

Can you **design a model** to describe how the **moon's motion** is related to its **phases**?

# Modeling Lunar Phases

## Background

**Phenomenon** One of the greatest achievements of our ancestors was learning to make sense of the repeating patterns in the phases of the moon. People began organizing time and planning major events, such as planting and harvesting crops, according to these cycles, resulting in the earliest stages of human civilization.

In this investigation, you will design a model, using available materials, to show the relationship between the moon's motion around Earth and the moon's phases.

## Materials

(per pair)

- bright flashlight
- one small foam ball
- one large foam ball
- sharpened pencils or skewers

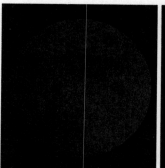
New Moon

First Quarter

Full Moon

Third Quarter

# Plan Your Investigation

☐ **Demonstrate** Go online for a downloadable worksheet of this lab.

☐ 1. You will model each view of the moon that is shown in the diagram. Look at the images of the moon. What do you think causes the differing amounts of lit moon in each image? Remember that the moon reflects light from the sun. Then think about the materials in the list. What do you think each material could represent in your model?

☐ 2. Start by discussing how you could model the view called *First Quarter*. Decide where you could position the flash-light and foam balls to show the sun, Earth, and moon in orbit. Where will you position the moon so an observer on Earth would see the first quarter moon? (Hint: Observe that during the first quarter phase, the right side of the moon is lit and the left side is dark.)

☐ 3. The next phase after first quarter is full moon. Based on this information, decide how to model the moon's orbit around Earth. In other words, in which direction does the moon orbit Earth?

☐ 4. Decide how to model the full moon, the third quarter, and the new moon. Where in its orbit does the moon take on each shape as seen from Earth?

☐ 5. Record your plans for modeling the phases of the moon. Include sketches or drawings that will help you to construct your model. Review your plans with your teacher before building and testing your model.

## Plan

## Sketches

# Analyze and Interpret Data

1. **Develop Models** In your model, where did you place the flashlight, large foam ball, and small foam ball to model the first quarter moon?

..............................................................................................................
..............................................................................................................
..............................................................................................................
..............................................................................................................
..............................................................................................................

2. **Patterns** Compare and contrast your models of the first quarter moon and the third quarter moon. What causes these shapes to look different to an observer on Earth?

..............................................................................................................
..............................................................................................................
..............................................................................................................
..............................................................................................................
..............................................................................................................

3. **Apply Scientific Reasoning** At the first and third quarter phases, the moon's shape appears as half a circle. Why do you think these phases are called *quarter* phases and not *half* phases?

..............................................................................................................
..............................................................................................................
..............................................................................................................
..............................................................................................................
..............................................................................................................

4. **Construct an Explanation** One lunar cycle includes all of the lunar phases. One lunar cycle is about one month long. Use evidence from your model to describe how the motions of the moon lead to lunar phases that occur in a lunar cycle.

..............................................................................................................
..............................................................................................................
..............................................................................................................
..............................................................................................................
..............................................................................................................

# TOPIC
# 10

# Solar System and the Universe

**LESSON 1**
Solar System Objects
**uInvestigate Lab:** Pulling Planets

**LESSON 2**
Learning About
the Universe
**uInvestigate Lab:** Space Exploration
  Vehicle

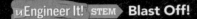 **uEngineer It!** STEM **Blast Off!**

**LESSON 3**
Stars
**uInvestigate Lab:** How Far Is That Star?

**LESSON 4**
Galaxies
**uInvestigate Lab:** Model the Milky Way

**NGSS PERFORMANCE EXPECTATIONS**
**MS-ESS1-2** Develop and use a model to describe
the role of gravity in the motions within galaxies
and the solar system.
**MS-ESS1-3** Analyze and interpret data to
determine scale properties of objects in the solar
system.

How do astronomers use telescopes and space probes to study the universe?

**GO ONLINE** to access your digital course.

 VIDEO

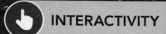 INTERACTIVITY

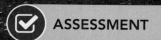 VIRTUAL LAB

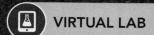 ASSESSMENT

 eTEXT

 APP

**HANDS-ON LAB**

*u***Connect** Develop a model to compare Earth's size to the size of the other planets.

## The Essential Question

### What kind of data and evidence help us to understand the universe?

For thousands of years, people have stared at and studied the sky. Some use tools such as diagrams, telescopes, cameras, and lasers to assist them. Some have even traveled beyond Earth to take a better look. Why do you look at the sky? Why do you think others do?

.............................................................................

.............................................................................

.............................................................................

.............................................................................

# Quest KICKOFF

## How do we look for things that can't be seen?

 **STEM** **Phenomenon** Telescopes and other technology allow astronomers and astrophysicists to collect data on objects in the universe. In this Quest activity, you will help with the hiring of three astronomers for a new observatory. Their specialties include asteroids, extraterrestrial life, and dark matter. In digital activities, you will investigate the work that asteroid, extraterrestrial, and dark matter hunters do. By applying what you have learned, you will develop persuasive advertisements for these positions.

**👆 INTERACTIVITY**

Searching for a Star

**MS-ESS1-2** Develop and use a model to describe the role of gravity in the motions within galaxies and the solar system.

**MS-ESS1-3** Analyze and interpret data to determine scale properties of objects in the solar system.

 **NBC LEARN** ▶ VIDEO

After watching the Quest Kickoff video, which examines the work of an astronomer who searches for life on planets outside our solar system, think about the qualities that make for a skilled astronomer. What scientific attitudes are important to the work of an astronomer such as the one in the video? Record your thoughts.

### Qualities of a Skilled Astronomer

1 .................................................................

2 .................................................................

3 .................................................................

4 .................................................................

# Quest CHECK-IN

### IN LESSON 1

**STEM** What have astronomers learned about our solar system? Think about the skills and tools an astronomer needs to study our solar system and the universe.

 **INTERACTIVITY**

Space Invaders

# Quest CHECK-IN

### IN LESSON 2

How do astronomers study distant objects? Explore how astronomers are able to detect asteroids and the dangers these objects pose to Earth.

 **INTERACTIVITY**

Anybody Out There?

### IN LESSON 3

How do astronomers classify stars? Consider how studying stars helps astronomers in the search for extraterrestrial life.

Telescopes and other equipment in this observatory allow astronomers to learn more about the properties of and relationships among our close neighbors in space as well as distant galaxies.

## Quest FINDINGS

# Complete the Quest!

Apply what you've learned about the work astronomers do by creating a persuasive job advertisement.

 **INTERACTIVITY**

Reflect on Searching for a Star

## Quest CHECK-IN

### IN LESSON 4

STEM How do astronomers know that dark matter exists? Explore the ways in which astronomers study something that cannot be seen.

 **INTERACTIVITY**

Searching for the Unseen

# ① Solar System Objects

## Guiding Questions

- How do the characteristics of the planets, moons, and smaller objects in the solar system compare?
- What is the role of gravity in the motions of planets, moons, and smaller objects in the solar system?
- What are the relationships between the sun and the planets in the solar system?

## Connections

**Literacy** Integrate With Visuals

**Math** Convert Measurement Units

MS-ESS1-2, MS-ESS1-3

## Vocabulary

solar system
astronomical unit
sun
planet
moon
asteroid
meteoroids
comets

## Academic Vocabulary

features

 **VOCABULARY APP**

Practice vocabulary on a mobile device.

### Quest CONNECTION

Recognize how knowing the characteristics of asteroids would help an asteroid hunter monitor and predict possible asteroid strikes.

## Connect It!

✏ **Put an X on the object in the center of the solar system. Draw a circle around Earth.**

**Use Models** List all the objects you can identify.

.................................................................................................

.................................................................................................

**Apply Scientific Reasoning** What do the curved lines in the illustration represent? How can you tell?

.................................................................................................

.................................................................................................

# Understanding the Solar System

Our home, Earth, is a planet. Earth is just one of many objects that make up our solar system. The **solar system** consists of the sun, the planets, their moons, and a variety of smaller objects. Each object in the solar system has a unique set of **features**. The sun is at the center of the solar system, with other objects orbiting around it. The force of the sun's gravitational pull keeps objects in their orbits around it. The strength of the gravitational force between any two objects in the solar system depends on their masses and the distance between them.

**HANDS-ON LAB**

Model the movements of planets around the sun.

**Academic Vocabulary**

The term *feature* can be used to mean a trait or characteristic. What are some features of the mode of transportation you use to get to school each day?

......................................
......................................
......................................
......................................

**Objects in the Solar System**

**Figure 1** In the solar system, planets and other objects orbit the sun.

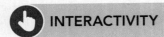

**INTERACTIVITY**

Explore the scale of distances in the solar system.

## Distances in the Solar System

Distances between objects in the solar system are so large that they are not easily measured in meters or kilometers. Instead, scientists frequently use a unit called the **astronomical unit** (AU). One astronomical unit equals the average distance measured from the center of the sun to the center of Earth, which is about 150,000,000 kilometers. The entire solar system extends more than 100,000 AU from the sun.

# Math Toolbox

## Converting Units of Distance

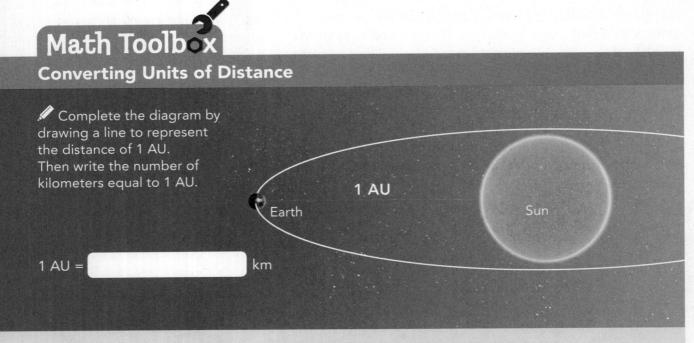

✏ Complete the diagram by drawing a line to represent the distance of 1 AU. Then write the number of kilometers equal to 1 AU.

1 AU = [          ] km

1 AU    Earth    Sun

The distances between objects in the solar system are vast. As a result, scientists use the larger value of the astronomical unit to make the numbers easier to work with.

To give you some perspective, the combined length of about 18 football fields is equal to 1 mi. One mile is about 1.6 km. That means 1 AU is equal to 1,650,000,000,000 football fields!

1. **Convert Measurement Units** Jupiter, the largest planet in our solar system, is about 630,000,000 km from Earth. About how many AU is Jupiter from Earth?

   .............................................................................................

2. **Apply Mathematical Concepts** Develop your own conversion between AU and a common distance such as the length of a football field. How many of your common units is equal to 1 AU?

   .............................................................................................

   .............................................................................................

   .............................................................................................

**Comparing the Sun and Planets** Our solar system has the sun at its center. The **sun** is a gaseous body much larger than anything else in the solar system. In fact, the sun accounts for about 99.85 percent of the entire mass of the solar system. Despite being more than a million times the volume of Earth, our sun is actually a very ordinary mid-sized star. Astronomers have used telescopes to observe stars that are a thousand times more massive than the sun. Our ordinary star is expected to continue burning for another five billion years.

A **planet** is round, orbits the sun, and has cleared out the region of the solar system along its orbit. The four inner planets, including Earth, are closer to the sun, small, and made mostly of rock and metal. The four outer planets are farther from the sun, very large, and made mostly of gas and liquid. Like Earth, each planet has a "day" and a "year." A planet's day is the time it takes to rotate on its axis. A planet's year is the time it takes to orbit the sun.

✓READING CHECK **Summarize Text** How do the inner and outer planets differ?

.........................................................................

.........................................................................

.........................................................................

▶ **VIDEO**
Learn about distances in the solar system.

**HANDS-ON LAB**

✐**Investigate** Develop a model to describe the role of gravity in the solar system.

**Comparing the Sun and Earth**
**Figure 2** 🖊 Circle the word that correctly completes each statement in the table.

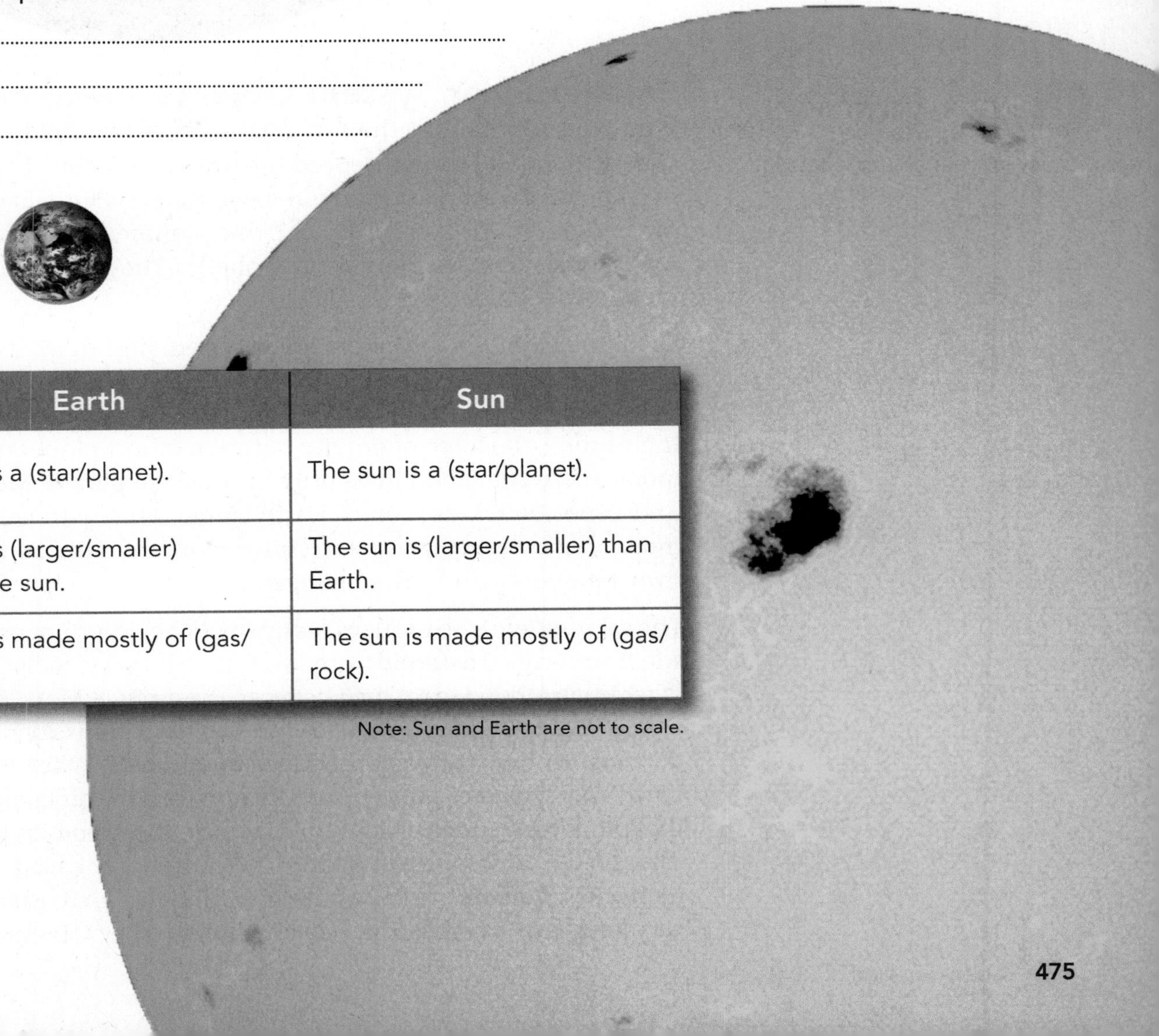

| Earth | Sun |
|---|---|
| Earth is a (star/planet). | The sun is a (star/planet). |
| Earth is (larger/smaller) than the sun. | The sun is (larger/smaller) than Earth. |
| Earth is made mostly of (gas/rock). | The sun is made mostly of (gas/rock). |

Note: Sun and Earth are not to scale.

## Pluto and Ida

**Figure 3** Pluto (right) was considered the ninth planet in our solar system for many years. Astronomers now classify it as a dwarf planet. Asteroid Ida (top), identified in 1884, is the first observed asteroid with a moon.

⊕ **INTERACTIVITY**

Investigate the factors that affect the interactions of astronomical bodies.

**Smaller Solar System Objects** A dwarf planet is an object that orbits the sun and has enough gravity to be spherical, but it has not cleared the area of its orbit. There are five known dwarf planets in our solar system: Pluto, Eris, Ceres, Makemake (MAH keh MAH keh), and Haumea (how MAY uh). As scientists observe more distant objects, they may identify more dwarf planets.

Six of the eight planets in our solar system host at least one natural satellite, or **moon**. A natural satellite is a celestial body in orbit. Just as the sun's gravitational pull keeps the planets in their orbits, the force of gravity between a host planet and its moon keeps the moon in its orbit around the planet. Mercury and Venus both lack moons. Earth comes next, with just one moon. Jupiter and Saturn each have more than 60! Some dwarf planets also have satellites.

The solar system also includes many smaller objects that orbit the sun. Some, called **asteroids**, are small, mostly rocky bodies, many of which are found in an area between the orbits of Mars and Jupiter. **Figure 3** shows an asteroid named Ida. Chunks of rock or dust smaller than asteroids are called **meteoroids**. When entering Earth's atmosphere, a meteoroid's friction with the air creates heat that produces a streak of light called a meteor. Meteoroids that pass through the atmosphere and hit Earth's surface are called meteorites. **Comets** are loose balls of ice and rock that usually have very long, narrow orbits. They develop tails as they orbit the sun.

# Structure of the Sun

Recall that the sun is a gaseous body much larger than anything else in our solar system. The sun contains no solid surface, unlike our own planet. About three fourths of the sun's mass is hydrogen, and about one fourth is helium. The hydrogen and helium are in the form of plasma, a fourth state of matter. Plasma is a very hot fluid-like gas consisting of electrically-charged particles. However, like Earth, the sun has an interior and an atmosphere.

HANDS-ON LAB

Design a model of the sun's layers.

**The Sun's Interior** The interior of the sun includes the convection zone, the radiative zone, and the core. **Figure 4** shows the sun's interior.

**Inside the Sun**

**Figure 4** 🖉 The interior of the sun has three main layers. Draw an arrow to indicate how energy created at the sun's core travels.

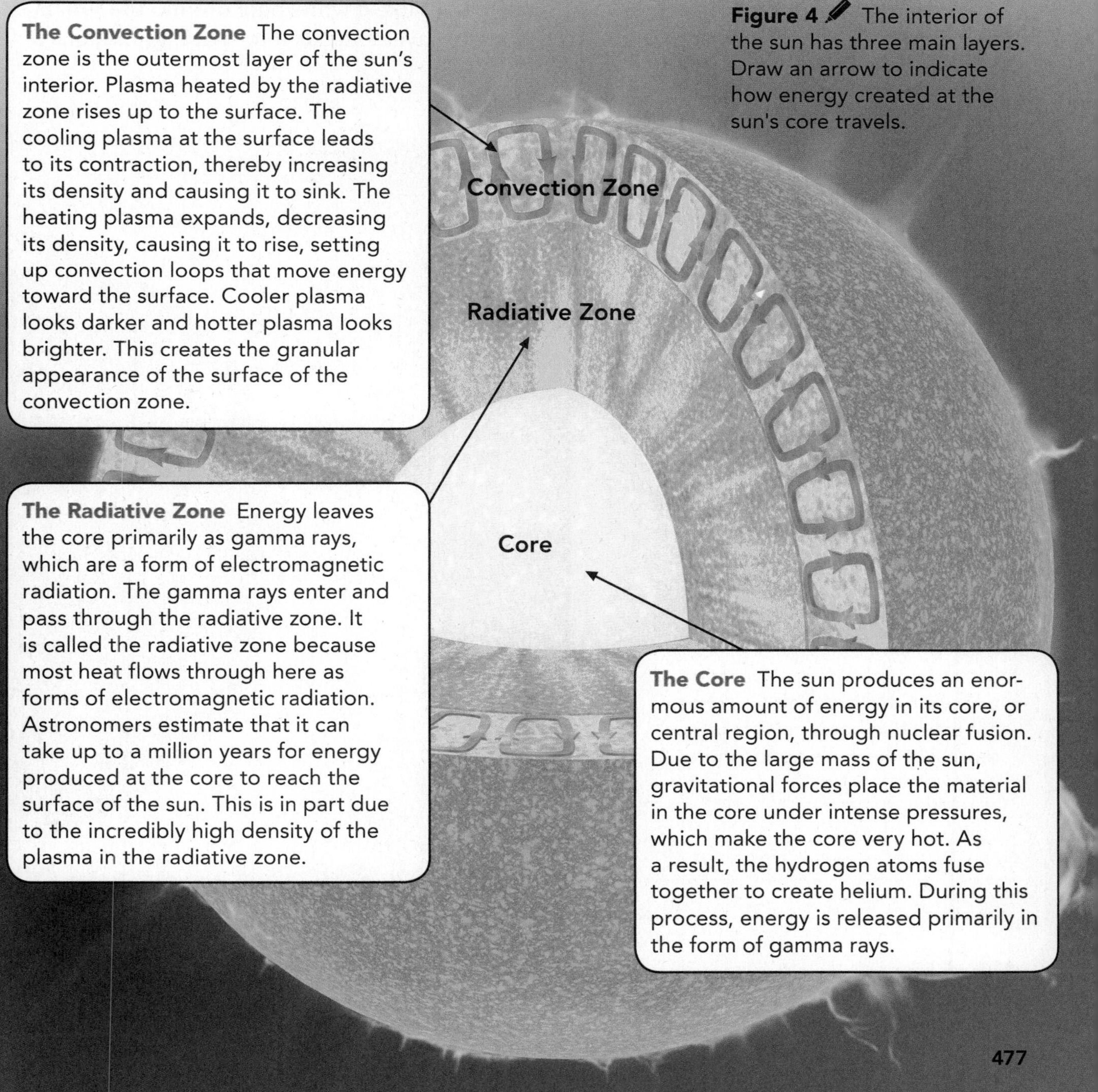

**The Convection Zone** The convection zone is the outermost layer of the sun's interior. Plasma heated by the radiative zone rises up to the surface. The cooling plasma at the surface leads to its contraction, thereby increasing its density and causing it to sink. The heating plasma expands, decreasing its density, causing it to rise, setting up convection loops that move energy toward the surface. Cooler plasma looks darker and hotter plasma looks brighter. This creates the granular appearance of the surface of the convection zone.

Convection Zone

Radiative Zone

Core

**The Radiative Zone** Energy leaves the core primarily as gamma rays, which are a form of electromagnetic radiation. The gamma rays enter and pass through the radiative zone. It is called the radiative zone because most heat flows through here as forms of electromagnetic radiation. Astronomers estimate that it can take up to a million years for energy produced at the core to reach the surface of the sun. This is in part due to the incredibly high density of the plasma in the radiative zone.

**The Core** The sun produces an enormous amount of energy in its core, or central region, through nuclear fusion. Due to the large mass of the sun, gravitational forces place the material in the core under intense pressures, which make the core very hot. As a result, the hydrogen atoms fuse together to create helium. During this process, energy is released primarily in the form of gamma rays.

## The Sun's Atmosphere

The Sun's Atmosphere The sun's atmosphere extends far into space, as shown in **Figure 5**. Like the sun's interior, the atmosphere is composed primarily of hydrogen and helium, and consists of three main layers—the photosphere, the chromosphere, and the corona.

The inner layer of the sun's atmosphere is called the photosphere (FOH tuh sfeer). The plasma in this layer is dense enough to be visible and directly observed. A reddish glow is sometimes visible around the edge of the photosphere. Often, this glow can be seen at the beginning and end of a total solar eclipse. This glow comes from the chromosphere, the middle layer of the sun's atmosphere. The Greek word chroma means "color," so this layer is the "color sphere." The outer layer of the atmosphere, which looks like a white halo around the sun, is called the corona. This layer extends into space for millions of kilometers.

## Model It!

### The Sun's Atmosphere

**Figure 5** This image is a combination of two photographs of the sun. One shows the sun's surface and was taken through a special filter that shows the sun's features. The other shows the corona and was taken during an eclipse.

1. **Use Models** ✏ On the image, label the photosphere and the corona. Shade in and label the area of the chromosphere.

2. **Develop Models** ✏ Think about how you could use commonly available materials to make a model of the sun's atmosphere. Label the layers with the materials you would use to represent them.

3. **Identify Limitations** Describe two ways the materials you chose are limited in how accurately they represent the sun's atmosphere.

.................................................................

.................................................................

.................................................................

.................................................................

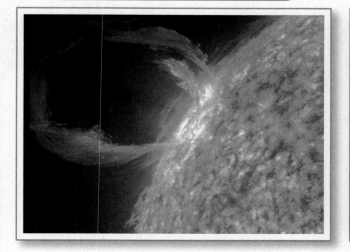

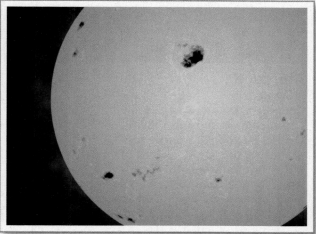

# Features of the Sun

Astronomers have used special telescopes, satellites, and space probes to study the structure and features of the sun. The most visible features are sunspots, prominences, and solar flares.

**Sunspots** Astronomers studying the sun have observed dark areas on the sun's surface. These sunspots are areas of plasma that are cooler than the plasma around them. The cooler plasma gives off less light, resulting in the dark spots. The number of sunspots varies in a regular cycle that peaks every 11 years and corresponds to an increase in the amount of light energy given off by the sun.

Observations of the changing positions of sunspots indicate that the sun rotates, or spins on its axis. Unlike the solid Earth, which has a single rate of rotation, the sun rotates faster at its equator than near its poles.

**Prominences** Sunspots often occur in pairs. Huge loops of plasma that are polarized, called prominences, often link different parts of sunspot regions. Particles following these magnetic forces flow out and back on the sun's surface. You can compare sunspots and prominences in **Figure 6**.

**Solar Flares** Sometimes the loops in sunspot regions suddenly connect, releasing large amounts of magnetic energy. The energy heats plasma on the sun to millions of degrees Celsius, causing it to erupt into space. These eruptions are called solar flares.

☑ READING CHECK **Read and Comprehend** When prominences join, they cause (sunspots/solar flares).

**An Active Star**
**Figure 6** Different types of photographs show the sun's different features. Label the two images above as either sunspots or prominences.

 **INTERACTIVITY**

Explore the structure of the sun.

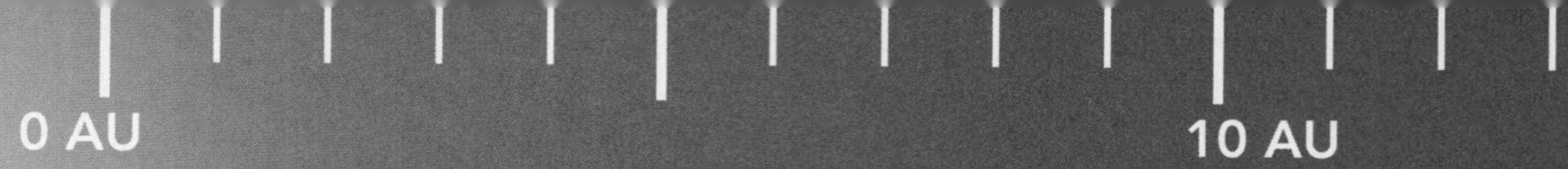

**0 AU** | | | | | | | | | | | | | | **10 AU**

### Mercury
**Mass:** $0.330 \times 10^{24}$ kg
**Equatorial Diameter:** 4,879 km
**Distance from the sun:** 0.39 AU
**Orbital period:** 88.0 Earth days
**Moons:** 0
**Mean Temperature:** 167°C
**Atmospheric Composition:** None (thin exosphere made up of atoms blasted off surface by solar wind)

During the day, temperatures on Mercury can reach 430°C. But without a real atmosphere, temperatures at night plunge to –170°C.

### Earth
**Mass:** $5.97 \times 10^{24}$ kg
**Equatorial Diameter:** 12,756 km
**Distance from the sun:** 1 AU
**Orbital period:** 365.26 Earth days
**Moons:** 1
**Mean Temperature:** 15°C
**Atmospheric Composition:** nitrogen, oxygen, trace amounts of other gases

Our planet is the only object in the solar system known to harbor life, mainly due to the fact that liquid water exists on its surface.

### Venus
**Mass:** $4.87 \times 10^{24}$ kg
**Equatorial Diameter:** 12,104 km
**Distance from the sun:** 0.72 AU
**Orbital period:** 224.7 Earth days
**Moons:** 0
**Mean Temperature:** 464°C
**Atmospheric Composition:** carbon dioxide (with sulfuric acid clouds)

Most planets and moons in the solar system rotate from west to east. Venus, oddly, rotates from east to west.

### Mars
**Mass:** $0.642 \times 10^{24}$ kg
**Equatorial Diameter:** 6,792 km
**Distance from the sun:** 1.52 AU
**Orbital period:** 687 Earth days
**Moons:** 2
**Mean Temperature:** −63°C
**Atmospheric Composition:** mainly carbon dioxide, with nitrogen and argon

The red planet is home to the largest volcano in the solar system, Olympus Mons.

### The Solar System
**Figure 7** ✏ The planets' sizes are shown to scale, but their distances from the sun are not. Use the data provided to mark the position of each planet on the distance scale.

**Describe Patterns** Examine the data about each planet. What patterns do you observe?

.......................................................................................................

.......................................................................................................

.......................................................................................................

.......................................................................................................

## Jupiter

**Mass:** $1,898 \times 10^{24}$ kg
**Equatorial Diameter:** 142,984 km
**Distance from the sun:** 5.20 AU
**Orbital period:** 4,331 Earth days
**Moons:** 67
**Mean Temperature:** −110°C
**Atmospheric Composition:** mostly hydrogen with some helium

The Great Red Spot is one of the most noticeable features of Jupiter. This storm is so huge that two to three Earths could fit inside it.

## Uranus

**Mass:** $86.8 \times 10^{24}$ kg
**Equatorial Diameter:** 51,118 km
**Distance from the sun:** 19.20 AU
**Orbital period:** 30,589 Earth days
**Moons:** 27
**Mean Temperature:** −195°C
**Atmospheric Composition:** hydrogen, helium, and a small amount of methane

Viewed from Earth, Uranus rotates top to bottom instead of side to side. This is because the planet's axis of rotation is tilted at an angle about 90 degrees from vertical.

## Saturn

**Mass:** $568 \times 10^{24}$ kg
**Equatorial Diameter:** 120,536 km
**Distance from the sun:** 9.55 AU
**Orbital period:** 10,747 Earth days
**Moons:** 62
**Mean Temperature:** −140°C
**Atmospheric Composition:** mostly hydrogen with some helium

The particles that make up Saturn's majestic rings range in size from grains of dust to ice and rock that may measure several meters across.

## Neptune

**Mass:** $102 \times 10^{24}$ kg
**Equatorial Diameter:** 49,528 km
**Distance from the sun:** 30.05 AU
**Orbital period:** 59,800 Earth days
**Moons:** 14
**Mean Temperature:** −200°C
**Atmospheric Composition:** hydrogen, helium, and a small amount of methane

This planet just might be the windiest place in the solar system. Winds on Neptune can reach speeds of 2,000 kph.

✓ **READING CHECK** **Integrate Visuals** How does the size of the sun compare to the sizes of the planets?

......................................................................................................................

......................................................................................................................

## Literacy Connection

**Integrate With Visuals**
Use the information in the text to write a caption for the top left image in **Figure 8**.

...............................................................

...............................................................

...............................................................

## Forming the Solar System

**Figure 8** ✏ The solar system formed from a cloud of gas and other materials. Write the numbers 1 through 4 to put the images in order and represent how the solar system formed.

# Solar System Formation

Scientists think the solar system formed at a minimum of 4.6 billion years ago from a cloud of hydrogen, helium, rock, ice, and other materials. The first step in the formation of the solar system occurred as the force of gravity began to pull together materials in the cloud. A rotating disk of gas, ice, and dust formed as the cloud material was drawn toward the central mass. As more material was pulled into the disk's center, it became more dense, pressures increased, and as a result, the center grew hot.

Eventually, temperature and pressures became so high that hydrogen atoms combined to form helium. This process, called nuclear fusion, releases large amounts of energy in the form of electromagnetic radiation, which includes sunlight.

Around the sun, bits of rock, ice, and gas began to pull together first from electrostatic charges, or electrical forces that do not flow. As the objects grew larger, gravity pulled them together. The rock and ice formed small bodies called planetesimals (plan uh TES suh muhllz). These planetesimals collided with each other and eventually created most of the objects that we see in the solar system, shown in **Figure 8**. The inner planets that formed closer to the sun were relatively smaller in size and mass. Their weak gravity, combined with the hot environment, resulted in dry, rocky bodies that were unable to hold onto light gases such as helium and hydrogen. Farther away from the sun, ice combined with rock and metal in the cooler environment. The outer planets that formed were more massive. As a result, gravity exerted a strong pull on hydrogen and helium gases, forming the gas giants we know today.

# ☑ LESSON 1 Check

MS-ESS1-2, MS-ESS1-3

1. **Cause and Effect** What is responsible for the intense heat and pressure in the sun's core?

..................................................................................

..................................................................................

..................................................................................

2. **Summarize Text** Describe the formation of the solar system.

..................................................................................

..................................................................................

..................................................................................

..................................................................................

..................................................................................

..................................................................................

..................................................................................

..................................................................................

..................................................................................

..................................................................................

3. **Distinguish Relationships** What is the relationship between a planet's distance from the sun and the length of its year? Explain.

..................................................................................

..................................................................................

..................................................................................

..................................................................................

..................................................................................

..................................................................................

4. **Compare and Contrast** Compare and contrast asteroids, comets, and meteroids.

..................................................................................

..................................................................................

..................................................................................

..................................................................................

..................................................................................

5. **Apply Scientific Reasoning** Explain why you think the solar system could or could not have formed without gravity.

..................................................................................

..................................................................................

..................................................................................

..................................................................................

## Quest CHECK-IN

**In this lesson, you discovered the characteristics of planets, moons, and smaller solar system objects. You also learned how the sun and other parts of the solar system were formed.**

Explain How do you think understanding the formation of the solar system can help to explain the presence of smaller solar system objects, such as asteroids?

..................................................................................

..................................................................................

..................................................................................

## 👆 INTERACTIVITY

Space Invaders

**Go online** to explore more about the characteristics of asteroids and how scientists monitor and predict their possible strikes. Then list experience that an ideal applicant for a job at the observatory would have.

MS-ESS1-3

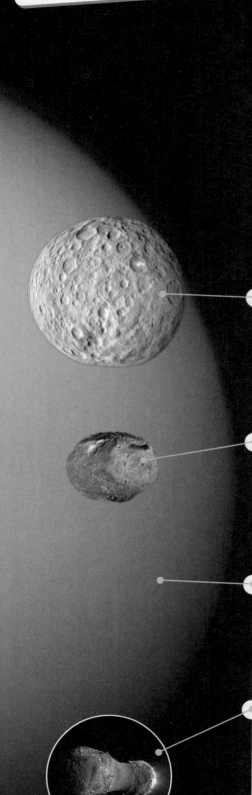

# Comparing
# Solar System Objects

Small solar system objects far from Earth—such as comets, dwarf planets, and asteroids—have been observed for centuries. Only in recent years have astronomers been able to make observations from up close, thanks to technological advances in telescopes and spacecraft.

## Ceres

A dwarf planet in the asteroid belt between Mars and Jupiter, Ceres takes 4.6 Earth years to revolve around the sun. It is about 2.8 AU from the sun. Ceres has a core of water ice and a rocky crust made of different salts. Its crust is marked by numerous impact craters.

## Vesta

An asteroid in the same asteroid belt as Ceres, Vesta is made of hardened lava. About 1 percent of Vesta was blasted into space when another object collided with it, leaving a crater 500 kilometers wide. Vesta is about 530 km wide, though it is not spherical in shape.

## Titan

The largest moon around Saturn, Titan has an icy surface with rivers of liquid methane and ethane. It is 9.54 AU from the sun. With a radius of 2,575 km, it is larger than Earth's moon. Its mass is $1.3455 \times 10^{23}$ kg.

## Hartley 2

A comet that visits the inner solar system every 6.5 years, Hartley 2, also known as 103P, is an icy mass that spins around one axis while tumbling around another. At its closest distance, Hartley 2 is about 1.05 AU from the sun, or 0.05 AU from Earth's orbit. The outer reaches of Hartley 2's orbit takes it about 5.9 AU from the sun. The comet loses some of its icy mass each time it passes near the sun.

Complete the table that summarizes the characteristics of four small objects of the solar system. Then use the information you have gathered to answer the following questions.

| | Ceres | Vesta | Titan | Hartley 2 |
|---|---|---|---|---|
| Classification | Dwarf planet | Asteroid | | |
| Mass (kg) | $9.47 \times 10^{20}$ | $2.67 \times 10^{20}$ | | $3 \times 10^{11}$ |
| Diameter (km) | 952 | | 5,150 | 0.16 (nucleus) |
| Distance from Sun (AU) | | 2.5 | | |
| Composition | | | | Ice and carbon dioxide |

1. **Classify** Why is Vesta considered an asteroid while its "sister" Ceres is classified by astronomers as a dwarf planet?

..................................................................................................................

..................................................................................................................

2. **Apply Scientific Reasoning** Titan's average distance from the sun is 9.54 AU, which is the same as Saturn's average distance from the Sun. Why doesn't Titan crash into Saturn?

..................................................................................................................

..................................................................................................................

3. **Develop Models** Suppose you are given a diagram that shows the position of the planets from the sun and their relative sizes. You are asked to add the four smaller solar system objects in the chart to the model. Which of the objects' characteristics would be easier to represent in the model? Which characteristics would be difficult to represent?

..................................................................................................................

..................................................................................................................

..................................................................................................................

..................................................................................................................

# 2  Learning About the Universe

## Guiding Questions

- How does the electromagnetic spectrum help scientists learn about the universe?
- How do scientists use technology to learn about the universe?

## Connection

**Literacy**  Determine Central Ideas

MS-ESS1-3

## Vocabulary

electromagnetic radiation
visible light
spectrum
wavelength
telescope

## Academic Vocabulary

complement

**VOCABULARY APP**

Practice vocabulary on a mobile device.

**Quest CONNECTION**

Think about the ways technology provides tools to help scientists search for signs of extraterrestrial life.

## Connect It!

**Study the photo and answer the questions.**

Use Models  What are some of the objects you see?

........................................................................................

Apply Scientific Reasoning  How do you think astronomers took this image?

........................................................................................

........................................................................................

# Collecting Space Data

With advances in engineering and technology, humans discover more about the universe every year. Data from telescopes, satellites, and other instruments based both on Earth and in space are opening up the mysteries of the universe to people on Earth.

**The Electromagnetic Spectrum** All objects in space emit, or give off, energy. This energy is known as **electromagnetic radiation**, or energy that can travel in the form of waves. Astronomers use instruments and tools, such as telescopes, that detect electromagnetic radiation to collect data and produce images of objects in space, such as the one in **Figure 1.**

There are many types of electromagnetic radiation, but visible light is the type that is most familiar to you. **Visible light** is the light you can see. If you've ever observed light shining through a prism, then you know that the light separates into different colors with different wavelengths, called a visible light **spectrum**. When you look at the moon or a star with the naked eye or through a telescope, you are observing visible light.

There are many forms of electromagnetic radiation that we cannot see. They include radio waves, infrared radiation, ultraviolet radiation, X-rays, and gamma rays. These waves are classified by **wavelength**, or the distance between the crest of one wave and the crest of the next wave. Radio waves have the longest wavelengths and gamma rays have the shortest wavelengths.

**HANDS-ON LAB**

Determine how lenses affect the appearance of objects seen at a distance.

 **INTERACTIVITY**

Explore how astronomers analyze data collected by telescopes, satellites, and probes.

## Literacy Connection

**Determine Central Ideas** Underline the sentence that states the central idea of the text.

## A Distant Galaxy

**Figure 1** This image of the distant galaxy NGC 1512 is made up of several images taken by NASA's Hubble Space Telescope. This telescope is able to detect different types of objects in space.

## Optical Telescopes

Objects in space give off all types of electromagnetic radiation. **Telescopes** are instruments that collect and focus light and other forms of electromagnetic radiation. Telescopes make distant objects appear larger and brighter. Some are based on Earth and others can be found floating in space. Optical telescopes use lenses and mirrors to collect and focus visible light. There are two main types of optical telescopes. Reflecting telescopes primarily use mirrors to collect light. Refracting telescopes use multiple lenses to collect light.

## Other Telescopes

Scientists also use non-optical telescopes to **complement** data obtained by other methods. These telescopes collect different types of electromagnetic radiation. Radio telescopes, such as the ones in **Figure 2**, detect radio waves from objects in space. Most radio telescopes have curved, reflecting surfaces. These surfaces focus faint radio waves the way the mirror in a reflecting telescope focuses light waves. Radio telescopes need to be large to collect and focus more radio waves because radio waves have long wavelengths. Other kinds of telescopes produce images in the infrared and X-ray portions of the spectrum.

**✓ READING CHECK** **Determine Central Ideas** Why do astronomers rely on different types of telescopes?

.................................................................................................

.................................................................................................

**Academic Vocabulary**
What does it mean when images in a book complement the text?

......................................................

**Radio Telescope**

**Figure 2** These radio telescopes are located in Owens Valley, California.

**Apply Concepts** Why are radio telescopes so large?

......................................................

......................................................

**Space Probes** Since humans first began exploring space, only 27 people have landed on or orbited the moon. Yet, during this period, astronomers have gathered a great deal of information about other parts of the solar system. Most of this information has been collected by space probes. A space probe is a spacecraft that carries scientific instruments to collect and transmit data, but has no human crew.

Each space probe is designed for a specific mission. Some are designed to land on a certain planet, such as the Mars rovers. Others are designed to fly by and collect data about planets and other bodies in the solar system.

**Data from Probes** Each space probe has a power system to produce electricity and a communication system to send and receive signals. Probes often carry scientific instruments to perform experiments. Some probes, called orbiters, are equipped to photograph and analyze the atmosphere of a planet. Other probes, called landers, are equipped to land on a planet and analyze the materials on its surface. Telescopes, satellites, astronauts, and probes have all contributed to our growing knowledge of the solar system and our universe. Space exploration is now limited only by technology, our imaginations, and the availability of funding.

HANDS-ON LAB

☑**Investigate** Design and build a model of a space exploration vehicle.

☑READING CHECK **Determine Meaning** Why do you think spacecraft that carry instruments to collect data about objects in space are called probes?

..................................................................................................

..................................................................................................

**Plan It!**

### Space Probe Mission

**Use Models** The flowchart shows the stages of a space probe mission to Mars. Write captions to describe the stages of the space probe mission.

.......................... .......................... .......................... ..........................

.......................... .......................... .......................... ..........................

.......................... .......................... .......................... ..........................

.......................... .......................... .......................... ..........................

# History of Space Exploration

The advent of rocket technology in the 1940s led to a new era of space exploration, detailed in the timelines in **Figure 3** and **Figure 4**. Astronomers were no longer bound to ground-based observations, as humans, telescopes, and space probes were sent into space.

## 1947 Fruit Flies Launched into Space

Uncertain of the effects of space-travel on organisms, NASA begins experimentation on the effects of space exposure by launching a container of fruit flies into space to see how it affects them. Their container parachutes back to Earth and the fruit flies are recovered alive and in apparent good health.

## 1957 Laika Goes to Space

The Soviet Union also seeks to test the effects of space-travel on living organisms. The Soviets launch a dog named Laika into space on board a small craft called *Sputnik II.* She was the first animal ever to orbit Earth. Sadly, she died in space during the mission.

## 1940s

## 1950s

## 1957 *Sputnik I*

The Soviet Union launches *Sputnik I,* Earth's first artificial satellite, on October 4, 1957. This tiny craft, about the size of a beach ball and weighing little more than 80 kg, orbits Earth in 98 minutes. Its launch marks the start of the space age and a fierce space-race between the United States and the Soviet Union.

## 1958 *Explorer I*

The United States launches its first artificial satellite into space on January 31, 1958. Although the *Sputnik* crafts carried radio technology to signal where they were, *Explorer I* is the first satellite to carry scientific instruments into space. Its instruments help to detect and study the Van Allen Belts, strong belts of charged particles trapped by Earth's magnetic field.

## 1973 Skylab

Long before the International Space Station (ISS), NASA builds America's first space station, Skylab, in 1973. It orbits Earth until 1979 with the objective of helping scientists to develop science-based manned space missions. Weighing more than 77,000 kg, Skylab I includes a workshop, a solar observatory, and systems to allow astronauts to spend up to 84 days in space.

## 1961 First Person to Orbit Earth

On April 12, 1961, Soviet Yuri Gagarin becomes the first person to travel into space and orbit Earth. His 108-minute mission circles the Earth once and reaches a maximum altitude of about 300 kilometers.

## 1977 Voyager 1 & 2

One of the greatest missions to explore our solar system is led by twin space-probes called *Voyager 1* and *Voyager 2*. The two spacecraft are the first human-made objects to visit the planets of the outer solar system. Their instruments help scientists to explore and study Jupiter, Saturn, Uranus, Neptune, and many of their moons.

# 1960s

# 1970s

## 1962 *Mariner 2* to Venus

NASA launches *Mariner 2* toward Venus on August 27, 1962. It is the first human-made object to study another planet from space. As *Mariner 2* flies by Venus, its sensors send back data on the Venusian atmosphere, magnetic field, and mass. Its instruments also take measurements of cosmic dust and solar particles before and after passing the planet.

## 1969 Moon Landing

Three American astronauts travel to the moon aboard *Apollo 11*. As Michael Collins pilots the command module *Columbia* above, Neil Armstrong and Buzz Aldrin land the lunar module *Eagle* on the moon and become the first humans to walk on its surface.

## Space Exploration from the 1940s to the 1970s

**Figure 3** 🖉 Early space exploration involved some missions that carried people and some that did not. In each circle on the timeline, write *U* if the mission was unmanned, or *M* if the mission was manned.

📓 **Write About It** Scientists sent animals into space before they ever considered sending humans. In your science notebook, explain why you think humans were sent only after animals went into space.

## 1981  The Space Shuttles

First lifting off in 1981, the U.S. space shuttle is able to take off like a rocket and land like a plane, making it the first reusable spacecraft. Over the next 30 years, a fleet of five shuttles will be built and fly 135 missions carrying astronauts and cargo into space. Boasting a large cargo bay and lots of room for a crew, the shuttles make it possible for astronauts to launch and repair satellites, conduct research, and assist in the building of the ISS.

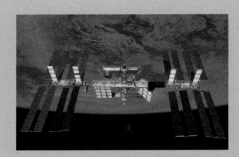

## 1998  The International Space Station (ISS)

Construction begins on the ISS, which requires more than 115 space flights to build. With a mass of nearly 420,000 kg, the ISS is almost five times larger than Skylab. About the size of a football field, it is the largest human-made structure ever built in space. A truly international effort, the ISS is a space-based laboratory and observatory used by scientists from around the world to conduct research that requires or focuses on the conditions found in space.

## 1980s

## 1990s

## 1990  Hubble Space Telescope

Carried aboard the space shuttle *Discovery* on April 24, 1990, the Hubble Space Telescope is the first space observatory located in space. Orbiting about 550 km above Earth and its blurry atmosphere, Hubble uses advanced visible-light optical technology to study the most distant objects in our solar system—stars and exoplanets in the Milky Way, as well as the farthest galaxies in the universe.

## 1997  Cassini-Huygens

A joint project between the United States and Europe, the Cassini mission launches on October 15, 1997, on a 3.5-billion-km journey to study Saturn, its ring system, and its many moons. Cassini also carries the Huygens Probe, which captures photos of Saturn's largest moon, Titan, while landing on its surface. The mission's many discoveries include rivers and lakes of liquid hydrocarbons on Titan's surface, making it the only known place in the solar system besides Earth where matter exists as a liquid on the surface.

## 2003 Mars Exploration Rovers

In 2003, NASA launches two rovers—*Spirit* and *Opportunity*—to land on and explore Mars. Their missions are to search for signs of past life. Using wheels to move around, instruments to drill and test rock and soil samples, and several sophisticated cameras, the rovers help scientists find evidence that Mars was once a wet, warm world capable of supporting life.

## 2009 Kepler

Seeking to answer the question of how unique our solar system is, NASA launches the Kepler Space Telescope in 2009, with instruments specially designed to search for planets outside our solar system. The Kepler mission focuses on studying a small part of the sky, counting the number and type of exoplanets it finds, and then using those data to calculate the possible number of exoplanets in our galaxy.

## 2000s                    Present

## 2003 Spitzer Space Telescope

In August of 2003, NASA launches the Spitzer Space Telescope. Spitzer uses an 85-cm infrared telescope capable of seeing heat to peer into regions of space that visible-light telescopes such as the Hubble have difficulty seeing or seeing through. Using Spitzer, scientists can more easily study exoplanets, giant clouds of cool molecular gas and organic molecules, and the formation of new stars.

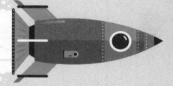

### Space Exploration from the 1980s to Present

**Figure 4** 🖍 As space exploration evolved, missions changed in focus to studying more distant objects. Continue to write *U* for unmanned missions and *M* for manned missions.

**Identify** Describe any patterns you observe in the development of space exploration.

.................................................
.................................................
.................................................
.................................................
.................................................

## 2012 Voyager 1 Leaves the Solar System

On August 25, 2012, *Voyager 1* leaves the area of the sun's influence and enters interstellar space, becoming the first human-made object to leave the solar system. It continues to assist scientists by transmitting data on its location and the density of plasma it encounters at the boundaries of our solar system.

1. **Determine Differences** Contrast the electromagnetic radiation used by radio telescopes and optical telescopes.

.........................................................
.........................................................
.........................................................
.........................................................

2. **Communicate** Identify a spacecraft operated by human beings and describe how it helped add to our knowledge of space.

.........................................................
.........................................................
.........................................................
.........................................................
.........................................................

3. **Connect to Technology** Which space technology used today contributes the most to our understanding of distant stars? Explain your answer.

.........................................................
.........................................................
.........................................................
.........................................................

4. **Synthesize Information** ✎ Choose two tools that astronomers use to learn more about objects in the universe. Draw a Venn diagram to compare and contrast how the tools function and the kinds of data they collect.

# Quest CHECK-IN

**In this lesson, you learned how scientists use technology to study the universe. You also discovered how the electromagnetic spectrum helps scientists to learn about objects in the universe.**

**Construct Arguments** What kinds of technology do you think would be most helpful when looking for signs of extraterrestrial life? Explain your answer.

.........................................................
.........................................................
.........................................................

 **INTERACTIVITY**

Anybody Out There?

**Go online** to find out more about what extraterrestrial-life hunters look for and the technology they use. Then identify the technology with which an ideal applicant for a job at the observatory should be familiar.

MS-ESS1-3

# BLAST OFF!

INTERACTIVITY

Launch a Space Probe

## How do you get a
space probe into outer space?
You engineer it! Rocket
technology shows us how.

**The Challenge:** To get a
space probe on its way to Pluto
and beyond.

**Phenomenon** In 2006, the *New Horizons* space probe was launched from Cape Canaveral, Florida. The probe was destined for the outer reaches of our solar system, studying the dwarf planet Pluto in a flyby encounter from 2015 to 2016. The Atlas V rocket was used to launch the probe on its long, 4-billion-km (2.5-billion-mile), journey. This powerful rocket, like many other rockets used to launch satellites and probes into space, is made up of two major sections called stages.

The payload carries the *New Horizons* space probe and the second-stage Centaur engine.

The Atlas V booster is the main part of the rocket that helps thrust the craft upward and releases it from Earth's gravitational pull.

The solid booster rockets provide additional thrust and then fall away not long after the launch.

An Atlas V rocket on the launchpad.

## DESIGN CHALLENGE

Can you design and build a model of a rocket? Go to the Engineering Design Notebook to find out!

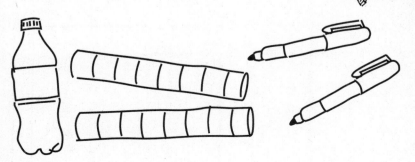

## Guiding Questions

- What are the properties of a star?
- How do scientists classify stars?
- What is the role of gravity in the formation of a star?

## Connections

**Literacy** Determine Central Ideas

**Math** Represent Relationships

MS-ESS1-2

## Vocabulary

nebula
protostar
white dwarf
supernova
apparent
  brightness
absolute brightness

## Academic Vocabulary

analyze

 **VOCABULARY APP**

Practice vocabulary on a mobile device.

**Quest CONNECTION**

Consider how understanding the properties and formation of stars can help scientists locate objects such as asteroids or dark matter.

## Connect It!

🖊 **Write an X in the circle that points to the location of the brightest stars in the Orion Nebula.**

**Apply Scientific Reasoning** Why do you think the Orion Nebula is called a stellar nursery?

..................................................................................................................................

..................................................................................................................................

..................................................................................................................................

..................................................................................................................................

# Formation and Development of Stars

Stars do not last forever. Each star forms, changes during its life span, and eventually dies. Star formation begins when gravity causes the gas and dust from a nebula to contract and become so dense and hot that nuclear fusion starts. How long a star lives depends on its mass.

All stars start out as parts of nebulas, such as the one in **Figure 1**. A **nebula** is a large cloud of gas and dust containing an immense volume of material. A star, on the other hand, is made up of a large amount of gas in a relatively small volume.

In the densest part of a nebula, gravity pulls gas and dust together. A contracting cloud of gas and dust with enough mass to form a star is called a **protostar**. *Proto-* means "first" in Greek, so a protostar is the first stage of a star's formation. Without gravity to contract the gas and dust, a protostar could not form.

Nuclear fusion is the process by which atoms combine to form heavier atoms. In the sun, for example, gravity causes hydrogen atoms to combine and form helium. During nuclear fusion, an enormous amount of energy is released. Nuclear fusion begins in a protostar.

## Literacy Connection

**Determine Central Ideas**
As you read, look for ways that a nebula and a protostar are similar and different. Write your answers below.

.................................................................

.................................................................

.................................................................

.................................................................

.................................................................

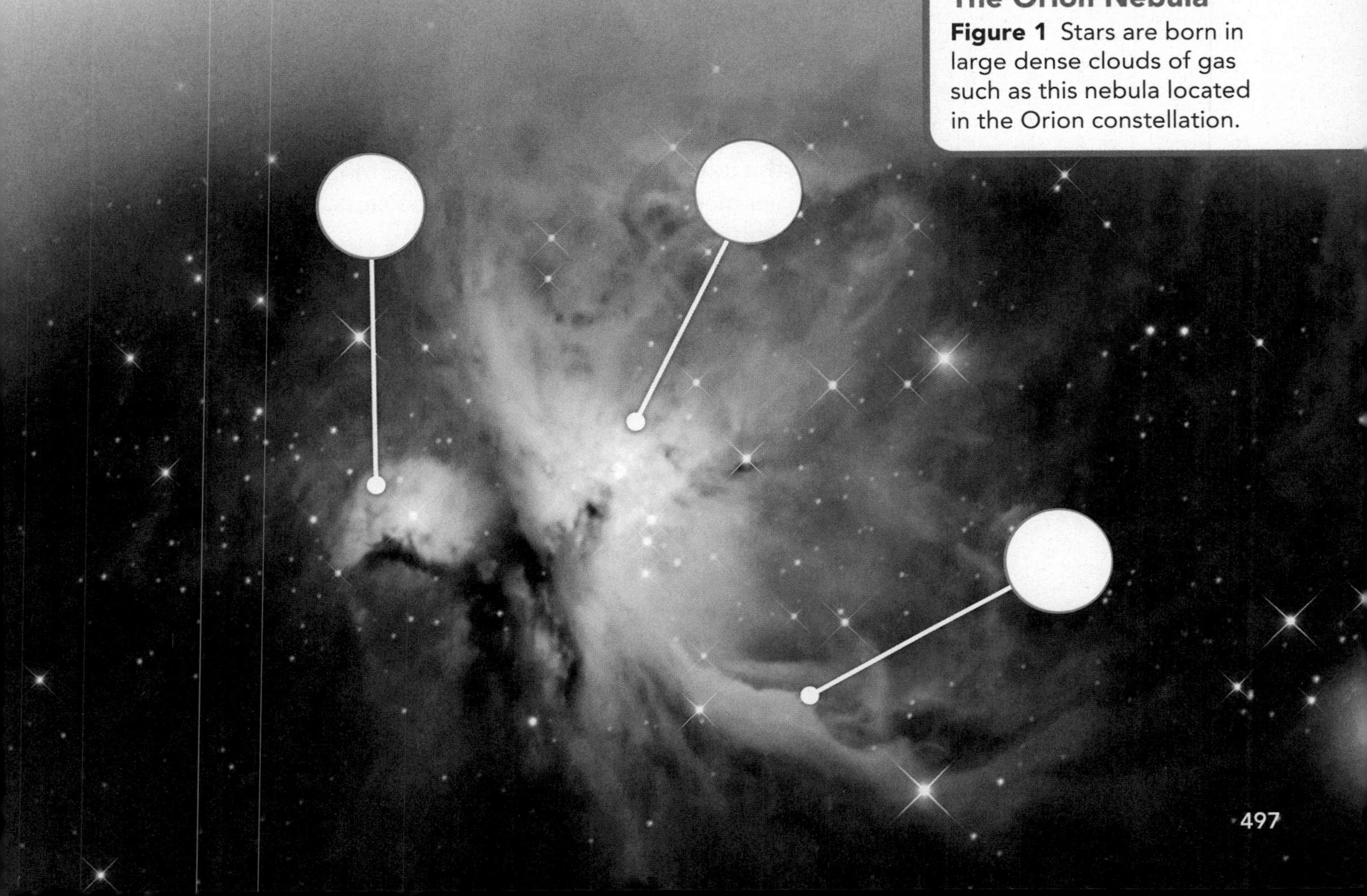

## The Orion Nebula
**Figure 1** Stars are born in large dense clouds of gas such as this nebula located in the Orion constellation.

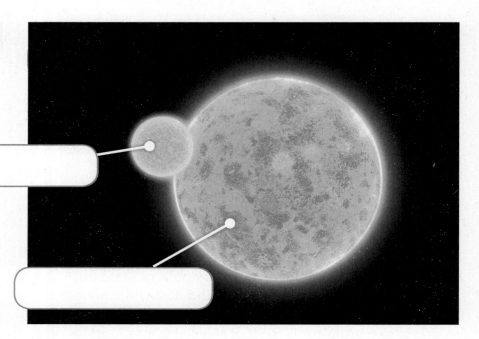

## Star Mass and Life Span

**Figure 2** ✏ How long a star lasts depends on its mass. Look at the yellow and blue stars. Label the star that has more mass and the star that has less mass. Predict which star will last longer by drawing an X on that star.

**Cite Evidence** Explain your prediction.

.................................................

.................................................

.................................................

.................................................

# Life Span

The properties and life span of every star are the result of how massive it is. Each star's mass is determined by how much gas and dust condensed to form its protostar.

How long a star lasts is directly related to its mass and how quickly it uses that mass as fuel. It may seem that stars with more mass would last longer than stars with less mass. But the reverse is true. Stars are like cars. A small car has a small gas tank, but it also has a small engine that burns gas slowly. A large car has a larger gas tank, but its large engine burns gas rapidly. The small car can travel farther on a smaller tank of gas than the larger car with a large tank. Small-mass stars use up their fuel more slowly than large-mass stars, so they last much longer.

Generally, stars that have less mass than our sun use their fuel slowly and can last for up to 200 billion years. A medium-mass star like the sun will last for about 10 billion years. The sun is about 4.6 billion years old, so it is about halfway through its life span. The yellow star in **Figure 2** is similar to the sun.

Stars that have more mass than the sun, such as the blue star shown in **Figure 2**, may last only about 10 million years. That may seem like a very long time, but it is only one-tenth of one percent of the life span of our sun.

☑ **READING CHECK** **Determine Central Ideas** Describe how a star's life span is related to its size.

.................................................................................

.................................................................................

.................................................................................

**White Dwarfs** When a star begins to run out of fuel, its core shrinks and its outer portion expands. Depending on its mass, the star becomes either a red giant or a supergiant. Red giants and supergiants evolve in very different ways.

Low-mass stars and medium-mass stars take billions of years to use up their fuel. As they start to run out of fuel, their outer layers expand, and they become red giants. Eventually, the outer parts grow larger still and drift out into space, forming a glowing cloud of gas called a planetary nebula. The blue-white core that is left behind cools and becomes a **white dwarf**.

White dwarfs are about the size of Earth but about one million times more dense than the sun. White dwarfs have no fuel, but they glow faintly from leftover energy. After billions of years, a white dwarf stops glowing. Then it is a black dwarf.

**Supernovas** The evolution of a high-mass star is quite different. These stars quickly procede into brilliant supergiants. When a supergiant runs out of fuel, it explodes suddenly. Within hours, the star blazes millions of times brighter. The explosion is called a **supernova**. After a supernova, some of the material from the star expands into space. This material may become part of a nebula. This nebula can then contract to form a new, partly recycled star. Nuclear fusion creates heavy elements. A supernova provides enough energy to create the heaviest elements. Astronomers think that the matter in the solar system came from a gigantic supernova. If so, this means that most of the matter around you was created in a star, and all matter on Earth except hydrogen is a form of stardust.

**VIDEO**

Discover how a star begins its life.

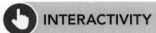
**INTERACTIVITY**

Examine the life cycle of a star.

**White Dwarf**
**Figure 3** The Hubble Space Telescope captured this image of a white dwarf. The white dot in the center is the dense remaining core of the star. The glowing cloud of gas surrounds the white dwarf and eventually blows off all its outer layers.

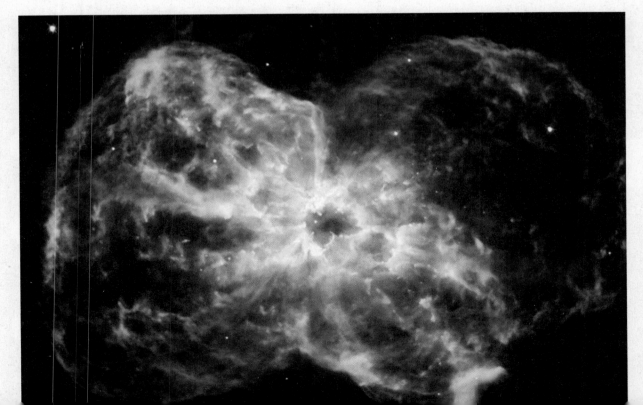

**Neutron Stars, Pulsars, and Black Holes** After a supergiant explodes, some of the material from the star is left behind. This material may form a neutron star. Neutron stars are even smaller and denser than white dwarfs. A neutron star may contain as much as three times the mass of the sun but be only about 25 kilometers in diameter—the size of a city.

In 1967, Jocelyn Bell, a British astronomy student working with Antony Hewish, detected an object in space that appeared to give off regular pulses of radio waves. Soon, astronomers concluded that the source of the radio waves was a rapidly spinning neutron star. Spinning neutron stars are called pulsars, short for pulsating radio sources. Some pulsars spin hundreds of times per second!

The most massive stars—those that have more than 10 times the mass of the sun—may become black holes when they die. A black hole is an object with gravity so strong that nothing, not even light, can escape. After a very massive star dies in a supernova explosion, the gravity of the remaining mass can be so strong that it pulls the gases inward, packing it into a smaller and smaller space. The star's gas becomes squeezed so hard that the star converts into a black hole. The extreme gravity near a black hole, which is surrounded by large volumes of gas, will turn the gas into super-fast spinning disks around its equator and jets of plasma from its poles.

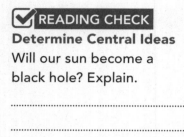

**READING CHECK**

**Determine Central Ideas**
Will our sun become a black hole? Explain.

........................................................

........................................................

........................................................

**Stages of Star Development**
**Figure 4** ✏ Fill in the missing stages on the diagram.

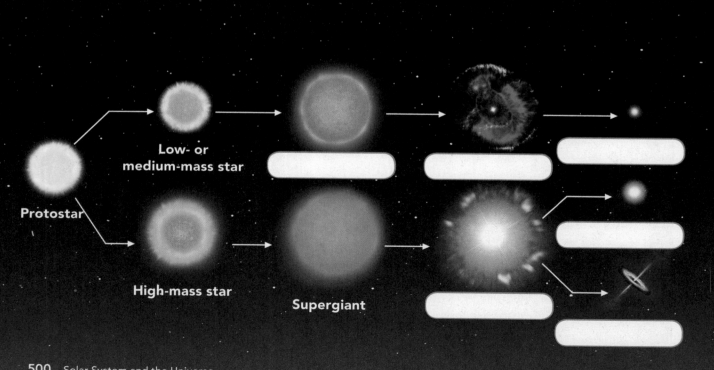

Protostar

Low- or medium-mass star

High-mass star

Supergiant

| Temperature and Star Color | |
|---|---|
| Approximate surface temperature (Kelvins) | Star color |
| 30,000 – 60,000 K | Blue stars |
| 10,000 – 30,000 K | Blue-white stars |
| 7,500 – 10,000 K | White stars |
| 6,000 – 7,500 K | Yellow-white stars |
| 5,000 – 6,000 K | Yellow stars |
| 3,500 – 5,000 K | Yellow-orange stars |
| <3,500 K | Red stars |

Source: Australia Telescope National Facility

## Star Color and Temperature

**Figure 5** A star's surface temperature determines its color. Look at the two stars in **Figure 2**. Use the information in the table to determine which of those two stars has the greater surface temperature. How much hotter is it than the other star?

.............................................

.............................................

.............................................

.............................................

.............................................

**Write About It** Trace the evolution of a neutron star.

## Star Properties

All stars are huge spheres of super-hot, glowing gas called plasma. The exact composition of this plasma varies from star to star, but it is made mostly of hydrogen. Many stars also contain varying amounts of elements such as helium, oxygen, and carbon. During its life, a star produces energy through the process of nuclear fusion, which generates energy from the process of combining atoms into larger atoms. Most stars do this by combining hydrogen atoms to form helium atoms, slowly changing their compositions over time. A star's size and composition affect its physical characteristics. Astronomers classify stars according to their physical characteristics, including color, temperature, size, composition, and brightness.

**Color and Temperature** If you look at the night sky, you can see slight differences in the colors of the stars. A star's color indicates its surface temperature. The coolest stars—with a surface temperature of less than 3,500 K—appear red. Our yellow sun has an average temperature of about 5,500 K. The hottest stars, with surface temperatures ranging from 30,000 K to 60,000 K, appear bluish.

**Size** Many stars in the sky are about the size of our sun. Some stars—a minority of them—are much, much larger. These very large stars are called giant stars or supergiant stars. Most stars are smaller than the sun. White dwarf stars are about the size of Earth. Neutron stars are even smaller, only about 25 kilometers in diameter.

A scientist is studying an unknown liquid in her lab. Describe a test that she could conduct to analyze a property of the liquid.

....................................................

....................................................

....................................................

....................................................

....................................................

## Chemical Composition

Stars vary in their chemical composition. The chemical composition of most stars is about 73 percent hydrogen, 25 percent helium, and 2 percent other elements by mass. Recall that nuclear fusion is the process that powers stars. This process involves the fusing of atoms to form larger atoms. In stars, this process usually involves the fusing of two hydrogen atoms to form one helium atom. As the star uses up its hydrogen, it then begins to fuse helium together, forming carbon when it reaches 100,000,000 K.

Astronomers use spectrographs to determine the elements found in stars. A spectrograph breaks light into colors and produces an image of the resulting spectrum. Today, most large telescopes have spectrographs to **analyze** light.

The gases in a star's atmosphere absorb some wavelengths of light produced within the star. When the star's light is seen through a spectrograph, each absorbed wavelength appears as a dark line on a spectrum. Each chemical element absorbs light at particular wavelengths. Just as each person has a unique set of fingerprints, each element has a unique set of spectral lines for a given temperature.

## Model It

### Star Spectra

**Figure 6** The spectra below are from four different elements. By comparing a star's spectrum with the spectra of known elements, astronomers can identify the elements in a star. Each star's spectrum is an overlap of the spectra from the individual elements.

**Use Models** Identify the elements with the strongest lines in Stars A and B.

**Develop Models** ✏ Star C is made up of the elements hydrogen and sodium. Draw lines to model the spectrum of a star with this composition.

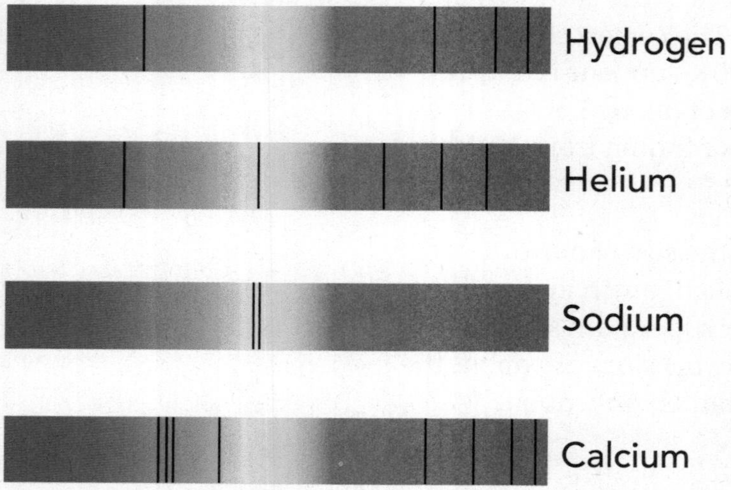

Hydrogen

Helium

Sodium

Calcium

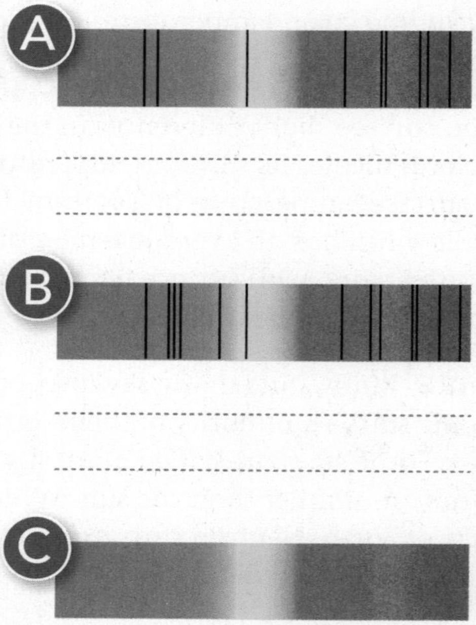

A

----------------------------------------

----------------------------------------

B

----------------------------------------

----------------------------------------

C

**Brightness** Stars also differ in their brightness, or the amount of light they give off. The brightness of a star depends upon both its size and temperature. A larger star tends to be brighter than a smaller star. A hotter star tends to be brighter than a cooler star.

Astronomers use a unit called the light-year to measure the distances of stars. A light-year is the distance that light travels in one year, or about 9.46 trillion kilometers. How bright a star appears depends on both its distance from Earth and how bright the star truly is. Because of these two factors, the brightness of a star is described in two ways: apparent brightness and absolute brightness.

A star's **apparent brightness** is its brightness as seen from Earth. Astronomers can measure apparent brightness fairly easily using electronic devices. However, astronomers can't tell how much light a star gives off just from the star's apparent brightness. Just as a flashlight looks brighter the closer it is to you, a star looks brighter the closer it is to Earth. For example, the sun looks very bright. Its apparent brightness does not mean that the sun gives off more light than all other stars. The sun looks so bright simply because it is so close to Earth.

A star's **absolute brightness** is the brightness the star would have if it were at a standard distance from Earth. Finding a star's absolute brightness is more complex than finding its apparent brightness. An astronomer must first find out both the star's apparent brightness and its distance from Earth. The astronomer can then calculate the star's absolute brightness.

**☑ READING CHECK Determine Central Ideas** Our sun is a an average-sized star, yet appears brighter than others we can see. Explain why.

........................................................................

........................................................................

........................................................................

........................................................................

## Apparent and Absolute Brightness

**Figure 7** ✎ The three stars Alnitak, Alnilam, and Mintaka in the constellation Orion all seem to have the same apparent brightness from Earth. But Alnilam is actually farther away than the other two stars. Write an asterisk (*) next to the name of the star that has the greatest absolute brightness.

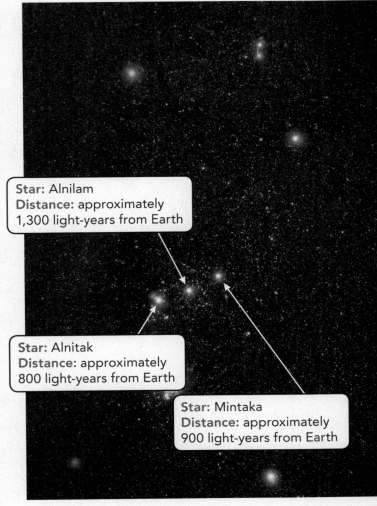

Star: Alnilam
Distance: approximately 1,300 light-years from Earth

Star: Alnitak
Distance: approximately 800 light-years from Earth

Star: Mintaka
Distance: approximately 900 light-years from Earth

# Classifying Stars

About 100 years ago, two scientists working independently made the same discovery. Both Ejnar Hertzsprung (EYE nahr HURT sprung) in Denmark and Henry Norris Russell in the United States made graphs to help them to determine whether the temperature and the absolute brightness of stars are related. They plotted the surface temperatures of stars on the x-axis and their absolute brightness on the y-axis. The points formed a pattern. The graph they made is called the Hertzsprung-Russell diagram, or H-R diagram.

Astronomers use H-R diagrams to classify stars and to understand how stars change over time. The diagram in the Math Toolbox shows how most of the stars in the H-R diagram form a diagonal area called the main sequence. More than 90 percent of all stars, including the sun, are main-sequence stars. Within the main sequence, the surface temperature increases as absolute brightness increases. Hot bluish stars occur at the left of an H-R diagram and cooler reddish stars are at the right.

## Math Toolbox

### Classify Stars by Their Properties

The H-R diagram shows the relationship between surface temperature and absolute brightness of stars.

1. **Interpret Graphs** ✎ Circle the words that correctly complete the following sentence: Sirius B is a (hot/cool) star with (high/low) brightness.

2. **Represent Relationships** ✎ Place the following stars on the H-R diagram and record their classifications below.

   **Star A:** Red-orange, 5,000 K, high brightness

   ......................................................

   **Star B:** Yellow, 6,000 K, medium brightness

   ......................................................

   **Star C:** White, 10,000 K, low brightness

   ......................................................

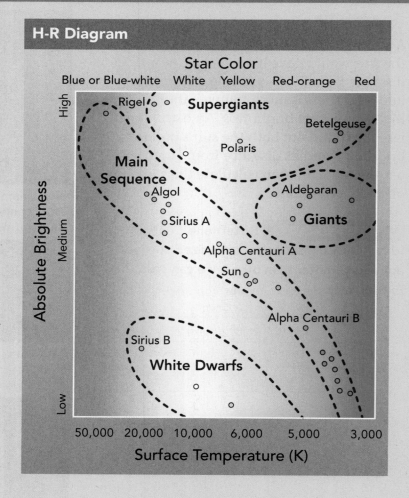

MS-ESS1-2

**1. Identify** What are three properties astronomers use to describe stars?

.......................................................................

.......................................................................

.......................................................................

.......................................................................

.......................................................................

**2. Predict** Which of the following will the sun eventually become: a white dwarf, neutron star, or a black hole? Explain your answer.

.......................................................................

.......................................................................

.......................................................................

.......................................................................

.......................................................................

**3. Apply Scientific Reasoning** New stars are forming in a part of space known as NGC 346. Explain what is occurring there and the role gravity plays in the formation of these stars.

.......................................................................

.......................................................................

.......................................................................

.......................................................................

.......................................................................

.......................................................................

**Use the H-R diagram in the Math Toolbox activity to help you answer Questions 4 through 6.**

**4. Interpret Diagrams** The star Procyon B has a surface temperature of 7,500 K and a low absolute brightness. What type of star is it?

.......................................................................

.......................................................................

.......................................................................

**5. Interpret Data** Stars X and Y are both bluish main sequence stars. Star X has a higher absolute brightness than star Y. How do their temperatures compare? Explain your answer.

.......................................................................

.......................................................................

.......................................................................

.......................................................................

**6. Model** ✏ Explain why our sun is classified as a main sequence star. Then, in the space below, model the life span of our sun from its birth to its eventual final stage. Include labels that describe its color and size at each stage of your model.

.......................................................................

.......................................................................

.......................................................................

.......................................................................

# (4) Galaxies

## Guiding Questions

- How can we determine the sizes of and distances between stars and galaxies?
- What makes up galaxies of different sizes and shapes?

## Connections

**Literacy** Summarize Text

**Math** Use Mathematical Representations

MS-ESS1-2

## Vocabulary

galaxy
universe
light-year
big bang

## Academic Vocabulary

determine

 **VOCABULARY APP**

Practice vocabulary on a mobile device.

### Quest CONNECTION

Think about the various ways that scientists might be able to study things that cannot be directly observed.

## Connect It!

✏ **Place an X on the spiral galaxies you see in this image of deep space.**

Explain  Based on what you see, how do you think scientists measure the distances between objects in space?

........................................................................................................

........................................................................................................

Apply Scientific Reasoning  What are some challenges that you think scientists face when trying to study other galaxies?

........................................................................................................

........................................................................................................

........................................................................................................

# From Stars to Galaxies

The brightest and largest spots of light that you see in **Figure 1** are galaxies. There are estimated to be billions of galaxies, and each of these galaxies is made up of many billions of stars. Measuring the distances between Earth and these objects poses a challenge to astronomers because the distances are so vast.

**Parallax** When trying to determine the distance to nearby stars and other objects, astronomers measure the object's apparent motion in the sky as Earth is on opposite sides of its orbit around the sun. This apparent motion in the object against distant background stars is called parallax.

Parallax is best used to measure the distance to nearby stars. The parallax of objects that are extremely far away is too small to be useful in obtaining an accurate measurement.

**HANDS-ON LAB**

**Investigate** Develop a model of the Milky Way.

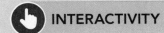

**INTERACTIVITY**

Find out how Hollywood goes to space.

### Deep in Space

**Figure 1** The universe is enormous, almost beyond imagination. This image was captured by the Hubble Space Telescope in 1995 while peering into one of the darkest regions of space as seen from Earth. Astronomers were amazed to see more than 3,000 galaxies in the tiny patch of sky captured by the orbiting observatory.

## Star Systems
Many stars are part of groups of two or more stars, called star systems. Star systems that have two stars are called double stars or binary stars. Groups of three or more stars are called multiple star systems.

Often one star in a binary system is much brighter and more massive than the other. Even if only one star can be seen from Earth, astronomers can often detect its dimmer partner by observing the effects of its gravity. As a dim companion star revolves around a bright star, its gravity causes the bright star to wobble. In 1995, astronomers first discovered an exoplanet—one outside our own solar system—revolving around a star. Again, they detected the planet by observing the effect the planet's gravity had on the star it orbited.

## Model It!

### Eclipsing Binary Stars
**Figure 2** A dim star may pass in front of a brighter star and block it. A system in which one dim star eclipses the light from another periodically is called an eclipsing binary. Scientists can measure the brightness of the brighter star and determine when the dim star is eclipsing it.

Develop Models ✏ Use the information in the graph to complete the missing panels in the diagram. Indicate the positions of each of the stars in the binary system.

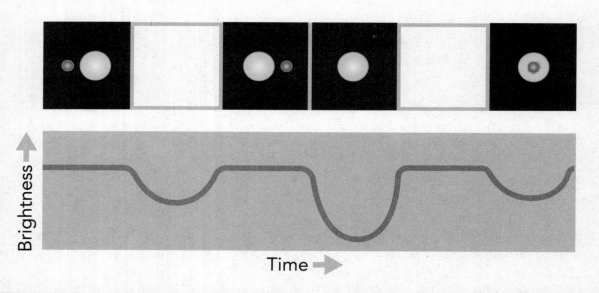

## Star Clusters

Many stars belong to larger groupings called clusters. All of the stars in a particular cluster formed from the same nebula at about the same time. An open cluster looks loose and disorganized. These clusters may contain up to a few thousand stars. They also contain a lot of gas and dust. Globular clusters are large groupings of older stars. They are round and may have more than a million stars.

## Galaxies

A **galaxy** is a group of single stars, star systems, star clusters, dust, and gas bound together by gravity. **Figure 3** shows several common types of galaxies. Spiral galaxies appear to have a bulge in the middle and arms that spiral outward like pinwheels. Our solar system is located in a spiral galaxy that we have named the Milky Way. Elliptical galaxies are rounded but may be elongated and slightly flattened. They contain billions of stars but have little gas or dust between the stars. Stars are no longer forming inside them, so they contain only old stars. Irregular galaxies do not have regular shapes. They are smaller than spiral or elliptical galaxies. They contain young, bright stars and include a lot of gas and dust to form new ones. Quasars are active, young galaxies with black holes at their center. Gas spins around the black hole, heats up, and glows.

**Kinds of Galaxies**
**Figure 3** 🖊 From what you know about the shapes of galaxies, label each galaxy.

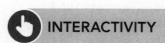 INTERACTIVITY

Explore the different types of galaxies.

✅ **READING CHECK** **Summarize Text** How are stars, star systems, star clusters, and galaxies related?

.................................................................................

.................................................................................

509

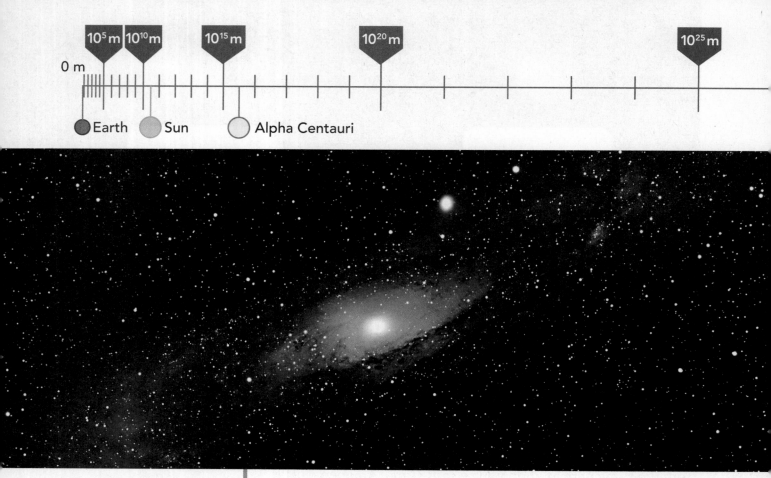

The distance scale: 0 m, $10^5$ m, $10^{10}$ m, $10^{15}$ m, $10^{20}$ m, $10^{25}$ m. Earth, Sun, and Alpha Centauri are marked along the scale.

## The Andromeda Galaxy

**Figure 4** 🖉 Our nearest galactic neighbor is a giant spiral galaxy similar to the Milky Way called the Andromeda Galaxy. It is 2.5 × $10^{22}$ meters away. Draw where the Andromeda Galaxy should appear on the distance scale shown.

# The Universe

Astronomers define the **universe** as all of space and everything in it. They study objects as close as the moon and as far away as quasars, the farthest known objects in the universe. Their research also looks at incredibly large objects, such as clusters of galaxies that are millions of light-years across. They also study tiny particles, such as the atoms within stars.

**Light-Years** Distances to the stars are so large that meters are not very practical units. In space, light travels at a speed of about 300,000,000 meters per second. A **light-year** is the distance that light travels in one year, about 9.46 trillion kilometers. The light-year is a unit of distance, not time. Imagine it this way. If you bicycle at a speed of 10 kilometers per hour, it would take you 1 hour to go to a mall 10 kilometers away. You could say that the mall is "1 bicycle-hour" away.

**Scientific Notation** As shown in **Figure 4**, the numbers that astronomers use are often very large or very small, so they frequently use scientific notation to describe sizes and distances in the universe. Scientific notation uses powers of ten to write very large or very small numbers in shorter form. Each number is written as the product of a number between 1 and 10 and a power of 10.

## The Scale of the Universe

Human beings have wondered about the size and distance of the night sky throughout history. Aristarchus of Samos began questioning how far the moon was from Earth as early as the third century BCE. He used the shadow of Earth on the moon during a lunar eclipse to come up with a figure for the distance that was surprisingly accurate.

Edmond Halley is a well-known early astronomer who honed his skills in the 1600s and 1700s. He found a way to measure the distance to the sun and to the planet Venus. He did this by closely observing and measuring the shift of Venus in the sky. His discoveries helped later scientists to **determine** a more accurate scale of the entire solar system.

✓ READING CHECK **Determine Central Ideas** What is the reason astronomers choose to write the measurements of the universe in scientific notation?

.................................................................................

.................................................................................

**Academic Vocabulary**

What difficulties did scientists have when they tried to determine the size of the universe? Explain some ways you can determine the size of something.

.........................................................

.........................................................

.........................................................

.........................................................

.........................................................

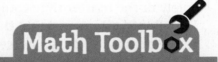

## Math Toolbox

### Scientific Notation

One light-year is about 9,460,000,000,000 km. To express this number in scientific notation, first insert a decimal point in the original number to write a number between one and ten. To determine the power of ten, count the number of places that the decimal point moved. Because there are 12 digits after the first digit, the distance be written as $9.46 \times 10^{12}$ km.

**Use Mathematical Representations** Convert the following numbers from light-years to km. Then express the numbers using scientific notation.

The Andromeda Galaxy is the closest major galaxy to the Milky Way. It is about 2,500,000 light-years from our galaxy, and its diameter is estimated to be 220,000 light-years.

2,500,000 light-years = ................................................................

220,000 light-years = ................................................................

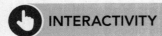

**INTERACTIVITY**

Design a hierarchical model of a galaxy.

**VIDEO**

Find out more about the big bang theory.

**Literacy Connection**

**Summarize Text** What is dark matter?

..............................................

..............................................

..............................................

..............................................

# Understanding the Universe

Astronomers theorize that the universe began between 13.77 and 13.82 billion years ago. At that time, the part of the universe we can see was no larger than the period at the end of this sentence.

**The Big Bang** The universe then exploded in what has been called the **big bang**. The big bang theory states that the universe formed in an instant, billions of years ago, in an enormous explosion. New observations lead many astronomers to conclude that the universe is expanding and will likely expand forever.

**The Future of the Universe** In the 1920s, American astronomer Edwin Hubble discovered that almost all galaxies are moving away from Earth and from each other. Hubble's law states that the farther away a galaxy is, the faster it is moving away from us.

Other researchers believe that the force of gravity will begin to pull the galaxies back together into a reverse big bang. The universe would be crushed in an enormous black hole, called the big crunch.

Until recently, astronomers assumed that the universe consisted solely of the matter they could observe directly. But astronomer Vera Rubin discovered that the matter astronomers can see may make up as little as ten percent of the mass in the galaxies. The rest exists in the form of dark matter. Dark matter is matter that does not give off electromagnetic radiation. It cannot be seen directly. However, its presence can be inferred by observing the effect of its gravity on visible objects within a rotating galaxy.

In the late 1990s, astronomers observed that the expansion of the universe appeared to be accelerating. Astronomers infer that a mysterious new force, which they call dark energy, may be causing the expansion of the universe to increase.

☑ **READING CHECK** **Determine Central Ideas** How does Hubble's law support the big bang theory?

..............................................................................................................

..............................................................................................................

..............................................................................................................

..............................................................................................................

## How the Universe Formed

**Figure 5** This diagram illustrates how astronomers theorize that the universe began and will continue. How does the idea of an expanding universe support the big bang theory?

..............................................................
..............................................................
..............................................................
..............................................................
..............................................................
..............................................................
..............................................................

Big Bang

Today

Time →

# ☑ LESSON 4 Check

MS-ESS1-2

**1. Identify** What are the four types of galaxies?

....................................................................

....................................................................

....................................................................

....................................................................

**2. Understanding Main Ideas** How can astronomers detect a binary star if only one of the two stars is visible from Earth?

....................................................................

....................................................................

....................................................................

....................................................................

....................................................................

**3. Interpret and Calculate Data** The speed of light is $3.0 \times 10^8$ m/s when expressed in scientific notation. How would you express this in real numbers?

....................................................................

....................................................................

....................................................................

**4. Apply Concepts** A friend uses an analogy of raisins in rising bread dough to describe galaxies in the expanding universe. Is your friend correct? Explain.

....................................................................

....................................................................

....................................................................

....................................................................

....................................................................

....................................................................

**5. Estimate** Based on what astronomers currently know, how old is our universe?

....................................................................

....................................................................

....................................................................

....................................................................

....................................................................

....................................................................

# Quest CHECK-IN

**In this lesson, you learned about how astronomers determine the distances between objects. You also learned about how they think the universe began and how it will continue in the future.**

Draw Conclusions Why is it important for astronomers to be able to make inferences when interpreting data about things they cannot observe directly?

....................................................................

....................................................................

....................................................................

....................................................................

....................................................................

....................................................................

## ✋ INTERACTIVITY

Searching for the Unseen

**Go online** to explore how scientists know dark matter exists even though they cannot see it. Then begin developing the job descriptions for the new positions at the observatory.

MS-ESS1-2

# Traveling Through the
# Milky Way

The Milky Way is a spiral galaxy 100,000 light-years wide. Our solar system is a small speck on one of the arms that spirals out from the center of the galaxy. Just as the planets of our solar system revolve around the sun due to gravity, the entire solar system orbits the center of the Milky Way due to the force of gravity.

Our solar system moves at 240 kilometers per second around the center of the Milky Way. At this speed, it takes 250 million Earth years for our solar system to travel all the way around!

Modern astronomy uses sophisticated tools to measure distances among objects in the Milky Way, and also to identify those objects. The Kepler space telescope, launched into Earth's orbit in 2009, has helped astronomers identify thousands of exoplanets, or planets outside our solar system. The discovery of exoplanets has helped astronomers understand that our solar system is just one of many that travels around the center of the Milky Way. Astronomers have even identified areas and exoplanets of the Milky Way that could have the right conditions to support life.

**MY DISCOVERY**

Search for the term *Milky Way* in an online search engine to learn more about our galaxy. What might happen to the solar system without the gravitational force exerted by the center of the galaxy?

The Milky Way is a spiral galaxy like the one shown here.

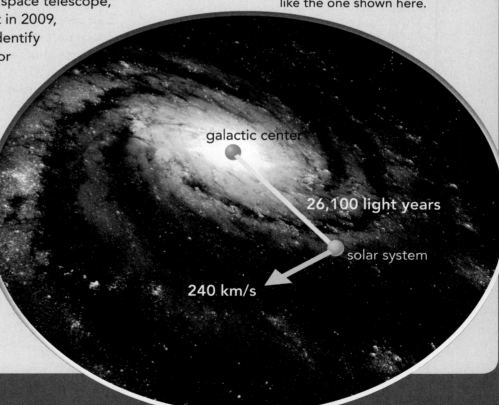

galactic center

26,100 light years

solar system

240 km/s

# ☑TOPIC 10 Review and Assess

## 1 Solar System Objects

MS-ESS1-2, MS-ESS1-3

**1.** What characteristic do all the inner planets have in common?
   **A.** ring system     **B.** liquid water
   **C.** rocky surface     **D.** thick atmosphere

**2.** All the gas giants are surrounded by
........................................................ made up of small
particles to very large chunks of ice and dust.

**3.** One astronomical unit is equal to the distance
from ............................... to ...............................

**4.** **Compare and Contrast** Compare the conditions that led to the formation of the inner planets with those that led to the formation of the outer planets.

...............................................................
...............................................................
...............................................................
...............................................................
...............................................................
...............................................................
...............................................................
...............................................................
...............................................................
...............................................................
...............................................................
...............................................................
...............................................................
...............................................................
...............................................................
...............................................................
...............................................................

## 2 Learning About the Universe

MS-ESS1-3

**5.** Which object is the largest?
   **A.** Earth     **B.** Saturn
   **C.** Jupiter     **D.** the sun

**6.** A student is making a model of the sun's interior. Which feature should the student represent in the convection zone?
   **A.** gas erupting into space
   **B.** gases rising and sinking
   **C.** radiation moving outward
   **D.** nuclear fusion producing energy

**7.** Which technology makes it possible for people to live and work in space for long periods?
   **A.** space probe     **B.** space station
   **C.** radio telescope     **D.** optical telescope

**8.** **Analyze Benefits** In 1981, the first space shuttle was launched from Cape Canaveral. Which statement describes an advantage that space shuttles have compared to earlier space probes and capsules?
   **A.** Space shuttles can travel beyond Earth's orbit.
   **B.** Space shuttles are inexpensive to build.
   **C.** Space shuttles can be used more than once.
   **D.** Space shuttles can travel beyond the solar system.

**9.** **Apply Concepts** Describe one kind of telescope and how you could use it to learn about an object in space.

...............................................................
...............................................................
...............................................................
...............................................................
...............................................................
...............................................................

**10.** Telescopes work by collecting and focusing different forms of ...............................
radiation.

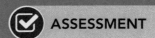

## 3 Stars

MS-ESS1-2

**11.** Using the H-R diagram, astronomers classify stars using which two star properties?
A. color and composition
B. size and surface temperature
C. surface temperature and absolute brightness
D. surface temperature and apparent brightness

**12.** Which property indicates a star's temperature?
A. size
B. color
C. composition
D. brightness

**13.** A .................................................................. forms when .................................................................. pulls together the gas and dust in the densest part of a nebula.

**14. Develop Models** ✏ Draw a flow chart to model the stages in the life span of a high-mass star.

## 4 Galaxies

MS-ESS1-2

**15.** In what kind of star system does one star sometimes block the light from another?
A. open cluster
B. globular cluster
C. quasar system
D. eclipsing binary

**16.** What is the name of the explosion that began the universe?
A. solar nebula
B. big bang
C. dark matter
D. supernova

**17.** What is dark matter?
A. matter that can be seen directly
B. matter that does not give off electromagnetic radiation
C. matter that makes up about 10 percent of the mass of the universe
D. matter that has no effect on other objects

**18. Compare and Contrast** How do open clusters and globular clusters differ in terms of numbers of stars?

..................................................................................................

..................................................................................................

**19. Analyze Systems** Determine the hierarchy of the universe in a list, starting with stars.

..................................................................................................

..................................................................................................

..................................................................................................

..................................................................................................

..................................................................................................

..................................................................................................

..................................................................................................

..................................................................................................

..................................................................................................

MS-ESS1-2

## Evidence-Based Assessment

Willa is developing a model to help her study gravity. She wants to understand that role that gravity plays in keeping objects in the solar system in orbit around the sun. She plans on using some household materials to model a gravity well.

A gravity well is a representation of the gravitational field or pull of an object in space. A massive object like the sun has a deep gravity well. A less massive object, such as an asteroid, has a very shallow gravity well.

Willa stretches plastic wrap across a large hoop to represent the "fabric" of space. She has one large clay ball, some small marbles, and tiny ball bearings.

When Willa places the clay ball on the plastic, she observes that it sinks into the plastic and forms a well. When she places a marble or bearing near the ball, Willa observes the marble roll along the surface of the plastic toward the ball.

1. **Develop Models** In Willa's model, which of the following solar system objects does the large clay ball represent?
   - (A) the sun
   - B. a planet
   - C. a moon
   - D. an asteroid

2. **Apply Concepts** Willa tests her model by placing the large clay ball, a single marble, and a single ball bearing one at at time on the plastic. Which object creates the deepest well? How can these observations be applied to solar system objects? Explain.

   ...............................................................

   ...............................................................

   ...............................................................

   ...............................................................

   ...............................................................

   ...............................................................

   ...............................................................

   ...............................................................

   ...............................................................

3. **Identify Limitations** How does Willa's model show that gravity keeps objects in the solar system in orbit around the sun? What are the limitations of her model? Do objects in the solar system behave like they would in the model? Explain.

   ...............................................................

   ...............................................................

   ...............................................................

   ...............................................................

   ...............................................................

   ...............................................................

   ...............................................................

   ...............................................................

4. **Construct Explanations** How can Willa use the materials and her model to explain why objects that are very far from the sun do not orbit it?

   ...............................................................

   ...............................................................

   ...............................................................

   ...............................................................

   ...............................................................

   ...............................................................

   ...............................................................

   ...............................................................

   ...............................................................

# Quest FINDINGS

## Complete the Quest!

**Phenomenon** You learned what it takes to be an asteroid hunter, an extraterrestrial life hunter, and a dark matter hunter. Apply the knowledge you gained to write advertisements to attract great candidates to the new observatory.

**Cause and Effect** Think about the three different types of scientists needed. Why might it be important for them to use models in their investigations?

   ...............................................................

   ...............................................................

   ...............................................................

   ...............................................................

▶ **INTERACTIVITY**

Reflect on Searching for a Star

# Scaling Down the Solar System

How can you **build scale models** of **volcanoes** from three **planets** to show which one is largest?

## Background

**Phenomenon** Mauna Loa in Hawaii is currently the largest active volcano on Earth. But is it the largest volcano in the solar system? Sapas Mons on Venus and Olympus Mons on Mars are two other volcanoes that can be viewed from Earth with telescopes. Scientists use scale models to help them answer questions about landforms on other planets. In this investigation, you will make scale models of volcanoes found on different planets in our solar system.

## Materials

(per group)

- calculator
- graph paper
- a variety of common craft materials, such as construction paper, tape, glue, craft sticks, modeling clay, foam, cotton balls, and markers
- metric ruler

## Safety

Be sure to follow all safety guidelines provided by your teacher. The Safety Appendix of your textbook provides more details about the safety icons.

Mauna Loa, Hawaii

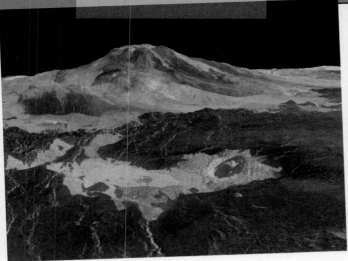

Sapas Mons

Olympus Mons

# Procedure

1. Examine the images of the three volcanoes that are found on different planets in our solar system. Research the volcanoes to find out about their heights, diameters, and any other distinguishing characteristics. In the space provided on the next page, create a data table to record the names of the volcanoes, their locations, their heights (in km), and their diameters (in km).

2. Determine an appropriate scale for your models. This decision is affected by two factors: how big an area you need to model and how much detail you want to show. If you need to show a large area, then you would want to choose a smaller scale to avoid the model becoming too big. But at smaller scales, models are limited in the amount of detail they can show. Consider the details you want to show and how large or small you want the models to be. Take into account the greatest and smallest values in your data table. Choose a scale that will allow you to represent these values in the models appropriately.

   Record the scale that you will use for your models.

   1 km = _____

3. ✂ You will construct a three-dimensional model of each volcano from construction paper, modeling clay, or other available materials.

4. Draw a sketch to show your plans. Your sketch should indicate the scale of your models. It also should clearly identify the materials you will use in each part of your models. After obtaining your teacher's approval, follow your plan to construct your models to scale.

## HANDS-ON LAB

и**Demonstrate** Go online for a downloadable worksheet of this lab.

Data Table

Model Sketch

# Analyze and Interpret Data

1. **Evaluate Reasoning** Could you have used a different scale for each volcano to represent their relative sizes? Explain.

.................................................................................

.................................................................................

2. **Evaluate Claims** Suppose someone suggested that you add a scale model of a human to your volcano models. Is this a reasonable or unreasonable suggestion? Use the scale of the models to construct your answer. (*Note: The height of a typical adult human is slightly less than 2 m, or 0.002 km.*)

.................................................................................

.................................................................................

.................................................................................

.................................................................................

3. **Use Models** When you are studying models of different solar system objects, how does identifying the scale of each model help you to compare and understand their sizes and features?

.................................................................................

.................................................................................

.................................................................................

.................................................................................

.................................................................................

4. **Identify Limitations** Compare your models to the photographs of each volcano. What are some of the advantages of your models over the photographs? What are some of the disadvantages?

.................................................................................

.................................................................................

.................................................................................

.................................................................................

5. **Apply Concepts** Using the scale models created by your class, compare characteristics such as the size and shape of the three different volcanoes found on Venus, Earth, and Mars. What can you infer about the three planets from this analysis?

.................................................................................

.................................................................................

.................................................................................

SEP.1, SEP.8

# The Meaning of Science

## Science Skills

Science is a way of learning about the natural world. It involves asking questions, making predictions, and collecting information to see if the answer is right or wrong.

The table lists some of the skills that scientists use. You use some of these skills every day. For example, you may observe and evaluate your lunch options before choosing what to eat.

📓 **Reflect** Think about a time you misplaced something and could not find it. Write a sentence defining the problem. What science skills could you use to solve the problem? Explain how you would use at least three of the skills in the table.

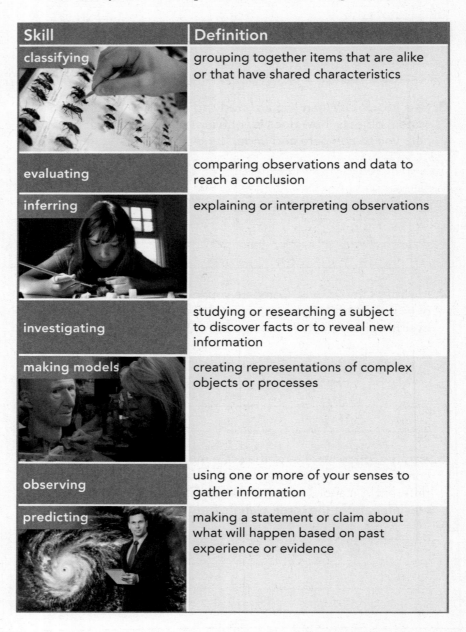

| Skill | Definition |
|---|---|
| classifying | grouping together items that are alike or that have shared characteristics |
| evaluating | comparing observations and data to reach a conclusion |
| inferring | explaining or interpreting observations |
| investigating | studying or researching a subject to discover facts or to reveal new information |
| making models | creating representations of complex objects or processes |
| observing | using one or more of your senses to gather information |
| predicting | making a statement or claim about what will happen based on past experience or evidence |

# Scientific Attitudes

Curiosity often drives scientists to learn about the world around them. Creativity is useful for coming up with inventive ways to solve problems. Such qualities and attitudes, and the ability to keep an open mind, are essential for scientists.

When sharing results or findings, honesty and ethics are also essential. Ethics refers to rules for knowing right from wrong.

Being skeptical is also important. This means having doubts about things based on past experiences and evidence. Skepticism helps to prevent accepting data and results that may not be true.

Scientists must also avoid bias—likes or dislikes of people, ideas, or things. They must avoid experimental bias, which is a mistake that may make an experiment's preferred outcome more likely.

# Scientific Reasoning

Scientific reasoning depends on being logical and objective. When you are objective, you use evidence and apply logic to draw conclusions. Being subjective means basing conclusions on personal feelings, biases, or opinions. Subjective reasoning can interfere with science and skew results. Objective reasoning helps scientists use observations to reach conclusions about the natural world.

Scientists use two types of objective reasoning: deductive and inductive. Deductive reasoning involves starting with a general idea or theory and applying it to a situation. For example, the theory of plate tectonics indicates that earthquakes happen mostly where tectonic plates meet. You could then draw the conclusion, or deduce, that California has many earthquakes because tectonic plates meet there.

In inductive reasoning, you make a generalization from a specific observation. When scientists collect data in an experiment and draw a conclusion based on that data, they use inductive reasoning. For example, if fertilizer causes one set of plants to grow faster than another, you might infer that the fertilizer promotes plant growth.

**Make Meaning**
Think about a bias the marine biologist in the photo could show that results in paying more or less attention to one kind of organism over others. Make a prediction about how that bias could affect the biologist's survey of the coral reef.

**Write About It**
Suppose it is raining when you go to sleep one night. When you wake up the next morning, you observe frozen puddles on the ground and icicles on tree branches. Use scientific reasoning to draw a conclusion about the air temperature outside. Support your conclusion using deductive or inductive reasoning.

SEP.1, SEP.2, SEP.3, SEP.4, CCC.4

# Science Processes

## Scientific Inquiry

**Write About It**
Describe a question that you posed, formally or informally, about an event in your life that you needed to investigate or resolve. Write the hypothesis you developed to answer your question, and describe how you tested the hypothesis.

Scientists contribute to scientific knowledge by conducting investigations and drawing conclusions. The process often begins with an observation that leads to a question, which is then followed by the development of a hypothesis. This is known as scientific inquiry.

One of the first steps in scientific inquiry is asking questions. However, it's important to make a question specific with a narrow focus so the investigation will not be too broad. A biologist may want to know all there is to know about wolves, for example. But a good, focused question for a specific inquiry might be "How many offspring does the average female wolf produce in her lifetime?"

A hypothesis is a possible answer to a scientific question. A hypothesis must be testable. For something to be testable, researchers must be able to carry out an investigation and gather evidence that will either support or disprove the hypothesis.

## Scientific Models

Models are tools that scientists use to study phenomena indirectly. A model is any representation of an object or process. Illustrations, dioramas, globes, diagrams, computer programs, and mathematical equations are all examples of scientific models. For example, a diagram of Earth's crust and mantle can help you to picture layers deep below the surface and understand events such as volcanic eruptions.

Models also allow scientists to represent objects that are either very large, such as our solar system, or very small, such as a molecule of DNA. Models can also represent processes that occur over a long period of time, such as the changes that have occurred throughout Earth's history.

Models are helpful, but they have limitations. Physical models are not made of the same materials as the objects they represent. Most models of complex objects or processes show only major parts, stages, or relationships. Many details are left out. Therefore, you may not be able to learn as much from models as you would through direct observation.

**Reflect** Identify the benefits and limitations of using a plastic model of DNA, as shown here.

# Science Experiments

An experiment or investigation must be well planned to produce valid results. In planning an experiment, you must identify the independent and dependent variables. You must also do as much as possible to remove the effects of other variables. A controlled experiment is one in which you test only one variable at a time.

For example, suppose you plan a controlled experiment to learn how the type of material affects the speed at which sound waves travel through it. The only variable that should change is the type of material. This way, if the speed of sound changes, you know that it is a result of a change in the material, not another variable such as the thickness of the material or the type of sound used.

You should also remove bias from any investigation. You may inadvertently introduce bias by selecting subjects you like and avoiding those you don't like. Scientists often conduct investigations by taking random samples to avoid ending up with biased results.

Once you plan your investigation and begin to collect data, it's important to record and organize the data. You may wish to use a graph to display and help you to interpret the data.

Communicating is the sharing of ideas and results with others through writing and speaking. Communicating data and conclusions is a central part of science.

Scientists share knowledge, including new findings, theories, and techniques for collecting data. Conferences, journals, and websites help scientists to communicate with each other. Popular media, including newspapers, magazines, and social media sites, help scientists to share their knowledge with nonscientists. However, before the results of investigations are shared and published, other scientists should review the experiment for possible sources of error, such as bias and unsupported conclusions.

**Write About It**
List four ways you could communicate the results of a scientific study about the health of sea turtles in the Pacific Ocean.

SEP.1, SEP.6, SEP.7, SEP.8

# Scientific Knowledge

## Scientific Explanations

Suppose you learn that adult flamingos are pink because of the food they eat. This statement is a scientific explanation—it describes how something in nature works or explains why it happens. Scientists from different fields use methods such as researching information, designing experiments, and making models to form scientific explanations. Scientific explanations often result from many years of work and multiple investigations conducted by many scientists.

## Scientific Theories and Laws

A scientific law is a statement that describes what you can expect to occur every time under a particular set of conditions. A scientific law describes an observed pattern in nature, but it does not attempt to explain it. For example, the law of superposition describes what you can expect to find in terms of the ages of layers of rock. Geologists use this observed pattern to determine the relative ages of sedimentary rock layers. But the law does not explain why the pattern occurs.

By contrast, a scientific theory is a well-tested explanation for a wide range of observations or experimental results. It provides details and describes causes of observed patterns. Something is elevated to a theory only when there is a large body of evidence that supports it. However, a scientific theory can be changed or overturned when new evidence is found.

**Write About It**
Choose two fields of science that interest you. Describe a method used to develop scientific explanations in each field.

**Compare and Contrast** Complete the table to compare and contrast a scientific theory and a scientific law.

| | Scientific Theory | Scientific Law |
|---|---|---|
| Definition | | |
| Does it attempt to explain a pattern observed in nature? | | |

# Analyzing Scientific Explanations

To analyze scientific explanations that you hear on the news or read in a book such as this one, you need scientific literacy. Scientific literacy means understanding scientific terms and principles well enough to ask questions, evaluate information, and make decisions. Scientific reasoning gives you a process to apply. This includes looking for bias and errors in the research, evaluating data, and identifying faulty reasoning. For example, by evaluating how a survey was conducted, you may find a serious flaw in the researchers' methods.

# Evidence and Opinions

The basis for scientific explanations is empirical evidence. Empirical evidence includes the data and observations that have been collected through scientific processes. Satellite images, photos, and maps of mountains and volcanoes are all examples of empirical evidence that support a scientific explanation about Earth's tectonic plates. Scientists look for patterns when they analyze this evidence. For example, they might see a pattern that mountains and volcanoes often occur near tectonic plate boundaries.

To evaluate scientific information, you must first distinguish between evidence and opinion. In science, evidence includes objective observations and conclusions that have been repeated. Evidence may or may not support a scientific claim. An opinion is a subjective idea that is formed from evidence, but it cannot be confirmed by evidence.

**Write About It**
Suppose the conservation committee of a town wants to gauge residents' opinions about a proposal to stock the local ponds with fish every spring. The committee pays for a survey to appear on a web site that is popular with people who like to fish. The results of the survey show 78 people in favor of the proposal and two against it. Do you think the survey's results are valid? Explain.

**Make Meaning**
Explain what empirical evidence the photograph reveals.

SEP.3, SEP.4

# Tools of Science

## Measurement

Making measurements using standard units is important in all fields of science. This allows scientists to repeat and reproduce other experiments, as well as to understand the precise meaning of the results of others. Scientists use a measurement system called the International System of Units, or SI.

For each type of measurement, there is a series of units that are greater or less than each other. The unit a scientist uses depends on what is being measured. For example, a geophysicist tracking the movements of tectonic plates may use centimeters, as plates tend to move small amounts each year. Meanwhile, a marine biologist might measure the movement of migrating bluefin tuna on the scale of kilometers.

Units for length, mass, volume, and density are based on powers of ten—a meter is equal to 100 centimeters or 1000 millimeters. Units of time do not follow that pattern. There are 60 seconds in a minute, 60 minutes in an hour, and 24 hours in a day. These units are based on patterns that humans perceived in nature. Units of temperature are based on scales that are set according to observations of nature. For example, 0°C is the temperature at which pure water freezes, and 100°C is the temperature at which it boils.

**✍ Write About It**
Suppose you are planning an investigation in which you must measure the dimensions of several small mineral samples that fit in your hand. Which metric unit or units will you most likely use? Explain your answer.

| Measurement | Metric units |
|---|---|
| **Length or distance** | meter (m), kilometer (km), centimeter (cm), millimeter (mm)<br>1 km = 1,000 m    1 cm = 10 mm<br>1 m = 100 cm |
| **Mass** | kilogram (kg), gram (g), milligram (mg)<br>1 kg = 1,000 g    1 g = 1,000 mg |
| **Volume** | cubic meter (m³), cubic centimeter (cm³)<br>1 m³ = 1,000,000 cm³ |
| **Density** | kilogram per cubic meter (kg/m³), gram per cubic centimeter (g/cm³)<br>1,000 kg/m³ = 1 g/cm³ |
| **Temperature** | degrees Celsius (°C), kelvin (K)<br>1°C = 273 K |
| **Time** | hour (h), minute (m), second (s) |

# Math Skills

Using numbers to collect and interpret data involves math skills that are essential in science. For example, you use math skills when you estimate the number of birds in an entire forest after counting the actual number of birds in ten trees.

Scientists evaluate measurements and estimates for their precision and accuracy. In science, an accurate measurement is very close to the actual value. Precise measurements are very close, or nearly equal, to each other. Reliable measurements are both accurate and precise. An imprecise value may be a sign of an error in data collection. This kind of anomalous data may be excluded to avoid skewing the data and harming the investigation.

Other math skills include performing specific calculations, such as finding the mean, or average, value in a data set. The mean can be calculated by adding up all of the values in the data set and then dividing that sum by the number of values.

| Hour | Number of Ducks Observed at a Pond |
| --- | --- |
| 1 | 12 |
| 2 | 10 |
| 3 | 2 |
| 4 | 14 |
| 5 | 13 |
| 6 | 10 |
| 7 | 11 |

**Calculate** The data table shows how many ducks were seen at a pond every hour over the course of seven hours. Is there a data point that seems anomalous? If so, cross out that data point. Then, calculate the mean number of ducks on the pond. Round the mean to the nearest whole number.

# Graphs

Graphs help scientists to interpret data by helping them to find trends or patterns in the data. A line graph displays data that show how one variable (the dependent or outcome variable) changes in response to another (the independent or test variable). The slope and shape of a graph line can reveal patterns and help scientists to make predictions. For example, line graphs can help you to spot patterns of change over time.

Scientists use bar graphs to compare data across categories or subjects that may not affect each other. The heights of the bars make it easy to compare those quantities. A circle graph, also known as a pie chart, shows the proportions of different parts of a whole.

**Write About It**
You and a friend record the distance you travel every 15 minutes on a one-hour bike trip. Your friend wants to display the data as a circle graph. Explain whether or not this is the best type of graph to display your data. If not, suggest another graph to use.

SEP.1, SEP.2, SEP.3, SEP.6

# The Engineering and Design Process

Engineers are builders and problem solvers. Chemical engineers experiment with new fuels made from algae. Civil engineers design roadways and bridges. Bioengineers develop medical devices and prosthetics. The common trait among engineers is an ability to identify problems and design solutions to solve them. Engineers use a creative process that relies on scientific methods to help guide them from a concept or idea all the way to the final product.

## Define the Problem

To identify or define a problem, different questions need to be asked: *What are the effects of the problem? What are the likely causes? What other factors could be involved?* Sometimes the obvious, immediate cause of a problem may be the result of another problem that may not be immediately apparent. For example, climate change results in different weather patterns, which in turn can affect organisms that live in certain habitats. So engineers must be aware of all the possible effects of potential solutions. Engineers must also take into account how well different solutions deal with the different causes of the problem.

**Reflect** Write about a problem that you encountered in your life that had both immediate, obvious causes as well as less-obvious and less-immediate ones.

DEFINE the problem

Develop POSSIBLE SOLUTIONS

DESIGN AND BUILD a solution

REDESIGN AND RETEST your solution

**ENGINEERING** *Design Process*

COMMUNICATE your solution

TEST AND EVALUATE your solution

As engineers consider problems and design solutions, they must identify and categorize the criteria and constraints of the project.

Criteria are the factors that must be met or accomplished by the solution. For example, a gardener who wants to protect outdoor plants from deer and rabbits may say that the criteria for the solution are "plants are no longer eaten" and "plant growth is not inhibited in any way." The gardener then knows the plants cannot simply be sealed off from the environment, because the plants will not receive sunlight and water.

The same gardener will likely have constraints on his solution, such as budget for materials and time that is available for working on the project. By setting constraints, a solution can be designed that will be successful without introducing a new set of problems. No one wants to spend $500 on materials to protect $100 worth of tomatoes and cucumbers.

## Develop Possible Solutions

After the problem has been identified, and the criteria and constraints identified, an engineer will consider possible solutions. This often involves working in teams with other engineers and designers to brainstorm ideas and research materials that can be used in the design.

It's important for engineers to think creatively and explore all potential solutions. If you wanted to design a bicycle that was safer and easier to ride than a traditional bicycle, then you would want more than just one or two solutions. Having multiple ideas to choose from increases the likelihood that you will develop a solution that meets the criteria and constraints. In addition, different ideas that result from brainstorming can often lead to new and better solutions to an existing problem.

**Make Meaning**
Using the example of a garden that is vulnerable to wild animals such as deer, make a list of likely constraints on an engineering solution to the problem you identified before. Determine if there are common traits among the constraints, and identify categories for them.

## Design a Solution

Engineers then develop the idea that they feel best solves the problem. Once a solution has been chosen, engineers and designers get to work building a model or prototype of the solution. A model may involve sketching on paper or using computer software to construct a model of the solution. A prototype is a working model of the solution.

Building a model or prototype helps an engineer determine whether a solution meets the criteria and stays within the constraints. During this stage of the process, engineers must often deal with new problems and make any necessary adjustments to the model or prototype.

## Test and Evaluate a Solution

Whether testing a model or a prototype, engineers use scientific processes to evaluate their solutions. Multiple experiments, tests, or trials are conducted, data are evaluated, and results and analyses are communicated. New criteria or constraints may emerge as a result of testing. In most cases, a solution will require some refinement or revision, even if it has been through successful testing. Refining a solution is necessary if there are new constraints, such as less money or available materials. Additional testing may be done to ensure that a solution satisfies local, state, or federal laws or standards.

**Make Meaning** Think about an aluminum beverage can. What would happen if the price or availability of aluminum changed so much that cans needed to be made of a new material? What would the criteria and constraints be on the development of a new can?

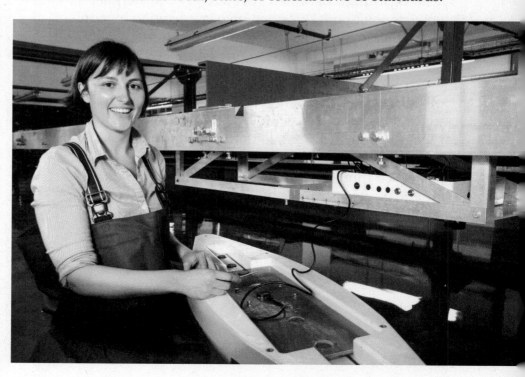

A naval architect sets up a model to test how the the hull's design responds to waves.

# Communicate the Solution

Engineers need to communicate the final design to the people who will manufacture the product. This may include sketches, detailed drawings, computer simulations, and written text. Engineers often provide evidence that was collected during the testing stage. This evidence may include graphs and data tables that support the decisions made for the final design.

If there is feedback about the solution, then the engineers and designers must further refine the solution. This might involve making minor adjustments to the design, or it might mean bigger modifications to the design based on new criteria or constraints. Any changes in the design will require additional testing to make sure that the changes work as intended.

# Redesign and Retest the Solution

At different steps in the engineering and design process, a solution usually must be revised and retested. Many designs fail to work perfectly, even after models and prototypes are built, tested, and evaluated. Engineers must be ready to analyze new results and deal with any new problems that arise. Troubleshooting, or fixing design problems, allows engineers to adjust the design to improve on how well the solution meets the need.

**Communicate** Suppose you are an engineer at an aerospace company. Your team is designing a rover to be used on a future NASA space mission. A family member doesn't understand why so much your team's time is taken up with testing and retesting the rover design. What are three things you would tell your relative to explain why testing and retesting are so important to the engineering and design process?

........................................................................................................................

........................................................................................................................

........................................................................................................................

........................................................................................................................

........................................................................................................................

........................................................................................................................

........................................................................................................................

........................................................................................................................

........................................................................................................................

## Safety Symbols

These symbols warn of possible dangers in the laboratory and remind you to work carefully.

 **Safety Goggles** Wear safety goggles to protect your eyes in any activity involving chemicals, flames or heating, or glassware.

 **Lab Apron** Wear a laboratory apron to protect your skin and clothing from damage.

 **Breakage** Handle breakable materials, such as glassware, with care. Do not touch broken glassware.

 **Heat-Resistant Gloves** Use an oven mitt or other hand protection when handling hot materials, such as hot plates or hot glassware.

 **Plastic Gloves** Wear disposable plastic gloves when working with harmful chemicals and organisms. Keep your hands away from your face, and dispose of the gloves according to your teacher's instructions.

 **Heating** Use a clamp or tongs to pick up hot glassware. Do not touch hot objects with your bare hands.

 **Flames** Before you work with flames, tie back loose hair and clothing. Follow your teacher's instructions about lighting and extinguishing flames.

 **No Flames** When using flammable materials, make sure there are no flames, sparks, or other exposed heat sources present.

 **Corrosive Chemical** Avoid getting acid or other corrosive chemicals on your skin or clothing or in your eyes. Do not inhale the vapors. Wash your hands after the activity.

 **Poison** Do not let any poisonous chemical come into contact with your skin, and do not inhale its vapors. Wash your hands when you are finished with the activity.

 **Fumes** Work in a well-ventilated area when harmful vapors may be involved. Avoid inhaling vapors directly. Test an odor only when directed to do so by your teacher, and use a wafting motion to direct the vapor toward your nose.

 **Sharp Object** Scissors, scalpels, knives, needles, pins, and tacks can cut your skin. Always direct a sharp edge or point away from yourself and others.

 **Animal Safety** Treat live or preserved animals or animal parts with care to avoid harming the animals or yourself. Wash your hands when you are finished with the activity.

 **Plant Safety** Handle plants only as directed by your teacher. If you are allergic to certain plants, tell your teacher; do not do an activity involving those plants. Avoid touching harmful plants such as poison ivy. Wash your hands when you are finished with the activity.

 **Electric Shock** To avoid electric shock, never use electrical equipment around water, when the equipment is wet, or when your hands are wet. Be sure cords are untangled and cannot trip anyone. Unplug equipment not in use.

 **Physical Safety** When an experiment involves physical activity, avoid injuring yourself or others. Alert your teacher if there is any reason you should not participate.

 **Disposal** Dispose of chemicals and other laboratory materials safely. Follow the instructions from your teacher.

 **Hand Washing** Wash your hands thoroughly when finished with an activity. Use soap and warm water. Rinse well.

 **General Safety Awareness** When this symbol appears, follow the instructions provided. When you are asked to develop your own procedure in a lab, have your teacher approve your plan.

## Using a Laboratory Balance

The laboratory balance is an important tool in scientific investigations. Different kinds of balances are used in the laboratory to determine the masses and weights of objects. You can use a triple-beam balance to determine the masses of materials that you study or experiment with in the laboratory. An electronic balance, unlike a triple-beam balance, is used to measure the weights of materials.

The triple-beam balance that you may use in your science class is probably similar to the balance depicted in this Appendix. To use the balance properly, you should learn the name, location, and function of each part of the balance.

### Triple-Beam Balance

The triple-beam balance is a single-pan balance with three beams calibrated in grams. The back, or 100-gram, beam is divided into ten units of 10 grams each. The middle, or 500-gram, beam is divided into five units of 100 grams each. The front, or 10-gram, beam is divided into ten units of 1 gram each. Each gram on the front beam is further divided into units of 0.1 gram.

**Apply Concepts** What is the greatest mass you could find with the triple-beam balance in the picture?

.......................................................

**Calculate** What is the mass of the apple in the picture?

.......................................................

**The following procedure can be used to find the mass of an object with a triple-beam balance:**

1. Place the object on the pan.

2. Move the rider on the middle beam notch by notch until the horizontal pointer on the right drops below zero. Move the rider back one notch.

3. Move the rider on the back beam notch by notch until the pointer again drops below zero. Move the rider back one notch.

4. Slowly slide the rider along the front beam until the pointer stops at the zero point.

5. The mass of the object is equal to the sum of the readings on the three beams.

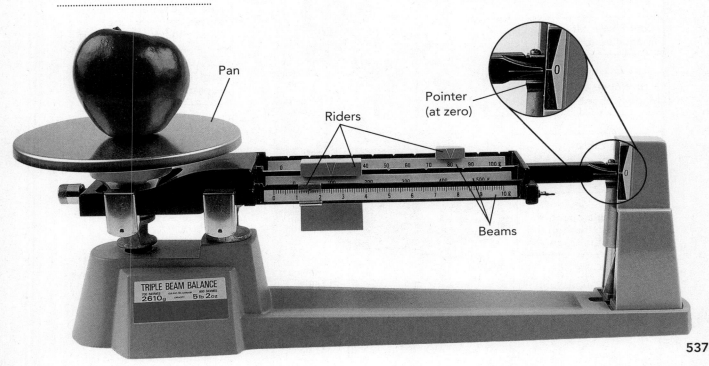

Pan

Riders

Pointer (at zero)

Beams

TRIPLE BEAM BALANCE
700 SERIES    SEARS HOLMBERG    800 SERIES
2610 g    CAPACITY    5 lb 2 oz

# APPENDIX C

## Using a Microscope

The microscope is an essential tool in the study of life science. It allows you to see things that are too small to be seen with the unaided eye.

You will probably use a compound microscope like the one you see here. The compound microscope has more than one lens that magnifies the object you view.

Typically, a compound microscope has one lens in the eyepiece (the part you look through). The eyepiece lens usually magnifies 10×. Any object you view through this lens will appear 10 times larger than it is.

A compound microscope may contain two or three other lenses called objective lenses. They are called the low-power and high-power

objective lenses. The low-power objective lens usually magnifies 10×. The high-power objective lenses usually magnify 40× and 100×.

To calculate the total magnification with which you are viewing an object, multiply the magnification of the eyepiece lens by the magnification of the objective lens you are using. For example, the eyepiece's magnification of 10× multiplied by the low-power objective's magnification of 10× equals a total magnification of 100×.

Use the photo of the compound microscope to become familiar with the parts of the microscope and their functions.

### The Parts of a Microscope

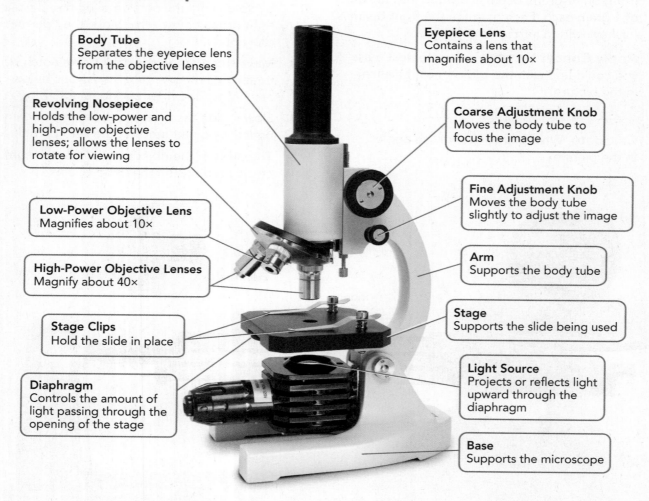

**Body Tube**
Separates the eyepiece lens from the objective lenses

**Revolving Nosepiece**
Holds the low-power and high-power objective lenses; allows the lenses to rotate for viewing

**Low-Power Objective Lens**
Magnifies about 10×

**High-Power Objective Lenses**
Magnify about 40×

**Stage Clips**
Hold the slide in place

**Diaphragm**
Controls the amount of light passing through the opening of the stage

**Eyepiece Lens**
Contains a lens that magnifies about 10×

**Coarse Adjustment Knob**
Moves the body tube to focus the image

**Fine Adjustment Knob**
Moves the body tube slightly to adjust the image

**Arm**
Supports the body tube

**Stage**
Supports the slide being used

**Light Source**
Projects or reflects light upward through the diaphragm

**Base**
Supports the microscope

## Using the Microscope

**Use the following procedures when you are working with a microscope.**

1. To carry the microscope, grasp the microscope's arm with one hand. Place your other hand under the base.

2. Place the microscope on a table with the arm toward you.

3. Turn the coarse adjustment knob to raise the body tube.

4. Revolve the nosepiece until the low-power objective lens clicks into place.

5. Adjust the diaphragm. While looking through the eyepiece, adjust the mirror until you see a bright white circle of light. **CAUTION:** Never use direct sunlight as a light source.

6. Place a slide on the stage. Center the specimen over the opening on the stage. Use the stage clips to hold the slide in place. **CAUTION:** Glass slides are fragile.

7. Look at the stage from the side. Carefully turn the coarse adjustment knob to lower the body tube until the low-power objective almost touches the slide.

8. Looking through the eyepiece, very slowly turn the coarse adjustment knob until the specimen comes into focus.

9. To switch to the high-power objective lens, look at the microscope from the side. Carefully revolve the nosepiece until the high-power objective lens clicks into place. Make sure the lens does not hit the slide.

10. Looking through the eyepiece, turn the fine adjustment knob until the specimen comes into focus.

## Making a Wet-Mount Slide

**Use the following procedures to make a wet-mount slide of a specimen.**

1. Obtain a clean microscope slide and a coverslip. **CAUTION:** Glass slides and coverslips are fragile.

2. Place the specimen on the center of the slide. The specimen must be thin enough for light to pass through it.

3. Using a plastic dropper, place a drop of water on the specimen.

4. Gently place one edge of the coverslip against the slide so that it touches the edge of the water drop at a 45° angle. Slowly lower the coverslip over the specimen. If you see air bubbles trapped beneath the coverslip, tap the coverslip gently with the eraser end of a pencil.

5. Remove any excess water at the edge of the coverslip with a paper towel.

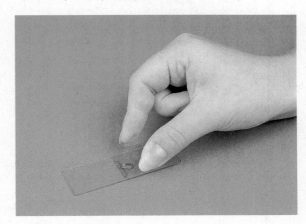

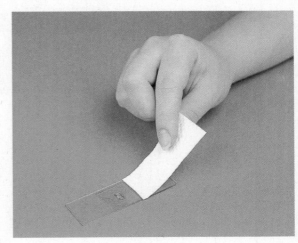

## Periodic Table of Elements

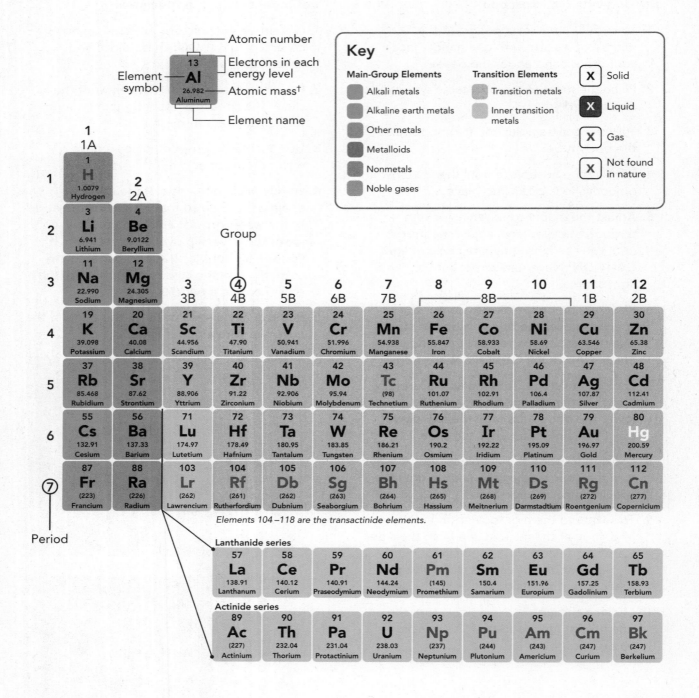

Elements 104–118 are the transactinide elements.

†The atomic masses in parentheses are the mass numbers of the longest-lived isotope of elements for which a standard atomic mass cannot be defined.

| 18 8A |
|---|
| 2 **He** 4.0026 Helium |

| 13 3A | 14 4A | 15 5A | 16 6A | 17 7A | |
|---|---|---|---|---|---|
| 5 **B** 10.81 Boron | 6 **C** 12.011 Carbon | 7 **N** 14.007 Nitrogen | 8 **O** 15.999 Oxygen | 9 **F** 18.998 Fluorine | 10 **Ne** 20.179 Neon |
| 13 **Al** 26.982 Aluminum | 14 **Si** 28.086 Silicon | 15 **P** 30.974 Phosphorus | 16 **S** 32.06 Sulfur | 17 **Cl** 35.453 Chlorine | 18 **Ar** 39.948 Argon |
| 31 **Ga** 69.72 Gallium | 32 **Ge** 72.59 Germanium | 33 **As** 74.922 Arsenic | 34 **Se** 78.96 Selenium | 35 **Br** 79.904 Bromine | 36 **Kr** 83.80 Krypton |
| 49 **In** 114.82 Indium | 50 **Sn** 118.69 Tin | 51 **Sb** 121.75 Antimony | 52 **Te** 127.60 Tellurium | 53 **I** 126.90 Iodine | 54 **Xe** 131.30 Xenon |
| 81 **Tl** 204.37 Thallium | 82 **Pb** 207.2 Lead | 83 **Bi** 208.98 Bismuth | 84 **Po** (209) Polonium | 85 **At** (210) Astatine | 86 **Rn** (222) Radon |
| 113 **Nh** (284) Nihonium | 114 **Fl** (289) Flerovium | 115 **Mc** (288) Moscovium | 116 **Lv** (292) Livermorium | 117 **Ts** (294) Tennessine | 118 **Og** (294) Oganesson |

| 66 **Dy** 162.50 Dysprosium | 67 **Ho** 164.93 Holmium | 68 **Er** 167.26 Erbium | 69 **Tm** 168.93 Thulium | 70 **Yb** 173.04 Ytterbium |
|---|---|---|---|---|
| 98 **Cf** (251) Californium | 99 **Es** (252) Einsteinium | 100 **Fm** (257) Fermium | 101 **Md** (258) Mendelevium | 102 **No** (259) Nobelium |

# GLOSSARY

## A

**absolute age** The age of a rock given as the number of years since the rock formed. (303)

**absolute brightness** The brightness a star would have if it were at a standard distance from Earth. (503)

**acceleration** The rate at which velocity changes. (133)

**acid** A substance that tastes sour, reacts with metals and carbonates, and turns blue litmus paper red. (49)

**adaptation** An inherited behavior or physical characteristic that helps an organism survive and reproduce in its environment. (245)

**alternative energy** Clean energy sources that do not come from fossil fuels. (412)

**amphibian** A vertebrate whose body temperature is determined by the temperature of its environment, and that lives its early life in water and its adult life on land. (322)

**apparent brightness** The brightness of a star as seen from Earth. (503)

**artificial selection** The process by which humans breed only those organisms with desired traits to produce the next generation; selective breeding. (217)

**asteroid** One of the rocky objects revolving around the sun that is too small and numerous to be considered a planet. (476)

**astronomical unit** A unit of distance equal to the average distance between Earth and the sun, about 150 million kilometers. (474)

**atom** The basic particle from which all elements are made; the smallest particle of an element that has the properties of that element. (6)

**atomic mass** The average mass of all the isotopes of an element. (18)

**atomic number** The number of protons in the nucleus of an atom. (11)

**autosomal chromosomes** The 22 pairs of chromosomes that are not sex chromosomes. (206)

**axis** An imaginary line that passes through a planet's center and its north and south poles, about which the planet rotates. (441)

## B

**base** A substance that tastes bitter, feels slippery, and turns red litmus paper blue. (52)

**big bang** The initial explosion that resulted in the formation and expansion of the universe. (512)

## C

**cascade effect** An unforeseen chain of events caused by a disturbance in a system. (410)

**cell cycle** The series of events in which a cell grows, prepares for division, and divides to form two daughter cells. (185)

**chemical change** A change in which one or more substances combine or break apart to form new substances. (80)

**chemical symbol** A one- or two-letter abbreviation for an element (19)

**chromatid** The structure formed when a chromosome divides during meiosis (190)

**chromosome** A threadlike structure within a cell's nucleus that contains DNA that is passed from one generation to the next. (185)

**climate** The average annual conditions of temperature, precipitation, winds, and clouds in an area. (385)

**climate change** A sudden or gradual change in Earth's climate. (396)

**clone** An organism that is genetically identical to the organism from which it was produced. (221)

**closed system** A system in which no matter is allowed to enter or leave. (95)

**coevolution** The process by which two species evolve in response to changes in each other over time. (264)

**colloid** A mixture containing small, undissolved particles that do not settle out. (71)

**comet** A loose collection of ice and dust that orbits the sun, typically in a long, narrow orbit. (430, 476)

**competition** The struggle between organisms to survive as they attempt to use the same limited resources in the same place at the same time. (251)

**compound** A substance made of two or more elements chemically combined in a specific ratio, or proportion. (30)

**conduction** The transfer of thermal energy from one particle of matter to another. (348)

**constellation** A pattern or grouping of stars that people imagine to represent a figure or object. (431)

**convection** The transfer of thermal energy by the movement of a fluid. (348)

**Coriolis effect** The effect of Earth's rotation on the direction of winds and currents. (357)

**corrosive** The way in which acids react with some metals so as to wear away the metal. (50)

**covalent bond** A chemical bond formed when two atoms share electrons. (42)

**current** A large stream of moving water that flows through the oceans. (363)

## D

**DNA** Deoxyribonucleic acid; the genetic material that carries information about an organism and is passed from parent to offspring. (195)

**dominant allele** An allele whose trait always shows up in the organism when the allele is present. (175)

**ductile** A term used to describe a material that can be pulled out into a long wire. (33)

## E

**eclipse** The partial or total blocking of one object in space by another. (455)

**El Niño** An abnormal climate event that occurs every two to seven years in the Pacific Ocean, causing changes in winds, currents, and weather patterns for one to two years. (366)

**electromagnetic radiation** The energy transferred through space by electromagnetic waves. (487)

**electromagnetic wave** A wave made up of a combination of a changing electric field and a changing magnetic field. (343)

**electron** A tiny, particle that moves around the outside of the nucleus of an atom. (7)

**ellipse** An oval shape, which may be elongated or nearly circular; the shape of the planets' orbits. (435)

**embryo** The young organism that develops from a zygote. (272)

**endosymbiosis** A relationship in which one organism lives inside another organism's cells. (287)

**endothermic reaction** A reaction that absorbs energy. (84)

**equinox** Either of the two days of the year on which neither hemisphere is tilted toward or away from the sun. (444)

**era** One of the three long units of geologic time between the Precambrian and the present. (316)

**evolution** Change over time; the process by which modern organisms have descended from ancient organisms. (239)

**exothermic reaction** A reaction that releases energy, usually in the form of heat. (84)

**extinct** Term used to refer to a group of related organisms that has died out and has no living members. (274)

## F

**fitness** How well an organism can survive and reproduce in its environment. (259)

**force** A push or pull exerted on an object. (123)

**fossil** The preserved remains or traces of an organism that lived in the past. (242, 305)

**fossil fuel** Energy-rich substances formed from the remains of organisms. (400)

**fossil record** All the fossils that have been discovered and what scientists have learned from them. (267)

**friction** The force that two surfaces exert on each other when they rub against each other. (124)

## G

**galaxy** A huge group of single stars, star systems, star clusters, dust, and gas bound together by gravity. (509)

**gene therapy** The process of replacing an absent or faulty gene with a normal working gene to treat a disease or medical disorder. (220)

**genetic engineering** The transfer of a gene from the DNA of one organism into another organism, in order to produce an organism with desired traits. (218)

**genome** The complete set of genetic information that an organism carries in its DNA. (222)

**genotype** An organism's genetic makeup, or allele combinations. (180)

**geocentric** Term describing a model of the universe in which Earth is at the center of the revolving planets and stars. (434)

**geologic time scale** A record of the geologic events and life forms in Earth's history. (313)

**global warming** A gradual increase in the Earth's average temperature. (399)

**gravity** The attractive force between objects; the force that moves objects downhill. (124, 445)

**greenhouse effect** The trapping of heat near a planet's surface by certain gases in the planet's atmosphere. (346, 395)

**greenhouse gas** A gas in Earth's atmosphere that absorbs heat leaving Earth's surface. (395)

**group** Elements in the same vertical column of the periodic table; also called family. (24)

# GLOSSARY

## H

**heliocentric** Term describing a model of the solar system in which Earth and the other planets revolve around the sun. (435)

**heredity** The passing of traits from parents to offspring. (173)

**homologous structures** Structures that are similar in different species and that have been inherited from a common ancestor. (272)

## I

**indicator** A compound that changes color in the presence of an acid or a base. (51)

**inertia** The tendency of an object to resist a change in motion. (142, 446)

**invertebrate** An animal without a backbone. (321)

**ion** An atom or group of atoms that has become electrically charged. (40)

**ionic bond** The attraction between ions with opposite charges. (41)

**isotope** An atom with the same number of protons and a different number of neutrons from other atoms of the same element. (12)

## J

**jet stream** Band of high-speed winds about 10 kilometers above Earth's surface. (359)

## L

**La Niña** A climate event in the eastern Pacific Ocean in which surface waters are colder than normal. (366)

**land breeze** The flow of air from land to a body of water. (355)

**law of conservation of mass** The principle that the total amount of matter is neither created nor destroyed during any chemical or physical change. (94)

**law of superposition** The geologic principle that states that in horizontal layers of sedimentary rock, each layer is older than the layer above it and younger than the layer below it. (304)

**law of universal gravitation** The scientific law that states that every object in the universe attracts every other object. (445)

**light-year** The distance that light travels in one year, about 9.46 trillion kilometers. (510)

**luster** The way a mineral reflects light from its surface. (33)

## M

**malleable** A term used to describe material that can be hammered or rolled into flat sheets. (33)

**mammal** A vertebrate whose body temperature is regulated by its internal heat, and that has skin covered with hair or fur and glands that produce milk to feed its young. (324)

**mass extinction** When many types of living things become extinct at the same time. (323)

**mass number** The sum of protons and neutrons in the nucleus of an atom. (12)

**mechanism** The natural process by which something takes place. (249)

**meiosis** The process that occurs in the formation of sex cells (sperm and egg) by which the number of chromosomes is reduced by half. (189)

**messenger RNA** Type of RNA that carries copies of instructions for the assembly of amino acids into proteins from DNA to ribosomes in the cytoplasm. (199)

**meteor** A streak of light in the sky produced by the burning of a meteoroid in Earth's atmosphere. (430)

**meteoroid** A chunk of rock or dust in space, generally smaller than an asteroid. (476)

**mitosis** The second stage of the cell cycle during which the cell's nucleus divides into two new nuclei and one set of DNA is distributed into each daughter cell. (191)

**mixture** Two or more substances that are together in the same place but their atoms are not chemically bonded. (69)

**molecule** A neutral group of two or more atoms held together by covalent bonds. (42)

**moon** A natural satellite that orbits a planet. (476)

**motion** The state in which one object's distance from another is changing. (121)

**mutation** Any change in the DNA of a gene or a chromosome. (208)

## N

**natural resource** Anything naturally occuring in the environment that humans use. (100)

**natural selection** The process by which organisms that are best adapted to their environment are most likely to survive and reproduce. (251)

**neap tide** The tide with the least difference between consecutive low and high tides. (457)

**nebula** A large cloud of gas and dust in space. (497)

**net force** The overall force on an object when all the individual forces acting on it are added together. (125)

**neutralization** A reaction of an acid with a base, yielding a solution that is not as acidic or basic as the starting solutions were. (53)

**neutron** A small particle in the nucleus of the atom, with no electrical charge. (10)

**newton** A unit of measure that equals the force required to accelerate 1 kilogram of mass at 1 meter per second per second. (123)

**nonpolar bond** A covalent bond in which electrons are shared equally. (43)

**nucleus** The central core of an atom which contains protons and neutrons. (8)

## O

**open system** A system in which matter can enter from or escape to the surroundings. (95)

**orbit** The path of an object as it revolves around another object in space. (442)

## P

**pedigree** A tool that geneticists use to map out the inheritance of traits. (188)

**penumbra** The part of a shadow surrounding the darkest part. (455)

**period** 1. A horizontal row of elements in the periodic table. (22); 2. One of the units of geologic time into which geologists divide eras. (316)

**periodic table** An arrangement of the elements showing the repeating pattern of their properties. (18)

**phase** One of the different apparent shapes of the moon as seen from Earth. (451)

**phenotype** An organism's physical appearance, or visible traits. (180)

**physical change** A change that alters the form or appearance of a material but does not make the material into another substance. (79)

**planet** An object that orbits a star, is large enough to have become rounded by its own gravity, and has cleared the area of its orbit. (429, 475)

**polar bond** A covalent bond in which electrons are shared unequally. (43)

**polyatomic ion** An ion that is made of more than one atom. (40)

**polymer** A long chain of molecules made up of repeating units. (102)

**probability** A number that describes how likely it is that a particular event will occur. (177)

**product** A substance formed as a result of a chemical reaction. (80)

**protein** Large organic molecule made of carbon, hydrogen, oxygen, nitrogen, and sometimes sulfur. (284)

**protein synthesis** The process by which amino acids link together to form proteins. (198)

**proton** A small, positively charged particle that is found in the nucleus of an atom. (8)

**protostar** A contracting cloud of gas and dust with enough mass to form a star. (497)

# GLOSSARY

## R

**radiation** The transfer of energy by electromagnetic waves. (348)

**radioactive dating** The process of determining the age of an object using the half-life of one or more radioactive isotopes. (308)

**radioactive decay** The process in which the nuclei of radioactive elements break down, releasing fastmoving particles and energy. (307)

**reactant** A substance that enters into a chemical reaction. (80)

**reactivity** The ease and speed with which an element combines, or reacts, with other elements and compounds. (32)

**recessive allele** An allele that is hidden whenever the dominant allele is present. (175)

**reference point** A place or object used for comparison to determine whether an object is in motion. (121)

**relative age** The age of a rock compared to the ages of other rocks. (303)

**reptile** A vertebrate whose temperature is determined by the temperature of its environment, that has lungs and scaly skin, and that lays eggs on land. (322)

**revolution** The movement of an object around another object. (442)

**rotation** The spinning motion of a planet on its axis. (441)

## S

**salt** An ionic compound made from the neutralization of an acid with a base. (53)

**satellite** An object that orbits a planet. (429)

**scientific theory** A well-tested explanation for a wide range of observations or experimental results. (246)

**sea breeze** The flow of cooler air from over an ocean or lake toward land. (355)

**semiconductor** A substance that can conduct electric current under some conditions. (35)

**sex chromosomes** The pair of chromosomes carrying genes that determine whether a person is biologically male or female. (206)

**sex-linked gene** A gene carried on a sex chromosome. (209)

**sexual selection** A type of natural selection that acts on an organism's ability to get the best possible mate. (263)

**slope** The steepness of a graph line; the ratio of the vertical change (the rise) to the horizontal change (the run). (131)

**solar system** The system consisting of the sun and the planets and other objects that revolve around it. (473)

**solstice** Either of the two days of the year on which the sun reaches its greatest distance north or south of the equator. (444)

**solubility** A measure of how much solute can dissolve in a given solvent at a given temperature. (74)

**solute** The part of a solution that is dissolved by a solvent. (72)

**solution** A mixture containing a solvent and at least one solute that has the same properties throughout; a mixture in which one substance is dissolved in another. (72)

**solvent** The part of a solution that is usually present in the largest amount and dissolves a solute. (72)

**species** A group of similar organisms that can mate with each other and produce offspring that can also mate and reproduce. (239)

**spectrum** The range of wavelengths of electromagnetic waves. (487)

**speed** The distance an object travels per unit of time. (129)

**spring tide** The tide with the greatest difference between consecutive low and high tides. (457)

**star** A ball of hot gas, primarily hydrogen and helium, that undergoes nuclear fusion. (429)

**sun** A large, gaseous body at the center of the solar system. (475)

**supernova** The brilliant explosion of a dying supergiant star. (499)

**suspension** A mixture in which particles can be seen and easily separated by settling or filtration. (71)

**synthetic** Created or manufactured by humans; not found occuring in nature (99)

## T

**telescope** An optical instrument that forms enlarged images of distant objects. (488)

**thermal energy** The total kinetic and potential energy of all the particles of an object. (347)

**tide** The periodic rise and fall of the level of water in the ocean. (456)

**transfer RNA** Type of RNA in the cytoplasm that carries an amino acid to the ribosome during protein synthesis. (199)

# U

**umbra**  The darkest part of a shadow. (455)

**unconformity**  A gap in the geologic record that shows where rock layers have been lost due to erosion. (306)

**universe**  All of space and everything in it. (510)

# V

**valence electron**  The electrons that are in the highest energy level of an atom and that are involved in chemical bonding. (30)

**variation**  Any difference between individuals of the same species. (205)

**velocity**  Speed in a given direction. (132)

**vertebrate**  An animal with a backbone. (322)

**visible light**  Electromagnetic radiation that can be seen with the unaided eye. (487)

# W

**wavelength**  The distance between two corresponding parts of a wave, such as the distance between two crests. (487)

**weight**  A measure of the force of gravity acting on an object. (155)

**white dwarf**  The blue-white hot core of a star that is left behind after its outer layers have expanded and drifted out into space. (499)

**wind**  The horizontal movement of air from an area of high pressure to an area of lower pressure. (353)

## W

**Wallace, Alfred Russel,** 251
**Water, bodies of,** 387
**Wavelength, 487**–488
**Weather**
   and climate change, 407,
    410–411
   and ocean currents, 365, 366
   and winds, 355–359
   *See also* **Climate; Winds**
**Weight, 155**
   and gravity, 445
**Wet-mount slides,** 539
**White dwarf, 499**
**Wind turbines,** 361
**Wind vanes,** 354

**Winds,** 349, **353**–359
   as climate factor, 388–389
   and Coriolis effect, 357
   global, 356–359
   land and sea, 355
   local, 355
   measuring, 354
   naming, 354
   and ocean currents, 364
   prevailing, 388
   seasonal, 389
**Writing Skills.** *See* **Science Notebook**

## X

**X-rays,** 487, 488

# ACKNOWLEDGEMENTS

## Photographs

Photo locators denoted as follows: Top (T), Center (C), Bottom (B), Left (L), Right (R), Background (Bkgd)
**Front Cover**: Hubble Telescope/Stocktrek/Getty Images
**Back Cover**: blank notes and papers Marinello/DigitalVision Vectors/Getty Images

### Front Matter
iv: Clari Massimiliano/Shutterstock; ix: Buffy1982/Fotolia; vi: Alexander Cher/Shutterstock; vii: HTU/Shutterstock; viii: Matteo Arteni/Shutterstock; x: tonyz20/Shutterstock; xi: Sinclair Stammers/Science Photo Library/Getty Images; xii: UniversalImagesGroup/Getty Images; xiii: Michael Turner/Alamy Stock Photo; xiv: Chris Cook/Science Source; xv: John A. Davis/Shutterstock; xvi: Brian J. Skerry/National Geographic/Getty Images; xvii: Steve Byland/Shutterstock

### Topic 1
xviii: Alexander Cher/Shutterstock; 002: Peter Dazeley/Iconica/Getty Images; 004: vodolaz/Fotolia; 007: Bon Appetit/Alamy Stock Photo; 011: David Tipling/DigitalVision/Getty Images; 014: John S. Zeedick/Hulton Archive/Getty Images; 016: Billy Hustace/Photographer's Choice/Getty Images; 018: Chip Clark/Fundamental Photographs; 022 BC: photoeverywhere/Fotolia; 022 BL: SPL/Science Source; 022 BR: Asturcon/Shutterstock; 024 BC: SPL/Science Source; 024 CL: SPL/Science Source; 024 CR: Burmakin Andrey/123RF; 025 BL: SPL/Science Source; 025 BR: SPL/Science Source; 025 CL: SeDmi/Shutterstock; 025 CR: Tom Grundy/Shutterstock; 026 C: Charles D. Winters/Science Source; 026 CL: Courtesy of NASA/SDO and the AIA, EVE, and HMI science teams/NASA; 026 CR: blackpixel/Shutterstock; 028: GL Archive/Alamy Stock Photo; 033 Bkgrd: sakda2527/Fotolia; 033 BL: dgool/123RF; 033 BR: Matthew Howard/123RF; 033 CR: Eddie Phantana/Shutterstock; 035: dpa picture alliance archive/Alamy Stock Photo; 037 CR: generalfmv/iStock/Getty Images; 037 TR: CERN/MCT/Newscom; 038: Lightspringd/Shutterstock; 041 Bkgrd: Radu/Fotolia; 041 C: Andrew Lambert Photography/Science Source; 041 CL: SPL/Science Source; 042: Charles D. Winters/Science Source; 043 BL: Ryan McVay/Photodisc/Getty Images; 043 BR: michaelstephan-fotografie/Shutterstock; 044: Sciencephotos/Alamy Stock Photo; 045: Sciencephotos/Alamy Stock Photo; 048: Martyn Williams/Alamy Stock Photo; 049: Robert Harding/Alamy Stock Photo; 050: Alessia Pierdomenico/Bloomberg/Getty Images; 051 BL: 256261/Shutterstock; 051 TR: Gilbert S. Grant/Science Source; 052 BCL: Focal Point/Shutterstock; 052 BR: Nikola Bilic/Shutterstock; 052 TC: Lana Langlois/Shutterstock; 052 TR: Petr Malyshev/Fotolia; 053: Oleksandr Lysenko/Alamy Stock Photo; 060: Alexey Protasov/Fotolia; 061: Andrew Lambert Photography/Science Source

### Topic 2
064: HTU/Shutterstock; 065: Anita Patterson Peppers/Shutterstock; 066: Steve Hix/Getty Images; 068: djgis/Shutterstock; 069: Alexander Bark/Shutterstock; 071 BC: Gareth Boden/Pearson Education Ltd.; 071 BL: Jim West/The Image Works; 071 T: DarKinG/Shutterstock; 074: Alexey Lysenko/Shutterstock; 075: imageBROKER/Alamy Stock Photo; 077: Jake Lyell/Alamy Stock Photo; 078: Lew

Robertson/Photographer's Choice/Getty Images; 081: Richard Megna/Fundamental Photographs; 084 TC: Charles D. Winters/Science Source; 084 TR: serezniy/123RF; 087: MG-PicturesProd/Shutterstock; 089 BL: John Lund/The Image Bank/Getty Images; 089 BR: Interfoto/Hermann Historica/akg-images; 090: Anastasios71/Shutterstock; 093: Chepko Danil Vitalevich/Shutterstock; 095 BC: Patrick Moynihan/pyronious/Getty Images; 095 BR: vlorzor/Fotolia; 096: 123RF; 098: Vidady/Fotolia; 099 BCR: gamjai/Fotolia; 099 CL: thewet/Fotolia; 099 R: Feng Yu/Alamy Stock Photo; 101 BC: Thomas J. Peterson/Alamy Stock Photo; 101 CL: Shyripa Alexandr/Shutterstock; 101 TL: naretev/Fotolia; 102 BL: Mau Horng/Shutterstock; 102 L: monticello/Shutterstock; 103 BR: Nils Z/Shutterstock; 103 TL: Borodin Denis/Shutterstock; 104 BL: Oscar Dominguez/Alamy Stock Photo; 104 BR: Nigel Wilkins/Alamy; 106 Bkgrd: Alain Machet/Alamy Stock Photo; 106 CR: Roman.S-Photographer/Shutterstock; 106 TR: loonger/E+/Getty Images; 112: jordeangjelovik/Shutterstock; 113: Charles D. Winters/Science Source

### Topic 3
116: Matteo Arteni/Shutterstock; 118: Heiner Heine/imageBROKER/Alamy Stock Photo; 120: Seth K. Hughes/Image Source/Alamy Stock Photo; 122: Marcio Jose Bastos Silva/Shutterstock; 123 CR: WilleeCole Photography/Shutterstock; 123 TCR: Sonya Etchison/Fololia; 123 TR: dmussman/iStock/Getty Images; 124 BL: gbh007/Getty Images; 124 BR: Monkey Business Images/Shutterstock; 128: Ian Lishman/Juice Images/Getty Images; 130: Scott A. Miller/ZUMA Press/Newscom; 131: Jim Zuckerman/Alamy Stock Photo; 132: Emma Yacomen/Alamy Stock Photo; 134 TC: WING/UPPA/Photoshot/Newscom; 134 TL: John Ewing/Portland Press Herald/Getty Images; 134 TR: Jim Cummins/The Image Bank/Getty Images; 138 Bkgrd: hkeita/Shutterstock; 138 CL: BLACKDAY/Shutterstock; 140: lsantilli/123RF; 142 CL: Janet Horton/Alamy Stock Photo; 142 TL: Hero Images/Alamy Stock Photo; 143: Sorin Papuc/Alamy Stock Photo; 144: omgimages/123RF; 145 BL: Janet Horton/Alamy Stock Photo; 145 C: Jiang Dao Hua/Shutterstock; 146: imageBROKER/Alamy Stock Photo; 147 B: D. Trozzo/Alamy Stock Photo; 147 TR: full image/Fotolia; 149 CR: ScofieldZa/Shutterstock; 149 TCR: Barry Blackburn/Shutterstock; 150: kuznetsov_konsta/Fotolia; 154: Robert Daly/OJO Images/Getty Images; 159 B: Andrey Volodin/Alamy Stock Photo; 159 CR: koya979/Fotolia; 164: Jason O. Watson (Sports)/Alamy Stock Photo; 165: Gary Hamilton/Icon SMI/Icon Sport Media/Getty Images

### Topic 4
168: Buffy1982/Fotolia; 171 Bkgrd: Tim Gainey/Alamy Stock Photo; 171 TR: luis abrantes/Shutterstock; 173 Bkgrd: draleksun/Fotolia; 173 C: Biosphoto/SuperStock; 173 CL: Alan J. S. Weaving/ardea/AGE Fotostock; 174 CL: Laurent Geslin/Nature Picture Library; 174 TL: cbimages/Alamy Stock Photo; 176: Les Gibbon/Alamy Stock Photo; 177 BL: Sujata Jana/EyeEm/Getty Images; 177 TR: Visions Pictures/AGE Fotostock; 178: Kadmy/Fotolia; 179: Danita Delimont/Alamy Stock Photo; 180: kali9/Getty Images; 182: Svetlana Foote/Alamy Stock Photo; 186: Martin Shields/Alamy Stock Photo; 187: James Steidl/Shutterstock; 188: Martin Shields/Alamy Stock Photo; 194: cuppyuppycake Creative/Getty Images; 203 BR: MixAll Studio Creative/Getty Images; 203 TR: Miodrag

Gajic/Getty Images; 214: eriklam/123RF; 216: REUTERS/Alamy Stock Photo; 218 BL: Eye of Science/Science Source; 218 TR: Coneyl Jay/Getty Images; 219: Clive Gee/AP Images; 220: M. Watson/ardea/AGE Fotostock; 228: sheilaf2002/Fotolia; 229: eurobanks/Fotolia

## Topic 5

234: tonyz20/Shutterstock; 235: John Cancalosi/Alamy Stock Photo; 236: Blickwinkel/Alamy Stock Photo; 239 Bkgrd: jo Crebbin/Shutterstock; 239 CR: Loop Images Ltd/Alamy Stock Photo; 240: Fototeca Gilardi/akg-images; 242 T: Holmes Garden Photos/Alamy Stock Photo; 242 TCL: Russell Shively/Shutterstock; 244 BC: Westend61/Getty Images; 244 BR: Brian Kushner/Alamy Stock Photo; 246: Visual China Group/Getty Images; 248 TC: Pises Tungittipokai/Shutterstock; 248 TL: Nature Photographers Ltd/Alamy Stock Photo; 248 TR: Oli Scarff/AFP/Getty Images; 249: Nature Photographers Ltd/Alamy Stock Photo; 250: IrinaK/Shutterstock; 252: kali9/Getty Images; 253 TC: Patricia Isaza; 253 TL: Zeljko Radojko/Shutterstock; 254: IrinaK/Shutterstock; 255 BCR: All Canada Photos/Alamy Stock Photo; 255 TCR: Reuters/Ulises Rodriguez/Alamy Stock Photo; 256: imageBROKER/Alamy Stock Photo; 261: Blickwinkel/Alamy Stock Photo; 262 BC: Sailorr/Shutterstock; 262 TC: Bazzano Photography/Alamy Stock Photo; 262 TR: Angel DiBilio/Shutterstock; 263: Angel DiBilio/Shutterstock; 264: Martin Shields/Alamy Stock Photo; 265: vodolaz/Fotolia; 266 BC: YAY Media AS/Alamy Stock Photo; 266 BR: wwing/Getty Images; 267 BC: Scott Camazine/Alamy Stock Photo; 267 BL: The Science Picture Company/Alamy Stock Photo; 267 BR: Fabian von Poser/Getty Images; 268: Bildagentur Zoonar GmbH/Shutterstock; 270 BC: Steve Vidler/Alamy Stock Photo; 270 BR: Pedro Bernardo/Shutterstock; 273 CR: Barry Mansell/Nature Picture Library; 273 TR: Michelle Gilders/Alamy Stock Photo; 274: Saverio Gatto/Alamy Stock Photo; 276: Julia Clarke/Department of Geological Sciences/The University of Texas at Austin; 278: Vlad61/Shutterstock; 280: vitstudio/Shutterstock; 283: Abeselom Zerit/Shutterstock; 284: Pallava Bagla/Getty Images; 287 B: Don Johnston/Getty Images; 287 CR: BGSmith/Shutterstock; 289: John Cancalosi/Science Source; 292 BL: Gallinago_media/Shutterstock; 292 BR: CLS Digital Arts/Shutterstock; 293: J Hindman/Shutterstock

## Topic 6

298: Sinclair Stammers/Science Photo Library/Getty Images; 300: James L. Amos/Science Source; 302: Jim in SC/Shutterstock; 304 BL: Carol Dembinsky/Dembinsky Photo Associates/Alamy Stock Photo; 304 BR: Chris Curtis/Shutterstock; 310: greenfire/Fotolia; 312: Mark Godden/Shutterstock; 314 BL: Chase Studio/Science Source; 314 BR: Ralf Juergen Kraft/Shutterstock; 315 BR: Catmando/Shutterstock; 315 TC: DEA/G. Ciglioni/Getty Images; 315 TL: Jean-Philippe Delobelle/Alamy Stock Photo; 315 TR: Kevin Schafer/Alamy Stock Photo; 316: Biophoto Associates/Science Source; 319: James King-Holmes/Science Source; 320: Laurie O'Keefe/Science Source; 322: MarcelClemens/Shutterstock; 323 TL: John Cancalosi/Alamy Stock Photo; 323 TR: Sabena Jane Blackbird/Alamy Stock Photo; 324 BR: Herschel Hoffmeyer/Shutterstock; 324 TL: Stocktrek Images, Inc./Alamy Stock Photo; 326 B: The Natural History Museum/The Image Works; 326 TL: Jerry Young/Dorling Kindersley;

327 BC: Andreas Meyer/123RF; 327 C: Bedrock Studios/Dorling Kindersley; 327 TC: Chase Studio/Science Source; 329 B: Sean Pavone/Alamy Stock Photo; 329 TR: Alan Novelli/Getty Images; 334: Jonathan Blair/Getty Images; 335: Adwo/Shutterstock

## Topic 7

338: UniversalImagesGroup/Getty Images; 340: dan_prat/Getty Images; 342: Louise Murray/Robert Harding/Getty Images; 349: Iakov Kalinin/Shutterstock; 351: NASA; 352: Ian Brown/Alamy Stock Photo; 354: id1974/123RF; 355 BL: efesenko/Fotolia; 355 BR: Polifoto/Fotolia; 362: Andrey Armyagov/Shutterstock; 366: Stuart Rankin/NOAA; 367: Geraldas Galinauskas/Shutterstock; 370: Kevin Kelley/Getty Images; 376: vermontalm/Fotolia

## Topic 8

380: Michael Turner/Alamy Stock Photo; 382: Paul Prescott/Alamy Stock Photo; 383: K. Arjana/Shutterstock; 384: marcaletourneux/Fotolia; 386 B: Karim Agabi/Science Source; 386 TR: Dorling Kindersley/Getty Images; 390: The Whiteview/Shutterstock; 391: Michael Runkel/Alamy Stock Photo; 393 BR: Goddard Space Flight Center/Scientific Visualization Studio/NASA; 393 TR: Goddard Space Flight Center/Scientific Visualization Studio/NASA; 394: Paulo Nabas/Shutterstock; 397: AFP/Getty Images; 400 BL: David Noton Photography/Alamy Stock Photo; 400 BR: Science Source; 401 BR: Aeropix/Alamy Stock Photo; 401 TL: Blickwinkel/Alamy Stock Photo; 401 TR: Blaize Pascall/Alamy Stock Photo; 406: Westend61/Getty Images; 411 Bkgrd: Volodymyr Goinyk/Shutterstock; 411 CL: Gece33/Getty Images; 411 TR: Ashley Cooper/Getty Images; 413: Lonely Planet Images/Getty Images; 420: Joel Sartore/National Geographic/Getty Images

## Topic 9

424: Chris Cook/Science Source; 426: Paul Lindsay/Alamy Stock Photo; 428: Scott Stulberg/Getty Images; 430: Halley Multicolor Camera Team, Giotto Project, ESA; 432: Alan Dyer/VWPics/Alamy Stock Photo; 438: AF Fotografie/Alamy Stock Photo; 440: Triff /NASA/Shutterstock; 444: David Clapp/Shutterstock; 445: NASA/Getty Images; 449 Bkgrd: eFesenko/Shutterstock; 449 CR: iStock/Getty Images; 450: David M. Schrader/Shutterstock; 452: Quaoar/Shutterstock; 454 BL: Chris Collins/Shutterstock; 454 CL: Oorka/Shutterstock; 464: Quaoar/Shutterstock; 465: Claudio Divizia/Shutterstock

## Topic 10

468: John A. Davis/Shutterstock; 470: Blickwinkel/Alamy Stock Photo; 475 B: Ivann/Shutterstock; 475 CL: Robert_S/Shutterstock; 476 TL: JPL/NASA; 476 TR: NASA/Shutterstock; 479 TL: NASA; 479 TR: Ivannn/Shutterstock; 484 BL: JPL-Caltech/UMD/NASA; 484 CL: JPL-Caltech/UCAL/MPS/DLR/IDA/NASA; 484 L: NASA; 484 TL: NASA; 488: Hubble & NASA/S. Smartt/ESA/NASA; 490: European Space Agency; 491: Comstock Images/Getty Images; 492 BR: NASA; 492 CR: Sovfoto/UIG/Getty Images; 492 TR: Sovfoto/UIG/Getty Images; 493 BC: John Baran/Alamy Stock Photo; 493 TR: NASA; 494 BL: NASA & ESA; 494 CL: Everett Historical/Shutterstock; 494 TR: Stocktrek Images/Alamy Stock Photo; 495 BL: JPL/NASA; 495 CR: Tim Jacobs/NASA; 495 TL: NASA; 500: peresanz/Shutterstock; 503: NASA/S.Dupuis/Alamy Stock

# ACKNOWLEDGEMENTS

Photo; 507: Igordabari/Shutterstock; 510: G. Illingworth, D. Magee, and P. Oesch, University of California, Santa Cruz; R. Bouwens, Leiden University; and the HUDF09 Team/ESA/NASA; 514: Albert Barr/Shutterstock; 519: NASA; 524: Dhoxax/Getty Images; 525 TL: JPL/NASA; 525 TR: Stocktrek Images/Getty Images

## End Matter
524 BCL: Philippe Plailly & Elisabeth Daynes/Science Source; 524 BL: EHStockphoto/Shutterstock; 524 TCL: Cyndi Monaghan/Getty Images; 524 TL: Javier Larrea/AGE Fotostock; 525: WaterFrame/Alamy Stock Photo; 526: Africa Studio/Shutterstock; 527: Jeff Rotman/Alamy Stock Photo; 528: Grant Faint/Getty Images; 529: Ross Armstrong/Alamy Stock Photo; 530: Geoz/Alamy Stock Photo; 533: Martin Shields/Alamy; 534: Nicola Tree/Getty Images; 535: Regan Geeseman/NASA; 536: Pearson Education Ltd.; 537: Pearson Education Ltd.; 538 BR: Pearson Education Ltd.; 538 CR: Pearson Education Ltd.

# Take Notes

# Take Notes

Use this space for recording notes and sketching out ideas.

# Take Notes

Use this space for recording notes and sketching out ideas.

# Take Notes

Use this space for recording notes and sketching out ideas.

# Take Notes

Use this space for recording notes and sketching out ideas.